Lecture Notes in Computer Science 15696

Founding Editors

Gerhard Goos
Juris Hartmanis

W0111607

Advanced Research in Computing and Software Science
Subline of Lecture Notes in Computer Science

More information about this series at https://link.springer.com/bookseries/558

Arie Gurfinkel · Marijn Heule
Editors

Tools and Algorithms for the Construction and Analysis of Systems

31st International Conference, TACAS 2025
Held as Part of the International Joint Conferences
on Theory and Practice of Software, ETAPS 2025
Hamilton, ON, Canada, May 3–8, 2025, Proceedings, Part I

 Springer

Editors
Arie Gurfinkel
University of Waterloo
Waterloo, ON, Canada

Marijn Heule
Carnegie Mellon University
Pittsburgh, PA, USA

ISSN 0302-9743   ISSN 1611-3349 (electronic)
Lecture Notes in Computer Science
ISBN 978-3-031-90642-8   ISBN 978-3-031-90643-5 (eBook)
https://doi.org/10.1007/978-3-031-90643-5

This Springer imprint is published by the registered company Springer Nature Switzerland AG
The registered company address is: Gewerbestrasse 11, 6330 Cham, Switzerland

If disposing of this product, please recycle the paper.

ETAPS Foreword

Welcome to the 28th ETAPS! ETAPS 2025 took place in Hamilton, Canada. It is the first time ETAPS was held outside of Europe.

ETAPS 2025 was the 28th instance of the International Joint Conferences on Theory and Practice of Software. ETAPS is an annual federated conference established in 1998, and consists of four conferences: ESOP, FASE, FoSSaCS, and TACAS. Each conference has its own Program Committee (PC) and its own Steering Committee (SC). The conferences cover various aspects of software systems, ranging from theoretical computer science to foundations of programming languages, analysis tools, and formal approaches to software engineering. Organizing these conferences in a coherent, highly synchronized conference programme enables researchers to participate in an exciting event, having the possibility to meet many colleagues working in different directions in the field, and to easily attend talks of different conferences. On the weekend before the main conference, numerous satellite workshops took place that attracted many researchers from all over the globe.

ETAPS 2025 received 329 submissions in total, 106 of which were accepted, yielding an overall acceptance rate of 32.2%. I thank all the authors for their interest in ETAPS, all the reviewers for their reviewing efforts, the PC members for their contributions, and in particular the PC (co-)chairs for their hard work in running this entire intensive process. Last but not least, my congratulations to all authors of the accepted papers!

ETAPS 2025 featured the unifying invited speakers Ina Schaefer (Karlsruhe Institute of Technology, Germany) and Matthew B. Dwyer (University of Virginia, USA), and the invited speakers Amal Ahmed (Northeastern University, USA) for ESOP and José Meseguer (University of Illinois Urbana-Champaign, USA) for FASE. Invited tutorials were provided by Suguman Bansal (Georgia Institute of Techology, USA) on reinforcement learning from logical specifications and Arun Ross (Michigan State University, USA) on biometrics.

ETAPS 2025 was organized by McMaster University. The Faculty of Engineering at McMaster University has a reputation for innovative programs, cutting-edge research, leading faculty, and aspiring students. It has earned a strong reputation as a center for academic excellence and innovation. The Faculty has approximately 180 faculty members, along with close to 4,500 undergraduate and 1,000 graduate students. The local organization team consisted of Claudio Menghi and Mark Lawford (general chairs), Melissa Alzaeim (event organizer), Alan Wassyng and Angelo Gargantini (workshop chairs), Sébastien Mosser and Matt Luckcuck (publicity chairs), Patrizio Pelliccione (sponsor chair), Silvia Bonfanti and Andrea Bombarda (web chairs), Jacques Carette and Christos Tsigkanos (local proceedings chair), Lena Liberale and Martin von Mohrenschildt (finance chairs), Damiano Torre and Lina Marsso (registration chairs), and Vera Pantelic and Denise Geiskkovitch (student volunteer chairs).

ETAPS 2025 is further supported by the following associations and societies: ETAPS e.V., EATCS (European Association for Theoretical Computer Science), EAPLS (European Association for Programming Languages and Systems), and EASST (European Association of Software Science and Technology).

The ETAPS Steering Committee consists of an Executive Board, and representatives of the individual ETAPS conferences, as well as representatives of EATCS, EAPLS, and EASST. The Executive Board consists of Marieke Huisman (Twente, chair), Andrzej Wąsowski (Copenhagen), Thomas Noll (Aachen), Jan Kofroň (Prague), Barbara König (Duisburg-Essen), Arnd Hartmanns (Twente), Caterina Urban (Inria), Jan Křetínský (Munich), Elizabeth Polgreen (Edinburgh), and Lenore Zuck (Chicago).

Other members of the steering committee are: Elvira Albert (Madrid), Maurice ter Beek (Pisa), Nathalie Bertrand (Rennes), Dirk Beyer (Munich), Artur Boronat (Leicester), Luís Caires (Lisboa), Ferruccio Damiani (Torino), Gordon Fraser (Passau), Arie Gurfinkel (Waterloo), Reiner Hähnle (Darmstadt), Reiko Heckel (Leicester), Marijn Heule (Pittsburgh), Sebastian Junges (Nijmegen), Joost-Pieter Katoen (Aachen and Twente), Guy Katz (Jerusalem), Delia Kesner (Paris), Fabrice Kordon (Paris), Robbert Krebbers (Nijmegen), Kim Guldstrand Larsen (Aalborg), Mark Lawford (Hamilton), Claudio Menghi (Hamilton and Bergamo), Stefan Milius (Erlangen-Nürnberg), Andrzej Murawski (Oxford), Corina Păsăreanu (Ames), Laure Petrucci (Paris), Peter Y.A. Ryan (Luxembourg), Don Sannella (Edinburgh), Viktor Vafeiadis (Kaiserslautern), and Anton Wijs (Eindhoven).

I would like to take this opportunity to thank all authors, keynote speakers, attendees, organizers of the satellite workshops, and Springer Nature for their support. ETAPS 2025 was also generously supported by Tourism Hamilton and the Tutte Institute for Mathematics and Computing. I hope you all enjoyed ETAPS 2025.

Finally, a big thanks to Claudio, Mark and Melissa and their local organization team for all their enormous efforts to make ETAPS a fantastic event.

May 2025

Marieke Huisman
ETAPS SC Chair
ETAPS e.V. President

Preface

This three-volume proceedings contains the papers presented at the 31st International Conference on Tools and Algorithms for the Construction and Analysis of Systems (TACAS 2025). TACAS 2025 was part of the 28th International Joint Conferences on Theory and Practice of Software (ETAPS 2025), which was held in Hamilton, Ontario, Canada.

TACAS is a forum for researchers, developers and users interested in rigorous tools and algorithms for the construction and analysis of systems. The conference aims to bridge the gaps between different communities with this common interest and to support them in their quest to improve the utility, reliability, flexibility, and efficiency of tools and algorithms for building systems. TACAS 2025 interleaves and integrates various disciplines, including formal verification of software and hardware systems, static analysis, probabilistic programming, program synthesis, concurrency, testing, simulations, verification of machine learning/autonomous systems, Cyber-Physical Systems, SAT/SMT solving, automated and interactive theorem proving, and proof checking.

There were four submission categories for TACAS 2025:

1. **Regular research papers** identifying and justifying a principled advance to the theoretical foundations for the construction and analysis of systems.
2. **Case study papers** describing the application of techniques developed by the community to a single problem or a set of problems of practical importance, preferably in a real-world setting.
3. **Regular tool papers** presenting a novel tool or a new version of an existing tool built using novel algorithmic and engineering techniques.
4. **Tool demonstration papers** demonstrating a new tool or application of an existing tool on a significant case-study.

Regular research, case study, and regular tool paper submissions were restricted to 16 pages, whereas tool demonstration papers were restricted to 6 pages, excluding the bibliography and appendices.

TACAS 2025 received 148 submissions, consisting of 103 regular research papers, 6 case study papers, 29 regular tool papers, and 10 tool demonstration papers. Each submission was assigned for review to at least three Program Committee (PC) members, who made use of sub-reviewers. Regular research papers were reviewed as double-blind, whereas case study, regular tool, and tool-demonstration papers were reviewed using a single-blind reviewing process.

As in previous years, authors had the option to submit an artifact alongside their paper. For TACAS 2025, artifact submission was mandatory for regular tool and tool demonstration papers, and optional for regular research and case study papers. Artifacts could include tools, models, proofs, or any other data necessary to validate the paper's results. The Artifact Evaluation Committee (AEC), which was composed of 89 members of the community, was responsible for reviewing these submissions, assessing their documentation, usability, and, most importantly, whether the results presented in the corresponding paper could be successfully reproduced. Most evaluations were conducted using a standardized virtual machine or a Docker image to ensure consistency, except in cases where specific hardware or software requirements applied. Artifact evaluation at TACAS 2025 was carried out in two rounds. The first round, which took place alongside the work of the Program Committee (PC), involved the mandatory evaluation of regular tool and tool demo papers. The decisions of the AEC were shared with the PC and factored into their discussions. The second round focused on the voluntary evaluation of regular research and case study papers and was conducted after paper acceptance notifications were issued. In both rounds, each artifact received three reviews, and authors had the opportunity to anonymously communicate with the AEC to resolve technical issues. In total, 65 artifacts (39 were mandatory as they were associated with tool papers, and 26 were voluntary) were evaluated for their availability, functionality, and re-usability. Papers with successfully assessed artifacts were awarded one or more badges which are placed on the first page of the corresponding paper, certifying the relevant claims and properties of the tool.

Selected papers were requested to provide a rebuttal in case a PC review gave rise to questions. Using the review reports and rebuttals, the PC had a thorough discussion on each paper. For regular tool and tool demonstration papers, the PC also discussed the corresponding artifact, using the AEC recommendations. As a result, the PC decided to accept 46 papers, out of which there were 28 regular research papers, 11 regular tool papers, 3 case study papers, and 4 tool demonstration papers. This corresponds to an overall acceptance rate of 31%.

TACAS 2025 also hosted SV-COMP 2025, the 14th International Competition on Software Verification. This event evaluated 62 tools for automatic verification of C and Java programs and 18 tools for witness validation, where 35 verification and 13 validation tools were registered and actively supported by development teams. The TACAS 2025 proceedings contain a competition report by the SV-COMP chairs and 13 short papers selected by the competition jury. One short paper deals with reproduction aspects of the competition and the remaining short papers describe 12 out of the tools participating with active team support. The 13 short papers were reviewed by a separate program committee (jury); each was assessed by at least four jury members. Two sessions in the TACAS 2025 program were reserved for SV-COMP: (1) a presentation session with a report by the competition chairs and summaries by the development teams of participating tools, and (2) an open community meeting in the second session.

We would like to thank everyone who helped to make TACAS 2025 successful. We thank the authors for submitting their papers to TACAS 2025. The PC members and additional reviewers did an excellent job in reviewing papers: they provided detailed reports and engaged in the PC discussions. We thank the TACAS steering committee, and especially its chair, Joost-Pieter Katoen, for his valuable advice. We are grateful to the ETAPS steering committee, and in particular its chair, Marieke Huisman, for supporting our changes and suggestions on the TACAS 2025 review process and final program. We also acknowledge the invaluable support provided by the EasyChair developers. Lastly, we would like to thank the overall organization team of ETAPS 2025.

May 2025

Arie Gurfinkel
Marijn Heule
PC Chairs

Daniela Kaufmann
Mark Santolucito
AEC Chairs

Dirk Beyer
Jan Strejček
SV-COMP Chairs

Organization

Program Committee Chairs

Arie Gurfinkel   University of Waterloo, Canada
Marijn Heule   Carnegie Mellon University, USA

Program Committee

Erika Abraham	RWTH Aachen University, Germany
Elvira Albert	Universidad Complutense de Madrid, Spain
Cyrille Valentin Artho	KTH Royal Institute of Technology, Sweden
Haniel Barbosa	Universidade Federal de Minas Gerais, Brazil
Clark Barrett	Stanford University, USA
Dirk Beyer	LMU Munich, Germany
Armin Biere	University of Freiburg, Germany
Nikolaj Bjørner	Microsoft, USA
Roderick Bloem	Graz University of Technology, Austria
Rose Bohrer	Worcester Polytechnic Institute, USA
Borzoo Bonakdarpour	Michigan State University, USA
Mingshuai Chen	Zhejiang University, China
Mila Dalla Preda	University of Verona, Italy
Rayna Dimitrova	CISPA Helmholtz Center for Information Security, Germany
Grigory Fedyukovich	Florida State University, USA
Hadar Frenkel	Bar Ilan University, Israel
Alberto Griggio	Fondazione Bruno Kessler, Italy
Ichiro Hasuo	National Institute of Informatics, Japan
Holger Hermanns	Saarland University, Germany
Alan J. Hu	University of British Columbia, Canada
Sebastian Junges	Radboud University, Netherlands
Temesghen Kahsai	Amazon, USA
Joost-Pieter Katoen	RWTH Aachen University, Germany
Guy Katz	Hebrew University of Jerusalem, Israel
Umang Mathur	National University of Singapore, Singapore
Anastasia Mavridou	KBR/NASA Ames Research Center, USA
Kuldeep S. Meel	University of Toronto, Canada
Magnus O. Myreen	Chalmers University of Technology, Sweden

Nina Narodytska	VMware Research by Broadcom, USA
Jorge A. Navas	Certora, USA
Laura Nenzi	University of Trieste, Italy
Aina Niemetz	Stanford University, USA
André Platzer	Karlsruhe Institute of Technology, Germany
Elizabeth Polgreen	University of Edinburgh, UK
Kristin Yvonne Rozier	Iowa State University, USA
Christian Schilling	Aalborg University, Denmark
Anne-Kathrin Schmuck	Max Planck Institute for Software Systems, Germany
Natasha Sharygina	USI, Switzerland
Sharon Shoham	Tel Aviv University, Israel
Xujie Si	University of Toronto, Canada
Mihaela Sighireanu	Université Paris-Saclay, CNRS, ENS Paris-Saclay, France
Tanel Tammet	Tallinn University of Technology, Estonia
Yong Kiam Tan	Institute for Infocomm Research (I^2R), A*STAR and Nanyang Technological University, Singapore
Silvia Lizeth Tapia Tarifa	University of Oslo, Norway
Cesare Tinelli	University of Iowa, USA
Hazem Torfah	Chalmers University of Technology, Sweden
Yakir Vizel	Technion, Israel
Tomas Vojnar	Masaryk University and Brno University of Technology, Czech Republic
Jingbo Wang	University of Southern California, USA
Georg Weissenbacher	TU Wien, Austria
Anton Wijs	Eindhoven University of Technology, Netherlands
Sarah Winkler	Free University of Bozen-Bolzano, Italy
Haoze Wu	Amherst College, USA

Artifact Evaluation Committee Chairs

| Daniela Kaufmann | TU Wien, Austria |
| Mark Santolucito | Barnard College at Columbia University, USA |

Artifact Evaluation Committee

| Mohammad Afzal | TCS Research Pune and IIT Bombay India, India |
| Mohammad M. Ahmadpanah | Chalmers University of Technology, Sweden |

Hichem Rami Ait El Hara	OCamlPro/Université Paris-Saclay, France
Ashwani Anand	Max Planck Institute for Software Systems, Kaiserslautern, Germany
Bruno Andreotti	Universidade Federal de Minas Gerais, Brazil
Åsmund Aqissiaq Arild Kløvstad	University of Oslo, Norway
Paulína Ayaziová	Masaryk University, Czech Republic
Anna Becchi	Fondazione Bruno Kessler, Italy
Raven Beutner	CISPA Helmholtz Center for Information Security, Germany
Alberto Bombardelli	Fondazione Bruno Kessler, Italy
Konstantin Britikov	USI, Switzerland
Marco Campion	Inria & École Normale Supérieure ∣ Université PSL, France
Filip Cano	Graz University of Technology, Austria
Falke Carlsen	Aalborg Universityi, Denmark
Abha Chaudhary	Binghamton University (SUNY), USA
Lei Chen	HKUST (GZ), China
Siyu Chen	Purdue University, USA
Weiyi Chen	Purdue University, USA
Robin Coutelier	TU Wien, Austria
Vlad Constantin Craciun	BitDefender, UAIC, Romania
Leyi Cui	Columbia University, USA
Charles de Haro	École Normale Supérieure ∣ Université PSL, France
Rafael Dewes	CISPA Helmholtz Center for Information Security, Germany
Oyendrila Dobe	Amazon Web Services, USA
Aoyang Fang	Chinese University of Hong Kong, Shenzhen, China
Mathias Fleury	University of Freiburg, Germany
Rui Ge	University of British Columbia, Canada
Pritam Gharat	Microsoft Research, USA
Pablo Gordillo	Universidad Complutense de Madrid, Spain
Jan Heemstra	Eindhoven University of Technology, Netherlands
Philippe Heim	CISPA Helmholtz Center for Information Security, Germany
Maximilian Heisinger	JKU Linz, Austria
Alejandro Hernández-Cerezo	Complutense University of Madrid, Spain
Matthias Hetzenberger	TU Wien, Austria
Nikolaus Holzer	Columbia University, USA
Petra Hozzová	Czech Technical University, Czech Republic
Guangyu Hu	Hong Kong University of Science and Technology (HKUST), China

Miguel Isabel	Universidad Politécnica de Madrid, Spain
Omri Isac	Hebrew University of Jerusalem, Israel
Tobias John	University of Oslo, Norway
Basel Khouri	Technion, Israel
Elad Kinsbruner	Technion, Israel
Paul Kobialka	University of Oslo, Norway
Tomáš Kolárik	USI, Switzerland
Wietze Koops	Lund University, Sweden and University of Copenhagen, Denmark
Martin Kristjansen	Aalborg University, Denmark
Marco Lewis	Inria, France
Changyue Li	Chinese University of Hong Kong, China
Xuyang Li	Purdue University, USA
Jing Liu	University of California, Irvine, USA
Yonghui Liu	Monash University, Australia
Nils Lommen	RWTH Aachen University, Germany
Filip Macák	Brno University of Technology, Czech Republic
Benedikt Maderbacher	Graz University of Technology, Austria
Kaushik Mallik	IMDEA Software Institute, Spain
Baoluo Meng	GE Aerospace Research, USA
Srinidhi Nagendra	Max Planck Institute for Software Systems, Germany
Tobias Nießen	TU Wien, Austria
Andy Oertel	Lund University and University of Copenhagen, Denmark
Elizaveta Pertseva	Stanford, USA
Anja Petković Komel	TU Wien, Austria
Mark Peyrer	JKU Linz, Austria
Jyoti Prakash	University of Passau, Germany
Juliane Päßler	University of Oslo, Norway
Arshia Rafieioskouei	Michigan State University, USA
Idan Refaeli	Hebrew University of Jerusalem, Israel
Simon Robillard	Université de Montpellier, France
Clara Rodriguez Nuñez	Complutense University of Madrid, Spain
Raven Rothkopf	Barnard College, USA
Neea Rusch	Augusta University, USA
Kartik Sabharwal	University of Iowa, USA
Tobias Seufert	University of Freiburg, Germany
Abhishek Singh	Tel Aviv University, Israel
Mallku Soldevila	Universidade Federal de Minas Gerais, Brazil
Reza Soltani	University of Twente, Netherlands
Yusen Su	University of Waterloo, Canada

Geoff Sutcliffe	University of Miami, USA
Joseph Tafese	University of Waterloo, Canada
Gefei Tan	Northwestern University, USA
Yun Chen Tsai	National Institute of Informatics, Japan
Divyesh Unadkat	Synopsys Inc., India
Christoph Wernhard	University of Potsdam, Germany
Aosen Xiong	University of Waterloo, Canada
Beyazit Yalcinkaya	University of California, Berkeley, USA
Jiong Yang	Georgia Institute of Technology, USA
Bohan Zhang	Binghamton University, USA
Yi Zhou	Carnegie Mellon University, USA

SV-COMP Organization

Chairs

Dirk Beyer	LMU Munich, Germany
Jan Strejček	Masaryk University, Czechia

Benchmark Quality Assurance

Zsófia Ádám	BUTE, Budapest, Hungary
Raphaël Monat	Inria and University of Lille, France
Simmo Saan	University of Tartu, Estonia
Frank Schüssele	University of Freiburg, Germany

Benchmark Categories

Thomas Lemberger	LMU Munich, Germany

Infrastructure

Philipp Wendler	LMU Munich, Germany (BenchExec)
Po-Chun Chien	LMU Munich, Germany (BenchCloud)
Marek Jankola	LMU Munich, Germany (BenchCloud)
Henrik Wachowitz	LMU Munich, Germany (FM-Weck)
Matthias Kettl	LMU Munich, Germany (Competition Scripts)
Marian Lingsch-Rosenfeld	LMU Munich, Germany (WitnessLint)

Reproducibility

Levente Bajczi   BUTE, Budapest, Hungary

SV-COMP Program Committee and Jury

Dirk Beyer (Co-chair)	LMU Munich, Germany
Jan Strejček (Co-chair)	Masaryk University, Czechia
Zsófia Ádám	BUTE, Budapest, Hungary
Paulína Ayaziová	Masaryk University, Czechia
Levente Bajczi	BUTE, Budapest, Hungary
Manuel Bentele	University of Freiburg, Germany
Martin Blicha	University of Lugano, Switzerland
Lei Bu	Nanjing University, China
Marek Chalupa	ISTA, Austria
Zhenbang Chen	National University of Defense Technology, China
Po-Chun Chien	LMU Munich, Germany
Tomáš Dacík	Brno University of Technology, Czechia
Priyanka Darke	Tata Consulting Services, India
Daniel Dietsch	University of Freiburg, Germany
Marcel Ebbinghaus	University of Freiburg, Germany
Gidon Ernst	LMU Munich, Germany
Fei He	Tsinghua University, China
Matthias Heizmann	University of Freiburg, Germany
Falk Howar	TU Dortmund, Germany
Soha Hussein	Ain Shams University, Egypt
Martin Jonáš	Masaryk University, Czechia
Dominik Klumpp	University of Freiburg, Germany
Marian Lingsch-Rosenfeld	LMU Munich, Germany
Nils Lommen	RWTH Aachen, Germany
Nils Loose	University of Luebeck, Germany
Viktor Malík	Brno University of Technology, Czechia
Ravindra Metta	Tata Consulting Services, India
Raphaël Monat	Inria and University of Lille, France
Hernán Ponce de León	Huawei Dresden Research Center, Germany
Matthew Richards	University of New South Wales, Australia
Simmo Saan	University of Tartu, Estonia
Peter Schrammel	Diffblue Ltd., UK
Frank Schüssele	University of Freiburg, Germany
Vesal Vojdani	University of Tartu, Estonia

Henrik Wachowitz   LMU Munich, Germany
Tong Wu   University of Manchester, UK

TACAS Steering Committee

Dirk Beyer   LMU Munich, Germany
Dana Fisman   Ben-Gurion University, Israel
Holger Hermanns   Universität des Saarlandes, Germany
Joost-Pieter Katoen (Chair)   RWTH Aachen/Universiteit Twente,
                                      Germany/Netherlands
Kim G. Larsen   Aalborg University, Denmark
Corina Păsăreanu   NASA Ames, USA

Additional Reviewers

Abou El Wafa, Noah   Fesefeldt, Ira
Anand, Ashwani   Fleury, Mathias
Ang, Zhendong   Frankel, Guy
Antal, László   Frenkel, Eden
Arceri, Vincenzo   Frohn, Florian
Assolini, Nicola   Froleyks, Nils
Baier, Daniel   Gamboa Guzman, Laura P.
Banerjee, Subarno   Garagiola, Nazareno
Bassan, Shahaf   Gehnen, Christina
Berthon, Raphaël   Geng, Chuqin
Blicha, Martin   Gerlach, Carolina
Bork, Alexander   Gozzi, Riccardo
Bovy, Eline   Gstrein, Bernhard
Brand, Sebastiaan   Hamza, Ameer
Britikov, Konstantin   Hansen, Jonas
Butte, Julia   Haring, Johannes
Campion, Marco   Heemstra, Jan
Cano, Filip   Heim, Philippe
Chen, Xin   Holík, Lukáš
Dacík, Tomáš   Hsu, Tzu-Han
Dalleiger, Sebastian   Iosif, Radu
Dengler, Gabriel   Isac, Omri
Dewes, Rafael   Jankola, Marek
Elad, Neta   Johannsen, Chris
Elboher, Yizhak   Kabra, Aditi
Eshghie, Mojtaba   Katis, Andreas
Fazekas, Katalin   Kettl, Matthias

Klinkenberg, Lutz
Kløvstad, Åsmund Aqissiaq Arild
Kobialka, Paul
Koenighofer, Bettina
Kolárik, Tomáš
Kovács, József
Krogmeier, Paul
Köhl, Maximilian Alexander
Labbaf, Faezeh
Larraz, Daniel
Laurent, Jonathan
Lemberger, Thomas
Lengal, Ondrej
Li, Yixuan
Li, Zhiyang
Lingsch-Rosenfeld, Marian
Lorch, Robert
Lotan, Raz
Luque Cerpa, Alejandro
Maderbacher, Benedikt
Malík, Viktor
Miao, Mingkai
Nalbach, Jasper
Nayak, Satya Prakash
Negrini, Luca
Noll, Thomas
Novozhilov, Sergei
Otoni, Rodrigo
Panja, Promit
Patault, Paul
Perez-Lopez, Áron Ricardo
Pertseva, Elizaveta
Pferscher, Andrea
Pinto, Alessandro
Pollitt, Florian
Pranger, Stefan
Preiner, Mathias
Promies, Valentin
Päßler, Juliane
Pîrlea, George
Qian, Long
Quatmann, Tim
Rafieioskouei, Arshia
Raha, Ritam
Refaeli, Idan

Reynolds, Andrew
Riley, Daniel
Rogalewicz, Adam
Rosentrater, Alec
Saglam, Irmak
Sangnier, Arnaud
Saveri, Gaia
Schlatte, Rudolf
Schlichtkrull, Anders
Schmidt, Andreas
Schreiber, Dominik
Schurr, Hans-Jörg
Shankar, Raghav
Sierra, Sebastian
Silvetti, Simone
Skurka, Antonina
Sogokon, Andrew
Soldevila, Mallku
Sun, Yutao
Tan, Grace
Tappler, Martin
Trtík, Marek
Tschaikowski, Max
Tsiskaridze, Nestan
Vaandrager, Frits
van den Haak, Lars B.
van der Vegt, Marck
Varanasi, Sarat Chandra
Wachowitz, Henrik
Wang, Zhongyi
Wang, Zili
Wendler, Philipp
Winkler, Tobias
Wu, Min
Yang, Jiong
Yang, Mingqi
Ye, Leiqi
Yu, Hengzhi
Zavalia, Lucas
Zhang, David
Zhao, Huan
Zhou, Xiaqing
Zimmer, Dominic
Zimmermann, Martin

Contents – Part I

LTL

Verification 1

Contents – Part II

Equivalence Checking

Games

Contents – Part III

14th Competition on Software Verification (SV-COMP 2025)

Program Analysis

On Stability in a Happens-Before Propagator for Concurrent Programs (Reproducibility Study)

Levente Bajczi[✉][ID], Csanád Telbisz[ID], Dániel Szekeres[ID], and András Vörös[ID]

Department of Artifical Intelligence and Systems Engineering,
Budapest University of Technology and Economics, Budapest, Hungary
{bajczi,vori}@mit.bme.hu

Abstract. Analyzing concurrent programs often involves reasoning about happens-before relations, handled by dedicated SMT theory solvers. Recently, preventative propagation rules have been introduced for consistency models to avoid unnecessary computations. This paper analyses the reproducibility of a recently published paper regarding a conflict-avoiding happens-before propagator. We show that the underlying axioms are insufficient for supporting sequential consistency. We find that the algorithm can leave out constraints on event ordering (even considering the original axioms), impacting the accuracy of verification. We show a simple counterexample to the stability claim in the paper. Two revisions of the algorithm are presented, and a proof on the correctness of these approaches respective of the original axioms is shown. The tool implementing the original algorithm is examined to ascertain how it circumvents wrong results. It is found that it deviates from the published algorithm. We show that an unmodified algorithm (via a patch in the implementing tool) causes incorrect results. We also show that our revised algorithm can be implemented efficiently in an independent verification tool.

Keywords: verification · formal methods · software verification

1 Introduction

DEAGLE [1,2] won the error-reachability-based CONCURRENCYSAFETY category of the software verification competition SV-COMP for two consecutive years in 2022 [3] and 2023 [4]. This has motivated us to research the underlying algorithms in detail, in hopes of implementing (and hopefully, improving) the state-of-the-art techniques that led DEAGLE to victory. One aspect of the algorithm found in DEAGLE is the consistency-preserving propagation of happens-before orders [5].

This research was partially funded by the EKÖP-24-{2,3} New National Excellence Program under project numbers EKÖP-24-2-BME-118, EKÖP-24-3-BME-213 and EKÖP-24-3-BME-159, and the Doctoral Excellence Fellowship Programme under project numbers 400434/2023, 400443/2023; funded by the NRDI Fund of Hungary. This work was partially supported by project no. 2022-1.2.4-EUREKA-2023-00013 under the 2022-1.2.4 EUREKA funding scheme from the the National Research, Development and Innovation Fund of Hungary.

A. Gurfinkel and M. Heule (Eds.): TACAS 2025, LNCS 15696, pp. 3–19, 2025.
https://doi.org/10.1007/978-3-031-90643-5_1

However, we found our implementation of the published algorithm faulty, yet DEAGLE produced no wrong results in 2022, and only one incorrect result in 2023. Therefore, we constructed a *reproducibility study* in hopes of uncovering the reason for this discrepancy. Our contributions in this paper concerning the reproducibility of the published results are the following:

- We analyze the published algorithm theoretically, and provide a counterexample to its *stability* claim (see Section 3), and dispute its applicability for *sequential consistency (SC)* (see Section 3.4)
- We propose two ways of fixing the algorithm, and prove the *stability* claim for both (see Section 4)
- We formulate actionable research questions to validate the applicability of the proposed approach(es) compared to the previous state of the art (see Section 5)
- We devise and implement experiments to answer the research questions (see Section 5.1)
- We evaluate the experimental data and answer the research questions, thus also providing an answer to the *reproducibility* premise of our paper (see Section 5.2, while also discussing the threats to the validity of our results (see Section 5.3)

We hope that our contributions and insights in this paper will save potential tool developers from experiencing the same contrariety between theory and practice, thus being able to build better-performing competing verification tools.

2   Happens-Before Relations in Concurrent Software

The formal verification of concurrent software is often reduced to reasoning about *happens-before* relations [6,7] (defined as a partial order on program instructions), utilized by many Satisfiability Modulo Theories (SMT) based verification tools both for strictly sequential, as well as weak memory software-hardware systems [8,9,5]. In most cases, either a dedicated theory solver, or an encoding to a pre-existing theory (supported by the underlying SMT solver backend) is applied.

The idea behind these techniques is the following. Instead of applying the semantics of asynchronous concurrency directly (i.e., any of the threads may advance from a state of the program, therefore we must analyze all possible orders), we treat global memory accesses as *events*, for which we must find a (partially defined) sequence they can be ordered in. Suitable orders are *consistent* with the execution semantics of the platform. Then, we pair *read* events to *write* events, which we call the *read-from* (rf) relation, meaning the *read* event returned the value written by the *write* event. Furthermore, we employ conventional analyses to explore the state space of the individual threads, treating *reads* as reading values from their *rf*-paired *write* accesses.

Because values returned by these *read* accesses might be used in guards of conditional statements, and in turn, the accesses to encode as events depend on the execution of these conditionals, one cannot completely separate the event graph and local analyses. However, in the context of this work, we presume that the local analyses already rely on SMT solvers, that can be utilized to handle the events and their relations. Some approaches encode this in a theory supported by the SMT solver [10], and others rely on custom theory solvers integrated with the SMT engine [8,9,5].

2.1 Consistency-Preserving Propagation

Satisfiability Modulo Theories (SMT) is the problem of deciding whether a value assignment to symbols exists that satisfies a first-order formula within formal *theories* [11]. SMT solvers utilize *theory solver* backends to handle the different supported theories (such as real numbers, integers, or arrays), and recently, even user-defined theory solvers (*user propagators*) have become possible to implement [12]. Generally, a dedicated theory solver must implement three procedures [11]:

- *Propagation*: Given a set of facts, derive consequences and add them to the set of known facts
- *Consistency checking*: Decide whether a certain set of facts are consistent with the background theory
- *Conflict clause generation*: If a set of facts is *inconsistent* with the background theory, determine which (minimal) subset is responsible for the inconsistency.

However, *Sun et al.* recently developed a framework of *preventative* propagation rules for sequential consistency that always result in consistent models, and thus, there is no need for either *consistency checking* or *conflict clause generation* [5]. This novel approach greatly boosts verification performance due to the decreased need for backtracking in the solver.

Unfortunately, part of the published algorithm contains an oversight, which results in missing crucial constraints on the event ordering (in case of certain sequences of decisions in the solver backend). We aim to revise this algorithm, and discuss its influence on the overall performance of the algorithm.

3 Instability in Propagation

In this paper, program verification based on event propagation assumes a loop-free program in concurrent static single assignment (CSSA) form [13], and an error property ρ_{error} (e.g., a designated "bad" program location, or some variable valuation representing an erroneous state) [5].

In this section, we start by summarizing the work of Sun et al. [5]. This work is not our contribution to claim, and for a more contextualized explanation, we direct the Reader to the original paper [5]. Here we introduce the core concepts and notations, which are necessary for understanding our contributions in later sections.

3.1 Value Encoding in SMT

First, we encode the value assignments of the program in the formula ρ_{va} by taking each *write* access with its accompanying *guard* (i.e., its enabling condition; the conjunction of all decisions the program must have taken in order for the event to execute). Given a guard grd_{w_i}, and assuming w_i sets variable v_i with CSSA index k to $expr_i$, then $grd_{w_i} \Rightarrow v_i^k = expr_i$. Consequently, ρ_{va} is the conjunction of all such implications.

Similarly, we must encode the *read* accesses in the program. Because the value of the *read* operations depend on their *rf*-paired *write* operation, we introduce a boolean variable rf_{ij} for each same-address events w_i and r_j. Then, if rf_{ij} is *true*, we know that $v_i = v_j$, grd_{w_i}, and grd_{r_j} hold. To encode all *reads*, ρ_{rf-val} [9] is the conjunction of all $rf_{ij} \Rightarrow grd_{w_i} \wedge grd_{r_j} \wedge v_i = v_j$. Furthermore, because all *reads* must be paired with a *write*, we know that if a grd_{r_i} holds, then $\exists j.rf_{ij}$. We encode this in $\rho_{rf-some}$ [9].

3.2 Ordering Constraint Encoding

Furthermore, we must encode the *ordering constraints* of the program. Due to causality, all *read* operations paired with a *write* operation must happen after the associated *write* operation (this is the *rf*-ordering set $\prec_{rf}$, a subset of the happens-before ordering set $\prec$). For sequential consistency, all *program order* (i.e., the actual instruction order in the program source) constraints are preserved, and are thus added to $\prec$ as ρ_{ppo}. For both of these sets, we use the same notation as a predicate, meaning $i \prec j := (i,j) \in \prec$. We also encode the relationship that $\forall (i,j).i \prec_{rf} j \iff rf_{ij}$ as ρ_{rf-ord}.

3.3 Decision Procedure

We must decide if $\rho_{va} \wedge \rho_{error} \wedge \rho_{rf-val} \wedge \rho_{rf-some} \wedge \rho_{rf-ord} \wedge \rho_{ppo}$ is satisfiable. If yes, we return the resulting model as the *counterexample* to the original problem. If not, we have proven the safety of the program.

This satisfiability check will need to check whether any candidate model would result in a cycle being formed in the transitive closure of the $\prec$ relation. Because all elements of $\prec$ denote a *happens-before* relation, this would mean that an element precedes itself, which is impossible, thus rendering the candidate inconsistent. To achieve this, we can implement a *propagation* module for the SMT solver, which will be called every time the decision procedure fixes a value for a given expression that influences the ordering sets. For us, these expressions will either be the rf_{ij} variables, or the guard expressions grd_k. We then perform *derivation* on the current elements of $\prec$ and $\prec_{rf}$ by applying the following axioms:

1. *transitivity* axiom: $(e_1 \prec e_2) \wedge (e_2 \prec e_3) \Rightarrow (e_1 \prec e_3)$
2. *from-read* axiom [9] for same-address events:
   $(w_1 \prec_{rf} r) \wedge (w_1 \prec w_2) \wedge grd_{w_2} \Rightarrow (r \prec w_2)$

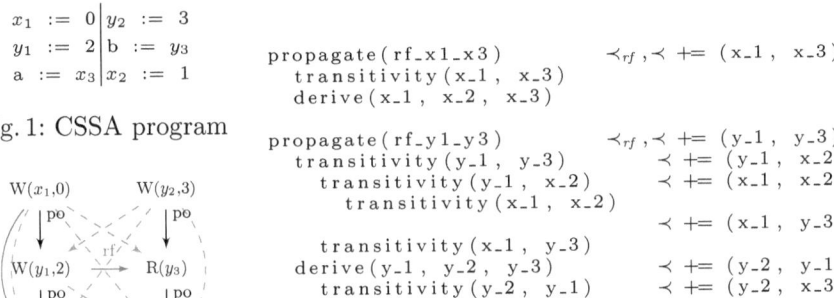

$$x_1 := 0 \mid y_2 := 3$$
$$y_1 := 2 \mid b := y_3$$
$$a := x_3 \mid x_2 := 1$$

Fig. 1: CSSA program

```
propagate ( rf_x1_x3 )                    ≺_rf , ≺ += ( x_1 ,  x_3 )
  transitivity ( x_1 ,   x_3 )
  derive ( x_1 ,   x_2 ,   x_3 )

propagate ( rf_y1_y3 )                     ≺_rf , ≺ += ( y_1 ,   y_3 )
  transitivity ( y_1 ,   y_3 )                   ≺ += ( y_1 ,   x_2 )
  transitivity ( y_1 ,   x_2 )                   ≺ += ( x_1 ,   x_2 )
  transitivity ( x_1 ,   x_2 )
                                                 ≺ += ( x_1 ,   y_3 )
  transitivity ( x_1 ,   y_3 )
  derive ( y_1 ,   y_2 ,   y_3 )                 ≺ += ( y_2 ,   y_1 )
  transitivity ( y_2 ,   y_1 )                   ≺ += ( y_2 ,   x_3 )
  transitivity ( y_2 ,   x_3 )
```

Fig. 3: A trace of Algorithm 1 over Figure 1

Fig. 2: Final $\prec$, $\prec_{rf}$

3. *write-serialization* axiom [5] for same-address events:

$$(w_1 \prec_{rf} r) \wedge (w_2 \prec r) \wedge grd_{w_2} \Rightarrow (w_2 \prec w_1)$$

The algorithm for propagation is shown in Algorithm 1, taken from *Sun et al.'s Algorithm 2: Theory Propagation*[1] [5]. Then, either conventional consistency checking and conflict clause generation follows, or the *preventative reasoning* step introduced by *Sun et al.* [5]. The claim these solutions build upon is that after propagation, $\prec$ is *stable*, i.e., it contains all elements derivable by applying theory axioms. Using the example CSSA program in Figure 1 and the accompanying trace in Figure 3, we show a counterexample to this claim: x_3 and x_2 are not ordered in $\prec$ as shown in Figure 2, therefore any order may be taken. However, because $x_1 \prec_{rf} x_3$ and $x_1 \prec x_2$, Axiom 2 would order x_2 after x_3, yet this is not encoded in $\prec$. Therefore, we conclude that the state of $\prec$ is *not* always stable after propagation. This may (and will) lead to incorrect results.

3.4   Happens-Before Orders for Sequential Consistency

In this paper, we use the same axioms as *Sun et al.* [5] for the ordering constraints, and thus, for the happens-before order propagation. However, we must discuss the applicability of said axioms on *Sequential Consistency*, the most strict memory model targeted in the original paper (besides its relaxed versions *Total Store Ordering (TSO)* and *Partial Store Ordering (PSO))*.

Consider the happens-before graph (including rf, po, and generic $\prec$ relations) in Figure 4:

- We cannot apply the *transitivity* axiom any further, because all such relations have already been discovered (shown in gray).

---

[1] There are some typos in the original paper's Algorithm 2: in lines 31-33, e should be e'. These are minor mistakes and are fixed here.

Algorithm 1 Original Theory Propagation Algorithm [5], with typos fixed

Input: l: Positive literal
1: **proc** PROPAGATE(l)
2:     **if** l is rf_{ij} **then**
3:         $w_i, r_j :=$ write and read of rf_{ij}
4:         $\prec_{rf} \leftarrow \prec_{rf} \cup \{(w_i, r_j)\}$
5:         $\prec \leftarrow \prec \cup \{(w_i, r_j)\}$
6:         TRANSITIVITY(w_i, r_j)
7:         **foreach** w_k s.t. grd_k **do**
8:             **if** (w_i, w_k, r_j) same-addr. **then**
9:                 DERIVE(w_i, w_k, r_j)
10:             **end if**
11:         **end foreach**
12:     **else if** l is grd_k **then**
13:         $w_k :=$ write of grd_k
14:         **foreach** $(w_i, r_i) \in \prec_{rf}$ **do**
15:             **if** (w_i, w_k, r_j) same-addr. **then**
16:                 DERIVE(w_i, w_k, r_j)
17:             **end if**
18:         **end foreach**
19:     **end if**
20: **end proc**

Input: w_i, w_k, r_j: $w_i \prec_{rf} r_j, grd_k$
1: **proc** DERIVE(w_i, w_k, r_j)
2:     **if** $w_k \prec r_j$ **then**
3:         $\prec \leftarrow \prec \cup \{(w_k, w_i)\}$
4:         TRANSITIVITY(w_k, w_i)
5:     **else if** $w_i \prec w_k$ **then**
6:         $\prec \leftarrow \prec \cup \{(r_j, w_k)\}$
7:         TRANSITIVITY(r_j, w_k)
8:     **end if**
9: **end proc**

Input: e_1, e_2: $e_1 \prec e_2$
1: **proc** TRANSITIVITY(e_1, e_2)
2:     **foreach** $(e_2, e_3) \in \prec$ **do**
3:         **if** $(e_1, e_3) \notin \prec$ **then**
4:             $\prec \leftarrow \prec \cup \{(e_1, e_3)\}$
5:             TRANSITIVITY(e_1, e_3)
6:         **end if**
7:     **end foreach**
8:     **foreach** $(e_0, e_1) \in \prec$ **do**
9:         **if** $(e_0, e_2) \notin \prec$ **then**
10:             $\prec \leftarrow \prec \cup \{(e_0, e_2)\}$
11:             TRANSITIVITY(e_0, e_2)
12:         **end if**
13:     **end foreach**
14: **end proc**

- We cannot apply the *from-read* axiom, because that would require an *rf*-edge beginning with a *write* that has a successor *write* with the same address, and no such pair exists.
- We cannot apply the *write-serialization* axiom either, because that would require an *rf*-edge ending with a *read* that has a predecessor *write* with the same address, and no such pair exists.

Therefore, according to the axioms, we are finished with deriving happens-before relations, and as we found no cycles, the execution is deemed *allowed*. However, adding *any* order between the writes to z (shown in **bold**) makes a cycle (via the *reads* to z in the last two threads, when all axioms are applied again after adding either order between the writes), and therefore, this execution is not actually allowed over SC. Therefore, we conclude that the axioms are not

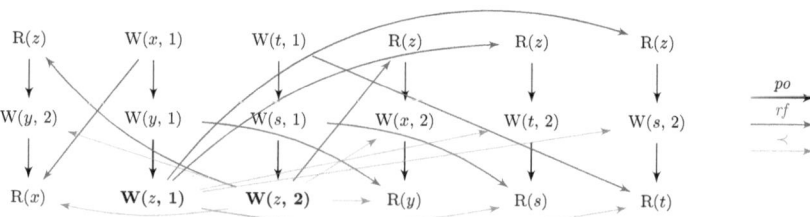

Fig. 4: Counterexample for the applicability of *Sun et al.*'s axioms [5] for Sequential Consistency (SC). Example taken from [14], Fig. 1c.

suitable for determining SC-consistency. Therefore, in this paper, we cannot claim we verify SC concurrency, but rather, a somewhat weaker memory model, called *Weak Sequential Consistency* [14].

Fixing this issue can be done post-propagation, by trying to serialize all writes in the program, and reporting the execution *inconsistent* with SC if this cannot be done. However, this scales exponentially with the number of same-variable writes, which we expect, as the problem (VSC-Read) is NP-complete [15][2]. Therefore, we exclude this fix from our solution proposals in Section 4, and focus on satisfying the axioms as they are written by *Sun et al.* [5], and show they are still not fulfilled.

4   Fixing Stability of the Propagation

To fix the stability problems of $\prec$ after the propagation step, we propose two solutions:

Retrospective approach We repeat PROPAGATE in Algorithm 1 until its applications of all axioms no longer produce new relations.

Prospective approach We patch Algorithm 1 to disallow non-stable $\prec$ outputs by analyzing and fixing its procedures, thus achieving stability by construction.

4.1   Fixing Stability Retrospectively

In order to achieve *stability*, i.e., a state of $\prec$ where the theory axioms can no longer add new relations, the simplest method is to apply this definition directly by wrapping PROPAGATE in the procedure in Algorithm 2. Because this will not return until $\prec$ stops changing, we can be sure that all axioms are fully applied and therefore, stability is achieved. However, as evident from Algorithm 2, this comes at the price of complexity: we need to iterate over $\prec$ and $\prec_{rf}$ repeatedly.

4.2   Fixing Stability Prospectively

To avoid the expensive option of fixing stability retrospectively, the alternative is to fix it *prospectively*, i.e., by applying the axioms only on recent additions to the orders. This was also the goal of *Sun et al.* [5], and hence Algorithm 1 needs only some minor modifications to realize this.

The main problem with Algorithm 1 is that DERIVE is not re-called even though the conditions $w_k \prec r_j$ and $w_i \prec w_k$ may change during later calls to any of the procedures when new elements are added to $\prec$. Therefore, as shown in Figure 3, when DERIVE is first called with $(w_i, w_k, r_j) = (x_1, x_2, x_3)$, it checks whether $w_k \prec r_j$ (which is false with $x_2 \prec x_3$), and $w_i \prec w_k$ (which is also false

---

[2] Note: the originally published algorithm is polynomial (every edge is added at most once to the event graph) [5], and therefore, cannot be the solution to this problem.

Algorithm 2 Retrospective algorithm

Input: l: Positive literal
1: **proc** PROPAGATEWRAPPER(l)
2:     PROPAGATE(l)
3:     **while** $\prec$ not fix **do**
4:         **foreach** $(e_1, e_2) \in \prec$ **do**
5:             TRANSITIVITY(e_1, e_2) // Axiom 1
6:         **end foreach**
7:         **foreach** $(w_i, r_j) \in \prec_{rf}$ **do**
8:             **foreach** w_k *s.t.* grd_k **do**
9:                 **if** (w_i, w_k, r_j) same-addr. **then**
10:                     DERIVE(w_i, w_k, r_j) // Axiom 2, 3
11:                 **end if**
12:             **end foreach**
13:         **end foreach**
14:     **end while**
15: **end proc**

---

with $x_1 \prec x_2$), then returns without adding anything to the order. Later, when propagating $rf_{y_1 y_3}$, during the call to TRANSITIVITY(y_1, x_2), the pair (x_1, x_2) is added to $\prec$, making the else if condition retroactively true for the DERIVE call above, but it is never checked again. Thus, $x_3 \prec x_2$ is missed, $\prec$ is unstable, and we mistakenly allow some executions that would never be observable on the execution platform.

To fix this issue, one solution is to re-call DERIVE every time a new relation is added to $\prec$ that could influence the conditions therein. This means that all same-address (w_k, r_j) and (w_i, w_k) relations are subject to this rule, for all previously checked triples (w_i, w_k, r_j). Because we know that DERIVE is only ever called with same-address events for which $w_i \prec_{rf} r_j$ also holds, we already have access to the set of already checked triples. Therefore we introduce a helper procedure, ADDTOORDER, and change Algorithm 1 to always call this procedure instead, when any other procedure adds a new element to $\prec$. The updated algorithm can be seen in Algorithm 3. Notice that checking the nonexistence of the new pair in $\prec$ is also included in ADDTOORDER, leading to it no longer being necessary in other procedures.

Theorem 1. *After executing Algorithm 3 with any l positive literal, then given $\prec$ is stable, $\prec$ remains stable.*

To prove stability, we must show that all three axioms are fully applied to $\prec$ when PROPAGATE returns.

Lemma 1. *Axiom 1 is fully applied (may no longer be used to derive new relations) when PROPAGATE returns.*

Proof. The full application of Axiom 1 is always given, as after every addition to $\prec$ (line 3), the procedure TRANSITIVITY is called, which adds all events that

Algorithm 3 Revised Theory Propagation Algorithm

Input: l: Positive literal
1: **proc** PROPAGATE(l)
2:    **if** l is rf_{ij} **then**
3:        $w_i, r_j :=$ write and read of rf_{ij}
4:        $\prec_{rf} \leftarrow \prec_{rf} \cup \{(w_i, r_j)\}$
5:        ADDTOORDER(w_i, r_j)
6:        **foreach** w_k s.t. grd_k **do**
7:            **if** (w_i, w_k, r_j) same-addr. **then**
8:                DERIVE(w_i, w_k, r_j)
9:            **end if**
10:        **end foreach**
11:    **else if** l is grd_k **then**
12:        $w_k :=$ write of grd_k
13:        **foreach** $(w_i, r_i) \in \prec_{rf}$ **do**
14:            **if** (w_i, w_k, r_j) same-addr. **then**
15:                DERIVE(w_i, w_k, r_j)
16:            **end if**
17:        **end foreach**
18:    **end if**
19: **end proc**

Input: e_1, e_2: Events
1: **proc** ADDTOORDER(e_1, e_2)
2:    **if** $(e_1, e_2) \notin \prec$ **then**
3:        $\prec \leftarrow \prec \cup \{(e_1, e_2)\}$
4:        TRANSITIVITY(e_1, e_2)
5:        **if** (e_1, e_2) same-addr. **then**
6:            **if** e_1 is write, e_2 is read **then**
7:                **foreach** $(w, e_2) \in \prec_{rf}$ **do**
8:                    DERIVE(w, e_1, e_2)
9:                **end foreach**
10:            **else if** e_1 is write, e_2 is write **then**
11:                **foreach** $(e_1, r) \in \prec_{rf}$ **do**
12:                    DERIVE(e_1, e_2, r)
13:                **end foreach**
14:            **end if**
15:        **end if**
16:    **end if**
17: **end proc**

Input: w_i, w_k, r_j: $w_i \prec_{rf} r_j, grd_k$
1: **proc** DERIVE(w_i, w_k, r_j)
2:    **if** $w_k \prec r_j$ **then**
3:        ADDTOORDER(w_k, w_i)
4:    **end if**
5:    **if** $w_i \prec w_k$ **then**
6:        ADDTOORDER(r_j, w_k)
7:    **end if**
8: **end proc**

Input: e_1, e_2: $e_1 \prec e_2$
1: **proc** TRANSITIVITY(e_1, e_2)
2:    **foreach** $(e_2, e_3) \in \prec$ **do**
3:        ADDTOORDER(e_1, e_3)
4:    **end foreach**
5:    **foreach** $(e_0, e_1) \in \prec$ **do**
6:        ADDTOORDER(e_0, e_2)
7:    **end foreach**
8: **end proc**

are $\prec$-before the first event as being $\prec$-before the second element as well; and events $\prec$-after the second event as being $\prec$-after the first element as well. This is the definition of Axiom 1.

Lemma 2. *Axiom 2 and Axiom 3 are fully applied (may no longer be used to derive new relations) when* PROPAGATE *returns.*

Proof. Axiom 2 as per its definition can derive new elements of $\prec$ when either grd_k becomes *true*, or a new same-address *write-write* pair is added to $\prec$, or a new pair is added to $\prec_{rf}$. In addition, Axiom 3 can also derive new elements when a new same-address *write-read* pair is added to $\prec$. Therefore, when:

1. grd_k becomes *true*, we must examine all $w \prec_{rf} r$ elements for which the premise of Axiom 2 may hold with w_k, i.e., $w \prec w_k$. Therefore, DERIVE(w, w_k, r) is called with all $(w, r) \in \prec_{rf}$ (line 15 in PROPAGATE), and checks whether $w \prec w_k$ holds (line 5), after which it adds the new derived element (r, w_k) to $\prec$;

2. a new same-address *write-write* pair (w_1, w_2) is added to $\prec$, we must examine all $w_1 \prec_{rf} r$ pairs. We know grd_{w_2} holds because it could not have been added to $\prec$ otherwise, so we call DERIVE(w_1, w_2, r) (in line 12 of ADDTOORDER), which, because $w_1 \prec w_2$ (in line 5), adds (r, w_2) to $\prec$;

3. a new same-address *write-read* pair (w, r) is added to $\prec$, we must examine all such $w_2 \prec_{rf} r_2$ pairs where r is r_2. We know grd_{w_2} holds because it could

not have been added to $\prec_{rf}$ otherwise, so we call DERIVE(w_2, w, r) (in line 8 of ADDTOORDER), which, because $w \prec r$ (in line 2), adds (w, w_2) to $\prec$;

4. a new pair (w, r) is added to $\prec_{rf}$, we must examine all same-address *write-write* (w_1, w_2) (for Axiom 2, where w_1 is w) and *write-read* (w_2, r_2) (for Axiom 3, where r_2 is r) pairs in $\prec$. In both cases, grd_{w_2} must hold. Therefore, we must look at all guard-enabled same-address *writes*, and call DERIVE(w, w_2, r) (in line 8 of PROPAGATE), which will add both the consequence of Axiom 2 (in line 6), and the consequence of Axiom 3 (in line 3), given their premises are fulfilled (lines 5 and 2, respectively)[3].

Because for every possible change in the terms of the premises of Axiom 2 and Axiom 3 the premises are checked and the consequences are applied, both axioms are fully applied.

5   Empirical Evaluation

In order to determine the performance impact and efficacy of the two proposed solutions, we formulated the following experimental research questions:

ERQ1 How does the performance change among the original, the retrospective, and the prospective algorithm in an isolated, *clean* implementation?

ERQ2 How does the practical implementation in the tool corresponding to the original *Sun et al.* publication [5] (DEAGLE) circumvent *false* results, given the theoretical issue with Algorithm 1?

ERQ3 How does the performance and efficacy of the revised algorithms (both the prospective and the retrospective) transfer to another verification tool (THETA [16])?

ERQ4 How does the performance change among the retrospective and the prospective algorithm when integrated in a model checking tool?

Additionally, we formulate the premise of our paper as a research question:

RQ Is the stability claim by *Sun et al.* [5] supported theoretically, and reproducible in practice?

5.1   Experimental Setup

We used the CONCURRENCYSAFETY-MAIN category of SV-COMP [4] to measure verification performance throughout the experiments. We relied on BENCHEXEC [17] to provide accurate and reproducible performance measurements.

---

[3] In the original algorithm presented in Algorithm 1, the check for Axiom 2 and Axiom 3 were mutually exclusive in DERIVE. We believe this is faulty, and have therefore changed it here.

Isolated Implementation We transformed a simple (i.e., pointerless and arrayless) subset of the SV-COMP CONCURRENCYSAFETY-MAIN category's tasks into the CSSA form suitable for the algorithms above, with an unrolling bound of 2. Then, we used the original algorithm (in Algorithm 1) to generate a consistent rf-assignment for each task. We then replayed the order of rf-assignments in the two algorithms proposed in Section 4. We measured time, and the size of $\prec$ after propagation. There were 22 tasks where there was a discrepancy in the size of $\prec$ among the original and the two revised algorithms (on average, 6.9%), in which cases more traces are thought to be possible than in reality, possibly leading to false unsafe verdicts (see Figure 1). The two revised algorithms always produced the same size $\prec$, as expected, empirically supporting the soundness proof in Section 4.2. In these 22 instances, the performance of the three algorithms is visible in Figure 5. We can see that the retrospective solution is much slower than the original (on average, by 240%), and that the prospective approach is consistently a bit slower (on average, by 16%).

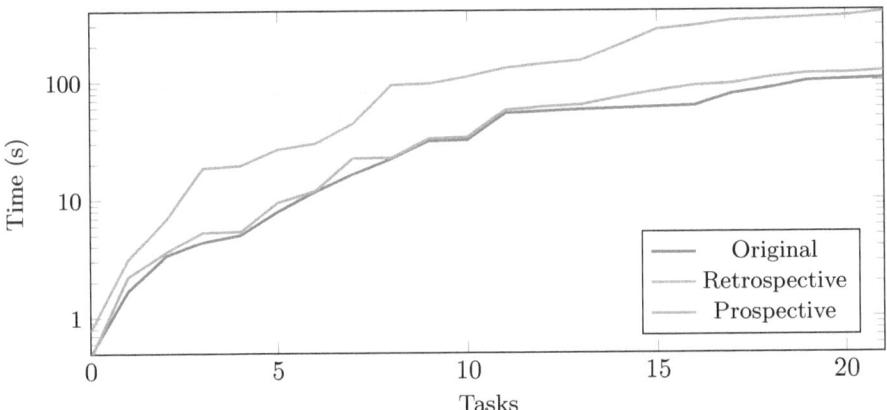

Fig. 5: Quantile plot of execution times for the isolated implementation

Implementation in Deagle We used the publicly available source code of DEAGLE[4] for this part of the experimental evaluation. We also ran our experiments with the SV-COMP'24 binary release [2]. We used 900 seconds of timeout in the experiments.

We used the entire CONCURRENCYSAFETY-MAIN category of SV-COMP with 713 tasks. The results can be seen in Figure 6, showing a verdict-based comparison.

We first ran our experiments with the binary release [2] and an unmodified version of the source code. We found that the binary release solved marginally

---

[4] https://github.com/thufv/Deagle/commit/19e267151cca620cb1d24bc109a451b8a0e617f8

fewer tasks, but produced *no incorrect verdicts*. However, the source release solved marginally more tasks, but produced 14 incorrect verdicts. We compared the logs of these two configurations, and found the lines "USE SV-COMP UN-WINDING STRATEGY: X" differ between the two configurations, varying between 2 and 100. This leads us to believe that there is a discrepancy in the way the unwinding strategy is selected between the two versions, which leads to the slight difference in solved tasks and can cause false results, because DEAGLE accepts a bounded proof of safety as an overall safety proof. There is one notable exception, PTHREAD-RACE-CHALLENGES/THREAD-LOCAL-VALUE.YML, which is correctly determined to be *safe* by the binary version with 5 unwindings, but incorrectly classified as *unsafe* by the source version with 2 unwindings. This means that there may be further differences between the versions.

We examined the source code of DEAGLE to find out how it is possible that with a faulty implementation, there can still exist a version (the binary release) which circumvents all incorrect results. We found that in the CLOSURE-SOLVER.CC file there is a ONE_MORE_TIME flag in the PROPAGATE() function[5] that checks for newly added edges, and recursively calls PROPAGATE again, until a fixpoint (no new edges) is reached. This closely resembles what we call the *retrospective* approach.

Because this is not aligned with the algorithm of the original publication, we removed this flag. Besides this flag, we found no other meaningful difference between the published algorithm and the source. We ran the experiments with this version as well, and its results are included in Figure 6. A lot of tasks run afoul of an assertion in this configuration, causing an overall dip in solved tasks, but this is not (directly) the problem of the originally published algorithm, just a side effect. However, even with this smaller sample size, the nominal number of incorrect verdicts still grew: there were 20 tasks that this version solved incorrectly, out of which 14 could still be solved by the source code, unpatched version.

	binary release (retrospective)	source code (retrospective)	patched (original)
correct	**618**	**628**	**236**
true	320	332	165
false	298	296	71
incorrect	**0**	**14**	**20**
true	0	10	4
false	0	4	16

Fig. 6: Verification efficacy of DEAGLE's binary release, source code release, and patched version

---

[5] https://github.com/thufv/Deagle/blob/19e267151cca620cb1d24bc109a451b8a0e617f8/minisat-2.2.1/minisat/core/ClosureSolver.cc#L452

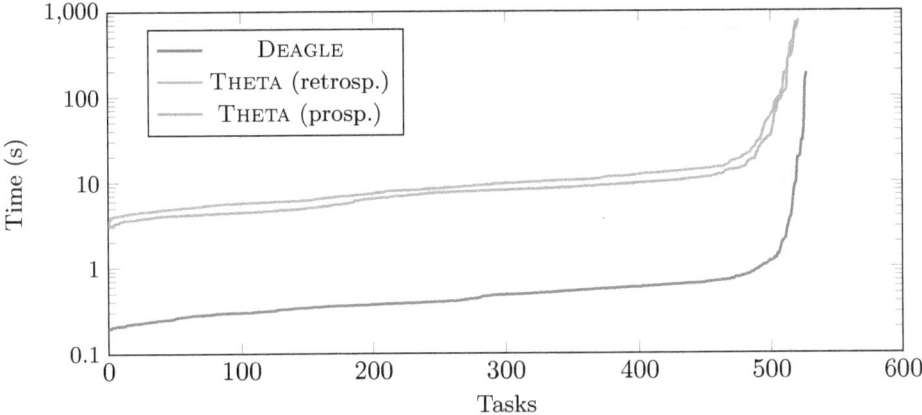

Fig. 7: Quantile plot of execution times for THETA vs. DEAGLE

Implementation in Theta We implemented a version of the prospective, as well as the retrospective algorithm in THETA [16] (as an independent model checker tool). We compare its experimental results with the best performing, source-based, unpatched version of DEAGLE. The results can be seen as a quantile plot in Figure 7. THETA produced 2 wrong results due to insufficient loop unrollings, and DEAGLE produced 14 wrong results, presumably due to similar issues. These verdicts are not included in the quantile plot. Furthermore, THETA does not support certain elements of the C language in its frontend, and therefore we excluded these tasks to preserve a fair comparison.

We can see (in Figure 7) that the two tools produce almost the same number of correct verdicts (528 for DEAGLE and 522/520 for the retrospective/prospective version of THETA), with similar performance characteristics. The offset in performance (in our opinion) is down to THETA being a non-native, JVM-based application, while Deagle is a compiled, native program. We can further see that while the prospective algorithm consistently outperformed the retrospective one, it did so only marginally, and even ended up solving two tasks fewer.

5.2   Evaluation of Experiments

Based on our results reported in Section 5.1, we can answer the three experimental research questions.

ERQ1 As shown in Section 5.1, the original (faulty) algorithm is the fastest, the prospective algorithm is slightly slower (by around 16%), and the retrospective algorithm is much slower (by around 240%).

ERQ2 As shown in Section 5.1, the published algorithm [5] and the implementation in the published source code differ in containing a flag to re-run PROPAGATE() when necessary (akin to our proposed *retrospective* solution). Without this patch, the original algorithm produces (more) wrong results.

ERQ3 The performance and efficacy of the algorithm transfers suitably to independent tools, as shown with our implementation in the THETA model checking framework.

ERQ4 As shown in Figure 7, the prospective algorithm is slightly faster than the retrospective algorithm. The difference is far less pronounced than with the clean, isolated implementation (Section 5.1).

Additionally, we can answer **RQ** as well. The claim that after propagation, the state of the execution graph is *stable*, is not supported theoretically, as shown with our counterexample in Figure 3. In practice, the stability *is* reproducible, but only with a modified algorithm, containing a supporting flag, as uncovered in Section 5.1. Without this patch, the stability after running the algorithm is not guaranteed, and can cause real-life problems, as the newly incorrect verdicts in Section 5.1 showcase.

5.3   Threats to Validity

As one of the main contributions of this paper is the experiment design and its analysis, the factors that threaten the validity of this experiment are presented in this section.

Internal Validity. Consistency and accuracy of the experiments were ensured by using the BenchExec framework [17]. Memory consumption statistics may deviate between executions due to the managed nature of some languages used in developing the tested tools, therefore, such metrics are not used. CPU time and, therefore, solved tasks may be influenced by external factors such as other processes or environmental temperature fluctuations, therefore, minute differences are disregarded.

External Validity. The results of the experiments are at risk of not being generalizable due to the relatively low number of benchmarks used throughout the experiments. Furthermore, we as authors do not have access to the most up-to-date source code of DEAGLE which was used to compile the competition binary. Additionally, we are not familiar with the whole DEAGLE code base, which may mean we missed crucial implementation details in the tool. Also, we were not able to meaningfully circumvent the assertion violation using our patched version when trying to achieve an implementation close to the published one, and therefore, the majority of test cases were excluded in that analysis.

Construct Validity. To justify the type of metrics used in the evaluation of the experiments, we considered the main use cases these tools would face should they be used in the approach described in this paper. Academic competitions such as SV-COMP [4] reflect the performance of tools after careful tuning of them while constantly re-testing on the same benchmark set. Therefore, our results may not be easily reproduced on a different benchmark set.

6 Conclusion and Future Work

In this paper, we have shown that the *Basic algorithm* published by *Sun et al.* [5] contains a problem where some $\prec$ elements are not discovered given a set of axioms for weak sequential consistency. Their algorithm is the basis of the software verification tool DEAGLE [5] that was the winner of the concurrency category of SV-COMP 2022 [3] and 2023 [4] which highlights the importance of the approach and the need for its improvement. We have proposed two solutions to this problem, a retrospective and a prospective algorithm, and have proven the post-propagation stability property of both. Using empirical data, we can conclude that in some circumstances the issue materializes in real-life problems as well, but there is a performance impact of using the revised algorithms. We found the prospective algorithm does not impact performance as much as the retrospective, but we could only show a significant difference in an isolated environment. We further found that the original implementing tool, DEAGLE, already contains a way to circumvent the problem, by utilizing a solution resembling our retrospective approach. We show that without this modification of the algorithm, DEAGLE does produce wrong results on verification tasks. We also showed that our proposal transfers to other model checkers as well, by showing that an implementation in the THETA [16] model checking framework achieved similar results to that of DEAGLE. Finally we have analyzed the empirical results and answered the premise of our reproducibility study: *the claims of the paper are not substantiated either theoretically, or in practice.*

References

1. F. He, Z. Sun, and H. Fan, "Deagle: An SMT-based Verifier for Multi-threaded Programs (Competition Contribution)," in *Tools and Algorithms for the Construction and Analysis of Systems*, D. Fisman and G. Rosu, Eds.   Cham: Springer International Publishing, 2022, pp. 424–428.
2. Z. Sun, "Deagle for SV-COMP 2024," Nov. 2023. [Online]. Available: https://doi.org/10.5281/zenodo.10207348
3. D. Beyer, "Progress on Software Verification: SV-COMP 2022," ser. Lecture Notes in Computer Science, D. Fisman and G. Rosu, Eds., vol. 13244.   Springer, 2022, pp. 375–402. [Online]. Available: https://doi.org/10.1007/978-3-030-99527-0_20
4. D. Beyer, "Competition on Software Verification and Witness Validation: SV-COMP 2023," ser. Lecture Notes in Computer Science, S. Sankaranarayanan and N. Sharygina, Eds., vol. 13994.   Springer, 2023, pp. 495–522. [Online]. Available: https://doi.org/10.1007/978-3-031-30820-8_29

5. Z. Sun, H. Fan, and F. He, "Consistency-preserving propagation for SMT solving of concurrent program verification," *Proc. ACM Program. Lang.*, vol. 6, no. OOPSLA2, oct 2022. [Online]. Available: https://doi.org/10.1145/3563321

6. J. Alglave, L. Maranget, S. Sarkar, and P. Sewell, "Fences in weak memory models (extended version)," *Formal Methods Syst. Des.*, vol. 40, no. 2, pp. 170–205, 2012. [Online]. Available: https://doi.org/10.1007/s10703-011-0135-z

7. J. Alglave, D. Kroening, and M. Tautschnig, "Partial Orders for Efficient Bounded Model Checking of Concurrent Software," in *Computer Aided Verification*, N. Sharygina and H. Veith, Eds.   Berlin, Heidelberg: Springer Berlin Heidelberg, 2013, pp. 141–157.

8. T. Haas, R. Meyer, and H. Ponce de León, "CAAT: consistency as a theory," *Proc. ACM Program. Lang.*, vol. 6, no. OOPSLA2, oct 2022. [Online]. Available: https://doi.org/10.1145/3563292

9. F. He, Z. Sun, and H. Fan, "Satisfiability modulo ordering consistency theory for multi-threaded program verification," in *Proceedings of the 42nd ACM SIGPLAN International Conference on Programming Language Design and Implementation*, ser. PLDI 2021.   New York, NY, USA: Association for Computing Machinery, 2021, p. 1264–1279. [Online]. Available: https://doi.org/10.1145/3453483.3454108

10. H. Ponce-de León, F. Furbach, K. Heljanko, and R. Meyer, "Dartagnan: Bounded Model Checking for Weak Memory Models (Competition Contribution)," in *Tools and Algorithms for the Construction and Analysis of Systems*, A. Biere and D. Parker, Eds.   Cham: Springer International Publishing, 2020, pp. 378–382.

11. C. Barrett and C. Tinelli, *Satisfiability Modulo Theories*.   Cham: Springer International Publishing, 2018, pp. 305–343. [Online]. Available: https://doi.org/10.1007/978-3-319-10575-8_11

12. N. Bjørner, C. Eisenhofer, and L. Kovács, "Satisfiability Modulo Custom Theories in Z3," in *Verification, Model Checking, and Abstract Interpretation*, C. Dragoi, M. Emmi, and J. Wang, Eds.   Cham: Springer Nature Switzerland, 2023, pp. 91–105.

13. C. Wang, S. Kundu, M. Ganai, and A. Gupta, "Symbolic Predictive Analysis for Concurrent Programs," in *FM 2009: Formal Methods*, A. Cavalcanti and D. R. Dams, Eds.   Berlin, Heidelberg: Springer Berlin Heidelberg, 2009, pp. 256–272.

14. R. Zennou, M. F. Atig, R. Biswas, A. Bouajjani, C. Enea, and M. Erradi, "Boosting Sequential Consistency Checking Using Saturation," in *Automated Technology for Verification and Analysis - 18th International Symposium, ATVA 2020, Hanoi, Vietnam, October 19-23, 2020, Proceedings*, ser. Lecture Notes in Computer Science, D. V. Hung and O. Sokolsky, Eds., vol. 12302.   Springer, 2020, pp. 360–376. [Online]. Available: https://doi.org/10.1007/978-3-030-59152-6_20

15. P. B. Gibbons and E. Korach, "Testing shared memories," *SIAM Journal on Computing*, vol. 26, no. 4, pp. 1208–1244, 1997.

16. T. Tóth, A. Hajdu, A. Vörös *et al.*, "Theta: a Framework for Abstraction Refinement-Based Model Checking," in *17th Conference on Formal Methods in Computer-Aided Design*, D. Stewart and G. Weissenbacher, Eds., 2017, pp. 176–179.

17. D. Beyer, S. Löwe, and P. Wendler, "Reliable benchmarking: requirements and solutions," *Int. J. Softw. Tools Technol. Transf.*, vol. 21, no. 1, pp. 1–29, 2019.

Inferring Incorrectness Specifications for Object-Oriented Programs

Wenhua Li[1]([✉]), Quang Loc Le[2], Yahui Song[1], and Wei-Ngan Chin[1]

[1] National University of Singapore, Singapore, Singapore
liwenhua@comp.nus.edu.sg
[2] University College London, London, UK

Abstract. Incorrectness logic (IL) based on under-approximation is effective at finding real program bugs. The prior work utilises bi-abductive specification inference mechanism to infer IL specifications for analysing large-scale C projects. However, this approach does not work well with object-oriented (OO) programs because it does not account for *class inheritance* and *method overriding*. In our work, we present an IL specification inference system that tackles these issues. At its core, we encode type information in our bi-abductive reasoning and propagate *type constraints* throughout the analysis. The direct benefit is that we can efficiently identify bugs caused by improper usage of the casting operator, which cannot be handled by the existing specification inference. Meanwhile, our system can reduce false positives while finding more true bugs because of not losing OO-type information. Furthermore, we model dynamic dispatching calls by inferring *dynamic specifications*, where the possible types of the calling object at runtime are bounded by the *type constraints*. We prototype our system in ILoop and evaluate it using real-world projects. Experimental results show that it finds 400% more class-cast-exceptions compared with Error Prone and improves the precision of finding null-pointer-exceptions by 27.0% compared with Pulse.

1 Introduction

Incorrectness Logic (IL) [31], as a dual to Hoare logic (HL), is an effective and principled approach for proving the presence of bugs. A recent work [20] implements a tool called Pulse-X to infer IL specifications within the Meta/Infer framework and aims at real bug detection for large C-based projects. In Pulse-X, IL with its extension via Incorrectness Separation Logic (ISL) are used together with bi-abduction [12] to infer specifications automatically. Pulse-X has been shown to be effective in finding bugs in real-world projects such as OpenSSL.

The current IL bi-abductive inference mechanism [20] only associates every variable with its declared type during the analysis. However, this is inadequate for modelling OO programs. In OO programming, types form class hierarchies and declared types encompass themselves and all their subclasses. Consequently, a method could accept multiple types during the real execution. These characteristics create challenges for the existing inference mechanism.

Firstly, it cannot handle the casting operation, which is widely used in OO programs. The casting operation is in the form of $(C)\,e$, which casts the source

© The Author(s) 2025
A. Gurfinkel and M. Heule (Eds.): TACAS 2025, LNCS 15696, pp. 20–39, 2025.
https://doi.org/10.1007/978-3-031-90643-5_2

type of the value by evaluating expression e to type C. Casting operations can cause system failures, i.e., class-cast-exception (CCE), at run-time when the source type is not a subtype of C. Research [14,19,24,30] has shown that the CCE stands as one of the most pervasive bugs in OO programs. Unfortunately, the current approach could not analyse casting operations as it cannot recognise object type possibilities. In addition, a lack of OO-type information leads to false positives, as some bugs will only occur if some type constraints are satisfied. However, as variables are type-insensitive in [20], it may report infeasible bugs.

Furthermore, because this mechanism uses fixed types, each method call, e.g., $x.mn(\bar{y})$, is considered to be statically dispatched. Then, the analysis could be imprecise. Suppose the type declared for x is an interface; it could not find a specification as mn does not have an implementation in the interface. If the declared type of x is a normal class, it loses precision due to the ignorance of subtypes and method overriding in OO programs. Considering these unsolved issues are crucial in OO programs, the current inference approach must be advanced.

Incorrectness Logic and Bi-abduction. $[p]\ S\ [\epsilon{:}q]$ denotes an IL triple. Here, $\epsilon \in \{ok, er\}$ captures symbolic traces of successful or error outcomes. Intuitively, an IL triple is valid if every program state satisfying the postcondition is reachable from some program states satisfying the precondition. A key feature of IL is that it allows dropping execution paths while ensuring all described paths are true in actual executions. Hence, an error postcondition $[er{:}\ ...]$ stands for true bugs. A bi-abduction problem [12] $p * m \vdash_{bi} q * f$ is to abduce a missing formula m, which is necessary to execute a command and calculate an unchanged frame f. Bi-abductive reasoning can generate HL specifications automatically. As IL is dual to HL, Pulse-X adapts bi-abduction to infer IL specifications due to the flipped consequence rule. Specifically, the IL bi-abduction problem is $q * f \vdash_{bi} p * m$ where m is inferred via frame calculation. Pulse-X analyses each method starting from the typical formula $emp \wedge true$, while in our system, the initial condition will record all declared type information. Our system builds up and propagates *type constraints* throughout the reasoning, accommodating the bug finding for CCEs and recording the possible types for dynamic dispatching in real executions.

Errors in OO Programs and Error Reporting. In this work, we target CCEs and null-pointer-exceptions (NPEs), which occur when trying to access a null pointer that does not point to an object. For NPEs, not all the *possible errors* are of programmers' interest. For example, the method $foo(A\ a)\{a.mn()\}$ can trigger an NPE when null is given as its input. The programmer may reason that a will rarely be null and decide to ignore this possible NPE.

To systematically decide if an error is worth reporting and reduce false positives, Le et al. [20] defined *manifest bugs*, which persistently occur regardless of the input values, and *latent bugs* which only occur for some input values. Following the convention, in this work, we also target manifest bugs for NPEs. Pulse-X may generate multiple specifications for one analysed method. Each specification is associated with one path of the program. However, to determine manifest bugs, they examine specifications individually while ignoring the bugs that exist in multiple paths. We propose a *merging* mechanism which generalises the reporting strategies to discover more true bugs. In addition, dynamic dispatching calls introduce a large set of paths, as each possible type leads to a different set of paths, which worsens the path explosion problem. The proposed *merging* mechanism can mitigate the problem by combining compatible specifications. The mechanism reduces the path space without sacrificing path information. On the other hand, we argue that latent CCEs are also worth reporting. For example, the programmers may not be aware of the entire class hierarchy and ignore some type possibilities for input objects. Some inputs are fine, but those ignored objects could be dangerous, especially when the code is re-used or used externally. Hence, we further relax the reporting criteria which covers a larger set of interesting bugs. Our contributions are:

- We propose an IL specification inference system for OO programs. Our system is type-sensitive, such that it can effectively reason about OO features and find bugs which cannot be handled by the existing inference system.
- We propose bug reporting criterion for both NPEs and CCEs. The NPEs reporting criteria is a generalisation of the existing work via *merging* and the *merging* mechanism can also mitigate the path explosion issue.
- We implement the inference mechanism in a tool called ILoop. Our experimental results show that our tool outperforms the state-of-the-art tools. The source code of the ILoop is available from [8].

2   Motivating Examples

Our motivation examples demonstrate that our approach can effectively detect CCEs, and increase the precision of the existing static analysis for OO programs.

2.1   Detecting Class-Cast-Exceptions

Fig. 1 shows a *possible* casting error found by ILoop. The input of this method is a *COSBase* object. In the if branch, the developer uses an *instanceof* operator to guard the casting (*COSObject*) o. However, in the else branch, the developer directly casts the object o to *COSDictionary*, which may cause a runtime exception as there exist classes that are neither subtypes of *COSObject* nor *COSDictionary*. This issue has been existing for more than ten years, and fixed by the developer recently (June, 2024). To identify this bug, ILoop starts with an initial program state, $\phi_0 = (ty(o) \prec : COSBase)$, meaning that the input type of o is *COSBase* or *COSBase*'s subclasses. At line 4, ILoop extends the state with the type constraint: $\phi_1 = (ty(o) \not\prec : COSObject)$. When analysing line 4, ILoop

```
1  private COSDictionary toDictionary(COSBase o){
2    if (o instanceof COSObject){
3        return (COSDictionary)((COSObject)o).getObject();}
4    else{return (COSDictionary)o;}} //may cause a run-time error
```

Fig. 1. A Casting Error Found in an Open-Source Project Pdfbox [6]

explores the possibility of CCEs, which is when $\phi_2 = (ty(o) \not\prec : COSDictionary)$. Since ϕ_2 does not contradict to the current state, ILoop infers an error specification with a precondition containing $\phi_0 \wedge \phi_1 \wedge \phi_2$.

2.2   Increasing Bug-finding Precision

ILoop is more accurate than the state-of-the-art tool Pulse, the commercial version of Pulse-X, by reducing false positives while finding more true positives.

Reduce False Positives. As shown in Fig. 2, Pulse reports a bug at line 2, which calls the method defined at line 4 by passing *null* as the second argument. As the second formal argument, object *icon* is dereferenced at line 7 to access its method *getImage()*; and if *icon* is *null*, there is an NPE. Hence, Pulse reports this error.

However, as this method call is under an *instanceof* checking and *null* is not an instance of any class, *icon*'s value will never be *null* at line 7. Therefore, there is no NPE. ILoop avoids such false positives by inferring specifications containing precise type constraints. The precondition inferred for entering the if branch at line 7 contains a condition $ty(icon) \prec : ImageIcon$. Then, ILoop finds that the method call at line 2 does not take this precondition as a valid call since $icon = null$. Thus, ILoop does not report any NPEs here.

```
1  public ErrorDialog(JComponent owner, Throwable t){
2     this(owner, null, t); } // this is a false positive NPE
3
4  public ErrorDialog(JComponent owner, Icon icon, Throwable t){
5     ...
6     if (icon instanceof ImageIcon){
7        setIconImage(((ImageIcon) icon).getImage());}
8     else {...}}
```

Fig. 2. A (Simplified) False Positive Reported by Pulse [4]

Find True Positives. Fig. 3 presents a buggy program from Infer's test repository [17]. Unfortunately, this bug has existed in this repository for several years but still cannot be found by its toolchain. There are two classes declared in this example where B is a subclass of A. B overrides the method *foo()* such that *A.foo()* returns a new *Object* instance, while *B.foo()* returns *null*. The method *dyn_mn* takes the object o as the input, and o could be either an instance of A or an instance of B. The method executes normally if it has type A but throws an NPE if it has type B. Pulse could not detect such bugs as it only analyses the case where o is type A and fails to consider the other possible type B. In

```
1  class A {Object foo() {return new Object();}}
2  class B extends A { @Override Object foo() {return null;}}
3  void dyn_mn(A o) {o.foo().toString();}
4  void buggy(B b) {dyn_mn(b);}  // this is a true bug
```

Fig. 3. A True NPE in Infer's Test Repository

addition, this bug becomes manifest in method *buggy* at line 4 as it calls method *dyn_mn* by always passing a B type instance as an input. However, Pulse does not support the reasoning for the dynamic dispatching call shown in the example, i.e., the specification of the overriding method in the subclass is missing. As such, it could not derive the error specification for *buggy*. This example highlights the need for a systematic method to catch and report such bugs in OO programs.

In our approach, ILoop infers the *static specifications* for both $A.foo()$ and $B.foo()$ according to their implementations, respectively. Meanwhile, ILoop composes a *dynamic specification* for $A:foo()$ from the earlier inferred static specifications of both A and B. The notation $A:foo()$ means that *foo* is dynamically dispatched. ILoop utilises the dynamic specification to cover the behaviour when o is type B in *dyn_mn* and captures the missing bug in *buggy*.

3   Target Language and Specification Language

$$
\begin{array}{rclcrcl}
\mathcal{P} & ::= & \overline{cdef}; & \qquad cdef & ::= & class\ C_1\ extends\ C_2\ \{\overline{t\ f};\ \overline{meth}\} \\
\tau & ::= & int \mid bool \mid void & & t & ::= & C \mid \tau \\
meth & ::= & t\ mn\ (\overline{t}\ \overline{x})\ \{S\} & & v & ::= & const \mid x \\
S & ::= & skip \mid e \mid t\ x; S \mid S; S \mid S+S \mid S^* \\
e & ::= & \multicolumn{5}{l}{v \mid x{:=}e \mid y := x.f \mid x.f{:=}y \mid error() \mid new\ C(\overline{x}) \mid} \\
& & \multicolumn{5}{l}{x.mn(\overline{y}) \mid x\ instanceof\ C \mid (C)\ x \mid assume(b)}
\end{array}
$$

Fig. 4. A Core Object-Oriented Language

Fig. 4 presents our target OO language, which is call by value and uses single inheritance. The entire class hierarchies of a program are constructed via *extends* keyword. *Object* is an implicit superclass of all classes; $x, y...$ range over variables. The *const* represents the constant values. Following the encoding convention [31,20], we represent conditionals as $(assume(b); S_1)+(assume(\neg b); S_2)$ where b is a Boolean value and $+$ is a non-deterministic choice between two statements; and *while* is encoded as $(assume(b); S)^*; assume(\neg b)$ where $*$ is the Kleene star iteration. The semantics of the core language can be found in our technical report [27].

Fig. 5 presents the syntax of the specification language, where $\kappa_1 * \kappa_2$ presents two non-overlapping heaps via separation conjunction $*$; $x.f \mapsto e$ means the field f of x points to e and $x:C$ means the run-time type of x stored in the heap is C. We use a simplified notation $x \mapsto C\langle \overline{f} : \overline{e} \rangle$ to denote a constructed heap object. $x \mapsto C\langle \overline{f} : \overline{e} \rangle$ is a point-to predicate where the object x has the exact type C and the fields $\overline{f}$ from C points to $\overline{e}$. We may shorten it to $x \mapsto C\langle \overline{f} \rangle$ for simplicity in some following sections. By default, we know which class a field f belongs to.

$$
\begin{array}{rcl}
p, q, f, m, F & ::= & (\kappa \wedge \phi) \mid p \vee p \mid \exists x.p \\
\kappa & ::= & emp \mid x.f \mapsto e \mid x:C \mid x \mapsto C\langle \overline{f} : \overline{e} \rangle \mid \kappa_1 * \kappa_2 \\
\phi & ::= & true \mid false \mid x{=}e \mid x{<}e \mid \phi_1 \wedge \phi_2 \mid \phi_1 \vee \phi_2 \mid \neg \phi \mid \phi_1 {\Rightarrow} \phi_2 \mid \\
& & C_1{=}C_2 \mid C_1 {\prec} C_2 \mid ty(x){=}C \mid ty(x){\prec}C \mid ty(x){\in}\{C_1, \ldots, C_n\}
\end{array}
$$

Fig. 5. An Assertion Logic for OOP

Lastly, ϕ stands for pure arithmetic constraints. In contrast to the prior works [35,20], we do not have the notation $x\nmapsto$ called "negative heap", as we do not have explicit memory management, such as $free()$ to de-allocate objects from heaps. In addition, we have a set of extra terms to constrain the types in our pure logic. The type of an object is immutable throughout its lifetime. We can use those terms to constrain the allocated type. For example, $ty(x)=C$ means the run-time type of x is exactly C while $ty(x)\prec:C$ ($ty(x)=C \vee ty(x) \prec C$) can be used when x's type is either C or its subclasses.

4   Specification Inference

We semantically define IL triples [31] via program transitions. A configuration is a pair (S,σ) where S is a program and σ is a program state, i.e., the valuation of both memory stacks and heaps. A program transition is a binary relation $\rightsquigarrow$ on configurations. Relation $(S,\sigma)\rightsquigarrow(S',\sigma')$ holds if the execution of the statement in the configuration (S,σ) results in the new configuration (S',σ'). We define $\rightsquigarrow^*$, the reflexive-transitive closure of $\rightsquigarrow$, to capture finite executions. We assume all terminating executions end at a *skip* statement. We use $\sigma \in [\![p]\!]$ to denote that the program state σ satisfy the assertion p. Finally, $T_{sp} \models [p]\, S\, [\epsilon{:}q]$ denotes a valid IL triple, where T_{sp} is a context storing the specifications for the analyzed methods. Formally,

$$T_{sp} \models [p]\, S\, [\epsilon{:}q]\ \textit{iff}\ \forall \sigma.\, \sigma \in q,\ \exists \sigma'.\, \sigma' \in p\ \textit{s.t.}\ (S,\sigma)\rightsquigarrow^*(skip,\sigma)$$
$$\textit{with the specification context } T_{sp}\ \textit{and}\ \epsilon \in \{ok, er\}.$$

4.1   IL Triples For OO Statements and Type Constraint Propagation

Fig. 6 presents a set of valid IL triples [26] for primitive OO program statements. As these triples hold without context T_{sp}, we omit it here. Rules **Skip**, **Read** and **Write** are standard. Rule **Assume** allows us to back-propagate the Boolean expression to the precondition as a path condition. There are three possibilities for the *instanceof* operation. Rule **InsNull** states that *null* is not an instance of

$\models [emp]\, skip\, [ok{:}\ emp]$ **Skip** $\models [x.f\mapsto e_1 \wedge y=e_2]\, y{:}=x.f\ [ok{:}\ x.f\mapsto e_1 \wedge y=e_1]$ **Read**

$\models [x=null]\, y{:}=x.f\ [er{:}\ x=null]$ **NullRead** $\models [x.f\mapsto e]\, x.f{:}= y\ [ok{:}\ x.f\mapsto y]$ **Write**

$\models [x=null]\, x.f{:}=y\ [er{:}\ x=null]$ **NullWrite** $\models [emp\wedge b]\, assume(b)\ [ok{:}\ emp\wedge b]$ **Assume**

$\models [emp]\, error()\ [er{:}\ emp]$ **Error** $\models [x=null]\, x\ instanceof\ C\ [ok{:}\ x=null\wedge\neg res]$ **InsNull**

$\models [x\neq null \wedge ty(x)\prec:C]\ x\ instanceof\ C\ [ok{:}\ x\neq null \wedge ty(x)\prec:C \wedge res]$ **InsT**

$\models [x\neq null \wedge ty(x)\nprec:C]\ x\ instanceof\ C\ [ok{:}\ x\neq null \wedge ty(x)\nprec:C \wedge \neg res]$ **InsF**

$\models [x=null]\ (C)\ x\ [ok{:}\ x=null \wedge res=x]$ **CastNull**

$\models [x\neq null \wedge ty(x)\prec:C]\ (C)\ x\ [ok{:}\ x\neq null \wedge ty(x)\prec:C \wedge res=x]$ **CastOk**

$\models [x\neq null \wedge ty(x)\nprec:C]\ (C)\ x\ [er{:}\ x\neq null \wedge ty(x)\nprec:C]$ **CastEr**

Fig. 6. Primitive IL Triples For OO Statements

```
public synchronized boolean equals (final Object other) {
```
$[\,...ty(other) \prec: Object \wedge \boxed{ty(other) \prec: AbsHis} \wedge ty(other) \not\prec: DblHis\,]$
```
if (other instanceof AbsHis) {
```
$[ok\!: \,...ty(other) \prec: Object \wedge ty(other) \prec: AbsHis \wedge ty(other) \not\prec: DblHis\,]$
```
    DblHis otherHis = (DblHis) other;
```
$[er\!: \,...ty(other) \prec: Object \wedge ty(other) \prec: AbsHis \wedge ty(other) \not\prec: DblHis]$

Fig. 7. Finding a CCE [7], via Type Constraint Propagation

any class. If x is allocated, it can either be or not be an instance of C, denoted by rules **InsT** and **InsF**. Similarly, there are three possibilities for casting, and one leads to CCEs. We use the default res in poststate q to denote the result being returned from an expression e in $[p]e[\epsilon:q]$.

Based on primitive IL triples, specification inference allows us to generate specifications for bigger code blocks [20,37], which consist of primitive statements. We show that such a mechanism can be applied to propagate type constraints according to program statements, which are critical for analysing OO programs. For example, statement $if\,(x\,instanceof\,C)\,...\,else\,...$ results two possible specifications: $ty(x)\prec:C$ for the if branch and $ty(x)\not\prec:C$ for the else branch. Type constraints indicate the possible types for an object at run-time.

The example in Fig. 7 is taken from an open-source project HdrHistogram and fixed by the developer [7]. For simplicity, we only show the typing part of the inferred specification. The initial state before the if statement is $\phi_0 = (ty(other)\prec:Object)$, obtained from the method signature. The (boxed) constraint $\phi_1 = (ty(other)\prec:AbsHis)$ (according to the if condition) is back propagated to form the precondition for entering the if branch, i.e., $\phi_0 \wedge \phi_1$. For the casting operation at line 5, ILoop infers $\phi_2 = (ty(other) \not\prec: DblHis)$ ($highlighted$) as the missing formula which leads to an error postcondition. As the accumulated type constraint is satisfiable when reaching the $post$, i.e., $(\phi_0 \wedge \phi_1 \wedge \phi_2) \neq false$, it indicates that this error is on a feasible path. The states at line 2 and line 6 form an error specification for this method. In fact, $AbsHis$ and $DblHis$ are two unrelated classes, and this bug was caused by a typo from the programmer.

4.2   Inference Relations

We now discuss how to automatically achieve IL specification inference for OO programs. Given a statement S, we use the following relation $T_{sp} \vdash [p]?[m]\ S\ [\epsilon:q]$ to infer a missing formula m which is necessary to execute S and computes the corresponding postcondition $[\epsilon:q]$ with a given precondition p. T_{sp} is the specification table which initially contains the primitive rules in Fig. 6. For each analysed method, its inferred specifications are stored in T_{sp}, and used to further infer the specifications for the rest of the methods. Instead of using a standard $emp \wedge true$ symbolic heap [12,20] when analysing a new method, the inference is initialized with a precondition p that records the declared type for each input object. For example, given a method definition of class C: $t_0\ mn\ (args)\ \{S\}$, the precondition for reasoning S is initialized as follows:

$$p = (\bigwedge_{(C_i'\, x_i)\, \in\, args} (x_i = null \lor ty(x_i) \prec: C')) \land ty(this) = C$$

The rest of the inference relations are presented in Fig. 8. The system performs forward symbolic executions. During the inference, the bi-abduction obligations in the form of $q * f \vdash_{bi} p * m$ are solved by the approaches in [12], where the missing resource m is inferred through frame calculation, and the *anti-frame* f carried is abduced. **ASSIGN-VAR** performs standard Floyd's forward assignment rule. **LOCAL** picks fresh variables to represent locally declared variables in specifications. The "default_value(v_t)" means the default value when a variable of type t is declared. **CHOICE** rule is design for non-deterministic choice $+$ which paths could be split. **SEQ** performs the sequential composition. In **SEQ2**, $mod(S)$ returns the set of variables modified in the program S and $fv(f)$ is the set of free variables in formula f. The **UNROLLING** rule is designed Kleene star iterations S^* which allows it to unroll non-deterministically. In this work, we use upper-

ASSIGN−VAR

$$\dfrac{\begin{array}{c} vars = (\bigwedge\limits_{\forall y_i.y_i \in pvar(e)} y_i = e_i) \land x = x' \\ vars * f \vdash_{bi} p * m \\ q = \exists x'.(m * p)[x'/x] \land x = e[x'/x] \end{array}}{T_{sp} \vdash [p]?[m]\ x := e\ [ok:q]}$$

LOCAL

$$\dfrac{fresh(o) \quad default\_value(v_t)}{T_{sp} \vdash [p \land o = v_t]?[m]\ S[o/x]\ [\epsilon:q]}$$
$$\dfrac{}{T_{sp} \vdash [p]?[m]\ t\ x; S\ [\epsilon: \exists o.\ q]}$$

VAL−VAR

$$\dfrac{q = p \land res = v}{T_{sp} \vdash [p]?[m]\ v\ [ok:q]}$$

CHOICE1

$$\dfrac{T_{sp} \vdash [p]?[m]\ S_1\ [\epsilon:q]}{T_{sp} \vdash [p]?[m]\ S_1 + S_2\ [\epsilon:q]}$$

CHOICE2

$$\dfrac{T_{sp} \vdash [p]?[m]\ S_2\ [\epsilon:q]}{T_{sp} \vdash [p]?[m]\ S_1 + S_2\ [\epsilon:q]}$$

SEQ1

$$\dfrac{T_{sp} \vdash [p]?[m]\ S_1\ [er:q]}{T_{sp} \vdash [p]?[m]\ S_1; S_2\ [er:q]}$$

SEQ2

$$\dfrac{\begin{array}{c} T_{sp} \vdash [p_1]?[m_1]\ S_1\ [ok:q_1] \\ T_{sp} \vdash [p_2]?[m_2]\ S_2\ [\epsilon::q_2] \\ (p_2 * m_2) * f \vdash_{bi} q_1 * m \\ mod(S_1) \cap fv(m) = mod(S_2) \cap fv(f) = \emptyset \end{array}}{T_{sp} \vdash [p_1]?[m_1 * m]\ S_1; S_2\ [\epsilon:q_2 * f]}$$

CONSEQUENCE

$$\dfrac{p' \Rightarrow p \quad T_{sp} \vdash [p']?[m]\ S\ [\epsilon:q'] \quad q \Rightarrow q'}{T_{sp} \vdash [p]?[m]\ S\ [\epsilon:q]}$$

FRAME

$$\dfrac{T_{sp} \vdash [p]?[m]\ S\ [\epsilon:q] \quad mod(S) \cap fv(f) = \emptyset}{T_{sp} \vdash [p * f]?[m]\ S\ [\epsilon:q * f]}$$

UNROLLING

$$\dfrac{T_{sp} \vdash [p]?[m]\ skip + (S; S^*)\ [\epsilon:q]}{T_{sp} \vdash [p]?[m]\ S^*\ [\epsilon:q]}$$

ERR−CALL

$$\dfrac{m = (x = null)}{T_{sp} \vdash [p]?[m]\ x.mn\ [er:p]}$$

CALL-STATIC

$$\dfrac{\begin{array}{c} ty\_constraints(x) \implies ty(x) = C \\ ST(C.mn(\bar{w})) = ([p']\_[\epsilon:q']) \in T_{sp} \\ p'[x/this, \bar{y}/\bar{w}] * f \vdash_{bi} p * m \\ q = q'[x/this, \bar{y}/\bar{w}] \end{array}}{T_{sp} \vdash [p]?[m]\ x.mn(\bar{y})\ [\epsilon:q * f]}$$

CALL-DYNAMIC

$$\dfrac{\begin{array}{c} DY(C : mn(\bar{w})) \in T_{sp} \\ DY(C : mn(\bar{w})) \land ty\_constraints(x) = [p']\_[\epsilon:q'] \\ p'[x/this, \bar{y}/\bar{w}] * f \vdash_{bi} p * m \\ q = q'[x/this, \bar{y}/\bar{w}] \end{array}}{T_{sp} \vdash [p]?[m]\ x.mn(\bar{y})\ [\epsilon:q * f]}$$

Fig. 8. Specification Inference Relations

bounded loop unrolling. The inference process terminates once it reaches an *er* postcondition.

Method Calls. There are two kinds of calls: CALL-STATIC and CALL-DYNAMIC are for static and dynamic calls, respectively. In our language, both the method calls are in the form of $x.mn(\bar{y})$ (we omit the arguments and use $x.mn$ for simplicity). We use $ty\_constraints(x)$ to denote the set of all type assertions of x in the pre-state formula. We say that this call can be statically determined if there is only one type possibility for x. For example, x is locally initialized by $new\ C(...)$, then $ty(x) = C$. In this case, we use the static specification for this call. Static specifications are directly inferred through the inference relations for each method by analysing its concrete implementation. We store the inferred specifications in T_{sp} and can be retrieved by $ST(C.mn)$. Note that we use CALL−STATIC to process the primitive statements shown in Fig. 6.

Dynamic Specifications. On the other hand, if the type of x is not statically determined, $x.mn$ is dynamically dispatched. We use $C.mn$ for the mn implementation in class C, and $C:mn$ to denote the set of mn implementations in C and its subclasses. Specifications for such $C:mn$ are dynamic specifications, denoted by $DY(C:mn)$. A natural way to derive dynamic specifications is to collect the static specifications of mn in all C', where $C' \prec : C$. Formally,

Definition 1. *Given class C and its subclasses, let $C:mn$ be the set of implementations of mn in these classes. The dynamic specification, denoted by $DY(C:mn)$, is defined as follows:*

$$DY(C:mn) = \bigwedge_{\forall C_i \prec : C} ST(C_i.mn).$$

The derived dynamic specifications will also be stored in T_{sp}. To find a correct dynamic specification for a dynamically dispatched call $x.mn$, we need to follow these steps: 1) Find the least positive type constraint of x (we call a type constraint $ty(x) \prec : C$, $ty(x) \not\prec : C$ as positive constraint and negative constraint, respectively). Let it be $ty(x) \prec : C_l$. By least positive type constraint, we mean that C_l is not the superclass of any other C in the other positive type constraints; 2) Find $DY(C_l:mn)$; 3) Trim $DY(C_l:mn)$ by removing specifications of infeasible types according to the negative type constraints. Examples can be found in [27].

Note that constructors are special methods that only require static specifications. When analysing a constructor $C(...)$, the initial precondition p contains an allocated heap object (all uninitialized fields are null at the beginning) with the exact type $ty(...) = C$. Upon an *ok* termination, its reference is implicitly returned. We define the soundness of our inference mechanism in Theorem 1.

Theorem 1 (Soundness of the Inference Relations). *For all $T_{sp}, p, M, S, \epsilon, q$, if the inference relations conclude that $T_{sp} \vdash [p]?[M]\ S\ [\epsilon:q]$, then $T_{sp} \models [p * M]\ S\ [\epsilon:q]$.*

5   Bug Reporting

We aim to create a practical analyser with low false positives and high true positives. This section outlines our efforts to achieve this for OO programs.

5.1   Merging

Prior work [20] defines manifest bugs and latent bugs. In a nutshell, latent bugs are context-dependent, which will not always occur. In contrast, manifest bugs occur regardless of the calling context and should be reported to the user. In particular, to find manifest bugs, the previous tool classifies an *er* triple as manifest if its precondition is $emp \wedge true$ or *relaxed-manifest* if its precondition contains heap-allocated variables without any pure constraints. Otherwise, it is classified as a latent bug. However, this approach only reports a subset of manifest bugs as they examine specifications individually and hence may miss manifest bugs amongst multiple paths. We show such an example in Fig. 9, where class B extends class A, and two branches are rejoining at the $error()$ statement. Hence, the error occurs regardless of the type of the input x.

We may infer two specifications for each branch separately. The error occurs in both the if branch and the else branch. However, using the previous approach, we will find that the inferred specifications contain path conditions $ty(x) \prec: B$ and $ty(x) \not\prec: B$, respectively.

```
void goo(A x) {
    if (x instanceof B){skip;}
    else {skip;}
    error();}
```

Fig. 9. A Manifest Bug

Therefore, we need to classify the triples in both branches as latent bugs and not report them to the user. To reduce such false negatives, we propose a merging mechanism which can join the *preconditions* of the specifications for the two branches so that this bug can be classified as a manifest bug.

On the other hand, the construction of dynamic specifications requires capturing specifications from multiple classes, which leads to path explosion for method calls. An under-approximating analyser will drop excessive specifications once the limit is reached. Although sacrificing precision, path dropping helps achieve scalability. Our merging mechanism can combine static specifications to form a more concise dynamic specification without losing path information. By doing this, we can slow down the path growth. Therefore, we enhance analysis precision via merging from two perspectives: 1) merging *preconditions* from error specifications to find more true bugs; and 2) merging static specifications to form dynamic specifications and slow down the path dropping.

Merging Mechanism We first defined *c-hierarchy* predicate in Definition 2 to model the class hierarchy in OO programs. Each *c-hierarchy* predicate has a tree-like structure where T is its root (superclass) with some subtrees (subclasses). A *c-hierarchy* predicate can model the full/partial class inheritance.

Definition 2 (*C-hierarchy* Predicate). *A c-hierarchy predicate is a disjunctive set of objects in the following form:*

$$D := \emptyset \mid T(\bar{f}, \bar{D})$$

A non-empty c-hierarchy *predicate pointed by x is defined as follows:*

$$x \mapsto T(\bar{f}, \bar{D}) \stackrel{def}{=} x \mapsto T\langle \bar{f} \rangle \ \vee \bigvee_{T_i(\bar{f}_i, \bar{D}_i) \in \bar{D}} x \mapsto T_i(\bar{f}{+}{+}\bar{f}_i, \bar{D}_i)$$

Recall that $x \mapsto T\langle \bar{f} \rangle$ indicates that x points to a heap object with exact type T. For $T(\bar{f}, \bar{D})$, T is the superclass name, $\bar{f}$ are the field mappings from T, and $\bar{D}$ is the predicates of some other classes directly extending T. The notation ++ is the appending operator. The subclasses (e.g., D_i) in a *c-hierarchy* predicate must always maintain the same state for field mappings inherited from the superclass (e.g., T). For example, $x \mapsto T_1(1, \{T_2(), T_3(2)\})$ means $x \mapsto T_1\langle 1 \rangle \vee x \mapsto T_2\langle 1 \rangle \vee x \mapsto T_3\langle 1, 2 \rangle$. A well-formed *c-hierarchy* predicate should respect the original class hierarchy from the program. Specifically, one *c-hierarchy* predicate must form a connected subgraph of the class hierarchy.

$$\frac{S \prec_d T}{var \mapsto S(\bar{f}_T{+}{+}\bar{f}_S, \bar{D}_S) * F * F' \ \vee \ var \mapsto T(\bar{f}_T, \bar{D}_T) * F * F_{@\bar{S}'}}{var \mapsto T(\bar{f}_T, \bar{D}_T{+}{+}S(\bar{f}_S, \bar{D}_S)) * F * F_{@\bar{S}'} * F'_{@S}} \text{ (Merging)}$$

This rule merges two formulae where *var* points to either a subclass or superclass *c-hierarchy* predicate, where $S \prec_d T$ means T is the direct superclass of S. The formula for the subclass S may contain an extra frame F' when *var* points to a subclass instance (e.g., the objects pointed by extension fields of subclasses). We tag this extra frame as $F'_{@S}$ to denote that F' is exclusively owned by the S *c-hierarchy* predicate after merging. Similarly, the formula for the superclass T may have already merged with some other direct subclasses $\bar{S}'$. Hence, it may contain some other tagged frames $F_{@\bar{S}'}$. These tagged frames will remain unchanged.

Note that the OO method's specifications will include *this* object, which denotes the current object. We merge two specifications from the superclass and the subclass using the above **Merging** rule for both *pre* and *post* by replacing *var* with *this*. This merging rule only merges formulae with the same F. In other words, we only merge the superclass and subclass specifications under the same path condition. We keep the specifications separate if the *pre* or *post* cannot be merged.

Merging makes the dynamic specification concise by simplifying a disjunctive form $P_1 \vee P_2$ to P_3 such that $P_3 = (P_1 \vee P_2)$ without loss of information. In the OO context, this happens quite often as a subclass usually behaves very similarly to its superclass. We illustrate the merging through the example in Fig. 10. Both *DblA* and *C* extend *A* where *DblA* overrides the original methods with a backup field to store the original value in field *val*. We infer static specifications for the three classes respectively: $[this \mapsto A\langle e \rangle]\_[ok: this \mapsto A\langle x \rangle]$ for A; $[this \mapsto DblA\langle e, b \rangle]\_[ok: this \mapsto DblA\langle x, e \rangle]$ for *DblA*;

```
1  class A {
2     int val;
3     void set(int x){
4        this.val = x;}}
5
6  class DblA extends A{
7     int bak;
8     void set(int x){
9        this.bak=this.val;
10       this.val = x;  }}
11
12 class C extends A {}
```

Fig. 10. A Merging Example

and $[this \mapsto C\langle e\rangle]_-[ok: this \mapsto C\langle x\rangle]$ for C. By using merging, the dynamic spec for $A : set$ can be obtained as:
$[this \mapsto A(e, \{DblA(b), C()\})]_-[ok: this \mapsto A(x, \{DblA(e), C()\})]$. Next, we define the generalised relaxed-manifest bug via merging.

Definition 3 (Relaxed-Manifest Bug). *Let E be a mapping from error statement S to the set of error specifications terminated at it. Then, S denotes a manifest bug if point 1 holds and point 3 holds after the merging described by point 2:*

1. $E(S) \neq \emptyset$ and $\forall spec \in E(S).\ sat(post(spec))$
2. $\forall spec \in E(S).\ pre(spec) \xrightarrow{merging\ steps} E_{pre}(S)$
3. $\exists p \in E_{pre}(S).\ \kappa \wedge \phi_{ty} \vdash p$

Where κ is the heap formula representing the possible heap resources without pure constraints. ϕ_{ty} represents the initial type constraints (constructed from the initial method signature) we mentioned earlier.

We require the postconditions in specifications to be satisfiable and $E(s)$ is non-empty. $E_{pre}(s)$ is the set of formulae formed by merging the *preconditions* from all specifications in $E(s)$ through the following steps repeatedly until the preconditions cannot be merged.

- Step 1: Merge all *vars* in *pres* with the same path condition by **merging** rule.
- Step 2: Combine the merged formulae using the $\vee$ calculus.

These steps are trying to check if an error happens in several paths. "Context-independent" bugs in the OO program should occur regardless of the types of input parameters as the types of input objects are the additional dimension of the calling context. In the actual implementation, we sometimes relax this requirement. If there is no *instanceof* or casting throughout the method, we will report a bug that occurs when the types of inputs are the same as the declared ones since programmers may not consider subclasses in this case.

Note that the merging for the dynamic specification formation and bug reporting are different. The former is the merging of multiple *specifications* across multiple methods (from different classes) while the latter happens within one method and we only merge *preconditions*. Both of them may need to use *c-hierarchy* predicates to represent heap objects.

5.2 Reporting Class-Cast-Exceptions

A statement $(C)\ e$ could cause a CCE if $ty\_constraints(e) \not\Rightarrow (ty(e) \prec: C)$ in the precondition. CCEs and NPEs share the following similarities: 1) The statement might not always trigger a runtime exception; 2) A guard can prevent the error (e.g., null checks for NPEs and *instanceof* checks for CCEs); 3) Without a guard, it's difficult to determine if an error should be reported, as the programmer may intentionally omit it based on their design, leading to potential false positives.

Since NPEs and CCEs exhibit similar characteristics, we can adopt the same methodology used for NPEs when addressing CCEs. However, our experimental findings indicate that this approach results in minimal detection of CCEs in real-world projects. There are two potential explanations for this. Firstly, programmers might not experience CCEs like NPEs; for instance, they may not pass a manifest-error object with incompatible types to methods. Secondly, CCEs could arise from external libraries with inaccessible source code or through code reuse. Programmers may lack awareness of the complete class hierarchy, leading them to overlook certain input object possibilities while coding. Even though only a certain kind of inputs can lead to CCEs, they could be in the interests of the programmers. According to a prior survey [30], 50% of the casting operations are unguarded by the *instanceof* checking which risks the programs. Is the casting operation safe when the programmers are aware of using *instanceof* checking? Our primary thought is that if CCEs still occur when programmers realise to do type filtering by using *instanceof*, it might be a mistake and we should alert the programmer about such a mistake. When we apply this strategy, we find some true CCEs in real-world projects, such as the examples in Fig. 1 and Fig. 7. We formally define the reporting criteria for CCEs in Definition 4.

Definition 4 (CCE Reporting Criteria). *An er triple is reportable if: It ends at a casting operation $C(e)$ and the postcondition is satisfiable; and*

- *It satisfies Definition 3; or*
- *e is an initialized object such that $ty(e) = C'$ and $C' \not<: C$; or*
- *An instanceof operator has been applied on e before the casting operation.*

6   Implementation and Evaluation

Implementation. We build ILoop inside Infer's framework (version id: 5050294) with an additional 10K lines of OCaml codes. We utilise Infer's bi-abductive entailment solver to compute missing formulae and frames. ILoop is an under-approximating analyser for finding bugs in Java programs. It performs compositional reasoning and generates IL triples for error reporting. In particular, ILoop includes a function $compute(p, T_{sp}, mn(\bar{C}\ \bar{o}))$ as the predicate transformer. Given a method mn, this function takes the initial precondition p mentioned in Sect. 4.2 and the specification table as inputs. It then applies the inference relations in Sect. 4 to infer the preconditions and the postcondition $\epsilon': Q'$ of mn. Given a Java program, ILoop first generates static specifications for methods and then, ILoop reports bugs on error triples if they satisfy the criteria in Sect. 5. The dynamic specifications are computed on-demand to save resources i.e., ILoop infers dynamic specifications for a method only when the method is dynamically dispatched and called somewhere. The inferred specifications are stored in T_{sp}.

To reduce the possible high cost of satisfiability checking when merging formulae for error reporting, we design some heuristics which can identify a subset of bugs in the proposed mechanism. We inspect errors likely to manifest after merging, i.e., the error specifications occupy a large portion of paths when there is no path dropping. We use syntactic checks to filter pairs of triples that are more likely to be merged successfully. Using these heuristics, ILoop keeps more informative IL triples to assist with reportable bugs.

Evaluation. To conduct the experiments, we select a set of real-world programs as our benchmarks. In particular, the benchmarks are from a test case repository developed and maintained by Meta/Infer developers [17], Apache projects[1] and some popular code repositories which receive thousands of stars on Github. This Infer's repository contains challenging test cases and is accumulated in a real-world codebase. Some are for regression testing, and others for designing and testing new features of its tools, such as Pulse. The latter is beyond its capability, such as detecting CCEs. The experiments are designed to answer the following three research questions (RQ):

- RQ1: Is our approach capable of detecting CCEs in OO programs?
- RQ2: Are the detected CCEs containing false positives?
- RQ3: How does ILoop compare in performance with the state-of-the-art tool for detecting NPEs.

Table 1. CCEs Reported by ILoop and Error Prone. CCEs: number of CCEs reported. Fixed: the number of CCEs has been fixed according to the commits. Risky: the number of risky CCEs that have not been fixed in any commits. T: running time in seconds. The numbers in **red** indicate the false positives reported by ILoop.

#	Project		ILoop				Error Prone			
	Name	KLoc	CCEs	Fxied	Risky	T	CCEs	Fxied	Risky	T
1	Infer-c2dc303	11.4	2	0	2	11	0	0	0	2
2	pdfbox-a51dd40	12.1	4+1	2	2	42	0	0	0	28
3	ebean-b450227	20.7	3	0	3	40	3	0	3	42
4	HdrHistogram-9866a4c	27.2	1	1	0	27	1	1	0	5
5	jedis-febc027	33.9	1	1	0	20	0	0	0	12
6	spoon-9c1c3bf	46.5	6+1	2	4	43	0	0	0	33
7	classgraph-1310809180s	136.7	1	1	0	180	0	0	0	15
8	jfreechart-21922c1	292.6	1	0	1	32	0	0	0	30
9	Others	285.1	1+2	1	0	87	0	0	0	39
	Total	859.7	20+4	8	12	482	4	1	3	206

To answer RQ1, we summarize the experimental results on Table 1. Firstly, we compare the reported results with the Github commits. ILoop reports 24 CCEs in total and 8 (33.3%) are corrected by the developers. We examine the rest of the reports and find another 12 reports risky, especially when the code is used by someone unaware of the entire class hierarchy. Secondly, we compare ILoop with Error Prone (version 2.32.0), a popular static analyser developed by Google [2] for Java programs. Error Prone detects bugs through pattern recognition [3] and alerts users when the written code matches the pre-defined error patterns. Error Prone has reported four bugs which are the subset of ILoop's reports. One of the four is fixed by the developers while the other three match our risky reports. The results show that ILoop could effectively find more meaningful bugs in real-world programs.

To answer RQ2, as Table 1 shows, we conclude that there are 4 false positives. As the rules for reporting CCEs are designed to avoid false positives, the false

```
1  protected SettableBeanProperty constructSettableProperty(...){
2     ...
3     if (mutator instanceof AnnotatedMethod) {
4        prop = new MethodProperty((AnnotatedMethod) mutator);
5     } else {
6     // 08-Sep-2016, tatu: wonder if we should verify it is
         'AnnotatedField' to be safe?
7        prop = new FieldProperty((AnnotatedField) mutator);
8        // ILoop reports one error at line 7
```

Fig. 11. A (Simplified) False Positive Reported by ILoop [5]

positive rate is fairly low (16.7%). We manually investigate the reports, such as by referring to the developer's comments or using semantic analysis. We find that although some bugs can be syntactically triggered, they may not be of users' interests. Hence, we mark them as false positives. We show a false positive in Fig. 11. According to our proposed reporting strategy, line 7 may contain a casting error. This is because ILoop finds out that there exist some types that are neither the subtype of *AnnotatedMethod* nor *AnnotatedField* for object *mutator*. Hence, casting at line 7 could be risky. The developers seem aware of this issue and wrote a comment on line 6. The comment mentions that they should verify the correctness of this casting. However, the code has not been changed since the creation of this comment. Hence, *mutator* may not be an instance from the dangerous classes in an actual execution. It could be semantically safe.

Table 2. NPEs Reported by ILoop and Pulse. Op: the overlapping reports by both tools. $T_{OO,PL}$: running time in seconds. -FP: the number of false positives reduced by ILoop. +TP: the number of additional true bugs found by ILoop. +FP: the additional false positive reported by ILoop. -TP: the missed true bugs by ILoop. The commit ID of jackson-databind is 4a40123.

#	Project	KLoc	ILoop	T_{OO}	Pulse	T_{PL}	Op	-FP	+TP	+FP	-TP
1	Infer-c2dc303	11.4	96	11	89	10	89	0	7	0	0
2	pdfbox-606f916	21.6	48	44	50	41	44	3	4	0	3
3	spoon-5e77e89	33.5	9	101	11	96	6	5	2	1	0
4	ebean-b0ec23e	48.4	20	36	22	32	17	3	3	0	2
5	Botania-92f4863	77.4	21	47	18	39	18	0	3	0	0
6	ratis-8a50099	109.8	8	50	10	51	8	2	0	0	0
7	jackson-databind	210.3	6	47	12	18	6	6	0	0	0
8	picocli-a856a14	776.7	7	70	6	60	6	0	1	0	0
	Total	1289.1	215	406	218	347	194	19	20	1	5

To answer RQ3, we compare ILoop with Pulse (Infer version id: 5050294, July 2023). The results of our experiments are shown in Table 2. We analyse the bugs reported by both tools, categorizing them as true or false positives. Focusing on non-overlapping reports to highlight the differences between ILoop and Pulse, we find that ILoop eliminates an average of 16.9% of Pulse's false positives and identifies 10.1% new true positives. Together, these improvements lead to a 27.0% increase in precision. The missed true bugs and newly introduced false positives represent a small fraction of ILoop's reports and both tools exhibit similar running times. Overall, our findings demonstrate that our approach effectively enhances bug-finding precision.

7   Related Work and Conclusion

Incorrectness Logic. Applications of IL have been investigated in different domains, such as finding memory errors in large C projects [20], detecting data race/deadlock in concurrent programs [36], verifying quantum while-programs [15], detecting logical bugs in quantum programs [39], detecting forbidden graph structures and failing executions [34]. Similar to IL, other recent logics focusing on under-approximating reasoning include local completeness of abstract interpretation [11], outcome logic [40], and exact separation logic [29]. Unfortunately, none of them supports class inheritance and method overriding, except for [26]. [26] proposes a verification system for upholding Liskov substitution principle (LSP) in under-approximating reasoning. However, specifications must be manually provided in this system, and the lack of automation could limit its practicality in analysing large projects. Moreover, their work focuses on verification. It is hard for users to know if an error specification is risky or likely harmless. Our reporting criteria remedy this by only reporting dangerous error specifications automatically.

Formal Verification for OO programs. OO program verification via over-approximation has been extensively studied in various works: Verifying objects through dynamic frames to handle aliasing problem [18]; using supertype abstraction for concise and modular reasoning [28,23,21,22]; using separation logic and abstraction predicate for reasoning about abstract datatypes [32,38]; using class invariant to ensure the functional correctness of programs [16,9,25]. Later, two independent papers [13,33] propose the co-existence of static/dynamic specifications for OOP to uphold LSP while avoiding re-verification. Following the landscape of the proposals in [13,32,33,26], we propose our system for IL static/dynamic specification inference in OO programs.

Bugs in OO Programs. NPEs and CCEs are common bug types in OO programs. Error-prone is a pattern-based bug detector [2]. It supports CCE detection, but only finds CCEs in a specific way via pattern recognition [3]. In our work, we thoroughly study how to detect possible CCEs and our ILoop can effectively find more bugs. On the other hand, ILoop also outperforms another state-of-the-art Pulse in terms of finding NPEs as we model the OO features in our approach, such as class inheritance and method overriding. DOOP framework [10] performs pointer analysis for Java programs using Datalog, which potentially discovers CCEs when pointers are cast improperly. However, DOOP's analysis is not fully modular. It requires a *main* method as an entry point, and only pointers initialised can be checked. Such scenarios are the subsets of our CCE reporting criteria. DOOP could not find the errors like Fig. 1, Fig. 7.

Specification Inference via Bi-abduction. Bi-abduction [12] is a form of logical inference for separation logic that automates local reasoning. Bi-abduction generates *pre/post* based on *frame* and *anti-frame* formulae inference. Like the prior tool Pulse-X, we also make use of the bi-abduction technique in our specification inference process. Moreover, we incorporate type information analysis, which enables our tool to support class inheritance and method overriding. In addition, we propose the merging mechanism to support generalised error reporting, which improves the bug-finding precision.

Conclusion. Motivated by the question "How to generically and automatically infer IL specifications for object-oriented programs?", we demonstrate that carrying type information is crucial. Type constraints reveal runtime type possibilities, enabling static analysis of dynamic behaviours. Our system reasons about casting operations and infers static/dynamic specifications to effectively identify bugs in OO programs. Specifically, we formalise the *inference relations* to guarantee the validity of our inferred specifications. We also provide novel insights into bug reporting for OO programs, supporting both NPE and CCE detections through sound reasoning. Our approach establishes a formal foundation for IL-based bi-abductive inference in OO programs.

Acknowledgment. This work is supported by a Singapore Ministry of Education (MoE) Tier 3 grant "Automated Program Repair", MOE-MOET32021-0001. We thank anonymous reviewers for their insightful comments.

References

1. The apache software foundation. https://github.com/apache. Accessed: 2024-1-13.
2. Error prone: a static analysis tool for java that catches common programming mistakes. https://github.com/google/error-prone. Accessed: 2024-05-16.
3. Error prone patterns: a static analysis tool for java that catches common programming mistakes. https://errorprone.info/bugpatterns. Accessed: 2024-05-16.
4. A false positive. https://github.com/apache/pdfbox/blob/trunk/debugger/src/main/java/org/apache/pdfbox/debugger/ui/ErrorDialog.java. Accessed: 2024-02-16.
5. jackson-databind. https://github.com/FasterXML/jackson-databind/blob/4a401237adfe3fd4e417504176171f76464aae96/src/main/java/com/fasterxml/jackson/databind/deser/BeanDeserializerFactory.java. Accessed: 2024-10-13.
6. An open source java tool for working with pdf documents: Pdfbox. https://github.com/apache/pdfbox/commit/eaf3b9862e80f1065f59acce150b38dd66a007c7. Accessed: 2024-02-16.
7. Hdrhistogram - (commit id: 030aac1). https://github.com/HdrHistogram/HdrHistogram/commit/030aac1ea20b8c09e7c522a4594388534164d643, 12 2023. Accessed: 2023-12-20.
8. ILoop source code. https://github.com/liwenhual/infer, 2024.
9. Michael Barnett, Robert DeLine, Manuel Fähndrich, K Rustan M Leino, and Wolfram Schulte. Verification of object-oriented programs with invariants. *J. Object Technol.*, 3(6):27–56, 2004.

10. Martin Bravenboer and Yannis Smaragdakis. Strictly declarative specification of sophisticated points-to analyses. In Shail Arora and Gary T. Leavens, editors, *Proceedings of the 24th Annual ACM SIGPLAN Conference on Object-Oriented Programming, Systems, Languages, and Applications, OOPSLA 2009, October 25-29, 2009, Orlando, Florida, USA*, pages 243–262. ACM, 2009.
11. Roberto Bruni, Roberto Giacobazzi, Roberta Gori, and Francesco Ranzato. A correctness and incorrectness program logic. *J. ACM*, 70(2), mar 2023.
12. Cristiano Calcagno, Dino Distefano, Peter O'Hearn, and Hongseok Yang. Compositional shape analysis by means of bi-abduction. In *Proceedings of the 36th annual ACM SIGPLAN-SIGACT symposium on Principles of programming languages*, pages 289–300, 2009.
13. Wei-Ngan Chin, Cristina David, Huu Hai Nguyen, and Shengchao Qin. Enhancing modular oo verification with separation logic. In *Proceedings of the 35th Annual ACM SIGPLAN-SIGACT Symposium on Principles of Programming Languages*, POPL '08, pages 87–99, New York, NY, USA, 2008. Association for Computing Machinery.
14. Roberta Coelho, Lucas Almeida, Georgios Gousios, and Arie Van Deursen. Unveiling exception handling bug hazards in android based on github and google code issues. In *2015 IEEE/ACM 12th Working Conference on Mining Software Repositories*, pages 134–145. IEEE, 2015.
15. Yuan Feng and Sanjiang Li. Abstract interpretation, hoare logic, and incorrectness logic for quantum programs. *Information and Computation*, 294:105077, 2023.
16. C.A.R. Hoare. Proof of correctness of data representations. *Acta Informatica*, 1(4):271–281, 1972.
17. Infer. Infer's test repository. https://github.com/facebook/infer/blob/main/infer/tests/codetoanalyze/java/pulse. Accessed: 2023-8-20.
18. Ioannis T Kassios. Dynamic frames: Support for framing, dependencies and sharing without restrictions. In *FM 2006: Formal Methods: 14th International Symposium on Formal Methods, Hamilton, Canada, August 21-27, 2006. Proceedings 14*, pages 268–283. Springer, 2006.
19. Maria Kechagia and Diomidis Spinellis. Undocumented and unchecked: exceptions that spell trouble. In *Proceedings of the 11th Working Conference on Mining Software Repositories*, pages 312–315, 2014.
20. Quang Loc Le, Azalea Raad, Jules Villard, Josh Berdine, Derek Dreyer, and Peter W. O'Hearn. Finding real bugs in big programs with incorrectness logic. *Proc. ACM Program. Lang.*, 6(OOPSLA1), apr 2022.
21. Gary T Leavens and David A Naumann. Behavioral subtyping is equivalent to modular reasoning for object-oriented programs. *Department of Computer Science, Iowa State University, Ames, Iowa*, 50011:06–36, 2006.
22. Gary T Leavens and David A Naumann. Behavioral subtyping, specification inheritance, and modular reasoning. *ACM Transactions on Programming Languages and Systems (TOPLAS)*, 37(4):1–88, 2015.
23. Gary T Leavens and William E Weihl. Specification and verification of object-oriented programs using supertype abstraction. *Acta Informatica*, 32(8):705–778, 1995.
24. Junhee Lee, Seongjoon Hong, and Hakjoo Oh. Npex: Repairing java null pointer exceptions without tests. In *Proceedings of the 44th International Conference on Software Engineering*, pages 1532–1544, 2022.
25. K Rustan M Leino and Peter Müller. Object invariants in dynamic contexts. In *European Conference on Object-Oriented Programming*, pages 491–515. Springer, 2004.

26. Wenhua Li, Quang Loc Le, Yahui Song, and Wei-Ngan Chin. Incorrectness proofs for object-oriented programs via subclass reflection. In Chung-Kil Hur, editor, *Programming Languages and Systems - 21st Asian Symposium, APLAS 2023, Taipei, Taiwan, November 26-29, 2023, Proceedings*, volume 14405 of *Lecture Notes in Computer Science*, pages 269–289. Springer, 2023.

27. Wenhua Li, Quang Loc Le, Yahui Song, and Wei-Ngan Chin. Inferring incorrectness specifications for object-oriented programs (technical report). `https://github.com/liwenhua1/infer/blob/main/TACAS25.pdf`, 2024.

28. Barbara Liskov. Keynote address-data abstraction and hierarchy. In *Addendum to the proceedings on Object-oriented programming systems, languages and applications (Addendum)*, pages 17–34, 1987.

29. Petar Maksimović, Caroline Cronjäger, Andreas Lööw, Julian Sutherland, and Philippa Gardner. Exact Separation Logic: Towards Bridging the Gap Between Verification and Bug-Finding. In Karim Ali and Guido Salvaneschi, editors, *37th European Conference on Object-Oriented Programming (ECOOP 2023)*, volume 263 of *Leibniz International Proceedings in Informatics (LIPIcs)*, pages 19:1–19:27, Dagstuhl, Germany, 2023. Schloss Dagstuhl – Leibniz-Zentrum für Informatik.

30. Luis Mastrangelo, Matthias Hauswirth, and Nathaniel Nystrom. Casting about in the dark: An empirical study of cast operations in java programs. *Proceedings of the ACM on Programming Languages*, 3(OOPSLA):1–31, 2019.

31. Peter W. O'Hearn. Incorrectness logic. *Proc. ACM Program. Lang.*, 4(POPL):10:1–10:32, 2020.

32. Matthew Parkinson and Gavin Bierman. Separation logic and abstraction. In *Proceedings of the 32nd ACM SIGPLAN-SIGACT symposium on Principles of programming languages*, pages 247–258, 2005.

33. Matthew J Parkinson and Gavin M Bierman. Separation logic, abstraction and inheritance. *ACM SIGPLAN Notices*, 43(1):75–86, 2008.

34. Christopher M Poskitt. Incorrectness logic for graph programs. In *International Conference on Graph Transformation*, pages 81–101. Springer, 2021.

35. Azalea Raad, Josh Berdine, Hoang-Hai Dang, Derek Dreyer, Peter O'Hearn, and Jules Villard. Local reasoning about the presence of bugs: Incorrectness separation logic. In *International Conference on Computer Aided Verification*, pages 225–252. Springer, 2020.

36. Azalea Raad, Josh Berdine, Derek Dreyer, and Peter W O'Hearn. Concurrent incorrectness separation logic. *Proceedings of the ACM on Programming Languages*, 6(POPL):1–29, 2022.

37. Yahui Song, Xiang Gao, Wenhua Li, Wei-Ngan Chin, and Abhik Roychoudhury. Provenfix: Temporal property-guided program repair. *Proc. ACM Softw. Eng.*, 1(FSE):226–248, 2024.

38. Stephan van Staden, Cristiano Calcagno, and Bertrand Meyer. Verifying executable object-oriented specifications with separation logic. In *ECOOP 2010–Object-Oriented Programming: 24th European Conference, Maribor, Slovenia, June 21-25, 2010. Proceedings 24*, pages 151–174. Springer, 2010.

39. Peng Yan, Hanru Jiang, and Nengkun Yu. On incorrectness logic for quantum programs. *Proceedings of the ACM on Programming Languages*, 6(OOPSLA1):1–28, 2022.

40. Noam Zilberstein, Derek Dreyer, and Alexandra Silva. Outcome logic: A unifying foundation for correctness and incorrectness reasoning. *Proc. ACM Program. Lang.*, 7(OOPSLA1), apr 2023.

Performance Heuristics for GR(1) Realizability Checking and Related Analyses

Roy Yatskan, Ilia Shevrin, and Shahar Maoz[✉]

Tel Aviv University, Israel
maoz@cs.tau.ac.il

Abstract. Reactive synthesis is an automated process for deriving correct-by-construction reactive systems from temporal specifications. GR(1), in particular, is a popular LTL fragment that balances efficient synthesis complexity and expressiveness. In this paper, we present a set of novel heuristics to further improve the performance of GR(1) realizability checking and related algorithms, motivated by several observations. These heuristics include (1) discarding intermediate memory not required for many GR(1) algorithms, (2) setting good initial orders of variables and justice constraints, (3) improving the embedding of finite automata into GR(1) when supporting advanced language constructs, and (4) algorithm-specific heuristics for additional GR(1) analyses such as non-well-separation and inherent vacuity detection. We implemented these heuristics in the Spectra synthesizer, and extensively validated and evaluated them on well-known benchmarks consisting of hundreds of specifications. Our results show major performance gains, in particular, an average of realizability checking at least two times faster than the baseline.

1 Introduction

Reactive synthesis is an automated process for deriving correct-by-construction reactive systems from temporal specifications [41]. Unlike traditional approaches that involve manual system construction followed by model checking, synthesis directly generates an implementation guaranteed to satisfy the given specification, provided such an implementation exists.

We focus on GR(1) [9], a fragment of Linear Temporal Logic (LTL). GR(1) specifications comprise initial, safety, and justice assumptions and guarantees. Initial properties define the expected state at the outset, safety properties specify invariants for all states and transitions, and justice properties describe conditions that must be satisfied infinitely often in any infinite run. GR(1) has gained popularity and was implemented in several tools, e.g., RATSY [6], Slugs [17], and Spectra [32], thanks to its relatively efficient symbolic synthesis algorithm and expressive power, capable of representing almost all of the common specification patterns identified by Dwyer et al. [16,29]. Its balance of expressiveness and computational efficiency makes it suitable for a wide range of applications of reactive synthesis, e.g., in robotics [26,30].

© The Author(s) 2025
A. Gurfinkel and M. Heule (Eds.): TACAS 2025, LNCS 15696, pp. 40–59, 2025.
https://doi.org/10.1007/978-3-031-90643-5_3

In this paper, we present a set of novel heuristics designed to improve the performance of GR(1) realizability checking and related algorithms. Developing specifications is a long, iterative process, just like developing program code. Our focus is on reducing the computational cost of the actual algorithms used in specification development to improve the developer experience.

We start by making the following high-level observations:

- Many analyses used during specification development do not require the intermediate results of the GR(1) algorithm's fixed-point iterations. These are required only for controller construction, but not for analyses such as realizability checking, non-well-separation detection [25,31], inherent vacuity detection [34], and kind-realizability checking [22,28].
- The syntax of the specification, as written by developers, provides opportunities for deeper insight into the inner structure of the GR(1) game model and corresponding opportunities for performance improvements.
- High-level language constructs simplify writing and reading complex specifications but often introduce hidden costs, such as additional variables and constraints. Some of these may be unavoidable, but others may be redundant.

Based on these observations, we present concrete heuristics that target various aspects of GR(1) realizability checking and related analyses:

- A partial memoryless heuristics, which discards the parts of the memory accumulated during realizability checking that are not required for realizability checking and for previously presented heuristics from [19].
- Heuristics to set an initial order on the variables of the specification and an order on the specification's justice constraints, by embedding semantic information from the specification in a graph-based representation and using off-the-shelf graph algorithms to minimize graph bandwidth and compute the relative importance of nodes.
- Heuristics to improve the embedding of finite automata into GR(1), to enable more efficient addition of high-level constructs like patterns and triggers.
- Algorithm-specific heuristics for two important analyses beyond realizability checking, the detection of non-well-separation [25,31] and the detection of inherent vacuities [34] in GR(1) specifications.

All the heuristics we present are conservatively sound, that is, they never change the analysis result (except for one case, see Rem. 1). They only affect the computation's total memory and time. Moreover, all the heuristics we present are fully automatic and completely transparent to the developer who wrote the specification.

We have implemented our ideas on top of the Spectra GR(1) synthesizer [32]. We chose Spectra due to its support for GR(1) and related algorithms, its use of existing heuristics [19], and the thousands of specifications it offers for extensive evaluation. Additionally, Spectra's rich specification language includes high-level constructs such as counters, patterns [29], and triggers [5], allowing more expressive and readable specifications within GR(1).

We have validated and evaluated the implemented heuristics on benchmarks from the literature, including 3390 specifications from the SYNTECH benchmarks. Our results show major performance gains, in particular, an average of realizability checking at least two times faster than the baseline.

2   Background on GR(1) and Spectra

We provide a short background on GR(1) and Spectra, with references to relevant papers for more details and complete formal definitions.

2.1   GR(1)

Since LTL synthesis is computationally expensive (2EXPTIME-complete [41]), authors have suggested LTL fragments with more efficient synthesis algorithms, for example, GR(1) [9,40], whose expressive power covers most of the well-known LTL specification patterns [16,29]. GR(1) specifications include assumptions and guarantees about what needs to hold on all initial states, on all states and transitions (safety), and infinitely often on every run (justice). A GR(1) synthesis problem consists of the following elements [9]:

- $\mathcal{X}$ is a set of input variables controlled by the environment;
- $\mathcal{Y}$ is a set of output variables controlled by the system;
- θ^e is an assertion, i.e., a propositional logic formula, over $\mathcal{X}$ characterizing initial environment states;
- θ^s is an assertion over $\mathcal{V} = \mathcal{X} \cup \mathcal{Y}$ characterizing initial system states;
- ρ^e is an assertion over $\mathcal{V} \cup \mathcal{X}'$, with $\mathcal{X}'$ a primed copy of variables $\mathcal{X}$; given a state, ρ^e restricts the next input;
- ρ^s is an assertion over $\mathcal{V} \cup \mathcal{V}'$, with $\mathcal{V}'$ a primed copy of variables $\mathcal{V}$; given a state and input, ρ^s restricts the next output;
- $J^e_{i \in 1..n}$ is a set of assertions over $\mathcal{V}$ for the environment to satisfy infinitely often (called justice assumptions);
- $J^s_{j \in 1..m}$ is a set of assertions over $\mathcal{V}$ for the system to satisfy infinitely often (called justice guarantees).

GR(1) Realizability A GR(1) synthesis problem is strictly realizable iff the following LTL formula is realizable:

$$\phi_{sr} = (\theta_e \rightarrow \theta_s) \wedge (\theta_e \rightarrow G((H\rho_e) \rightarrow \rho_s))$$
$$\wedge\ (\theta_e \wedge G\rho_e \rightarrow (\bigwedge_{i=1}^{n} GFJ^e_i \rightarrow \bigwedge_{j=1}^{m} GFJ^s_j)) \tag{1}$$

GR(1) realizability can be checked using the 3-nested fixed-point algorithm shown in Alg. 1.

Algorithm 1 GR(1) game algorithm [9] to compute system winning states Z

1: $Z = \textbf{true}$
2: **while** not reached fixed-point of Z **do**
3:      **for** $j = 1$ **to** $|J^s|$ **do**
4:          $Y = \textbf{false}$; $cy = 0$
5:          **while** not reached fixed-point of Y **do**
6:              $start = J_j^s \wedge \bigcirc Z \vee \bigcirc Y$
7:              $Y = \textbf{false}$
8:              **for** $i = 1$ **to** $|J^e|$ **do**
9:                  $X = Z$ //better approx. than **true**, see [9]
10:                  **while** not reached fixed-point of X **do**
11:                      $X = start \vee (\neg J_i^e \wedge \bigcirc X)$
12:                  **end while**
13:                  $Y = Y \vee X$
14:                  $\texttt{X}[j][i][cy] \leftarrow X$
15:              **end for**
16:              $\texttt{Y}[j][cy\texttt{++}] \leftarrow Y$
17:          **end while**
18:          $Z = Y$
19:          $\texttt{Z}[j] = \texttt{Y}$
20:      **end for**
21: **end whilereturn** Z

2.2 Spectra

Spectra [32] is a specification language and a synthesis environment that includes a GR(1) synthesizer. It extends GR(1)'s Boolean variables to finite-type variables, e.g., enumerations and bounded integers. Beyond GR(1) with several performance heuristics [19], it includes extensions that are reduced into GR(1), e.g., patterns [29] and triggers [5], and comes with several analyses, e.g., well-separation detection [31] and repairs for unrealizable specifications [33]. Since 2015, Spectra has been used by hundreds of final-year CS undergrads in semester-long project classes at Tel Aviv University, specifying and executing robotic and other systems, resulting in the SYNTECH collection of specifications. Spectra is available from https://github.com/spectrasynthesizer.

Patterns and Triggers Dwyer et al. [16] have identified 55 LTL specification patterns considered common in industrial specifications. An example of a pattern is the property "p becomes true between q and r". Based on [29], a library of almost all of these 55 patterns has been added to Spectra by translating each pattern into a Büchi automaton and then using auxiliary variables, initial, safety, and justice constraints to embed it within the GR(1) specification.

Triggers are another Spectra language construct that aims to improve expressiveness and readability. Spectra triggers are similar to PSL triggers [18,23]. A trigger is a formula of the form $regexp1 \mid => regexp2$, where $regexp1$ and $regexp2$ are regular expressions (REs) over assertions on the specification's variables. *regexp1* is the prefix RE of the trigger, and *regexp2* is the suffix RE of the trigger. Roughly, the formula represents a conditional satisfaction such that whenever *regexp1* holds, *regexp2* should hold immediately afterward. Similar to the patterns mentioned above, the addition of triggers to Spectra is done by translating the trigger into a Büchi automaton and then using auxiliary variables, initial, safety, and justice constraints to embed it within the GR(1) specification. See [5].

Abstract Syntax of a Specification Some of the heuristics we present depend on the syntax of the specification. We repeat here the abstract syntax definition of a GR(1) specification, from [34].

Definition 1 (Abstract syntax of a specification). *A GR(1) specification is a tuple $Spec = \langle V_e, V_s, D, M_e, M_s \rangle$, where V_e and V_s are sets of environment and system variables respectively, $D : V_e \cup V_s \to Doms$ assigns a finite domain to each variable, and M_e and M_s are the environment and system modules. A module is a triplet $M = \langle I, T, J \rangle$ that contains sets of initial assertions $I = \{I_n\}_{n=1}^{i}$, safety assertions $T = \{T_n\}_{n=1}^{t}$, and justice assertions $J = \{J_n\}_{n=1}^{j}$ of the module, where $i = |I|, t = |T|$ and $j = |J|$. The set of elements of module $M = \langle I, T, J \rangle$ is $B_M = I \cup \{\mathbf{G}T_i\}_{i=1}^{t} \cup \{\mathbf{GF}J_i\}_{i=1}^{j}$.*

2.3 Binary Decision Diagrams (BDDs) and Variable Ordering

All computations described above are performed symbolically using manipulations on Boolean functions. These are implemented using Binary Decision Diagrams (BDDs) [12], which are concise representations for Boolean functions that allow for fast manipulation.

The performance of BDD manipulation algorithms is highly sensitive to the ordering of variables within the BDD [13]. Finding an optimal variable ordering for BDDs is NP-hard [10]. As a result, heuristic approaches are employed to discover good orderings. These approaches are divided into two categories: dynamic variable reordering methods targeting the BDD level independently of the model, and static variable ordering using model-specific information.

The most commonly used method is dynamic variable reordering using sifting [42], which iteratively refines the ordering during computation. While sifting has proven fast and effective, it does not always achieve optimal performance [39].

3 Performance Heuristics

For each heuristics, we discuss motivation and background, present the heuristics itself, and consider its expected impact. Some of the heuristics apply to the realizability checking algorithm itself. Others are applied during the construction of the game model before the fixed-point computation starts. The heuristics are independent, meaning each can be applied regardless of the others. That said, some are related in the sense that in the presence of one, another is expected to become more effective. All our heuristics are conservatively sound, meaning they don't alter the analysis result (except for one case, see Rem. 1). They only impact memory usage and computation time.

3.1   Memoryless Computation

The GR(1) synthesis algorithm, as presented in [9], retains fixed-point results throughout the computation process in order to facilitate the construction of a controller. This approach is implemented by default in notable GR(1) synthesizers like Spectra and Slugs [17]. However, for realizability checking alone, retaining these intermediate results is unnecessary.

Motivation Software development involves iterative steps of coding and debugging, just as specification development requires multiple cycles of realizability checks and refinements before finalizing the specification for controller construction. Ma'ayan and Maoz [27] recommend an iterative development scheme with frequent realizability checks, saving full synthesis for the final realizable specification, resulting in many checks without immediate controller construction.

Heuristics In [19], Firman et al. introduced several performance heuristics for GR(1) synthesis, including: sca: combined conjunction and existential abstraction; eun: early detection of unrealizability; efp: early detection of fixed-point; and fpr: fixed-point recycling.

Importantly, while the intermediate results are not necessary for realizability checking, some of the above heuristics rely on them. Specifically, efp requires saving the intermediate Z fixed-point BDDs, and fpr requires saving the intermediate X fixed-point BDDs. We therefore consider two alternative heuristics: **full memoryless**: discards the X, Y, and Z fixed-point BDDs, and utilizes only sca and eun heuristics; and **partial memoryless**: discards only the Y fixed-point BDDs, and fully utilizes the four heuristics.

Avoiding efp might lead to worse performance on some unrealizable specs, and avoiding fpr is expected to increase the lengths of fixed-point iterations. Following preliminary experiments on a small arbitrary subset of specifications from our corpus, which confirmed the above weaknesses of the full memoryless alternative, we decided to employ the partial memoryless alternative in our work.

Expected Impact We expect that our partial memoryless approach would reduce running times, not only thanks to faster sifting (or other dynamic reordering algorithms if used) but also thanks to a better variable ordering (intuitively, with fewer BDDs stored in memory, finding an effective ordering is easier).

3.2   Initial Static Variable Ordering

Motivation Considerable work has been done on static variable ordering for BDD-based models, e.g., [2,3,4,35]. To the best of our knowledge, it has not been attempted for GR(1) or LTL synthesis. We propose a static variable ordering heuristic that leverages GR(1) structure to put together semantically related variables. This creates a better starting point for the dynamic ordering method (specifically, sifting) used later in the GR(1) algorithm.

Heuristics Our approach follows ideas from [35], applied to our context of GR(1). We start by representing the GR(1) specification as a bipartite graph, where one set of nodes represents the specification's variables (both unprimed and primed), and the other set of nodes represents the constraints, including initial, safety, and justice assumptions and guarantees, the Spectra constructs (triggers, counters, patterns), and the multiple constraints derived from them. An edge between a variable and a constraint means that the variable appears in the constraint's support. The graph serves as an abstraction, only capturing relationships between specification elements and variables.

Next, we build the graph's adjacency matrix and apply an off-the-shelf implementation of the classic Cuthill-McKee algorithm [15] (technically, its commonly used reversed variant), to minimize the matrix's bandwidth, i.e., the distance of nonzeros to the diagonal of a matrix. Since Cuthill-Mckee only accepts symmetric matrices, we apply the symmetrization and de-symmetrization approach used in [35]. Reducing bandwidth roughly corresponds to our goal of making variables that are in the support of the same constraints closely ordered.

Expected Impact We hypothesize that complementing the dynamic ordering during the GR(1) algorithm with a good initial static ordering would positively impact performance. Minimizing the bandwidth is expected to put related variables (w.r.t. the constraints they appear in) close to each other.

That said, the initial ordering currently used by Spectra is not arbitrary - it follows the original variable declaration order from the specification and puts all unprimed and primed variables for each domain together. For human-written specifications, it is reasonable to assume that related variables are often close together in the specification file. Thus, currently implemented ordering may already be relatively effective, and it is not clear that our proposed heuristics would outperform it.

3.3   Justice Ordering

Motivation In GR(1) specifications, the environment and system justices represent fairness conditions. The order in which they are written in the specification doesn't affect its semantics. However, we have performed preliminary experiments showing that their computation order in the fixed-point algorithm can significantly impact performance. The current implementation in Spectra follows the order in which the justices are originally written in the specification.

We propose a method to order the environment justices and system justices, each set separately, based on their relative importance in the specification structure. We hypothesize that trying to reach the most important justices first will improve the algorithm's performance.

Heuristics To determine the relative importance of justices, we build a bipartite graph similar to the one presented earlier, i.e., where one set of nodes represents the specification's variables, and the other set represents the constraints (initial, safety, and justice assumptions and guarantees). An edge between a variable and a constraint means that the variable appears in the constraint's support.

To determine the importance of each justice, we use the eigenvalue centrality score (see, e.g., [11]), as implemented in the JGraphT [37] library. A popular adaption of eigenvalue centrality is PageRank [38]. We use the centrality score to reorder each set of justices, environment and system, in decreasing order.

Expected Impact Justice ordering is expected to positively affect the performance of the GR(1) realizability checking algorithm by potentially reaching fixed-points faster. Faster running time via a specific order is partly caused by a reduction in the total number of fixed-point iterations, as we have confirmed in our preliminary experiments.

Spectra already uses the order as it appears in the specification file. This order is already not random but typically based on the developer's natural intention to put the most important constructs first or to put related constructs close to one another. We ran preliminary experiments that showed that this order is already much better than a random one. Therefore, in our evaluation in Sect. 4, we compare our heuristics to the original order, and not to a random one.

Finally, observe that our suggested order may outperform the specification file's order not only by speeding up computation, but also by providing consistent performance, regardless of how the engineer chose to write the specification.

3.4   Simplified Automaton Embedding into GR(1)

Background and Motivation To allow for more concise specifications and easier expression of complex properties that capture LTL logic without a direct GR(1) equivalent (without additional variables), Spectra supports the use of specification patterns [16,29] and triggers [5]. This support is systematically done in Spectra by embedding generated automata into the game model, using auxiliary variables. Although this is done inside the synthesizer and is completely transparent to the specification developer, it adds variables and justice constraints to the game model. It thus increases the specification's complexity and state-space and in general results in a negative effect on performance.

Observation and Heuristics We observed that many of the specification patterns already defined in Spectra's patterns library and potentially many of the triggers written by developers are currently encoded using a Büchi automaton with a justice acceptance condition. However, many of them are actually safety properties that can be encoded with fewer states and potentially fewer variables. Specifically, we found that 36 of the 51 patterns in the library can be expressed without a justice condition.

```
1  pattern P_becomes_true_between_Q_and_R(p, q, r) {
2    var { S0, S1, S2} state;
3
4    -- initial assignments: initial state
5    state=S0;
6
7    -- safety this and next state
8    alw (
9    (state=S0 & ((!q & !p) | (q & r) | (!r & p) | (!q & r & p)) &
         next(state=S0)) |
10   (state=S0 & (q & !r & !p) & next(state=S1)) |
11   (state=S1 & (!r & p) & next(state=S0)) |
12   (state=S1 & (!r & !p) & next(state=S1)) |
13   (state=S1 & (r) & next(state=S2)) |
14   (state=S2 & TRUE & next(state=S2)));
15
16   -- equivalence of satisfaction
17   alwEv (state=S0 | state=S1);}
```

Listing 1. The example pattern before the application of our heuristics

Definition 2 (dead-end state). *Given an automaton, a dead-end state is a state from which no accepting state of the automaton is reachable.*

Spectra's library of patterns was created by translating the patterns given as LTL formulas into minimal deterministic Büchi automata. Therefore, when an LTL formula at hand represents a safety property, its automaton includes a single dead-end state.

Given an automaton representing a pattern, we first remove its dead-end state (and its incoming and outgoing transitions), if any. We then check whether the remaining states are all accepting, and if so, remove the justice from the pattern's representation for Spectra. Note that removing dead-end states does not change the language accepted by the automaton's embedding into GR(1). Moreover, when all states are accepting, the added justice becomes trivially true and is therefore redundant.

For example, the pattern "p becomes true between q and r" appears in Spectra's pattern library as shown in List. 1. In our new simplified automata library, the same pattern is defined as shown in List. 2. Specifically, note that the dead-end state S2 and the justice from line 17 in List. 1 have been removed.

Remark 1 (Effect on the Specification's Semantics). Interestingly, unlike all other heuristics we present in this work, this heuristics has a side effect on the semantics of the GR(1) specification. Specifically, due to the GR(1) semantics of strict realizability [9,25], where the system may avoid satisfying its justice guarantees as long as the environment does not satisfy its justice assumptions, a specification that was regarded as realizable before the application of our heuristics, due to non-well-separation, will become unrealizable after the application of our

```
 1  pattern P_becomes_true_between_Q_and_R(p, q, r) {
 2      var {S0, S1} state;
 3
 4      -- initial assignments: initial state
 5      state=S0;
 6
 7      -- safety this and next state
 8      alw (
 9      (state=S0 & ((!q & !p) | (q & r) | (!r & p) | (!q & r & p)) &
               next(state=S0)) |
10          (state=S0 & (q & !r & !p) & next(state=S1)) |
11          (state=S1 & (!r & p) & next(state=S0)) |
12          (state=S1 & (!r & !p) & next(state=S1)));}
```

Listing 2. The example pattern after the application of our heuristics

heuristics (the justice guarantee violation is replaced with a safety guarantee violation). This side effect is actually desirable, as it prevents the system from taking advantage of non-well-separation and forcing the environment into assumption violation. Indeed, it may happen in realizability checking but cannot happen in kind-realizability checking (see [22,28] and below).

Remark 2 (Simplification for Triggers). The embedding of triggers into GR(1) in Spectra allows a similar simplification. In the general case, the translation adds a justice constraint to ensure that once reaching *regexp2*, eventually the automaton will start waiting again for *regexp1*. However, intuitively, if *regexp2* includes no Kleene star or Kleene plus symbols (or an unbounded range), this eventuality is bounded (there is no cycle in the automaton corresponding to *regexp2*) and so the added justice is redundant. We thus apply a similar simplification heuristics of removing dead-ends and unnecessary justices to the automata generated by Spectra for triggers as well.

Expected Impact Based on the heuristics described above, out of the 51 Dwyer patterns defined in the Spectra library according to [29], 78.4% (40) had a dead-end state that can be removed, 70% (36) had a justice that can be removed, and 45% (23) resulted in the removal of one variable. The removal of a variable (one variable per pattern instance) makes the problem smaller. Moreover, the removal of justice(s) means fewer fixed-point loops to execute. Both the dead-end states and justice removals keep the semantics (see Rem. 1). Finally, applying the heuristics to the patterns library was done offline once, adding no overhead to realizability checking performance. Although applying them to triggers incurs a small overhead, it only affects a small automaton rather than the entire specification. Therefore, we expect these heuristics to improve performance.

3.5 Grouping of Auxiliary Variables

Motivation The original GR(1) setup does not explicitly handle auxiliary variables, but Spectra enhances it with high-level constructs such as patterns, triggers, and counters, which require auxiliary variables for embedding them within GR(1). We observe that these auxiliary variables are local, as they are used only by the constraints representing the pattern, trigger, or counter.

Heuristics Firman et al. [19] considered the grouping for each variable in V_e and V_s, in pairs of primed and unprimed. However, their evaluation showed that this variable grouping approach might worsen performance for some specifications. We suggest a different approach, grouping only auxiliary variables that correspond to the same high-level construct instance.

Expected Impact As the auxiliary variables added for each language construct instance are semantically closely related and are not used directly by any constraint outside the construct instance, we expect that their grouping based on the construct instance they belong to would reduce BDD sizes and speed up BDD operations. Grouping is also expected to reduce dynamic reordering times, as reordering is done at the group level and not at the level of each variable alone.

3.6 Heuristics for Additional GR(1) Specification Analyses

All the above heuristics are relevant not only to the GR(1) realizability checking algorithm but also to other existing analyses for GR(1) specifications: non-well-separation, kind-realizability, and inherent vacuity.

Well-separation [25,31] is a property of environment specifications that ensures the environment cannot be forced to violate its own assumptions, regardless of system behavior. Spectra includes an algorithm for detecting non-well-separated GR(1) specifications by reducing the problem to GR(1) realizability checking. We apply all the heuristics mentioned above to the non-well-separation detection in Spectra. Notably, detecting non-well-separation does not require guarantees, so we do not load them. We expect these heuristics to enhance the performance of non-well-separation detection.

Kind-realizability [22], following [28], uses a 4 fixed-points realizability checking algorithm that checks the existence of a strategy that ensures that the system does not exploit non-well-separated specifications, i.e., by forcing environment assumption violations. This 4 fixed-point algorithm, while capturing the concept of realizability in a more desired way, incurs significantly higher computational costs, as evident in experiments presented in [22,28]. This limits its use in practice. We apply all the above heuristics to the kind-realizability checking implemented in Spectra.

Inherent vacuity [20] deals with redundant elements in a specification. Spectra includes an implementation of inherent vacuity detection for GR(1) [34], specifically identifying assumptions, guarantees, and variable values whose removal from the specification will not change its semantics. We apply all the above heuristics to the inherent vacuity detection implemented in Spectra. We further observe that in the case of redundant environment variable values, there is no need for the system guarantees and therefore do not load them at all. The application of all these heuristics is expected to improve the performance of inherent vacuity detection.

4   Evaluation

4.1   Specification Corpus, Implementation, and Validation

Specification Corpus We used two main sources for specifications. First, the SYNTECH set of benchmarks, which includes specifications written by CS students during semester-long project classes between 2015 and 2023, modeling and executing or simulating many robotic and other systems. They include not only final specifications but also many intermediate versions from the specification development process, and so, e.g., many unrealizable specifications. The SYNTECH benchmarks have been used in the evaluation of many previous works, e.g., [5,14,19,22,27,36]. Second, Spectra versions of AMBA [7] and GenBuf [8], which are parametric specifications commonly used in the evaluation of GR(1) and related algorithms and are part of the SYNTCOMP benchmark [24].

The SYNTECH benchmark includes a total of 3390 specifications. We used 9 AMBA specifications (2 to 10 masters) and 14 GenBuf specifications (5 to 130 requests).

To evaluate the heuristics that relate to patterns and triggers, we focused on specific subsets of the SYNTECH specifications that already include at least one pattern or at least one trigger (but not necessarily ones that are amenable to our automata simplification heuristics). Out of the SYNTECH specs, 449 include at least one pattern and 173 of these include at least one pattern relevant to our heuristics. Similarly, 217 include at least one trigger and 176 of these include at least one trigger relevant to our heuristics (not all triggers in the benchmark can have their state/justice reduced; the heuristics applies only to triggers whose second SFA contains an unnecessary sink state, see Rem. 2). We name these SYNTECH-P and SYNTECH-T respectively.

To evaluate the heuristics that relate to well-separation, we used only the subset of realizable specifications from SYNTECH. We name it SYNTECH-R.

Implementation We have implemented our ideas on top of the Spectra GR(1) synthesizer [32] (with the heuristics of [19]), with a modified version of the CUDD BDD library, implemented in C [43]. The dynamic reordering method used is sifting. Other settings remain unchanged. We used the Cuthill-Mckee implementation available in the Boost C++ library [1].

Validation To validate the correctness of our ideas and implementation, we conducted extensive testing for each algorithm (GR(1), kind-realizability checking, well-separation, and inherent vacuity). Specifically, we compared the results from the public version of Spectra (i.e., without our heuristics), and our new implementation with heuristics, to check that they agree. We executed these tests on all specifications in our corpus.

The single case where the results may not agree, see Rem. 1, happened in realizability checking of exactly one specification that passed the lower bound filter (see below) from SYNTECH-T. As expected, it did not happen in the kind-realizability checks.

4.2   Experiment Setup and Reporting

We ran all experiments on an AWS t3.2xlarge instance (representing an ordinary laptop with up to 3.1GHz CPU and 32GB RAM) with Windows 10 64-bit OS, Java 11 64Bit, and CUDD 3 compiled for 64Bit, using one CPU core. Times we use are average values of 3 runs, measured in milliseconds. Although the algorithms we deal with are deterministic, we performed 3 runs as JVM garbage collection and the CUDD implementation of dynamic reordering add variance to running times. To simplify the presentation, we use a fixed table structure to report all results. We now explain the meaning of the columns in the table.

Columns Benchmark and #>60s: To focus on the cases where improving performance is more valuable, we filtered out from the experiment results for each benchmark all specifications where the original realizability checking by Spectra (with the heuristics of [19]) took less than 60 seconds. Column Benchmark presents the benchmark name and column #>60s shows how many of the specifications in this benchmark passed the lower bound filter. The remainder of the table refers to this number.

Columns R50%, R, and R<1: For each benchmark, we compute the geometric mean of the ratios between the time with the heuristics and the baseline time. That is, every number below 1.0 means that the heuristics had, on average, made the computation faster. The lower the number, the faster the heuristics relative to the baseline. We report two such average ratios, for the specifications whose baseline performance was slower than the median baseline performance and for the complete benchmark (after filtering and without timeouts, see below), in columns R50% and R resp. In addition, column R<1 reports the percentage of specifications (after filtering and without timeouts) for which the heuristics has improved running time, i.e., the percentage of specifications for which the ratio was below 1.0. The higher this percentage, the better the results compared to the baseline.

Columns B-TO and H-TO: To keep the cost of the experiments over hundreds of specifications reasonable, we set a timeout of 10 minutes for all experiments. When at least one of the algorithms, with or without the heuristics, reaches the

Heuristics vs. baseline	Benchmark	#>60s	R50%	R	R<1	B-TO	H-TO
Partial memoryless	SYNTECH	268	0.93	0.95	63%	14%	13%
vs. Spectra	AMBA+GenB	12	0.76	0.85	88%	42%	42%
Static variable ordering	SYNTECH	268	0.60	0.56	69%	15%	16%
vs. partial memoryless	AMBA+GenB	12	1.02	1.19	50%	33%	17%
Justice ordering	SYNTECH	268	0.91	0.97	55%	15%	14%
vs. partial memoryless	AMBA+GenB	12	0.67	0.80	25%	33%	42%
	SYNTECH-P	142	0.72	0.76	67%	12%	8%
Simp. auto. + aux. grp.	SYNTECH-T	90	0.52	0.70	74%	17%	14%
vs. partial memoryless	AMBA	9	0.05	0.17	89%	44%	0%
WS vs. part. mem.	SYNTECH-R	197	0.78	0.86	77%	1%	1%
Inh. vac. vs. part. mem.	SYNTECH	268	0.54	0.68	98%	1%	0%

Table 1. Results for individual heuristics (measuring realizability checking times except the last two rows which refer to non-well-separation and inherent vacuity)

Analysis	Benchmark	#>60s	R50%	R	R<1	B-TO	H-TO
Real. check	SYNTECH	268	0.45	0.49	80%	16%	12%
	AMBA+GenBuf	12	0.35	0.60	83%	42%	0%
Well-sep.	SYNTECH-R	197	0.62	0.75	83%	0%	0%
	AMBA+GenBuf	12	0.14	0.27	100%	8%	0%
Kind. real.	SYNTECH	268	0.46	0.57	79%	53%	42%
	AMBA+GenBuf	12	0.20	0.48	67%	33%	0%

Table 2. Results for all heuristics together vs. Spectra

timeout, we do not count it in the computed average ratios. Instead, in columns B-TO and H-TO we report the percentage of specifications that resulted in a timeout for the baseline and for the heuristics respectively.

Minor differences between the results in the two tables are expected as they report results from separate executions of the experiments and thus slightly different baselines.

4.3 Results

We aim to assess the impact of each heuristic on the performance of realizability checking and other analyses. Since the partial memoryless heuristic is expected to affect all algorithms, we first evaluate it against the original Spectra implementation. This partial memoryless version serves as a baseline for subsequent experiments, allowing us to evaluate the additional impact of the other heuristics. We conclude the report with a comparison of all our heuristics against the original Spectra implementation (without the partial memoryless heuristics). In all cases, we use Spectra with all the heuristics from [19].

The evaluation of individual heuristics appears in Table 1.

Partial Memoryless Computation We observe that for 268 specifications of the SYNTECH benchmark, the baseline realizability checking time was more than 60 seconds, and for these specifications, the heuristics performed approximately 5% faster on average, was faster in about 2/3 of the specifications, and resulted in slightly less cases of timeout compared to the Spectra baseline.

As expected, the use of partial memory did not change the number of fixed-point iterations. The reduction in total variable reordering time is mixed, as we observed (not shown in the table) a 15% reduction for SYNTECH and a 2% percent increase for AMBA+GenBuf. This partly explains the improvement we see in performance.

Static Variable Ordering We observe that on the SYNTECH benchmark the heuristics performed at least 40% faster on average, was faster in about 2/3 of the specifications, and resulted in roughly the same number of timeouts. On AMBA+GenBuf, it performed slightly slower on average, but still was faster in half of the specifications, and resulted in fewer timeouts.

Justice Ordering On the SYNTECH benchmark, the heuristics was up to 9% faster on average, was faster in almost 2/3 of the specifications, and resulted in the same number of timeouts. On AMBA+GenBuf, it performed much better on average, but was faster in only a quarter of the specifications, and resulted in more timeouts.

Note that in this heuristics and the previous one, we compare against the original ordering used by Spectra, which is not arbitrary but follows the order in which the variables and justices appear in the specification. Thus, the competition is expected to be tough.

Simplified Automaton Embedding and Grouping of Auxiliary Variables for Patterns and Triggers We observe that the heuristics performed at least 24% faster on average, with higher improvements for originally slow computations. We also observed that the heuristic was faster in at least 2/3 of the specifications in each corpus and resulted in fewer timeouts.

The reductions in running times are partly explained by reductions in the number of X fixed-points iterations (not shown in the table), 9%, 33%, and 79% reduction in the SYNTECH-P, SYNTECH-T, and AMBA corpora respectively.

Interestingly, for AMBA the improvement was exceptional. We investigated it and found that the Spectra specification of AMBA, which aims to formalize the requirements from [21], uses multiple patterns, for readability. For instance, guarantee G2: *When a locked unspecified length burst starts, a new access does not start until the current master (i) releases the bus by lowering HBUSREQi*, which in [21] is formalized using a long LTL formula with the until operator (and several additional operators), is formalized in the Spectra specification, for every i from 0 to N, as

```
P_becomes_true_between_Q_and_R
(!hbusreq[i], locked_unspec_burst(i) & start, next(start));
```

These N patterns create redundant states and justice guarantees, which our heuristics detects and removes.

Heuristics for Additional Specification Analyses For non-well-separation detection (environment only), the heuristics performed at least 14% faster on average, and improved performance on 77% of the specifications.

For inherent vacuity detection (of redundant environment values), the heuristics performed at least 32% faster on average, and improved performance on at least 98% of the specifications.

All Heuristics Together Finally, Table 2 presents results for all heuristics together vs. Spectra, w.r.t. realizability checking, non-well-separation, and kind-realizability.

For the SYNTECH specifications realizability checking, we observe that our heuristics performed on average at least 2 times faster than Spectra, improved performance in 80% of the specifications, and resulted in less timeouts. For well-separation, we observe that our heuristics performed about 25% faster on average, and improved performance on 83% of the specifications. For kind-realizability, our heuristics performed at least 43% faster on average, improved performance in 79% of the specifications, and resulted in less timeouts.

We see similar and even mostly better results for the AMBA+GenBuf specifications.

The reductions in realizability checking running times are partly explained by the reductions in the number of X fixed-points iterations and the reductions in total variable reordering time - with R values of 0.85, 0.45 and R<1 values of 45%, 83% for these metrics respectively.

Why Do Some Specifications Resist Our Heuristics? We checked the characteristics of the 12% of specifications that reached the timeout despite the use of all heuristics (Table 2), compared to the other 88%, and found that the specifications in the first set have on average 42% more variables (101 compared to 70), 72% more pattern instances (1.9 / 1.1), 87% more trigger instances (1.5 / 0.8), and 43% more justice guarantees (6 / 4.2). A deeper analysis is required to better understand whether the challenge is primarily the size of these specifications and how additional heuristics may help.

5   Conclusion

We introduced heuristics to enhance the performance of GR(1) realizability checking and related algorithms. These heuristics are based on three observations: (1) many analyses in specification development do not require the intermediate results of the GR(1) algorithm's fixed-point iterations, (2) the syntax of the specification, as written by developers, reveals insights into the structure of the GR(1) game model, offering opportunities for performance improvements, and (3) while high-level language constructs can simplify the writing and reading of complex specifications, they often incur hidden, redundant costs.

We implemented the heuristics and evaluated them over a large corpus of hundreds of GR(1) specifications written in the Spectra language. The results showed that compared to the previous implementation of the Spectra synthesizer, based on [19], each of the heuristics alone and all of them together result in faster realizability checking and other related analyses.

Artifact An artifact is available in `https://doi.org/10.5281/zenodo.14616533`. It includes the benchmarks used in our evaluation, raw data, and scripts to run and reproduce the experiments.

Acknowledgements This research was supported by the Israel Science Foundation (grant No. 1954/23, SPECTACKLE) as well as by Len Blavatnik and the Blavatnik Family Foundation. The authors thank the anonymous reviewers and Rafi Shalom for helpful comments.

References

1. Boost C++ Libraries, `http://www.boost.org/`
2. Aloul, F., Markov, I., Sakallah, K.: Mince: A static global variable-ordering for SAT and BDD. In: International Workshop on Logic and Synthesis. pp. 1167–1172 (2001)
3. Aloul, F.A., Markov, I.L., Sakallah, K.A.: Force: a fast and easy-to-implement variable-ordering heuristic. In: Proceedings of the 13th ACM Great Lakes symposium on VLSI. pp. 116–119 (2003)
4. Amparore, E.G., Donatelli, S., Beccuti, M., Garbi, G., Miner, A.: Decision diagrams for petri nets: a comparison of variable ordering algorithms. Transactions on Petri Nets and Other Models of Concurrency XIII pp. 73–92 (2018)
5. Amram, G., Ma'ayan, D., Maoz, S., Pistiner, O., Ringert, J.O.: Triggers for reactive synthesis specifications. In: 45th IEEE/ACM International Conference on Software Engineering, ICSE 2023, Melbourne, Australia, May 14-20, 2023. pp. 729–741. IEEE (2023). `https://doi.org/10.1109/ICSE48619.2023.00070`
6. Bloem, R., Cimatti, A., Greimel, K., Hofferek, G., Könighofer, R., Roveri, M., Schuppan, V., Seeber, R.: RATSY - A new requirements analysis tool with synthesis. In: CAV. LNCS, vol. 6174, pp. 425–429. Springer (2010), `http://dx.doi.org/10.1007/978-3-642-14295-6_37`
7. Bloem, R., Galler, S., Jobstmann, B., Piterman, N., Pnueli, A., Weiglhofer, M.: Automatic hardware synthesis from specifications: A case study. In: 2007 Design, Automation & Test in Europe Conference & Exhibition. pp. 1–6. IEEE (2007)
8. Bloem, R., Galler, S., Jobstmann, B., Piterman, N., Pnueli, A., Weiglhofer, M.: Specify, compile, run: Hardware from PSL. Electronic Notes in Theoretical Computer Science **190**(4), 3–16 (2007)
9. Bloem, R., Jobstmann, B., Piterman, N., Pnueli, A., Sa'ar, Y.: Synthesis of Reactive(1) Designs. J. Comput. Syst. Sci. **78**(3), 911–938 (2012)

10. Bollig, B., Wegener, I.: Improving the variable ordering of OBDDs is NP-complete. IEEE Trans. Computers **45**(9), 993–1002 (1996). https://doi.org/10.1109/12.537122

11. Bonacich, P.: Some unique properties of eigenvector centrality. Social networks **29**(4), 555–564 (2007)

12. Bryant, R.E.: Graph-Based Algorithms for Boolean Function Manipulation. IEEE Trans. Computers **35**(8), 677–691 (1986)

13. Bryant, R.E.: Symbolic Boolean Manipulation with Ordered Binary-Decision Diagrams. ACM Comput. Surv. **24**(3), 293–318 (1992). https://doi.org/10.1145/136035.136043

14. Cavezza, D.G., Alrajeh, D., György, A.: Minimal assumptions refinement for realizable specifications. In: Bae, K., Bianculli, D., Gnesi, S., Plat, N. (eds.) FormaliSE@ICSE 2020: 8th International Conference on Formal Methods in Software Engineering, Seoul, Republic of Korea, July 13, 2020. pp. 66–76. ACM (2020). https://doi.org/10.1145/3372020.3391557

15. Cuthill, E.H., McKee, J.: Reducing the bandwidth of sparse symmetric matrices. In: Proceedings of the 24th national conference, ACM 1969, USA, 1969. pp. 157–172. ACM (1969). https://doi.org/10.1145/800195.805928

16. Dwyer, M.B., Avrunin, G.S., Corbett, J.C.: Patterns in property specifications for finite-state verification. In: ICSE. pp. 411–420. ACM (1999)

17. Ehlers, R., Raman, V.: Slugs: Extensible GR(1) synthesis. In: CAV. LNCS, vol. 9780, pp. 333–339. Springer (2016)

18. Eisner, C., Fisman, D.: A Practical Introduction to PSL. Series on Integrated Circuits and Systems, Springer (2006)

19. Firman, E., Maoz, S., Ringert, J.O.: Performance heuristics for GR(1) synthesis and related algorithms. Acta Informatica **57**(1-2), 37–79 (2020). https://doi.org/10.1007/s00236-019-00351-9

20. Fisman, D., Kupferman, O., Sheinvald-Faragy, S., Vardi, M.Y.: A framework for inherent vacuity. In: Chockler, H., Hu, A.J. (eds.) Hardware and Software: Verification and Testing, 4th International Haifa Verification Conference, HVC 2008, Haifa, Israel, October 27-30, 2008. Proceedings. Lecture Notes in Computer Science, vol. 5394, pp. 7–22. Springer (2008)

21. Godhal, Y., Chatterjee, K., Henzinger, T.A.: Synthesis of AMBA AHB from formal specification: a case study. Int. J. Softw. Tools Technol. Transf. **15**(5-6), 585–601 (2013). https://doi.org/10.1007/S10009-011-0207-9

22. Gorenstein, A., Maoz, S., Ringert, J.O.: Kind controllers and fast heuristics for non-well-separated GR(1) specifications. In: Proceedings of the 46th IEEE/ACM International Conference on Software Engineering, ICSE 2024, Lisbon, Portugal, April 14-20, 2024. pp. 28:1–28:12. ACM (2024). https://doi.org/10.1145/3597503.3608131

23. IEEE: IEC 62531:2012(E) (IEEE Std 1850-2010): Standard for Property Specification Language (PSL). Tech. rep., IEEE (2012). https://doi.org/10.1109/IEEESTD.2012.6228486

24. Jacobs, S., Perez, G.A., Abraham, R., Bruyere, V., Cadilhac, M., Colange, M., Delfosse, C., van Dijk, T., Duret-Lutz, A., Faymonville, P., Finkbeiner, B., Khalimov, A., Klein, F., Luttenberger, M., Meyer, K., Michaud, T., Pommellet, A., Renkin, F., Schlehuber-Caissier, P., Sakr, M., Sickert, S., Staquet, G., Tamines, C., Tentrup, L., Walker, A.: The reactive synthesis competition (syntcomp): 2018-2021 (2024), https://arxiv.org/abs/2206.00251

25. Klein, U., Pnueli, A.: Revisiting synthesis of GR (1) specifications. In: Haifa Verification Conference. Lecture Notes in Computer Science, vol. 6504, pp. 161–181. Springer (2010)
26. Kress-Gazit, H., Fainekos, G.E., Pappas, G.J.: Temporal-logic-based reactive mission and motion planning. IEEE Trans. Robotics **25**(6), 1370–1381 (2009)
27. Ma'ayan, D., Maoz, S.: Using Reactive Synthesis: An End-to-End Exploratory Case Study. In: 45th IEEE/ACM International Conference on Software Engineering. pp. 742–754. IEEE (2023). https://doi.org/10.1109/ICSE48619.2023.00071
28. Majumdar, R., Piterman, N., Schmuck, A.K.: Environmentally-friendly GR (1) synthesis. In: International Conference on Tools and Algorithms for the Construction and Analysis of Systems. pp. 229–246. Springer (2019)
29. Maoz, S., Ringert, J.O.: GR(1) synthesis for LTL specification patterns. In: ESEC/FSE. pp. 96–106. ACM (2015)
30. Maoz, S., Ringert, J.O.: Synthesizing a Lego Forklift Controller in GR(1): A Case Stud. In: Cerný, P., Kuncak, V., Madhusudan, P. (eds.) Proceedings Fourth Workshop on Synthesis, SYNT 2015, San Francisco, CA, USA, 18th July 2015. EPTCS, vol. 202, pp. 58–72 (2015). https://doi.org/10.4204/EPTCS.202.5
31. Maoz, S., Ringert, J.O.: On well-separation of GR (1) specifications. In: Proceedings of the 2016 24th ACM SIGSOFT International Symposium on Foundations of Software Engineering. pp. 362–372 (2016)
32. Maoz, S., Ringert, J.O.: Spectra: a specification language for reactive systems. Software and Systems Modeling **20**(5), 1553–1586 (2021)
33. Maoz, S., Ringert, J.O., Shalom, R.: Symbolic repairs for GR(1) specifications. In: Atlee, J.M., Bultan, T., Whittle, J. (eds.) Proceedings of the 41st International Conference on Software Engineering, ICSE 2019, Montreal, QC, Canada, May 25-31, 2019. pp. 1016–1026. IEEE / ACM (2019). https://doi.org/10.1109/ICSE.2019.00106
34. Maoz, S., Shalom, R.: Inherent vacuity for GR(1) specifications. In: ESEC/FSE. pp. 99–110. ACM (2020)
35. Meijer, J., Pol, J.: Bandwidth and wavefront reduction for static variable ordering in symbolic reachability analysis. In: Proceedings of the 8th International Symposium on NASA Formal Methods - Volume 9690. p. 255–271. NFM 2016, Springer-Verlag, Berlin, Heidelberg (2016)
36. Menghi, C., Tsigkanos, C., Pelliccione, P., Ghezzi, C., Berger, T.: Specification patterns for robotic missions. IEEE Trans. Software Eng. **47**(10), 2208–2224 (2021). https://doi.org/10.1109/TSE.2019.2945329
37. Michail, D., Kinable, J., Naveh, B., Sichi, J.V.: JGraphT — A Java Library for Graph Data Structures and Algorithms. ACM Trans. Math. Softw. **46**(2) (May 2020)
38. Page, L., Brin, S., Motwani, R., Winograd, T.: The PageRank Citation Ranking: Bringing Order to the Web. Tech. rep., Stanford Digital Library Technologies Project (1998)
39. Panda, S., Somenzi, F.: Who are the variables in your neighbourhood. In: Proceedings of IEEE International Conference on Computer Aided Design (ICCAD). pp. 74–77 (1995). https://doi.org/10.1109/ICCAD.1995.479994
40. Piterman, N., Pnueli, A., Sa'ar, Y.: Synthesis of reactive (1) designs. In: International Workshop on Verification, Model Checking, and Abstract Interpretation. pp. 364–380. Springer (2005)
41. Pnueli, A., Rosner, R.: On the Synthesis of a Reactive Module. In: POPL. pp. 179–190. ACM Press (1989)

42. Rudell, R.: Dynamic variable ordering for ordered binary decision diagrams. In: Lightner, M.R., Jess, J.A.G. (eds.) Proceedings of the 1993 IEEE/ACM International Conference on Computer-Aided Design, 1993, Santa Clara, California, USA, November 7-11, 1993. pp. 42–47. IEEE Computer Society / ACM (1993). https://doi.org/10.1109/ICCAD.1993.580029
43. Somenzi, F.: CUDD: CU Decision Diagram Package Release 2.3. 0. University of Colorado at Boulder **621** (1998)

Stream-Based Monitoring of Algorithmic Fairness

Jan Baumeister(✉) ⓘ, Bernd Finkbeiner ⓘ, Frederik Scheerer ⓘ,
Julian Siber ⓘ, and Tobias Wagenpfeil ⓘ

CISPA Helmholtz Center for Information Security, Saarbrücken, Germany
{jan.baumeister, finkbeiner, frederik.scheerer, julian.siber,
tobias.wagenpfeil}@cispa.de

Abstract. Automatic decision and prediction systems are increasingly deployed in applications where they significantly impact the livelihood of people, such as for predicting the creditworthiness of loan applicants or the recidivism risk of defendants. These applications have given rise to a new class of *algorithmic-fairness* specifications that require the systems to decide and predict without bias against social groups. Verifying these specifications statically is often out of reach for realistic systems, since the systems may, e.g., employ complex learning components, and reason over a large input space. In this paper, we therefore propose stream-based monitoring as a solution for verifying the algorithmic fairness of decision and prediction systems at runtime. Concretely, we present a principled way to formalize algorithmic fairness over temporal data streams in the specification language RTLola and demonstrate the efficacy of this approach on a number of benchmarks. Besides synthetic scenarios that particularly highlight its efficiency on streams with a scaling amount of data, we notably evaluate the monitor on real-world data from the recidivism prediction tool COMPAS.

1 Introduction

Machine learning is used to automate an increasing number of critical decisions pertaining to people's opportunities in areas such as loan or job application [19], healthcare [41], and criminal sentencing [5]. It is of vital interest that these decision and prediction systems adhere to societies' shared values and, hence, they should in particular not discriminate against members of protected social groups, e.g., based on attributes such as gender or perceived ethnicity. Since the machine-learned systems are trained from historical data, they often inherit the historical human bias present in these data sets. So far, this usually was revealed by posterior analyses after the systems have been deployed for years [37,38] and hence have already produced harmful results. In this paper, we propose stream-based monitoring of algorithmic fairness properties as a way to alleviate this situation, and to significantly reduce the impact unfair decisions have on people that are subject to learned decision and prediction systems. Unlike static verification of these systems, which is often intractable due to their complex learning components and large input space, monitors are lightweight and can be deployed alongside the machine-learned systems, raising awareness once they are

A. Gurfinkel and M. Heule (Eds.): TACAS 2025, LNCS 15696, pp. 60–81, 2025.
https://doi.org/10.1007/978-3-031-90643-5_4

sufficiently sure of unfair behavior. While this does not avert all decisions made by an unfair system, we show empirically that it can still significantly reduce the number of decisions made by an unfair system by alerting practicioners early.

1.1 Motivating Example

As a motivating example, we consider the COMPAS tool developed by Northpointe [37]. COMPAS predicts the recidivism risk of defendants in criminal trials in order to assist judges in, e.g., setting bond amounts or in sentencing during trial. Hence, the system gives a prediction on how likely a person is to commit a(nother) crime, and this predic-

date	event	id	group	risk	...
2013-01-02	SCREEN	0	A	HIGH	...
2013-01-02	SCREEN	1	B	LOW	...
2013-01-03	RECID.	1	-	-	...
2013-01-03	SCREEN	2	B	HIGH	...
...	...	...	...	...	...

Fig. 1: Data streams for an example of recidivism risk assessment with COMPAS [37].

tion has a direct impact on criminal sentencing. A retrospective investigation by ProPublica into the predictions by COMPAS during 2013 and 2014 in Broward County, Florida, revealed that the tool is significantly biased against defendants perceived as black [5]. For instance, the false positive rate for black defendants was found to be significantly higher than for white defendants, i.e., black defendants were more likely classified with a high risk of re-offending, without actually committing a crime in the near future. The ultimate vision of our work is that, instead of such a posterior analysis of algorithmic fairness, runtime monitors are deployed that assess the fairness of decision and prediction systems during their execution, in order to raise awareness of unfair treatment early and in this way mitigate unproportional harm put on groups due to an unfair bias. To illustrate our monitoring approach, we will consider a simplified version of the risk assessment setting as shown in Figure 1. This table shows a number of events describing an execution of the COMPAS system that is defined on data streams such as event or id. For example, the first row describes that on the 2nd of January 2013, an individual of group A was screened via COMPAS and assessed to have a high risk of recidivism. A (simplified) algorithmic-fairness specification compares certain conditional probabilities associated with the different groups:

$$\left| \mathbb{P}(\text{HIGH} \mid \text{A}, \text{RECIDIVISM}) - \mathbb{P}(\text{HIGH} \mid \text{B}, \text{RECIDIVISM}) \right| \le \epsilon \ .$$

This condition states that the probability of a re-offending member of group A to be labeled as high-risk is not too far (less than ϵ) from the probability of a re-offending member of group B to be labeled as high-risk. Hence, it compares the *true positive rates* between the two groups. In this paper, we show how we can use the stream-based monitoring language RTLola to process such data streams and in this way analyze the algorithmic fairness of their underlying system in real-time. The main idea is to automatically partition the stream events into independent trials and to construct RTLola specifications that estimate the conditional probabilities associated with algorithmic-fairness specifications.

1.2   Outline and Contributions

The challenges in our stream-based setting are twofold: First, we observe only a single execution of the system but require a larger number of independent trials to reliably estimate the conditional probabilities. Second, the independent trials and also the fairness definitions contain a real-time component. We address the first challenge in Section 3 by defining a principled way to extract individual trials based on a predefined dependence relation between stream events. In Section 4, we then describe how this can be implemented in the specification language RTLola. We show how we can estimate conditional probabilities over these trials with RTLola, and address the second challenge: RTLola naturally supports reasoning about real-time events, and hence we can use it to collect stream events that are spread throughout time and calculate their relative delay, which allows us to express certain intricacies of algorithmic-fairness specifications, such as an upper time bound between relevant events. We evaluate this RTLola compilation in a case study including both synthetic and real-world benchmarks. For the former, we present a benchmark generator that models application scenarios at a company and a seminar assignment at a university. In both cases, we can easily scale, e.g., the number of applicants, which serves as a stress test for our implementation and allows a thorough comparison with more traditional approaches based on databases. We show that RTLola significantly outperforms database approaches, which suggests that stream-based monitoring is the tool of choice for settings with high data throughput. Moreover, synthetic benchmarks allow us to set a ground truth for the fairness of the decision system, and we show that our monitoring approach can detect unfair systems without raising too many false alarms on fair systems. As a real-world benchmark, we consider the aforementioned recidivism prediction tool COMPAS [5]. Unlike the synthetic benchmarks, this is also an example of a prediction system, such that more complex specifications become relevant. We show that RTLola is able to express these specifications succinctly and effectively alert to unfairness in the prediction system early. All experiments can be found in Section 5.

Contributions. To summarize, we make the following contributions:

- We formalize the estimation of probabilities from single executions in stream-based monitoring.
- We implement RTLola monitors that allow the monitoring of a wide range of algorithmic-fairness specifications from the literature.
- We present a generator for constructing challenging benchmarks related to algorithmic fairness in job application and university admission.
- We perform an extensive experimental evaluation on these synthetic benchmarks, as well as on a real-world data set from the COMPAS tool.

1.3   Related Work

Efforts of the machine learning community generally aim more at improving the fairness of learned models than rigorously verifying it [35]. Three categories of mechanisms stand out, namely Pre-Processing [30,22], In-Processing [1,31], and Post-Processing [38,17]. Our work on monitoring algorithmic fairness is an orthogonal effort that allows us to audit learned systems even when their training process cannot be influenced, as we treat the learned system as a black box. We present a general approach based on RTLola and encode popular fairness properties, such as *equalized odds*. These techniques can also be used to encode other fairness properties such as *equal opportunity* [26] or *counterfactual fairness* [32].

Related to our effort of verifying and testing fairness, a variety of different approaches in the formal methods community exist: Udeshi et al. [43] propose an automated and directed testing technique to generate discriminatory inputs for machine learning models. FairTest [42] is a framework for specifying and testing algorithmic fairness. A similar approach is given by Bastiani et al. [7] by using adaptive concentration inequalities to design a scalable sampling technique for providing fairness guarantees. Albarghouthi et al. [3] transform fairness properties as probabilistic program properties and develop an SMT-based technique to verify fairness of decision-making programs. Albarghouthi and Vinitsky [4] propose a white-box monitoring technique based on adding annotations in a program, but they cannot reason about temporal properties, unlike our approach. To certify individual fairness, Rouss et al. [39] introduce a local property that coincides with robustness within a particular distance metric. Another approach is to repair biased decision systems with a program repair technique [2]. Teuber and Beckert [40] have made an intriguing connection between secure information-flow and algorithmic fairness, and use information-flow tools for verifying fairness of white-box programs. Henzinger et al. propose monitoring of *probabilistic specification expressions (PSEs)* [27] and extensions [29] for monitoring algorithmic fairness properties [28]. Baum et al. [8] combine monitoring and input generation for a probabilistic falsification technique aimed at individual fairness. Cano et al. [14] propose fairness shields that combine monitoring and enforcement of fairness properties. In our work, we show that it is possible to use the widely studied formalism of stream-based monitoring languages [9] to go even further by additionally considering temporal aspects of fairness such as delays between relevant events. Notably, this is possible without any pre-processing of the stream-events that may be needed for, e.g., PSEs, as this is already handled by stream-based monitoring languages. These languages predate the PSE approach by decades [18] and have already proven useful in diverse areas such as unmanned aircraft [10,11] and network monitoring [21]. We use RTLola in this paper, but the general ideas may also be adapted to other stream-based languages, such as TeSSLa [16] or Striver [25].

The usage of opaque machine-learning models in high-stake scenarios has sparked scholarly debate on its ethics [13,34], as well as extensive governmental regulation [6,15]. Given that these models promise to be more accurate [33] and ultimately even more impartial than human decision makers, there seems to be a clear trend toward further adoption. As we show here, RTLola can be a useful tool for alleviating unintended negative side effects of this trend by promoting effective monitoring of the decision system during deployment.

2   Preliminaries

We briefly recall the necessary background on probability theory, algorithmic fairness and stream-based monitoring with RTLola.

2.1   Probability Theory

A *probability space* is a tuple $(\Omega, \mathcal{E}, \mathbb{P})$, where Ω is a *sample space* and $\mathcal{E}$ is a σ-*algebra* over Ω, i.e., we have $\emptyset \in \mathcal{E}$, $A \in \mathcal{E} \implies \bar{A} \in \mathcal{E}$, and $A_0, A_1, \ldots \in \mathcal{E} \implies \bigcup_{i=0}^{\infty} A_i \in \mathcal{E}$. Finally, $\mathbb{P}$ is a *probability measure* $\mathcal{E} \to \mathbb{R}$, i.e., a non-negative function with $\mathbb{P}(\Omega) = 1$, $\mathbb{P}(\emptyset) = 0$ that satisfies countable additivity: For any sequence of pairwise disjoint events $A_0, A_1, \ldots \in \mathcal{E}$ we have that $\mathbb{P}(\bigcup_{i=0}^{\infty} A_i) = \Sigma_{i=0}^{\infty} \mathbb{P}(A_i)$. A *random variable* is a function $X : (\Omega, \mathcal{E}) \to (\Gamma, \mathcal{V})$ that maps elements of the sample space Ω to some set Γ equipped with the σ-algebra $\mathcal{V}$, such that $X^{-1}(B) \in \mathcal{E}$ for all $B \in \mathcal{V}$. Such an X induces a probability measure on $(\Gamma, \mathcal{V})$ as $\mathbb{P}(B) = \mathbb{P}(X^{-1}(B))$ for all $B \in \mathcal{V}$. Lastly, the *conditional probability* of some $A \in \mathcal{E}$ given some $B \in \mathcal{E}$ is defined as $\mathbb{P}(A \mid B) = \frac{\mathbb{P}(A \cap B)}{\mathbb{P}(B)}$.

2.2   Algorithmic Fairness

Algorithmic fairness is an umbrella term for several specifications that have recently been put forward for decision and classification systems [38]. The general idea is to compare the probabilities of certain good and bad events between social groups, e.g., we may require the probability of a loan request being accepted conditioned on the applicant being in group A to be not too far from the same probability conditioned on the applicant being in group B. In the following, we introduce the fairness specifications considered in this work, as they have been proposed in the literature. Note that these pure definitions do not consider timing issues such as the good outcome being obtained within a certain bound.

The simplest fairness specification is *demographic parity*, which requires the probabilities of good outcomes conditioned on the different groups to differ no more than the predefined parameter ϵ.

Definition 1 (Demographic Parity [20]). *A decision system for the binary decision A satisfies demographic parity, iff*

$$\big| \mathbb{P}(A = 1 \mid G = 1) - \mathbb{P}(A = 1 \mid G = 0) \big| \leq \epsilon .$$

The value of G represents the group a person belongs to (e.g., male or female), while A indicates the positive outcome. Demographic parity ensures that positive outcomes are assigned to the two groups at a similar rate, but it does not consider background factors that may be relevant to assess the fairness of a system. For instance, men and women may apply unproportionally to different departments of a university, such that the admission process of the university appears to be unfair while the same processes of the individual departments are fair.[1] If the

---

[1] This observation has been termed *Simspon's Paradox* by Colin Blyth [12].

existence of such confounding variables is known, it may be more appropriate to use a fairness measure such as *conditional statistical parity*.

Definition 2 (Conditional Statistical Parity [17]). *A decision system for the binary decision A satisfies conditional statistical parity, iff*

$$\left| \mathbb{P}(A = 1 \mid L = 1, G = 1) - \mathbb{P}(A = 1 \mid L = 1, G = 0) \right| \leq \epsilon .$$

Conditional statistical parity states, similar to demographic parity, that people from different groups should have an equal probability of positive outcomes. Additionally, it further conditions the probability on other legitimate factors L, e.g., confounding variables such as the department that students apply to. These factors have to be determined a priori and are based on the background knowledge of the specifier.

While the above parity measures define a notion of fairness for decision systems with binary outcomes, many fairness issues arise also for prediction systems that, e.g. classify the recidivism risk of defendants in criminal trials [5]. Fairness of such systems is more accurately described by comparing the true and false positive rates between groups, as done by the *equalized-odds* fairness measure.

Definition 3 (Equalized Odds [26]). *A prediction system $\hat{Y}$ for the outcome Y satisfies equalized odds, iff*

$$\left| \mathbb{P}(\hat{Y} = 1 \mid G = 1, Y = 0) - \mathbb{P}(\hat{Y} = 1 \mid G = 0, Y = 0) \right| \leq \epsilon \ and$$
$$\left| \mathbb{P}(\hat{Y} = 1 \mid G = 1, Y = 1) - \mathbb{P}(\hat{Y} = 1 \mid G = 0, Y = 1) \right| \leq \epsilon .$$

Here, $\hat{Y}$ describes the predicted value, while Y is the true value of an outcome to be predicted. Hence, the equalized-odds measure requires the differences between the false positive rates (FPR) and the differences between the true positive rates (TPR) of all pairs of groups to be within a predefined bound ϵ.

2.3   Stream-based Monitoring with RTLola

In this work, we use the stream-based specification language RTLola to monitor the previously described fairness definitions. RTLola uses stream-equations to translate streams of input data to output streams and trigger conditions that describe violations of the specification. We illustrate the RTLola language with a small example and refer for more details to [9,10,23].

Example 1 (RTLola Example).

```
1  input user_id : UInt64, value : Int64
2  output amount(user)
3      spawn with user_id
4      eval when user_id = user with value + amount(user).last(or: 0)
5  trigger @value amount.aggregate(over_instances: all, using:
       max).defaults(to: 0) > 500 "Upper Limit Violation"
6  trigger @1Hz value.aggregate(over: 1s, using: count) > 5 "Too many
       transactions"
```

The specification declares two input streams describing a transaction to a user: The input stream `user_id` encodes a unique identifier for each user and `value` represents the amount. Next, the output stream `amount` sums up the values per user using parameterization. With parameterization, the output stream describes a set of instances and the specification can refer to each instance with the parameter, in this example the parameter `user`. The spawn declaration describes when a new instance is added to this set, in our case for every new `user_id`. The eval declaration describes for each instance when a new value is computed with the `when`-clause and the computation of this value with the `with`-clause. Here, each instance of the `amount` stream is computed when the `user_id` is equal to the instance parameter and the new value is computed as the sum of the previous value of this instance and the current value of the `value`-stream. The first trigger then aggregates over all instances of the `amount` stream, takes the maximum value, and compares this value against a threshold. Since in theory this access could fail, we need to provide a default value. If this condition is true, the generated monitor for this specification emits the corresponding trigger message. The second trigger checks the number of transactions over the last five seconds, illustrating the real-time capabilities of RTLola.

The semantics of RTLola is defined over a collection of timed data streams and intuitively checks whether the values in the collection correspond to the computed values for the stream equation. Additionally, it validates that the time is monotone.

Definition 4 (Data Streams). *A collection of timed data streams* $\omega \in \mathbb{W}$ *over a set of input streams* $ID^\uparrow$ *and output streams* $ID^\downarrow$ *is the combination of a StreamMap and a TimeMap.*

$$Stream := InstanceID \rightarrow Time \rightarrow \mathbb{V}_\perp$$
$$StreamMap := ID^\uparrow \uplus ID^\downarrow \rightarrow Stream$$
$$TimeMap := Time \rightarrow \mathbb{R}$$
$$\mathbb{W} := StreamMap \times TimeMap$$

Figure 2 gives an intuition on the data stream representation based on the specification in Example 1. The *TimeMap* is a total function from the discrete timestamps, indicated at the top of the figure, to a real-time value. In the examples, the first three events arrive at the timestamps 0.6, 0.8, and 2.4. Given $\omega = (streams, times) \in \mathbb{W}$, we use $\omega(t) := times(t)$ to get the real-time value of a discrete timestamp $t \in Time$. The *StreamMap* assigns each stream identifier and instance to an infinite sequence of optional values, where $\perp$ indicates that the stream instance does not produce a value. In our example, $\omega(user\_id)(\top)$ represents the infinite sequence of the input stream, and $\omega(user\_id)(\top)(1)$ returns the value of the input stream at time 1. Note that we use $\top$ as the instance identifier if the stream is not parameterized, i.e., only one stream instance exists in the *StreamMap*. In contrast, the output stream `amount` is parameterized, such that different instances (e.g., $\omega(amount)(1)$) exist. Formally, infinite sequences are represented by total functions, and we define

Time	0	1	2	...
TimeMap	$\omega(0) = 0.6$	$\omega(1) = 0.8$	$\omega(2) = 2.4$	...
StreamMap				
Stream $\omega(user\_id)$				
$\omega(user\_id)(\top)$	$\omega(user\_id)(\top)(0) = 2$	$\omega(user\_id)(\top)(1) = 0$	$\omega(user\_id)(\top)(2) = 2$	...
Stream $\omega(amount)$				
$\omega(amount)(0)$	$\omega(amount)(0)(0) = \bot$	$\omega(amount)(0)(1) = 2$	$\omega(amount)(0)(2) = \bot$	...
$\omega(amount)(1)$	$\omega(amount)(1)(0) = \bot$	$\omega(amount)(1)(1) = \bot$	$\omega(amount)(1)(2) = \bot$	...
$\omega(amount)(2)$	$\omega(amount)(2)(0) = 3$	$\omega(amount)(2)(1) = \bot$	$\omega(amount)(2)(2) = 5$	...

Fig. 2: The data streams exemplified on the specification from Example 1.

the access functions $\omega(sid) := streams(sid)$ for the stream $sid \in \text{ID}^\uparrow \uplus \text{ID}^\downarrow$, $\omega(sid)(i) := streams(sid)(i)$ to access stream instances $i \in InstanceID$ of stream sid, and $\omega(sid)(i)(t)$ for the stream instance value at discrete timestamp t.

The set of *stream events* of ω is defined as $Events(\omega) := \{(r, f) \mid \forall sid \in \text{ID}^\uparrow \uplus \text{ID}^\downarrow, i \in InstanceID. \, \omega(sid)(i)(\omega^{-1}(r)) = f(sid)(i)\} \subseteq \mathbb{E}_\omega := \mathbb{R} \times (\text{ID}^\uparrow \uplus \text{ID}^\downarrow \to InstanceID \to \mathbb{V}_\bot)$. Hence, $\mathbb{E}_\omega$ denotes the set of all conceivable stream events over the datatypes defined by ω, while $Events(\omega)$ denotes the concrete events appearing in ω. For our example above, $Events(\omega)$ would map each real-time timestamp to the corresponding column in the figure.

3   Statistical Estimates from Data Streams

In this section, we outline the formal background for our RTLola specifications that estimate algorithmic fairness properties. We first describe how to extract multiple samples from a single execution of our system, we then describe how to use random variables to describe fairness properties in this setting, and lastly how we estimate the probability of events over these random variables.

3.1   Extracting Independent Trials from Data Streams

The central challenge in our setting is that we observe only a single execution of the system under scrutiny but want to perform a statistical estimation that naturally gets more accurate the more samples become available. We utilize the fact that in our applications, the single system execution describes a number of independent trials pertaining to the specification we care about, e.g., a single execution of the COMPAS tool for assessing the recidivism risk of defendants describes a large number of independent risk screenings. Hence, we propose a principled way to extract multiple samples from the observed system execution. At its core lies the definition of the probability space $(\Omega_\omega, \mathcal{E}_\omega, \mathbb{P}_\omega)$ associated with the data streams $\omega \in \mathbb{W}$. The sample space Ω_ω is constructed as the set of all possible sequences of dependent events, which we identify through a *dependence relation* $\delta \subseteq \mathbb{E}_\omega^2$. This predefined δ is an equivalence relation over the stream events $\mathbb{E}_\omega$ whose equivalence classes define the possible sets of events that form mutually independent trials. Elements of the sample space Ω_ω are ordered subsets of such dependent events: $\Omega_\omega := \{E_0 \dots E_n \in E^n \mid \forall 0 \le i \le j \le n. \, t(E_i) \le t(E_j) \wedge \delta(E_i, E_j)\}$ and we take $\mathcal{E}_\omega$ simply as the powerset of Ω_ω, while $\mathbb{P}_\omega$ is unknown to us.

Example 2. Consider the COMPAS recidivism risk assessment tool described in Section 1.1 and the corresponding data streams illustrated in Figure 1. We assume that the outcomes of individual screenings do not affect each other, and hence define the dependence relation such that two events are dependent if they refer to the same defendant (identified through the stream id), i.e., $\delta := \{(E_0, E_1) \mid E_0(\mathtt{id}) = E_1(\mathtt{id})\}$. Consequently, the data streams ω illustrated in Figure 1 describe the following samples $s_{0,1,2} \in \Omega_\omega$.

$$s_0 = (0.0, \mathtt{SCREEN}, 0, \mathtt{A}, \mathtt{HIGH}) \dots$$
$$s_1 = (0.0, \mathtt{SCREEN}, 1, \mathtt{B}, \mathtt{LOW})(1.0, \mathtt{RECIDIVISM}, 1, \text{-}, \text{-}) \dots$$
$$s_2 = (1.0, \mathtt{SCREEN}, 2, \mathtt{B}, \mathtt{HIGH}) \dots$$

Hence, our dependence relation δ partitions the data streams of the system into independent sequences of stream events, that naturally grow the more events are produced by the system. Note that the first components in the stream events with the values 0.0 and 1.0 encode the dates, i.e., **2013-01-02** and **2013-01-03**, via the *StreamMap* as outlined in Definition 4.

3.2 Defining Indicator Variables

Having defined our probability space through a dependence relation δ, the next step is to define Bernoulli random variables $X : \Omega_\omega \to \{0, 1\}$ that serve as indicator variables for the events relevant to algorithmic fairness.

Example 3. For instance, we may want to specify equalized odds (Definition 3) for the COMPAS risk assessment tool from Section 1.1. We may naturally define the prediction $\hat{Y}$ for a defendant associated with the sample ω as $\hat{Y}(\omega) := \exists i. \, \omega(\mathtt{event})(i) = \mathtt{SCREEN} \wedge \omega(\mathtt{risk})(i) = \mathtt{HIGH}$, and similarly, the true outcome is defined as $Y(\omega) := \exists i. \, \omega(\mathtt{event})(i) = \mathtt{RECIDIVISM}$. Here, we quantify over the time stamps i. Membership to, e.g., group A is captured by $G_{\mathtt{A}}(\omega) := \exists i. \, \omega(\mathtt{event})(i) = \mathtt{SCREEN} \wedge \omega(\mathtt{group})(i) = \mathtt{A}$. It is also possible to define a sanity check as an additional variable that we condition on. For example, we may only consider recidivism events that happen less than two years after a screening event, as this is the specific time horizon that the COMPAS tool is targeting [5,37]. We can achieve this by utilizing the real-time information of the stream events with the variable $Y_{<2y} := \exists i, j. \, \omega(\mathtt{event})(i) = \mathtt{SCREEN} \wedge \omega(\mathtt{event})(j) = \mathtt{RECIDIVISM} \wedge \omega(j) - \omega(i) < 730.0$. Hence the FPR part of a specification of equalized odds with $\epsilon = 0.1$ is:

$$\varphi := \left| \mathbb{P}(\hat{Y} = 1 \mid G_{\mathtt{A}} = 1, Y_{<2y} = 1) - \mathbb{P}(\hat{Y} = 1 \mid G_{\mathtt{A}} = 0, Y_{<2y} = 1) \right| \le 0.1 \; .$$

3.3   Maximum A Posteriori Estimation

Since during monitoring we obtain samples sequentially, the first samples have an unproportionally large impact on the assessment of fairness at the start of monitoring, since the estimation of the conditional probabilities in a formula like φ only gets more robust over time. Hence, we use methods from Bayesian statistics to control the trigger behavior of the monitor at the start of an execution: *maximum a posteriori (MAP)* estimation [36] allows us to take a prior belief about the conditional probabilities that make up the fairness specifications into consideration, as well as a degree of confidence therein. Formally, for every conditional probability $\Theta = \mathbb{P}(A \mid B)$ in our specification we require a prior γ and a confidence κ. Then, the estimate $\hat{\Theta}$ is given as:

$$\hat{\Theta} = \frac{S_{A \cap B} + \gamma(\omega)\kappa}{S_B + \kappa} ,$$

where $S_{A \cap B}$ is the number of samples that satisfy A and B, while S_B is the number of samples satisfying B. The parameters γ, κ and ϵ suffice to achieve sufficient initial robustness of the monitor, which we demonstrate experimentally in Section 5. The longer the observed system execution gets and the more samples become available, the less influence these parameters have on the monitor verdict.

Dynamic Updating of the Prior Belief. While MAP is a standard method from statistics, we face unique challenges when dynamically analyzing data streams, since we only have limited knowledge about the monitored system. Certain background knowledge like how many free places and applicants emerge during the execution may change the prior belief we have about the conditional probabilities. For instance, we may know that a university always fills all seminars with students, but the chance of an individual student's application to be accepted of course still depends on the number of seminar places and the number of other students applying. To account for such dynamic updates to the prior belief, we consider the prior γ to be a function of the data streams ω, such that it may be defined, e.g., as the ratio of places and applying students.

4   Implementation in RTLola

This section describes the implementation of the fairness definitions from Section 2.2 in the stream-based specification language RTLola. In general, each fairness specification follows the same structure: First, we extract information on independent trials from the input data and store it in parameterized streams that directly correspond to the indicator variables that are relevant in a given fairness specification. These variables can use the full power of RTLola expressions such as stream aggregations and real-time properties. We then build accumulators that are used in estimating the conditional probabilities. Last, we define trigger conditions that indicate that the estimates violate the fairness specification.

4.1   Implementation of Equalized Odds for the COMPAS Tool

We illustrate this principle by discussing the implementation of equalized odds (cf. Example 3). The RTLola specification for this fairness property, in the context of the COMPAS system, is shown in Figure 3. The specification is defined over input data streams that encode the relevant events of the COMPAS system as described in Section 1.1: The "SCREEN" event includes the unique identifier of a defendant in the input stream id, their group attribute in the input stream group and the COMPAS score describing the predicted likelihood of that person re-offending in the input stream score. The COMPAS score is an integer value between 0 and 10 as in the original data set. We use the same classification of any score above 6 as high risk as used by ProPublica [5] in the original investigation. If the defendant re-offends, the second event "RECIDIVISM" is given to the monitor together with the identifier of the defendant. The timestamps of these events are implicitly included through RTLola.

Storing Independent Trials in Parameterized Streams. The specification uses three parameterized output streams to store the relevant information of independent trials, where the parameter i identifies the trial, e.g., an individual defendant. The streams are days_per, has_re and tp_event. Each of these streams has a lifecycle of exactly 730 days after screening the defendant. In RTLola, this lifecycle is represented with the spawn, starting the lifecycle with the first occurrence for each identifier, and the close declaration, ending the lifecycle when the associated condition is satisfied. The output stream days_per counts the number of days after the screening of the defendant and the output stream has_re maps a "RECIDIVISM" event to the defendant. Then, the output stream tp_event synchronizes all information about one defendant after 730 days. This realizes the extraction of independent trials as described formally in Section 3.1. For example, the indicator variable $Y_{<2y}$ is described with the second clause of the eval-when declaration of the stream using stream aggregation (line 18), i.e., has_re(i).aggregate(over: 730d, using: ∃). This expression checks if the defendant re-offended during a timeframe of 730 days using stream aggregation and follows the definition from Example 3. The stream tp_event is additionally parametrized with the group and the score of the defendant from which we can derive the indicator variables G_A and C directly. After the indicator variables are computed and used by the accumulators as described in the following paragraph, we close these stream instances to free the underlying memory since their value is not required after the first use of the variable.

Accumulator Variables and MAP Estimation. The specification then stores the accumulated information for each group using stream parameterization, where this time the parameter g identifies the group associated with the stream. It uses the stream abs_re to count the number of defendants that re-offendend in a given group (line 22). Similarly, the stream abs_hr_re counts the number of re-offenders per group that were scored as high-risk by COMPAS (line 26). The parameterized stream tp_ratio then computes for each group the true-positive ratio $\mathbb{P}(\hat{Y} = 1 \mid G = g, Y = 1)$, i.e., the probability that a person was

```
1   input event : String
2   input id : Int64
3   input group : String
4   input score : Int64
5
6   /// Defendant Information
7   output days_per(i)
8     spawn with id
9     eval @Global(1d) with days_per(i).last(or: 0) + 1
10    close when days_per(i) = 730
11  output has_re(i)
12      spawn with id
13      eval when id == i with event == "RECIDIVISM"
14      close @Global(1d) when days_per(i).hold(or: 0) = 730
15  output tp_event(i, g, s)
16    spawn with (id, group, score)
17    eval @Global(1d)
18      when days_per(i).hold(or: 0) = 730 ∧ has_re(i).aggregate(over:
              730d, using: ∃) with s > 6
19    close @Global(1d) when days_per(i).hold(or: 0) = 730
20
21  /// TP Ratio
22  output abs_re(g) : UInt64
23      spawn with group
24      eval @Global(1d) with abs_re(g).last(or: 100) +
25        tp_event.aggregate(over_instances: All(ii, ig, is => ig = g),
              using: count)
26  output abs_hr_re(g) : UInt64
27    spawn with group
28    eval @Global(1d) with abs_hr_re(g).last(or: 50) +
29        tp_event.aggregate(over_instances: All(ii, ig, is => ig = g),
              using: sum)
30  output tp_ratio(g)
31      spawn with group
32      eval when abs_re(g) != 0
33          with cast<UInt64, Float64>(abs_hr_re(g)) / cast<UInt64,
              Float64>(abs_re(g))
34
35  /// Equalized Odds: True Positive
36  trigger @1d tp_ratio.aggregate(over_instances: all, using:
          max).defaults(to: 0.0) - tp_ratio.aggregate(over_instances: all,
          using: min).defaults(to: 0.0) > 0.1
```

Fig. 3: RTLola specification computing and checking the differences of the true positive ratios between all groups, which makes up one half of the equalized-odds specification for the COMPAS data set.

assigned a high-risk score under the condition that this person has re-offended. To encode the MAP estimation from Section 3.3, we assign the `abs_re` and `abs_hr_re` streams different default values when accessing the previous value, which effectively initializes the streams with these default values at the first time point. Finally, the trigger (line 36) encodes a violation of the fairness definition using the following underlying formula:

$$max_{g \in G}\{\mathbb{P}(\hat{Y} = 1 \mid G = g, Y = 1)\} - min_{g \in G}\{\mathbb{P}(\hat{Y} = 1 \mid G = g, Y = 1)\} \leq \epsilon.$$

Here, G is the set of all groups. Hence, this formula takes the maximum difference between *any* two groups and compares it against the threshold ϵ. This suffices to infer a violation in all cases. Additionally, the exact values of the ratios can be read from the parameterized streams such as `tp_ratio`. The full specification for equalized odds extends this principle to the false positive ratio by defining parameterized streams `abs_not_re` to count the defendants per group that did not re-offend, `abs_hr_not_re` to count the number of these that were screened high-risk, and `fp_ratio` for the resulting ratio. Additionally, the trigger condition is extended to account for all pairs of parameters of the `fp_ratio` stream. The experimental results of running this specification on the COMPAS data from the original ProPublica investigation can be found in Section 5.2.

5   Case Studies

We specified all algorithmic fairness requirements defined in Section 2.2 with RTLola in a similar way as outlined for equalized odds in Section 4. In this section, we report on experiments with these fairness specifications in a variety of settings[2]. We first consider synthetically constructed data streams related to hiring and application scenarios that allow us to study the utility and efficiency of the approach under varying assumptions. Afterward, we consider data from the COMPAS recidivism risk assessment tool discussed in Section 1.1 to assess the utility of our tool in a real-world setting. The experiments were conducted with Ubuntu 24.04, a 4-core Intel i5 2.30GHz processor, as well as 8GB of memory.

5.1   Synthetic Scenarios

Our two synthetic scenarios deal with hiring done by a company and seminar assignments at a university. For the hiring scenario, we make the simplifying assumption that the company has no fixed limit on the number of employees it can hire. For the seminar assignment, we assume that each seminar has a fixed number of places. Both scenarios are synthesized from a generator script that allows us to specify and scale a number of interesting parameters such as the number of applicants and seminars, as well as the number of places per seminar. The input streams of both scenarios encode the individual applicants and events related to them, i.e., there is an event for an applicant with a specific

---

[2] Our artifact is available on Zenodo: https://doi.org/10.5281/zenodo.14627198.

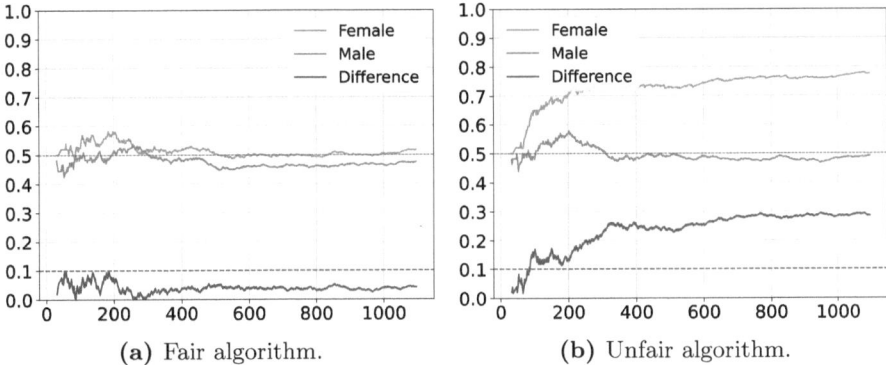

Fig. 4: Demographic parity of hiring algorithms. The Female and Male lines correspond to the estimates $\hat{\Theta}_{F,M}$ for women and men, respectively. The Difference line shows the absolute difference between these ratios, while the dashed red line at 0.1 indicates the threshold parameter ϵ (cf. Definition 1).

id, gender, and *qualification.* For the seminar assignment system, also an input *seminar* to indicate which seminar the applicant applies to, such that we can also monitor conditional statistical parity in addition to demographic parity. Further, seminars have a predefined maximum number of places. Additionally, there is a separate input stream *accepted* that gives the IDs of accepted applicants. The generator allows to specify which decision algorithm should be used. We discuss these with the experimental results in the following.

Company Hiring. This scenario modeling a hiring system at a company consists of truly independent trials. We can adjust the probabilities $\Theta_F = \mathbb{P}(A = 1 \mid F = 1)$ and $\Theta_M = \mathbb{P}(A = 1 \mid M = 1)$ with which women and men get accepted, respectively. In this way, we can compare the monitoring outcome of a hiring system that is unfair by construction to a truly fair one. In the unfair system, we set the probability to be accepted for men to $\Theta_M = 0.5$ and for women to $\Theta_F = 0.2$, while both are 0.5 in the fair system. We then monitor for demographic parity (cf. Definition 1). The prior (cf. Section 3.3) is set to 0.5 with a confidence of 24 (a more detailed discussion on how to set these parameters follows in the next paragraph). Graphs for the estimated conditional probabilities $\hat{\Theta}_{F,M}$, their difference, and the trigger condition (based on $\epsilon = 0.1$) are depicted in Figure 4. As we can see, the fair algorithm stabilizes far below the trigger threshold. The diffuse behavior at the start, which usually would result in a number of false alarms, is held back by our MAP approach, such that no triggers are thrown. In contrast, after around time point 85, the unfair algorithm constantly raises triggers indicating unfairness, as the difference of the conditional probabilities stabilizes far above the threshold of 0.1, overpowering the prior belief. These results confirm that monitoring can adequately discern between unfair and fair systems after a reasonably small number of decisions has been made.

University Application. How to choose the right parameters? We now show that synthetic experiments can be an effective way to choose the confidence κ and threshold ϵ. We consider different decision-making algorithms for distributing places to applicants. This lets us explore how the different parameters influence the number of triggers on different algorithms. The first algorithm is *First Come*

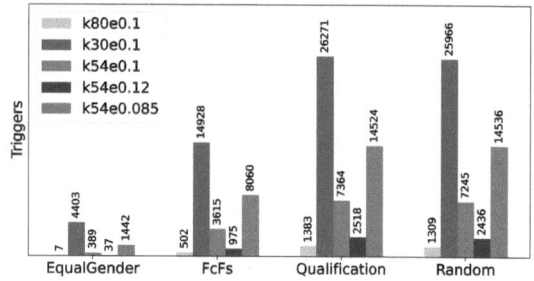

Fig. 5: Number of triggers thrown for different values of confidence κ (k) and threshold ϵ (e).

First Served (FCFS), which accepts the first people applying regardless of other attributes. The second is *Randomize*, which picks randomly in the pool of applicants for a given seminar. The third algorithm, called *Qualification*, picks the most qualified people for each seminar. The last algorithm is *EqualGender*, which tries to ensure the same acceptance rates for all groups in the long run. Note that demographic parity does not take into account additional attributes such as the qualification, and hence the fairness of, e.g., the Qualification algorithm completely depends on the randomization of the qualification values. Similarly, the fairness of FCFS depends on the application times which are generated randomly. In Figure 5, we compare the number of thrown triggers for the different parameters on two thousand generated scenarios for every algorithm with a hundred applicants each. Our specification of demographic parity with parameters $\kappa = 54$ and $\epsilon = 0.085$ gets violated 1031 times over all the scenarios generated with the EqualGender algorithm (which have 200000 distinct events). A general trend that can be inferred from Figure 5 is that parameter values that are too low lead to a large amount of triggers. Finding the right parameters requires estimating how many applicants are expected, and selecting them to achieve a desired contrast between the different algorithms on the simulated scenarios. For instance, a confidence of 80 and threshold of 0.1 results in 187× as many triggers on the random algorithm than on the EqualGender algorithm, while a confidence of 30 and threshold of 0.1 results only in around 6× as many triggers on the random algorithm.

Runtime Comparison. It is a viable question to ask what advantages monitoring with a stream-based specification language has over a simple database implementation. Therefore, we have compared our approach with a naïve implementation using SQLite, and an advanced implementation using RisingWave [44], a state-of-the-art streaming database [24]. For the databases we first defined a SQL query that encodes the fairness specifications and returns a Boolean value, similar to an RTLola trigger. During execution we then iteratively update the database with new events. Crucially, the streaming database is optimized for such incremental computations and only updates the changed values in the query. This is a similar approach to the RTLola monitor, which also incrementally and effi-

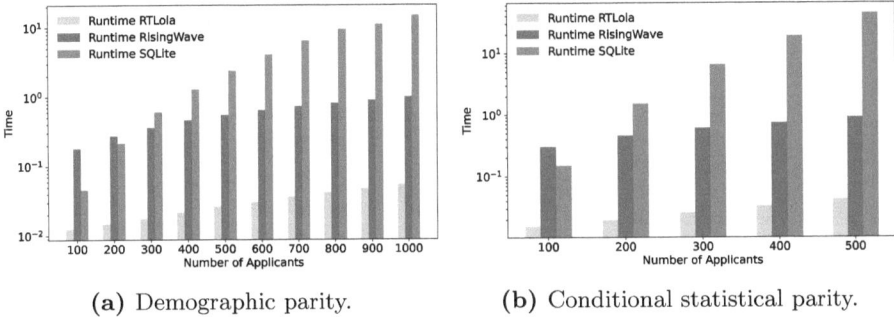

(a) Demographic parity.   **(b)** Conditional statistical parity.

Fig. 6: Runtime comparison between monitoring and database implementations. The bars report the average runtime over ten generated scenarios.

ciently updates its valuation upon encountering new events. We have generated seminar application scenarios with a varying number of applicants and report the average runtime of the three approaches in Figure 6. We stopped at 500 applicants in the case of conditional statistical parity because the SQLite approach already took more than 100 seconds. The results show that RTLola is faster than the database approaches in our scenarios. As a side result, we also see that the streaming database RisingWave outperforms the SQLite implementation on all but the smallest inputs, which is even more pronounced for conditional statistical parity. Monitoring with RTLola still significantly outperforms even the advanced streaming database approach. This runtime advantage gets particularly important for systems meant to be deployed at a large scale, such as the COMPAS recidivism risk assessment tool.

5.2 Monitoring Fairness of the COMPAS Tool

We revisit the motivating example from Section 1.1 to study the utility of our approach on real-world data from the recidivism risk prediction tool COMPAS. We use the same data set of COMPAS screenings between 2013 and 2014 in Broward County, Florida, which was also used by ProPublica [5] in their original investigation. We converted their original data into streams that are temporally ordered to simulate online monitoring of the COMPAS tool. We then executed our RTLola monitor with the equalized-odds specification as outlined in Section 4 for every combination of social groups. We used a confidence κ of 100, prior $\gamma(\omega) = 0.5$ and a threshold $\epsilon = 0.1$. In Figure 7, we illustrate the probability estimates and corresponding differences for African-American and European-American defendants. Note that the first two years are not shown, as a false positive result can only be definitely inferred after two years without recidivism, since this is the prediction horizon of the COMPAS tool as outlined in the COMPAS user guide [37]. As we can see, once the first two years have passed and the first definite outcomes can be inferred, unfairness can be established after less than a month, since the false positive rates of the groups quickly diverge. Since

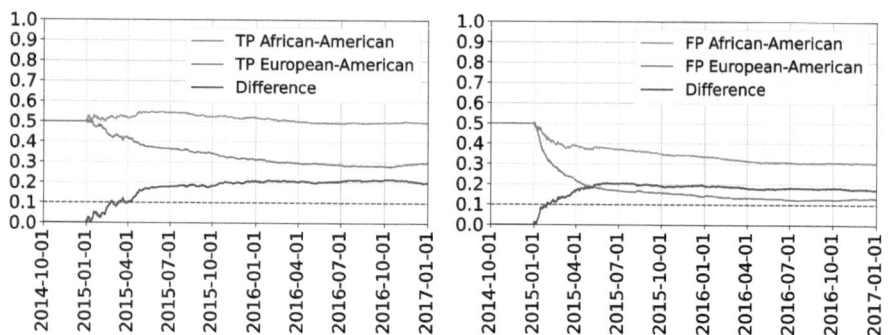

Fig. 7: True positive rates (TP) and false positive rates (FP) of African-American and European-American defendants while monitoring equalized odds on the COMPAS data set [5]. The dashed red line shows threshold ϵ.

such tools are deployed over a long time-horizon, these initial two years without verdict bear comparatively little weight. Moreover, the judgment is robust and stays far above the threshold afterward. This experiment with data from the COMPAS tool shows that stream-based monitoring can be a viable method to detect unfairness of prediction systems early, and hence reduce the number of unfair decisions and predictions.

6   Conclusion

We have studied the monitoring of algorithmic fairness with the stream-based specification language RTLola. This language not only allows us to encode the estimation of conditional probabilities inherent to algorithmic-fairness specifications but also the timing requirements common to real-world applications where these specifications are crucial. We have demonstrated this exemplarily with the COMPAS tool that is used to predict the recidivism risk of defendants. Moreover, we have contributed a benchmark generator for constructing synthetic scenarios related to job application and university admission scenarios and have used these scenarios for an extensive evaluation of our approach, which shows that it is able to detect the ground truth reliably and efficiently. In the future, we plan on leveraging RTLola's innate capabilities for reasoning about data and time to express even more complex algorithmic-fairness specifications dealing with, e.g., expected values of credit scores or response times.

Acknowledgments. This work was partially supported by the DFG in project 389792660 (TRR 248 – CPEC) and by the ERC Grant HYPER (No. 101055412). Funded by the European Union. Views and opinions expressed are however those of the authors only and do not necessarily reflect those of the European Union or the European Research Council Executive Agency. Neither the European Union nor the granting authority can be held responsible for them.

References

1. Agarwal, A., Beygelzimer, A., Dudík, M., Langford, J., Wallach, H.M.: A reductions approach to fair classification. In: Dy, J.G., Krause, A. (eds.) Proceedings of the 35th International Conference on Machine Learning, ICML 2018, Stockholmsmässan, Stockholm, Sweden, July 10-15, 2018. Proceedings of Machine Learning Research, vol. 80, pp. 60–69. PMLR (2018), `http://proceedings.mlr.press/v80/agarwal18a.html`
2. Albarghouthi, A., D'Antoni, L., Drews, S.: Repairing decision-making programs under uncertainty. In: Majumdar, R., Kuncak, V. (eds.) Computer Aided Verification - 29th International Conference, CAV 2017, Heidelberg, Germany, July 24-28, 2017, Proceedings, Part I. Lecture Notes in Computer Science, vol. 10426, pp. 181–200. Springer (2017). `https://doi.org/10.1007/978-3-319-63387-9_9`,
3. Albarghouthi, A., D'Antoni, L., Drews, S., Nori, A.V.: Fairsquare: probabilistic verification of program fairness. Proc. ACM Program. Lang. 1(OOPSLA), 80:1–80:30 (2017). `https://doi.org/10.1145/3133904`
4. Albarghouthi, A., Vinitsky, S.: Fairness-aware programming. In: danah boyd, Morgenstern, J.H. (eds.) Proceedings of the Conference on Fairness, Accountability, and Transparency, FAT* 2019, Atlanta, GA, USA, January 29-31, 2019. pp. 211–219. ACM (2019). `https://doi.org/10.1145/3287560.3287588`
5. Angwin, J., Larson, J., Mattu, S., Kirchner, L.: Machine bias. there's software used across the country to predict future criminals. and it's biased against blacks. ProPublica (2016), `https://www.propublica.org/article/machine-bias-risk-assessments-in-criminal-sentencing`
6. Artificial intelligence act (regulation (EU) 2024/1689), official journal version of 13 june 2024, `http://data.europa.eu/eli/reg/2024/1689/oj` (Accessed: 28.01.2024)
7. Bastani, O., Zhang, X., Solar-Lezama, A.: Probabilistic verification of fairness properties via concentration. Proc. ACM Program. Lang. 3(OOPSLA), 118:1–118:27 (2019). `https://doi.org/10.1145/3360544`
8. Baum, K., Biewer, S., Hermanns, H., Hetmank, S., Langer, M., Lauber-Rönsberg, A., Sterz, S.: Taming the AI monster: Monitoring of individual fairness for effective human oversight. In: Neele, T., Wijs, A. (eds.) Model Checking Software - 30th International Symposium, SPIN 2024, Luxembourg City, Luxembourg, April 8-9, 2024, Proceedings. Lecture Notes in Computer Science, vol. 14624, pp. 3–25. Springer (2024). `https://doi.org/10.1007/978-3-031-66149-5_1`
9. Baumeister, J., Finkbeiner, B., Kohn, F., Scheerer, F.: A tutorial on stream-based monitoring. In: Platzer, A., Rozier, K.Y., Pradella, M., Rossi, M. (eds.) Formal Methods - 26th International Symposium, FM 2024, Milan, Italy, September 9-13, 2024, Proceedings, Part II. Lecture Notes in Computer Science, vol. 14934, pp. 624–648. Springer (2024). `https://doi.org/10.1007/978-3-031-71177-0_33`
10. Baumeister, J., Finkbeiner, B., Kohn, F., Schirmer, S., Torens, C., Löhr, F., Manfredi, G.: Monitoring unmanned aircraft: Specification, integration, and lessons-learned. In: Computer Aided Verification - 36th International Conference, CAV 2024, Montreal, Canada, July 22-27, 2024 (2024)

11. Baumeister, J., Finkbeiner, B., Schirmer, S., Schwenger, M., Torens, C.: Rtlola cleared for take-off: Monitoring autonomous aircraft. In: Lahiri, S.K., Wang, C. (eds.) Computer Aided Verification - 32nd International Conference, CAV 2020, Los Angeles, CA, USA, July 21-24, 2020, Proceedings, Part II. Lecture Notes in Computer Science, vol. 12225, pp. 28–39. Springer (2020). https://doi.org/10.1007/978-3-030-53291-8_3

12. Blyth, C.R.: On simpson's paradox and the sure-thing principle. Journal of the American Statistical Association **67**(338), 364–366 (1972). https://doi.org/10.1080/01621459.1972.10482387

13. Bostrom, N., Yudkowsky, E.: The ethics of artificial intelligence, p. 316–334. Cambridge University Press (2014)

14. Cano, F., Henzinger, T.A., Könighofer, B., Kueffner, K., Mallik, K.: Fairness shields: Safeguarding against biased decision makers. CoRR **abs/2412.11994** (2024). https://doi.org/10.48550/ARXIV.2412.11994

15. Colorado senate bill 24-205, https://leg.colorado.gov/sites/default/files/2024a_205_signed.pdf (Accessed: 28.01.2024)

16. Convent, L., Hungerecker, S., Leucker, M., Scheffel, T., Schmitz, M., Thoma, D.: Tessla: Temporal stream-based specification language. In: Massoni, T., Mousavi, M.R. (eds.) Formal Methods: Foundations and Applications - 21st Brazilian Symposium, SBMF 2018, Salvador, Brazil, November 26-30, 2018, Proceedings. Lecture Notes in Computer Science, vol. 11254, pp. 144–162. Springer (2018). https://doi.org/10.1007/978-3-030-03044-5_10

17. Corbett-Davies, S., Pierson, E., Feller, A., Goel, S., Huq, A.: Algorithmic decision making and the cost of fairness. In: Proceedings of the 23rd ACM SIGKDD International Conference on Knowledge Discovery and Data Mining, Halifax, NS, Canada, August 13 - 17, 2017. pp. 797–806. ACM (2017). https://doi.org/10.1145/3097983.3098095

18. D'Angelo, B., Sankaranarayanan, S., Sánchez, C., Robinson, W., Finkbeiner, B., Sipma, H.B., Mehrotra, S., Manna, Z.: LOLA: runtime monitoring of synchronous systems. In: 12th International Symposium on Temporal Representation and Reasoning (TIME 2005), 23-25 June 2005, Burlington, Vermont, USA. pp. 166–174. IEEE Computer Society (2005). https://doi.org/10.1109/TIME.2005.26

19. Dastin, J.: Amazon scraps secret ai recruiting tool that showed bias against women (2018), https://www.reuters.com/article/idUSKCN1MK0AG/ (Accessed: 19.04.2024)

20. Dwork, C., Hardt, M., Pitassi, T., Reingold, O., Zemel, R.S.: Fairness through awareness. In: Goldwasser, S. (ed.) Innovations in Theoretical Computer Science 2012, Cambridge, MA, USA, January 8-10, 2012. pp. 214–226. ACM (2012). https://doi.org/10.1145/2090236.2090255

21. Faymonville, P., Finkbeiner, B., Schirmer, S., Torfah, H.: A stream-based specification language for network monitoring. In: Falcone, Y., Sánchez, C. (eds.) Runtime Verification - 16th International Conference, RV 2016, Madrid, Spain, September 23-30, 2016, Proceedings. Lecture Notes in Computer Science, vol. 10012, pp. 152–168. Springer (2016). https://doi.org/10.1007/978-3-319-46982-9_10

22. Feldman, M., Friedler, S.A., Moeller, J., Scheidegger, C., Venkatasubramanian, S.: Certifying and removing disparate impact. In: Cao, L., Zhang, C., Joachims, T., Webb, G.I., Margineantu, D.D., Williams, G. (eds.) Proceedings of the 21th ACM SIGKDD International Conference on Knowledge Discovery and Data Mining, Sydney, NSW, Australia, August 10-13, 2015. pp. 259–268. ACM (2015). https://doi.org/10.1145/2783258.2783311

23. Finkbeiner, B., Kohn, F., Schledjewski, M.: Leveraging static analysis: An IDE for rtlola. In: André, É., Sun, J. (eds.) Automated Technology for Verification and Analysis - 21st International Symposium, ATVA 2023, Singapore, October 24-27, 2023, Proceedings, Part II. Lecture Notes in Computer Science, vol. 14216, pp. 251–262. Springer (2023). https://doi.org/10.1007/978-3-031-45332-8_13

24. Fragkoulis, M., Carbone, P., Kalavri, V., Katsifodimos, A.: A survey on the evolution of stream processing systems. VLDB J. **33**(2), 507–541 (2024). https://doi.org/10.1007/S00778-023-00819-8

25. Gorostiaga, F., Sánchez, C.: Striver: Stream runtime verification for real-time event-streams. In: Colombo, C., Leucker, M. (eds.) Runtime Verification - 18th International Conference, RV 2018, Limassol, Cyprus, November 10-13, 2018, Proceedings. Lecture Notes in Computer Science, vol. 11237, pp. 282–298. Springer (2018). https://doi.org/10.1007/978-3-030-03769-7_16

26. Hardt, M., Price, E., Srebro, N.: Equality of opportunity in supervised learning. In: Lee, D.D., Sugiyama, M., von Luxburg, U., Guyon, I., Garnett, R. (eds.) Advances in Neural Information Processing Systems 29: Annual Conference on Neural Information Processing Systems 2016, December 5-10, 2016, Barcelona, Spain. pp. 3315–3323 (2016), https://proceedings.neurips.cc/paper/2016/hash/9d2682367c3935defcb1f9e247a97c0d-Abstract.html

27. Henzinger, T.A., Karimi, M., Kueffner, K., Mallik, K.: Monitoring algorithmic fairness. In: Enea, C., Lal, A. (eds.) Computer Aided Verification - 35th International Conference, CAV 2023, Paris, France, July 17-22, 2023, Proceedings, Part II. Lecture Notes in Computer Science, vol. 13965, pp. 358–382. Springer (2023). https://doi.org/10.1007/978-3-031-37703-7_17

28. Henzinger, T.A., Karimi, M., Kueffner, K., Mallik, K.: Runtime monitoring of dynamic fairness properties. In: Proceedings of the 2023 ACM Conference on Fairness, Accountability, and Transparency, FAccT 2023, Chicago, IL, USA, June 12-15, 2023. pp. 604–614. ACM (2023). https://doi.org/10.1145/3593013.3594028

29. Henzinger, T.A., Kueffner, K., Mallik, K.: Monitoring algorithmic fairness under partial observations. In: Katsaros, P., Nenzi, L. (eds.) Runtime Verification - 23rd International Conference, RV 2023, Thessaloniki, Greece, October 3-6, 2023, Proceedings. Lecture Notes in Computer Science, vol. 14245, pp. 291–311. Springer (2023). https://doi.org/10.1007/978-3-031-44267-4_15

30. Kamiran, F., Calders, T.: Data preprocessing techniques for classification without discrimination. Knowl. Inf. Syst. **33**(1), 1–33 (2011). https://doi.org/10.1007/S10115-011-0463-8

31. Kamishima, T., Akaho, S., Asoh, H., Sakuma, J.: Fairness-aware classifier with prejudice remover regularizer. In: Flach, P.A., Bie, T.D., Cristianini, N. (eds.)

Machine Learning and Knowledge Discovery in Databases - European Conference, ECML PKDD 2012, Bristol, UK, September 24-28, 2012. Proceedings, Part II. Lecture Notes in Computer Science, vol. 7524, pp. 35–50. Springer (2012). https://doi.org/10.1007/978-3-642-33486-3_3

32. Kusner, M.J., Loftus, J.R., Russell, C., Silva, R.: Counterfactual fairness. In: Guyon, I., von Luxburg, U., Bengio, S., Wallach, H.M., Fergus, R., Vishwanathan, S.V.N., Garnett, R. (eds.) Advances in Neural Information Processing Systems 30: Annual Conference on Neural Information Processing Systems 2017, December 4-9, 2017, Long Beach, CA, USA. pp. 4066–4076 (2017), https://proceedings.neurips.cc/paper/2017/hash/a486cd07e4ac3d270571622f4f316ec5-Abstract.html

33. Lin, Z., Jung, J., Goel, S., Skeem, J.: The limits of human predictions of recidivism. Science Advances **6**(7) (2020). https://doi.org/10.1126/sciadv.aaz0652

34. Matthias, A.: The responsibility gap: Ascribing responsibility for the actions of learning automata. Ethics and Information Technology **6**(3), 175–183 (2004). https://doi.org/10.1007/s10676-004-3422-1

35. Mehrabi, N., Morstatter, F., Saxena, N., Lerman, K., Galstyan, A.: A survey on bias and fairness in machine learning. ACM Comput. Surv. **54**(6), 115:1–115:35 (2022). https://doi.org/10.1145/3457607

36. Mitchell, T.M.: Machine learning, International Edition. McGraw-Hill Series in Computer Science, McGraw-Hill (1997), https://www.worldcat.org/oclc/61321007

37. Northpoint Inc. d/b/a equivant: Practitioner's guide to compas core, https://archive.epic.org/algorithmic-transparency/crim-justice/EPIC-16-06-23-WI-FOIA-201600805-COMPASPractionerGuide.pdf (Accessed: 11.10.2024)

38. Pessach, D., Shmueli, E.: Algorithmic Fairness, pp. 867–886. Springer International Publishing, Cham (2023). https://doi.org/10.1007/978-3-031-24628-9_37

39. Ruoss, A., Balunovic, M., Fischer, M., Vechev, M.T.: Learning certified individually fair representations. In: Larochelle, H., Ranzato, M., Hadsell, R., Balcan, M., Lin, H. (eds.) Advances in Neural Information Processing Systems 33: Annual Conference on Neural Information Processing Systems 2020, NeurIPS 2020, December 6-12, 2020, virtual (2020), https://proceedings.neurips.cc/paper/2020/hash/55d491cf951b1b920900684d71419282-Abstract.html

40. Teuber, S., Beckert, B.: An information-flow perspective on algorithmic fairness. In: Wooldridge, M.J., Dy, J.G., Natarajan, S. (eds.) Thirty-Eighth AAAI Conference on Artificial Intelligence, AAAI 2024, Thirty-Sixth Conference on Innovative Applications of Artificial Intelligence, IAAI 2024, Fourteenth Symposium on Educational Advances in Artificial Intelligence, EAAI 2014, February 20-27, 2024, Vancouver, Canada. pp. 15337–15345. AAAI Press (2024). https://doi.org/10.1609/AAAI.V38I14.29458

41. Thomas, D., Ravi, K.: The potential for artificial intelligence in healthcare. Future Healthc Journal **6** (2019). https://doi.org/10.7861/futurehosp.6-2-94

42. Tramèr, F., Atlidakis, V., Geambasu, R., Hsu, D.J., Hubaux, J., Humbert, M., Juels, A., Lin, H.: Fairtest: Discovering unwarranted associations in data-driven applications. In: 2017 IEEE European Symposium on Security and Privacy, EuroS&P 2017, Paris, France, April 26-28, 2017. pp. 401–416. IEEE (2017). https://doi.org/10.1109/EuroSP.2017.29

43. Udeshi, S., Arora, P., Chattopadhyay, S.: Automated directed fairness testing. In: Huchard, M., Kästner, C., Fraser, G. (eds.) Proceedings of the 33rd ACM/IEEE International Conference on Automated Software Engineering, ASE 2018, Montpellier, France, September 3-7, 2018. pp. 98–108. ACM (2018). https://doi.org/10.1145/3238147.3238165
44. Wang, Y., Liu, Z.: A sneak peek at risingwave: a cloud-native streaming database. In: Zhou, Y., Chrysanthis, P.K., Gulisano, V., Zacharatou, E.T. (eds.) 16th ACM International Conference on Distributed and Event-based Systems, DEBS 2022, Copenhagen, Denmark, June 27 - 30, 2022. pp. 190–193. ACM (2022). https://doi.org/10.1145/3524860.3543284

ATP and Rewriting

Augmenting Model-Based Instantiation with Fast Enumeration

Lydia Kondylidou[1]($\boxtimes$)(iD), Andrew Reynolds[2](iD), and Jasmin Blanchette[1](iD)

[1] Ludwig-Maximilians-Universität München, Munich, Germany
{l.kondylidou,jasmin.blanchette}@lmu.de
[2] The University of Iowa, Iowa City, USA
andrew.j.reynolds@gmail.com

Abstract. Satisfiability modulo theories (SMT) solvers rely on various quantifier instantiation strategies to support first- and higher-order logic. We introduce MBQI-Enum, an approach that extends model-based quantifier instantiation (MBQI) with syntax-guided synthesis (SyGuS) techniques. Our approach targets first-order theories without well-established quantifier instantiation techniques and higher-order quantifiers that can benefit from instantiations with λ-terms. By incorporating a SyGuS enumerator, our approach generates a broader set of candidate instantiations, including identity functions and terms containing uninterpreted symbols, thereby improving the effectiveness of MBQI.

1 Introduction

Satisfiability modulo theories (SMT) solvers combine a Boolean satisfiability (SAT) solver with decision procedures for interpreted theories. Several SMT solvers, including Bitwuzla [16], Boolector [17], cvc5 [2], veriT [7], and Z3 [15], also support quantifiers via Skolemization and instantiation. With complete instantiation strategies, SMT solvers offer a semidecision procedure for first-order logic with theories. SMT has also been partly extended to higher-order logic [4].

Quantifier instantiation is a technique whereby quantified variables in a formula are instantiated with ground terms until a contradiction is found or all necessary instantiations have been generated. Consider the unsatisfiable axiom $(\forall x.\ \mathsf{p}\ x) \wedge \neg \mathsf{p}\ \mathsf{b}$. The SAT solver first finds a model that makes $\forall x.\ \mathsf{p}\ x$ true and $\mathsf{p}\ \mathsf{b}$ false, taken as black boxes. Then the quantifier instantiation strategy of the SMT solver might heuristically instantiate x with a, resulting in the formula $(\forall x.\ \mathsf{p}\ x) \Longrightarrow \mathsf{p}\ \mathsf{a}$, which is conjoined with the axiom. Next, the SAT solver finds a new model that also makes $\mathsf{p}\ \mathsf{a}$ true. At this point, the instantiation strategy might instantiate x with b, resulting in $(\forall x.\ \mathsf{p}\ x) \Longrightarrow \mathsf{p}\ \mathsf{b}$. Since the SAT solver cannot make $\mathsf{p}\ \mathsf{b}$ both true and false at the same time, the axiom conjoined with the two additional formulas is unsatisfiable at the SAT level, meaning that the original axiom is unsatisfiable in the SMT logic.

One successful instantiation strategy is model-based quantifier instantiation (MBQI) [9]. Briefly, it iteratively refines a candidate model constructed from the quantifier-free part of the problem. This model guides the generation of new

© The Author(s) 2025
A. Gurfinkel and M. Heule (Eds.): TACAS 2025, LNCS 15696, pp. 85–103, 2025.
https://doi.org/10.1007/978-3-031-90643-5_5

terms for instantiating quantifiers, reducing the search space. MBQI is complete for certain fragments and tends to generate small models for satisfiable problems. But it also has some limitations: First, MBQI instantiates quantifiers only with terms that denote values in a theory. In particular, it does not consider the problem's uninterpreted symbols when creating instantiations, leading it to miss some useful instantiations. Second, for higher-order problems, MBQI cannot generate function terms that return an argument, such as the identity $\lambda x.\ x$.

Another instantiation strategy, which addresses these limitations, is syntax-guided instantiation (SyQI) [18]. This constructs a grammar for each universally quantified variable according to its type and uses enumerated terms derived from the grammar as instantiations. Its main weakness is that although it is model-based like MBQI, it uses a less scalable approach to refining models that centers around syntactic constraints.

In this paper, we propose a new strategy, MBQI-Enum, that combines the strengths of MBQI and SyQI. Specifically, our strategy augments the set of instantiations created from the MBQI model with instantiations generated by a syntax-guided synthesis (SyGuS) grammar. It incorporates uninterpreted symbols gathered from the problem. For higher-order problems, it also considers λ-abstractions as potential instantiations. In this way, we exploit the fast model-finding capabilities of MBQI and the diversity of terms considered by SyQI.

Our work shares some similarities with Preiner et al. [21], but their approach was limited to selected first-order theories and did not handle higher-order logic. Our approach is resolutely pragmatic; it does not aim at completeness, which can be achieved using other instantiation strategies.

As an example where λ-terms are needed, consider the unsatisfiable problem consisting of the axiom $\forall z.\exists x,y.\ z\ x\ y \neq x$, where z ranges over binary functions. Running cvc5 with strategies such as MBQI and higher-order E-matching [4] leads the solver to give up early. By contrast, with our strategy, cvc5 immediately finds a contradiction based on the substitution $\{z \mapsto \lambda x, y.\ x\}$. Indeed, if we instantiate z with $\lambda x, y.\ x$ in the axiom and β-reduce, we obtain $x \neq x$.

We implemented MBQI-Enum in cvc5. Our empirical evaluation finds that the strategy increases the number of solved problems for a benchmark suite consisting of various first-order SMT-LIB files by a noticeable margin. Our approach is especially useful to solve unsatisfiable problems involving theories without well-established quantifier instantiation techniques. We can also report substantial gains on higher-order TPTP benchmarks. The raw evaluation data are publicly available online.[3] Our source code, along with instructions for reproducing the experiments, is also available online.[4]

2   Preliminaries

Our work relies on the following pillars: higher-order logic, SMT with quantifiers, MBQI, and SyQI.

---

[3] https://doi.org/10.5281/zenodo.14627782
[4] https://doi.org/10.5281/zenodo.14604430

Higher-Order Logic. Monomorphic higher-order logic [1, 10], also called simple type theory [8], generalizes classical first-order logic by allowing quantification over functions. The syntax distinguishes between types and terms. Types τ are either base types κ or applications of the function arrow $\rightarrow$ to two types: $\tau_1 \rightarrow \tau_2$. The type of Booleans is denoted by o.

The term language is based on Church's simply typed λ-calculus, where terms t, e are inductively defined as variables w, x, y, z, $\ldots$, function symbols p, f, constants a, b, c, term applications $t\, t'$, and λ-abstractions $\lambda x.\, t$, where x is the bound variable and t is the body. A variable is free in a term if it is not bound by a λ-abstraction. We let $\bar{x}$ stand for $x_1, x_2, \ldots, x_n$, where $n \geq 1$. Terms are syntactically equal modulo α-, β-, and η-conversion, meaning, for example, that $(\lambda x.\, x)\, \mathsf{c}$ is equal to c. Throughout this work, we assume that terms are expressed in η-long β-normal form, meaning that η-expansion and β-reduction have been applied exhaustively. The type of a term t is of the form $\tau_1 \rightarrow \cdots \rightarrow \tau_n \rightarrow \tau$, where τ_i are the argument types and τ is the result type. If τ is of type o, which is the distinguished Boolean type, we call t a predicate. A term of type o is called a formula.

SMT with Quantifiers. Traditionally, SMT solvers work on problems in first-order logic, but they have partly been extended to higher-order logic [4], and in this paper we consider both first- and higher-order problems. SMT solvers that support quantifiers typically do so via a combination of Skolemization and instantiation: Universal quantifiers occurring negatively can be Skolemized; universal quantifiers occurring positively are instantiated heuristically; and existential quantifiers are expressed in terms of $\forall$ using the equivalence $(\exists x.\, \phi) \iff \neg(\forall x.\, \neg\phi)$. To simplify the presentation, we will assume that formulas are in a normal form where possibly negated $\forall$-quantifiers all appear in a cluster at the top level—e.g., $\forall x, y.\, \neg \forall z.\, \mathsf{p}\, x\, y\, z$.

Let $\mathcal{T}$ be a theory for a set of interpreted symbols, and let F be the input formula over $\mathcal{T}$. The goal is to find a model of F or derive a contradiction. If F does not contain quantifiers, the quantifier-free part of the SMT solver searches for a $\mathcal{T}$-satisfiable set L of literals that propositionally satisfies F. If such an L exists, F is $\mathcal{T}$-satisfiable (i.e., satisfiable with respect to $\mathcal{T}$); otherwise, F is $\mathcal{T}$-unsatisfiable.

If the formula F contains quantifiers, the quantifier-free solver cannot be directly applied. In the SMT solver's main loop, presented in Algorithm 1, the SMT solver tries to find a set L of literals whose atoms come from F and that propositionally satisfies F. Briefly, L is partitioned into a set E of ground literals and two sets of quantified literals, Q_p and Q_n. The ground literals within E must be $\mathcal{T}$-satisfiable, Q_p consists of formulas of the form $\forall \bar{x}.\, \phi$, and Q_n consists of formulas of the form $\neg \forall \bar{x}. \phi$. If the solver is unable to find such an L, it concludes that the formula F is $\mathcal{T}$-unsatisfiable.

On the other hand, if a set L of literals is found, new lemmas A are generated through the instantiation and Skolemization rounds. The instantiation round generates *instantiation lemmas*—that is, lemmas of the form $q_i \implies q_i\sigma$—from the sets Q_p and E. For each $q_i \in Q_\mathsf{p}$, an instantiation strategy computes

---

Algorithm 1 The main SMT loop

1: **function** SMT-LOOP(F)
2:     find a set of literals L where
3:         — $L \models_{\mathrm{p}} F$, where L's atoms are a subset of atoms(F)
4:         — L can be partitioned into $(E, Q_{\mathrm{p}}, Q_{\mathrm{n}})$, where
5:             — E is ground and $\mathcal{T}$-satisfiable
6:             — Q_{p} consists of universally quantified atoms
7:             — Q_{n} consists of negated universally quantified atoms
8:     **if** no such L exists **then**
9:         **return** unsat
10:    $A \leftarrow$ INSTANTIATION-ROUND(Q_{p}, E) $\cup$ SKOLEMIZATION-ROUND(Q_{n})
11:    **if** $A = \emptyset$ **then**
12:        **return** sat
13:    **else**
14:        **return** SMT-LOOP($F \cup A$)
15: **function** INSTANTIATION-ROUND($\{q_1, \ldots, q_n\}, E$)
16:    $I \leftarrow \emptyset$
17:    **for each** $i \in \{1, \ldots, n\}$ **do**
18:        $I \leftarrow I \cup \{q_i \Longrightarrow q_i\sigma \mid \sigma \in$ INSTS(q_i, E)$\}$
19:    **return** I
20: **function** INSTS(q_i, E)
21:    **return** a set of substitutions for q_i based on (q_i, E)
22: **function** SKOLEMIZATION-ROUND($\{\neg q_1, \ldots, \neg q_n\}$)
23:    $K \leftarrow \emptyset$
24:    **for each** $i \in \{1, \ldots, n\}$ **do**
25:        $K \leftarrow K \cup \{\neg q_i \Longrightarrow \neg q_i\sigma_{k,i}\}$, where $\sigma_{k,i}$ maps to Skolem constants for q_i
26:    **return** K

---

substitutions σ for every top-level variable in q_i mapping them to terms. The Skolemization round generates *Skolemization lemmas* from the set Q_{n}—that is, lemmas of the form $\neg q_i \Longrightarrow \neg q_i\sigma_{j,i}$, where $\sigma_{j,i}$ instantiates every top-level variable in q_i with a Skolem constant. (We abuse notation and write $(\forall \bar{x}.\ \phi)\sigma$ to mean $\phi\sigma$, syntactically conflating quantifier instantiation and substitution.) The lemmas are then added to the original formula F, and the SMT loop is called recursively. On line 12 of Algorithm 1, we assume that the instantiation strategy denoted by INSTS is *model-sound*, meaning that if INSTS returns an empty set of substitutions, it indicates that the formula F is $\mathcal{T}$-satisfiable.

We now define the instantiation strategy INSTS starting with a naive approach. Subsequently, we will introduce more advanced techniques, including MBQI and SyQI, followed by our strategy, MBQI-Enum. These strategies can replace the naive approach to improve the solver's efficiency.

Definition 2. An *instantiation strategy* takes as input a set of ground terms E and a quantified formula q of the form $\forall \bar{x}.\ \phi$, and outputs a set of grounding substitutions $\{\sigma_1, \ldots, \sigma_m\}$, where the variables mapped by σ_i are exactly the variables in $\bar{x}$ for each $i \in \{1, \ldots, m\}$.

Example 3. Let a : *Int* and p : *Int* → *Bool*. Let F be the formula $(\forall y.\, \mathsf{p}\, y) \land \neg\mathsf{p}\,\mathsf{a}$, where y : *Int*. In the SMT loop, the sets $E = \{\neg\mathsf{p}\,\mathsf{a}\}$, $Q_\mathsf{p} = \{\forall y.\, \mathsf{p}\, y\}$, and $Q_\mathsf{n} = \emptyset$ are defined. The naive instantiation strategy produces substitutions mapping y to terms from E of the same type as y, as shown below:

$q \in Q_\mathsf{p}$	$\mathrm{INSTS}(E, q)$
$\forall y.\, \mathsf{p}\, y$	$\{\{y \mapsto \mathsf{a}\}\}$

The instantiation lemma $(\forall y.\, \mathsf{p}\, y) \Longrightarrow \mathsf{p}\,\mathsf{a}$ is added to F. Now, the quantifier-free solver finds a contradiction.

The most widely used strategy for quantifier instantiation is *E-matching* [14]. This is a heuristic and typically incomplete technique that chooses substitutions by matching ground terms with *patterns*. In Example 3, the ground term p a matches p y for substitution $\{y \mapsto \mathsf{a}\}$, and hence this substitution is returned by the strategy. Over the past decade, SMT solvers have been extended with more sophisticated approaches. *Conflict-based instantiation* [26] is another incomplete technique that attempts to find a single instantiation that would induce a ground conflict, before resorting to E-matching. *MBQI* [9] is a technique for finding instantiations that refute a candidate model, and is typically run when E-matching saturates. This strategy is also able to answer "$\mathcal{T}$-satisfiable" when no such instantiation can be found. *Enumerative instantiation* [22] is an alternative to MBQI that focuses on finding instantiations over the current set of ground terms that are not entailed in the current context. This has similar properties to MBQI but is more tailored for unsatisfiable instances.

Quantifier instantiation strategies that target specific theories have also been proposed. *Counterexample-guided instantiation* [24] is complete for specific theories with quantifiers that admit quantifier elimination, such as linear arithmetic and bit vectors. *SyQI* [18] is a more general purpose strategy that uses syntax-guided synthesis for enumerating instantiations and is effective for theories that otherwise do not have well-established instantiation strategies.

MBQI. MBQI iteratively refines a candidate model M constructed from the quantifier-free part of the problem. As shown in Algorithm 4, the strategy replaces function symbols in the body ϕ of the quantified formula with their interpretation in M. If $\neg\phi^M$ is $\mathcal{T}$-satisfiable, this means that a model M' exists, and the strategy returns the substitution $\{y_1 \mapsto y_1^{M'}, \ldots, y_n \mapsto y_n^{M'}\}$, where $y_i^{M'}$ represents a term denoting the interpretation for the variable y_i in M'.

Example 5. Let a : *Int* and p : *Int* → *Bool*. Let F be the input formula

$$(\forall y.\, \mathsf{p}\, y) \land 0 < \mathsf{a} < 2 \land \neg\mathsf{p}\,\mathsf{a}$$

where y : *Int*. In the SMT loop, our set of literals L is partitioned into $E = \{0 < \mathsf{a} < 2, \neg\mathsf{p}\,\mathsf{a}\}$, $Q_\mathsf{p} = \{\forall y.\, \mathsf{p}\, y\}$, and $Q_\mathsf{n} = \emptyset$. MBQI builds a model M from E—assume $\mathsf{a}^M = 1$ and $\mathsf{p}^M = \lambda x.\, x \neq 1$. (We abuse notation by denoting values using λ-terms.) It then considers the negation of the body of the quantified

---

Algorithm 4 The MBQI strategy

1: **function** INSTS_MBQI(q, E)
2:     **assume** q is $\forall y_1, \ldots, y_n.\ \phi$
3:     **let** M be a model of E
4:     **if** $\neg \phi^M$ is unsatisfiable **then**
5:         **return** $\emptyset$
6:     **let** M' be a model of $\neg \phi^M$
7:     **return** $\{\{y_1 \mapsto y_1^{M'}, \ldots, y_n \mapsto y_n^{M'}\}\}$

---

formula in Q_{p} under the interpretation M, which is $\neg (\lambda x.\ x \neq 1)\ y$, which simplifies to $y = 1$ and has a model M' where $y^{M'} = 1$. Thus, MBQI generates the substitution $\{y \mapsto 1\}$, from which the instantiation lemma $(\forall y.\mathsf{p}\ y) \implies \mathsf{p}\ 1$ is constructed and added to F. Now, the quantifier-free solver finds a contradiction.

Example 6. Let $\mathsf{f} : Int \to Int \to Bool$. Let F be the higher-order formula

$$\forall x, y.\ y\ x \neq y\ (\mathsf{f}\ x)$$

where $x : Int$ and $y : Int \to Int$. The set L is partitioned into sets $E = \emptyset$, $Q_{\mathrm{p}} = \{\forall x, y.\ y\ x \neq y\ (\mathsf{f}\ x)\}$, and $Q_{\mathrm{n}} = \emptyset$. MBQI constructs a model M for E such that $\mathsf{f}^M = \lambda z.\ 0$. It then considers the negation of the body of the quantified formula in Q_{p} under the interpretation M. This is $\neg y\ x \neq y\ ((\lambda z.\ 0)\ x)$, which simplifies to $y\ x = y\ 0$ and has a model M' where $x^{M'} = 0$ and $y^{M'} = \lambda z.\ 0$. Thus, it generates the substitution $\{x \mapsto 0,\ y \mapsto \lambda z.\ 0\}$ based on the candidate model. Now, the quantifier-free solver finds a contradiction. Indeed, if we instantiate x and y with this substitution and β-reduce, we obtain $0 \neq 0$.

SyQI. SyQI uses SyGuS to choose instantiation terms. It aims to synthesize a term t for a variable x in a given formula $\forall x.\ \mathsf{p}\ x$ such that $\neg \mathsf{p}\ t$ holds. Each quantified variable is associated with a SyGuS grammar. The main advantage of SyQI is that, unlike MBQI, it does not require theory-specific quantifier instantiation procedures. The only parts that depend on the theory are the grammar and the $\mathcal{T}$-satisfiability check for the generated instances.

3   The Method

The core idea behind our new instantiation strategy, MBQI-Enum, is to integrate a SyGuS enumerator within MBQI, thereby enabling the generation of a broader set of candidate instantiations for quantified variables.

Instantiation Strategy. Instead of restricting instantiations to ground terms derived from the current MBQI model, our strategy uses a SyGuS grammar to produce additional candidate instantiations. This grammar is not limited to ground terms with the types of the quantified variables; rather, it incorporates uninterpreted symbols gathered from the entire formula. As a result, it generates a more extensive and comprehensive language of terms.

For each quantified variable in a formula, our strategy performs iterative term enumeration. It generates candidate substitutions from the extended grammar and tests each enumerated term within the formula. For each enumerated term, the strategy tries to apply it as an instantiation for the quantified variable. For higher-order problems, it also considers λ-abstractions as candidate instantiations. If the strategy produces a useless instance according to the current model, it continues to the next candidate until a suitable instantiation is found or all possibilities are exhausted.

When none of the candidate instantiations derived from the SyGuS enumeration prove successful, MBQI-Enum reverts to the original MBQI model-derived instantiation. This fallback mechanism ensures that our strategy can in principle solve any problem that MBQI can solve.

Our initial motivation for developing MBQI-Enum was to increase cvc5's success rate on higher-order problems. Nevertheless, incorporating uninterpreted symbols gathered from the entire formula extends our approach's applicability to first-order problems using various SMT theories.

Our approach is presented in Algorithm 7. The strategy starts by invoking MBQI to generate a set of initial substitutions Σ, since the goal is to postprocess the substitutions generated by MBQI using a SyGuS enumerator. If Σ is empty, the strategy immediately returns an empty set, indicating that no valid instantiation could be found. Otherwise, it proceeds by initializing Σ to contain a single substitution σ. Next, it generates additional substitutions by extending the current one using the SyGuS enumerator.

Our strategy then iterates over the quantified variables y_i in the formula q to instantiate. For each variable, it constructs a grammar G_i used to guide the enumeration of candidate terms for substituting y_i. The enumeration starts by · generating terms from G_i in a sequential manner. For each term e, the strategy creates a new substitution σ' by mapping y_i to e in the current substitution σ. It then checks whether the negation of the body ϕ under σ' is $\mathcal{T}$-satisfiable. This check serves to maintain the invariant that the negation of the body of the quantified formula, after applying the current substitution, remains $\mathcal{T}$-satisfiable. In other words, we want to ensure that the generated instantiation refutes the current model (cf. line 6 of Algorithm 4). If it does, σ is updated to σ', and the strategy moves on to the next variable. Once all variables have been considered, the strategy returns the refined substitution σ.

Choice of Grammar. Term enumeration is based on a SyGuS grammar. Choosing an appropriate grammar for each quantified variable is crucial for selecting the correct instantiations. Our strategy builds a set S of symbols based on three Boolean options: *syms_global*, *ext_vars*, and *syms_local*. These options specify which symbols from the formula F will be included when constructing the SyGuS grammar.

If no options are enabled, the set S is empty. If *syms_global* is enabled, all function symbols from the entire formula F are contained in S. If *ext_vars* is

---

Algorithm 7 The MBQI-Enum strategy

1: **function** INSTS_MBQI_FAST_SYGUS(q, E)
2:     **assume** q is $\forall y_1, \ldots, y_n. \phi$
3:     **let** $\Sigma \leftarrow$ INSTS_MBQI(q, E)
4:     **if** $\Sigma = \emptyset$ **then**
5:         **return** $\emptyset$
6:     **else**
7:         **let** $\Sigma \leftarrow \{\sigma\}$
8:     **for each** $i \in \{1, \ldots, n\}$ **do**
9:         **let** $G_i \leftarrow$ CHOOSE_GRAMMAR(q, y_i)
10:         **for each** $j \in \{1, 2, \ldots\}$ **do**
11:             **let** $e \leftarrow$ GET_ENUM_TERM(G_i, j)
12:             **if** e does not exist **then**
13:                 **break**
14:             $\sigma' \leftarrow \sigma[y_i \mapsto e]$
15:             **if** $\neg \phi \sigma'$ is sat **then**
16:                 $\sigma \leftarrow \sigma'$
17:                 **break**
18:     **return** σ
19: **function** CHOOSE_GRAMMAR(q, y_i)
20:     **let** F be the original input formula
21:     **let** $S \leftarrow \emptyset$
22:     **if** option_syms_global **then**
23:         $S \leftarrow S \cup \text{symbols}(F)$
24:     **if** option_syms_local **then**
25:         $S \leftarrow S \cup \text{symbols}(q)$
26:     **if** option_ext_vars **then**
27:         $S \leftarrow S \cup \{y_{i+1}, \ldots, y_n\}$
28:     **return** grammar that generates terms of the same sort as y_i over symbols in S

---

enabled, S is augmented with bound variables from the formula q that are not yet instantiated. Finally, if *syms_local* is enabled, the set S also contains function symbols specifically from q. Based on these settings, our approach constructs a grammar that generates terms over the symbols in S, while ensuring that these terms are well-typed with respect to the type of y_i.

For higher-order variables, since we use η-long β-normal form, it is sufficient to consider only grammars that generate λ-abstractions. The variables bound by these λ-abstractions are considered terminal symbols of the grammar that generates the abstraction's body. For example, for a function variable whose arity is n and whose arguments are of the same base type as its return type, we add grammar rules of this form:

$$A ::= \lambda x_1, \ldots, x_n. B$$
$$B ::= x_1 \mid \cdots \mid x_n$$

Moreover, there will be additional rules for B and possibly for some of the grammar's other nonterminal symbols. This ensures that any λ instantiations are formed by enumerating the body B over the bound variables $x_1, \ldots, x_n$.

Example 8. Let $a : Int$ and $p : Int \to Bool$. Let F be the input formula

$$(\forall y. \neg p\,(y\,a)) \wedge p\,a$$

where $y : Int \to Int$. The set L is partitioned into $E = \{p\,a\}$, $Q_p = \{\forall y. \neg p\,(y\,a)\}$, and $Q_n = \emptyset$. MBQI generates substitutions such as $\{y \mapsto \lambda x.\,0\}$, $\{y \mapsto \lambda x.\,1\}, \ldots$. As a result, the solver does not terminate. In contrast, MBQI-Enum augments these instantiations based on enumeration. On the first iteration of the SMT loop, MBQI-Enum considers the set $\Sigma = \{\{y \mapsto \lambda x.\,0\}\}$ consisting of the first substitution generated by MBQI. MBQI-Enum first constructs a grammar for y. The set of symbols S is empty. The grammar is

$$\mathcal{A} ::= \lambda x.\,\mathcal{B}$$
$$\mathcal{B} ::= x \mid 0 \mid 1 \mid \mathcal{B} + \mathcal{B} \mid \mathcal{B} - \mathcal{B} \mid \mathsf{ite}(\mathcal{B}, \mathcal{B}, \mathcal{B})$$
$$\mathcal{C} ::= \mathsf{true} \mid \mathsf{false} \mid \mathcal{B} = \mathcal{B} \mid \mathcal{B} \le \mathcal{B} \mid \neg \mathcal{C} \mid \mathcal{C} \wedge \mathcal{C} \mid \mathcal{C} \vee \mathcal{C}$$

Next, MBQI-Enum enumerates terms derived from the grammar and creates the substitution $\sigma' = \{y \mapsto \lambda x.\,x\}$ by updating σ with the enumerated term $\lambda x.\,x$ from the grammar. The strategy then checks whether the negation of the body of the quantified formula after applying σ' is $\mathcal{T}$-satisfiable. Indeed, if we instantiate y with $\lambda x.\,x$ and β-reduce, we obtain $p\,a$, which is $\mathcal{T}$-satisfiable. The substitution σ is then updated to $\{y \mapsto \lambda x.\,x\}$ and returned. Back in the SMT loop, the instantiation lemma $(\forall y. \neg p\,(y\,a)) \implies \neg p\,a$ is added to F. Now, the quantifier-free solver finds a contradiction.

The candidate substitutions generated by MBQI-Enum (M) are listed below:

Iter.	$q \in Q_p$	E	$M(q, E)$	New E
1	$\forall y. \neg p\,(y\,a)$	$\{p\,a\}$	$\{\{y \mapsto \lambda x.\,x\}\}$	$\{p\,a, \neg p\,a\}$

The first column shows the number of the SMT loop iteration. The second column shows the quantified formula q, and the third column shows the set E of ground literals before every iteration. The fourth column shows the possible selection of substitutions of y that are considered with MBQI-Enum, and the fifth column shows the set E after every iteration.

In this example, MBQI-Enum was able to terminate in the first iteration, since it found a substitution for y that immediately leads to a refutation, whereas MBQI considers a repeating pattern of instantiations that leads to a timeout.

Another useful candidate substitution would have been $\{y \mapsto \lambda x.\,a\}$. MBQI-Enum would have found this substitution as well if it had not terminated after finding $\{y \mapsto \lambda x.\,x\}$.

In an informal, preliminary evaluation on higher-order TPTP benchmarks, we determined that the most successful configuration enables *ext_vars* and *syms_local* and leaves *syms_global* disabled. The following examples are based on this configuration.

Example 9. Let $p : Int \to Bool$ and $f : Int \to Int$. Let F be the input formula

$$\forall y. \, \neg \forall z. \, \neg p \, (y \, z) \lor p \, (f \, z)$$

where $y : Int \to Int$ and $z : Int$. The set L is partitioned into sets $E = \emptyset$, $Q_p = \{\forall y. \, \neg \forall z. \, \neg p \, (y \, z) \lor p \, (f \, z)\}$, and $Q_n = \emptyset$. MBQI generates substitutions such as $\{y \mapsto \lambda x. \, 0\}, \{y \mapsto \lambda x. \, 1\}, \ldots$, and the solver goes on forever. In contrast, MBQI-Enum adds the first substitution generated by MBQI, $\{y \mapsto \lambda x. \, 0\}$, to the set Σ and proceeds to postprocess it. Our strategy first constructs a grammar for y using the function symbols from q. The set of symbols used is $S = \{f, p\}$. The grammar is

$$\mathcal{A} ::= \lambda x. \, \mathcal{B}$$
$$\mathcal{B} ::= x \mid f \, \mathcal{B} \mid 0 \mid 1 \mid \mathcal{B} + \mathcal{B} \mid \mathcal{B} - \mathcal{B} \mid \text{ite}(\mathcal{C}, \mathcal{B}, \mathcal{B})$$
$$\mathcal{C} ::= \text{true} \mid \text{false} \mid \mathcal{B} = \mathcal{B} \mid \mathcal{B} \leq \mathcal{B} \mid p \, \mathcal{B} \mid \neg \mathcal{C} \mid \mathcal{C} \land \mathcal{C} \mid \mathcal{C} \lor \mathcal{C}$$

In the first iteration, MBQI-Enum generates the substitution $\sigma = \{y \mapsto \lambda x. \, x\}$. The instantiation lemma $(\forall y. \, \neg \forall z. \, \neg p \, (y \, z) \lor p \, (f \, z)) \implies \neg \forall z. \, \neg p \, z \lor p \, (f \, z)$ is added to F. The set L is now partitioned into $E = \emptyset$, $Q_p = \{\forall y. \, \neg \forall z. \, \neg p \, (y \, z) \lor p \, (f \, z)\}$, and $Q_n = \{\neg \forall z. \, \neg p \, z \lor p \, (f \, z)\}$. Next, the quantifier in Q_n is Skolemized. The Skolemization lemma $(\neg \forall z. \neg p \, z \lor p \, (f \, z)) \implies p \, sk_1 \land \neg p \, (f \, sk_1)$ is added to F. As a result, the set E is updated to $\{p \, sk_1, \neg p \, (f \, sk_1)\}$.

In the next iteration, the substitution σ is modified to $\{y \mapsto \lambda x. \, f \, x\}$, incorporating the enumerated term $\lambda x. \, f \, x$ from the grammar. The instantiation lemma $(\forall y. \, \neg \forall z. \, \neg p \, (y \, z) \lor p \, (f \, z)) \implies \neg \forall z. \, \neg p \, (f \, z) \lor p \, (f \, z)$ is then added to F. After Skolemization, the set E is augmented with $\{p \, (f \, sk_2), \neg p \, (f \, sk_2)\}$. The quantifier-free solver finds a contradiction. Indeed, if we instantiate y with $\lambda x. \, f \, x$ in F, β-reduce, and Skolemize z, we obtain $p \, (f \, sk_2) \land \neg p \, (f \, sk_2)$.

The candidate substitutions generated by MBQI-Enum (M) are listed below:

Iter.	$q \in Q_p$	E	$M(q, E)$	New E
1	$\forall y. \, \neg \forall z. \, \neg p \, (y \, z) \lor p \, (f \, z)$	$\emptyset$	$\{\{y \mapsto \lambda x. \, x\}\}$	$\{p \, sk_1, \neg p \, (f \, sk_1)\}$
2	$\forall y. \, \neg \forall z. \, \neg p \, (y \, z) \lor p \, (f \, z)$	$\{p \, sk_1, \neg p \, (f \, sk_1)\}$	$\{\{y \mapsto \lambda x. \, f \, x\}\}$	$\{p \, sk_1, \neg p \, (f \, sk_1)$ $p \, (f \, sk_2), \neg p \, (f \, sk_2)\}$

In this example, our strategy terminated in the second iteration, whereas MBQI would lead the solver to time out.

Example 10. In this example, our strategy is run with and without the *syms_global* option enabled. Let u be an uninterpreted sort, and let $a : u$ and $b : u$. Let F be the input formula

$$(\forall x, y, z. \, x \, y = x \, z) \land a \neq b$$

where $x : (u \to u) \to u$, $y : u \to u$, and $z : u \to u$. The set L is partitioned into $E = \{a \neq b\}$, $Q_p = \{\forall x, y, z. \, x \, y = x \, z\}$, and $Q_n = \emptyset$. MBQI-Enum fails to construct a grammar for a variable x, y, or z that has any terms of the same type as the variable. As a result, it cannot generate any substitutions, and the solver gives up early. In contrast, when the *syms_global* option is enabled in MBQI-Enum, function symbols from the entire formula F are used to construct a grammar for each variable x, y, and z. For these variables, the set of symbols is $\{a, b\}$. The grammar for x follows:

$$A ::= \lambda w.\ B$$
$$B ::= w\ B \mid a \mid b \mid \mathrm{ite}(C, B, B)$$
$$C ::= \mathrm{true} \mid \mathrm{false} \mid B = B \mid \neg C \mid C \wedge C \mid C \vee C$$

(Since w is of unary function type, we pass an argument corresponding to the nonterminal B in the second grammar rule.) The grammar for y and z follows:

$$A ::= \lambda w.\ B$$
$$B ::= w \mid a \mid b \mid \mathrm{ite}(C, B, B)$$
$$C ::= \mathrm{true} \mid \mathrm{false} \mid B = B \mid \neg C \mid C \wedge C \mid C \vee C$$

Our strategy then enumerates terms derived from the grammar and builds the substitutions $\{x \mapsto \lambda w.\ w\ b\}, \{y \mapsto \lambda w.\ w\}$, and $\{z \mapsto \lambda w.\ a\}$. The instantiation lemma $(\forall x, y, z.\ x\ y = x\ z) \implies b = a$ is added to F. Now, the quantifier-free solver finds a contradiction. Indeed, if we instantiate x with $\lambda w.\ w\ b$, y with $\lambda w.\ w$, and z with $\lambda w.\ a$ in F and β-reduce, we obtain $a = b \wedge a \neq b$.

The candidate substitutions generated by MBQI-Enum (M) are listed below:

Iter.	$q \in Q_p$	E	$M(q, E)$	New E
1	$\forall x, y, z.\ x\ y = x\ z$	$\{a \neq b\}$	$\emptyset$	$\{a \neq b\}$

The same information is provided for MBQI-Enum with the option *syms_global* enabled (M+g) below:

Iter.	$q \in Q_p$	E	$(M{+}g)(q, E)$	New E
1	$\forall x, y, z.\ x\ y = x\ z$	$\{a \neq b\}$	$\{\{x \mapsto \lambda w.\ w\ b\},$ $\{y \mapsto \lambda w.\ w\},$ $\{z \mapsto \lambda w.\ a\}\}$	$\{a \neq b, a = b\}$

In this example, MBQI-Enum with *syms_global* was able to terminate in the first iteration, since it found a substitution for the quantified variables that leads to a refutation. By contrast, default MBQI-Enum does not terminate since it cannot build any substitutions.

4   Implementation and Heuristics

We implemented MBQI-Enum as an extension of cvc5's implementation of MBQI. Our strategy is invoked after the current MBQI strategy returns a candidate instantiation (line 3 of Algorithm 7).

For each variable, our algorithm chooses a grammar (line 9) and initializes a term enumeration data structure. Since the choice of the grammar is fixed over the course of solving, the grammar is constructed only once. Our implementation uses the utility for fast SyGuS enumeration described by Reynolds et al. [23] as a black box. Since the grammar for each variable is fixed, we can cache the enumeration and invoke this utility only on line 11 of Algorithm 7, when j is larger than the number of terms we have generated on a previous run, where we notice that a term that was skipped in a previous call to this method may be incorporated into instantiations on later calls.

On line 15 of Algorithm 7, we use cvc5's ability to call a copy of itself as a subsolver. As an optimization, this satisfiability check can be avoided if the query to check simplifies to "true" or "false."

5   Evaluation

We extensively evaluated our cvc5 implementation of MBQI-Enum on both higher- and first-order benchmarks.

Setup. As the base configuration, we use the setup that we found to be the most successful in a preliminary evaluation: MBQI-Enum with the options *ext_vars* and *syms_local* enabled by default. We denote this configuration by cvc5[M].

We first compare the performance of the base configuration against traditional instantiation techniques: cvc5[e], which uses enumerative instantiation [22]; cvc5[s], which uses SyQI [18]; cvc5[c], which uses counterexample-guided instantiation [24]; and cvc5[m], which uses MBQI [9].

Additionally, for higher-order problems, we also include a comparison with the state-of-the-art provers Vampire [6] and Zipperposition [28]. For Vampire, we used its portfolio mode, while Zipperposition was run in its so-called "best" mode, since it does not include a portfolio.

Next, we compare the base configuration on first-order benchmarks with three state-of-the-art SMT solvers: Z3 [15], the only SMT solver besides cvc5 that supports all the logics handled by our implementation; Bitwuzla [16], which supports only logics without arithmetic; and Boolector [17], which implements the most closely related approach to ours, counterexample-guided model synthesis [21], but focuses only on the theory of bit vectors.

Finally, we compare the performance of all four MBQI-Enum configurations on both higher-order and first-order problems. In this evaluation, we toggled one option at a time: cvc5[M−x] denotes MBQI-Enum with *ext_vars* disabled, cvc5[M−ℓ] denotes MBQI-Enum with *syms_local* disabled, and cvc5[M+g] denotes MBQI-Enum with *syms_global* enabled.

We performed all experiments on a system with a 40-core Intel Xeon Silver 4114 processor at 2.20 GHz and with 192 GB of RAM using Debian Bookworm as the operating system. We used a time limit of 60 seconds for each benchmark.

Table 1. MBQI-Enum vs. other strategies and provers on TPTP TH0 benchmarks

	Vampire	Zipperposition	cvc5[e]	cvc5[s]	cvc5[m]	cvc5[M]
Satisfiable	6	0	72	78	121	**129**
Unsatisfiable	**1757**	1499	1643	1304	1637	1670
Total	1763	1499	1715	1382	1758	**1799**
Unknown	0	0	350	38	127	59
Timeouts	999	1263	697	1342	877	904

Table 2. MBQI-Enum configurations on TPTP TH0 benchmarks

	cvc5[M]	cvc5[M−x]	cvc5[M−ℓ]	cvc5[M+g]
Satisfiable	**129**	**129**	122	**129**
Unsatisfiable	1670	1665	1655	**1672**
Total	1799	1794	1777	**1801**
Unknown	59	65	88	56
Timeouts	904	903	897	905

Higher-Order Problems. The higher-order part of the experiments was carried out on monomorphic higher-order problems (TH0) from version 9.0.0 of the TPTP library [27]. The benchmark set consists of 2762 problems. From the 3962 TH0 problems, we excluded 1200 benchmarks that one or more systems could not parse (e.g., because they use arithmetic).

The results are summarized in Table 1. In this and the following tables, bold indicates the most successful system. Notably, our approach achieves the highest total count of solved benchmarks, surpassing the nearest competitor by 36 solved problems. Overall, it outperforms all other cvc5 strategies as well as Zipperposition in higher-order logic and solves 87 fewer unsatisfiable problems than Vampire. Our strategy's advantage over Zipperposition likely stems from using Zipperposition's "best" mode instead of a portfolio. Remarkably, our strategy manages to solve 129 satisfiable problems, whereas Vampire solves only 6, and Zipperposition none.

Although our approach is based on both MBQI and SyQI, it is considerably stronger than either of those techniques used individually. Specifically, compared with MBQI, which was until now the most successful strategy in cvc5, MBQI-Enum solves an additional 41 problems without any losses. When compared with SyQI, our strategy solves 417 more benchmarks while also incurring no losses.

Table 2 shows the evaluation of the different configurations of MBQI-Enum on higher-order problems. We see that all three options are beneficial, but for *syms_global* the difference is only two problems. (In our preliminary evaluation, we had found *syms_global* to be slightly harmful, which is why we disabled it by default.)

First-Order Problems. The experiments on first-order problems were conducted on the SMT-LIB benchmarks [5] from April 2024, focusing on logics that support quantifiers. We included logics involving theories such as floating-point arithmetic, linear and nonlinear arithmetic, and bit vectors. Overall, we consider the logics BV (bit vectors), FP (floating-point arithmetic), LIA (linear integer arithmetic), LRA (linear real arithmetic), NIA (nonlinear integer arithmetic), NRA (nonlinear real arithmetic), and their combinations: BVFP, BVFPLRA, and FPLRA. We also incorporate ABV (arrays and bit vectors) and UFBV (uninterpreted functions with bit vectors). In total, our benchmark set consists of 21 605 problems.

Table 3. MBQI-Enum vs. other techniques and solvers on SMT-LIB benchmarks

Library	Boolector SAT	UNSAT	Bitwuzla SAT	UNSAT	Z3 SAT	UNSAT	cvc5[e] SAT	UNSAT	cvc5[s] SAT	UNSAT	cvc5[c] SAT	UNSAT	cvc5[m] SAT	UNSAT	cvc5[M] SAT	UNSAT
BV	585	4980	**642**	5066	547	5001	202	4836	313	4911	437	**5190**	611	4835	594	5076
SAT+UNSAT	5565		**5708**		5548		5038		5224		5627		5446		5670	
ABV			378	47	387	103	21	**930**	618	237	17	90	**790**	135	731	157
ABVFP			24	0	29	2	10	**3**	15	0	13	0	**31**	0	**31**	0
ABVFPLRA			32	1	**55**	**3**	14	2	18	1	18	2	41	2	42	2
BVFP			**179**	**12**	164	5	26	12	102	3	106	0	167	4	169	7
BVFPLRA			**233**	25	205	18	80	**25**	119	24	111	24	220	24	226	**25**
FP			**130**	2176	17	1802	113	1591	99	2040	116	2015	115	2059	116	**2223**
FPLRA			**37**	0	23	0	20	0	24	0	22	0	**37**	0	36	0
UFBV			26	120	**43**	103	8	103	9	108	8	52	23	84	21	105
Subtotal			1681	7447	1470	7037	494	7502	1317	7324	848	7373	**2035**	7143	1966	**7595**
SAT+UNSAT			9128		8507		7996		8641		8221		9178		**9561**	
LIA					140	230	12	170	**150**	236	**150**	**266**	**150**	167	149	239
LRA					**760**	**1361**	468	1117	478	1130	593	1303	545	1123	557	1161
NIA					65	**144**	16	43	49	45	64	**144**	67	47	**80**	61
NRA					**3**	**3806**	1	3802	1	3785	**3**	3801	**3**	3712	**3**	3802
Total					2438	12578	991	12634	1995	12520	1658	**12887**	**2800**	12192	2755	12858
SAT+UNSAT					15016		13625		14515		14545		14992		**15613**	

The results, summarized in Table 3, show that our approach performs remarkably well against all other cvc5 configurations, as well as against Boolector, Bitwuzla, and Z3, across all SMT logics. Notably, it achieves the highest total count of benchmarks solved, surpassing the nearest competitor by 597 solved problems. Our strategy solves the most satisfiable problems in ABVFP and NIA and achieves the highest number of unsatisfiable benchmarks solved in FP.

For the evaluated SMT theories, our strategy is a clear improvement over previous instantiation strategies. When compared with MBQI, it successfully solves an additional 701 problems while incurring a loss of 79 problems across all logics. The raw evaluation data also reveals a notable reduction in timeouts, decreasing from 3491 to 2343.

Our strategy also substantially outperforms enumerative instantiation and SyQI across most benchmark categories. Both of these strategies share an enumerative nature. The former relies on evolving ground terms within the current context, while the latter employs a fixed grammar derived from the initial set of terms. Overall, enumerative instantiation and SyQI perform clearly better than

Table 4. MBQI-Enum configurations in SMT-LIB benchmarks

Library	cvc5[M]		cvc5[M−x]		cvc5[M−ℓ]		cvc5[M+g]	
	SAT	UNSAT	SAT	UNSAT	SAT	UNSAT	SAT	UNSAT
ABV	731	157	731	157	647	135	**737**	**159**
ABVFP	31	0	31	0	31	0	**32**	0
ABVFPLRA	**42**	2	**42**	2	41	2	38	2
BV	594	5076	594	5075	**616**	4843	600	**5087**
BVFP	169	**7**	169	**7**	167	4	**176**	2
BVFPLRA	226	**25**	226	**25**	220	24	**231**	**25**
FP	**116**	**2223**	**116**	**2223**	115	2092	**116**	**2223**
FPLRA	36	0	36	0	**37**	0	36	0
LIA	149	**239**	149	**239**	**150**	167	149	**239**
LRA	**557**	**1157**	**557**	**1157**	546	1129	**557**	**1157**
NIA	**80**	**61**	**80**	**61**	68	47	78	56
NRA	3	**3802**	3	**3802**	3	3712	3	**3802**
UFBV	21	**105**	21	**105**	**24**	89	17	99
Total	2755	**12 858**	2755	12 857	2665	12 244	**2771**	12 854

MBQI on unsatisfiable benchmarks (+442), but they underperform on satisfiable benchmarks (−805). This highlights the need for a hybrid approach that combines model-based and enumerative techniques. Our strategy incorporates the enumerative aspects of SyQI while enhancing the model-based features of MBQI to generate instantiations. This is likely why it outperforms all the mentioned configurations. Our strategy also matches or outperforms counterexample-guided instantiation in most logics. However, in logics such as LRA, counterexample-guided instantiation is expected to perform better due to its specialized handling of such theories.

Compared with Boolector, our strategy outperforms it on both satisfiable and unsatisfiable benchmarks, solving 105 more benchmarks overall. Compared with Bitwuzla and Z3, our approach performs very well across various logics, often closely matching or even surpassing both competitors. Overall, our strategy solves 433 more benchmarks than Bitwuzla and 597 more than Z3 in total. Bitwuzla is generally stronger for satisfiable problems, which is not surprising because MBQI-Enum is primarily designed for deriving contradictions. Z3's higher success rate for real arithmetic is likely attributable to its well-established instantiation strategies for these theories.

Finally, the evaluation of the various configurations of MBQI-Enum on first-order SMT-LIB benchmarks across different theories is shown in Table 4. We see that most configurations perform similarly; however, MBQI-Enum without the *syms_local* option enabled shows significantly poorer performance.

In summary, our approach is highly effective on first-order SMT-LIB benchmarks, solving the highest number of benchmarks. With refinements tailored to specific logics, we suspect that its performance could be improved further.

6   Related Work

Mainstream approaches for quantifier instantiation in SMT are typically centered around E-matching [14]. Conflict-based instantiation [3,11,26] can improve the solver's ability to answer "$\mathcal{T}$-unsatisfiable" by prioritizing instantiations that induce quantifier-free conflicts. As a whole, these techniques are generally incomplete and do not target specific background theories. For satisfiable instances, Ge and de Moura [9] introduced MBQI, which is complete for certain fragments. Finite model finding [25] is a variant of this technique that targets quantified formulas whose domains are small and finite. Approaches for quantified formulas in higher-order logic are discussed by Barbosa et al. [4], but, in contrast to this work, they are based on (higher-order) E-matching.

Other approaches for higher-order logic, notably in Vampire [6] and Zipperposition [28], rely on superposition. Vampire has been initially extended to handle higher-order reasoning using applicative first-order logic with combinators. Since this proved insufficient for problems requiring complex unifiers, its superposition calculus was later enhanced with native λ-abstractions and a depth-bounded version of higher-order unification [6]. As for Zipperposition, it also uses a superposition calculus that directly supports higher-order terms. It tackles the challenge of higher-order unification by using techniques such as pattern unification and heuristics to manage undecidability issues.

Certain background theories admit quantifier elimination, which can be handled using domain-specific instantiation strategies. Specifically, efficient and complete instantiation procedures have been developed for quantified linear arithmetic [24] and quantified bit vectors [19]. These techniques require specific knowledge of the background theory.

Other recent works on quantifier instantiation have pursued enumeration as a pragmatic means for discovering useful instantiations. Reynolds et al. [22] introduced enumerative instantiation as an alternative to MBQI, which primarily focused on first-order logic in the empty theory. This technique has been further studied in more recent works, where more advanced selection strategies are used for instantiations, including those based on machine learning [12,13,20].

The closest related works to ours are counterexample-guided model synthesis [21] and SyQI [18], which both focus on enumerative approaches for finding useful instantiations in rich background logics. The former was implemented in the Boolector [17] solver; it was limited to selected first-order theories and did not handle higher-order logic. The latter work can potentially be used for any theory but does not leverage MBQI for guiding the instantiation procedure. Our evaluation shows that our MBQI-Enum strategy generally outperforms SyQI overall.

7   Conclusion

We presented a new strategy, MBQI-Enum, for instantiating quantifiers in SMT solvers. It extends MBQI with the SyGuS enumerator, thereby augmenting the number of instantiations considered at every iteration. The main strength of our strategy is that it combines the fast model-finding capabilities of MBQI and the diversity of terms considered by SyQI. MBQI generates very specific instances; by resorting to a grammar, the terms in our instantiations are more abstract and therefore tend to lead to more useful instances. We implemented the strategy in cvc5 and found that it helps solve many first- and higher-order problems from SMT-LIB and TPTP for which cvc5 previously either timed out or gave up early.

Several aspects of our approach present opportunities for future work. First, we could improve performance by enhancing the quantifier-free solver to better integrate with our instantiation approach. Moreover, although our instantiation technique is designed to be generic, we could tailor it to individual SMT logics. Finally, we could develop more sophisticated instantiation strategies for higher-order logic. By designing methods that can more intelligently navigate the space of enumerated terms, we should be able to improve the solver's ability to handle complex higher-order problems.

Acknowledgments. We thank the anonymous reviewers for their helpful comments. We also thank Pascal Fontaine and Mark Summerfield, who provided many comments on earlier drafts.

This research was cofunded by the European Union (ERC, Nekoka, 101083038). Views and opinions expressed are however those of the authors only and do not necessarily reflect those of the European Union or the European Research Council. Neither the European Union nor the granting authority can be held responsible for them.

References

1. Andrews, B.: An Introduction to Mathematical Logic and Type Theory: To Truth Through Proof, vol. 27. Springer, 2nd edn. (2002)
2. Barbosa, H., Barrett, C., Brain, M., Kremer, G., Lachnitt, H., Mann, M., Mohamed, A., Mohamed, M., Niemetz, A., Nötzli, A., Ozdemir, A., Preiner, M., Reynolds, A., Sheng, Y., Tinelli, C., Zohar, Y.: cvc5: A versatile and industrial-strength SMT solver. In: Fishman, D., Rosu, G. (eds.) TACAS 2022. LNCS, vol. 13243, pp. 415–442 (2022)
3. Barbosa, H., Fontaine, P., Reynolds, A.: Congruence closure with free variables. In: Legay, A., Margaria, T. (eds.) TACAS 2017, Part II. LNCS, vol. 10206, pp. 214–230. Springer (2017)
4. Barbosa, H., Reynolds, A., Ouraoui, D.E., Tinelli, C., Barrett, C.: Extending SMT solvers to higher-order logic. In: Fontaine, P. (ed.) CADE 2019. LNCS, vol. 11716, pp. 35–54. Springer (2019)
5. Barrett, C., Fontaine, P., Tinelli, C.: The satisfiability modulo theories library (SMT-LIB) (2016)
6. Bhayat, A., Suda, M.: A higher-order Vampire (short paper). In: Benzmüller, C., Heule, M.J.H., Schmidt, R.A. (eds.) IJCAR 2024. LNCS, vol. 14739, pp. 75–85. Springer (2024)
7. Bouton, T., de Oliveira, D.C.B., Déharbe, D., Fontaine, P.: veriT: An open, trustable and efficient SMT-solver. In: Schmidt, R.A. (ed.) CADE 2009. LNCS, vol. 5663, pp. 151–156. Springer (2009)

8. Church, A.: A formulation of the simple theory of types. Journal of Symbolic Logic **5**(2), 56–68 (1940)
9. Ge, Y., de Moura, L.: Complete instantiation for quantified formulas in satisfiabiliby modulo theories. In: Bouajjani, A., Maler, O. (eds.) CAV 2009. LNCS, vol. 5643, pp. 306–320. Springer (2009)
10. Gordon, M.J.C.: Introduction to the HOL system. In: Archer, M., Joyce, J.J., Levitt, K.N., Windley, P.J. (eds.) TPHOL 1991. pp. 2–3. IEEE (1991)
11. Hoenicke, J., Schindler, T.: Incremental search for conflict and unit instances of quantified formulas with E-matching. In: Henglein, F., Shoham, S., Vizel, Y. (eds.) VMCAI 2021. LNCS, vol. 12597, pp. 534–555. Springer (2021)
12. Jakubův, J., Janota, M., Piotrowski, B., Piepenbrock, J., Reynolds, A.: Selecting quantifiers for instantiation in SMT. In: Graham-Lengrand, S., Preiner, M. (eds.) SMT 2023. CEUR Workshop Proceedings, vol. 3429, pp. 71–77. CEUR-WS.org (2023)
13. Janota, M., Barbosa, H., Fontaine, P., Reynolds, A.: Fair and adventurous enumeration of quantifier instantiations. In: FMCAD 2021. pp. 256–260. IEEE (2021)
14. de Moura, L., Bjørner, N.: Efficient E-matching for SMT solvers. In: Pfenning, F. (ed.) CADE 2007. LNCS, vol. 4603, pp. 183–198. Springer (2007)
15. de Moura, L., Bjørner, N.: Z3: An efficient SMT solver. In: Ramakrishnan, C.R., Rehof, J. (eds.) TACAS 2008. LNCS, vol. 4963, pp. 337–340. Springer (2008)
16. Niemetz, A., Preiner, M.: Bitwuzla. In: Enea, C., Lal, A. (eds.) CAV 2023. LNCS, vol. 13965, pp. 3–17. Springer (2023)
17. Niemetz, A., Preiner, M., Biere, A.: Boolector 2.0. Journal on Satisfiability, Boolean Modeling and Computation **9**, 53–58 (2014)
18. Niemetz, A., Preiner, M., Reynolds, A., Barrett, C., Tinelli, C.: Syntax-guided quantifier instantiation. In: Groote, J.F., Larsen, K.G. (eds.) TACAS 2021. LNCS, vol. 12652, pp. 145–163. Springer (2021)
19. Niemetz, A., Preiner, M., Reynolds, A., Barrett, C.W., Tinelli, C.: Solving quantified bit-vectors using invertibility conditions. In: Chockler, H., Weissenbacher, G. (eds.) CAV 2018, Part II. LNCS, vol. 10982, pp. 236–255. Springer (2018)
20. Piepenbrock, J., Janota, M., Urban, J., Jakubův, J.: First experiments with neural cvc5. In: Bjørner, N.S., Heule, M., Voronkov, A. (eds.) LPAR 2024. EPiC Series in Computing, vol. 100, pp. 264–277. EasyChair (2024)
21. Preiner, M., Niemetz, A., Biere, A.: Counterexample-guided model synthesis. In: Legay, A., Margaria, T. (eds.) TACAS 2017. LNCS, vol. 10205, pp. 264–280. Springer (2017)
22. Reynolds, A., Barbosa, H., Fontaine, P.: Revisiting enumerative instantiation. In: Beyer, D. (ed.) TACAS 2018. LNCS, vol. 10806, pp. 112–131. Springer (2018)
23. Reynolds, A., Barbosa, H., Nötzli, A., Barrett, C.W., Tinelli, C.: cvc4sy: Smart and fast term enumeration for syntax-guided synthesis. In: Dillig, I., Tasiran, S. (eds.) CAV 2019, Part II. LNCS, vol. 11562, pp. 74–83. Springer (2019)
24. Reynolds, A., Deters, M., Kuncak, V., Tinelli, C., Barrett, C.: Counterexample-guided quantifier instantiation for synthesis in SMT. In: Kroening, D., Păsăreanu, C.S. (eds.) CAV 2015. LNCS, vol. 9207, pp. 198–216. Springer (2015)
25. Reynolds, A., Tinelli, C., Goel, A., Krstić, S.: Finite model finding in SMT. In: Sharygina, N., Veith, H. (eds.) CAV 2013. LNCS, vol. 8044, pp. 640–655. Springer (2013)
26. Reynolds, A., Tinelli, C., de Moura, L.: Finding conflicting instances of quantified formulas in SMT. In: FMCAD 2014. pp. 195–202. IEEE (2014)
27. Sutcliffe, G.: The TPTP problem library and associated infrastructure—from CNF to TH0, TPTP v6.4.0. Journal of Automated Reasoning **59**(4), 483–502 (2017)

28. Vukmirović, P., Bentkamp, A., Blanchette, J., Cruanes, S., Nummelin, V., Tourret, S.: Making higher-order superposition work. Journal of Automated Reasoning **66**(4), 541–564 (2022)

Pantograph: A Machine-to-Machine Interaction Interface for Advanced Theorem Proving, High Level Reasoning, and Data Extraction in Lean 4

Leni Aniva(✉)[iD], Chuyue Sun[iD], Brando Miranda[iD], Clark Barrett[iD],
and Sanmi Koyejo[iD]

Stanford University, Stanford, USA
{aniva,chuyues,brando90,barrettc,sanmi}@stanford.edu

Abstract. *Machine-assisted theorem proving* refers to the process of conducting structured reasoning to automatically generate proofs for mathematical theorems. Recently, there has been a surge of interest in using machine learning models in conjunction with proof assistants to perform this task. In this paper, we introduce Pantograph, a tool that provides a versatile interface to the Lean 4 proof assistant and enables efficient proof search via powerful search algorithms such as Monte Carlo Tree Search. In addition, Pantograph enables high-level reasoning by enabling a more robust handling of Lean 4's inference steps. We provide an overview of Pantograph's architecture and features. We also report on an illustrative use case: using machine learning models and proof sketches to prove Lean 4 theorems. Pantograph's innovative features pave the way for more advanced machine learning models to perform complex proof searches and high-level reasoning, equipping future researchers to design more versatile and powerful theorem provers.

1 Introduction

Proof assistants are used for a variety of tasks requiring strong guarantees and rigorous reasoning. High-profile applications include formal verification of computer systems (e.g., seL4 [10]) and formalization of mathematics (e.g., [7]). Among proof assistants, Lean 4 has recently accumulated significant momentum both among mathematicians and non-mathematicians. Its Mathlib library [14], for example, is an extensive effort to formalize many branches of mathematics and contains many non-trivial mathematical definitions and theorems.

A common challenge shared by all proof assistants is that completing proofs is tedious and requires manual effort and expertise. Machine learning offers one potential avenue for addressing this challenge. Indeed, recent years have seen several major efforts dedicated to using machine learning to automatically search for proofs in proof assistants (e.g., [21], [22], [5], [6], [12], [11], [8], [9], [20]). While these efforts have produced promising results, many proofs are still beyond the reach of machine learning-based automation.

In order to continue to make progress in this area, several challenges need to be addressed. One of these challenges is the need for better interfaces between

© The Author(s) 2025
A. Gurfinkel and M. Heule (Eds.): TACAS 2025, LNCS 15696, pp. 104–123, 2025.
https://doi.org/10.1007/978-3-031-90643-5_6

proof assistants and machine learning systems. In this paper, we introduce **Pantograph**,[1] an API and Read-Eval-Print Loop (REPL) for Lean 4, whose primary goal is to provide a convenient interface for training and evaluating theorem proving agents. The name "Pantograph" alludes to the process of recording a proof during proof search.[2]

The main motivation for creating Pantograph is to overcome the limitations of the interface provided by the Lean 4 Language Server Protocol (LSP), which is the standard interface provided for interactive use by a human user. Although the LSP provides interactive feedback for a human operator of Lean 4, it suffers from a number of problems as a machine interface. The LSP interface requires its user to keep track of positions of a cursor in text, and a machine user would be burdened with tracking these redundant data. Moreover, there is no straightforward way to extract tactic training data from the LSP interface or sketch out a proof to be finished by automation tactics. In contrast, Pantograph is designed from the ground up as an efficient and convenient interface for machine (and especially machine learning) agents.

The main contributions of Pantograph are:

1. Unlike prior work, the user can decide to solve goals independently. This enables more powerful search algorithms such as Monte Carlo Tree Search (MCTS), which have been successful in other domains (e.g., AlphaGo and AlphaZero [17,18]), achieving superhuman performance on complex games like Go, Chess, and Shogi.[3] To do this, Pantograph handles metavariable coupling, which is a phenomenon that complicates tree search [13].

2. In contrast to prior work in Lean 4 [23], Pantograph supports the use of the advanced reasoning steps (called tactics) have, let, conv, and calc. These tactics are crucial for supporting high-level reasoning strategies like proof sketching [8].

3. Pantograph fully supports essential data extraction tasks (e.g., it can extract the before- and after-goal states of tactic executions, which are usually not available in raw Lean 4 scripts). In addition, Pantograph introduces several novel data extraction capabilities, including the ability to extract entire proof scripts with associated comments, which can be used for tasks like autoformalization, and the important ability to extract proof representations as programs, which allows for one-shot prediction of proofs.

4. Pantograph provides feedback from partially executed conv and calc tactics, which was not possible in preceding works.

5. Pantograph allows the user to resume an incomplete proof containing the sorry keyword in Lean 4. This is useful for machine learning models which produce a proof draft before resolving the details in the proofs.

---

[1] https://github.com/stanford-centaur/PyPantograph

[2] A Pantograph is a mechanism for recording the movement of a pen while drawing in order to create a copy.

[3] Although these board games are not equally difficult, the state-of-the-art algorithms for these board games all involve MCTS.

6. By making use of the novel features listed above, Pantograph can be used to support the draft-sketch-proof (DSP) approach [8]. An evaluation of this approach on the important MiniF2F benchmark [24] in Lean 4 is provided in Section 5. To our knowledge, this is the first implementation of DSP in Lean 4.

As additional evidence of its usefulness, before this paper was even published, research groups in both academia and industry were already using Pantograph for machine-assisted theorem proving.

The rest of the paper is organized as follows. In Section 2, we cover background material on proof assistants and tree search. We then discuss related work in Section 3. Section 4 gives an overview of the architecture and main features of Pantograph. Section 5 illustrates and evaluates Pantograph's capabilities through an implementation of DSP in Lean 4. Finally, Section 6 concludes.

2   Background

2.1   The Lean 4 Proof Assistant

A *proof assistant* is a computer program that can formulate and check formal mathematical proofs. This includes Lean 4 [15], Coq [19], Isabelle [16], Aya [3], and many others. These programs operate by formulating mathematics as expressions and checking the validity of the expressions via type-theoretic rules. Proof assistants may differ in a number of ways, including their syntax and the underlying variant of type theory they use. In the language of a proof assistant, every definition, theorem, or proof is a value with a type. A value is represented by an **expression**. A proof of a theorem is a term whose type is the theorem. A proof assistant checks the validity of a proof of a theorem by evaluating its type and checking that it matches the statement of the theorem. It does this using a set of type deduction rules.

For example, the commutativity of the logical OR ($\vee$) operation can be written as the expression:

$$\forall (p : \mathsf{Prop}), \forall (q : \mathsf{Prop}), \forall (h : p \vee q), q \vee p. \tag{1}$$

This statement says that if p and q are Boolean propositions (of type Prop in Lean 4), then, given the hypothesis h of type $p \vee q$, we can conclude $q \vee p$.

The notation in (1) is more verbose than what mathematicians typically use. This is because proof assistants require the utmost unambiguity. However, informally, the above expression could also be written using the more concise notation:

$$\forall p, q.\, p \vee q \rightarrow q \vee p$$

A proof of (1) is an expression whose type is given by (1). For example,

$$\lambda (p, q : \mathsf{Prop})(h : p \vee q)$$
$$\mapsto \vee.\, \mathrm{cases}\, h \,(\lambda h_p : p \mapsto \vee.\, \mathrm{inr}\, h_p)\,(\lambda h_q : q \mapsto \vee.\, \mathrm{inl}\, h_q)$$

is a proof of the commutativity of OR. The type of a λ-expression is a $\forall$-expression. The λ's in the expression correspond to the three $\forall$'s in the statement of the commutativity theorem. Intuitively, this expression says that when $p \vee q$ is assumed to be true, proving $q \vee p$ requires proving $q \vee p$ when p is true and also when q is true. This is signified by the special function $\vee$. cases, which is provided by Lean 4 as part of the support for the $\vee$ operator. It represents the fact that deriving any value from $p \vee q$ requires two functions, one to handle the case when p is true, and one to handle the case when q is true.

Assuming p is true, $\vee$. inr generates a proof of $q \vee p$ from a proof of the right operand p ($\vee$. inl is similar but requires a proof of the left operand q).

Expressions can also be constructed incrementally. For example, we could postulate that the following expression has the type shown in Expression (1):

$$?1 := \lambda(p : \mathsf{Prop}) \mapsto ?2[p]$$

Then ?2 must have the type

$$?2 : \forall(q : \mathsf{Prop}), \forall(h : p \vee q), q \vee p \qquad \left\{ p : \mathsf{Prop} \right. \qquad (2)$$

Here, ?1 and ?2 are *metavariables*. A **metavariable** is a variable, possibly unassigned, with a **context**. A **goal** (also called a **hole**) is an unassigned metavariable. When writing proofs in Lean 4, the sorry keyword can be used as a placeholder for a hole. A **free variable** in the *context* of a metavariable (e.g., the variable p above) references a value assumed to be true for this metavariable. ?2 is a goal. The **proof state** consists of all metavariables, both those that are unassigned (i.e., the goals) and those that are assigned.

Proof expressions, while easy for the proof assistant to check, are difficult for a human operator to write. Thus, some proof assistants such as Lean 4 also provide an alternative interface for theorem proving, in which a proof can be executed via a series of *tactics*. A **tactic** changes the proof state by assigning an expression, possibly containing new goals, to a goal in the current state. In Lean 4, a tactic can transform one goal into a finite number of subgoals. A tactic that generates no subgoals *solves* the parent goal. If all subgoals produced by a tactic are solved, the goal is solved as well. For example, suppose a variable ?1 has the type shown in Expression (1). Executing the intro tactic on ?1 results in the *assignment* $?1 := \lambda(p : \mathsf{Prop}) \mapsto ?2[p]$, where ?2 has the type in Expression (2). ?2 becomes the new goal that must be solved.

Some tactics can create interdependent metavariables. This is known as **metavariable coupling** [13]. For example, in order to prove

$$\exists(x : \mathbb{N}), 2x + 5 \leq 10$$

one would need to invoke the Exists.intro lemma, which creates the following goals in Lean 4:

$$?x : \mathbb{N}$$
$$2?x + 5 \leq 10$$

where the second goal is now coupled to the first, since any solution of the first goal will necessarily affect the second.

2.2   Tree Search

Tree Search refers to the process of searching through a tree, each of whose nodes represents a potential solution to a problem, attempting to find the best possible solution [4]. **Monte Carlo Tree Search** (**MCTS**) is a class of tree search algorithms where in each iteration a leaf node from the current search tree is selected and expanded. The selection of this leaf node is driven by the **policy** of the tree search algorithm.

MCTS is used by AlphaGo [18] and AlphaZero [17] for playing board games and by HyperTree [11] for proof search in Lean 3.

The tree structure that results from using tactics to prove theorems in Lean 4 is called an *and-or tree* and contains two types of nodes: *goals* (Or), where solving at least one descendant suffices to solve the goal, and *goal states* (And) produced by tactics, where solving all descendants is required. A Lean 4 proof begins with a single goal. A full proof tree for the commutativity of OR is shown in Figure 1. When applying Monte Carlo Tree Search two theorem proving, two functions are required: the **policy function** decides which node (i.e., goal) to explore next, and the **tactic function** decides which tactic to use on that goal.

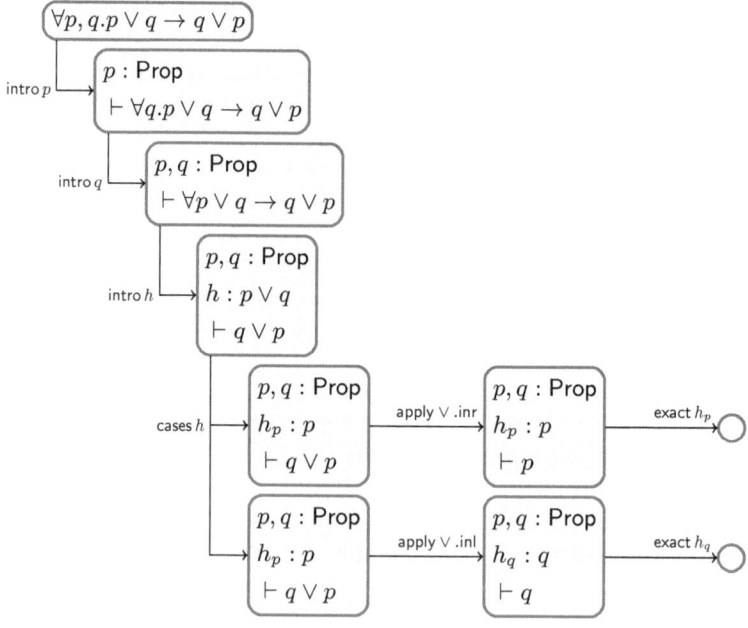

Fig. 1: A proof tree for Expression (1)

The main motivation for creating Pantograph is to create an interface that can easily be used by machine learning systems aiming to exploit this incremental tree structure to conduct mathematical reasoning. Potential applications of

Pantograph include automatic verified program generation, rigorous reasoning for language models, and autoformalization of mathematics results.

3   Related Work

The closest related work is **LeanDojo** [23], which provides a Python interface for machine interaction with Lean 4. A user can use this interface to execute tactics on a current proof state in a Lean 4 process. LeanDojo can be used to save and resume proof states. LeanDojo can also run commands such as `#eval` and `#check` and extract goal-tactic pairs over an existing proof.

Pantograph has several key architectural improvements over LeanDojo. First of all, it is written entirely in Lean 4. This removes the need for external dependencies (such as Docker) and also improves the speed of interaction. Also, some tactics not supported by LeanDojo, such as `have`, are available in Pantograph. Other tactics, such as `conv` and `calc`, can only be used monolithically to solve goals in LeanDojo, whereas Pantograph supports incremental exploration using these tactics, allowing a user to obtain feedback at each step, even if a goal is not solved. Moreover, Pantograph efficiently handles the problem of metavariable coupling (see Section 4.3), empowering ML models to work on interdependent proof branches without risking inconsistency.

Like LeanDojo, Pantograph can extract information from existing proofs, including training data based on triples of goal states, tactics, and post-tactic goal states. It can also extract comment data and arbitirary expressions, both of which may be useful as additional training data.   However, LeanDojo's data extraction and proof execution units are essentially separate, which makes it impossible to extract an incomplete proof and resume from it, whereas Pantograph supports this use case.

In [11], Lample et al. implement the aforementioned and-or tree search structure to solve goals in Lean 3. In this work, the relation between goals and tactics is a *hypertree*. This enables efficient proof search via a variant of Monte Carlo Tree Search. The policy and tactic functions are both provided by Large Language Models (LLMs). Pantograph is compatible with this approach, as it gives the user control over both policy and tactic functions.

Draft-Sketch-Prove (DSP) [8] is a *neural theorem prover* which uses an approach based on *drafting*. Instead of directly generating Lean 4 tactics, the neural theorem prover generates intermediate goals in an informal language (draft). Then it translates these goals into Isabelle (sketch), and finally a *hammer* tactic from Isabelle solves the goals (prove). Pantograph's drafting feature supports this technique as well, allowing the Draft-Sketch-Prove algorithm to be implemented in Lean 4 (see Section 4.6).

Aesop [13] is a proof automation (*hammer*) tactic based on tree-search. Aesop is not based on machine learning and takes metavariable coupling into account when solving goals. When a goal gets solved in Aesop, all of the goals coupled to this goal are brought back into scope. This is known as *copying*. Pantograph's

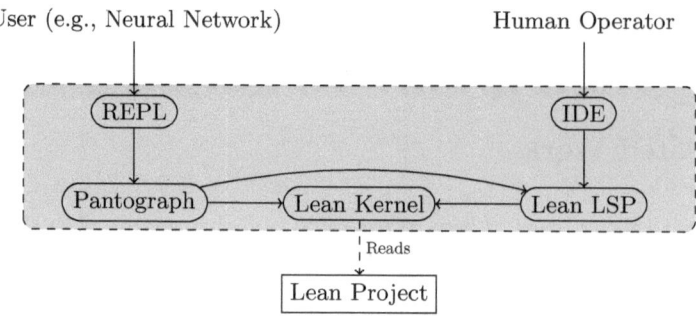

Fig. 2: System architecture of Pantograph. A solid arrow indicates that the component at the arrow source calls functions in the component that is the arrow's target. A human operator interacts with Lean 4's kernel via the IDE, but a machine learning agent can interact via one of Pantograph's interfaces.

approach to metavariable coupling is based on Aesop's technique, but extends it by allowing the user to determine which metavariable to solve next.

CoqGym [22] is similar to LeanDojo but for the Coq theorem prover instead of Lean 4. CoqGym stores proofs in a tree structure and allows the user agent to execute tactics. Optionally, CoqGym can serialize proof terms into S-expressions. These same features are supported by Pantograph, but for Lean 4. Pantograph also has some features unsupported by CoqGym, such as the ability to implement draft-sketch-prove and to handle metavariable coupling.

4   Architecture and Features

Pantograph is implemented entirely in Lean 4 with no external dependencies. Figure 2 shows an overview of the operation of Pantograph. The user, which is often a machine learning model, calls Pantograph's functions via one of its interfaces. Pantograph provides three interfaces: (i) a Python interface called PyPantograph; (ii) a REPL via the **pantograph-repl** executable; and (iii) a library via the C Foreign Function Interface (FFI). When the user executes a tactic, Pantograph calls the Lean 4 kernel's `Elab.Tactic.evalTactic` function. Internally, many of Lean 4's functions are *monads*, which are abstract structures enabling state manipulation in an otherwise functional language. Lean 4's monad hierarchy (from the order of most to least general) has the order `IO`, `CoreM`, `MetaM`, `Elab.TermElabM`, and `Elab.Tactic.TacticM`. Figure 3 outlines the most important functions called during the execution of a tactic via Pantograph.

Other features of Pantograph call into the Lean 4 Language Server Protocol (LSP), the Lean 4 parser, and the Lean 4 compiler. In particular, Pantograph intercepts the Lean 4 compiler state when it processes Lean 4 source code, enabling it to extract information that is otherwise only available via the IDE.

In the rest of this section, we provide details about the features available in Pantograph. We discuss Pantograph's support for the following features: (i) both

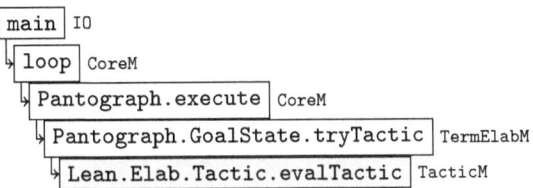

Fig. 3: Call hierarchy in Pantograph during the execution of a normal tactic. The text on the right indicates the Lean 4 monad each function runs in.

expression-based and tactic-based proof; (*ii*) tree search; (*iii*) custom handling of metavariable coupling; (*iv*) the extraction of tactic training data; and (*v*) drafting.

4.1   Expressions and Tactics

Pantograph enables AI agents to use the same tactics as a human operator can while interacting with Lean. Human-written proofs in Lean 4 (e.g., in Mathlib) are often a mixture between expressions and tactics. As mentioned above, tactics are used to reduce a goal to one or more new subgoals. To see how expressions can be used, consider the following example.

```
example : exists x, x + 2 = 8 := by
  let a : Nat := 3 * 2
  exists a
```

In this example, the required witness for x is directly constructed as the expression $3 \cdot 2$. Pantograph supports seamlessly switching between expression-based and tactic-based proof by providing a custom `expr` tactic. This tactic takes an expression $e[?1, ?2, \ldots]$ and assigns it to the current goal. The holes $?1, ?2, \ldots$ then become the new goals.

There are 3 views of a proof:

1. **Presentation View**: A proof written for presentation and verification. Coupling does not exist. It may contain values with puzzling origins such as complex bounds that are not apparent before reading the entire proof.
2. **Search View**: A proof viewed as the trajectory of a proof search agent traverses through while finding the proof. It may contain backtracking, coupling, and goal selection.
3. **Kernel View**: A proof viewed as a set of metavariables.

Pantograph enables agents to operate in the search view and handles proofs internally in the kernel view.

Lean 4 includes sophisticated tactics, like `conv` and `calc`, which are *composite* in the sense that they are used to compose sequences of other tactics. While these tactics can be executed monolithically by supplying the full sequence of tactics to be composed, human operators of Lean 4 often rely on Lean 4's interactive interface to *incrementally* explore possible sequences, obtaining feedback at each step. Pantograph provides a command called `goal.tactic`, which can partially execute a `conv` or `calc` tactic and provide feedback from this partial execution. As an example, consider the following use of the `calc` tactic, which is used in Lean 4 to compose a series of transitivity steps.

```
example (a b c : Nat) : a + b = b + c := by
  calc a + b = a + a := sorry
    _ = b + b := sorry
  sorry
```

Here, the goal `a + b = b + c` is not provable by `calc`, but a user can still partially execute the tactic by applying just the first line and seeing what the result is. In this case, the result of executing just the first line results in the following new goal.

```
a b c : Nat
|- a + a = b + c
```

Pantograph supports this partial execution model and can return the new goal shown above.

Pantograph also supports the `have` and `let` tactics. These tactics define temporary expressions in a local scope and are indispensable when developing proofs by hand. For example, consider the following snippet.

```
example (n: Nat), n + 0 = 0 + n := by
  have h1 : n + 0 = n := sorry
  sorry
```

The use of `have` introduces a new expression and a new goal. The two `sorry` expressions create two holes corresponding to the two goals shown below.

```
n : Nat
|- n + 0 = n
n : Nat
h1 : n + 0 = n
|- n + 0 = 0 + n
```

The Pantograph repository contains documentation and examples for these tactics.

In order to be friendly towards searching methods such as Monte Carlo Tree Search [4], Pantograph provides an interface for incrementally executing tactics. If a tactic creates more than one goal, it is called a *branching* tactic. When more than one goal exists in a proof state, Pantograph provides the option to choose which goal to apply a tactic to.

If a tactic cannot execute for some reason, Pantograph outputs an error message corresponding to what a human operator would see during interaction with Lean's LSP.

4.2   Tree Search

As mentioned above, tree search is a common search technique and is utilized in various proof search approaches such as HyperTree [11] and Aesop [13]. Since each tactic produces zero or more goals, the search structure of applying tactics to goals can be viewed as an And-Or tree (in the absence of metavariable coupling, see Section 4.3). When the current proof state has multiple goals, Pantograph allows the user to choose which goal to attempt next, i.e., it allows user-defined policy functions.

This naturally leads to the question of the fate of sibling goals. Suppose there are two goals [?1, ?2] in the current proof state, and the user applies a tactic to ?1, generating ?3. The status of ?2 depends on the *automatic mode* option. Automatic mode is turned on by default, which means sibling goals are carried forward to the next proof state. Hence, with automatic mode on, the next proof state would contain [?3, ?2], with all goals present and active. If the user disables automatic mode, the proof state instead becomes [?3]. The goal ?2 becomes *dormant*. Dormant goals are unassigned metavariables that do not appear in the current proof state. Note that dormant goals are an artifact of Pantograph's manual tree search capability: they do not occur when using Lean 4 through the interactive interface. Dormant goals must either be tracked by the user or

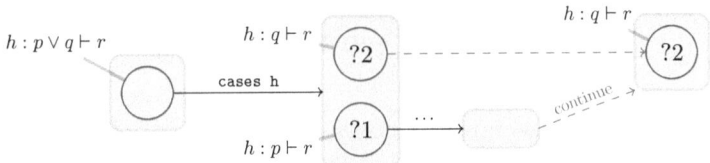

Fig. 4: ?2 becomes dormant after a tactic is applied to ?1. It must be brought back into scope with `goal.continue` before the proof can finish. The ellipses (...) are plalceholders for some combination of tactics which eventually solves the descendant of ?1.

brought back into the proof state using the `goal.continue` command, as shown in Figure 4.

To summarize, in *automatic mode*, goals are immediately continued after a tactic execution. Goals will never become dormant in automatic mode. This provides a gym-like environment to its user. Users who wish to handle tree search manually should disable this mode.

4.3   Metavariable Coupling

Recall that a proof state may contain 0 or more goals, and metavariable coupling [13] refers to inter-dependencies between goals in a proof state. Metavariable coupling arises naturally in many contexts. For example, applying the transitivity axiom of $\leq_{\mathbb{N}}$ to the goal $2 \leq 5$ results in the following goals.

$$?1 : 2 \leq ?z$$
$$?2 : ?z \leq 5$$
$$?z : \mathbb{N}$$

Because $?z$ appears in all three goals, these goals are all coupled. This complicates proof search because if an assignment is made to z in one goal, it will propagate to all of the other coupled goals. In this case, the other two goals will no longer be coupled, but they will contain the assignment made to z.

Pantograph provides explicit information about which goals are coupled. Since there are multiple possible ways of handling coupling, the choice of what to do with the coupling is left to the user. One method employed by [13] is *copying*, where coupled goals are solved sequentially to avoid conflicts.

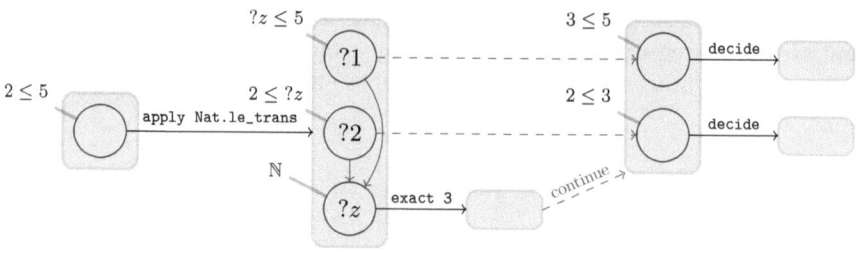

Fig. 5: In this diagram, rectangular boxes are proof states, and circles are goals. Each proof state has 0 or more goals. A state with no goals is considered solved. If all descendant goals of a state become solved, the state itself becomes solved.

Figure 5 gives a full example of the above proof, conducted with automatic mode *off*. The application of the transitivity tactic creates a proof state with three goals. Using the `exact 3` tactic on the $?z$ goal results in a solved proof state. Applying `goal.continue` then brings goals ?1 and ?2 back into the proof state, where they are no longer coupled. Each can be discharged with an additional tactic such as `decide`.

4.4   The Environment

All running instances of Lean 4, including instances running behind the LSP or the Pantograph front end, maintain a library of active symbols known as the *environment*. Internally, Lean 4 stores all theorem statements and proofs in the environment as expressions, regardless of how they were constructed. The user can extract the proof of any theorem in the current environment via `env.inspect`, which will produce an expression similar to Expression (1).

After a proof concludes, the user can extract the proof expression of the root proposition using the `goal.print` command. These expressions can then be inserted back into the current environment using the `env.add` command. Adding a lemma to the environment makes it accessible as a step in future proofs. Note that adding lemmas to the environment cannot be done while in the middle of an incomplete proof.

Like CoqGym [22], Pantograph can optionally output proof expressions in S-expression format by turning on the `printExprAST` option via `options.set`. The user can also change Lean 4's expression pretty-printing options by providing command line parameters to the Pantograph REPL. For example, to turn off all pretty-printing, use `--pp.all=true`.

4.5   Tactic Training Data

The Lean 4 community has produced several large collections of theorems with human-written formal proofs, e.g., Mathlib [14]. These collections can be used to train theorem proving agents. The `frontend.process` command runs the Lean 4 compiler on a Lean 4 file, collects all tactics in the file, and returns them as a list of (before, after, tactic) triplets. These triplets are conveniently presented in a format conducive to offline reinforcement learning training. Pantograph also outputs information about the starting and ending positions (in the file) of each Lean 4 command in case the user is interested in processing comments or other metadata. Below is an example of one extracted tactic triple.

```
{
    "goalBefore":"⊢ ∀(p, q : Prop), p ∨ q → q ∨ p ",
    "goalAfter":" p : Prop \n ⊢ ∀(q : Prop), p ∨ q → q ∨ p ",
    "tactic":"intro p"
}
```

4.6   Drafting

Drafting refers to a theorem proving technique which starts by generating a proof outline, instead of building a full proof step by step. A *draft* proof first consists of an overview with holes. Draft proofs are resolved by proving the individual goals corresponding to the holes in the proof. For example, consider the task of proving the commutativity of addition in Peano arithmetic. One approach would be to write a proof based on induction, using the inductive hypothesis $n + m = m + n$ to prove the inductive step $m + (n + 1) = (m + n) + 1$. As stated, this proof is not rigorous or detailed enough for Lean 4, but it *can* be written as a draft proof:

```
theorem add_comm : forall n m : Nat, n + m = m + n := by
    intros n m
    induction n with
    | zero =>
      have h_base: 0 + m = m := sorry
```

```
    have h_symm: m + 0 = m := sorry
    sorry
  | succ n ih =>
    have h_inductive: n + m = m + n := sorry
    have h_pull_succ_out_from_right: m + Nat.succ n = Nat.succ (m + n)
    := sorry
    sorry
```

The placeholders for intermediate goals have marked with the `sorry` keyword.

Pantograph supports drafting in two ways. The first is via the `have` tactic. This tactic introduces a lemma or intermediate claim and creates a new goal corresponding to the lemma.

The other way Pantograph supports drafting is via `sorry`-extraction. Pantograph can find all occurrences of `sorry` in a proof or definition and convert them to goals. For example, when `add_comm` from the above proof is fed into Pantograph's `frontend.process` command, it generates the following list of goals:

```
m : Nat
|- 0 + m = m
m : Nat
h_base : 0 + m = m
|- m + 0 = m
m : Nat
h_base : 0 + m = m
h_symm : m + 0 = m
|- 0 + m = m + 0
m : Nat
n : Nat
ih : n + m = m + n
|- n + m = m + n
m : Nat
n : Nat
ih : n + m = m + n
h_inductive : n + m = m + n
|- m + n.succ = (m + n).succ
m : Nat
n : Nat
ih : n + m = m + n
h_inductive : n + m = m + n
h_pull_succ_out_from_right : m + n.succ = (m + n).succ
|- n + 1 + m = m + (n + 1)
```

The user can then execute tactics on these goals as they see fit. This feature is appealing for machine learning agents, since it allows an agent (e.g., a Generative AI agent like an LLM) to effectively draft the next step of the proof without having to dive into details about its execution. If a sketch contains type errors that cannot be rectified, Pantograph forwards the error generated by the Lean 4 Kernel to the user.

4.7   Limitations

Pantograph is limited by the functionalities available in Lean. For example, if a tactic has a bug and discards a metavariable, Pantograph cannot catch the issue until the end of the proof. Anything that cannot be expressed in Lean's type system (e.g., Homotopy Type Theory (HoTT)) also cannot be expressed in Pantograph. Due to the tight coupling of Pantograph with Lean's internals, non-trivial engineering effort is required to update Pantograph when Lean undergoes a major version change.

Moreover, due to the user-defined nature of tactics, distributing computation via pickling of objects in Pantograph is not trivial. For example, if two branches of a proof executing on two different machines are concluded, Pantograph does not handle the algorithmically difficult problem of uniting the two branches.

5   Evaluation

In this section, we demonstrate that Pantograph has the necessary power to implement a Draft-Sketch-Prove (DSP) solver based on GPT-4o (which, notably, is not tuned for the task) and Aesop [8] (mentioned in Section 3). DSP works as follows: A formal mathematical problem is fed into a language model instance. The language model outputs a proof skeleton outlining the major steps of the formal proof. Then a proof automation tool, which does not use machine learning, fills in the holes.

We used both the GPT-4o [1] and the GPT-o1-preview [2] language models, with parameters given in Table 1, and ran on the theorem proving evaluation benchmark MiniF2F [24]. Each individual experiment works as follows. The language model is given the formal theorem statement from MiniF2F and is asked to generate a natural language proof. Next, the same model is provided with this natural language proof and asked to generate one or three formal proof sketches in Lean 4 (GPT-o1-preview is only asked to generate a single proof sketch, as it does not yet support multiple sketches). These sketches may contain the `sorry` keyword. The sketches are then fed into Pantograph's sorry-extraction command and turned into goals, which we try to solve one by one. To attempt to solve the goals, we use the following Lean 4 tactics as hammers: `aesop` [13], `simp`, and `linarith` (from Mathlib [14]).

Parameter	Value
Max tokens	2048
Top P	0.95
Temperature	0.8

Table 1: LLM parameters for DSP Experiment

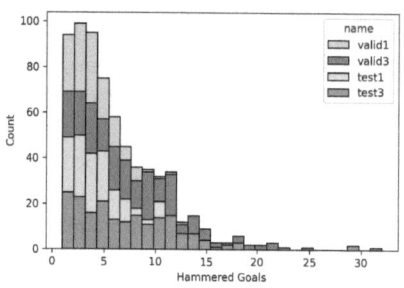
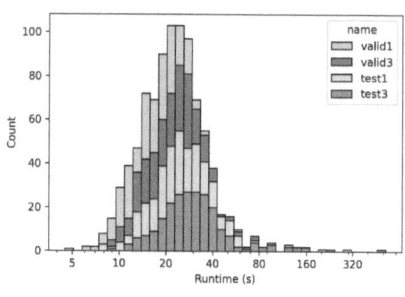

(a) Number of goals generated for the hammer tactic

(b) Total Runtime

Fig. 6: Hammer invocations and runtimes of DSP on the validation and test sets of MiniF2F using the GPT-4o model. The name of the legend refers to the dataset split (validation or test) and the number of sketches used to solve the dataset split.

Having built the DSP solver, the results are shown Table 2. They are not state of the art but are better than expected since we conducted no training. The drafting feature of Pantograph made this easy to implement. We show results on both the Validation and Test subsets of the MiniF2F benchmark set, both with one and three proof sketch(es). We report the overall success rate, and the average number of hammer invocations and the average runtime per benchmark. Our best configuration uses GPT-4o and three requested sketches. For this configuration, the DSP system out of the box successfully proved 28% of the theorems from MiniF2F [24]. Since Lean and Isabelle have different type systems, we do not do a comparison with the Isabelle implementation of DSP.

Benchmark Set	Validation			Test		
Requested Sketches (Model)	1 (4o)	1 (o1)	3 (4o)	1 (4o)	1 (o1)	3 (4o)
Success Rate (%)	12.7	10.9	23.6	14.7	16.0	**28.4**
Hammer Invocations	4.17	5.38	7.93	4.46	5.72	7.34
Runtime (s)	17.25	73.23	23.98	28.39	88.38	36.41

Table 2: DSP's proof success rate (in %) using the Pantograph interface on the MiniF2F formal theorem proving benchmark. We used GPT-4o (labeled 4o) and o1-preview (labeled o1) for the DSP experiments.

Figure 6 shows the result of the DSP experiment on the validation and test sets of the MiniF2F dataset. We plot the distribution of the number of hammer tactic invocations and the distribution of runtimes. The LLM nearly always outputs fewer than 10 goals per sketch. We also observe that running 3 sketches

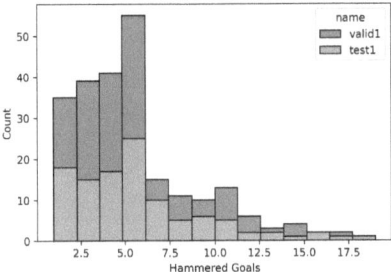
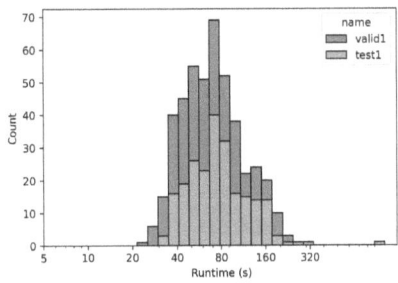

(a) Number of goals generated for the hammer tactic

(b) Total Runtime

Fig. 7: Hammer invocations and runtimes of DSP on the validation and test sets of MiniF2F using the o1-preview model. The name of the legend refers to the dataset split (validation or test) and the number of sketches used to solve the dataset split.

rather than 1 does not dramatically increase the runtime, indicating that the main performance bottleneck is the inference of the GPT-4o model.

In Figure 7, we show a similar plot for the o1-preview model. This model cannot generate multiple sketches. We observe that the runtime is much longer, likely due to the complex inference mechanism of the o1-preview model. However the success rate is either worse than or only marginally better than the GPT-4o model.

To our knowledge, these results represent the first successful implementation of DSP in Lean 4. We expect that the performance can be improved significantly by tuning parameters or using more refined models, but this work provides a baseline that can be built on and compared to in future work.

6   Conclusion

In this work, we introduce Pantograph, a Machine-to-Machine interaction library for Lean 4. We compare its features against existing tools used for training machine learning models for theorem proving, and we provide a list of its novel features. We also illustrate an application by implementing the first Lean 4 implementation of the Draft-Sketch-Prove approach.

In future work, we plan to use Pantograph to build and train various machine learning approaches for theorem proving. We also expect and hope that others will use it in interesting and novel ways and that these use cases will provide feedback for additional improvements and extensions of Pantograph.

Our evaluation also demonstrates one way that formal tools like Lean can be used to address potential harm from Language Models such as the one used in the evaluation section. Language models, though powerful, still face the problem of hallucination and generation of illogical results. These can be mitigated by applying formal techniques to the results produced of language models. The draft-sketch-prove experiment is an instance of this general idea, where proof automation formally checks the potentially incorrect result generated by an LLM. In the future, Pantograph could be used for other hybrid reasoning approaches combining generative AI and formal reasoning.

Acknowledgements

We thank Abdalrhman Mohamed for his input on Lean 4's expression system. We also thank Lean 4 Zulip chat users who answered our development questions. We thank Dr. Kim Morrison for the lean-training-data repository and examples of interacting with Lean 4's front end. We thank Dr. David Dill for his feedback in proofreading the paper. This work was funded in part by a gift from Amazon Web Services and by Centaur: the Stanford Center for Automated Reasoning.

Appendix

The prompt for the Draft part of the DSP experiment is

```
Draft an informal solution similar to the one below. The informal
solution will be used to sketch a formal proof in the Lean 4 Proof
Assistant.
Here are some examples:

Informal:
(*### Problem\n\n
[...nl/i problem text...]\n\n
### Solution\n\n
[...nl/i solution/draft text...]\n\n
*)\n\n

Informal:
(*### Problem\n\n
{nl_problem}
### Solution\n\n
[...Model Completion...]
```

The prompt for the Sketch part is

```
[... Translate informal draft to a formal sketch in Lean 4. Here are some
    examples: ...]
Informal:\n
(*### Problem\n\n
[...nl/i problem text...]\n\n
### Solution\n\n
[...nl/i solution/draft text...]\n\n
*)\n\n
```

```
Formal:\n
[...fl/i problem text...]
[...fl/i partial sketch text...]
\n\n

Informal:\n
(*### Problem\n\n
{nl_problem}
### Solution\n\n
{nl_solution}
*)\n\n
Formal:\n
{fl_problem}
[...Model Completion...]
```

References

1. Hello gpt-4o. https://openai.com/index/hello-gpt-4o/ (9 2024)
2. Introducing openai o1-preview. https://openai.com/index/introducing-openai-o1-preview/ (9 2024)
3. Aya developers: The aya proof assistant. https://www.aya-prover.org (2021)
4. Browne, C.B., Powley, E., Whitehouse, D., Lucas, S.M., Cowling, P.I., Rohlfshagen, P., Tavener, S., Perez, D., Samothrakis, S., Colton, S.: A survey of monte carlo tree search methods. IEEE Transactions on Computational Intelligence and AI in Games **4**(1), 1–43 (Mar 2012). https://doi.org/10.1109/TCIAIG.2012.2186810
5. Crouse, M., Abdelaziz, I., Makni, B., Whitehead, S., Cornelio, C., Kapanipathi, P., Srinivas, K., Thost, V., Witbrock, M., Fokoue, A.: A deep reinforcement learning approach to first-order logic theorem proving (2020)
6. Gauthier, T.e.a.: Tactictoe: Learning to prove with tactics. Journal of Automated Reasoning **65**(2), 257–286 (Feb 2021). https://doi.org/10.1007/s10817-020-09580-x, arXiv:1804.00596 [cs]
7. Hales, T., Adams, M., Bauer, G., Dang, T.D., Harrison, J., Le Truong, H., Kaliszyk, C., Magron, V., McLaughlin, S., Nguyen, T.T., et al.: A formal proof of the kepler conjecture. In: Forum of mathematics, Pi. vol. 5, p. e2. Cambridge University Press (2017)
8. Jiang, A.e.a.: Draft, sketch, and prove: Guiding formal theorem provers with informal proofs (Oct 2022). https://doi.org/10.48550/arXiv.2210.12283, https://arxiv.org/abs/2210.12283v2
9. Jiang, A.Q., Li, W., Tworkowski, S., Czechowski, K., Odrzygóźdź, T., Miłoś, P., Wu, Y., Jamnik, M.: Thor: Wielding hammers to integrate language models and automated theorem provers (2022)
10. Klein, G., Elphinstone, K., Heiser, G., Andronick, J., Cock, D., Derrin, P., Elkaduwe, D., Engelhardt, K., Kolanski, R., Norrish, M., et al.: sel4: Formal verification of an os kernel. In: Proceedings of the ACM SIGOPS 22nd symposium on Operating systems principles. pp. 207–220 (2009)
11. Lample, G., Lachaux, M.A., Lavril, T., Martinet, X., Hayat, A., Ebner, G., Rodriguez, A., Lacroix, T.: Hypertree proof search for neural theorem proving (2022)
12. Li, Z.e.a.: Graph contrastive pre-training for effective theorem reasoning. CoRR **abs/2108.10821** (2021), https://arxiv.org/abs/2108.10821

13. Limperg, J., From, A.H.: Aesop: White-box best-first proof search for lean. In: Proceedings of the 12th ACM SIGPLAN International Conference on Certified Programs and Proofs. p. 253–266. CPP 2023, Association for Computing Machinery, New York, NY, USA (2023). https://doi.org/10.1145/3573105.3575671, https://doi.org/10.1145/3573105.3575671

14. mathlib: The lean mathematical library. CoRR **abs/1910.09336** (2019), http://arxiv.org/abs/1910.09336

15. de Moura, L., Ullrich, S.: The lean 4 theorem prover and programming language. In: Platzer, A., Sutcliffe, G. (eds.) Automated Deduction – CADE 28. pp. 625–635. Springer International Publishing, Cham (2021)

16. Nipkow, T., Paulson, L.C., Wenzel, M.: Isabelle/HOL: a proof assistant for higher-order logic, vol. 2283. Springer Science & Business Media (2002)

17. Silver, D., Hubert, T., Schrittwieser, J., Antonoglou, I., Lai, M., Guez, A., Lanctot, M., Sifre, L., Kumaran, D., Graepel, T., Lillicrap, T., Simonyan, K., Hassabis, D.: A general reinforcement learning algorithm that masters chess, shogi, and go through self-play. Science **362**, 1140–1144 (12 2018). https://doi.org/10.1126/SCIENCE.AAR6404, https://www.science.org

18. Silver, D., Schrittwieser, J., Simonyan, K., Antonoglou, I., Huang, A., Guez, A., Hubert, T., Baker, L., Lai, M., Bolton, A., Chen, Y., Lillicrap, T., Hui, F., Sifre, L., Driessche, G.V.D., Graepel, T., Demis, H.: Mastering the game of go without human knowledge

19. The Coq Development Team: The Coq reference manual – release 8.19.0. https://coq.inria.fr/doc/V8.19.0/refman (2024)

20. Wang, H., Yuan, Y., Liu, Z., Shen, J., Yin, Y., Xiong, J., Xie, E., Shi, H., Li, Y., Li, L., Yin, J., Li, Z., Liang, X.: Dt-solver: Automated theorem proving with dynamic-tree sampling guided by proof-level value function. In: Proceedings of the 61st Annual Meeting of the Association for Computational Linguistics (Volume 1: Long Papers). p. 12632–12646. Association for Computational Linguistics, Toronto, Canada (Jul 2023). https://doi.org/10.18653/v1/2023.acl-long.706, https://aclanthology.org/2023.acl-long.706

21. Wang, M., Deng, J.: Learning to Prove Theorems by Learning to Generate Theorems. No. arXiv:2002.07019 (Oct 2020). https://doi.org/10.48550/arXiv.2002.07019, http://arxiv.org/abs/2002.07019, arXiv:2002.07019 [cs, stat]

22. Yang, K., Deng, J.: Learning to Prove Theorems via Interacting with Proof Assistants. No. arXiv:1905.09381 (May 2019). https://doi.org/10.48550/arXiv.1905.09381, http://arxiv.org/abs/1905.09381, arXiv:1905.09381 [cs, stat] type: article

23. Yang, K., Swope, A., Gu, A., Chalamala, R., Song, P., Yu, S., Godil, S., Prenger, R., Anandkumar, A.: LeanDojo: Theorem proving with retrieval-augmented language models. In: Neural Information Processing Systems (NeurIPS) (2023)

24. Zheng, K., Han, J.M., Polu, S.: Minif2f: a cross-system benchmark for formal olympiad-level mathematics. arXiv preprint arXiv:2109.00110 (2021)

Automated Analysis of Logically Constrained Rewrite Systems Using crest*

Jonas Schöpf$^{(\boxtimes)}$ and Aart Middeldorp

Department of Computer Science, University of Innsbruck, Innsbruck, Austria
{jonas.schoepf,aart.middeldorp}@uibk.ac.at

Abstract. We present crest, a tool for automatically proving (non-) confluence and termination of logically constrained rewrite systems. We compare crest to other tools for logically constrained rewriting. Extensive experiments demonstrate the promise of crest.

Keywords: Automation · Confluence · Termination · Term Rewriting · Logical Constraints.

1 Introduction

Term rewriting is a simple Turing-complete model of computation. Properties like confluence and termination are of key interest and numerous powerful tools have been developed for their analysis. Logically constrained term rewrite systems (LCTRSs for short) constitute a natural extension of term rewrite systems (TRSs) in which rules are equipped with logical constraints that are handled by SMT solvers, thereby avoiding the cumbersome encoding of operations on e.g. integers and bit vectors in term rewriting. LCTRSs, introduced by Kop and Nishida in 2013 [25], are useful for program analysis [8, 13, 23, 40]. They also developed Ctrl [26, 27], a tool for LCTRSs specializing in termination analysis and equivalence testing. Later, techniques for completion [39] and non-termination [33] analysis were added.

In this paper we describe crest, the Constrained REwriting Software Tool. The tool crest was first announced in [34] with support for a small number of confluence techniques. The new version described here includes numerous extensions:

- more advanced confluence techniques (introduced in [35]),
- automated non-confluence and termination analysis,
- support for fixed-sized bit vectors,
- transformation techniques based on splitting critical pairs and merging constrained rewrite rules, to further boost the confluence proving power.

---

* This research is funded by the Austrian Science Fund (FWF) project I5943.

A. Gurfinkel and M. Heule (Eds.): TACAS 2025, LNCS 15696, pp. 124–144, 2025.
https://doi.org/10.1007/978-3-031-90643-5_7

Extensive experiments show the strength of crest. The tool is open-source and available from http://cl-informatik.uibk.ac.at/software/crest.

The remainder of the paper is organized as follows. In the next section we recall important definitions pertaining to LCTRSs. Section 3 summarizes the main confluence and termination techniques implemented in crest. Automation details are presented in Section 4. The new transformation techniques are described in Section 5. In Section 6 we present our experiments, before concluding in Section 7 with suggestions for future extensions. We conclude this introductory section with mentioning other tools for LCTRSs.

Related Tools. We already mentioned Ctrl[1] which until 2023 was the only tool capable of analyzing confluence and termination of LCTRSs. It supports termination analysis [24], completion techniques [39], rewriting induction for equivalence testing of LCTRSs [13], and basic confluence analysis [27]. Unfortunately, it is neither actively maintained nor very well documented, which is one reason why the development of crest was started. Moreover, a branch[2] of the automated resource analysis tool TcT [4] performs complexity analysis on LCTRSs based on [40]. RMT by Ciobâcă et al. [7,8] is a newer tool for program analysis based on a variation of LCTRSs.

In the 2024 edition of the Confluence Competition[3] the tool CRaris,[4] developed by Nishida and Kojima, made its appearance. The tool implements weak orthogonality [25] and the Knuth–Bendix criterion for terminating LCTRSs [34]. For termination, it implements the dependency pair framework [24] and the singleton self-looping removal processor [29] for LCTRSs with bit vectors.

Also in 2024 Guo et al. [14, 15] announced Cora, a new open-source tool for termination analysis of logically constrained *simply-typed* term rewrite systems, which serve as a high-order generalization of LCTRSs. It employs static dependency pairs [28] with several base methods, including a variant of the higher-order recursive path order [18].

2 Logically Constrained Term Rewriting

Familiarity with the basic notions of term rewriting [5] is assumed. We assume a many-sorted signature $\mathcal{F} = \mathcal{F}_{\mathsf{te}} \cup \mathcal{F}_{\mathsf{th}}$ consisting of term and theory symbols together with a countably infinite set of variables $\mathcal{V}$. For every sort ι in $\mathcal{F}_{\mathsf{th}}$ we have a non-empty set $\mathcal{V}\mathsf{al}_\iota \subseteq \mathcal{F}_{\mathsf{th}}$ of value symbols, such that all $c \in \mathcal{V}\mathsf{al}_\iota$ are constants of sort ι. We demand $\mathcal{F}_{\mathsf{te}} \cap \mathcal{F}_{\mathsf{th}} \subseteq \mathcal{V}\mathsf{al}$ where $\mathcal{V}\mathsf{al} = \bigcup_\iota \mathcal{V}\mathsf{al}_\iota$. The set of terms constructed from function symbols in $\mathcal{F}$ and variables in $\mathcal{V}$ is by $\mathcal{T}(\mathcal{F}, \mathcal{V})$. A term in $\mathcal{T}(\mathcal{F}_{\mathsf{th}}, \mathcal{V})$ is called a *logical* term. Ground logical terms are mapped to values by an interpretation $\mathcal{J}$: $[\![f(t_1, \ldots, t_n)]\!] = f_{\mathcal{J}}([\![t_1]\!], \ldots, [\![t_n]\!])$. Logical terms of sort bool are called *constraints*. A constraint φ is *valid* if $[\![\varphi\gamma]\!] = \top$ for all

---

substitutions γ such that $\gamma(x) \in \mathcal{V}\mathsf{al}$ for all $x \in \mathcal{V}\mathsf{ar}(\varphi)$. Positions are sequences of positive integers to indicate subterms. The root of a term is denoted by the empty string ϵ. For a term s, its subterm at position p is given by $s|_p$. The set of positions in $s \in \mathcal{T}(\mathcal{F}, \mathcal{V})$ is denoted by $\mathcal{P}\mathsf{os}(s)$ whereas $\mathcal{P}\mathsf{os}_\mathcal{F}(s)$ is restricted to positions with function symbols in s. We write $\mathcal{V}\mathsf{ar}(s)$ for the set of variables in s. A *constrained rewrite rule* is a triple $\rho\colon \ell \to r\ [\varphi]$ where $\ell, r \in \mathcal{T}(\mathcal{F}, \mathcal{V})$ are terms of the same sort such that $\mathsf{root}(\ell) \in \mathcal{F}_{\mathsf{te}} \setminus \mathcal{F}_{\mathsf{th}}$ and φ is a constraint. We denote the set $\mathcal{V}\mathsf{ar}(\varphi) \cup (\mathcal{V}\mathsf{ar}(r) \setminus \mathcal{V}\mathsf{ar}(\ell))$ of *logical* variables in ρ by $\mathcal{L}\mathcal{V}\mathsf{ar}(\rho)$. We write $\mathcal{E}\mathcal{V}\mathsf{ar}(\rho)$ for the set $\mathcal{V}\mathsf{ar}(r) \setminus (\mathcal{V}\mathsf{ar}(\ell) \cup \mathcal{V}\mathsf{ar}(\varphi))$ of *extra* variables. A set of constrained rewrite rules is called an LCTRS. A substitution σ *respects* a rule $\rho\colon \ell \to r\ [\varphi]$, denoted by $\sigma \vDash \rho$, if $\mathcal{D}\mathsf{om}(\sigma) \subseteq \mathcal{V}\mathsf{ar}(\rho)$, $\sigma(x) \in \mathcal{V}\mathsf{al}$ for all $x \in \mathcal{L}\mathcal{V}\mathsf{ar}(\rho)$, and $\varphi\sigma$ is valid. Moreover, a constraint φ is respected by σ, denoted by $\sigma \vDash \varphi$, if $\sigma(x) \in \mathcal{V}\mathsf{al}$ for all $x \in \mathcal{V}\mathsf{ar}(\varphi)$ and $\varphi\sigma$ is valid. We call $f(x_1, \dots, x_n) \to y\ [y = f(x_1, \dots, x_n)]$ with a fresh variable y and $f \in \mathcal{F}_{\mathsf{th}} \setminus \mathcal{V}\mathsf{al}$ a *calculation rule*. The set of all calculation rules induced by the signature $\mathcal{F}_{\mathsf{th}}$ of an LCTRS $\mathcal{R}$ is denoted by $\mathcal{R}_{\mathsf{ca}}$ and we abbreviate $\mathcal{R} \cup \mathcal{R}_{\mathsf{ca}}$ to $\mathcal{R}_{\mathsf{rc}}$. A rewrite step $s \to_\mathcal{R} t$ satisfies $s|_p = \ell\sigma$ and $t = s[r\sigma]_p$ for some position p, constrained rewrite rule $\rho\colon \ell \to r\ [\varphi]$ in $\mathcal{R}_{\mathsf{rc}}$, and substitution σ such that $\sigma \vDash \rho$.

A *constrained term* is a pair $s\ [\varphi]$ consisting of a term s and a constraint φ. Two constrained terms $s\ [\varphi]$ and $t\ [\psi]$ are *equivalent*, denoted by $s\ [\varphi] \sim t\ [\psi]$, if for every substitution $\gamma \vDash \varphi$ with $\mathcal{D}\mathsf{om}(\gamma) = \mathcal{V}\mathsf{ar}(\varphi)$ there is some substitution $\delta \vDash \psi$ with $\mathcal{D}\mathsf{om}(\delta) = \mathcal{V}\mathsf{ar}(\psi)$ such that $s\gamma = t\delta$, and vice versa. Let $s\ [\varphi]$ be a constrained term. If $s|_p = \ell\sigma$ for some constrained rewrite rule $\rho\colon \ell \to r\ [\psi] \in \mathcal{R}_{\mathsf{rc}}$, position p, and substitution σ such that $\sigma(x) \in \mathcal{V}\mathsf{al} \cup \mathcal{V}\mathsf{ar}(\varphi)$ for all $x \in \mathcal{L}\mathcal{V}\mathsf{ar}(\rho)$, φ is satisfiable and $\varphi \Rightarrow \psi\sigma$ is valid then $s\ [\varphi] \to_\mathcal{R} s[r\sigma]_p\ [\varphi]$. The rewrite relation $\leadsto_\mathcal{R}$ on constrained terms is defined as $\sim \cdot \to_\mathcal{R} \cdot \sim$ and $s\ [\varphi] \leadsto_\mathcal{R}^p t\ [\psi]$ indicates that the rewrite step in $\leadsto_\mathcal{R}$ takes place at position p in s. Similarly, we write $s\ [\varphi] \leadsto_{\geqslant p} t\ [\psi]$ if the position in the rewrite step is below position p. We illustrate some of these concepts by means of a simple example which models the computation of the maximum of two integers.

Example 1. Consider the LCTRS $\mathcal{R}$ over the theory Ints with the rules

$$\alpha\colon \mathsf{max}(x, y) \to x\ [x \geqslant y] \qquad\qquad \beta\colon \mathsf{max}(x, y) \to y\ [y \geqslant x]$$

Here x and y are logical variables in both rules. There are no extra variables. The symbol max is the only term symbol. The theory symbols depend on the definition of Ints. As the goal is automation this usually consists of non-linear integer arithmetic as specified in the respective SMT-LIB theory.[5]

By applying the calculation rule $x_1 + x_2 \to y\ [y = x_1 + x_2]$ with substitution $\{x_1 \mapsto 3, x_2 \mapsto 2, y \mapsto 5\}$ followed by rule α we obtain

$$\mathsf{max}(3 + 2, 3) \to \mathsf{max}(5, 3) \to 5$$

---

[5] https://smtlib.cs.uiowa.edu/Theories/Ints.smt2

An example of constrained rewriting is given by

$$\mathsf{max}(3, 3 + x) \; [x \geqslant 0] \twoheadrightarrow \mathsf{max}(3, z) \; [x \geqslant 0 \wedge z = 3 + x]$$
$$\twoheadrightarrow z \; [x \geqslant 0 \wedge z = 3 + x]$$

One-step rewriting, i.e., rewriting a term using a single rule, was introduced above. The sufficient criteria for confluence, highlighted in the next section, heavily rely on the notation of parallel ($\twoheadrightarrow$) and multi-step ($\twoheadrightarrow$) rewriting following [35, Definition 3] and [34, Definition 8]. The former is capable of applying several rules at parallel positions in a step while the latter additionally allows recursive steps within the used matching substitutions of rules. A rewrite sequence consists of consecutive rewrite steps, independent of which kind. The reflexive and transitive closure of $\rightarrow$ is denoted by $\rightarrow^*$. Moreover, for arbitrary terms s and t we write $s \leftrightarrow t$ if $s \; (\leftarrow \cup \rightarrow) \; t$ and $s \downarrow t$ if there exists a term u such that $s \rightarrow^* u \; ^* \leftarrow t$.

3   Confluence and Termination

Termination and confluence are well-known properties in static program analysis. Both properties are in general undecidable. With respect to (logically constrained) term rewriting, a program is terminating whenever it does not admit an infinite rewrite sequence. Confluence states that $s \downarrow t$ whenever $t \; ^* \leftarrow s \rightarrow^* u$, for all terms s, t and u. Naively checking the properties is obviously not feasible. In (logically constrained) term rewriting there exist sufficient criteria that guarantee that these properties are satisfied for a given program. In the following we highlight key components of confluence and termination analysis for logically constrained rewrite systems.

The confluence methods implemented in crest are based on (parallel) critical pairs. These are defined as follows. Given a constrained rewrite rule ρ, we write $\mathcal{EC}_\rho$ for $\bigwedge \{x = x \mid x \in \mathcal{EV}ar(\rho)\}$. An *overlap* of an LCTRS $\mathcal{R}$ is a triple $\langle \rho_1, p, \rho_2 \rangle$ with rules $\rho_1 \colon \ell_1 \rightarrow r_1 \; [\varphi_1]$ and $\rho_2 \colon \ell_2 \rightarrow r_2 \; [\varphi_2]$, satisfying the following conditions: (1) ρ_1 and ρ_2 are variable-disjoint variants of rewrite rules in $\mathcal{R}_{\mathsf{rc}}$, (2) $p \in \mathcal{P}os_{\mathcal{F}}(\ell_2)$, (3) ℓ_1 and $\ell_2|_p$ unify with mgu σ such that $\sigma(x) \in \mathcal{V}al \cup \mathcal{V}$ for all $x \in \mathcal{LV}ar(\rho_1) \cup \mathcal{LV}ar(\rho_2)$, (4) $\varphi_1 \sigma \wedge \varphi_2 \sigma$ is satisfiable, and (5) if $p = \epsilon$ then ρ_1 and ρ_2 are not variants, or $\mathcal{V}ar(r_1) \not\subseteq \mathcal{V}ar(\ell_1)$. In this case we call $\ell_2 \sigma[r_1 \sigma]_p \approx r_2 \sigma \; [\varphi_1 \sigma \wedge \varphi_2 \sigma \wedge \psi \sigma]$ a *constrained critical pair* (CCP) obtained from the overlap $\langle \rho_1, p, \rho_2 \rangle$. Here $\psi = \mathcal{EC}_{\rho_1} \wedge \mathcal{EC}_{\rho_2}$. The peak

$$\ell_2 \sigma[r_1 \sigma]_p \; [\Phi] \leftarrow \ell_2 \sigma \; [\Phi] \rightarrow^\epsilon r_2 \sigma \; [\Phi]$$

with $\Phi = (\varphi_1 \wedge \varphi_2 \wedge \psi)\sigma$, from which the constrained critical pair originates, is called a *constrained critical peak*. The set of all constrained critical pairs of $\mathcal{R}$ is denoted by $\mathsf{CCP}(\mathcal{R})$. A constrained equation $s \approx t \; [\varphi]$ is *trivial* if $s\sigma = t\sigma$ for every substitution σ with $\sigma \vDash \varphi$. The trivial equations from $\mathcal{EC}_\rho$ are used in order to prevent loosing the information which (extra) variables are logical variables in the underlying rules of a CCP.

Example 2. Let us extend the LCTRS $\mathcal{R}$ from Example 1 with an additional rule modeling the commutativity of max:

$$\mathsf{max}(x, y) \to x \ [x \geqslant y] \quad \mathsf{max}(x, y) \to y \ [y \geqslant x] \quad \mathsf{max}(x, y) \to \mathsf{max}(y, x)$$

There are six constrained critical pairs, including the following two:

$$x \approx y \ [x \geqslant y \wedge y \geqslant x] \qquad\qquad x \approx \mathsf{max}(y, x) \ [x \geqslant y]$$

The left one is trivial, the one on the right becomes trivial after one rewrite step: $x \approx \mathsf{max}(y, x) \ [x \geqslant y] \to x \approx x \ [x \geqslant y]$. The remaining four pairs can be rewritten similarly.

Restricting the way in which constrained critical peaks are rewritten into trivial ones, yields different sufficient conditions for confluence of (left-)linear LCTRSs. We state the conditions below but refer to [25, 34, 35] for precise definitions:

(C1) (weak) orthogonality ([25, Theorem 4]),

(C2) joinable critical pairs for terminating LCTRSs ([34, Corollary 4]).

(C3) strong closedness for linear LCTRSs ([34, Theorem 2]),

(C4) (almost) parallel closedness for left-linear LCTRSs ([34, Theorem 4]),

(C5) (almost) development closedness for left-linear LCTRSs ([35, Corollary 1]).

The final confluence criterion implemented in crest is based on parallel critical pairs. Let $\mathcal{R}$ be an LCTRS, $\rho\colon \ell \to r \ [\varphi]$ a rule in $\mathcal{R}_{\mathsf{rc}}$, and $P \subseteq \mathcal{P}os_{\mathcal{F}}(\ell)$ a nonempty set of parallel positions. For every $p \in P$ let $\rho_p\colon \ell_p \to r_p \ [\varphi_p]$ be a variant of a rule in $\mathcal{R}_{\mathsf{rc}}$. Let $\psi = \mathcal{EC}_\rho \wedge \bigwedge_{p \in P} \mathcal{EC}_{\rho_p}$ and $\Phi = \varphi\sigma \wedge \psi\sigma \wedge \bigwedge_{p \in P} \varphi_p\sigma$. The peak $\ell\sigma[r_p\sigma]_{p \in P} \ [\Phi] \twoheadleftarrow\!\!\leftarrow \ell\sigma \ [\Phi] \to_{\mathcal{R}}^{\epsilon} r\sigma \ [\Phi]$ forms a *constrained parallel critical pair* $\ell\sigma[r_p\sigma]_{p \in P} \approx r\sigma \ [\Phi]$ if the following conditions are satisfied:

1. $\mathcal{V}ar(\rho_1) \cap \mathcal{V}ar(\rho_2) = \varnothing$ for different rules ρ_1 and ρ_2 in $\{\rho\} \cup \{\rho_p \mid p \in P\}$,
2. σ is an mgu of $\{\ell_p = \ell|_p \mid p \in P\}$ such that $\sigma(x) \in \mathcal{V}\mathsf{al} \cup \mathcal{V}$ for all $x \in \mathcal{LV}ar(\rho) \cup \bigcup_{p \in P} \mathcal{LV}ar(\rho_p)$,
3. $\varphi\sigma \wedge \bigwedge_{p \in P} \varphi_p\sigma$ is satisfiable, and
4. if $P = \{\epsilon\}$ then ρ_ϵ is not a variant of ρ or $\mathcal{V}ar(r) \not\subseteq \mathcal{V}ar(\ell)$.

A constrained peak forming a constrained parallel critical pair is called a *constrained parallel critical peak*. The set of all constrained parallel critical pairs of $\mathcal{R}$ is denoted by $\mathsf{CPCP}(\mathcal{R})$. The following sufficient condition for confluence is reported in ([35, Corollary 2]):

(C6) parallel closedness of parallel critical pairs for left-linear LCTRSs.

Conditions (C5) and (C6) do not subsume each other. Both generalize conditions (C1) – (C4). All these confluence criteria try to find a specific closing rewrite sequence starting from a constrained (parallel) critical pair—which is seen as a constrained equation—to a trivial constrained equation. For example, parallel closedness in (C4) involves showing that each constrained critical pair $s \approx t \ [\varphi]$ can be rewritten into a trivial constrained equation using a single parallel step $s \approx t \ [\varphi] \ \dottedplus_{\geqslant 1} \ s' \approx t \ [\varphi]$. Note that only the left part (s) is rewritten here and $s' \approx t \ [\varphi]$ is a trivial constrained equation. For (finite) terminating TRSs, confluence is decided by rewriting critical pairs to normal form [20]. For terminating LCTRSs confluence—even for a decidable theory—is undecidable [35], but rewriting constrained critical pairs to normal forms is still of value. This is used in (C2) above. We need however to adapt the notion of normal form for constrained terms.

Example 3. The LCTRS $\mathcal{R}$ over the theory Ints with rewrite rules

$$
\begin{array}{lll}
\mathsf{f}(x) \to \mathsf{g}(x) \ [x \geqslant 1] & \mathsf{g}(1) \to \mathsf{a} & \mathsf{h}(x) \to \mathsf{a} \ [x \leqslant 1] \\
\mathsf{f}(x) \to \mathsf{h}(x) \ [x \leqslant 2] & \mathsf{g}(x) \to \mathsf{b} \ [x \geqslant 2] & \mathsf{h}(x) \to \mathsf{b} \ [x > 1] \\
& \mathsf{g}(x) \to \mathsf{c} \ [x < 1] &
\end{array}
$$

admits one (modulo symmetry) constrained critical pair:

$$
\mathsf{g}(x) \approx \mathsf{h}(x) \ [x \geqslant 1 \wedge x \leqslant 2]
$$

None of the rules above are applicable, so this non-trivial constrained critical pair is in normal form with respect to $\to_{\mathcal{R}}$, but it would be wrong to conclude that $\mathcal{R}$ is not confluent; all substitutions σ that satisfy the constraint $x \geqslant 1 \wedge x \leqslant 2$ allow us to rewrite $(\mathsf{g}(x) \approx \mathsf{h}(x))\sigma$ to the trivial equations $\mathsf{a} \approx \mathsf{a}$ or $\mathsf{b} \approx \mathsf{b}$.

Definition 1. *Given an LCTRS $\mathcal{R}$, a constrained term $s \ [\varphi]$ is in* normal form *if and only if for all substitutions σ with $\sigma \vDash \varphi$ we have $s\sigma \to_{\mathcal{R}} t$ for no term t.*

Note that the constrained critical pair in Example 3 is not in normal form according to this definition. We present a simple sufficient condition for non-confluence. The easy proof can be found in the appendix of [37].

Lemma 1. *An LCTRS is* non-confluent *if there exists a constrained critical pair that rewrites to a non-trivial constrained equation in normal form.*

We will resume the analysis of Example 3 in Section 5. Termination plays an important role in the analysis of LCTRSs. crest implements the following methods reported in the papers by Kop and Nishida [24, 25]:

(T1) dependency graph ([24, Theorems 4 & 5]),
(T2) recursive path order ([25, Theorem 5]),
(T3) value criterion ([24, Theorem 10]),
(T4) reduction pairs ([24, Theorem 12]).

Method (T1) computes the strongly connected components in the dependency graph, and transforms the input LCTRS into so-called DP problems, which can be analyzed independently. It lies at the heart of the dependency pair framework [19] implemented in most termination tools for TRSs. Methods (T2) and (T4) are LCTRS variants of well-known methods for TRSs [3, 9]. Two further methods implemented in Ctrl are ported to crest:

(T5) subterm criterion

(T6) special value criterion

While (T5) is a well-known termination method for DP problems originating from TRSs [17], (T3) and (T6) are specific to LCTRSs. Method (T5) operates on the syntactic structure of dependency pairs and ignores the constraints. In method (T3) dependency pair symbols are also projected to a direct argument but then a strict decrease with respect to the constraint is required. For example, the rule $f(x) \rightarrow f(x-1)\,[x > 0]$ cannot be handled by (T5), but as $x > 0$ implies the strict decrease $x \succ x - 1$ for a suitable well-founded relation $\succ$, (T3) applies. Method (T6) is an extension of (T3) in which linear combinations of arguments are considered. Methods (T3) and (T6) are adapted to the higher-order LCTRS setting in [14, Sections 4.2 & 4.3].

4   Automation

Our tool crest is written in Haskell and the current version consists of roughly 12000 lines of code. Core modules like SMT solving use a fork of the simple-smt package[6] and the rewriting modules are inspired by the term-rewriting package.[7] In the following we provide some details of the key components.

Input Format. crest operates on LCTRSs in the new ARI format[8] [1] adopted by the Confluence Competition (CoCo) and also partly by the Termination Competition.[9] Problems in the ARI database are given a unique number which we will use throughout this paper to address specific LCTRSs. An example problem is given in Fig. 1. The ARI database format requires sort annotations for variables appearing as an argument of a polymorphic predicate. If this sort can be inferred at a different position then this can be ignored for crest. For example, consider the rule $f(x = y, x) \rightarrow z\,[z = x+1]$ with $f\colon \mathsf{Bool} \rightarrow \mathsf{Int} \rightarrow \mathsf{Int}$, $+\colon \mathsf{Int} \rightarrow \mathsf{Int} \rightarrow \mathsf{Int}$ and $=\colon A \rightarrow A \rightarrow \mathsf{Bool}$ with a polymorphic sort A. In the ARI database all variables need concrete sort annotation. For crest no sort annotation is necessary as all the sorts of variables can be inferred from the sort of f.

Theory symbols are those that are defined in a specific SMT-LIB theory, however, for fixed-sized bit vectors crest additionally supports function symbols defined in the SMT-LIB logic QF_BV.[10] In addition to LCTRSs also plain TRSs and many-sorted TRSs are supported.

Pre-Processing. After parsing its input and assigning already known sorts to function symbols and variables we apply a basic type inference algorithm. Some function symbols in the core theory, which provides basic boolean functions, like

---

[6] https://hackage.haskell.org/package/simple-smt

[7] https://hackage.haskell.org/package/term-rewriting

[8] https://project-coco.uibk.ac.at/ARI/lctrs.php

[9] https://termination-portal.org/wiki/Termination_Portal

[10] https://smt-lib.org/logics-all.shtml#QF_BV

```
(format LCTRS :smtlib 2.6)
(theory Ints)
(fun f (-> Int Int Int))
(fun g (-> Int Int Int))
(fun c (-> Int Int Int))
(fun h (-> Int Int))
(rule (f x y) (h (g y (* 2 2))) :guard (and (<= x y) (= y 2)))
(rule (f x y) (c 4 x) :guard (<= y x))
(rule (g x y) (g y x))
(rule (c x y) (g 4 2) :guard (not (= x y)))
(rule (h x) x)
```

Fig. 1. ARI file 1528 (without sort annotations and meta information).

"=" have a polymorphic sort. Therefore we need to infer unknown sorts in order to obtain a fully sorted LCTRS. This is required as sort information must be present for the declaration of variables in the SMT solver. During the parsing phase crest parses the respective theory from an internal representation of the SMT-LIB specification. Currently the theory of integers, reals, fixed-sized bit vectors and a combination of integers and reals are supported. Subsequently crest preprocesses the LCTRS by moving values in the left-hand sides of the rewrite rules into the constraints (by applying the transformation described in [34, Definition 13]). Afterwards it merges as many rules as possible following Definition 3 in Section 5.

Rewriting. One of the key components is the rewriting module which provides functionality to perform rewriting on constrained terms. This module computes rewrite sequences of arbitrary length, using single steps, parallel rewrite steps [35, Definition 7] and multisteps [35, Definition 5]. Calculation steps are modeled in an obvious way; whenever we have a term $s[f(s_1, \ldots, s_n)]$ $[\varphi]$ with $s_1, \ldots, s_n \in$ $\mathcal{V}al \cup \mathcal{V}ar(\varphi)$ and $f \in \mathcal{F}_{\mathsf{th}}$, then we produce $s[x]$ $[\varphi \wedge x = f(s_1, \ldots, s_n)]$ for a fresh variable x. In some cases single rule steps need more care because of the lack of equivalence steps in rewrite sequences. For rules with variables that do not occur in the left-hand side, the matching substitution of the left-hand side does not provide an instantiation. However, those variables are logical and need to be instantiated with values. This is achieved by adding the constraint of the rule and its extra variables to the resulting constrained term after it has been confirmed that for those variables an instantiation exists. We illustrate this in the following example.

Example 4. Consider the constrained rule $\rho\colon \mathsf{f}(x) \to y$ $[x \geqslant 0 \wedge x > y]$, the constrained term $\mathsf{f}(z)$ $[z = 2]$ and the matching substitution $\{x \mapsto z\}$ between the left-hand side of ρ and $\mathsf{f}(z)$. The variable y is not part of the matching substitution and thus crest rewrites $\mathsf{f}(z)$ $[z = 2]$ to y $[z = 2 \wedge z \geqslant 0 \wedge z > y]$. Using the constrained rule $\rho'\colon \mathsf{f}(x) \to y$ $[x \geqslant 0]$ from the same constrained term would give y $[z = 2 \wedge z \geqslant 0 \wedge y = y]$.

SMT. SMT solving is a key component in the analysis of LCTRSs and SMT solvers are heavily used during the analysis. In order for SMT solving to not form a bottleneck some care is needed. Again, each different analysis method is equipped with its own SMT solver instance started at the beginning of the analysis. Afterwards such an instance runs until the method has finished. In between, it waits for SMT queries, hence we avoid several restarts of this instance. Constraints are modeled as regular terms of sort boolean and can be checked for satisfiability and validity. Each of those checks runs in its own context (using push and pop commands) in order to avoid any interference with previous queries. Currently crest utilizes Z3 [30] as the default SMT solver, as it turned out to be the most reliable during development. Nevertheless, crest provides the (experimental) possibility to use Yices [10] and CVC5 [6].

Confluence. The computation of constrained critical pairs follows the definition and constrained parallel critical pairs are computed in a bottom up fashion by collecting all possible combinations of parallel steps. Then the various methods to conclude confluence are applied on those pairs. If a method fails on a constrained critical pair then, using Definition 2, the constrained critical pair is split. The logical constraint used in splitting is taken from a matching rule. The various methods run concurrently in order to prevent starvation of methods because of pending SMT solver queries. The first method which succeeds returns the result and all others, including their SMT solver instances, are terminated. We adopt heuristics to bound the number of rewrite steps in the closing sequences. The method that posed the biggest challenge to automation is the 2-parallel closedness [35, Definition 11] needed for (C6) as we cannot simply use an arbitrary parallel step starting from the right-hand side but need to synthesize a parallel step over a set of parallel positions that adheres to the variable condition present in the definition.

Termination. The choices in the parameters of the subterm criterion (T5) and the recursive path order (T2) are modeled in the SMT encoding. Similarly, for the value criterion (T3) first all possible projections are computed. Then an SMT encoding based on the given rules and theory is constructed and a model of the encoding (if it exists) delivers suitable projections that establish termination. An explicit boolean flag in the SMT encoding determines if a strict or weak decrease is achieved. The special variant with projections to suitable linear combinations (T6) encodes this by attaching unknown constants to the projected arguments and summing them up. Those unknowns are then determined by the SMT solver. The (special) value criterion is currently restricted to the theory of integers as suitable well-founded orderings are required. For the integer theory we use $n \succ m$ if $n > m \wedge n \geqslant 0$ holds.

Method (T4) receives a DP problem as input and tries to transform it into a smaller one by orienting strictly as many dependency pairs as possible. It is parameterized by a list of termination methods which are applied on the DP problem. The first one which succeeds determines the remaining problem to be solved. Before trying to solve the latter, (T1) is used to decompose it into smaller problems.

Features. Via the command-line arguments several features of crest can be accessed. This includes control over the number of threads in the concurrent setup, the overall timeout of the analysis, or if proof output and debug output should be printed. Furthermore, (parallel) critical pairs or the dependency graph approximation of a given LCTRS problem can be computed. The interface also offers a way to transform an LCTRS into a fully sorted LCTRS in the ARI format. In order to alter the default strategy for the analysis, crest offers a very basic strategy language to specify which methods should be used. Detailed information is provided in the usage information of the supplemented artifact.

5   Improving the Analysis via Transformations

In this section we present new transformations which are especially useful for confluence analysis. These transformations operate on either rules or constrained critical pairs and split or unify those based on their constraints.

Splitting Constrained Critical Pairs

If a constrained critical pair has more than one instance, which is almost always the case, and they cannot all be rewritten by a single rule, then we are not able to perform any rewrite step. To overcome this problem we propose a simple method to split constrained critical pairs.

Definition 2. *Given an LCTRS $\mathcal{R}$, a constrained critical pair $\rho: s \approx t\ [\varphi] \in \mathsf{CCP}(\mathcal{R})$ and a constraint $\psi \in \mathcal{T}(\mathcal{F}_{th}, \mathsf{Var}(\varphi))$, the set $\mathsf{CCP}(\mathcal{R})_\rho^\psi$ is defined as*
$(\mathsf{CCP}(\mathcal{R}) \setminus \{\rho\}) \cup \{s \approx t\ [\varphi \wedge \psi], s \approx t\ [\varphi \wedge \neg\psi]\}$.

The following key lemma states that after splitting critical pairs, all confluence methods are still available. The proof is given in the appendix of [37].

Lemma 2. *If $t\ _\mathcal{R}\leftarrow s \rightarrow_\mathcal{R} u$ then $t \downarrow_\mathcal{R} u$ or $t \leftrightarrow_{\mathsf{CCP}_\rho^\psi(\mathcal{R})} u$.*

We illustrate the lemma on the LCTRS in Example 3.

Example 5. Consider the CCP $\mathsf{g}(x) \approx \mathsf{h}(x)\ [\varphi]$ with $\varphi: x \geqslant 1 \wedge x \leqslant 2$ from Example 3. It is neither in normal form nor trivial. Since the subterm $\mathsf{g}(x)$ matches the left-hand side of the rule $\mathsf{g}(x) \rightarrow \mathsf{a}\ [x = 1]$ (which is how crest renders the rule $\mathsf{g}(1) \rightarrow \mathsf{a}$), and the combined constraint $\varphi \wedge x = 1$ is satisfiable, the CCP is split into

$$\mathsf{g}(x) \approx \mathsf{h}(x)\ [\varphi \wedge x = 1] \quad \text{and} \quad \mathsf{g}(x) \approx \mathsf{h}(x)\ [\varphi \wedge x \neq 1]$$

The left one rewrites to the trivial constrained equation $\mathsf{a} \approx \mathsf{a}\ [\varphi \wedge x = 1]$ using the rules $\mathsf{g}(x) \rightarrow \mathsf{a}\ [x = 1]$ and $\mathsf{h}(x) \rightarrow \mathsf{a}\ [x \leqslant 1]$. The right one is rewritten to $b \approx b \; [\varphi \wedge x \neq 1]$ using the rules $g(x) \to b \; [x \leqslant 2]$ and $h(x) \to b \; [x > 1]$. Hence the LCTRS $\mathcal{R}$ is locally confluent by Lemma 2. Using RPO with the precedence $f > g > h > a > b > c$, termination of $\mathcal{R}$ is easily shown and hence $\mathcal{R}$ is confluent.

The following example shows that constrained critical pairs may be split infinitely often before local confluence can be verified.

Example 6. Consider the LCTRS $\mathcal{R}$ over the theory Ints consisting of the rules

$$
\begin{array}{ll}
a \to f(n) \; [n \geqslant 0] & a \to g(n) \; [n \geqslant 0] \\
f(n) \to b \quad\; [n = 0] & g(n) \to b \quad\; [n = 0] \\
f(n) \to f(m) \; [n > 0 \wedge 2 * m = n] & g(n) \to g(m) \; [n > 0 \wedge 2 * m = n] \\
f(n) \to f(m) \; [n > 0 \wedge 2 * m + 1 = n] & g(n) \to g(m) \; [n > 0 \wedge 2 * m + 1 = n]
\end{array}
$$

This LCTRS has a constrained critical pair $f(n) \approx g(m) \; [n \geqslant 0 \wedge m \geqslant 0 \wedge n = n \wedge m = m]$ originating from a. To show confluence of $\mathcal{R}$ we would need to split the pair in order to make rules applicable for joining a specific instance. However, there are infinitely many instances with pairwise different joining sequences.

The next example shows that splitting also helps to prove non-confluence.

Example 7. Consider the LCTRS $\mathcal{R}$ in Example 3. By changing the constraint of the rule $f(x) \to g(x) \; [x \geqslant 1]$ to $[x \geqslant 0]$ we obtain a non-confluent LCTRS. This is shown by splitting the constrained critical pair $g(x) \approx h(x) \; [x \geqslant 0 \wedge x \leqslant 2]$, and subsequently showing that $g(x) \approx h(x) \; [x < 1 \wedge x \geqslant 0 \wedge x \leqslant 2]$ rewrites to the non-trivial normal form $c \approx a \; [x < 1 \wedge x \geqslant 0 \wedge x \leqslant 2]$.

Merging Constrained Rewrite Rules

Next we discuss the merging of constrained rewrite rules. The idea here is that rewrite steps may become possible after merging similar rules.

Definition 3. *Let $\rho_i \colon \ell_i \to r_i \; [\varphi_i]$ for $i = 1, 2$ be variable-disjoint rewrite rules in an LCTRS $\mathcal{R}$. Suppose there exists a renaming σ such that $\ell_1 = \ell_2\sigma$, $r_1 = r_2\sigma$ and $\mathcal{V}\text{ar}(\varphi_1) = \mathcal{V}\text{ar}(\varphi_2\sigma)$. The LCTRS $\mathcal{R}_{\rho_1}^{\rho_2}$ is defined as*

$$
(\mathcal{R} \setminus \{\rho_1, \rho_2\}) \cup \{\ell_1 \to r_1 \; [\varphi_1 \vee \varphi_2\sigma]\}
$$

The easy proof of the following lemma is omitted.

Lemma 3. *The relations $\to_{\mathcal{R}}$ and $\to_{\mathcal{R}_{\rho_1}^{\rho_2}}$ coincide.*

Example 8. The LCTRS $\mathcal{R}$ over the theory Ints consisting of the rewrite rules

$$
\begin{array}{lll}
f(x) \to 2 \quad\; [1 \leqslant x \wedge x \leqslant 3] & g(x) \to h(x) & h(x) \to y \; [x = 2 \wedge y = x] \\
f(x) \to g(x) \; [2 \leqslant x \wedge x \leqslant 4] & & h(x) \to y \; [x = 3 \wedge y = 2]
\end{array}
$$

admits the constrained critical pair $2 \approx g(x)$ $[1 \leqslant x \wedge x \leqslant 3 \wedge 2 \leqslant x \wedge x \leqslant 4]$. After rewriting the subterm $g(x)$ to $h(x)$, no further step is possible because the rewrite rules for h are not applicable. However, if we merge the two rules for h into

$$h(x) \rightarrow y \, [(x = 2 \wedge y = x) \vee (x = 3 \wedge y = 2)]$$

we can proceed as $1 \leqslant x \wedge x \leqslant 3 \wedge 2 \leqslant x \wedge x \leqslant 4$ implies $((x = 2 \wedge y = x) \vee (x = 3 \wedge y = 2))\sigma$ for $\sigma(y) = 2$. This is exactly how crest operates.

6 Experimental Evaluation

In this section we show the progress of crest since the start of its development in early 2023. Initial experiments of an early prototype of crest were reported in [34]. In the following tables the prototype of [34] is denoted by prototype. Since then more criteria for (non-)confluence and termination were added, and parts of the tool infrastructure were completely revised. Detailed results are available from the website of crest and the artifact of the experiments at the Zenodo repository [36].

All experiments were performed using the benchexec[11] benchmarking framework which is also used in the StarExec cluster. The benchmark hardware consists of several Intel Xeon E5-2650 v4 CPUs having a base clock speed of 2.20GHz, amounting in total to 64 cores and 128 GB of RAM. As benchmarks we use the problems in the new ARI database[12] in addition to the examples from this paper.

Tool Setup. Each tool receives an ARI benchmark as input and should return either "YES" (property was proved), "NO" (property was disproved) or "MAYBE" (don't know) as the first line of its output. In the tables we represent those with ✓, ✗ and ?, respectively. The fourth category depicted by † denotes that the translation from the ARI format to the input format of the respective tool failed. In order to have a realistic setup, a tool has 4 cores including 8 GB of RAM available for each run. Each tool has 60 seconds to solve a problem before it is killed. Since we have no information about how many threads the other tools use, in the experiments we use CPU time over wall-clock time in order to have a fair comparison.

Our tool crest is split into different binaries depending on the analysis. The most important ones are crest-cr for confluence and crest-sn for termination. We use those two including an additional flag to allow at most 8 threads for the concurrent setup. The default strategy for confluence uses all methods concurrently and where specific methods are tested we restrict to those using our strategy flag. For the default termination setup we use reduction pairs including

---

[11] https://github.com/sosy-lab/benchexec/
[12] https://ari-cops.uibk.ac.at/ARI/

Table 1. Confluence analysis of examples.

tool	1	2	3	6	7	8
crest	✓	✓	✓	?	✗	✓
CRaris	?	?	?	?	?	?
Ctrl	✓	?	?	?	?	?
prototype	✓	✓	?	?	?	?

dependency graph analysis, recursive path order, (special) value criterion and subterm criterion.

Cora, Ctrl and the prototype of [34] do not accept the ARI format as input. We have developed transformation tools which (try to) transform an ARI benchmark into their respective input. This might not always be possible, hence the transformation tool might fail, which is the reason why we do not distinguish tool (parse) errors from "MAYBE".

Examples. In Table 1 we compare the LCTRS confluence tools on the examples in this paper. crest only fails on Example 6, which is a confluent LCTRS, but for which no automatable method is known.

Confluence Competition. The last (2024) Confluence Competition[13] hosted the first LCTRS category, with crest and CRaris as participants. The former achieved 67 confluence and 26 non-confluence proofs on a total of 100 selected problems from the ARI database. CRaris, which does not (yet) implement techniques for non-confluence achieved 54 confluence proofs. Currently, crest is the only tool utilizing a criterion for non-confluence of LCTRSs.

Confluence. All confluence criteria implemented in crest, except (C2), require left-linearity. For (C3) right-linearity is also required. Left- and right-linearity is checked only on the non-logical variables. Table 2 presents a summary of the confluence methods implemented in crest. The full set of benchmarks consists

---

[13] https://project-coco.uibk.ac.at/2024/index.php

```
(format LCTRS :smtlib 2.6)
(theory Ints)
(fun f (-> Int Int))
(fun g (-> Int Int Int))
(fun a Int)
(rule (f a) (g 4 4))
(rule a (g (+ 1 1) (+ 3 1)))
(rule (g x y) (f (g z y)) :guard (= z (- x 2)))
```

Fig. 2. ARI file 1529 (without sort annotations and meta information).

Table 2. Confluence analysis using methods in crest on 107 LCTRSs.

criterion	solved	time (AVG)	time (total)
termination and joinable critical pairs (C2)	50	4.55 s	487 s
orthogonality (C1)	62	0.10 s	11 s
weak orthogonality (C1)	65	0.12 s	13 s
strongly closed critical pairs (C3)	56	1.21 s	129 s
parallel closed critical pairs (C4)	66	0.44 s	47 s
almost parallel closed critical pairs (C4)	70	11.03 s	1180 s
development closed critical pairs (C5)	66	0.39 s	42 s
almost development closed critical pairs (C5)	71	2.06 s	220 s
parallel closed parallel critical pairs (C6)	71	13.93 s	1490 s
all confluence methods (C1)–(C6)	72	8.40 s	899 s
non-confluence (Lemma 1)	26	1.96 s	210 s
methods (C1)–(C6) + (Lemma 1)	98	1.84 s	197 s
total solved	98	—	—

of the 107 problems in the ARI database. crest can prove in a full run with all methods enabled 72 confluent and 26 non-confluent. Of the remaining 9 problems, 2 result in "MAYBE" and 7 in a timeout. Interesting to observe is that (almost) development closedness is way faster than (almost) parallel closedness, which may be due to the fact that less multi-steps than parallel steps are needed to turn a constrained critical pair into a trivial one. The number 72 is explained by the fact that (C5) and (C6) are incomparable: (C5) succeeds on the problem in Fig. 1 but fails on the one in Fig. 2, while the opposite holds for (C6).

In Table 3 we compare all confluence tools on the same 107 LCTRS problems. Ctrl supports only weak orthogonality and CRaris in addition the Knuth–Bendix criterion. Overall crest is able to solve 92 % of the LCTRS problems in the current ARI database and this percentage is reached even if the timeout is restricted to

Table 3. Confluence analysis of LCTRS tools on 107 LCTRSs.

tool	✓	✗	?	†	solved	time (AVG)	time (total)
CRaris	58	0	49	—	54 %	0.13 s	14 s
crest	72	26	9	—	92 %	1.84 s	197 s
Ctrl	54	0	49	4	50 %	0.17 s	18 s
prototype	67	0	37	3	63 %	1.14 s	122 s
total solved	72	26	—	—	92 %	—	—

Table 4. Termination analysis using methods in crest on 107 LCTRSs.

method	solved	time (AVG)	time (total)
DP graph (T1)	9	0.08 s	9 s
recursive path order (T2)	27	0.11 s	12 s
recursive path order (T1), (T2)	28	0.11 s	12 s
subterm criterion (T1), (T5)	12	0.12 s	13 s
value criterion (T1), (T3)	34	0.13 s	14 s
special value criterion (T1), (T6)	70	0.12 s	13 s
reduction pairs no SVC (T1)–(T5)	37	0.14 s	15 s
default (T1)–(T6)	74	0.15 s	16 s
total solved	74	—	—

10 seconds. The prototype of [34] supports the methods (C1), (C3), (C4) and proves 67 (63 %) confluent within 122 seconds.

Termination. In Table 4 we compare the different termination methods in crest. The "dependency graph" method corresponds to (T1) with a check for the absence of SCCs, "recursive path order" corresponds to (T2), "subterm criterion" to (T5), "(special) value criterion" to (T3) ((T6)) and "reduction pairs" to (T4). The methods annotated with (T1) work on DP problems and are applied after an initial dependency graph analysis. The method "reduction pairs no SVC" uses (T2), (T3) and (T5) and "default" includes additionally (T6). The latter constitutes the current default setup in crest.

We continue the evaluation by comparing crest to other termination tools for LCTRSs. For this comparison we use the higher-order tool Cora and Ctrl. The experiments in Table 5 show that the tools are comparable in strength on the LCTRS benchmarks in the ARI database, which is not that surprising as the implemented methods are similar. All tools together prove 73 % of the LCTRSs in the ARI database terminating. All those tools fail on the bit vector problem in Fig. 3 whereas CRaris is able to prove termination (Naoki Nishida, personal

Table 5. Termination analysis of LCTRS tools on 107 LCTRSs.

tool	✓	?	†	solved	time (AVG)	time (total)
Cora	71	30	6	66 %	2.47 s	264 s
crest	74	33	—	69 %	0.15 s	16 s
Ctrl	74	29	4	69 %	0.96 s	103 s
total solved	78	—	—	73 %	—	—

```
(format LCTRS :smtlib 2.6)
(theory FixedSizeBitVectors)
(fun cnt (-> (_ BitVec 4) (_ BitVec 4)))
(fun u1 (-> (_ BitVec 4) (_ BitVec 4) (_ BitVec 4) (_ BitVec 4)))
(rule (cnt x) (u1 x #b0000 #b0000) )
(rule (u1 x i z) (u1 x (bvadd i #b0001) (bvadd z #b0001))
  :guard (bvult i x)))
(rule (u1 x i z) z :guard (not (bvult i x))))
```

Fig. 3. ARI file 1605 (without sort annotations and meta information).

communication). A fork of the official version of Ctrl[14] implements the technique of [33] for non-termination of LCTRSs. Initial experiments reveal that it succeeds to prove non-termination of 8 problems in Table 5.

Term Rewrite Systems. In the final experiment we compare crest with the state-of-the-art in automated confluence proving for TRSs. After parsing an input TRS, crest attaches a single sort to all function symbols and variables, and adds an empty constraint to all rules. At this point the TRS can be analyzed as an LCTRS. We compare crest to the latest winner of the TRS category in the Confluence Competition, CSI [32], on the 566 TRS benchmarks in the ARI database. The results can be seen in Table 6. Keeping in mind that there is some overhead in the analysis of crest on TRSs as all its methods are geared towards the constrained setting, the 31 % mark is not a bad result. Here it is important to note that CSI has been actively developed over a ten-year period and utilizes many more confluence methods—there is several decades of research on confluence analysis of TRSs while LCTRS confluence analysis is still in its infancy.

7   Conclusion and Future Work

In this paper we presented crest, an open-source tool for automatically proving (non-)confluence and termination of LCTRSs. Detailed experiments were provided to show the power of crest.

---

[14] https://github.com/bytekid/ctrl

Table 6. Confluence analysis of crest and CSI on 566 TRSs.

tool	✓	✗	?	solved	time (AVG)	time (total)
crest	100	73	393	31 %	15.87 s	8980 s
CSI	259	192	115	80 %	6.25 s	3540 s
total solved	259	192	—	80 %	—	—

```
(format LCTRS :smtlib 2.6)
(theory Reals)
(fun sumroot (-> Real Real))
(fun sqrt (-> Real Real))
(rule (sumroot x) 0.0 :guard (>= 0.0 x))
(rule (sumroot x) (+ (sqrt x) (sumroot  (- x 1.0))))
  :guard (not (>= 0.0 x)))
```

Fig. 4. ARI file 1549 (without meta information).

In order to further strengthen the (non-)confluence analysis in crest we plan to adapt powerful methods like order-sorted decomposition [12] and redundant rules [31, 38] for plain term rewriting to the constrained setting. Labeling techniques [41] are also on the agenda. The same holds for termination analysis. Natural candidates are matrix interpretations [11] as well as the higher-order methods in [14]. Especially termination problems on real values, like the one in Fig. 4, should be supported in future. Also non-termination analysis of LCTRSs [33] is of interest. Completion, which is supported in Ctrl [39], is another topic for a future release of crest. In a recent paper [2] the semantics of LCTRSs is investigated. In that context, concepts like checking consistency of constrained theories are relevant, which are worthy to investigate from an automation viewpoint.

Since constrained rewriting is highly complex [35, Section 3], a formalization of the implemented techniques in a proof assistant like Isabelle/HOL is important. The recent advances in the formalization and subsequent certification of advanced confluence techniques [16, 21, 22] for plain rewriting in connection with the transformation in [35, Section 4] make this a realistic goal.

Finally, to improve the user experience we aim at a convenient web interface and a richer command-line strategy.

Code and Availability Statement. The source code and data that support the contributions of this work are freely available in the Zenodo repository "crest - Constrained REwriting Software Tool: Artifact for TACAS 2025" at https://doi.org/10.5281/zenodo.13969852 [36]. The authors confirm that the data supporting the findings of this study are available within the paper and the artifact.

Acknowledgments. We thank Fabian Mitterwallner for valuable discussions on automation. We are grateful to the authors of the tools used in the experiments for their help in obtaining executables and useful insights about their usage. The insightful comments and suggestions provided by the reviewers greatly improved the presentation of the paper.

Disclosure of Interests. The authors have no competing interests to declare that are relevant to the content of this article.

References

1. Aoto, T., Hirokawa, N., Kim, D., Kojima, M., Middeldorp, A., Mitterwallner, F., Nishida, N., Saito, T., Schöpf, J., Shintani, K., Thiemann, R., Yamada, A.: A new format for rewrite systems. In: Proc. 12th International Workshop on Confluence. pp. 32–37 (2023), available at http://cl-informatik.uibk.ac.at/iwc/iwc2023.pdf
2. Aoto, T., Nishida, N., Schöpf, J.: Equational theories and validity for logically constrained term rewriting. In: Rehof, J. (ed.) Proc. 9th International Conference on Formal Structures for Computation and Deduction. Leibniz International Proceedings in Informatics, vol. 299, pp. 31:1–31:21 (2024). https://doi.org/10.4230/LIPIcs.FSCD.2024.31
3. Arts, T., Giesl, J.: Termination of term rewriting using dependency pairs. Theoretical Computer Science **236**, 133–178 (2000). https://doi.org/10.1016/S0304-3975(99)00207-8
4. Avanzini, M., Moser, G., Schaper, M.: TcT: Tyrolean Complexity Tool. In: Chechik, M., Raskin, J.F. (eds.) Proc. 22nd International Conference on Tools and Algorithms for the Construction and Analysis of Systems. Lecture Notes in Computer Science, vol. 9636, pp. 407–423 (2016). https://doi.org/10.1007/978-3-662-49674-9_24
5. Baader, F., Nipkow, T.: Term Rewriting and All That. Cambridge University Press (1998). https://doi.org/10.1017/CBO9781139172752
6. Barbosa, H., Barrett, C.W., Brain, M., Kremer, G., Lachnitt, H., Mann, M., Mohamed, A., Mohamed, M., Niemetz, A., Nötzli, A., Ozdemir, A., Preiner, M., Reynolds, A., Sheng, Y., Tinelli, C., Zohar, Y.: cvc5: A versatile and industrial-strength SMT solver. In: Fisman, D., Rosu, G. (eds.) Proc. 28th International Conference on Tools and Algorithms for the Construction and Analysis of Systems. Lecture Notes in Computer Science, vol. 13243, pp. 415–442 (2022). https://doi.org/10.1007/978-3-030-99524-9_24
7. Ciobâcă, S., Lucanu, D., Buruiană, A.S.: Operationally-based program equivalence proofs using LCTRSs. Journal of Logical and Algebraic Methods in Programming **135**, 100894 (2023). https://doi.org/10.1016/j.jlamp.2023.100894
8. Ciobâcă, S., Lucanu, D.: A coinductive approach to proving reachability properties in logically constrained term rewriting systems. In: Galmiche, D., Schulz, S., Sebastiani, R. (eds.) Proc. 9th International Joint Conference on Automated Reasoning. Lecture Notes in Artificial Intelligence, vol. 10900, pp. 295–311 (2018). https://doi.org/10.1007/978-3-319-94205-6_20
9. Dershowitz, N.: Orderings for term-rewriting systems. Theoretical Computer Science **17**(3), 279–301 (1982). https://doi.org/10.1016/0304-3975(82)90026-3
10. Dutertre, B.: Yices 2.2. In: Biere, A., Bloem, R. (eds.) Proc. 26th International Conference on Computer Aided Verification. Lecture Notes in Computer Science, vol. 8559, pp. 737–744 (2014). https://doi.org/10.1007/978-3-319-08867-9_49
11. Endrullis, J., Waldmann, J., Zantema, H.: Matrix interpretations for proving termination of term rewriting. Journal of Automated Reasoning **40**(2-3), 195–220 (2007). https://doi.org/10.1007/s10817-007-9087-9
12. Felgenhauer, B., Middeldorp, A., Zankl, H., van Oostrom, V.: Layer systems for proving confluence. ACM Transactions on Computational Logic **16**(2:14), 1–32 (2015). https://doi.org/10.1145/2710017
13. Fuhs, C., Kop, C., Nishida, N.: Verifying procedural programs via constrained rewriting induction. ACM Transactions on Computational Logic **18**(2), 14:1–14:50 (2017). https://doi.org/10.1145/3060143

14. Guo, L., Hagens, K., Kop, C., Vale, D.: Higher-order constrained dependency pairs for (universal) computability. In: Královič, R., Kučera, A. (eds.) Proc. 49th International Symposium on Mathematical Foundations of Computer Science. Leibniz International Proceedings in Informatics, vol. 306, pp. 57:1–57:15 (2024). https://doi.org/10.4230/LIPIcs.MFCS.2024.57

15. Guo, L., Kop, C.: Higher-order LCTRSs and their termination. In: Weirich, S. (ed.) Proc. 33rd European Symposium on Programming. Lecture Notes in Computer Science, vol. 14577, pp. 331–357 (2024). https://doi.org/10.1007/978-3-031-57267-8_13

16. Hirokawa, N., Kim, D., Shintani, K., Thiemann, R.: Certification of confluence-and commutation-proofs via parallel critical pairs. In: Timany, A., Traytel, D., Pientka, B., Blazy, S. (eds.) Proc. 13th ACM SIGPLAN International Conference on Certified Programs and Proofs. pp. 147–161. ACM (2024). https://doi.org/10.1145/3636501.3636949

17. Hirokawa, N., Middeldorp, A.: Dependency pairs revisited. In: van Oostrom, V. (ed.) Proc. 15th International Conference on Rewriting Techniques and Applications. Lecture Notes in Computer Science, vol. 3091, pp. 249–268 (2004). https://doi.org/10.1007/978-3-540-25979-4_18

18. Jouannaud, J.P., Rubio, A.: The higher-order recursive path ordering. In: Proc. 14th Annual ACM/IEEE Symposium on Logic in Computer Science. pp. 402–411 (1999). https://doi.org/10.1109/LICS.1999.782635

19. Jürgen, Thiemann, R., Schneider-Kamp, P.: The dependency pair framework: Combining techniques for automated termination proofs. In: Baader, F., Voronkov, A. (eds.) Proc. 11th International Conference on Logic for Programming, Artificial Intelligence, and Reasoning. Lecture Notes in Computer Science, vol. 3452, pp. 301–331 (2005). https://doi.org/10.1007/978-3-540-32275-7_21

20. Knuth, D.E., Bendix, P.B.: Simple word problems in universal algebras. In: Computational Problems in Abstract Algebra, pp. 263–297. Pergamon Press (1970). https://doi.org/10.1016/B978-0-08-012975-4.50028-X

21. Kohl, C., Middeldorp, A.: A formalization of the development closedness criterion for left-linear term rewrite systems. In: Krebbers, R., Traytel, D., Pientka, B., Zdancewic, S. (eds.) Proc. 12th ACM SIGPLAN International Conference on Certified Programs and Proofs. pp. 197–210 (2023). https://doi.org/10.1145/3573105.3575667

22. Kohl, C., Middeldorp, A.: Formalizing almost development closed critical pairs. In: Naumowicz, A., Thiemann, R. (eds.) Proc. 14th International Conference on Interactive Theorem Proving. Leibniz International Proceedings in Informatics, vol. 268, pp. 38:1–38:8 (2023). https://doi.org/10.4230/LIPIcs.ITP.2023.38

23. Kojima, M., Nishida, N.: From starvation freedom to all-path reachability problems in constrained rewriting. In: Hanus, M., Inclezan, D. (eds.) Proc. 25th International Symposium on Practical Aspects of Declarative Languages. Lecture Notes in Computer Science, vol. 13880, pp. 161–179 (2023). https://doi.org/10.1007/978-3-031-24841-2_11

24. Kop, C.: Termination of LCTRSs. CoRR **abs/1601.03206** (2016). https://doi.org/10.48550/ARXIV.1601.03206

25. Kop, C., Nishida, N.: Term rewriting with logical constraints. In: Fontaine, P., Ringeissen, C., Schmidt, R.A. (eds.) Proc. 9th International Symposium on Frontiers of Combining Systems. Lecture Notes in Artificial Intelligence, vol. 8152, pp. 343–358 (2013). https://doi.org/10.1007/978-3-642-40885-4_24

26. Kop, C., Nishida, N.: Automatic constrained rewriting induction towards verifying procedural programs. In: Garrigue, J. (ed.) Proc. 12th Asian Symposium on Programming Languages and Systems. Lecture Notes in Computer Science, vol. 8858, pp. 334–353 (2014). https://doi.org/10.1007/978-3-319-12736-1_18

27. Kop, C., Nishida, N.: Constrained Term Rewriting tooL. In: Davis, M., Fehnker, A., McIver, A., Voronkov, A. (eds.) Proc. 20th International Conference on Logic for Programming, Artificial Intelligence, and Reasoning. Lecture Notes in Artificial Intelligence, vol. 9450, pp. 549–557 (2015). https://doi.org/10.1007/978-3-662-48899-7_38

28. Kusakari, K., Sakai, M.: Enhancing dependency pair method using strong computability in simply-typed term rewriting. Applicable Algebra in Engineering, Communication and Computing **18**(5), 407–431 (2007). https://doi.org/10.1007/S00200-007-0046-9

29. Matsumi, A., Nishida, N., Kojima, M., Shin, D.: On singleton self-loop removal for termination of LCTRSs with bit-vector arithmetic. CoRR **abs/2307.14094** (2023). https://doi.org/10.48550/arXiv.2307.14094

30. de Moura, L., Bjørner, N.: Z3: An efficient SMT solver. In: Ramakrishnan, C.R., Rehof, J. (eds.) Proc. 14th International Conference on Tools and Algorithms for the Construction and Analysis of Systems. Lecture Notes in Computer Science, vol. 4963, pp. 337–340 (2008). https://doi.org/10.1007/978-3-540-78800-3_24

31. Nagele, J., Felgenhauer, B., Middeldorp, A.: Improving automatic confluence analysis of rewrite systems by redundant rules. In: Fernández, M. (ed.) Proc. 26th International Conference on Rewriting Techniques and Applications. Leibniz International Proceedings in Informatics, vol. 36, pp. 257–268 (2015). https://doi.org/10.4230/LIPIcs.RTA.2015.257

32. Nagele, J., Felgenhauer, B., Middeldorp, A.: CSI: New evidence — a progress report. In: de Moura, L. (ed.) Proc. 26th International Conference on Automated Deduction. Lecture Notes in Artificial Intelligence, vol. 10395, pp. 385–397 (2017). https://doi.org/10.1007/978-3-319-63046-5_24

33. Nishida, N., Winkler, S.: Loop detection by logically constrained term rewriting. In: Piskac, R., Rümmer, P. (eds.) Proc. 10th International Conference on Verified Software: Theories, Tools, and Experiments. Lecture Notes in Computer Science, vol. 11294, pp. 309–321 (2018). https://doi.org/10.1007/978-3-030-03592-1_18

34. Schöpf, J., Middeldorp, A.: Confluence criteria for logically constrained rewrite systems. In: Pientka, B., Tinelli, C. (eds.) Proc. 29th International Conference on Automated Deduction. Lecture Notes in Artificial Intelligence, vol. 14132, pp. 474–490 (2023). https://doi.org/10.1007/978-3-031-38499-8_27

35. Schöpf, J., Mitterwallner, F., Middeldorp, A.: Confluence of logically constrained rewrite systems revisited. In: Benzmüller, C., Heule, M.J., Schmidt, R.A. (eds.) Proc. 12th International Joint Conference on Automated Reasoning. Lecture Notes in Artificial Intelligence, vol. 14740, pp. 298–316 (2024). https://doi.org/10.1007/978-3-031-63501-4_16

36. Schöpf, J., Middeldorp, A.: crest - Constrained REwriting Software Tool: Artifact for TACAS 2025 (Oct 2024). https://doi.org/10.5281/zenodo.13969852

37. Schöpf, J., Middeldorp, A.: Automated analysis of logically constrained rewrite systems using crest. CoRR **abs/2501.05240** (2025). https://doi.org/10.48550/arXiv.2501.05240

38. Shintani, K., Hirokawa, N.: Compositional confluence criteria. Logical Methods in Computer Science **20**(1) (2024). https://doi.org/10.46298/lmcs-20(1:6)2024

39. Winkler, S., Middeldorp, A.: Completion for logically constrained rewriting. In: Kirchner, H. (ed.) Proc. 3rd International Conference on Formal Structures for Computation and Deduction. Leibniz International Proceedings in Informatics, vol. 108, pp. 30:1–30:18 (2018). https://doi.org/10.4230/LIPIcs.FSCD.2018.30
40. Winkler, S., Moser, G.: Runtime complexity analysis of logically constrained rewriting. In: Fernández, M. (ed.) Proc. 30th International Symposium on Logic-Based Program Synthesis and Transformation. Lecture Notes in Computer Science, vol. 12561, pp. 37–55 (2021). https://doi.org/10.1007/978-3-030-68446-4_2
41. Zankl, H., Felgenhauer, B., Middeldorp, A.: Labelings for decreasing diagrams. Journal of Automated Reasoning **54**(2), 101–133 (2015). https://doi.org/10.1007/s10817-014-9316-y

Multiparty Session Typing, Embedded

Sung-Shik Jongmans(✉)🄳

University of Groningen, Groningen, The Netherlands
s.s.t.q.jongmans@rug.nl

Abstract. Multiparty session typing (MPST) is a method to make concurrent programming simpler. The idea is to use type checking to automatically detect safety and liveness violations of implementations relative to specifications. In practice, the premier approach to combine MPST with mainstream languages—in the absence of native support—is based on *external DSLs* and associated tooling.
In contrast, we study the question of how to support MPST by using *internal DSLs*. Answering this question positively, this paper presents the mpst.embedded library: it leverages Scala's lightweight form of dependent typing, called match types, to embed MPST directly into Scala. Our internal-DSL-based approach avoids programming friction and leaky abstractions of the external-DSL-based approach for MPST.

1 Introduction

Background With the advent of multicore processors, multithreaded programming—a notoriously error-prone enterprise—has become increasingly important.

Because of this, mainstream languages have started to offer core support for higher-level *communication* primitives besides lower-level *synchronisation* primitives (e.g., Clojure, Go, Kotlin, Rust). The idea has been to add *message passing* as an abstraction for *shared memory*, as—supposedly—*channels* are easier to use than *locks*. Yet, empirical research shows that "message passing does not necessarily make multithreaded programs less error-prone than shared memory" [33].

One of the core challenges is as follows: given a specification S of the *communication protocols* that an implementation I should fulfil, how to prove that I is *safe* and *live* relative to S? Safety means "bad" communication actions never happen: if a communication action happens in I, then it is allowed to happen by S. Liveness means "good" communication actions eventually happen.

Multiparty session typing (MPST) MPST [16] is a method to automatically prove safety and liveness of communication protocol implementations relative to specifications. The idea is to write specifications as *behavioural types* [1, 19] against which implementations are type-checked. Formally, the central theorem is that well-typedness at compile-time implies safety and liveness at run-time. Over the past 10–15 years, much progress has been made, including the development of many tools to combine MPST with mainstream languages (e.g., F# [29], F⋆ [36], Go [5], Java [17,18], OCaml [20], Rust [26,27], Scala [2,6,12,30], and TypeScript [28]). Fig. 1 visualises the idea behind MPST in more detail:

© The Author(s) 2025
A. Gurfinkel and M. Heule (Eds.): TACAS 2025, LNCS 15696, pp. 145–164, 2025.
https://doi.org/10.1007/978-3-031-90643-5_8

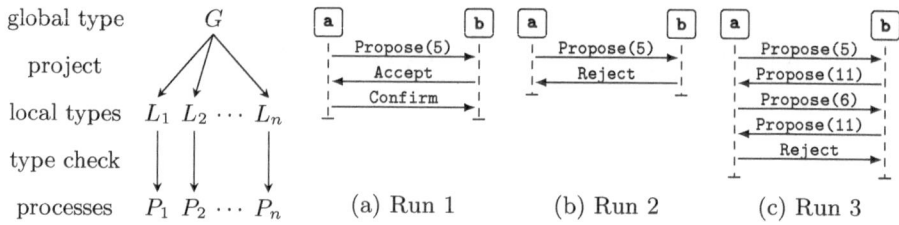

global type G

project

local types $L_1\ L_2 \cdots L_n$

type check

processes $P_1\ P_2 \cdots P_n$ (a) Run 1   (b) Run 2   (c) Run 3

Fig. 1: MPST   Fig. 2: A few possible runs of the Negotiation protocol

1. First, a protocol among roles $r_1, \ldots, r_n$ is implemented as a session of processes $P_1, \ldots, P_n$ (concrete), while it is specified as a *global type* G (abstract). The global type models the behaviour of all processes together.
2. Next, G is decomposed into local types $L_1, \ldots, L_n$ by *projecting* G onto each role. Each local type models the behaviour of one process alone.
3. Last, safety and liveness are verified by *type-checking* each P_i against L_i.

Example 1. The *Negotiation* protocol, originally defined in the MPST literature by Neykova et al. [29], consists of roles *Alice* and *Bob*. Fig. 2 shows three possible runs. First, a proposal is communicated from Alice to Bob. Next, its acceptance, rejection, or a counter-proposal is communicated from Bob to Alice. Next:

- In case of an acceptance, a confirmation is communicated from Alice to Bob.
- In case of a rejection, the protocol ends.
- In case of a counter-proposal, its acceptance, rejection, or another counter-proposal is communicated from Alice to Bob. And so on.

The following recursive **global type** specifies the protocol:

$$G = \mathbf{a} \rightarrow \mathbf{b}:\texttt{Propose(Int)}.\mu X.\mathbf{b} \rightarrow \mathbf{a}: \begin{cases} \texttt{Accept}.\mathbf{a} \rightarrow \mathbf{b}:\texttt{Confirm}.\checkmark \\ \texttt{Reject}.\checkmark \\ \texttt{Propose}.\mathbf{a} \rightarrow \mathbf{b}: \begin{cases} \texttt{Accept}.\mathbf{b} \rightarrow \mathbf{a}:\texttt{Confirm}.\checkmark \\ \texttt{Reject}.\checkmark \\ \texttt{Propose(Int)}.X \end{cases} \end{cases}$$

Global type $p \rightarrow q:\{t_i.G_i\}_{1 \leq i \leq n}$ specifies the communication of a value of data type t_i from role p to role q, followed by G_i, for some $1 \leq i \leq n$; we omit braces when $n = 1$. Global type $\checkmark$ specifies termination. The following recursive **local type, projected from the global type,** specifies Bob (Alice is similar):

$$L_\mathbf{b} = \mathbf{ab}?\texttt{Propose(Int)}.\mu X.\mathbf{ba}! \begin{cases} \texttt{Accept}.\mathbf{ab}?\texttt{Confirm}.\checkmark \\ \texttt{Reject}.\checkmark \\ \texttt{Propose}.\mathbf{ab}? \begin{cases} \texttt{Accept}.\mathbf{ba}!\texttt{Confirm}.\checkmark \\ \texttt{Reject}.\checkmark \\ \texttt{Propose(Int)}.X \end{cases} \end{cases}$$

Local types $pq!\{t_i.L_i\}_{1 \leq i \leq n}$ and $pq?\{t_i.L_i\}_{1 \leq i \leq n}$ specify the send and receive of a value of data type t_i from role p to role q, followed by L_i, for some $1 \leq i \leq n$; we omit braces when $n = 1$. Local type $\checkmark$ specifies termination. The following **process, well-typed by the local type,** implements a version of Bob:

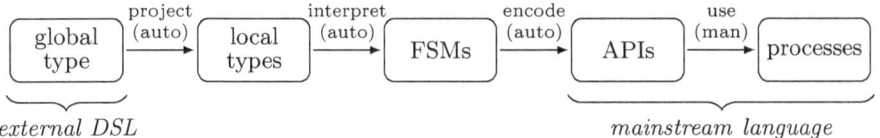

Fig. 3: Workflow of external-DSL-based MPST tools

$$P_b = s[\![ab]\!]?\_:\texttt{Propose(Int)} \ .$$

$$\mathbf{loop}_s \ s[\![ab]\!]!\texttt{propose(11)} \ . \ s[\![ab]\!]? \begin{cases} \_:\texttt{Accept} \ . \ s[\![ab]\!]!\texttt{confirm} \ . \ \mathbf{0} \\ \_:\texttt{Reject} \ . \ \mathbf{0} \\ \_:\texttt{Propose(Int)} \ . \ \mathbf{recur}_s \end{cases}$$

Process $x[\![pq]\!]!e$ implements the send of the value of expression e from role p to role q, followed by P, in session x. Process $x[\![pq]\!]?\{x_i{:}t_i.P_i\}_{1\leq i\leq n}$ implements the receive of a value of data type t_i into variable x_i, followed by P_i, in session x, for some $1\leq i\leq n$; we omit braces when $n=1$. Process $\mathbf{0}$ implements termination. Processes $\mathbf{loop}_x \ P$ and $\mathbf{recur}_x$ implement iteration in session x. □

In practice [34], the premier approach to combine MPST with mainstream languages—in the absence of native support—is based on: (1) external DSLs[1] to write global types; (2) associated tooling to generate corresponding code in mainstream languages, including Scribble [17,18], its extensions [5,8,9,26–30,36], StMungo [25], mpstpp [24], vScr [35], Pompset [6], Teatrino [2], and Oven [12].

The key ideas of the external-DSL-based approach were originally conceived by Deniélou, Hu, and Yoshida. It is based on two insights: local types can be interpreted as *finite-state machines* (FSM) [10,11], where states and transitions model sends and receives; FSMs can be encoded as object-oriented *application programming interfaces* (API) [17,18], where classes and methods model states and transitions. Fig. 3 visualises the workflow. First, the programmer writes a global type in a DSL; this is the input of the MPST tool. Next, the MPST tool projects the global type to local types, interprets the local types as FSMs, and encodes the FSMs as APIs in the mainstream language; this is the output of the MPST tool. Last, the programmer uses the APIs to write processes.

Example 2. Fig. 4 shows a global type for Negotiation (cf. G in Exmp. 1), written in the external DSL of Scribble. Statement t `from` p `to` q specifies the communication of a value of data type t from p to q. Statement `choice at` r `{` G_1 `}` `or` $\cdots$ `or` `{` G_k `}` specifies a choice among $G_1,\ldots,G_k$ made by r.

Fig. 5 shows the FSM for Bob, derivable from Fig. 4. Transition labels $pq!t$ and $pq?t$ specify the send and receive of a value of data type t from p to q.

Fig. 6 shows a *callback-based API* for Bob in Scala, derivable from Fig. 5. Trait Si in the API corresponds with state i of the FSM; methods of trait Si

---

[1] A *domain-specific language* (DSL) is either *external* or *internal*. External DSLs are stand-alone languages with their own dedicated syntax, while internal DSLs are embedded languages into a *general-purpose language* (GPL) with syntax inherited from that GPL. Both approaches have advantages and disadvantages [13].

```
Propose from A to B; rec X {
  choice at B
        { Accept   from B to A;
          Confirm from A to B; }
    or { Reject   from B to A; }
    or { Propose from B to A;
        choice at A
              { Accept   from A to B;
                Confirm from B to A; }
          or { Reject   from A to B; }
          or { Propose from A to B;
               continue X; } } }
```

Fig. 4: Global type for Negotiation (Scribble)

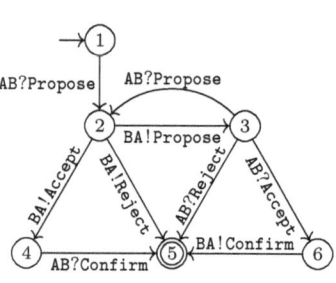

Fig. 5: FSM for Bob

```
trait Loop[S]:
  def loop(f: ((S => S5, S) => S5)): S5

trait S1:
  def recvFromA(f: (Propose, S2) => S5): S5

trait S2 extends Loop[S2]:
  def sendToA(v: Accept,  f: S4 => S5): S5
  def sendToA(v: Reject,  f: S5 => S5): S5
  def sendToA(v: Propose, f: S3 => S5): S5

trait S3 extends Loop[S3]:
  def recvFromA(f1: (Accept,  S6) => S5,
                f2: (Reject,  S5) => S5,
                f3: (Propose, S2) => S5): S5

... // traits S4, S5, and S6
```

Fig. 6: Callback-based API for Bob (Scala)

```
class Propose(val x: Int)
class Accept
class Reject
class Confirm

val v = new Propose(11)

def bob(s1: S1): S5 =
  s1.recvFromA((x, s2) =>
    s2.loop((recur, s2) =>
      s2.sendToA(v, s3 =>
        s3.recvFromA(
          (_, s6) =>
            s6.sendToA(...),
          (_, s5) => s5,
          (_, s2) =>
            recur(s2))))))
```

Fig. 7: Process for Bob

correspond with transitions of state i. Traits S2 and S3 also extend trait Loop to be able to start callback-based iteration in states 2 and 3 (i.e., these are the only states on a cycle in the FSM) in a type-sound manner. We note that each method and each callback returns a value of type S5 to ensure that the program can terminate only when the final state has been reached.

To demonstrate the usage of the API, Fig. 7 shows a process for Bob (cf. P in Exmp. 1). The idea is to write a function, bob, that consumes an "initial state object" s1 as input and produces a "final state object" s5 as output. First, the only communication action that can be performed, is the one for which s1 has a method (receiving). When that method is called, the actual receive is performed, and the callback is called with the received value x and a fresh "successor state object" s2. Next, the only communication actions that can be performed, are the ones for which s2 has a method (sending). And so on.   □

This work The external-DSL-based approach is well-established in the MPST literature: it is used in all MPST tools [5, 6, 8, 9, 12, 17, 18, 20, 24–30, 35, 36] that support *classical* MPST as in Fig. 1 (global types and projection; fully automatic; static up-to linearity). However, despite the major impact, it has two weaknesses:

Programming friction: The usage of an external DSL to specify protocols as global types causes programming friction. In general, this is a well-document-ed issue with external DSLs (e.g., [13]): new syntax needs to be learned; new tools to edit DSL code need to be adopted; extra effort is needed to intermix DSL code with the mainstream language.

Leaky abstractions: As demonstrated in Exmp. 2, APIs generated by MPST tools leak internal details: global types are essentially declarative, whereas the FSMs that seep through the APIs are essentially imperative. This repre-sentational gap causes dissonance between the level of abstraction at which global types are produced by the programmer (before API generation), and the level of abstraction at which local types are consumed by that same programmer *in terms of FSMs* (after API generation).

To avoid these weaknesses, we explore a different approach and study the question of how to support classical MPST by using *internal DSLs*. Answer-ing this question positively, we present the `mpst.embedded` library: it leverages Scala's "lightweight form of dependent typing" [3], called *match types*, to embed global/local types directly into Scala. As a result, `mpst.embedded` offers a fric-tionless interface between global/local types and processes (i.e., no new syntax, editors, or other tools need to be adopted). Moreover, `mpst.embedded` avoids leaky abstractions by not relying on FSMs; global/local types are first-class citizens.

In this way, `mpst.embedded` is the first internal-DSL-based MPST tool that supports all key aspects of classical MPST as in Fig. 1 (unlike Imai et al. [20], who do not support n-ary choice and require extra manual work to guide projection). This is a significant contribution, because: (a) internal DSLs have advantages over external DSLs, but (b) it is far from obvious how to build an internal DSL for MPST in a mainstream language without native support for session types.

Technically, to apply classical MPST and offer static guarantees, some form of compile-time computation is needed. This is the role of match types. They are essentially match expressions at the type level, which are evaluated by the Scala compiler as part of its static analysis, and which we use in this work to embed MPST theory. That is, the Scala compiler can check the typing rules of MPST theory by evaluating carefully crafted match types.

First, through extensive examples, we give an overview of the capabilities of `mpst.embedded` (Sect. 2 and Sect. 3). Next, we present technical details (Sect. 4). Last, we conclude this paper with related work and future work (Sect. 5).

2   A Tour of `mpst.embedded`: Basic Features

Global types Fig. 8 (top rows) shows the correspondence between global types in `mpst.embedded` and in MPST theory. In `mpst.embedded`, each global type G is built from classes `Com`, `End`, `Loop`, and `Recur`. The third type parameter of `Com` is an n-ary product type, called "the branches". Type parameter X of `Loop` is bound in type parameter G to the whole `Loop[X, G]`, to embed a recursive type. Each role p or q, and each recursion variable X, is a Scala *string literal type* (e.g., `"foo"` is a type with one inhabitant, `"foo"`). Each data type t is a Scala type.

Global types:
Com$[p$, q, $((t_1, G_1), \ldots, (t_n, G_n))]$, $p{\to}q{:}\{t_i.G_i\}_{1\leq i\leq n}$,
End, Loop$[X$, $G]$, Recur$[X]$ $\checkmark$, $\mu X.G$, X
Local types:
Send$[p$, q, $((t_1, L_1), \ldots, (t_n, L_n))]$, $pq!\{t_i.L_i\}_{1\leq i\leq n}$,
Recv$[p$, q, $((t_1, L_1), \ldots, (t_n, L_n))]$, $pq?\{t_i.L_i\}_{1\leq i\leq n}$,
End, Loop$[X$, $L]$, Recur$[X]$ $\checkmark$, $\mu X.L$, X
Processes
x.send$(q$, e, $(\_) \Rightarrow P)$, $x[\![pq]\!]!e$,
x.recv$(p$, $((x_1: t_1, \_) \Rightarrow P_1, \ldots, (x_n: t_n, \_) \Rightarrow P_n))$, $x[\![pq]\!]?\{x_i{:}t_i.P_i\}_{1\leq i\leq n}$,
x.loop$(($recur, $\_) \Rightarrow P)$, recur(x) $\mathbf{loop}_x\,P$, $\mathbf{recur}_x$

Fig. 8: Correspondence between mpst.embedded (left) and MPST theory (right)

Example 3. Fig. 9 shows a global type for Negotiation (cf. G in Exmp. 1). $\square$

Local types and projection Fig. 8 (middle rows) shows the correspondence between local types in mpst.embedded and in MPST theory. We add that local types can be computed from global types fully automatically and statically via type Proj: the Scala compiler reduces Proj$[G, r]$ to the projection of G onto r.

Example 4. Fig. 10 shows a local type for Bob (cf. L_b in Exmp. 1). Alternatively, it can be computed by having the Scala compiler reduce Proj$[$S, "B"$]$. $\square$

Processes and type checking Fig. 8 (bottom rows) shows the correspondence between processes in mpst.embedded and in MPST theory. In mpst.embedded, each process is a sequence of calls to methods send, recv, loop, and recur of class Local. This generic class has two type parameters: one to represent a role (enacted by the process), and another one to represent a local type (with which the process must comply). In turn, instances of Local are obtained through calls to method init of class Global. This generic class has one type parameter to represent a global type (with which all processes must comply). Method init consumes a role, initialises the session for it, and produces a Local object for it. Calls to init are *blocking*: they return only when *all* processes have called init.

Intuitively, Global and Local objects represent executable sessions from the global and local perspective, leveraging the same abstractions as the global and local types by which they are parametrised (no leaky abstractions).

Example 5. Fig. 11 shows processes for Alice and Bob on lines 1–19 and 21–31 (cf. P in Exmp. 1), plus session initiation on lines 33–35. We make three remarks:

– The process for Bob looks similar to Fig. 7. However, Fig. 11 is defined in terms of communication actions in a session (Local objects), whereas Fig. 7 is defined in terms of transitions of an FSM (Si objects).

```
1 type S =
2   Com["A", "B", ((Propose,
3     Loop["X",
4       Com["B", "A", (
5         (Accept,  Com["A", "B", ((Confirm, End))]),
6         (Reject,  End),
7         (Propose, Com["A", "B", (
8           (Accept,  Com["B", "A", ((Confirm, End))]),
9           (Reject,  End),
10          (Propose, Recur["X"]))])))]])))]
```

Fig. 9: Global type for Negotiation

```
1 type `S@B` = // equivalent to Proj[S, "B"] -- S is defined in Fig. 9
2   Recv["A", "B", ((Propose,
3     Loop["X",
4       Send["B", "A", (
5         (Accept,  Recv["A", "B", ((Confirm, End))]),
6         (Reject,  End),
7         (Propose, Recv["A", "B", (
8           (Accept,  Send["B", "A", ((Confirm, End))]),
9           (Reject,  End),
10          (Propose, Recur["X"]))])))]])))]
```

Fig. 10: Local type for Bob

```
1 def alice(
2     s: Local["A", Proj[S, "A"]] // S is defined in Fig. 9
3     ): Local["A", End] =
4   s.send("B", new Propose(5), s =>
5     s.recv("B", (
6       (_, s) => s.send("B", new Confirm, s => s),
7       (_, s) => s,
8       (v, s) =>
9         if
10          v.x < 11
11        then
12          s.send("B", new Accept, s =>
13            s.recv("B", (_, s) => s))
14        else
15          s.send("B", new Propose(6), s =>
16            s.recv("B", (
17              (_, s) => s.send("B", new Confirm, s => s),
18              (_, s) => s,
19              (_, s) => s.send("B", new Reject, s => s)))))))
20
21 def bob(
22     s: Local["B", `S@B`] // `S@B` is defined in Fig. 10
23     ): Local["B", End] =
24   s.recv("A", (_, s) =>
25     s.loop((recur, s) =>
26       // val error = s // redundant line -- only used in Exmp. 6
27       s.send("A", new Propose(11), s =>
28         s.recv("A", (
29           (_, s) => s.send("A", new Confirm, s => s),
30           (_, s) => s,
31           (_, s) => recur(s)))))
32
33 val s = new Global[S]
34 val _ = new Thread(() => { alice(s.init["A"]); () }).start
35 val _ = new Thread(() => { bob  (s.init["B"]); () }).start
```

Fig. 11: Processes for Alice and Bob

– The process for Bob exactly mimics the recursive structure of local type `˙S@B˙`. Such mimicry is not a general requirement for well-typed processes, as demonstrated by the process for Alice: instead of exactly mimicking the recursive structure of `Proj[S, "A"]` (which has a similar recursive structure as `S` in Fig. 9), it mimics two *unfoldings* of `Proj[S, "A"]`, followed by termination. That is, lines 5–15 in Fig. 11 comply with the first unfolding, while lines 16–19 comply with the second unfolding, without entering a loop.   □

Using `mpst.embedded`, the Scala compiler statically checks for each call α on a `Local` object, parametrised by local type L, whether or not α complies with L. If not, the Scala compiler reports an error. In this way, `mpst.embedded` assures that well-typedness at compile-time implies safety and liveness at run-time, modulo linear usage of `Local` objects (checked dynamically), and modulo non-terminating/exceptional behaviour (unchecked). These **two provisos** are standard for MPST tools. As the type parameters of `Local` objects are erased at compile-time, only generic `Local` objects exist at run-time.

Example 6. The following protocol violations are reported at compile-time:

– In Fig. 11, replace line 29 with one of the following:
```
(_, s) => s.send("A", new Reject, s => s),  // wrong data type
(_, s) => s.send("C", new Confirm, s => s), // wrong receiver
(_, s) => s.recv("A", (_, s) => s),         // wrong communication action
```
– In Fig. 11, uncomment line 26 and replace line 31 with:
```
(_, s) => recur(error))))))                 // wrong recursive type
```

The following protocol violation is reported as an error at run-time:

– In Fig. 11, replace line 31 with:
```
(_, s) => { recur(s); recur(s) })))))       // linearity violation
```

The technical report [22] contains a screenshot of error reporting.   □

Besides protocol violations, additionally, basic well-formedness violations of global types are reported as errors at compile-time; they are checked as part of the instantiation of generic class `Global` (e.g., Fig. 11, line 33). For instance, for `Com[p, q, ((t_1, G_1), ..., (t_n, G_n))]`, we always require $p \neq q$ and $n \geq 1$.

3   The Tour, Continued: Advanced Features

Full merging To project global types, an auxiliary partial operator to *merge* local types—the projections—is needed. There are two variants [31]: "plain" (basic) and "full" (advanced). Plain merge is *relatively easy* to support, but it works for *few* local types, so many global types cannot be projected. Conversely, full merge works for *many* local types, but it is *relatively hard* to support. For instance, Imai et al. [20] support only manual full merge (i.e., the programmer must write extra protocol-specific code to guide the computation of projections). In contrast, `mpst.embedded` supports automatic full merge via type `Merg`: the Scala compiler reduces `Merg[L_1, L_2]` to the full merge of L_1 and L_2.

```
1 type S =
2   Com["B1", "S", ((String,
3     Com["S", "B1", ((Int,
4       Com["S", "B2", ((Int,
5         Com["B1", "B2", ((Int,
6           T))])])])])]
7
8 type T =
9   Com["B2", "B1", (
10    (Ok,
11      Com["B2", "S", ((Ok,
12        Com["B2", "S", ((String,
13          Com["S", "B2", ((Date,
14            End))])])])]),
15    (Quit,
16      Com["B2", "S", ((Quit,
17        End))])])]
```

Fig. 12: Global type for Two-Buyer

```
1 type `S@S` = // equiv. Proj[S, "S"]
2   Recv["B1", "S", ((String,
3     Send["S", "B1", ((Int,
4       Send["S", "B2", ((Int,
5         // ignore Int from B1 to B2
6           `T@S`))])])])]
7
8 type `T@S` = // equiv. Proj[T, "S"]
9   Merg[(
10    // ignore Ok from B2 to B1
11      Recv["B2", "S", ((Ok,
12        Recv["B2", "S", ((String,
13          Send["S", "B2", ((Date,
14            End))])])])],
15    // ignore Quit from B2 to B1
16      Recv["B2", "S", ((Quit,
17        End))])]
```

Fig. 13: Local type for Seller

```
1 def seller(
2   s: Local["S", Proj[S, "S"]]
3   ): Local["S", End] =
4   s.recv("B1", (_, s) =>
5     val v = 11
6     s.send("B1", v, s =>
7       s.send("B2", v, s =>
8         s.recv("B2", (
9           (_: Ok, s) =>
10            s.recv("B2", (_, s) =>
11              val q: "B2" = "B2"
12              val v = new Date
13              s.send(q, v, s => s)),
14          (_: Quit, s) => s)))))
```

Fig. 14: Process for Seller

```
1 // one session between B1, B2, and S
2 type S = ... // Fig. 12
3 type T = ... // Fig. 12
4
5 // another session between B2 and B3
6 type U =
7   Com["B2", "B3", ((Int,
8     Com["B2", "B3", ((Delegatee,
9       Com["B3", "B2", (
10        (Ok, End),
11        (Quit, End))])])])]
12
13 type Delegatee =
14   Local["B2", Proj[T, "B2"]]
```

Fig. 15: Global types for Three-Buyer

```
1 def buyer2( // Three-Buyer version
2   s: Local["B2", Proj[S, "B2"]],
3   u: Local["B2", Proj[U, "B2"]]
4   ): Local["B2", End] =
5   s.recv("S", (x, s) =>
6     s.recv("B1", (y, s) =>
7       u.send("B3", x - y, u =>
8         u.send("B3", s, u =>
9           u.recv("B3", (
10            (_, u) => u, ...))))))
```

Fig. 16: Process for Buyer2

```
1 def buyer3(
2   u: Local["B3", Proj[U, "B3"]]
3   ): Local["B3", End] =
4   u.recv("B2", (_, u) =>
5     u.recv("B2", (s, u) =>
6       val v = new Quit
7       u.send("B2", v, u =>
8         s.send("B1", v, s =>
9           s.send("S", v, s => s))
10        u)))
```

Fig. 17: Process for Buyer3

Example 7. The *Two-Buyer* protocol, originally defined in the MPST literature by Honda et al. [16], consists of roles *Buyer1*, *Buyer2*, and *Seller*: "[Buyer1 and Buyer2] wish to buy an expensive book from Seller by combining their money. Buyer1 sends the title of the book to Seller, Seller sends to both Buyer1 and Buyer2 its quote, Buyer1 tells Buyer2 how much she can pay, and Buyer2 either accepts the quote or rejects the quote by notifying Seller." We use an extended version defined by Coppo et al. [7], in which Buyer2 notifies not only Seller about acceptance/rejection, but also Buyer1. In the case of acceptance, Buyer2 sends his address to Seller, and Seller sends back the delivery date to Buyer2.

Fig. 12 and Fig. 13 show a global type for Two-Buyer and a local type for Seller (split into S/S@S and T/T@S for presentational reasons.) First, we note that the communication from Buyer1 to Buyer2 on line 5 in the global type has no counterpart on line 5 in the local type; as Seller does not participate in the communication, it is simply skipped in the projection. Second, we note that the communication from Buyer2 to Buyer1 on line 9 in the global type is ignored, too, but the projections of the two branches do need to be combined into one. This is achieved by having the Scala compiler reduce

> `Merg[Recv["B2", "S", ((Ok, ...))], Recv["B2", "S", ((Quit, ...))]]`

to `Recv["B2", "S", ((Ok, ...), (Quit, ...))]`.

Fig. 14 shows a process for Seller. It demonstrates that merging is a type-level concept, hidden from the programmer: the Scala compiler reduces `Merg[...]` and type-checks the code against the result transparently.   □

Delegation Sessions are *higher-order*: Local object s for a first session can be *delegated* between processes via Local object u for a second session, by sending s via u. In the presence of delegation, within each session, well-typedness at compile-time continues to imply safety and liveness at run-time (modulo the "two provisos"; page 152). However, between sessions, liveness is not assured; supporting this would require substantial extra technical machinery [7], so none of the existing MPST tools support it.

Example 8. The *Three-Buyer* protocol, originally defined in the MPST literature by Coppo et al. [7], consists of roles *Buyer1*, *Buyer2*, *Buyer3*, and *Seller*. It resembles the Two-Buyer protocol, except that Buyer2 can ask Buyer3 to enact his role on his behalf—unbeknownst to Buyer1 and Seller—through delegation.

Fig. 15 shows global types for Three-Buyer. Global type S specifies the first sub-protocol among Buyer1, Buyer2, and Seller; it is identical to the global type for Two-Buyer. Global type U specifies the second sub-protocol between Buyer2 and Buyer3. Notably, line 8 specifies the delegation from Buyer2 to Buyer3.

Fig. 16 shows a process for Buyer2: on lines 1–4, Local objects for two sessions are consumed as inputs (to engage in two sub-protocols); on lines 5–6, the first session is used; on lines 7–10, the second session is used; on line 8, the remainder of the first session is delegated via the second session. Similarly, Fig. 17 shows a process for Buyer3: on lines 1–3, a Local object for the first session is consumed as input; on line 5, a Local object for the second session is received.

The process for Seller is exactly the same in Three-Buyer as in Two-Buyer (Fig. 14). In particular, Seller does not know that it communicates with Buyer3 instead of Buyer2. Thus, delegation is hidden from each role not involved.   □

Generic global types By embedding global/local types as Scala types, Scala's built-in mechanism of type parametrisation is readily available. This allows the programmer to write *generic global types* with type parameters for roles (common in external-DSL-based MPST tools) and sub-protocols (novel of `mpst.embedded`).

```
1 type T[P <: Role, Q <: Role] =    6 type U[P <: Role, Q <: Role, G <: GType] =
2   Com[P, Q, ((Propose,            7   Com[P, Q, (
3     Loop["X",                     8     (Accept,   Com[Q, P, ((Confirm, End))]),
4       U[Q, P,                     9     (Reject,   End),
5         U[P, Q, Recur["X"]]]])]  10     (Propose,  G))]
```

Fig. 18: Generic global types for Negotiation

$$p \to q:\{t_i.G_i\}_{i \in I} \upharpoonright p = pq!\{t_i.G_i \upharpoonright r\}_{i \in I}$$

$$p \to q:\{t_i.G_i\}_{i \in I} \upharpoonright q = pq?\{t_i.G_i \upharpoonright r\}_{i \in I}$$

$$p \to q:\{t_i.G_i\}_{i \in I} \upharpoonright r = \sqcap\{G_i \upharpoonright r\}_{i \in I} \quad \text{if } r \notin \{p, q\}$$

$$\checkmark \upharpoonright r = \checkmark$$

$$\mu X.G \upharpoonright r = \mu X.(G \upharpoonright r)$$

$$X \upharpoonright r = X$$

Fig. 19: Projection in MPST theory

Example 9. To alleviate the repetitive feel of Fig. 9, Fig. 18 shows generic global types that leverage type parameters. Type U generically specifies the communication of an acceptance, rejection, or counter-proposal from P to Q (type parameters for roles), followed by G (type parameter for a sub-protocol) in case of a counter-proposal; it can be instantiated twice to replace lines 5–7 and lines 8–10 in Fig. 9. This is done in type T, which generically specifies a role-parametric version of the whole S in Fig. 9. Thus, T["A", "B"] is equivalent to S in Fig. 9.   □

Consistency mpst.embedded also supports explicit *consistency checking* of sets of local types. Details can be found in the technical report [22], as they are rather technical/subtle. We do evaluate consistency checking times in Sect. 4.3, though.

4   Technical Details

As mpst.embedded closely follows MPST theory, and as it uses unique parts of the Scala type system, first, we summarise a few essential preliminaries (Sect. 4.1). Next, we describe our embedding of MPST into Scala (Sect. 4.2).

This section focusses on the basic features of Sect. 2. It allows us to keep the necessary background on MPST theory simple and succinct, while still being able to explain the general ideas of the embedding into the Scala type system in sufficient depth. The advanced features of Sect. 3 are based on more complex theoretical concepts, but their embedding follows similar general ideas.

4.1   Preliminaries

MPST theory We summarise the theory behind classical MPST (Fig. 1):

Global types, local types, and processes: The syntax was defined and explained in Fig. 8 (right column) and Exmp. 1.
Projection: Let $G \upharpoonright r$ denote the projection of G onto r; it is defined in Fig. 19. The projection of a communication yields a send if r is the sender, a receive if r is the receiver, or the full merge—denoted by $\sqcap$—of the projected branches otherwise (i.e., r does not participate in the communication).

$$\frac{\Gamma \vdash e : t_j \text{ and } \Gamma, x : L_j \vdash P, \text{ for some } j \in I}{\Gamma, x : pq!\{t_i.L_i\}_{i \in I} \vdash x[\![pq]\!]!e.P} \text{ [SEND]} \qquad \frac{\text{only } \checkmark \text{ local types in } \Gamma}{\Gamma \vdash \mathbf{0}} \text{ [TERM]}$$

$$\frac{\Gamma, x : L_i, x_i : t_i \vdash P_i, \text{ for each } i \in I}{\Gamma, x : pq?\{t_i.L_i\}_{i \in I}) \vdash x[\![pq]\!]?\{x_i{:}t_i.P_i\}_{i \in I}} \text{ [RECV]} \qquad \frac{\Gamma, x : L[\mu X.L/X] \vdash P}{\Gamma, x : \mu X.L \vdash P} \text{ [UNFOLD]}$$

Fig. 20: Type checking in MPST theory (excerpt)

Type checking: Let $\Gamma \vdash P$ denote well-typedness of P in typing environment Γ; it is defined in Fig. 20. Rule [SEND] states that a send from p to q in x is well-typed when the local type of x specifies a send, e is well-typed by t_j, and P is well-typed after setting the local type of x to L_j in the typing environment, for some j. Rule [RECV] states that a receive from p to q in x is well-typed when the local type of x specifies a receive, and P_i is well-typed after setting the local type of x to L_i in the typing environment, for each i. Thus, there is asymmetry: for sending, only one send specified must be implemented, but for receiving, each receive specified must be implemented.

Central theorem: Static well-typedness implies dynamic safety and liveness.

Match types in Scala The main feature of the Scala type system that we take advantage of in mpst.embedded is *match types*. We explain it with an example. Suppose that we need to write a function to convert Ints and Booleans:

```
type IntOrBoolean = Int | Boolean // type alias for a union type
def convert(x: IntOrBoolean): IntOrBoolean = x match {
  case i: Int => i == 1; case b: Boolean => if b then 1 else 0 }
```

However, return type IntOrBoolean is not precise enough. For instance, the Scala compiler fails to prove that convert(5) && false is safe, as it cannot infer that convert(5) is Boolean. What is missing, is a relation between the actual type of x (e.g., Int) and the return type (e.g., Boolean). Match types define such relations.

1. First, we redefine the signature of convert as follows:

   ```
   def convert[T <: IntOrBoolean](x: T): Convert[T] = ... // same as before
   ```

   Thus, we introduce a type parameter T (subtype of IntOrBoolean) and declare x to be T. Also, we declare the return value to be of match type Convert[T].
2. Next, the idea is to define Convert[T] in such a way that the relation between the actual type of x and the return type can be inferred, as follows:

   ```
   type Convert[T] = T match { case Int => Boolean; case Boolean => Int }
   ```

   The Scala compiler *reduces* every occurrence of Convert[T] to Int or Boolean, depending on the instantiation of T (e.g., Convert[Int] is reduced to Boolean).
3. Last, for instance, the Scala compiler correctly succeeds/fails to type-check convert(5) && false (safe) and convert(5) && 6 (unsafe).

Thus, match types are a "lightweight form of dependent typing" [3], to perform "type-level programming". In the remainder, we use the following built-ins:

```
1 type Proj[G, R] = G match
2   case End            => End
3   case Com[R, q, b] => Send[R, q, Map[b, [E] =>> (Head[E], Proj[Last[E], R])]]
4   case Com[p, R, b] => Recv[p, R, Map[b, [E] =>> (Head[E], Proj[Last[E], R])]]
5   case Com[_, _, b] => MergAll[Map[b, [E] =>> Proj[Last[E], R]]]
6   case Loop[x, g]   => Loop[x, Proj[g, R]]
7   case Recur[x]       => Recur[x]
```

Fig. 21: Projection in `mpst.embedded`

- `Head[(T1, ..., Tn)]` and `Last[(T1, ..., Tn)]` reduce to `T1` and `Tn`.
- `Map[(T1, ..., Tn), F]` reduces to `(F[T1], ..., F[Tn])`. We note that `F` can be a *type lambda* of the form `[X] => ... /*do something with X */`.

4.2   Embedding MPST into Scala

Global types, local types, processes As explained in Sect. 2, and as shown in Fig. 8, global types and local types are implemented as classes, while processes are implemented as methods of class `Local`. The communication infrastructure for processes is based on concurrent queues. However, a transport layer for distributed processes is also possible (orthogonal concern).

Projection Fig. 21 shows match type `Proj`. It is used to have the Scala compiler fully automatically and statically compute local types (e.g., line 2 in Fig. 11).

Match type `Proj` has two type parameters: a global type `G` and a role `R` (cf. $G \upharpoonright r$). To reduce `Proj[G, R]`, the Scala compiler matches `G` to a global type constructor, and it produces a local type **exactly as defined in Fig. 19**. By convention, lower case letters in patterns are *type variables*; they are bound to types as part of the matching algorithm. For instance, on lines 3–5 in Fig. 21, `b` is bound to a product type of the form `((T1, G1), ..., (Tn, Gn))`, where each `Ti` is a data type, and each `Gi` is a global type. When `b` is passed to `Map` on lines 3–4, it is converted into `((T1, Proj[G1, R]), ..., (Tn, Proj[Gn, R]))`. Alternatively, when `b` is passed to `Map` on line 5, it is converted into `(Proj[G1, R], ..., Proj[Gn, R])`, which is subsequently passed to `MergAll`; this is a helper match type that reduces to the full merge of all local types in the product type.

Type checking Fig. 22 shows an excerpt of class `Local` related to type checking. The idea is to have the Scala compiler reduce match types `SendCallback` and `RecvCallbacks` to fully automatically and statically compute the *expected types* of the callback arguments of methods `send` and `recv`, given a local type L. The reduction succeeds, and the actual callback argument is well-typed by the expected type, *if, and only if,* the communication action is well-typed by L **exactly as defined in Fig. 20**. Otherwise, the Scala compiler reports an error. In this way, `mpst.embedded` implements the same MPST typing rules as in Fig. 20 in terms of Scala match type reduction, and it provides the same assurances (modulo the "two provisos"; page 152):

```
1  class Local[R, L] private (val r: R, val net: Network) extends UseOnce:
2    def send[Q, D](q: Q, d: D, f: SendCallback[Q, D, L]): Local[R, End] = ...
3    def recv[P](p: P, fs: RecvCallbacks[P, L]): Local[R, End] = ...
4
5    type SendCallback[Q, D, L] = L match
6      case Send[R, q, b] => q match
7        case Q => (Local[R, App[b, D]] => Local[R, End])
8      case Loop[x, l] => SendCallback[Q, D, Substitute[l, L, x]]
9
10   type RecvCallbacks[P, L] = L match
11     case Recv[p, R, b] => p match
12       case P => Map[b, [E] =>> (Head[E], Local[R, Last[E]]) => Local[R, End]]
13     case Loop[x, l] => RecvCallbacks[P, Substitute[l, L, x]]
14
15   ... // function loop and type LoopCallback
```

Fig. 22: Type checking in `mpst.embedded` (excerpt)

- if, at compile-time, each process is well-typed by its projection,
- then, at run-time, the session of all processes is safe and live,
- modulo linear usage of `Local` objects (checked dynamically),
- modulo non-terminating/exceptional behaviour (unchecked).

We now explain `send` and `recv`. Regarding `send`, Fig. 20 states that a send is well-typed if the local type specifies it directly (rule [SEND]) or indirectly (rule [UNFOLD]). These cases correspond precisely to the two cases in `SendCallback`:

- Lines 6–7 state that a send is well-typed if the sender, receiver, and data type match the send of the local type L, and if the callback is a function that consumes a `Local` object, parametrised by the selected branch of L, namely `App[b, D]`. We note that `App[((T1, L1), ..., (Tn, Ln)),Ti]` reduces to `Li`.
- Line 8 states that a send is also well-typed when it is well-typed by the unfolding of the local type. We note that `Substitute[L1, L2, X]` reduces to a version of L1 in which each occurrence of `Recur[X]` is replaced with L2.

Regarding `recv`, similarly, Fig. 20 states that a receive is well-typed if the local type specifies the receive directly (rule [RECV]) or indirectly (rule [UNFOLD]). Due to the asymmetry between sends and receives, `SendCallback` (singular) reduces to a single function type, while `RecvCallbacks` (plural) reduces to a product of function types, computed using `Map`. Besides that, they follow the same ideas.

4.3 Evaluation and Discussion

Compile-time performance To validate the practical feasibility of using `mpst.embedded`, we systematically measured the type checking times during *non-incremental* compilation of all examples in Sect. 2 and Sect. 3, as well as twelve additional examples from the MPST literature [7,30,31] and the Scribble repository [14].[2] This is a representative set of protocols, previously developed by other

---

[2] Run-time performance (e.g., latency/throughput) depends on the transport mechanism for message passing, which is orthogonal to the contributions of this paper.

Table 1: Type checking times in milliseconds, reported as $\mu \pm \sigma$, where μ is the average (of 31 measurements), and where σ is the standard deviation

protocol	type checking without consistency	type checking with consistency	difference[†]
Negotiation (Exmp. 5)	$1,399 \pm 118$ ms	$1,254 \pm 36$ ms	-145 ± 125 ms
Negotiation (Exmp. 9)	$1,299 \pm 85$ ms	$1,240 \pm 22$ ms	-60 ± 88 ms
Two-Buyer (Exmp. 7)	$1,399 \pm 31$ ms	$1,658 \pm 50$ ms	258 ± 59 ms
Three-Buyer (Exmp. 8)	$1,489 \pm 57$ ms	$1,728 \pm 50$ ms	239 ± 76 ms
Three-Buyer [7]	$1,341 \pm 57$ ms	$1,622 \pm 71$ ms	280 ± 78 ms
OAuth2 Fragment [31]	713 ± 24 ms	*inconsistent*	*inconsistent*
Rec. Two-Buyers [31]	775 ± 24 ms	*inconsistent*	*inconsistent*
Rec. Map/Reduce [31]	$1,016 \pm 45$ ms	*inconsistent*	*inconsistent*
MP Workers [31]	891 ± 27 ms	*inconsistent*	*inconsistent*
Game [30]	$1,095 \pm 35$ ms	$1,338 \pm 29$ ms	243 ± 46 ms
Adder [14]	763 ± 21 ms	781 ± 19 ms	18 ± 28 ms
Booking [14]	$1,099 \pm 35$ ms	*inconsistent*	*inconsistent*
Fibonacci [14]	759 ± 22 ms	779 ± 17 ms	20 ± 28 ms
HTTP [14]	$1,703 \pm 41$ ms	$1,838 \pm 77$ ms	134 ± 88 ms
Loan Application [14]	879 ± 48 ms	1132 ± 29 ms	253 ± 56 ms
SMTP [14]	$1,726 \pm 70$ ms	2079 ± 128 ms	353 ± 146 ms

[†] The difference between type checking times *without* consistency $\mu_1 \pm \sigma_1$ and *with* consistency $\mu_2 \pm \sigma_2$ are reported as $\mu \pm \sigma$, where $\mu = \mu_2 - \mu_1$ and $\sigma = \sqrt{\sigma_1^2 + \sigma_2^2}$.

researchers (including the protocols in our examples in Sect. 2 and Sect. 3), of various sizes, that exercise all aspects of classical MPST theory.[3]

To measure only the protocol-related type checking times, the processes contained almost no computation code; just communication actions in compliance with the protocol. The measurements were obtained using an Intel i7-8569U processor (4 physical/4 virtual cores at 2.8 GHz) and 16 GB of memory, running macOS 14.0, OpenJDK 18.0.2, and Scala 3.3.1. We ran the measurements with consistency checking disabled and enabled, to be able to study the difference.

Table 1 shows the results, averaged over 31 runs per protocol. We make two main observations. First, without consistency checks, the type checking times seem sufficiently low for the usage of `mpst.embedded` to be practically feasible: less than two seconds for the biggest protocol in our benchmark set (SMTP). Moreover, our measurements were obtained using non-incremental compilation and, as such, constitute an upper bound on the expected type checking delays when using incremental compilation. Anecdotally, in our development environment (Visual Studio Code 1.87 with the Metals 1.30 extension for Scala pro-

---

[3] That is, the theory as originally defined by Honda et al. [16], but presented in the more recent style of, e.g., Scalas–Yoshida [31], including the full merge operator.

gramming), when using incremental compilation, the type checking delays were significantly lower (<100 ms) than those in Table 1, and not disruptive at all.

Second, with consistency checks (i.e., five examples violate consistency; this was expected), the results show that some overhead is added, but it does not make the usage of `mpst.embedded` infeasible (<500 ms). Also, when using incremental compilation, the type checking delays continued to not get in the way.

Experience The implementation of the benchmark set turned out to be, in its own right, a validation activity to experience whether or not the type checker catches all mistakes in practice. This is because, until a protocol implementation is finished, it does not comply with the specification yet. Thus, all until the end, the type checker reports errors to point out missing pieces. This guidance by the type checker effectively prevented us from making unintended programming mistakes, especially when writing the implementations of HTTP and SMTP (which are the more complicated protocols in our benchmark set). It would be interesting to try to reproduce these anecdotal findings in a larger user study.

Expressiveness Our benchmark set shows that `mpst.embedded` is feature-complete relative to classical MPST theory,[3] with full merging (e.g., the OAuth2 fragment requires full merge), as intended. Moreover, while the ability to write *generic* global types does not add expressive power in the formal sense, it enables better *reuse* of global types and serves as an abstraction/composition mechanism: it allows large protocols to be split into separate smaller sub-protocols—specified as generically as possible to maximise the opportunity for reuse—which can then be "invoked" from each other with concrete arguments. Such generic sub-protocols can also be packaged into libraries and shared between projects.

5   Conclusion

Related work Closest to our approach in this paper is the work by Imai et al. [20]. They developed an internal DSL in OCaml to specify protocols and verify processes based on MPST. However, their tool does *not* support all key aspects of classical MPST as in Fig. 1: it supports only binary choices instead of n-ary choices (e.g., Exmp. 1, which has ternary choices, is not supported), and it is not fully automatic (i.e., Imai et al. require the programmer to manually write extra protocol-specific code to project global types). In contrast, `mpst.embedded` supports n-ary choices and is fully automatic.

Another related tool is the Discourje library [15], which offers an MPST-based internal DSL in Clojure. However, Discourje does all verification dynamically, whereas `mpst.embedded` performs all verification statically up-to linearity.

There are four existing tools to combine MPST with Scala: *Scribble-Scala* [30], *Pompset* [6], *Teatrino* [2], and *Oven* [12]. Table 2 summarises the differences:

- *DSLs to specify protocols as global types:* Scribble-Scala, Pompset, and Teatrino are based on the external DSL of Scribble, while Oven is based on an external DSL for regular expressions.

Table 2: Comparison of MPST tools for Scala

	DSL	projection	interpretation	encoding
Scribble-Scala [30]	external	syntactic	FSMs	lchannels
Pompset [6]	external	syntactic	pomsets	vanilla Scala
Teatrino [2]	external	syntactic	–	Effpi
Oven [12]	external	semantic	FSMs	vanilla Scala
mpst.embedded	internal	syntactic	–	vanilla Scala

– *Projection of global types:* Scribble-Scala, Pompset, and Teatrino apply the classical *structural* projection operator (defined in terms of the syntax of global types; Sect. 4.2), while Oven applies a non-classical *behavioural* projection operator (defined in terms of the operational semantics of global types). The latter has additional expressive power to support the usage of regular expressions as global types [23].
– *Interpretation of local types:* Different from Fig. 3, Pompset uses *partially-ordered multisets* instead of FSMs as an intermediate operational model, while Teatrino directly encodes local types as APIs in Scala.
– *Encoding as APIs:* The APIs generated by Scribble-Scala and Teatrino are built on top of the existing libraries lchannels and Effpi (discussed in more detail below), while Pompset and Oven do not rely on such existing libraries.

Besides these existing tools to combine multiparty session typing with Scala (including global types and projection), there also exist libraries to combine binary session typing with Scala (excluding global types and projection), namely lchannels [30] and *Effpi* [32]. Conceptually, as mpst.embedded targets multiparty instead of binary, it is not really comparable to lchannels and Effpi. Technically, moreover, lchannels and Effpi do not use match types.

Future work Many extensions of MPST theory have been proposed. We are keen to explore which of them can be incorporated in mpst.embedded using match types. For instance, an important feature that we believe is compatible with mpst.embedded and match types is *parameterised MPST with indexed roles* as developed by Castro et al. [5]. Another feature that seems representable using match types, is *MPST with refinements* along the lines of Zhou et al. [36]. In contrast, a feature that seems prohibitively difficult to incorporate, is *timed MPST* [4]: match types seem unsuitable to statically offer real-time guarantees.

Data Availability Statement

The artifact is available on Zenodo [21]. It contains: (1) mpst.embedded; (2) the examples in the paper; (3) reproduction instructions for our evaluation.

References

1. Ancona et al., D.: Behavioral types in programming languages. Foundations and Trends in Programming Languages **3**(2-3), 95–230 (2016)
2. Barwell, A.D., Hou, P., Yoshida, N., Zhou, F.: Designing asynchronous multiparty protocols with crash-stop failures. In: ECOOP. LIPIcs, vol. 263, pp. 1:1–1:30. Schloss Dagstuhl - Leibniz-Zentrum für Informatik (2023)
3. Blanvillain, O., Brachthäuser, J.I., Kjaer, M., Odersky, M.: Type-level programming with match types. Proc. ACM Program. Lang. **6**(POPL), 1–24 (2022)
4. Bocchi, L., Yang, W., Yoshida, N.: Timed multiparty session types. In: CONCUR. LNCS, vol. 8704, pp. 419–434. Springer (2014)
5. Castro, D., Hu, R., Jongmans, S., Ng, N., Yoshida, N.: Distributed programming using role-parametric session types in go: statically-typed endpoint apis for dynamically-instantiated communication structures. PACMPL **3**(POPL), 29:1–29:30 (2019)
6. Cledou, G., Edixhoven, L., Jongmans, S., Proença, J.: API generation for multiparty session types, revisited and revised using scala 3. In: ECOOP. LIPIcs, vol. 222, pp. 27:1–27:28. Schloss Dagstuhl - Leibniz-Zentrum für Informatik (2022)
7. Coppo, M., Dezani-Ciancaglini, M., Yoshida, N., Padovani, L.: Global progress for dynamically interleaved multiparty sessions. Math. Struct. Comput. Sci. **26**(2), 238–302 (2016)
8. Cutner, Z., Yoshida, N.: Safe session-based asynchronous coordination in rust. In: COORDINATION. Lecture Notes in Computer Science, vol. 12717, pp. 80–89. Springer (2021)
9. Cutner, Z., Yoshida, N., Vassor, M.: Deadlock-free asynchronous message reordering in rust with multiparty session types. In: PPoPP. pp. 246–261. ACM (2022)
10. Deniélou, P., Yoshida, N.: Multiparty session types meet communicating automata. In: ESOP. LNCS, vol. 7211, pp. 194–213. Springer (2012)
11. Deniélou, P., Yoshida, N.: Multiparty compatibility in communicating automata: Characterisation and synthesis of global session types. In: ICALP (2). LNCS, vol. 7966, pp. 174–186. Springer (2013)
12. Ferreira, F., Jongmans, S.: Oven: Safe and live communication protocols in scala, using synthetic behavioural type analysis. In: ISSTA. pp. 1511–1514. ACM (2023)
13. Fowler, M.: Domain-Specific Languages. The Addison-Wesley signature series, Addison-Wesley (2011)
14. GitHub, Inc: scribble-java/scribble-demos/scrib at ccb0e48d69c6e3088e746138099 c3183ca1ac79b · scribble/scribble-java, accessed January 2025, `https://github.com/scribble/scribble-java/tree/` `ccb0e48d69c6e3088e746138099c3183ca1ac79b/scribble-demos/scrib`
15. Hamers, R., Jongmans, S.: Discourje: Runtime verification of communication protocols in clojure. In: TACAS (1). LNCS, vol. 12078, pp. 266–284. Springer (2020)
16. Honda, K., Yoshida, N., Carbone, M.: Multiparty asynchronous session types. In: POPL. pp. 273–284. ACM (2008)
17. Hu, R., Yoshida, N.: Hybrid session verification through endpoint API generation. In: FASE. LNCS, vol. 9633, pp. 401–418. Springer (2016)
18. Hu, R., Yoshida, N.: Explicit connection actions in multiparty session types. In: FASE. LNCS, vol. 10202, pp. 116–133. Springer (2017)
19. Hüttel, H., Lanese, I., Vasconcelos, V.T., Caires, L., Carbone, M., Deniélou, P., Mostrous, D., Padovani, L., Ravara, A., Tuosto, E., Vieira, H.T., Zavattaro, G.: Foundations of session types and behavioural contracts. ACM Comput. Surv. **49**(1), 3:1–3:36 (2016)

20. Imai, K., Neykova, R., Yoshida, N., Yuen, S.: Multiparty session programming with global protocol combinators. In: ECOOP. LIPIcs, vol. 166, pp. 9:1–9:30. Schloss Dagstuhl - Leibniz-Zentrum für Informatik (2020)
21. Jongmans, S.: Multiparty session typing, embedded (artifact) (2025), `https://doi.org/10.5281/zenodo.14201951`
22. Jongmans, S.: Multiparty session typing, embedded (technical report) (2025), `https://doi.org/10.48550/arXiv.2501.17741`
23. Jongmans, S., Ferreira, F.: Synthetic behavioural typing: Sound, regular multiparty sessions via implicit local types. In: ECOOP. LIPIcs, vol. 263, pp. 42:1–42:30. Schloss Dagstuhl - Leibniz-Zentrum für Informatik (2023)
24. Jongmans, S., Yoshida, N.: Exploring type-level bisimilarity towards more expressive multiparty session types. In: ESOP. LNCS, vol. 12075, pp. 251–279. Springer (2020)
25. Kouzapas, D., Dardha, O., Perera, R., Gay, S.J.: Typechecking protocols with mungo and stmungo: A session type toolchain for java. Sci. Comput. Program. **155**, 52–75 (2018)
26. Lagaillardie, N., Neykova, R., Yoshida, N.: Implementing multiparty session types in rust. In: COORDINATION. LNCS, vol. 12134, pp. 127–136. Springer (2020)
27. Lagaillardie, N., Neykova, R., Yoshida, N.: Stay safe under panic: Affine rust programming with multiparty session types. In: ECOOP. LIPIcs, vol. 222, pp. 4:1–4:29. Schloss Dagstuhl - Leibniz-Zentrum für Informatik (2022)
28. Miu, A., Ferreira, F., Yoshida, N., Zhou, F.: Communication-safe web programming in typescript with routed multiparty session types. In: CC. pp. 94–106. ACM (2021)
29. Neykova, R., Hu, R., Yoshida, N., Abdeljallal, F.: A session type provider: compile-time API generation of distributed protocols with refinements in f#. In: CC. pp. 128–138. ACM (2018)
30. Scalas, A., Dardha, O., Hu, R., Yoshida, N.: A linear decomposition of multiparty sessions for safe distributed programming. In: ECOOP. LIPIcs, vol. 74, pp. 24:1–24:31. Schloss Dagstuhl - Leibniz-Zentrum fuer Informatik (2017)
31. Scalas, A., Yoshida, N.: Less is more: multiparty session types revisited. Proc. ACM Program. Lang. **3**(POPL), 30:1–30:29 (2019)
32. Scalas, A., Yoshida, N., Benussi, E.: Verifying message-passing programs with dependent behavioural types. In: PLDI. pp. 502–516. ACM (2019)
33. Tu, T., Liu, X., Song, L., Zhang, Y.: Understanding real-world concurrency bugs in go. In: ASPLOS. pp. 865–878. ACM (2019)
34. Yoshida, N.: Programming language implementations with multiparty session types. In: Active Object Languages: Current Research Trends, Lecture Notes in Computer Science, vol. 14360, pp. 147–165. Springer (2024)
35. Yoshida, N., Zhou, F., Ferreira, F.: Communicating finite state machines and an extensible toolchain for multiparty session types. In: FCT. LNCS, vol. 12867, pp. 18–35. Springer (2021)
36. Zhou, F., Ferreira, F., Hu, R., Neykova, R., Yoshida, N.: Statically verified refinements for multiparty protocols. Proc. ACM Program. Lang. **4**(OOPSLA), 148:1–148:30 (2020)

Model Checking

Sound Statistical Model Checking
for Probabilities and Expected Rewards*

Carlos E. Budde[1,2], Arnd Hartmanns[3], Tobias Meggendorfer[4],

Maximilian Weininger[5], and Patrick Wienhöft[6,7] ✉

[1] Technical University of Denmark, Lyngby, Denmark
[2] University of Trento, Trento, Italy
[3] University of Twente, Enschede, The Netherlands
[4] Lancaster University Leipzig, Germany
[5] Institute of Science and Technology Austria, Klosterneuburg, Austria
[6] Technical University Dresden, Germany · patrick.wienhoeft@tu-dresden.de
[7] Centre for Tactile Internet with Human-in-the-Loop (CeTI), Dresden, Germany

Abstract. Statistical model checking estimates probabilities and expectations of interest in probabilistic system models by using random simulations. Its results come with statistical guarantees. However, many tools use *unsound* statistical methods that produce incorrect results more often than they claim. In this paper, we provide a comprehensive overview of tools and their correctness, as well as of sound methods available for estimating probabilities from the literature. For expected rewards, we investigate how to bound the path reward distribution to apply sound statistical methods for bounded distributions, of which we recommend the Dvoretzky-Kiefer-Wolfowitz inequality that has not been used in SMC so far. We prove that even reachability rewards can be bounded in theory, and formalise the concept of limit-PAC procedures for a practical solution. The MODES SMC tool implements our methods and recommendations, which we use to experimentally confirm our results.

1 Introduction

Statistical model checking (SMC) [83] estimates quantities of interest by sampling a large number k of random runs from a compact executable model of a probabilistic system. Typical quantities of interest are reachability probabilities and expected rewards, to query for e.g. reliability or performance measures [12].

* This work was supported by the DFG through the Cluster of Excellence EXC 2050/1 (CeTI, project ID 390696704, as part of Germany's Excellence Strategy) and the TRR 248 (see perspicuous-computing.science, project ID 389792660), by the European Union's Horizon 2020 research and innovation programme under Marie Skłodowska-Curie grant agreements 101008233 (MISSION), 101034413 (IST-BRIDGE), and 101067199 (ProSVED), by the EU under NextGenerationEU projects D53D23008400006 (Smartitude) under MUR PRIN 2022 and PE00000014 (SERICS) under MUR PNRR, by the Interreg North Sea project STORM_SAFE, and by NWO VIDI grant VI.Vidi.223.110 (TruSTy).

© The Author(s) 2025
A. Gurfinkel and M. Heule (Eds.): TACAS 2025, LNCS 15696, pp. 167–190, 2025.
https://doi.org/10.1007/978-3-031-90643-5_9

A *sound* statistical model checker delivers results guaranteed to be *probably approximately correct* (PAC), i.e. it returns a confidence interval I with $|I| \leq 2\varepsilon$ ("ε-approximately correct") such that the probability for I to contain the (unknown) true value x is higher than a given confidence level γ ("probably correct").

When applied judiciously, SMC can perform extremely well [82] and easily beat probabilistic model checking (PMC) [10, 11] tools that rely on exhaustive state space exploration as well as partial exploration tools [5, 53, 64] in competitions when PAC results are allowed [26]. It is widely implemented in tools such as C-SMC [31], COSMOS [15], FIG [22], HYPEG [73], MODES [24] of the MODEST TOOLSET [46], MULTIVESTA [43, 79], PLASMA LAB [60], PRISM [55], SBIP [69], or UPPAAL SMC [37]. It has been applied to case studies ranging from hardware [63, 77] over biology [84] to cybersecurity [23, 57]. New SMC tools such as SMC STORM [56] are now being developed in industrial contexts.

However, as we detail in Table 1, many existing and new SMC implementations either are unsound (i.e. they do not deliver PAC guarantees), or inefficient (i.e. they use statistical methods that need unnecessarily many samples). The unsoundness is often due to computing confidence intervals via approaches that rely on the central limit theorem, while the inefficiency is notably due to the widespread use of the Okamoto bound [70] for estimating probabilities.

Our contribution is a comprehensive treatment of the problem of efficiently obtaining sound SMC results when estimating probabilities as well as expected rewards. We review the statistical methods available for probabilities in Sec. 3, which forms the basis for Table 1. For expected rewards, in Sec. 4, we provide a novel fully sound approach for the instantaneous and cumulative cases, prove that sound SMC is possible for reachability rewards in theory, and give a practically useful method. We implemented our methods and recommendations in the MODES SMC tool (Sec. 5) to experimentally confirm our findings in Sec. 6.

SMC for reachability **probabilities** comes down to estimating binomial proportions, a well-studied problem in statistics. Sound methods for **expected rewards**, on the other hand, have been an open problem. Here, we need to estimate the mean x of the path reward distribution μ, whose shape is unknown and which can have unbounded support. For this problem, no PAC statistical methods exist. Thus, to obtain a sound SMC approach for expected rewards, we must (1) use structural information to soundly reduce to case of bounded support $[a, b]$ to then (2) employ an appropriate statistical method for this case.

We review the methods available for Step 2 in Sec. 4.1, recommending the use of the Dvoretzky-Kiefer-Wolfowitz inequality (DKW) [39]. This inequality provides a very strong and versatile result that allows the derivation of useful confidence intervals for the mean even for conservative values for a and b, yet has been curiously ignored in the SMC community so far.

For Step 1, we distinguish two cases in Sec. 4.2: First, for (step- or time-bounded) **cumulative** and **instantaneous rewards**, we can derive safe and practical values for a and b given an upper bound on r_{max}, the highest reward assigned to any state, which can typically be obtained from the model's syntax. For (unbounded) **reachability rewards**, we introduce *bounding sets* that provide a means to ignore very large path rewards while introducing an error of at most $\varepsilon' < \varepsilon$. We prove that a bounding set can be obtained for every finite discrete-time Markov chain (DTMC), given only bounds on certain parameters of the DTMC which can typically be derived syntactically, too. Yet, the resulting bounding set is not practical, thus serving only as a proof of the possibility of sound SMC for reachability rewards. In practice, we propose to use the DKW to obtain guaranteed *lower bounds* that provably converge to x as $k \to \infty$.

Our focus is on *estimating* probabilities and *undiscounted* expected rewards given either k or an *absolute* error ε. We briefly comment on *hypothesis testing* where appropriate, referring the reader to dedicated works on hypothesis testing in SMC like Reijsbergen et al.'s [76] for more details, cautioning that they may not emphasise soundness. Undiscounted rewards are standard in verification while discounting is ubiquitous in machine learning. It is easy to obtain good bounds $[a, b]$ on discounted rewards and thus apply the methods we review in Sec. 4.1 efficiently. For rare events [78] or very large expected rewards, one may want to specify a *relative error* $\varepsilon \cdot x$; we mention some methods specific for this case.

We consider SMC as in the original papers by Younes and Simmons [83] and Hérault et al. [49], motivated by the state space explosion problem which PMC faces for finite-but-large models of realistic applications, and the lack of scalable PMC approaches for non-Markovian models like stochastic automata (IOSA) [36] or HPnGs [68]. Thus, we sample runs from a (mostly) black-box model using $\mathcal{O}(1)$ memory to estimate global quantities of interest. This is in contrast to "model-based SMC" [1,8,65], which aims to apply PMC-like methods to black-box systems with simulation access by *learning* a model, in particular its transition probabilities, requiring memory quadratic in the number of states.

Related soundness. The formal methods community values trustworthy results with clear guarantees on possible analysis errors. For example, after finding that the common stopping criterion of the value iteration algorithm can lead to arbitrarily wrong results [20,44], the problem was addressed in many settings [6,9, 14,40,47,54,75]. Yet, in SMC, the issue of soundness has received little attention. Only recently, a survey of sound and unsound methods for estimating probabilities appeared [65], which our recommendations in Sec. 3 are based on.

2   Background

We write $\mathbb{1}_{pred}$ for the indicator function of *pred*: $\mathbb{1}_{pred}(x) = 1$ if *pred*(x) else 0. A *probability distribution* over a countable set S is a function $\mu \colon S \to [0, 1]$ such that $\sum_{s \in S} \mu(s) = 1$. Its *support* is $spt(\mu) \stackrel{\text{def}}{=} \{\, s \in S \mid \mu(s) > 0 \,\}$.

Models. The assumption of SMC is that models are given in a higher-level formalism—like HPnGs [68], IOSA [36], JANI [25], MODEST [19,45], or the PRISM language [55]—that allows behaviours to be randomly sampled without having to create an in-memory state space. Their semantics are some form of Markov process; we focus on the special case of DTMCs to simplify the presentation. All our methods immediately apply in the general setting or can be extended.

Definition 1. *A discrete-time Markov chain (DTMC) is a tuple $\langle S, R, T, s_I \rangle$ of a finite set of states S, a reward function $R \colon S \to \mathbb{R}_{\geqslant 0}$, an initial state $s_I \in S$, and a transition function $T \colon S \to Dist(S)$ mapping each state to a probability distribution over successor states. A (finite) path π (π_{fin}) is (a prefix of) an infinite sequence $\pi = s_0 \, s_1 \ldots \in S^\omega$ such that $s_0 = s_I$ and $\forall i \colon T(s_i)(s_{i+1}) > 0$.*

A DTMC induces a probability measure $\mathbb{P}$ over sets of paths that, intuitively, corresponds to multiplying the probabilities along the path (see e.g. [13, Chp. 10]). Abusing notation, we also use π or π_{fin} to refer to the set of a path's states. We write $\pi[i]$ for s_i, the path's $(i+1)$-th state, and $idx(\pi, S') = \min\{i \in \mathbb{N} \mid s_i \in S'\}$ for the index of the first state in $S' \subseteq S$ on π, with $idx(\pi, S') = \infty$ if $\pi \cap S' = \varnothing$. We write $r_{max} \stackrel{\text{def}}{=} \max\{R(s) \mid s \in S\}$ for a DTMC's maximum reward and $p_{min} \stackrel{\text{def}}{=} \min(\{T(s)(s') \mid s, s' \in S\} \setminus \{0\})$ for its minimum probability. We assume that, from only the higher-level formalism's syntax, we can efficiently obtain bounds $\overline{|S|} \geq |S|$, $\overline{r}_{max} \geq r_{max}$, and $0 < \underline{p}_{min} \leq p_{min}$.

Properties. Every property to be model-checked can be cast as the expected value $\mathbb{E}(X)$ w.r.t. of $\mathbb{P}$ of a random variable X that maps paths to values in $\mathbb{R}_{\geqslant 0}$. We consider the following kinds of properties, some of which take a step bound $c \in \mathbb{N}$ or a set of *goal states* $G \subseteq S$ specified as part of the model:

$$P_{\Diamond G} \stackrel{\text{def}}{=} \mathbb{E}(\lambda \pi. \, \mathbb{1}_{G \cap \pi \neq \varnothing}) \qquad\qquad \textit{(reachability probability)}$$

$$P_{\Diamond G}^{\leq c} \stackrel{\text{def}}{=} \mathbb{E}(\lambda \pi. \, \mathbb{1}_{idx(\pi, G) \leq c}) \qquad\qquad \textit{(bounded reach. probability)}_\perp$$

$$E_{\leq c} \stackrel{\text{def}}{=} \mathbb{E}(\lambda \pi. \, \textstyle\sum_{i=0}^{c} R(\pi[i])) \qquad\qquad \textit{(cumulative reward)}_\perp$$

$$E_{\Diamond G} \stackrel{\text{def}}{=} \mathbb{E}(\lambda \pi. \, \textstyle\sum_{i=0}^{idx(\pi, G)} R(\pi[i])) \qquad\qquad \textit{(reachability reward)}$$

$$E_{\Diamond G}^{\leq c} \stackrel{\text{def}}{=} \mathbb{E}(\lambda \pi. \, \textstyle\sum_{i=0}^{\min\{idx(\pi, G), \, c\}} R(\pi[i])) \qquad\qquad \textit{(bounded and reach. reward)}_\perp$$

$$E_{=c} \stackrel{\text{def}}{=} \mathbb{E}(\lambda \pi. \, R(\pi[c])) \qquad\qquad \textit{(instantaneous reward)}_\perp$$

$$E_{=G} \stackrel{\text{def}}{=} \mathbb{E}(\lambda \pi. \, R(\pi[idx(\pi, G)])) \qquad\qquad \textit{(reach-instant reward)}$$

Rewards are obtained upon entering states. $E_{\Diamond G}$ and $E_{=G}$ are defined to be ∞ if $\mathbb{P}(\{\pi \mid idx(\pi, G) = \infty\}) > 0$ [41]. The properties marked $\perp$ are *bounded*; all others are *unbounded*. The former are typical for SMC, required by e.g. PLASMA LAB [60, Table 1] and SMC STORM [56, Sect. 2.1]. Unbounded reachability probabilities and rewards, on the other hand, are standard in PMC and dominate model collections like the Quantitative Verification Benchmark Set (QVBS) [48].

Statistical model checking. At its core, SMC is Monte Carlo simulation [2,52, 59]: randomly generate a predetermined number k of paths, or *simulation runs*, that give rise to samples $X_1, \ldots, X_k$ of the random variable X; then compute the empirical mean $\hat{X} \stackrel{\text{def}}{=} \frac{1}{k} \sum_{i=1}^{k} X_i$, and perform a *statistical evaluation* to obtain a confidence interval $I = [l, u] \ni \hat{X}$ at predetermined *confidence level* γ.

Simulation. How to obtain simulation runs is specific to each higher-level formalism. We only assume that a method *sample(M, prop)* exists that, given a model M, implements the random variable X of property *prop*, i.e. that (pseu-do-)randomly generates a path π_{fin} through M's semantics according to $\mathbb{P}$ that is long enough to evaluate X and returns $X(\pi_{fin})$. For bounded properties, the "long enough" criterion is straightforward: just generate paths of length c.

To end a simulation run for $P_{\diamond G}$, we must determine whether it entered a bottom strongly connected component (BSCC) without goal states. For $E_{\diamond G}$ and $E_{=G}$ to be finite, we must determine whether a non-goal BSCC *exists*. BSCCs can be detected statistically by sampling given some structural information (such as p_{min}) [7]. Yet this requires storing a set of visited states that can be as large as S, breaking the $\mathcal{O}(1)$ memory property of SMC. Additionally, some fraction of $1 - \gamma$ must be devoted to all these tests (see e.g. [35]). However, most verification models—such as those in the QVBS—are structured so that (i) for reachability probabilities, all BSCCs contain only one state, and (ii) the goal state sets in reachability rewards are reached with probability 1, which allows for an efficient but limited stopping criterion. We follow this assumption in this paper.

Statistical evaluation. If we repeat the SMC procedure m times to obtain confidence intervals $I_1, \ldots, I_m$, we find some of them might be incorrect, i.e. $\mathbb{E}(X) \notin I_i$ for some i; occasionally obtaining an "incorrect" result is the nature of a statistical approach based on sampling. The (a priori) probability for a correct result is the *coverage probability* $p_{cov}(k) = \lim_{m \to \infty} \frac{cov_m}{m}$, where cov_m denotes the amount of correct confidence intervals. We call an SMC procedure **sound** if it is guaranteed to provide *probably approximately correct* (PAC) results: Given k and confidence level γ, it has $p_{cov}(k) \geq \gamma$ while producing intervals of width $|I| \leq 2\varepsilon$. Then, the midpoint of this interval is ε-close to the true mean of X with high probability.

Sound SMC results are obtained by employing an appropriate *statistical (evaluation) method* (SM) that relates k (or the concrete X_i), γ, and ε to ensure the PAC requirement, with two values given and the third under control of the SM. We consider two settings: The **fixed-k** setting, where γ and k are given while ε is determined by the SM, and the **sequential** setting, where γ and ε are given so that the SM must determine k. In the latter, k can precomputed from γ and ε, or it can be determined by a *truly sequential* SM that continuously checks whether enough samples have been gathered to be γ-confident of an interval I with $|I| \leq 2\varepsilon$. We always assume γ to be given, a typical value being $\gamma = 0.95$.

3   Sound SMC for Probabilities

For probabilities, i.e. $P_{\diamond G}$ and $P_{\diamond G}^{\leq c}$, each simulation run is a Bernoulli trial with outcome $X_i \in \{0, 1\}$. Thus, the SM samples from a binomial distribution with success probability p. After k samples, it observed $k_s = \sum_{i=1}^{k} X_i$ successes and has empirical mean $\hat{p} = \frac{k_s}{k} = \hat{X}$. Constructing a γ-confidence interval around $\hat{p}$ is a well-studied problem in statistics, resulting in many SMs for this task. We often abbreviate $\delta = 1 - \gamma$ for readability.

Meggendorfer et al. [65, Sec. 3] survey SMs in the context of "model-based SMC" for Markov decision processes, where individual transition probabilities are estimated to "learn" the model. Methods for this specific case also apply to SMC for reachability (and other "qualitative" 0/1 properties) in DTMCs. Hence, we recap their survey of SMs, extending it with examples and plots. Moreover, [65] only considers the fixed-k setting, whereas we also discuss the sequential setting and hypothesis testing. Our survey is the basis for the tool comparison in Sec. 5, where we show that existing tools use unsound and/or inefficient methods.

3.1   Unsound Methods

Denote by $p_{cov}(k, p)$ the coverage probability that the SM at hand attains given success probability p. Many of the commonly used SMs for binomial proportions only guarantee an *average* coverage probability of γ, i.e. $\int_0^1 p_{cov}(k, p)\,\mathrm{d}p \geq \gamma$. This is not in line with the frequentist definition of a confidence interval and **not** sufficient for sound SMC, producing too many incorrect results for certain values of p. We instead require that $\inf_{p=0}^1 p_{cov}(k, p) \geq \gamma$.

As per [65], unsound methods include those based on the central limit theorem (CLT), in particular the textbook Wald interval, the Wilson score interval, the Agresti-Coull interval [3], the Arcsine interval, and the Logit interval.

The Wilson score interval with continuity correction (Wilson/CC) [67] complements the CLT by adding adjustment terms to improve coverage. However, Newcombe already observed slightly below-nominal coverage [67, Table II], and [65] confirms the insufficient coverage for high confidence levels and p close to 0 or 1.

Sequential setting. Given ε instead of k, Chow and Robbins [33] show that the coverage of constructing a Wald interval after every sample and terminating once this interval has half-width $\leq \varepsilon$ goes to γ as $\varepsilon \to 0$. For any concrete $\varepsilon > 0$, however, coverage $\geq \gamma$ may not be achieved and thus this procedure is not sound for SMC. Reijsbergen et al. [76] adapt it to perform hypothesis testing with some extra parameters that reduce, but do not eliminate, the chance for incorrect results. The sequential methods proposed by Chen [30] are *empirically* sound, i.e. they appear to produce sound results in practice, but soundness is not proven for p close to $\frac{1}{2}$, and even for p away from $\frac{1}{2}$ only as a one-sided version.

3.2   Sound Methods

Okamoto bound. In 1959, Okamoto [70] proved that, for binomial proportions, $\mathbb{P}(\hat{p} - p \geq \varepsilon) \leq e^{-2k\varepsilon^2}$. We want $\delta \leq \mathbb{P}(|\hat{p} - p| \geq \varepsilon)$, giving

$$\frac{\delta}{2} \leq e^{-2k\varepsilon^2} \quad \Leftrightarrow \quad \varepsilon \geq \sqrt{\frac{\ln \frac{2}{\delta}}{2k}} \quad \Leftrightarrow \quad k \geq \frac{\ln \frac{2}{\delta}}{2\varepsilon^2}$$

by distributing δ symmetrically. Thus the interval $I_{Oka} = [\hat{p} - \varepsilon, \hat{p} + \varepsilon]$ always has coverage $\geq \gamma$ when ε, k, and δ satisfy the above inequalities. This bound is also referred to as Hoeffding bound [50] after his more general inequality, see Sec. 4.1.

Clopper-Pearson interval. The "exact" binomial interval by Clopper and Pearson [34] guarantees coverage $\geq \gamma$ for all p. One of several ways to compute it is

$$I_{CP} = [B(\delta/2, k_s, k - k_s + 1), B(1 - \delta/2, k_s + 1, k - k_s)]$$

where $B(p, \alpha, \beta)$ is the p-quantile of the Beta(α, β) distribution.

Blyth-Still-Casella and Wang. The approaches of Blyth-Still-Casella [29] and Wang [81] are also sound and produce shortest intervals in a specific sense, but are intricate to implement and computationally very expensive.

Sequential setting. The Okamoto bound provides ε, k, or δ given the other two; thus it applies to the sequential setting, too. For the Clopper-Pearson interval, we use the recent result that its number of required samples is maximal when $\hat{p} = \frac{1}{2}$ [65]. Based on this worst case, we can precompute the smallest k where the interval width is $\leq 2\varepsilon$ and perform a fixed-k evaluation.

3.3   Discussion

Recipes for sequential SMs. The minimum k may depend on p; e.g. for Clopper-Pearson, lower k suffice for p close to 0 or 1. A truly sequential method could exploit this. Any fixed SM can be converted to truly sequential in the Chow-Robbins style by checking after every sample if half-width $\leq \varepsilon$ is met, resulting in methods like "sequential Clopper-Pearson". They however are **not sound** as in general sample mean $\hat{p}$ and precision $|I|$ are correlated [51].

We may first spend a fraction of the "error budget" δ to get a rough interval estimate of p, and then calculate the number of samples required (given the remaining part of δ) based on the worst case in this interval, e.g. the value closest to $\frac{1}{2}$ for Clopper-Pearson as in [21]. Jégourel et al.'s two-step approach [51] similarly uses the Massart bound which improves on Okamoto's if p is known to be away from $\frac{1}{2}$. While sound and better than precomputation, these are two-step (generalisable to n-step), not truly sequential, approaches.

Frey [42] calculates a δ^* a priori so that, if a confidence level of $\gamma^* = 1 - \delta^*$ is used in each iteration of a Chow-Robbins-style sequentialisation of a sound fixed SM, the overall coverage probability soundly comes out to γ. However, computing such a δ^* becomes very hard already for small k (around 100-1000). The ADASELECT [38] and EBSTOP [66] algorithms are sequential methods for the relative error setting, recently generalised by Parmentier and Legay [71].

Example 1 (Soundness). To evaluate SMs for probabilities, we can directly compute their coverage probabilities for binomial distributions (see [27, App. C]). To give a visual comparison of coverage probabilities highlighting the concern for soundness, we fix confidence level $\gamma = 0.9$ and calculate the coverage probabilities for various methods in Fig. 1. The top row shows $p_{cov}(50, p)$ as achieved by the unsound Wald, the sound-but-inefficient Okamoto, and the sound-and-recommended Clopper-Pearson interval. Indeed, the Wald interval does not attain coverage ≥ 0.9 for many values of p, while the others do. Similarly, the bottom row concerns the truly sequential setting with $\varepsilon = 0.05$ and shows that the coverage probabilities for the unsound Chow-Robbins and sequential Clopper-Pearson methods are sometimes below γ. For Chen's method, we confirm its empirical but unproven soundness.

Example 2 (Sample Efficiency). We also observe that Okamoto significantly overshoots the desired confidence, which increases the number of samples it

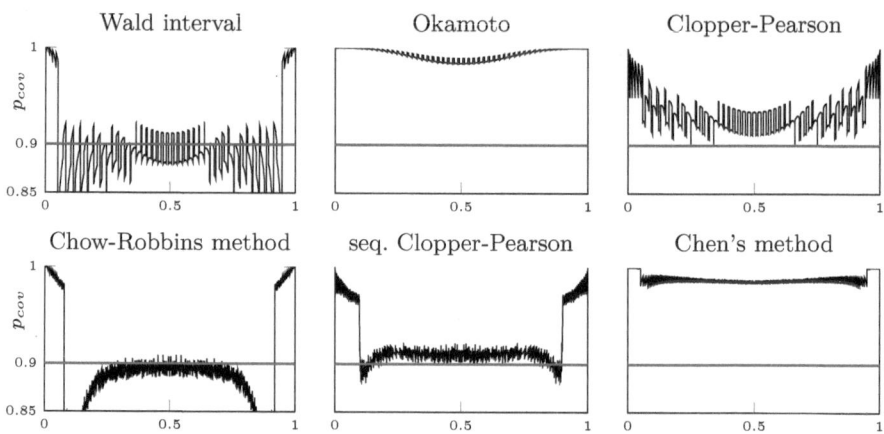

Fig. 1. Coverage for fixed (top, $k = 50$) and sequential methods (bottom, $\varepsilon = 0.05$).

requires. Indeed, I_{CP} always needs fewer samples than I_{Oka} experimentally [65, Sec. 3.3]. For example, with $\gamma = 0.95$ and $\varepsilon = 0.01$, we get a minimum k of 18 445 for Okamoto, independent of p or $\hat{p}$. For Clopper-Pearson, we get a worst-case k of 9 701; for k given and p closer to 0 or 1, we would in turn get much smaller ε.

Hypothesis testing. All methods that produce sound confidence intervals $I = [l, u]$ can be turned into sound hypothesis tests for deciding whether $p \sim p_t$ for a threshold p_t and $\sim \in \{\leq, \geq\}$: assuming $\sim$ is $\leq$, answer *yes* if $u \leq p_t$, *no* if $l \geq p_t$, and *unknown* otherwise. A dedicated and efficient method for hypothesis testing is the sequential probability ratio test (SPRT) [80]. It is sound if we consider its *indifference region* (an interval $[p - \varepsilon_i, p + \varepsilon_i]$ where the SPRT is allowed to give wrong answers) to fulfil the role of the ε error in our PAC requirement.

Our recommendation is to implement the Clopper-Pearson interval for $P_{\diamond G}$ and $P_{\diamond G}^{\leq c}$ in the fixed and sequential settings as it is proven sound *and* sample-efficient. In the sequential setting, a two-step approach can be considered. The Okamoto bound, employed by *most* tools using a sound method (Sec. 5), needs too many samples and produces overly conservative intervals: it should not be used for estimating probabilities. We highlight that our recommendations are independent of the underlying system dynamics and thus apply to SMC in general.

4   Sound SMC for Expected Rewards

For unbounded expected rewards, each simulation run is a sample from an unknown *path reward distribution* μ with outcomes in $[0, \infty)$. Given k samples, we want a PAC guarantee for the expected value $E_{\diamond G}$. In general, *no* SM can guarantee coverage for unknown distributions with unbounded support. Intuitively, k gives the SM an indication of how likely it is to have missed some paths; with

Fig. 2. High reward with low probability   **Fig. 3.** Unbounded path rewards

bounded support (e.g. for probabilities), this allows to quantify the uncertainty and thus ε. With unbounded support, outcomes with extremely low probability can dominate the expectation if they are even more extremely large. We discuss the general case in [27, App. A] and here provide an illustrative example.

Example 3. The DTMC in Fig. 2 has $E_{=\{t_1,t_2\}} = c$. If k is significantly lower than n, however, the SM likely only sees paths to t_2 and—if it is not sound—returns a confidence interval with an upper bound far below c.

When $spt(\mu) \subseteq [a, b]$, a number of sound SMs exists, which we survey below. Then, in Sec. 4.2, we avoid the general impossibility of the unbounded case in two ways. First, we exploit structural information about the DTMC to reduce to the bounded case. Second, we introduce a novel perspective by considering a new notion of statistically converging lower bounds.

4.1 Statistical Methods for Bounded Distributions

The textbook confidence interval for the mean of an unknown distribution is the *normal interval*: $I_{Norm} = \hat{X} \pm z_\delta \hat{\sigma}/\sqrt{k}$, where $\hat{\sigma}$ is the empirical standard deviation and z_δ the $(1 - \frac{\delta}{2})$-quantile of the standard normal distribution. (Obtaining z_δ via the Student's-t distribution with $k - 1$ degrees of freedom instead may work better for smaller k.) While asymptotic statement of Chow and Robbins about the normal interval also holds in the general, non-binomial setting, these methods are **not sound**. For example, on the DTMC of Fig. 2 with $n = 1000$, $c = 1$ and $k = 500$, we experimentally found I_{Norm} for $\gamma = 0.95$ to have a coverage probability of only $\approx 0.39 \ll 0.95$. Knowing bounds $[a, b]$ on the distribution's support, however, the sound methods we list below in this section are available.

Hoeffding's inequality. The Okamoto bound of Sec. 3.2 is a special case of Hoeffding's inequality, which actually bounds the sum of independent (not necessarily i.i.d.) bounded random variables [50]. It states that

$$\mathbb{P}(\hat{X} - \mathbb{E}(X) \geq \varepsilon) \leq e^{-\frac{2k\varepsilon^2}{(b-a)^2}}$$

and accordingly $\varepsilon \geq (b - a)\sqrt{(\ln 2/\delta)/2k}$ for the two-sided case by distributing δ equally. Note that Chernoff bounds [32] can be used to derive this inequality.

Bennett's and Bernstein's inequalities. Bennett's inequality can provide tighter bounds on a sum of random variables than Hoeffding's by taking the variance σ^2 into account [16]. However, not knowing the distribution, we do not know σ^2 either. We could insert bounds, a simple one being $\sigma^2 \leq \frac{1}{4}(b-a)^2$. Then, however,

Bennet's inequality is strictly worse than Hoeffding's [65, App. B]. Bernstein's inequality [17,18] is a relaxation of Bennet's that is easier to compute, but yields even wider intervals. Thus, in our setting, Hoeffding's inequality is preferable.

Dvoretzky-Kiefer-Wolfowitz(-Massart) inequality (DKW). The DKW [39, 62] relates the cumulative distribution function (cdf) $F(x) = \mathbb{P}(X \leq x)$ of the unknown distribution μ to the empirical cdf $\hat{F}(x) = \frac{1}{k} \sum_{i=1}^{k} \mathbb{1}_{X_i \leq x}$ as follows:

$$\mathbb{P}\left(\sup_{x \in \mathbb{R}} |\hat{F}(x) - F(x)| > \varepsilon\right) \leq 2e^{-2k\varepsilon^2}.$$

DKW is about thresholds, i.e. in our setting the probability of exceeding a certain reward. It characterizes a confidence band in which the real cdf lies with high probability. This can be used to derive bounds on the expected value by computing the expected values of the best- and worst-case cdfs within the confidence band. Formally, let C be a confidence band containing an uncountable set of cdfs; then with probability at least $1 - 2e^{-2k\varepsilon^2}$ we have

$$\min_{\underline{F} \in C} \mathbb{E}(Y \mid Y \sim \underline{F}) \leq \mathbb{E}(X) \leq \max_{\overline{F} \in C} \mathbb{E}(Y \mid Y \sim \overline{F}).$$

The cdfs minimising or maximising the expectation can be easily computed, as they are the upper and lower bound of the confidence band, respectively:

$$\underline{F}(x) = \min\left\{1, \hat{F}(x) + \sqrt{\tfrac{1}{2k} \ln \tfrac{2}{\delta}}\right\} \qquad \overline{F}(x) = \max\left\{0, \hat{F}(x) - \sqrt{\tfrac{1}{2k} \ln \tfrac{2}{\delta}}\right\}$$

Fig. 4 illustrates the DKW[8] for $[a, b] = [-3, 3]$, with F the smooth orange line, $\hat{F}$ the light blue step function in the center, and the outer purple step functions being $\underline{F}$ (to the left, with a higher probability for smaller outcomes) and $\overline{F}$ (to the right). All steps of $\underline{F}$ are the same as those of $\hat{F}$ except that we "map" the largest $\sqrt{(\ln 2/\delta)/2k}$ fraction of steps to the lower bound (i.e. at $x = a$). Similarly, $\overline{F}$ shifts probability mass into the upper bound b. In the worst case, the expectations of $\underline{F}$ or $\overline{F}$ coincide

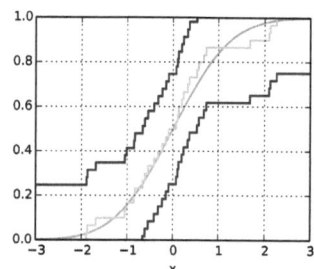

Fig. 4. The DKW cdfs

with Hoeffding, but provide a tighter confidence interval when few samples have an extremal value of a or b. Applying DKW is therefore especially advantageous when one of the a priori bounds a and b is very loose and samples are far above/below it. The best case is obtained when all samples coincide, where the width of confidence interval halves when using DKW as opposed to Hoeffding. In any case, the DKW interval is always contained in the Hoeffding interval.

Proposition 1. *For given confidence level γ and set of samples from a distribution with bounds $[a, b]$, let $[l_d, u_d]$ and $[l_h, u_h]$ be confidence intervals given by DKW and Hoeffing's inequality, respectively. Then $l_h \leq l_d < u_d \leq u_h$ and $\frac{u_h - l_h}{u_d - l_d} \leq 2$.*

DKW is also used by Phan et al. [58,72] with a view towards machine learning applications, who attribute its application to expected rewards to Anderson [4].

---

[8] Fig. 4 is based on file commons.wikimedia.org/wiki/File:DKW_bounds.svg (CC0).

Sequential setting and hypothesis testing. Hoeffding's inequality applies in the sequential setting in the same way as the Okamoto bound. For DKW, we could precompute k based on the worst case, but this coincides with Hoeffding. As mentioned, the Chow-Robbins scheme remains applicable and unsound. The ADASELECT algorithm we mentioned in Sec. 3.3 also works soundly for bounded distributions when a relative error is desired. For hypothesis testing, the SPRT in principle also applies to bounded distributions, and will in general perform better than the DKW for testing a single threshold. The latter's advantage is that it provides an entire confidence *band* around the cdf and thereby allows deriving the expected reward as well as probability bounds on *all* reward thresholds *at once*. In this way, the DKW can also be used to tackle quantile problems.

Our recommendation for estimating a bounded distribution is to use DKW in the fixed-k setting and resort to Hoeffding's inequality when given ε.

4.2   Bounding Expected Rewards

For a full sound SMC procedure for expected rewards, it remains to find the bounds $[a, b]$ on the path rewards. As rewards are non-negative, $a = 0$ is a safe lower bound (though larger a may give lower ε or k), leaving b to be determined.

Instantaneous and cumulative rewards. We know $\bar{r}_{max}$, an upper bound on the maximum state reward (Sec. 2). For instantaneous reward properties $E_{=c}$ and $E_{=G}$, a path's reward is at most $\max_{s \in S} R(s)$, making $b = \bar{r}_{max}$ the tightest safe upper bound we can give. For step-bounded reward properties $E_{\leq c}$ and $E_{\diamond G}^{\leq c}$, we can upper-bound the reward of a path $\pi = s_0 \ldots$ by $b = (c+1) \cdot \bar{r}_{max} \geq \sum_{i=0}^{c} R(s_i)$. Exploiting specific structures in higher-level languages may yield tighter bounds.

Reachability rewards. For unbounded reachability rewards $E_{\diamond G}$, we need to bound the accumulated path reward until visiting a state in G, i.e. $PR(\pi) = \sum_{i=0}^{idx(\pi, G)} R(\pi[i])$. We assume $\mathbb{E}(PR)$ to be finite, but PR can still be unbounded:

Example 4. Consider the very simple DTMC in Fig. 3. We have $E_{\diamond G} = \sum_{i=1}^{\infty} i \cdot (1/2)^i = 2$, but the reward of a single path is unbounded, since every reward $v \in \mathbb{N}$ is obtained with positive probability $(1/2)^v$.

This is not a degenerate case, but occurs whenever there exists a cycle with non-zero rewards. Consequently, we cannot directly apply the SMs from Sec. 4.1. Nevertheless, we can give meaningful estimations, by requiring additional knowledge or by relaxing the constraints on the result.

Bounding large values. As we cannot bound PR, we aim to bound the effect that large values have on $\mathbb{E}(PR)$. Let us work in a general setting, as follows:

Definition 2. *Let $(\Omega, \mathcal{F}, \mathbb{P})$ be a probability space, $X \colon \Omega \to \mathbb{R}_{\geq 0}$ a random variable with finite expectation, and $B \in \mathcal{F}$. We call B an ε-bounding set if (i) $\int_{\bar{B}} X \, d\mathbb{P} < \varepsilon$ (with $\bar{B} = \Omega \setminus B$), and (ii) $\forall \omega \in B \colon X(\omega) \in [a, b]$.*

(Concretely, X could be PR.) If B is a bounding set, then we can rewrite

$$\mathbb{E}(X) = \int_\Omega X \, d\mathbb{P} = \int_B X \, d\mathbb{P} + \int_{\overline{B}} X \, d\mathbb{P} < \int_B X \, d\mathbb{P} + \varepsilon.$$

Observe that $\int_B X \, d\mathbb{P} = \mathbb{E}(X^B)$, where $X^B(\omega) = X(\omega)$ if $X \in B$ else 0. Since we chose B such that $X(\omega) \in [a, b]$ for all $\omega \in B$, X^B clearly is bounded and we can apply our previous methods to obtain a statistical estimate of X^B. Inserting in the above equation then yields a bound on the overall expectation of X.

One possible choice for B would be $\{\omega \mid |X(\omega)| < t\}$ for a sufficiently large t. Such a t exists for any random variable with finite expectation by positivity and additivity of $\mathbb{P}$ (when $\mathbb{E}(X) = \int_\Omega X \, d\mathbb{P} < \infty$ we necessarily have $\lim_{t \to \infty} \int_{\{|X| > t\}} X \, d\mathbb{P} = 0$). However, without further assumptions we cannot derive such a t or any other kind of bounding set just by sampling. Thus, in the following we exploit that DTMCs give some structure to the random variable.

Geometric path lengths. While the value of PR in Ex. 4 can be arbitrarily large, as long as the expectation $\mathbb{E}(PR)$ is finite, this only happens with vanishingly low probabilities. This is the case for DTMCs (and many other Markov systems, see Remark 1) in general: Intuitively, the number of steps until G is reached is (roughly) geometrically distributed.

Lemma 1. *Let $\varepsilon > 0$. Choose q such that*

$$|S| \cdot \overline{r}_{max} \cdot (1 - (\underline{p}_{min})^{\overline{|S|}})^q \cdot (q - q(\underline{p}_{min})^{\overline{|S|}} + 1) \cdot (\underline{p}_{min})^{-\overline{|S|}} < \varepsilon.$$

Then $B = \lozenge^{\leq q \cdot \overline{|S|}} G = \{\pi \mid idx(\pi, G) \leq q \cdot \overline{|S|}\}$ is a bounding set.

Proof (Sketch). Every state s has a path of length at most $|S|$ to the goal G by assumption. Such a path has probability at least $(p_{min})^{|S|}$ and reward at most $|S| \cdot r_{max}$. Considering $|S|$ steps as an "episode", we can geometrically lower bound the probability to reach G after q episodes, and use this to upper bound the reward. See [27, App. B.1] for the full proof.

Corollary 1. *Given bounds $\overline{|S|} \geq |S|$, $0 < \underline{p}_{min} \leq p_{min}$, and $\overline{r}_{max} \geq r_{max}$, we can give PAC guarantees on $E_\lozenge G$.*

Remark 1. Due to the worst-case over-approximation involved, q is extremely large even for very small DTMCs and is thus not a practical solution. For example, a DTMC with 5 states, $p_{min} = 0.05$, and $r_{max} = 1$ with a desired bound $\varepsilon = 1$ requires $q > 10^8$. The value $(p_{min})^{-|S|}$ is closely related to the *mixing time* of a DTMC, see e.g. [61], which, in our setting, intuitively upper bounds the time until a goal state is reached with high probability. While often a coarse bound, there exists DTMCs for which it is tight [44, Fig. 3]. Determining better bounds on the mixing time (and thus q) requires knowledge of the DTMC's state space and transitions, which SMC explicitly does not have access to. For Markovian systems other than DTMCs, the geometric path lengths construction can also be used, provided we can obtain similar bounds; we conjecture that a sufficient condition is that the system is finite and goal states are reached almost surely.

Lower bounds. The inability to practically bound b means that we cannot gain confidence in an *upper* bound on $E_{\diamond}G$. However, since rewards are non-negative, we cannot miss any extreme "negative" events. Thus we at least want to derive meaningful *lower bounds*. Since 0 trivially is a correct lower bound, we need a definition of bounds being "close" to the true value. We propose the novel definition of *limit-PAC* lower bounds: they are not only (i) sound, but additionally require that (ii) given enough samples, they (unknowingly) become ε-close.

Definition 3. *Let X be a random variable. A procedure $\mathcal{A}$ yields* limit-PAC *lower bounds on $\mathbb{E}(X)$ if, for any confidence γ, the following two conditions hold: (i) For a collection of independent samples Ξ drawn from X, we have $\mathbb{P}(\mathcal{A}(\Xi, \gamma) \leq \mathbb{E}(X)) \geq \gamma$. (ii) For any precision $\varepsilon > 0$, there exists a threshold k_0 such that for a collection of independent samples Ξ drawn from X with $|\Xi| \geq k_0$, we have $\mathbb{P}(\mathbb{E}(X) - \varepsilon \leq \mathcal{A}(\Xi, \gamma) \leq \mathbb{E}(X)) \geq \gamma$.*

Remark 2. Classical procedures such as normal intervals do not provide limit-PAC bounds. While they may satisfy condition (ii) and provide enough coverage to satisfy condition (i) in the limit, they can be unsound for many sample sets Ξ that are not "sufficiently close to the limit."

We describe a procedure "DKW-$\mathbb{E}$-Lower" which provides limit-PAC lower bounds: For a given set of samples Ξ with $k = |\Xi|$, set $\chi_k = \sqrt{(\ln 2/1 - \gamma)/2k}$ (using χ instead of ε to avoid a clash of notation) and compute the empirical average over Ξ, however setting the largest χ_k fraction of samples to 0. This is equivalent to computing the expectation of the minimising cdf $\underline{F}(x)$ provided by the DKW (with width χ_k), as explained in Sec. 4.1.

Theorem 1. *For any non-negative, finite-expectation random variable X, DKW-$\mathbb{E}$-Lower gives limit-PAC lower bounds on $\mathbb{E}(X)$.*

Proof (sketch, full proof in [27, App. B.2]). Condition (i) holds by the DKW with coverage $\geq \gamma$ due to our choice of χ_k. For condition (ii), note that for every $\varepsilon/2$, we can find some bounding set $\{X > t\}$. Then for large enough Ξ, the difference between the actual expected value and the output of DKW-$\mathbb{E}$-Lower on $[0, t]$ can be bounded by $\varepsilon/2$ as in the bounded case (see Sec. 4.1), and on $[t, \infty)$ the difference is also bounded by $\varepsilon/2$ by definition of bounding sets.

Corollary 2. *DKW-$\mathbb{E}$-Lower gives limit-PAC lower bounds on $E_{\diamond}G$.*

Note that Theorem 1 directly extends to any random variable with a known lower bound, i.e. $X \in [a, \infty)$, by considering $X' = X - a$. Then $X' \geq 0$ and any limit-PAC estimation of X' also yields one for X, as $\mathbb{E}(X) = \mathbb{E}(X') + a$. Similarly, for $X \in (-\infty, a]$ we can give limit-PAC *upper* bounds.

5   Implementation

State of the art. In Table 1, we collect the results of an extensive survey of the SMs used by default in all current SMC tools we are aware of. It is based on

Table 1. Default statistical methods used in state-of-the-art SMC tools

Tool		For probabilities $p \in [0,1]$		For rewards $r \in [a,b]$	
Name	Ref.	fixed k	seq. ε	fixed k	seq. ε
C-SMC	[31]	**Okamoto**	—	—	—
Cosmos	[15]	**Clopper-Pearson**	Chow-Robbins	**Hoeffding**	Chow-Robbins
Fig	[22]*	Wilson w/o CC	seq. Student's-t	—	—
Hypeg	[74]	—	seq. Student's-t	—	—
MODES (prev.)	[24]*	**Okamoto**	Chen	Normal	Chow-Robbins
MultiVeSta	[43]	—	Chow-Robbins	—	Chow-Robbins
Plasma Lab	[60]*	**Okamoto**	**Okamoto**	**Hoeffding**	**Hoeffding**
Prism	[55]*	Student's-t	seq. Student's-t	Student's-t	seq. Student's-t
Sbip	[69]	Normal	**Okamoto**	—	—
SmcStorm	[56]	—	Chen	—	Chow-Robbins
Uppaal Smc	[37]*	**Clopper-Pearson**	seq. Clopper-P.	Student's-t	—
MODES v3.1.281		**Clopper-Pearson**	**Clopper-Pearson**	**DKW**	**Hoeffding**

the information available in their tool papers (column *Ref.*); for those marked
"*", we also tested a current version or consulted its documentation[9] for more
accurate information. The "seq." prefix for a method indicates a Chow-Robbins-
like procedure using an interval different from Wald's/the normal approximation-
based one. We highlight the provably sound methods in boldface. Entries "—"
indicate that the tool does not appear to support that setting.

We see that, in the fixed setting for probabilities, 5 of 8 tools choose a
sound method, although three of those use the inefficient Okamoto bound; in the
sequential setting, only 2 of 10 tools use a sound (but inefficient) method. For
expected rewards, Cosmos and Plasma Lab apply Hoeffding's inequality when
there is an obvious upper bound b, with Cosmos using information from its
higher-level formalism (e.g. a system's finite capacity bound when estimating the
average number of clients) for this purpose. In the general setting, in particular
for their respective variants of reachability rewards, Cosmos will build a normal
interval instead while Plasma Lab will return the estimate $\hat{X}$ only, without
error bounds. Overall, *no tool* implements a sound *and* efficient method for
probabilities in the sequential setting, nor for rewards in the fixed setting; those
tools that use Hoeffding for rewards only do so for very specific cases.

Sound SMC in MODES. We have implemented the recommendations we make
w.r.t. SMs for probabilities and the new methods we propose for soundly handling
expected rewards in the newest version of the MODES statistical model checker as
shown in the last row of Table 1. In particular, MODES uses the k-precomputation
based on the Clopper-Pearson interval in the sequential setting for probabilities,
and the DKW in the fixed setting for expected rewards, improving upon the
state of the art in soundness and sample efficiency. MODES supports $P_{\diamond G}^{\leq c}$, $P_{\diamond G}$,

---

[9] We used Fig 1.3, the previous version of MODES from the MODEST TOOLSET v3.1.265,
Prism 4.8.1, Uppaal Smc 5.0.0 with its online documentation as of 2024-10-09, and
the Plasma Lab 1.4.4 documentation from the Web Archive as of 2019-11-01.

$E_{\diamond G}^{\leq c}$, and $E_{\diamond G}$ properties. For $E_{\diamond G}^{\leq c}$ properties, it computes the upper bound as $b = (c+1) \cdot \bar{r}_{max}$. For $E_{\diamond G}$, it uses our new DKW-$\mathbb{E}$-Lower method by default. MODES also implements the Wilson/CC, Wald/normal, and Student's-t intervals, the Okamoto bound, Chen's methods, the Chow-Robbins approach, and the SPRT. Via a command-line parameter, the user can provide a preference list of these methods; for each property being analysed, MODES chooses the first in the list that can be applied to it. By default, it prefers sound over unsound and then efficient over less efficient methods, resulting in the first choices as in Table 1.

6   Experimental Evaluation

To evaluate SMs for probabilities, we can directly work with the binomial distribution as in Ex. 1. With expected rewards, however, the shape of the (unknown) reward distribution matters. We thus use our implementation in MODES on models from the QVBS [48] to evaluate the coverage probability, performance, and effectiveness of the methods we propose in Sec. 4 in a realistic setting. The code and scripts for reproduction are available online [28].

Experimental setup. We used MODES version 3.1.273[10]. We chose all DTMC and Markov decision process (MDP) models from the QVBS that contain an expected-reward property (except those that just ask for an expected number of transitions), excluding only the artificial *haddad-monmege* model plus *bluetooth* and *oscillators*, which MODES cannot handle for technical reasons (the former having multiple initial states, which MODES does not support[11], and the latter's syntax being too large to parse and compile[12]). We turn the MDP into DTMC by applying the PRISM language's DTMC semantics, which resolves all nondeterministic choices uniformly at random. The models are parametrised; we use up to four parameter valuations each, including the smallest and largest ones included in QVBS. A triple ⟨*model, parameter values, property*⟩ is a *benchmark instance*.

We consider all $E_{\diamond G}^{\leq c}$ and $E_{\diamond G}$ properties included with the models, the only $E_{\diamond G}^{\leq c}$ property being in the *resource-gathering* model. To be able to study the DKW and Hoeffding methods, we manually turn all $E_{\diamond G}$ into $E_{\diamond G}^{\leq c}$ by experimentally determining a small c that does not change the value of the property up to the third significant digit.[13] This in essence constitutes a manually-derived bounding

---

[10] MODES 3.1.273 implements all methods as described in Sec. 5, but uses Wilson/CC for probabilities by default. Version 3.1.281 defaults to Clopper-Pearson as in Table 1.

[11] Supporting multiple initial states, while natural for a PCTL model checker like PRISM, would require an SMC tool to perform a separate analysis starting from each initial state and thus defeat the scalability of SMC.

[12] The *oscillators* model explicitly encodes a large flat state space in the higher-level PRISM language's syntax, overwhelming MODES' parser that assumes its input to *compactly* encode a potentially large state space for SMC to sample runs from.

[13] We obtain reference results from the QVBS, if available, or via SMC with $k = 5 \cdot 10^6$. We determine a c as follows: Use SMC with $k = 10^6$ and some step bound c to obtain a value. If the three most significant digits of this value are equal to the reference result, stop and report c. Otherwise, increase c and repeat. All choices of c greater

set except we truncate rewards instead of setting them to 0. [27, App. D.1] lists the resulting 44 instances (including the values of c).

Coverage probabilities. While the normal interval and Chow-Robbins are unsound, it was not clear if this manifests on real models under typical k and ε. To investigate this, we implemented an empirical coverage test inside MODES: Given a benchmark instance, a confidence γ, step bound k, and a number m, it executes SMC with fixed k for m times, each time computing a γ-confidence interval. It counts w, the number of times the reference result was *wrong*, i.e. not in the computed confidence interval. Thus, we obtain the empirical coverage probability as $p_{cov} = \frac{w}{m}$, and compute a "meta" confidence interval $[l_{cov}, u_{cov}]$ around it using Clopper-Pearson.

In Table 2, we report the result of using this empirical coverage test choosing $\gamma = 0.95$, $k = 1000$, and $m = 5000$. We report the number of benchmark instances where the respective SM attained insufficient coverage $(p_{cov} < \gamma)$ in a statistically significant way $(u_{cov} < \gamma)$, as well

Table 2. Coverage over 44 instances ($\gamma = 0.95$)

SM	$u_{cov}{<}\gamma$	$p_{cov}{<}\gamma$	min p_{cov}	$\varnothing\, p_{cov}$
Normal	10	31	0.908	0.946
Student's-t	9	32	0.902	0.947
Hoeffding (k)	0	0	1	1
DKW	0	0	0.999	1.000
Chow-Robbins	16	24	0.723	0.937
Hoeffding (ε)	0	0	1	1

as the minimum min p_{cov} and average $\varnothing\, p_{cov}$ of the 44 coverage probabilities. Detailed results are in [27, App. D.2]. Hoeffding's inequality and the DKW produced only sound results as expected, although Hoeffding timed out (> 10 minutes) 39 times in the sequential setting. The unsound methods produce incorrect results much more often than they claim, with the insufficiency even being statistically significant in almost a quarter of the benchmark instances.

Performance. We next evaluate the performance of the two sound SMs available when $[a, b]$ is known. The runtime spent on the calculations involved with the SMs that we consider is negligible compared to that for generating sample paths. We thus compare the performance of Hoeffding's inequality and the DKW via the half-width ε of the interval returned given fixed $k = 500\,000$. The results are shown as a scatter plot in Fig. 5, where every point $\langle x, y \rangle$ (blue for DTMCs, orange for MDPs) is the result of one benchmark instance, stating that using

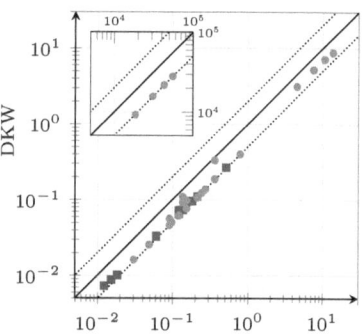

Fig. 5. Sound ε given k

Hoeffding's inequality resulted in $\varepsilon = x$ while the DKW gave $\varepsilon = y$. Note the logarithmic scale; points on the dotted diagonals mark 2× differences. We see that, as expected, the DKW consistently produces smaller intervals; the geometric mean of the ratios $\frac{\varepsilon \text{ for Hoeffding}}{\varepsilon \text{ for DKW}}$ over all 44 instances is 1.72, close to the

---

than the output of this procedure allow to approximate the result with precision 10^{-3}, in particular since in all QVBS models the target state is reached with probability 1.

theoretical maximum of 2 (see Proposition 1). Our upper bounds b computed as per Sec. 4.2 are rather loose, benefiting DKW and resulting in very asymmetric DKW intervals with a lower bound close to the true value and an upper bound similar to Hoeffding's.

Effectiveness. For unknown b as in $E_{\diamond G}$ properties, we test how quickly our novel DKW-$\mathbb{E}$-Lower method converges to the (usually unknown) true value by applying it to our 44 benchmark instances for $k = 10^i$ with $i \in \{2, 3, 4, 5, 6\}$. All results are in [27, App. D.3] and show behaviour similar to the three benchmark instances of Fig. 6 (from top to bottom: $\langle coupon, \langle 15, 4, 5 \rangle, exp\_draws \rangle$, $\langle resource\text{-}gathering, \langle 1300, 100, 100 \rangle, expgold \rangle$, and $\langle egl, \langle 5, 8 \rangle, messagesB \rangle$). The distance between the lower bound and the true value in most cases decreases by a factor between 2 and 3 on each step. Over all instances and steps, on average (geometric mean) the distance decreases by a factor of 2.6, which gives an indication of the practical convergence rate of the DKW-$\mathbb{E}$-Lower method.

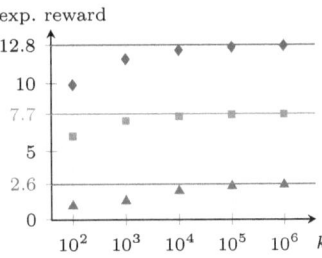

Fig. 6. DKW-$\mathbb{E}$-Lower

7   Conclusion

We raise attention to the issue of soundness in SMC given a state of the art where many tools use unsound statistical methods. For estimating probabilities, several sound methods exist, which have recently been compared in [65]. We summarised them as a reference for the SMC practitioner, and expanded upon [65] by looking into the sequential setting as well as adding coverage probability plots that highlight the level of (un)soundness at a glance and providing an overview of the methods employed by tools. For expected-reward properties, only two tools had (ad-hoc and inefficient) sound methods so far; we contribute a recommendation for the—apparently little-known—DKW and a thorough treatment of the problem of bounding the path reward distribution. While our proof that sound SMC is possible for reachability rewards is currently of theoretical use only, we expect our notion of bounding sets to be crucial for future practical solutions based on the identification of specific structural features of a model's state space or higher-level description. On the practical side, we formalised the notion of *limit-PAC* procedures, which we instantiate by the DKW-$\mathbb{E}$-Lower method that we show to give close bounds in practice. As immediate future work, our results can be extended to estimating rare event probabilities, where samples are in $[0, 1]$ or potentially unbounded depending on the rare event simulation method used. Our contributions should transfer to continuous-time Markov chains straightforwardly.

Data availability statement. The models, tools, and scripts to reproduce our experimental evaluation are archived and available at DOI 10.5281/zenodo.14743520 [28].

References

1. Agarwal, C., Guha, S., Kretínský, J., Muruganandham, P.: PAC statistical model checking of mean payoff in discrete- and continuous-time MDP. In: CAV (2). Lecture Notes in Computer Science, vol. 13372, pp. 3–25. Springer (2022). https://doi.org/10.1007/978-3-031-13188-2_1

2. Agha, G., Palmskog, K.: A survey of statistical model checking. ACM Trans. Model. Comput. Simul. **28**(1), 6:1–6:39 (2018). https://doi.org/10.1145/3158668

3. Agresti, A., Coull, B.A.: Approximate is better than "exact" for interval estimation of binomial proportions. The American Statistician **52**(2), 119–126 (1998). https://doi.org/10.2307/2685469

4. Anderson, T.W.: Confidence limits for the value of an arbitrary bounded random variable with a continuous distribution function. Bulletin of The International and Statistical Institute **43**, 249–251 (1969)

5. Ashok, P., Butkova, Y., Hermanns, H., Kretínský, J.: Continuous-time Markov decisions based on partial exploration. In: Lahiri, S.K., Wang, C. (eds.) 16th International Symposium on Automated Technology for Verification and Analysis (ATVA). Lecture Notes in Computer Science, vol. 11138, pp. 317–334. Springer (2018). https://doi.org/10.1007/978-3-030-01090-4_19

6. Ashok, P., Chatterjee, K., Daca, P., Kretínský, J., Meggendorfer, T.: Value iteration for long-run average reward in Markov decision processes. In: CAV (1). Lecture Notes in Computer Science, vol. 10426, pp. 201–221. Springer (2017). https://doi.org/10.1007/978-3-319-63387-9_10

7. Ashok, P., Daca, P., Kretínský, J., Weininger, M.: Statistical model checking: Black or white? In: Margaria, T., Steffen, B. (eds.) 9th International Symposium on Leveraging Applications of Formal Methods (ISoLA). Lecture Notes in Computer Science, vol. 12476, pp. 331–349. Springer (2020). https://doi.org/10.1007/978-3-030-61362-4_19

8. Ashok, P., Kretínský, J., Weininger, M.: PAC statistical model checking for markov decision processes and stochastic games. In: CAV (1). Lecture Notes in Computer Science, vol. 11561, pp. 497–519. Springer (2019). https://doi.org/10.1007/978-3-030-25540-4_29

9. Azeem, M., Evangelidis, A., Kretínský, J., Slivinskiy, A., Weininger, M.: Optimistic and topological value iteration for simple stochastic games. In: ATVA. Lecture Notes in Computer Science, vol. 13505, pp. 285–302. Springer (2022). https://doi.org/10.1007/978-3-031-19992-9_18

10. Baier, C.: Probabilistic model checking. In: Esparza, J., Grumberg, O., Sickert, S. (eds.) Dependable Software Systems Engineering, NATO Science for Peace and Security Series – D: Information and Communication Security, vol. 45, pp. 1–23. IOS Press (2016). https://doi.org/10.3233/978-1-61499-627-9-1

11. Baier, C., de Alfaro, L., Forejt, V., Kwiatkowska, M.: Model checking probabilistic systems. In: Clarke, E.M., Henzinger, T.A., Veith, H., Bloem, R. (eds.) Handbook of Model Checking, pp. 963–999. Springer (2018). https://doi.org/10.1007/978-3-319-10575-8_28

12. Baier, C., Haverkort, B.R., Hermanns, H., Katoen, J.P.: Performance evaluation and model checking join forces. Commun. ACM **53**(9), 76–85 (2010). https://doi.org/10.1145/1810891.1810912

13. Baier, C., Katoen, J.P.: Principles of model checking. MIT Press (2008)

14. Baier, C., Klein, J., Leuschner, L., Parker, D., Wunderlich, S.: Ensuring the reliability of your model checker: Interval iteration for Markov decision processes. In: CAV (1). Lecture Notes in Computer Science, vol. 10426, pp. 160–180. Springer (2017). https://doi.org/10.1007/978-3-319-63387-9_8

15. Ballarini, P., Barbot, B., Duflot, M., Haddad, S., Pekergin, N.: HASL: A new approach for performance evaluation and model checking from concepts to experimentation. Performance Evaluation **90**, 53–77 (2015). https://doi.org/10.1016/j.peva.2015.04.003

16. Bennett, G.: Probability inequalities for the sum of independent random variables. Journal of the American Statistical Association **57**(297), 33–45 (1962). https://doi.org/10.1080/01621459.1962.10482149

17. Bernstein, S.: On a modification of Chebyshev's inequality and of the error formula of Laplace. Ann. Sci. Inst. Sav. Ukraine, Sect. Math **1**(4), 38–49 (1924)

18. Bernstein, S.: Theory of Probability. 2 edn. (1934)

19. Bohnenkamp, H.C., D'Argenio, P.R., Hermanns, H., Katoen, J.P.: MoDeST: A compositional modeling formalism for hard and softly timed systems. IEEE Trans. Software Eng. **32**(10), 812–830 (2006). https://doi.org/10.1109/TSE.2006.104

20. Brázdil, T., Chatterjee, K., Chmelik, M., Forejt, V., Kretínský, J., Kwiatkowska, M.Z., Parker, D., Ujma, M.: Verification of Markov decision processes using learning algorithms. In: Cassez, F., Raskin, J.F. (eds.) 12th International Symposium on Automated Technology for Verification and Analysis (ATVA). Lecture Notes in Computer Science, vol. 8837, pp. 98–114. Springer (2014). https://doi.org/10.1007/978-3-319-11936-6_8

21. Bu, H., Sun, M.: Clopper-pearson algorithms for efficient statistical model checking estimation. IEEE Transactions on Software Engineering (01), 1–20 (2024). https://doi.org/10.1109/TSE.2024.3392720

22. Budde, C.E.: FIG: the Finite Improbability Generator v1.3. SIGMETRICS Perform. Evaluation Rev. **49**(4), 59–64 (2022). https://doi.org/10.1145/3543146.3543160

23. Budde, C.E.: Using statistical model checking for cybersecurity analysis. In: Skarmeta, A.F., Canavese, D., Lioy, A., Matheu, S.N. (eds.) First International Workshop on Digital Sovereignty in Cyber Security: New Challenges in Future Vision (CyberSec4Europe). Communications in Computer and Information Science, vol. 1807, pp. 16–32. Springer (2022). https://doi.org/10.1007/978-3-031-36096-1_2

24. Budde, C.E., D'Argenio, P.R., Hartmanns, A., Sedwards, S.: An efficient statistical model checker for nondeterminism and rare events. Int. J. Softw. Tools Technol. Transf. **22**(6), 759–780 (2020). https://doi.org/10.1007/S10009-020-00563-2

25. Budde, C.E., Dehnert, C., Hahn, E.M., Hartmanns, A., Junges, S., Turrini, A.: JANI: Quantitative model and tool interaction. In: Legay, A., Margaria, T. (eds.) 23rd International Conference on Tools and Algorithms for the Construction and Analysis of Systems (TACAS). Lecture Notes in Computer Science, vol. 10206, pp. 151–168 (2017). https://doi.org/10.1007/978-3-662-54580-5_9

26. Budde, C.E., Hartmanns, A., Klauck, M., Kretínský, J., Parker, D., Quatmann, T., Turrini, A., Zhang, Z.: On correctness, precision, and performance in quantitative verification – qcomp 2020 competition report. In: Margaria, T., Steffen, B. (eds.) 9th International Symposium on Leveraging Applications of Formal Methods (ISoLA). Lecture Notes in Computer Science, vol. 12479, pp. 216–241. Springer (2020). https://doi.org/10.1007/978-3-030-83723-5_15

27. Budde, C.E., Hartmanns, A., Meggendorfer, T., Weininger, M., Wienhöft, P.: Sound statistical model checking for probabilities and expected rewards. CoRR **abs/2411.00559** (2024). https://doi.org/10.48550/arXiv.2411.00559

28. Budde, C.E., Hartmanns, A., Meggendorfer, T., Weininger, M., Wienhöft, P.: Sound statistical model checking for probabilities and expected rewards (experimental reproduction package) (2025). https://doi.org/10.5281/zenodo.14743520
29. Casella, G.: Refining binomial confidence intervals. Canadian Journal of Statistics **14**(2), 113–129 (1986). https://doi.org/https://doi.org/10.2307/3314658
30. Chen, J.: Properties of a new adaptive sampling method with applications to scalable learning. Web Intell. **13**(4), 215–227 (2015). https://doi.org/10.3233/WEB-150322
31. Chenoy, A., Duchene, F., Given-Wilson, T., Legay, A.: C-SMC: A hybrid statistical model checking and concrete runtime engine for analyzing C programs. In: Laarman, A., Sokolova, A. (eds.) 27th International Symposium on Model Checking Software (SPIN). Lecture Notes in Computer Science, vol. 12864, pp. 101–119. Springer (2021). https://doi.org/10.1007/978-3-030-84629-9_6
32. Chernoff, H.: A Measure of Asymptotic Efficiency for Tests of a Hypothesis Based on the sum of Observations. The Annals of Mathematical Statistics **23**(4), 493–507 (1952). https://doi.org/10.1214/aoms/1177729330
33. Chow, Y.S., Robbins, H.: On the Asymptotic Theory of Fixed-Width Sequential Confidence Intervals for the Mean. The Annals of Mathematical Statistics **36**(2), 457–462 (1965). https://doi.org/10.1214/aoms/1177700156
34. Clopper, C., Pearson, E.: The use of confidence or fiducial limits illustrated in the case of the binomial. Biometrika **26**(4), 404–413 (1934). https://doi.org/10.1093/biomet/26.4.404
35. Daca, P., Henzinger, T.A., Kretínský, J., Petrov, T.: Faster statistical model checking for unbounded temporal properties. ACM Trans. Comput. Log. **18**(2), 12:1–12:25 (2017). https://doi.org/10.1145/3060139
36. D'Argenio, P.R., Monti, R.E.: Input/output stochastic automata with urgency: Confluence and weak determinism. In: Fischer, B., Uustalu, T. (eds.) 15th International Colloquium on Theoretical Aspects of Computing (ICTAC). Lecture Notes in Computer Science, vol. 11187, pp. 132–152. Springer (2018). https://doi.org/10.1007/978-3-030-02508-3_8
37. David, A., Larsen, K.G., Legay, A., Mikučionis, M., Poulsen, D.B.: Uppaal SMC tutorial. Int. J. Softw. Tools Technol. Transf. **17**(4), 397–415 (2015). https://doi.org/10.1007/s10009-014-0361-y
38. Domingo, C., Gavaldà, R., Watanabe, O.: Adaptive sampling methods for scaling up knowledge discovery algorithms. In: Discovery Science. Lecture Notes in Computer Science, vol. 1721, pp. 172–183. Springer (1999). https://doi.org/10.1007/3-540-46846-3_16
39. Dvoretzky, A., Kiefer, J., Wolfowitz, J.: Asymptotic Minimax Character of the Sample Distribution Function and of the Classical Multinomial Estimator. The Annals of Mathematical Statistics **27**(3), 642–669 (1956). https://doi.org/10.1214/aoms/1177728174
40. Eisentraut, J., Kelmendi, E., Kretínský, J., Weininger, M.: Value iteration for simple stochastic games: Stopping criterion and learning algorithm. Inf. Comput. **285**(Part), 104886 (2022). https://doi.org/10.1016/j.ic.2022.104886
41. Forejt, V., Kwiatkowska, M.Z., Norman, G., Parker, D.: Automated verification techniques for probabilistic systems. In: Bernardo, M., Issarny, V. (eds.) 11th International School on Formal Methods for the Design of Computer, Communication and Software Systems (SFM). Lecture Notes in Computer Science, vol. 6659, pp. 53–113. Springer (2011). https://doi.org/10.1007/978-3-642-21455-4_3
42. Frey, J.: Fixed-width sequential confidence intervals for a proportion. The American Statistician **64**(3), 242–249 (2010), https://www.jstor.org/stable/20799919

43. Gilmore, S., Reijsbergen, D., Vandin, A.: Transient and steady-state statistical analysis for discrete event simulators. In: IFM. pp. 145–160. Springer (2017). https://doi.org/10.1007/978-3-319-66845-1_10
44. Haddad, S., Monmege, B.: Interval iteration algorithm for mdps and imdps. Theor. Comput. Sci. **735**, 111–131 (2018). https://doi.org/10.1016/J.TCS.2016.12.003
45. Hahn, E.M., Hartmanns, A., Hermanns, H., Katoen, J.P.: A compositional modelling and analysis framework for stochastic hybrid systems. Formal Methods Syst. Des. **43**(2), 191–232 (2013). https://doi.org/10.1007/S10703-012-0167-Z
46. Hartmanns, A., Hermanns, H.: The Modest Toolset: An integrated environment for quantitative modelling and verification. In: Ábrahám, E., Havelund, K. (eds.) 20th International Conference on Tools and Algorithms for the Construction and Analysis of Systems (TACAS). Lecture Notes in Computer Science, vol. 8413, pp. 593–598. Springer (2014). https://doi.org/10.1007/978-3-642-54862-8_51
47. Hartmanns, A., Kaminski, B.L.: Optimistic value iteration. In: Lahiri, S.K., Wang, C. (eds.) 32nd International Conference on Computer Aided Verification (CAV). Lecture Notes in Computer Science, vol. 12225, pp. 488–511. Springer (2020). https://doi.org/10.1007/978-3-030-53291-8_26
48. Hartmanns, A., Klauck, M., Parker, D., Quatmann, T., Ruijters, E.: The quantitative verification benchmark set. In: Vojnar, T., Zhang, L. (eds.) 25th International Conference on Tools and Algorithms for the Construction and Analysis of Systems (TACAS). Lecture Notes in Computer Science, vol. 11427, pp. 344–350. Springer (2019). https://doi.org/10.1007/978-3-030-17462-0_20
49. Hérault, T., Lassaigne, R., Magniette, F., Peyronnet, S.: Approximate probabilistic model checking. In: Steffen, B., Levi, G. (eds.) 5th International Conference on Verification, Model Checking, and Abstract Interpretation (VMCAI). Lecture Notes in Computer Science, vol. 2937, pp. 73–84. Springer (2004). https://doi.org/10.1007/978-3-540-24622-0_8
50. Hoeffding, W.: Probability inequalities for sums of bounded random variables. Journal of the American Statistical Association **58**(301), 13–30 (1963). https://doi.org/10.1080/01621459.1963.10500830
51. Jégourel, C., Sun, J., Dong, J.S.: Sequential schemes for frequentist estimation of properties in statistical model checking. ACM Trans. Model. Comput. Simul. **29**(4), 25:1–25:22 (2019). https://doi.org/10.1145/3310226
52. Kretínský, J.: Survey of statistical verification of linear unbounded properties: Model checking and distances. In: ISoLA (1). Lecture Notes in Computer Science, vol. 9952, pp. 27–45 (2016). https://doi.org/10.1007/978-3-319-47166-2_3
53. Kretínský, J., Meggendorfer, T.: Of cores: A partial-exploration framework for Markov decision processes. Log. Methods Comput. Sci. **16**(4) (2020), https://lmcs.episciences.org/6833
54. Kretínský, J., Meggendorfer, T., Weininger, M.: Stopping criteria for value iteration on stochastic games with quantitative objectives. In: 38th Annual ACM/IEEE Symposium on Logic in Computer Science, LICS 2023, Boston, MA, USA, June 26-29, 2023. pp. 1–14. IEEE (2023). https://doi.org/10.1109/LICS56636.2023.10175771

55. Kwiatkowska, M.Z., Norman, G., Parker, D.: PRISM 4.0: Verification of probabilistic real-time systems. In: Gopalakrishnan, G., Qadeer, S. (eds.) 23rd International Conference on Computer Aided Verification (CAV). Lecture Notes in Computer Science, vol. 6806, pp. 585–591. Springer (2011). https://doi.org/10.1007/978-3-642-22110-1_47

56. Lampacrescia, M., Klauck, M., Palmas, M.: Towards verifying robotic systems using statistical model checking in STORM. In: Steffen, B. (ed.) Second International Conference on Bridging the Gap Between AI and Reality (AISoLA). Lecture Notes in Computer Science, vol. 15217, pp. 446–467. Springer (2024). https://doi.org/10.1007/978-3-031-75434-0_28

57. Lanotte, R., Merro, M., Zannone, N.: Impact analysis of coordinated cyber-physical attacks via statistical model checking: A case study. In: Huisman, M., Ravara, A. (eds.) 43rd IFIP WG 6.1 International Conference on Formal Techniques for Distributed Objects, Components, and Systems (FORTE). Lecture Notes in Computer Science, vol. 13910, pp. 75–94. Springer (2023). https://doi.org/10.1007/978-3-031-35355-0_6

58. Learned-Miller, E.G., Thomas, P.S.: A new confidence interval for the mean of a bounded random variable. CoRR **abs/1905.06208** (2019), https://arxiv.org/abs/1905.06208

59. Legay, A., Lukina, A., Traonouez, L.M., Yang, J., Smolka, S.A., Grosu, R.: Statistical model checking. In: Steffen, B., Woeginger, G.J. (eds.) Computing and Software Science – State of the Art and Perspectives, Lecture Notes in Computer Science, vol. 10000, pp. 478–504. Springer (2019). https://doi.org/10.1007/978-3-319-91908-9_23

60. Legay, A., Sedwards, S., Traonouez, L.M.: Plasma Lab: A modular statistical model checking platform. In: Margaria, T., Steffen, B. (eds.) 7th International Symposium on Leveraging Applications of Formal Methods (ISoLA). Lecture Notes in Computer Science, vol. 9952, pp. 77–93 (2016). https://doi.org/10.1007/978-3-319-47166-2_6

61. Levin, D.A., Peres, Y.: Markov chains and mixing times, vol. 107. American Mathematical Soc. (2017)

62. Massart, P.: The tight constant in the Dvoretzky-Kiefer-Wolfowitz inequality. The Annals of Probability **18**(3), 1269–1283 (1990). https://doi.org/10.1214/aop/1176990746

63. Mazurek, F., Tschand, A., Wang, Y., Pajic, M., Sorin, D.J.: Rigorous evaluation of computer processors with statistical model checking. In: 56th Annual IEEE/ACM International Symposium on Microarchitecture (MICRO). pp. 1242–1254. ACM (2023). https://doi.org/10.1145/3613424.3623785

64. Meggendorfer, T., Weininger, M.: Playing games with your PET: Extending the partial exploration tool to stochastic games. In: Gurfinkel, A., Ganesh, V. (eds.) Computer Aided Verification - 36th International Conference, CAV 2024, Montreal, QC, Canada, July 24-27, 2024, Proceedings, Part III. Lecture Notes in Computer Science, vol. 14683, pp. 359–372. Springer (2024). https://doi.org/10.1007/978-3-031-65633-0_16

65. Meggendorfer, T., Weininger, M., Wienhöft, P.: What are the odds? Improving the foundations of statistical model checking. CoRR **abs/2404.05424** (2024). https://doi.org/10.48550/arXiv.2404.05424

66. Mnih, V., Szepesvári, C., Audibert, J.Y.: Empirical Bernstein stopping. In: Cohen, W.W., McCallum, A., Roweis, S.T. (eds.) 25th International Conference on Machine Learning (ICML). ACM International Conference Proceeding Series, vol. 307, pp. 672–679. ACM (2008). https://doi.org/10.1145/1390156.1390241

67. Newcombe, R.G.: Two-sided confidence intervals for the single proportion: Comparison of seven methods. Statistics in medicine **17**(8), 857–872 (1998)

68. Niehage, M., Pilch, C., Remke, A.: Simulating hybrid Petri nets with general transitions and non-linear differential equations. In: 13th EAI International Conference on Performance Evaluation Methodologies and Tools (VALUETOOLS). pp. 88–95. ACM (2020). https://doi.org/10.1145/3388831.3388842

69. Nouri, A., Mediouni, B.L., Bozga, M., Combaz, J., Bensalem, S., Legay, A.: Performance evaluation of stochastic real-time systems with the $\mathcal{S}$BIP framework. International Journal of Critical Computer-Based Systems **8**(3-4), 340–370 (2018). https://doi.org/10.1504/IJCCBS.2018.096439

70. Okamoto, M.: Some inequalities relating to the partial sum of binomial probabilities. Annals of the Institute of Statistical Mathematics **10**(1), 29–35 (1959)

71. Parmentier, M., Legay, A.: Adaptive stopping algorithms based on concentration inequalities. In: Steffen, B. (ed.) Second International Conference on Bridging the Gap Between AI and Reality (AISoLA). Lecture Notes in Computer Science, vol. 15217, pp. 336–353. Springer (2024). https://doi.org/10.1007/978-3-031-75434-0_23

72. Phan, M., Thomas, P.S., Learned-Miller, E.G.: Towards practical mean bounds for small samples. In: Meila, M., Zhang, T. (eds.) 38th International Conference on Machine Learning (ICML). Proceedings of Machine Learning Research, vol. 139, pp. 8567–8576. PMLR (2021), https://proceedings.mlr.press/v139/phan21a.html

73. Pilch, C., Edenfeld, F., Remke, A.: HYPEG: Statistical model checking for hybrid Petri nets: Tool paper. In: Marin, A., Houdt, B.V., Casale, G., Petriu, D.C., Rossi, S. (eds.) 11th EAI International Conference on Performance Evaluation Methodologies and Tools (VALUETOOLS). pp. 186–191. ACM (2017). https://doi.org/10.1145/3150928.3150956

74. Pilch, C., Remke, A.: Statistical model checking for hybrid petri nets with multiple general transitions. In: DSN. pp. 475–486. IEEE Computer Society (2017). https://doi.org/10.1109/DSN.2017.41

75. Quatmann, T., Katoen, J.P.: Sound value iteration. In: Chockler, H., Weissenbacher, G. (eds.) 30th International Conference on Computer Aided Verification (CAV). Lecture Notes in Computer Science, vol. 10981, pp. 643–661. Springer (2018). https://doi.org/10.1007/978-3-319-96145-3_37

76. Reijsbergen, D., de Boer, P., Scheinhardt, W.R.W., Haverkort, B.R.: On hypothesis testing for statistical model checking. Int. J. Softw. Tools Technol. Transf. **17**(4), 377–395 (2015). https://doi.org/10.1007/S10009-014-0350-1

77. Roberts, R., Lewis, B., Hartmanns, A., Basu, P., Roy, S., Chakraborty, K., Zhang, Z.: Probabilistic verification for reliability of a two-by-two network-on-chip system. In: Lluch-Lafuente, A., Mavridou, A. (eds.) 26th International Conference on Formal Methods for Industrial Critical Systems (FMICS). Lecture Notes in Computer Science, vol. 12863, pp. 232–248. Springer (2021). https://doi.org/10.1007/978-3-030-85248-1_16

78. Rubino, G., Tuffin, B. (eds.): Rare Event Simulation using Monte Carlo Methods. Wiley (2009). https://doi.org/10.1002/9780470745403

79. Sebastio, S., Vandin, A.: MultiVeStA: statistical model checking for discrete event simulators. In: Horváth, A., Buchholz, P., Cortellessa, V., Muscariello, L., Squillante, M.S. (eds.) 7th International Conference on Performance Evaluation Methodologies and Tools (VALUETOOLS). pp. 310–315. ICST/ACM (2013). https://doi.org/10.4108/ICST.VALUETOOLS.2013.254377

80. Wald, A.: Sequential Tests of Statistical Hypotheses. The Annals of Mathematical Statistics **16**(2), 117–186 (1945). https://doi.org/10.1214/aoms/1177731118

81. Wang, W.: An iterative construction of confidence intervals for a proportion. Statistica Sinica **24**(3), 1389–1410 (2014), https://www.jstor.org/stable/24310993
82. Younes, H.L.S., Kwiatkowska, M.Z., Norman, G., Parker, D.: Numerical vs. statistical probabilistic model checking. Int. J. Softw. Tools Technol. Transf. **8**(3), 216–228 (2006). https://doi.org/10.1007/S10009-005-0187-8
83. Younes, H.L.S., Simmons, R.G.: Probabilistic verification of discrete event systems using acceptance sampling. In: Brinksma, E., Larsen, K.G. (eds.) 14th International Conference on Computer Aided Verification (CAV). Lecture Notes in Computer Science, vol. 2404, pp. 223–235. Springer (2002). https://doi.org/10.1007/3-540-45657-0_17
84. Zuliani, P.: Statistical model checking for biological applications. Int. J. Softw. Tools Technol. Transf. **17**(4), 527–536 (2015). https://doi.org/10.1007/S10009-014-0343-0

Efficient Evidence Generation for Modal μ-Calculus Model Checking

Anna Stramaglia$^{(\boxtimes)}$, Jeroen J. A. Keiren, Maurice Laveaux, and Tim A. C. Willemse

Department of Mathematics and Computer Science, Eindhoven University of Technology, Eindhoven, The Netherlands
{a.stramaglia, j.j.a.keiren, m.laveaux, t.a.c.willemse}@tue.nl

Abstract. Model checking is a technique to automatically establish whether a model of the behaviour of a system meets its requirements. Evidence explaining why the behaviour does (not) meet its requirements is essential for the user to understand the model checking result. Willemse and Wesselink showed that parameterised Boolean equation systems (PBESs), an intermediate format for μ-calculus model checking, can be extended with information to generate such evidence. Solving the resulting PBES is much slower than solving one without additional information, and sometimes even impossible. In this paper we develop a two-step approach to solving a PBES with additional information: we first solve its *core* and subsequently use the information obtained in this step to solve the PBES with additional information. We prove the correctness of our approach and we have implemented it, demonstrating that it efficiently generates evidence using both explicit and symbolic solving techniques.

Keywords: Model checking; modal μ-calculus; parameterised Boolean equation systems; counterexamples

1 Introduction

Model checking [1,8] is an automated technique for establishing whether user-defined requirements hold for (a model of) a system. The behaviour of the system is typically specified using a modelling language whose semantics is represented in terms of a *labelled transition system* or a *Kripke structure*. Requirements are expressed as formulas in LTL (linear temporal logic), or branching-time logics such as CTL (computation tree logic), CTL*, or the modal μ-*calculus*.

Given the description of the system and a temporal logic formula, a *model checker* answers the decision problem: 'Does (the model of) my system meet its requirement?'. The *yes / no* answer alone does not explain why the requirement is (not) satisfied. To this end, model checkers can provide evidence (often referred to as a *witness* or a *counterexample*) explaining the answer.

Model checking tools such as CADP [13] and mCRL2 [4] use *parameterised Boolean equation systems* (PBESs) to encode the μ-*calculus* model checking

© The Author(s) 2025
A. Gurfinkel and M. Heule (Eds.): TACAS 2025, LNCS 15696, pp. 191–210, 2025.
https://doi.org/10.1007/978-3-031-90643-5_10

problem [16]. In mCRL2, PBESs are first instantiated to a parity game (or Boolean equation system) [11,19,30] using a process similar to state space exploration. The resulting parity game is solved using standard algorithms such as the recursive algorithm [36]. Inspired by the work of Cranen et al. [10], Wesselink and Willemse showed that the encoding of the model checking problem to PBES can be extended with additional information such that evidence explaining the solution can be extracted [35]. The evidence subsequently allows for constructing a subgraph of the original state space that gives a minimal explanation of the outcome of the verification.

A fundamental problem in model checking is the *state-space explosion problem*: the size of the state space underlying a system model grows exponentially in the number of (parallel) components and state variables. Symbolic model checking [5,27] addresses this problem by using symbolic representations such as binary decision diagrams to compactly store the state space. These ideas have been extended to symbolically explore and solve the parity game underlying a PBES [3,4,19,24]. Symbolic PBES solvers are routinely used to solve the μ-calculus model checking problem for large models. For instance, the Workload Management System (WMS) model described in [31] and the Mechanical Lung Ventilator (MLV) model from [12] could only be verified using symbolic algorithms. However, in practice, the running time of solving PBESs with evidence information is so high that waiting for a solution is not an option.

Contributions. Our main contribution in this paper is a new approach for evidence generation from PBESs. Our approach first solves a PBES without additional information. As a second step, the solution of this PBES is used to simplify the solving of the PBES that does have additional information needed for evidence generation. We establish the correctness of the approach.

We have implemented our approach in the explicit PBES solver in mCRL2 [4], and added a hybrid approach, in which the first step is performed symbolically. This solution is then used to inform the explicit PBES solver in the second step.

We experimentally demonstrate the effectiveness of our new approaches. In particular, our experiments show that when the first step is done using the explicit solver, the performance is comparable with the original approach in [35]. When using the symbolic solver for the first step, our approach is able to efficiently generate evidence, also in the cases where this was not feasible before.

Related work. For a comprehensive overview of diagnostics for model checking, we refer to Busard's thesis [6]. We limit ourselves to the closest approaches providing evidence or diagnostics for the modal μ-calculus model checking problem. Such diagnostics have for instance been described using tableaux [21] and as two-player games [32]. There are several graph-based approaches describing evidence in the literature. Mateescu [26] describes evidence for the alternation free μ-calculus as a subgraph of an extended Boolean graph. Cranen et al. [9] describe *proof graphs*, that are an extension of support sets [34].

Symbolic solving of PBESs and parity games was studied in the context of LTSmin [19] and mCRL2 [24]. Symbolic model checking with evidence generation has been implemented for (Probabilistic) CTL in NuSMV [7] and PRISM [23].

Outline. Sect. 2 introduces the necessary background about the μ-calculus, PBESs, evidence generation, and a running example. In Sect. 3 we introduce a new approach to generate evidence from PBESs and prove its correctness. We evaluate the approach in Sect. 4 and conclude in Sect. 5.

2 Preliminaries

Our work is embedded in the context in which abstract data types are used to describe and reason about data, and we distinguish their syntax and semantics. We write data sorts with letters $D, E, \ldots$ and the semantics counterpart with $\mathbb{D}, \mathbb{E}, \ldots$. We require the presence of Booleans and natural numbers along with their usual operators. We use B to denote Booleans and N to denote natural numbers $\{0, 1, 2, 3, \ldots\}$, with semantic counterparts $\mathbb{B} = \{true, false\}$ and $\mathbb{N}$ respectively. For both sorts we use their semantics operation such as $\wedge$ and $+$ also for the syntactic counterparts. We use $\approx$ to syntactically represent equality. Furthermore, we have a set $\mathcal{D}$ of data variables $d, d_1, \ldots$. If a term is open we use the *data environment* δ that maps each variable in $\mathcal{D}$ to a value of the proper semantic domain. Given a term t, the interpretation function, under the context of a data environment δ, is denoted as $[\![t]\!]\delta$ which is evaluated in the standard way. We write $\delta[v/d]$ to denote that value v has been assigned to variable d, i.e., $\delta[v/d](d') = v$ if $d' = d$, and $\delta[v/d](d') = \delta(d')$ otherwise. We assume that every value $v \in \mathbb{D}$ can be represented by a closed term. With a slight abuse of notation, we also use v syntactically for this closed term.

2.1 Processes

In this paper, the behaviour of systems is modelled using *linear process equations* (LPEs) [15]. An LPE consists of a single process definition, parameterised with data, and condition-action-effect rules that may refer to local variables.

Definition 1. *A* linear process equation *is an equation of the following form:*

$$L(d \colon D) = +\{ \sum_{e_\alpha \colon E_\alpha} c_\alpha(d, e_\alpha) \to \alpha \cdot L(g_\alpha(d, e_\alpha)) \mid \alpha \in \mathcal{A}\}$$

where $+$ denotes a non-deterministic choice among the rules, $d \colon D$ is the state, $\alpha \in \mathcal{A}$ is an action label to which we associate local variable e_α of sort E_α; $c_\alpha(d, e_\alpha)$ is a condition, and term $g_\alpha(d, e_\alpha)$ describes the next state.

An LPE represents the (non-deterministic) choice to perform action $\alpha \in \mathcal{A}$ from a state represented by d, if condition $c_\alpha(d, e_\alpha)$ evaluates to *true* for some value e_α, which when executed updates the state to $g_\alpha(d, e_\alpha)$.

We typically write L instead of $L(d \colon D)$ when referring to an LPE and omit the sum when there is no local variable. The semantics of an LPE, with a closed term e as initial state, is a labelled transition system (LTS) denoted by $L(e)$.

Example 1. As a running example we consider a system whose behaviour is modelled by LPE L (left), where $a, b, c \in \mathcal{A}$, and its associated LTS (right), assuming the constant $M \approx 3$:

$$L(s : N) = \sum_{n:N} (s \approx 1 \wedge 0 < n < M) \to a \cdot L(s+n)$$
$$+ \sum_{n:N} (0 < n < s < M) \to b \cdot L(s-n)$$
$$+ (s \approx M) \to c \cdot L(s)$$

□

2.2 Modal μ-calculus

In this paper we consider requirements expressed as formulas in the modal μ-calculus [22].

Definition 2. *A μ-calculus formula φ is defined by the following grammar:*

$$\varphi ::= b \mid Y \mid \varphi_1 \wedge \varphi_2 \mid \varphi_1 \vee \varphi_2 \mid [\alpha]\varphi \mid \langle \alpha \rangle \varphi \mid \sigma X.\varphi$$

where b is a Boolean constant, $X, Y \in \mathcal{F}$ are fixpoint variables of some countable set $\mathcal{F}$, $\sigma \in \{\mu, \nu\}$ is a fixpoint, and $\alpha \in \mathcal{A}$ is an action.

We only consider formulas that are closed. That is, formulas in which no fixpoint variable Y occurs outside the scope of its binder. For instance, $\mu X.[a]X$ is allowed, but $\mu X.[a]Y$ is not allowed. For the denotational semantics of the μ-calculus we refer to the literature; see for instance [22].

Example 2. Consider the following μ-calculus formula:

$$\mu V.(\langle a \rangle V \vee \langle b \rangle V \vee \nu W.\langle c \rangle W).$$

This formula expresses that there is a finite path of a and b actions that ultimately ends with an infinite sequence of c-transitions. Intuitively, this formula holds for our running example: by executing action a to state 3 and subsequently executing the self-loop in state 3, such a path is produced.   □

2.3 Parameterised Boolean Equation Systems

Parameterised Boolean equation systems (PBESs) are systems of fixpoint equations parameterised with data, where the right-hand side is a predicate formula.

Definition 3. *Parameterised Boolean equation systems (PBESs) $\mathcal{E}$ and predicate formulas φ are syntactically defined as follows:*

$$\mathcal{E} ::= \epsilon \mid (\sigma X(d: D_X) = \varphi) \mathcal{E}$$
$$\varphi ::= b \mid X(e) \mid \varphi_1 \wedge \varphi_2 \mid \varphi_1 \vee \varphi_2 \mid \exists_{d:D}.\varphi \mid \forall_{d:D}.\varphi$$

where ϵ is the empty PBES, $\sigma \in \{\mu, \nu\}$ is a fixpoint sign, $X \in \mathcal{X}$ are predicate variables, d are data variables, and b and e are terms over data variables, where b is of sort B.

For equation $\sigma X(d\colon D_{\mathcal{X}}) = \varphi$, we write d_X and φ_X to denote parameter d and predicate formula φ, respectively. The set $\mathrm{bnd}(\mathcal{E})$ is the set of *bound* predicate variables occurring at the left-hand side of the equations in $\mathcal{E}$. We denote the set of predicate variables *occurring* in formula φ with $\mathrm{occ}(\varphi)$, and the predicate variables occurring in the right-hand sides of $\mathcal{E}$ with $\mathrm{occ}(\mathcal{E})$. A PBES $\mathcal{E}$ is *well-formed* if it has exactly one defining equation for each $X \in \mathrm{bnd}(\mathcal{E})$. It is *closed* if for every X, $\mathrm{occ}(\varphi_X) \subseteq \mathrm{bnd}(\mathcal{E})$, and the only free data variable in φ_X is d_X.

Example 3. Following the encoding of [16], the following PBES encodes whether $L(1)$ of Example 1 satisfies the μ-calculus formula of Example 2:

$$
\begin{aligned}
(\mu X(s\colon N) &= \exists_{n\colon N}.(s \approx 1 \wedge 0 < n < 3 \wedge X(s+n)) \\
&\vee \exists_{n\colon N}.(0 < n < s < 3 \wedge X(s-n)) \\
&\vee Y(s)) \\
(\nu Y(s\colon N) &= s \approx 3 \wedge Y(s))
\end{aligned}
$$

$\square$

Predicate formulas are interpreted in the context of a predicate environment η and data environment δ; see Table 1 for details.

A fixpoint semantics of PBESs is presented in [17]. Instead of the fixpoint semantics we here use the equivalent *proof graph* semantics provided in [9]. Given PBES $\mathcal{E}$, $\mathrm{sig}(\mathcal{E}) = \{X(v) \mid X \in \mathrm{bnd}(\mathcal{E}), v \in \mathbb{D}\}$ denotes the signature of $\mathcal{E}$, where $v \in \mathbb{D}$ is a value taken from the domain underlying the type of X. Every predicate variable $X \in \mathrm{bnd}(\mathcal{E})$ is assigned a number called *rank*; $\mathrm{rank}_{\mathcal{E}}(X)$ is *even* if and only if X is labelled with a greatest fixpoint, and $\mathrm{rank}_{\mathcal{E}}(X) \leq \mathrm{rank}_{\mathcal{E}}(Y)$ if X occurs before Y in $\mathcal{E}$.

Definition 4 ([9]). *Let $\mathcal{E}$ be a PBES and $\mathrm{G} = (V, E)$ be a directed graph, where $V \subseteq \mathrm{sig}(\mathcal{E})$ and $E \subseteq V \times V$. The graph G is a proof graph iff:*

- *for every $X(v) \in V$ and δ, $[\![\varphi_X]\!]\eta_{X(v)}\delta[v/d_X] = \mathit{true}$ with $\eta_{X(v)}(Y)(w) = \mathit{true}$ iff $\langle X(v), Y(w)\rangle \in E$ for all Y;*
- *for all infinite paths $X_1(v_1)X_2(v_2)\ldots$ through G, $\min\{\mathrm{rank}_{\mathcal{E}}(X) \mid X \in V^{\infty}\}$ is even, where V^{∞} is the set of predicate variables that occur infinitely often in the sequence.*

The first condition states that if all successors of $X(v) \in V$ in $\mathrm{G} = (V, E)$ together yield an environment that makes φ_X *true* when parameter d_X is assigned value v, then $X(v) = \mathit{true}$. The second condition ensures that the graph respects the parity condition typically associated with nested fixpoint formulas. The semantics of PBES $\mathcal{E}$ is now defined as follows [9].

Table 1: The interpretation function $[\![\varphi]\!]\eta\delta$ of predicate formula φ is its truth assignment in the context of δ and $\eta\colon \mathcal{X} \to 2^{\mathbb{D}}$, data and predicate environments.

$[\![b]\!]\eta\delta$	$= [\![b]\!]\delta$	$[\![X(e)]\!]\eta\delta$	$= \eta(X)([\![e]\!]\delta)$
$[\![\varphi \wedge \psi]\!]\eta\delta$	$= [\![\varphi]\!]\eta\delta$ and $[\![\psi]\!]\eta\delta$	$[\![\varphi \vee \psi]\!]\eta\delta$	$= [\![\varphi]\!]\eta\delta$ or $[\![\psi]\!]\eta\delta$
$[\![\exists_{d\colon D}.\varphi]\!]\eta\delta$	$=$ for some $v \in \mathbb{D}, [\![\varphi]\!]\eta\delta[v/d]$	$[\![\forall_{d\colon D}.\varphi]\!]\eta\delta$	$=$ for all $v \in \mathbb{D}, [\![\varphi]\!]\eta\delta[v/d]$

Definition 5. *The semantics of PBES $\mathcal{E}$ is a predicate environment $[\![\mathcal{E}]\!]$ such that $[\![\mathcal{E}]\!](X)(v)=true$ iff $X \in \mathrm{bnd}(\mathcal{E})$ and $X(v) \in V$ for some proof graph $G=(V,E)$.*

We use $\mathrm{PG}(\mathcal{E})$ to refer to a proof graph for PBES $\mathcal{E}$. An explanation of $X(v) = \textit{false}$ is given by means of a *refutation graph*, denoted as $\mathrm{NG}(\mathcal{E})$ for PBES $\mathcal{E}$, the dual of a proof graph, see [9]. Because of their duality we here outline our theory using proof graphs only.

PBESs are commonly solved using a process akin to state space exploration to obtain a parity game (or Boolean equation system) [11,19,30], and solving the resulting game. In practice, this process uses syntactic simplifications to reduce the number of vertices that are being generated in the parity game. A *lower bound* of the number of vertices that need to be explored instead relies on *semantic* dependencies. These are captured by *relevancy graphs* [25]. A relevancy graph contains a dependency $X(v) \to Y(w)$ if changing the truth value of $Y(w)$ can change the truth value of $\varphi_X[d_X := v]$. In the definition we write $\eta[b/X(e)]$ for the predicate environment satisfying $\eta[b/X(e)](Y)(f) = b$ if $X = Y$ and $e = f$, and $\eta[b/X(e)](Y)(f) = \eta(Y)(f)$ otherwise.

Definition 6 ([25]). *Let $\mathcal{E}$ be a PBES and $RG = (V, \to)$ be a directed graph, where*

- *$V \subseteq \mathrm{sig}(\mathcal{E})$ is a set of vertices,*
- *$\to \subseteq V \times V$ an edge relation such that for any $X(v) \in V$,*
  $X(v) \to Y(w)$ iff
  $\exists \eta, \delta. [\![\varphi_X]\!]\eta[true/Y(w)]\delta[v/d_X] \neq [\![\varphi_X]\!]\eta[false/Y(w)]\delta[v/d_X]$

We say that $RG = (V, \to)$ is a relevancy graph for $X(v)$ iff $X(v) \in V$.

In the remainder of the paper, we use the size of the relevancy graph as a proxy for estimating the effort required to solve a PBES.

Example 4. A proof graph for the PBES in Example 3 with initial vertex $X(1)$ is shown in Fig. 1a. It shows that vertices $X(1)$, $X(3)$ and $Y(3)$ are *true*, with the numbers above these vertices indicating their ranks, and the edges showing the required dependencies explaining this solution. The corresponding relevancy graph is shown in Fig. 1b. $\square$

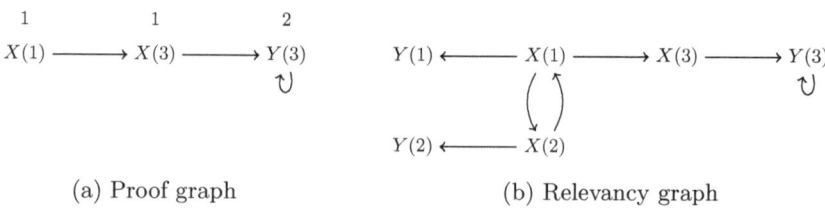

(a) Proof graph   (b) Relevancy graph

Fig. 1: Proof graph and relevancy graph for the PBES in Example 3.

Table 2: Translation to encode, given LPE L and $\sigma Z.\varphi$, the model checking problem $L(e) \models \sigma Z.\varphi$ into a PBES [35].

$$
\begin{array}{lll}
\mathbf{E}_L^c(b) & = \epsilon & \\
\mathbf{E}_L^c(Y) & = \epsilon & \\
\mathbf{E}_L^c(\varphi \oplus \psi) & = \mathbf{E}_L^c(\varphi)\,\mathbf{E}_L^c(\psi) & \text{for } \oplus \in \{\vee, \wedge\} \\
\mathbf{E}_L^c([\alpha]\varphi) & = \mathbf{E}_L^c(\varphi) & \\
\mathbf{E}_L^c(\langle\alpha\rangle\varphi) & = \mathbf{E}_L^c(\varphi) & \\
\mathbf{E}_L^c(\sigma X.\varphi) & = (\sigma X(d_L : D_L) = \mathbf{RHS}_L^c(\varphi))\,\mathbf{E}_L^c(\varphi) & \\
\mathbf{RHS}_L^c(b) & = b & \\
\mathbf{RHS}_L^c(Y) & = Y(d_L) & \\
\mathbf{RHS}_L^c(\varphi \oplus \psi) & = \mathbf{RHS}_L^c(\varphi) \oplus \mathbf{RHS}_L^c(\psi) & \text{for } \oplus \in \{\vee, \wedge\} \\
\mathbf{RHS}_L^c([\alpha]\varphi) & = \forall_{e_\alpha : E_\alpha}\,.\,c_\alpha(d, e_\alpha) \implies ((\mathbf{RHS}_L^c(\varphi)[g_\alpha(d, e_\alpha)/d] \wedge Z_\alpha^+(d, g_\alpha(d, e_\alpha))) & \\
& \qquad \vee Z_\alpha^-(d, g_\alpha(d, e_\alpha))) & \\
\mathbf{RHS}_L^c(\langle\alpha\rangle\varphi) & = \exists_{e_\alpha : E_\alpha}\,.\,c_\alpha(d, e_\alpha) \wedge ((\mathbf{RHS}_L^c(\varphi)[g_\alpha(d, e_\alpha)/d] \vee Z_\alpha^-(d, g_\alpha(d, e_\alpha))) & \\
& \qquad \wedge Z_\alpha^+(d, g_\alpha(d, e_\alpha))) & \\
\mathbf{RHS}_L^c(\sigma X.\varphi) & = X(d_L) & \\
\end{array}
$$

2.4 Model Checking and Evidence Generation

A μ-calculus model checking problem $L(e) \models \varphi$ can be encoded into a PBES using the translation proposed by Wesselink and Willemse [35]. Proof graphs and refutation graphs extracted from a PBES obtained by this encoding allow for generating evidence, in contrast to the encoding of [16]. The evidence generated from a proof graph is a *witness* that explains why the behaviour meets a requirement. Dually, the evidence generated from a refutation graph is a *counterexample* explaining why the requirement is violated. These two cases are fully symmetric for the μ-calculus. The translation scheme of the encoding $\mathbf{E}_L^c$ from [35] is in Table 2. The predicate variables Z_α^+ and Z_α^- in the right-hand sides $\mathbf{RHS}_L^c([\alpha]\varphi)$ and $\mathbf{RHS}_L^c(\langle\alpha\rangle\varphi)$ contain information about the action labels, the *transitions*. In particular, in a proof graph, a dependency on Z_α^+ indicates the α-transition is required for a *true* solution, whereas in a refutation graph, a dependency on Z_α^- indicates the α-transition is involved in the *false* solution.

In addition to the encoding of Table 2, for each action label α equations $\nu Z_\alpha^+(d : D, d' : D) = true$ and $\mu Z_\alpha^-(d : D, d' : D) = false$ are added to the equation system. These equations are solved and typically grouped at the end of the equation system. We write $\mathcal{Z}^+ \subseteq \mathcal{X}$ (resp. $\mathcal{Z}^- \subseteq \mathcal{X}$) for the set of predicate variables $\{Z_\alpha^+ \mid \alpha \in \mathcal{A}\}$ (resp. $\{Z_\alpha^- \mid \alpha \in \mathcal{A}\}$).

Theorem 1 ([35]). *Let $L(e)$ be an LPE, and $\sigma Z.\varphi$ be a closed μ-calculus formula. Then, $L(e) \models \sigma Z.\varphi$ if and only if $[\![\mathbf{E}_L^c(\sigma Z.\varphi)]\!](Z)([\![e]\!]) = true$.*

We usually write $\mathcal{E}$ for the PBES obtained from encoding $\mathbf{E}_L^c$. Specifically, $\mathcal{E} = \mathcal{E}_L \mathcal{E}_{\mathcal{Z}^+} \mathcal{E}_{\mathcal{Z}^-}$, where $\mathcal{E}_L$ contains the equations introduced by $\mathbf{E}_L^c$ and $\mathcal{E}_{\mathcal{Z}^+}$ (resp. $\mathcal{E}_{\mathcal{Z}^-}$) contains all equations of the shape $\nu Z_\alpha^+(d : D, d' : D) = true$ (resp. $\mu Z_\alpha^-(d : D, d' : D) = false$).

For the μ-calculus model checking problem $L(e) \models \varphi$, a proof graph allows for constructing an LTS $L_w(e)$ which is a subgraph of $L(e)$ that provides a minimal explanation of the validity of the model checking problem. This witness contains enough information to reconstruct the proof graph from which it was extracted; this dually holds for counterexamples and refutation graphs.

We show how we can extract a witness for our running example.

Example 5. Recall the LPE and μ-calculus formula from Examples 1 and 2. PBES $\mathcal{E}$ consists of the following equations.

$$
\begin{aligned}
(\mu X(s\colon N) \quad &= (\exists_{n\colon N}.(s \approx 1 \wedge 0 < n < 3 \wedge (X(s+n) \vee Z_a^-(s,s+n)) \\
&\quad \wedge Z_a^+(s,s+n))) \\
&\vee (\exists_{n\colon N}.(0 < n < s < 3 \wedge (X(s-n) \vee Z_b^-(s,s-n)) \\
&\quad \wedge Z_b^+(s,s-n))) \\
&\vee Y(s)) \\
(\nu Y(s\colon N) \quad &= s \approx 3 \wedge (Y(s) \vee Z_c^-(s,s)) \wedge Z_c^+(s,s)) \\
(\nu Z_a^+(s,s1\colon N) &= true)\ (\nu Z_b^+(s,s1\colon N) = true)\ (\nu Z_c^+(s,s1\colon N) = true) \\
(\mu Z_a^-(s,s1\colon N) &= false)\ (\mu Z_b^-(s,s1\colon N) = false)\ (\mu Z_c^-(s,s1\colon N) = false)
\end{aligned}
$$

The following proof graph for the PBES is found:

$$
Z_a^+(1,3) \xleftarrow{\ 2\ } X(1) \xrightarrow{\ 1\ } X(3) \xrightarrow{\ 1\ } Y(3) \xrightarrow{\ 2\ } Z_c^+(3,3)
$$

Predicate variables Z_a^+ and Z_c^+ encode information about which a-transitions and c-transitions in the LPE are involved in proving that the solution to the model checking problem is *true*. We filter the relevant vertices with information about evidence from the proof graph, here $Z_a^+(1,3)$ and $Z_c^+(3,3)$, and derive the following LPE (left) and *witness* LTS (right):

$$
\begin{aligned}
L_w(s\colon N) = \ &(s \approx 1) \rightarrow a \cdot L_w(3) \\
+ \ &(s \approx 3) \rightarrow c \cdot L_w(3)
\end{aligned}
$$

We remark that, by construction, this LTS is a subgraph of the LTS in Example 1, underlying the original specification. For the formal definition of witness and counterexample we refer to [35], for the concept of evidence to [10]. □

3   Improving Evidence Generation from PBESs

The encoding $\mathbf{E}_L^c$ results in a PBES from which evidence supporting the verdict of the model checking problem can be extracted. However, the additional information added to the right-hand sides of the equations significantly increases the effort needed to solve the PBES. We illustrate this using an example.

Example 6. The relevancy graph for PBES $\mathcal{E}$ from Example 5 is the following.

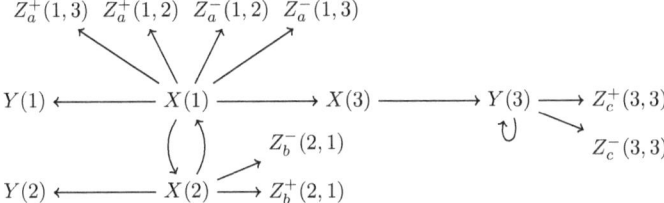

Note that it contains dependencies on $Z_a^+(1,n)$ and $Z_a^-(1,n)$ for all $n = 2,3$. By increasing the value of M, used in the LPE, to values larger than 3, the number of vertices can be increased to an arbitrary number. For instance, if $M \approx 1000$ then $X(1)$ will have 1998 dependencies related to action a. The number of dependencies related to action b will increase similarly.   □

Omitting the information from the PBES that is needed to generate evidence would result in the PBES from Example 3, whose much smaller relevancy graph was shown in Fig. 1b. The relevancy graphs of both PBESs illustrate a trade-off. On the one hand, solving the PBES in which information to generate evidence is omitted, denoted $core(\mathcal{E})$ (see Sect. 3.1), is (much) more efficient than solving $\mathcal{E}$. On the other hand, diagnostic information including the transitions is essential for understanding why a formula is (not) satisfied.

In the remainder of this section, we introduce a three-step approach that allows us to efficiently solve PBESs with additional information for evidence generation. An overview of the approach is presented in Fig. 2.

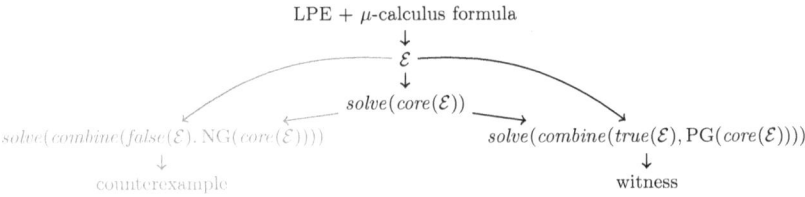

Fig. 2: Efficient evidence generation approach.

The case in which the solution to the PBES is *true*, and the one in which the solution is *false* are completely symmetric. In Fig. 2, we show the case where the solution is *false* in lighter colour. In view of the symmetry, here we focus on presenting the approach for the *true* case only. The three steps are as follows.

1. Remove the additional information from the PBES $\mathcal{E}$, and solve the resulting PBES $core(\mathcal{E})$ (see Sect. 3.1).
2. Use the solution of $core(\mathcal{E})$ to remove superfluous evidence information from the PBES, obtaining $true(\mathcal{E})$ (see Sect. 3.2).
3. Combine the proof graph for $core(\mathcal{E})$ with $true(\mathcal{E})$ to obtain a new PBES $combine(true(\mathcal{E}), \mathrm{PG}(core(\mathcal{E})))$, and solve this PBES (see Sect. 3.3).

The third step results in a solution and proof graph for the original PBES $\mathcal{E}$. In the remainder of this section, we address each of these steps in more detail.

We first introduce some auxiliary notation. We write $\lambda d_X : D_X.\varphi$ lifting predicate formula φ to a *predicate function* with the same parameters as predicate variable $X(d_X : D_X)$ [29]. The semantics is defined as $[\![\lambda d_X : D_X.\varphi]\!]\eta\delta = \lambda v \in \mathbb{D}_X.[\![\varphi]\!]\eta\delta[v/d_X]$. We use this lifting to substitute a predicate formula for a predicate variable. Given predicate formulas φ, ψ and predicate variable X, we write $\varphi[X := \lambda d_X : D_X.\psi]$ to denote that every occurrence of X is replaced with $\lambda d_X : D_X.\psi$ in φ. We write $\varphi[X := \psi_X, Y := \psi_Y]$ for the simultaneous substitution of X and Y ($X \neq Y$), and generalise this to $\varphi[X := \psi_X]_{X \in \mathcal{X}}$ to denote the simultaneous substitution of all $X \in \mathcal{X}$.

3.1   Solving a PBES Without Evidence Information

If we forego evidence, and focus on obtaining a solution for the model checking problem in terms of a *true/false* answer only, the amount of work can be reduced significantly. This motivates the first step in our approach.

The equations for the predicate variables in $\mathcal{Z}^+$ and $\mathcal{Z}^-$ in a PBES $\mathcal{E} = \mathcal{E}_L\mathcal{E}_{\mathcal{Z}^+}\mathcal{E}_{\mathcal{Z}^-}$ with information on evidence are solved. Therefore, $\mathcal{E}$ can be simplified by substituting in $\mathcal{E}_L$ all predicate variables in $\mathcal{Z}^+$ with *true* and all predicate variables in $\mathcal{Z}^-$ with *false*, without affecting the solution of $\mathcal{E}$. We refer to this as *core* PBES, defined as follows.

Definition 7. *Let* $\mathcal{E} = \mathcal{E}_L\mathcal{E}_{\mathcal{Z}^+}\mathcal{E}_{\mathcal{Z}^-}$. *Then*

$$core(\mathcal{E}) = \mathcal{E}_L[Z_a^+ := \lambda d : D_{Z_a^+}.true]_{Z_a^+ \in \mathcal{Z}^+}[Z_a^- := \lambda d : D_{Z_a^-}.false]_{Z_a^- \in \mathcal{Z}^-}\mathcal{E}_{\mathcal{Z}^+}\mathcal{E}_{\mathcal{Z}^-}$$

Example 7. Let PBES $\mathcal{E}$ be as in Example 5. Then $core(\mathcal{E})$ is obtained from this PBES by replacing the equations for X and Y by the corresponding equations from Example 3. Note the relevancy graph of the latter (see Fig. 1b) is much smaller than the one for $\mathcal{E}$ (see Example 6).   □

It follows immediately from standard results on PBESs [17] that the solution of the equations in $\mathcal{E}_L$ are preserved by transformation $core(\mathcal{E})$.

Lemma 1. *Let* $\mathcal{E} = \mathcal{E}_L\mathcal{E}_{\mathcal{Z}^+}\mathcal{E}_{\mathcal{Z}^-}$. *Then* $[\![\mathcal{E}]\!] = [\![core(\mathcal{E})]\!]$.

3.2   Removing Superfluous Evidence Information

Once we have established that the solution to $core(\mathcal{E})$, and hence $\mathcal{E} = \mathcal{E}_L\mathcal{E}_{\mathcal{Z}^+}\mathcal{E}_{\mathcal{Z}^-}$, is *true*, only the information for constructing a witness is relevant. We therefore remove the dependencies on predicate variables needed to construct counterexamples by substituting in $\mathcal{E}_L$ all predicate variables in $\mathcal{Z}^-$ with *false*. We refer to the resulting PBES as $true(\mathcal{E})$.

Definition 8. *Let* $\mathcal{E} = \mathcal{E}_L\mathcal{E}_{\mathcal{Z}^+}\mathcal{E}_{\mathcal{Z}^-}$. *Then*

$$true(\mathcal{E}) = \mathcal{E}_L[Z_a^- := \lambda d : D_{Z_a^-}.false]_{Z_a^- \in \mathcal{Z}^-}\mathcal{E}_{\mathcal{Z}^+}\mathcal{E}_{\mathcal{Z}^-}$$

By definition of $core(\mathcal{E})$ and $true(\mathcal{E})$, the following result follows immediately from the semantics [17].

Lemma 2. *Let* $\mathcal{E} = \mathcal{E}_L \mathcal{E}_{\mathbf{Z}^+} \mathcal{E}_{\mathbf{Z}^-}$. *Then* $[\![core(\mathcal{E})]\!] = [\![true(\mathcal{E})]\!]$.

Example 8. Recall that the solution of $core(\mathcal{E})$ of Example 7 is *true*. We use this to obtain the following PBES $true(\mathcal{E})$:

$$
\begin{aligned}
(\mu X(s\colon N) \quad &= (\exists_{n:N}.(s \approx 1 \wedge 0 < n < 3 \wedge X(s+n) \wedge Z_a^+(s, s+n))) \\
&\vee (\exists_{n:N}.(0 < n < s < 3 \wedge X(s-n) \wedge Z_b^+(s, s-n))) \\
&\vee Y(s)) \\
(\nu Y(s\colon N) \quad &= s \approx 3 \wedge Y(s) \wedge Z_c^+(s, s)) \\
(\nu Z_a^+(s, s1\colon N) &= true) \; (\nu Z_b^+(s, s1\colon N) = true) \; (\nu Z_c^+(s, s1\colon N) = true) \\
(\mu Z_a^-(s, s1\colon N) &= false) \, (\mu Z_b^-(s, s1\colon N) = false) \, (\mu Z_c^-(s, s1\colon N) = false)
\end{aligned}
$$

We obtain the corresponding relevancy graph by removing all vertices for Z_a^-, Z_b^- and Z_c^- and their incoming edges from the relevancy graph in Example 6.   □

3.3 Simplifying a PBES using Evidence Information

We now show how a proof graph can be used to further simplify the right-hand sides in a PBES. For this, recall that for a vertex $X(v)$ in the proof graph, the successors of $X(v)$ yield a predicate environment that makes $\varphi_X[d_X := v]$ true. Using this information, we can syntactically remove all dependencies that are not in the proof graph from the right-hand sides in a PBES, without affecting the solution. To achieve this, we define $combine(\mathcal{E}, G)$ as follows.

Definition 9. *Let* $\mathcal{E}$ *be a PBES, and* $G = (V, E)$ *be a proof graph. Then PBES combine$(\mathcal{E}, G)$ is obtained by replacing the right-hand side of every equation* $\sigma X(d_X : D_X) = \varphi_X$ *in* $\mathcal{E}$ *by the formula*

$$
\varphi_X[Y := \lambda e. \bigwedge_{v \in V_X} (d_X \approx v \implies e \in E_{X(v),Y} \wedge Y(e))]_{Y \in \mathcal{X} \setminus (\mathbf{Z}^+ \cup \mathbf{Z}^-)}
$$

where $V_X = \{v \in \mathbb{D} \mid X(v) \in V\}$ *contains all values* v *such that* $X(v)$ *is a vertex in* G, *and* $E_{X(v),Y} = \{w \in \mathbb{D} \mid \langle X(v), Y(w) \rangle \in E\}$ *contains all direct dependencies of* $X(v)$ *on* Y *in the proof graph.*

Intuitively, this retains only those dependencies in φ_X that according to the proof graph are needed to show that $X(v)$ is true, for any v.

Example 9. Recall the equation for X in PBES $true(\mathcal{E})$ from Example 8.

$$
\begin{aligned}
(\mu X(s\colon N) &= (\exists_{n:N}.(s \approx 1 \wedge 0 < n < 3 \wedge X(s+n) \wedge Z_a^+(s, s+n))) \\
&\vee (\exists_{n:N}.(0 < n < s < 3 \wedge X(s-n) \wedge Z_b^+(s, s-n))) \\
&\vee Y(s))
\end{aligned}
$$

The proof graph for $core(\mathcal{E})$ (see Fig. 1a) has vertices $V = \{X(1), X(3), Y(3)\}$ and edges $E = \{(X(1), X(3)), (X(3), Y(3)), (Y(3), Y(3))\}$. So, we infer $V_X = \{1, 3\}$, $V_Y = \{3\}$, $E_{X(1),X} = \{3\}$, $E_{X(1),Y} = E_{X(3),X} = \emptyset$, $E_{X(3),Y} = \{3\}$, $E_{Y(3),X} = \emptyset$, and $E_{Y(3),Y} = \{3\}$.

The right-hand side of the equation for X in $combine(true(\mathcal{E}), \text{PG}(core(\mathcal{E})))$, after β-reduction and simplification, is as follows.

$$(\mu X(s\colon N) = (\exists_{n:N}.(s \approx 1 \wedge 0 < n < 3$$
$$\wedge (s \approx 1 \implies (s+n) \in \{3\} \wedge X(s+n))$$
$$\wedge (s \approx 3 \implies (s+n) \in \emptyset \wedge X(s+n)) \wedge Z_a^+(s, s+n)))$$
$$\vee (\exists_{n:N}.(0 < n < s < 3$$
$$\wedge (s \approx 1 \implies (s-n) \in \{3\} \wedge X(s-n))$$
$$\wedge (s \approx 3 \implies (s-n) \in \emptyset \wedge X(s-n)) \wedge Z_b^+(s, s-n)))$$
$$\vee (s \approx 3 \implies s \in \{3\} \wedge Y(s)))$$

This simplifies further to

$$(\mu X(s\colon N) = (\exists_{n:N}.(s \approx 1 \wedge n \approx 2 \wedge X(s+n) \wedge Z_a^+(s, s+n)))$$
$$\vee (\exists_{n:N}.(0 < n < s < 3 \wedge Z_b^+(s, s-n)))$$
$$\vee (s \approx 3 \implies Y(s)))$$

If we also apply the corresponding substitution to the equation for Y and apply some simplification, we obtain the following PBES.

$$
\begin{aligned}
(\mu X(s\colon N) \quad &= (\exists_{n:N}.(s \approx 1 \wedge n \approx 2 \wedge X(s+n) \wedge Z_a^+(s, s+n))) \\
&\vee (\exists_{n:N}.(0 < n < s < 3 \wedge Z_b^+(s, s-n))) \\
&\vee (s \approx 3 \implies Y(s))) \\
(\nu Y(s\colon N) \quad &= s \approx 3 \wedge Y(s) \wedge Z_c^+(s, s)) \\
(\nu Z_a^+(s, s1\colon N) &= \mathit{true}) \ (\nu Z_b^+(s, s1\colon N) = \mathit{true}) \ (\nu Z_c^+(s, s1\colon N) = \mathit{true}) \\
(\mu Z_a^-(s, s1\colon N) &= \mathit{false}) \ (\mu Z_b^-(s, s1\colon N) = \mathit{false}) \ (\mu Z_c^-(s, s1\colon N) = \mathit{false})
\end{aligned}
$$

This PBES has the following relevancy graph, that no longer has dependencies on Z_b^+ and only a single dependency on Z_a^+, and is significantly smaller than the relevancy graph of Example 6:

$$Z_a^+(1,3) \longleftarrow X(1) \longrightarrow X(3) \longrightarrow Y(3) \longrightarrow Z_c^+(3,3)$$
$$\circlearrowleft$$

$\square$

In the example we have combined the PBES $\mathit{true}(\mathcal{E})$ with a proof graph for the strongly related PBES $\mathit{core}(\mathcal{E})$. Towards establishing the correctness of this transformation, we first prove the following technical lemma, that shows that the substitution of a single predicate variable in a proof graph like context does not change the solution. Proofs that are either sketched or omitted from this section are included in the extended version of this paper [33].

Lemma 3. *Let $V \subseteq \mathbb{D}$ be a set of values, Y a predicate variable, and $\{E_{v,Y} \subseteq \mathbb{D}\}_{v \in V}$ be a V-indexed family of sets of values. For every $v \in V$, predicate environment η such that $\eta(Y)(w) = \mathit{true}$ iff $w \in E_{v,Y}$, predicate formula φ, data variable d free in φ, and data environment δ, we have*

$$[\![\varphi]\!]\eta\delta[v/d] \implies [\![\varphi[Y := \lambda e. \bigwedge_{w \in V} (d \approx w \implies e \in E_{v,Y} \wedge Y(e))]\!]\eta\delta[v/d]$$

Proof. Fix, V, Y, $\{E_{v,Y} \subseteq \mathbb{D}\}_{v \in V}$, v and η as in the statement of the lemma. We proceed by induction on the structure of φ. Most cases are immediate, or follow from the induction hypothesis and the semantics of predicate formulas. We focus on the interesting case where $\varphi = Z(e')$ for some Z and e'. If $Z \neq Y$, the result is immediate, since the substitution has no effect. So, suppose $Z = Y$. We have to show that $[\![Y(e')]\!]\eta\delta[v/d]$ implies $[\![Y(e')[Y := \lambda e. \bigwedge_{w \in V}(d \approx w \implies e \in E_{v,Y} \wedge Y(e))]\!]\eta\delta[v/d]$.

Assume $[\![Y(e')]\!]\eta\delta[v/d]$ is *true*. Hence, $\eta(Y)([\![e']\!]\delta[v/d])$ is *true*, so by assumption, $[\![e']\!]\delta[v/d] \in E_{v,Y}$, and therefore $[\![e' \in E_{v,Y}]\!]\delta[v/d]$ is *true*. Similarly, it immediately follows that $[\![d \approx w]\!]\delta[v/d]$ is *true* iff $w = v$. So, it follows that $[\![\bigwedge_{w \in V}(d \approx w \implies e' \in E_{v,Y} \wedge Y(e'))]\!]\eta\delta[v/d]$ is *true*. Using the definition of substitution and β-reduction, it then follows that $[\![Y(e')[Y := \lambda e. \bigwedge_{w \in V}(d \approx w \implies e \in E_{v,Y} \wedge Y(e))]\!]\eta\delta[v/d]$ is also *true*. $\square$

We use this lemma to establish that the proof graph for $core(\mathcal{E})$ can easily be extended into a proof graph for $combine(true(\mathcal{E}), G)$. This shows that for values of interest to the original model checking problem, the result remains unchanged.

Proposition 1. *For every proof graph G for $core(\mathcal{E})$, there is a proof graph G' for $combine(true(\mathcal{E}), G)$ such that G is a subgraph of G'.*

Proof sketch. Let $G = (V, E)$ be a proof graph for $core(\mathcal{E})$. Define $G' = (V \cup V_{\mathcal{Z}^+}, E \cup (V \times V_{\mathcal{Z}^+}))$ with $V_{\mathcal{Z}^+} = \{Z_a^+(e_L, e_a, e'_L) \mid Z_a^+ \in \mathcal{Z}^+, e_L, e'_L \in \mathbb{D}_L, e_a \in \mathbb{D}_a\}$. Then G is a subgraph of G'.

We show G' is a proof graph for $combine(true(\mathcal{E}), G)$. For $Z_a^+(e_L, e_a, e'_L) \in V_{\mathcal{Z}^+}$, the condition on $\varphi_{Z_a^+}$ follows immediately. So, let $X(v) \in V$, and φ_X and $\psi_X = \varphi_X[Y := \lambda e. \bigwedge_{v \in V_X}(d_X \approx v \implies e \in E_{X(v),Y} \wedge Y(e))]_{Y \in \mathcal{X} \setminus (\mathcal{Z}^+ \cup \mathcal{Z}^-)}$ be the right-hand sides of X in $core(\mathcal{E})$ and $combine(true(\mathcal{E}), G)$, respectively. As G is a proof graph for $core(\mathcal{E})$, $[\![\varphi_X]\!]\eta_{X(v)}\delta[v/d_X]$ is *true*, where $\eta_{X(v)}$ is such that $\eta_{X(v)}(Y)(w) = true$ iff $\langle X(v), Y(w) \rangle \in E$. It follows from Lemma 3 that $[\![\psi_X]\!]\eta_{X(v)}\delta[v/d_X]$ is *true*, so G' is a proof graph for $combine(true(\mathcal{E}), G)$. $\square$

3.4   Providing Evidence for the Original PBES

The result that every proof graph G for $core(\mathcal{E})$ can be extended into a proof graph G' for $combine(true(\mathcal{E}), G)$ is sufficient to show that $combine(true(\mathcal{E}), G)$ does not change the solution of the PBES. However, G' may contain too many variables with evidence information, resulting in witnesses that are larger than needed. In practice, we therefore solve $combine(true(\mathcal{E}), G)$ again, leading to a proof graph that only contains the necessary dependencies on variables in $\mathcal{Z}^+$.

Correctness of our approach ultimately follows if a solution and proof graph obtained for PBES $combine(true(\mathcal{E}), G)$ are also a correct solution and proof graph for our original PBES $\mathcal{E}$. We first establish the following result.

Lemma 4. *Let $V \subseteq \mathbb{D}$ be a set of values, Y a predicate variable, and $\{E_{v,Y} \subseteq \mathbb{D}\}_{v \in V}$ be a V-indexed family of sets of values. For every $v \in V$, predicate environment η, formula φ, data variable d free in φ, and data environment δ,*

$$[\![\varphi[Y := \lambda e. \bigwedge_{w \in V}(d \approx w \implies e \in E_{v,Y} \wedge Y(e))]\!]\eta\delta[v/d] \implies [\![\varphi]\!]\eta\delta[v/d]$$

The proof is similar to that of Lemma 3. Note that where Lemma 3 considers every predicate environment η such that $\eta(Y)(w) = true$ iff $w \in E_{v,Y}$, in Lemma 4 there is no assumption on η. We now use Lemma 4 to establish that the proof graph computed for PBES $combine(true(\mathcal{E}), G)$ is also a proof graph for $\mathcal{E}$.

Theorem 2. *Let G be a proof graph for $core(\mathcal{E})$. Then every proof graph G' for $combine(true(\mathcal{E}), G)$ is also a proof graph for $\mathcal{E}$.*

Proof sketch. Let $G = (V, E)$ be a proof graph for $core(\mathcal{E})$ and $G' = (V', E')$ be a proof graph for $combine(true(\mathcal{E}), G)$.

For every X bound in $core(\mathcal{E})$, let φ_X be the right-hand side of X in $\mathcal{E}$. Let $\varphi_X^t = \varphi_X[Z_a^- := \lambda d\colon D_{Z_a^-}.false]_{Z_a^- \in \mathcal{Z}^-}$ be the right-hand side of X in $true(\mathcal{E})$. Also, let $\psi_X = \varphi_X^t[Y := \lambda e. \bigwedge_{v \in V_X}(d_X \approx v \implies e \in E_{X(v),Y} \wedge Y(e))]_{Y \in \mathcal{X} \setminus (\mathcal{Z}^+ \cup \mathcal{Z}^-)}$ be the right-hand side of X in $combine(true(\mathcal{E}), G)$.

Fix $X(v) \in V'$, then $[\![\psi_X]\!]\eta_{X(v)}\delta[v/d_X]$ is $true$ since G' is a proof graph for $combine(true(\mathcal{E}), G)$. It follows from Lemma 4 that $[\![\varphi_X^t]\!]\eta_{X(v)}\delta[v/d_X]$ is $true$, so G' is a proof graph for $true(\mathcal{E})$. As all variables in $\mathcal{Z}^-$ are $false$, any proof graph for $true(\mathcal{E})$ is a proof graph for $\mathcal{E}$, so G' is a proof graph for $\mathcal{E}$. $\square$

Hence, the proof graph computed using our approach is a proof graph for the original PBES $\mathcal{E}$, and the witness we extract from it is a witness for the model checking problem encoded by $\mathcal{E}$.

4   Implementation and Evaluation

The mCRL2 toolset [4] supports the original approach to extract evidence from PBESs [35] in the explicit model checking tool *pbessolve*. We have extended this tool with the approach described in Sect. 3. PBES $core(\mathcal{E})$ is explored and solved explicitly. Instead of precomputing $combine(true(\mathcal{E}), PG(core(\mathcal{E})))$, the corresponding right-hand sides are computed on-the-fly during explicit exploration. Solving is done using an explicit version of the recursive algorithm [36] that results in a *minimal* proof graph [35].

We have also extended the tool *pbessolvesymbolic*, that supports symbolic solving of PBESs [24], with a hybrid approach that enables evidence generation for symbolic model checking. In this approach, $core(\mathcal{E})$ is represented and solved symbolically. This results in a symbolic characterisation of $PG(core(\mathcal{E}))$. To obtain this proof graph, the symbolic implementation of the recursive algorithm [36] has been extended in such a way that an over-approximation of the proof graph is efficiently computed.[1] To reason symbolically about the underlying proof graph, the PBES must be in standard recursive form (SRF) [28], i.e., every right-hand side is either disjunctive or conjunctive. Any PBES can be transformed into this format. Exploring and solving $combine(true(\mathcal{E}), PG(core(\mathcal{E})))$ is done explicitly as before. The implementation here instead uses the symbolic proof graph to compute right-hand sides on-the-fly.

---

[1] The edge relation is over-approximated to achieve a compact symbolic representation, but it remains a valid proof graph (that is not necessarily minimal).

4.1 Experimental Setup

We evaluate the effectiveness of our approach using a number of mCRL2 spec-ifications with μ-calculus formulas. Each mCRL2 specification is linearised into an LPE, and combined with a μ-calculus formula into a PBES encoding the cor-responding model checking problem. To evaluate the effect of our improvements we compare the six different approaches to solve PBESs that are available in the mCRL2 toolset. For explicit model checking, we compare directly solving the PBES with information about evidence [35] (n-expl), and our own approach (expl). For symbolic model checking, the comparison is similar, but we use the symbolic algorithms from [24] to directly solve the PBESs with evidence (n-symb). We compare it to the hybrid implementation of our approach (symb). To illustrate the overhead of solving PBESs with information about evidence, we also include directly solving the PBES without that information explicitly [4,16] (noCE-expl), and symbolically (noCE-symb) [24].

The experiments are run using different types of models. This includes our running example scaled to $M = 1000$ (**witness1000**). We also use models based on industrial applications: the Storage Management System (**SMS**) and the Workload Management System (**WMS**) of the DIRAC Community Grid Solu-tion for the LHCb experiment at CERN [31]; the IEEE 1394 (**1394-fin**) inter-face standard that specifies a serial bus architecture for high-speed communi-cations [14]; two versions of the ERTMS Hybrid Level 3 train control system specification each with a different implementation of the Trackside System [2], *immediate update* (**ertms-hl3**) and *simultaneous update* (**ertms-hl3su**); and a Mechanical Lung Ventilator [12] (**MLV**). Moreover, we include a model of the onebit sliding window protocol (**onebit**) with buffers of size 2; and a model of the Hesselink's handshake register [18] (**hesselink**). For each of these models we verify requirements that are described in the corresponding papers.

The aforementioned models are selected taking into account different criteria. We include problems that hold (✓), and ones that do not hold (✗); problems for which the evidence is small, and ones for which it is large. We select problems that are well studied in the literature and for which the explicit and symbolic approach can be compared (**SMS, hesselink, 1394-fin, onebit**). Also, we in-clude all problems publicly available in mCRL2 that cannot be solved explicitly but only symbolically (**ertms-hl3su, ertms-hl3, MLV, WMS**). These are rep-resentative of the models we encounter in industrial applications.

All experiments are run 10 times, on a machine with 4 Intel 6136 CPUs and 3TB of RAM, running Ubuntu 20.04. We used a time-out of 1 hour (3600 sec-onds), and a memory limit of 64GB. For models **ertms-hl3**, **WMS** and **MLV** only the cases noCE-symb and symbolic were run 10 times. A preliminary exper-iment showed that all other cases either time-out or run out-of-memory. A repro-duction package is available in https://doi.org/10.5281/zenodo.14616612.

4.2 Results and Discussion

The results are presented in Table 3. We highlight the fastest run with evidence information for both the explicit and symbolic cases. We report the number of

Table 3: Experimental results for model checking, reporting number of vertices in the relevancy graph, and the mean total time over 10 runs (highlighted). For `expl` and `symb` we report the number of vertices in the relevancy graph after the second solving; the first solving results in the numbers reported in `noCE-expl` and `noCE-symb`, respectively. For every case, the fastest a) of `n-expl` and `expl`, and b) of `n-symb` and `symb` are highlighted.

	Result	noCE-expl	n-expl	expl	noCE-symb	n-symb	symb
witness1000							
canDobAlways	✓	2 000	1 001 002	5	2 000	–	5
		74.5s	170.3s	**74.6s**	251.0s	t-o	**247.1s**
SMS							
eventuallyDeleted	✗	25 206	195 406	1 503	27 506	–	2 443
		0.9s	4.7s	**1.1s**	1.7s	o-o-m	**2.1s**
noTransitFromDeleted	✗	16 106	187 338	28	18 886	504 726	68
		0.6s	3.6s	**0.8s**	1.7s	118.1s	**2.4s**
hesselink							
valuesCanBeRead	✓	1 093 760	3 325 184	2 209 472	1 093 760	–	2 209 472
		36.3s	**135.8s**	143.6s	21.5s	t-o	**133.0s**
1394-fin							
noDeadlockUpgrade	✓	377 138	1 034 224	705 681	377 138	–	705 681
		144.4s	**277.6s**	405.9s	26.1s	t-o	**310.9s**
noDoubleConfirmation	✓	565 708	1 222 794	894 251	565 708	–	894 251
		190.6s	**235.8s**	405.9s	9.0s	t-o	**240.8s**
noDeadlock	✓	188 569	845 655	517 112	188 569	–	517 112
		81.2s	**209.7s**	279.4s	27.2s	t-o	**245.2s**
onebit							
messCanBeOvertaken	✗	164 352	1 100 672	632 512	164 352	–	632 512
		7.1s	39.3s	**37.2s**	4.5s	o-o-m	**34.6s**
messReadInevSent	✗	153 984	1 090 304	4	153 984	–	112 981
		6.5s	31.2s	**6.8s**	3.5s	t-o	**8.0s**
noDeadlock	✓	81 920	1 018 240	550 080	81 920	–	550 080
		3.4s	31.7s	**29.0s**	2.3s	o-o-m	**27.9s**
ertms-hl3su							
detStabilisation	✓	–	–	–	11 973 823	–	–
		t-o	t-o	t-o	378.9s	t-o	o-o-m
termination	✗	188 865	–	13	196 593	–	29
		3 083.3s	t-o	**3 087.2s**	342.4s	t-o	**352.1s**
ertms-hl3							
termination	✗	–	–	–	321 421	–	90
		t-o	t-o	t-o	511.9s	t-o	**514.1s**
detStabilisation	✗	–	–	–	17 756 789	–	685
		t-o	t-o	t-o	364.9s	t-o	**406.0s**
MLV							
scenarioResumeVentilation	✓	–	–	–	6.15131e+23	–	5 950
		t-o	t-o	t-o	1 663.7s	t-o	**1 827.0s**
CONT38	✗	–	–	–	5.08225e+23	–	5 968
		t-o	t-o	t-o	1 519.8s	t-o	**1 565.0s**
WMS							
jobFailedToDone	✗	–	–	–	269 767 184	–	226
		t-o	o-o-m	t-o	20.8s	t-o	**28.1s**
noZombieJobs	✗	–	–	–	316 631 360	–	38
		t-o	o-o-m	t-o	24.7s	t-o	**56.2s**

vertices in the relevancy graph generated to solve the model checking problem and the mean total running time of ten runs in seconds ('t-o' for time-out, 'o-o-m' for out-of-memory). Standard deviation is typically below 10% of the mean.[2]

We focus our discussion on the approaches that support evidence generation. For the explicit implementation, our approach (`expl`) is typically comparable with the original approach (`n-expl`). In some cases, our approach reduces the running time of the verification in comparison with the original one, e.g., for model **onebit** and requirement *messReadInevSent*. In these cases the evidence is small, and the running time is similar to that of solving the PBES without additional information (`noCE-expl`). In other cases, `expl` has some overhead, e.g., for model **1394-fin** and requirement *noDoubleConfirmation*. Closer inspection suggests the evidence in these cases comprises most of the state space. Since our `expl` approach is a two-step approach, essentially the full exploration is performed twice, resulting in a larger running time. This suggests evidence should be typically generated if small; otherwise, a tool option could notify the user.

Moreover, the experiments show that our approach for evidence generation for symbolic model checking (`symb`) always outperforms the original approach (`n-symb`), enabling evidence generation for symbolic model checking, which was infeasible so far. Sometimes, the number of vertices after the second solving is larger due to the over-approximation of the proof graph symbolically extracted from $core(\mathcal{E})$. See, e.g., model **onebit** and requirement *messReadInevSent*.

5   Conclusion

In this paper we have described an approach to solving PBESs that allows for efficient evidence generation. Our approach solves a PBES without evidence information and uses its solution to simplify solving the PBES with evidence information described in [35]. We have established correctness of our approach, and implemented it in mCRL2 [4] as part of an explicit and a symbolic model checker. For explicit model checking, the performance is comparable to the original approach to evidence generation from [35]. If the counterexample is small, little overhead is incurred compared to solving the PBES without evidence information. Our approach makes evidence generation from PBESs efficient for symbolic checking, whereas this was not feasible before.

We plan to integrate our approach with other optimisations in the PBES solvers in mCRL2, and to preserve evidence information in static analysis techniques that are often used as preprocessing [20,29].

Acknowledgements This work was supported by the National Growth Fund through the Dutch 6G flagship project "Future Network Services", MACHI-NAIDE (ITEA3, No. 18030), and Cynergy4MIE (ChipsJU, No. 101140226).

---

[2] The SDs for the only cases where it exceeds 10% of the mean are: case `noCE-expl` **SMS** *eventuallyDeleted* and *noTransitFromDeleted*: 0.1; case `noCE-symb` **hesselink**: 3.2, **1394-fin** *noDoubleConfirmation*: 5.3 and *noDeadlock*: 4.9, **WMS** *noZombieJobs*: 3.0; and case `n-symb` **WMS** *jobFailedToDone*: 6.3 and *noZombieJobs*: 8.0.

References

1. Baier, C., Katoen, J.P.: Principles of model checking. MIT Press (2008)
2. Bartholomeus, M., Luttik, B., Willemse, T.A.C.: Modelling and analysing ERTMS hybrid level 3 with the mCRL2 toolset. In: FMICS. Lecture Notes in Computer Science, vol. 11119, pp. 98–114. Springer (2018). https://doi.org/10.1007/978-3-030-00244-2_7
3. Blom, S., van de Pol, J.: Symbolic reachability for process algebras with recursive data types. In: ICTAC. Lecture Notes in Computer Science, vol. 5160, pp. 81–95. Springer (2008). https://doi.org/10.1007/978-3-540-85762-4_6
4. Bunte, O., Groote, J.F., Keiren, J.J.A., Laveaux, M., Neele, T., de Vink, E.P., Wesselink, W., Wijs, A., Willemse, T.A.C.: The mCRL2 toolset for analysing concurrent systems - improvements in expressivity and usability. In: TACAS (2). Lecture Notes in Computer Science, vol. 11428, pp. 21–39. Springer (2019). https://doi.org/10.1007/978-3-030-17465-1_2
5. Burch, J.R., Clarke, E.M., McMillan, K.L., Dill, D.L., Hwang, L.J.: Symbolic model checking: 10^20 states and beyond. Inf. Comput. **98**(2), 142–170 (1992). https://doi.org/10.1016/0890-5401(92)90017-A
6. Busard, S.: Symbolic model checking of multi-modal logics: uniform strategies and rich explanations. Ph.D. thesis, Catholic University of Louvain, Louvain-la-Neuve, Belgium (2017), `https://hdl.handle.net/2078.1/186372`
7. Cimatti, A., Clarke, E.M., Giunchiglia, E., Giunchiglia, F., Pistore, M., Roveri, M., Sebastiani, R., Tacchella, A.: NuSMV 2: An opensource tool for symbolic model checking. In: CAV. Lecture Notes in Computer Science, vol. 2404, pp. 359–364. Springer (2002). https://doi.org/10.1007/3-540-45657-0_29
8. Clarke, E.M., Grumberg, O., Kroening, D., Peled, D.A., Veith, H.: Model checking, 2nd Edition. MIT Press (2018)
9. Cranen, S., Luttik, B., Willemse, T.A.C.: Proof graphs for parameterised boolean equation systems. In: CONCUR. Lecture Notes in Computer Science, vol. 8052, pp. 470–484. Springer (2013). https://doi.org/10.1007/978-3-642-40184-8_33
10. Cranen, S., Luttik, B., Willemse, T.A.C.: Evidence for fixpoint logic. In: CSL. LIPIcs, vol. 41, pp. 78–93. Schloss Dagstuhl - Leibniz-Zentrum für Informatik (2015). https://doi.org/10.4230/LIPICS.CSL.2015.78
11. van Dam, A., Ploeger, B., Willemse, T.A.C.: Instantiation for parameterised boolean equation systems. In: ICTAC. Lecture Notes in Computer Science, vol. 5160, pp. 440–454. Springer (2008). https://doi.org/10.1007/978-3-540-85762-4_30
12. van Dortmont, D., Keiren, J.J.A., Willemse, T.A.C.: Modelling and analysing a mechanical lung ventilator in mCRL2. In: ABZ. Lecture Notes in Computer Science, vol. 14759, pp. 341–359. Springer (2024). https://doi.org/10.1007/978-3-031-63790-2_27
13. Garavel, H., Lang, F., Mateescu, R., Serwe, W.: CADP 2011: a toolbox for the construction and analysis of distributed processes. Int. J. Softw. Tools Technol. Transf. **15**(2), 89–107 (2013). https://doi.org/10.1007/S10009-012-0244-Z
14. Garavel, H., Luttik, B.: Four formal models of IEEE 1394 link layer. In: MARS@ETAPS. EPTCS, vol. 399, pp. 21–100 (2024). https://doi.org/10.4204/EPTCS.399.5
15. Groote, J.F., Mousavi, M.R.: Modeling and Analysis of Communicating Systems. MIT Press (2014)

16. Groote, J.F., Willemse, T.A.C.: Model-checking processes with data. Sci. Comput. Program. **56**(3), 251–273 (2005). https://doi.org/10.1016/J.SCICO.2004.08.002
17. Groote, J.F., Willemse, T.A.C.: Parameterised boolean equation systems. Theor. Comput. Sci. **343**(3), 332–369 (2005). https://doi.org/10.1016/J.TCS.2005.06.016
18. Hesselink, W.H.: Invariants for the construction of a handshake register. Inf. Process. Lett. **68**(4), 173–177 (1998). https://doi.org/10.1016/S0020-0190(98)00158-6
19. Kant, G., van de Pol, J.: Efficient instantiation of parameterised boolean equation systems to parity games. In: GRAPHITE. EPTCS, vol. 99, pp. 50–65 (2012). https://doi.org/10.4204/EPTCS.99.7
20. Keiren, J.J.A., Wesselink, W., Willemse, T.A.C.: Liveness analysis for parameterised boolean equation systems. In: ATVA. Lecture Notes in Computer Science, vol. 8837, pp. 219–234. Springer (2014). https://doi.org/10.1007/978-3-319-11936-6_16
21. Kick, A.: Tableaux and witnesses for the μ-calculus. Tech. rep., Universitat Karlsruhe, Germany (1995)
22. Kozen, D.: Results on the propositional mu-calculus. Theor. Comput. Sci. **27**, 333–354 (1983). https://doi.org/10.1016/0304-3975(82)90125-6
23. Kwiatkowska, M.Z., Norman, G., Parker, D.: PRISM 4.0: Verification of probabilistic real-time systems. In: CAV. Lecture Notes in Computer Science, vol. 6806, pp. 585–591. Springer (2011). https://doi.org/10.1007/978-3-642-22110-1_47
24. Laveaux, M., Wesselink, W., Willemse, T.A.C.: On-the-fly solving for symbolic parity games. In: TACAS (2). Lecture Notes in Computer Science, vol. 13244, pp. 137–155. Springer (2022). https://doi.org/10.1007/978-3-030-99527-0_8
25. Liem, E.: Extraction of Invariants in Parameterised Boolean Equation Systems. Master's thesis, Eindhoven University of Technology (2023)
26. Mateescu, R.: Efficient diagnostic generation for boolean equation systems. In: TACAS. Lecture Notes in Computer Science, vol. 1785, pp. 251–265. Springer (2000). https://doi.org/10.1007/3-540-46419-0_18
27. McMillan, K.L.: Symbolic model checking. Kluwer (1993). https://doi.org/10.1007/978-1-4615-3190-6
28. Neele, T.: Reductions for parity games and model checking. Ph.D. thesis, Mathematics and Computer Science, Eindhoven University of Technology, The Netherlands (Sep 2020)
29. Orzan, S., Willemse, T.A.C.: Invariants for parameterised boolean equation systems. Theor. Comput. Sci. **411**(11-13), 1338–1371 (2010). https://doi.org/10.1016/J.TCS.2009.11.001
30. Ploeger, B., Wesselink, W., Willemse, T.A.C.: Verification of reactive systems via instantiation of parameterised boolean equation systems. Inf. Comput. **209**(4), 637–663 (2011). https://doi.org/10.1016/J.IC.2010.11.025
31. Remenska, D., Willemse, T.A.C., Verstoep, K., Templon, J., Bal, H.E.: Using model checking to analyze the system behavior of the LHC production grid. Future Gener. Comput. Syst. **29**(8), 2239–2251 (2013). https://doi.org/10.1016/J.FUTURE.2013.06.004
32. Stirling, C., Walker, D.: Local model checking in the modal mu-calculus. Theor. Comput. Sci. **89**(1), 161–177 (1991). https://doi.org/10.1016/0304-3975(90)90110-4
33. Stramaglia, A., Keiren, J.J.A., Laveaux, M., Willemse, T.A.C.: Efficient evidence generation for modal μ-calculus model checking (extended version) (2025), `https://arxiv.org/abs/2501.15938`

34. Tan, L., Cleaveland, R.: Evidence-based model checking. In: CAV. Lecture Notes in Computer Science, vol. 2404, pp. 455–470. Springer (2002). https://doi.org/10.1007/3-540-45657-0_37
35. Wesselink, W., Willemse, T.A.C.: Evidence extraction from parameterised boolean equation systems. In: ARQNL@IJCAR. CEUR Workshop Proceedings, vol. 2095, pp. 86–100. CEUR-WS.org (2018), https://ceur-ws.org/Vol-2095/paper6.pdf
36. Zielonka, W.: Infinite games on finitely coloured graphs with applications to automata on infinite trees. Theor. Comput. Sci. **200**(1-2), 135–183 (1998). https://doi.org/10.1016/S0304-3975(98)00009-7

Token Elimination in Model Checking of Petri Nets*

Nicolaj Ø. Jensen(✉)🆔, Kim G. Larsen🆔, and Jiří Srba🆔

Department of Computer Science, Aalborg University
Selma Lagerløfs Vej 300, 9220 Aalborg, Denmark
{noje,kgl,srba}@cs.aau.dk

Abstract. We propose a novel state-space reduction framework to improve the performance of model checking of Petri nets. We provide two instances of the framework: a static technique that considers only the structure of the net, and a dynamic technique that additionally considers the current marking. By analyzing impossible, visible, and directional effects of transitions, we identify places where tokens can be removed while preserving the property in question. Unlike structural reductions, our techniques modify only the current marking, allowing the net structure to be reused in multiple subproblems concurrently, which can be beneficial for example for CTL model checking. We prove the correctness of our techniques and implement them in the open-source tool TAPAAL, a repeated winner in the CTL category in the annual model checking contest (MCC). We measure our methods' performance on the MCC 2023 benchmark using the CTL categories and demonstrate that our methods reduce time and, especially, memory usage. Our dynamic method explores 39.3% fewer configurations on average and achieves two orders of magnitude speedup on at least one query on 23.7% of non-trivial models.

Keywords: Petri Nets · State-Space Reduction · Model Checking.

1 Introduction

The main obstacle of verifying properties of concurrent systems is the state-space explosion problem [8] that follows from the many possible interleavings of even simple subsystems and their composed intermediate states when run in parallel. The state space of a concurrent system is often exponentially larger than any of its constituent systems, and exploring every state to verify a property is intractable in practice. Therefore, many approaches have been developed to simplify systems structurally [7,8,22,26], to disregard equivalent traces through partial-order reductions [7,8,14,24,27], and to symbolically verify multiple states simultaneously [8,22,23]. We present a reduction that combines ideas from all the aforementioned methods to simplify the states and the amount of branching in the reduced system. The reduction is presented in the context of the weighted Petri net formalism with inhibitor arcs.

---

* Funded by the VILLUM INVESTIGATOR project S4OS.

A. Gurfinkel and M. Heule (Eds.): TACAS 2025, LNCS 15696, pp. 211–230, 2025.
https://doi.org/10.1007/978-3-031-90643-5_11

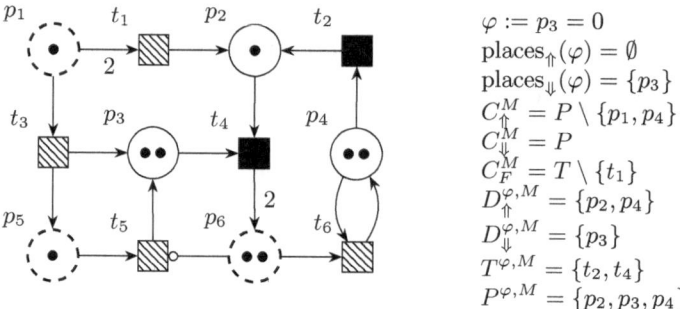

$$\varphi := p_3 = 0$$
$$\text{places}_\Uparrow(\varphi) = \emptyset$$
$$\text{places}_\Downarrow(\varphi) = \{p_3\}$$
$$C_\Uparrow^M = P \setminus \{p_1, p_4\}$$
$$C_\Downarrow^M = P$$
$$C_F^M = T \setminus \{t_1\}$$
$$D_\Uparrow^{\varphi,M} = \{p_2, p_4\}$$
$$D_\Downarrow^{\varphi,M} = \{p_3\}$$
$$T^{\varphi,M} = \{t_2, t_4\}$$
$$P^{\varphi,M} = \{p_2, p_3, p_4\}$$

Fig. 1: Example Petri net and sets computed by our technique for the depicted marking M and property φ. Solid transitions are in $T^{\varphi,M}$ and are the only ones that require firing to eventually satisfy φ from the given marking, if possible. Dashed places are not in $P^{\varphi,M}$ and can have their tokens removed without affecting whether EFφ holds. Arcs without weight annotation have weight 1.

Petri nets are directed bipartite graphs consisting of places (circles) and transitions (squares). Places can contain a number of tokens, and the token configuration across all places forms a state (a marking) of the Petri net. For a transition to fire, one or more tokens are required in each of its predecessor places, as firing it will remove a token from each predecessor place and add a token to each successor place, resulting in a new marking. In a weighted Petri net, the arcs are weighted, affecting how many tokens are removed and added. Inhibitor arcs, depicted with circle-headed arrows, are a special type of arc that prevent the transition at their head from firing if the number of tokens at the source place of the arc equals or exceeds the arc's weight. Petri nets are well suited for modeling parallel systems, where various discrete resources move from state to state, for example, packets in a network or tasks in a workflow system.

Consider the example Petri net illustrated in Figure 1 and let M denote the depicted marking. Now assume that we want to check whether it is possible to reach a marking with 0 tokens in place p_3, formally whether $M \models \text{EF}\varphi$ holds where $\varphi \equiv (p_3 = 0)$. It is possible to show that this property holds in multiple ways, e.g. firing the sequence $t_2t_4t_4$ will reach such a marking. However, some transitions and some tokens are unnecessary to demonstrate that the property holds. For example, the transition t_6 can always be omitted in such witness traces, and the number of tokens in p_6 is irrelevant since none of the shortest witness traces (those consisting of the fewest firings, i.e. $t_2t_4t_4$ and $t_4t_2t_4$) will not consume from p_6 anyway. Our approach in this paper computes a set of transitions $T^{\varphi,M}$ (solid squares in the example) such that if a trace to a φ-satisfying marking exists, then the shortest traces to such a marking consists exclusively of firings from this set. We use this set to identify a set of places $P^{\varphi,M}$, such that if marking M' matches M in these places but has 0 tokens elsewhere (elsewhere are dashed circles in the example), then it is guaranteed that the shortest witness traces are preserved, and thus $M' \models EF\varphi$ if and only if $M \models EF\varphi$.

Removing tokens from the reached markings during a state-space search has two major benefits: (i) two different markings where unimportant tokens are removed can become identical and this helps to reduce the size of the state space, and (ii) removing unimportant tokens disables unimportant transitions and hence reduces the branching degree of the state space.[1]

Our contributions. We present a novel on-the-fly technique that reduces the reachable state space by removing tokens from the explored markings. As a direct consequence of only modifying markings, our method is suitable where other techniques are not, e.g. in on-the-fly model checking. Our technique is also applicable to unrestricted (even unbounded) Petri nets—all theorems are proven in full generality. The termination of the state-space search is, of course, not guaranteed in such a case, but like many other reductions, our technique will reduce some infinite state spaces to finite ones.

We present two versions of our technique. The static version uses the structure of the net to compute visible effects, distinguishing between visible increases and decreases, and thus determines where tokens are invisible and can be removed. When using the static version, the set of visible places can be cached to reduce overhead. The dynamic version is a refinement that first, based on the current marking, approximates a set of transitions that can never be enabled in future markings. This allows us to disregard some impossible effects that would otherwise be structurally visible, limiting how visibility propagates in the net and resulting in more places where tokens can be removed.

Our techniques only preserve reachability properties, but due to their ability to be used in concurrent model checking, our experiments focus on Computation Tree Logic (CTL) [8] where reachability sub-properties often must be checked, potentially with many different initial markings. Structural reductions that only preserve reachability properties cannot be used in this context, whereas our reduction can. We implement our techniques in the popular model checker TAPAAL, and evaluate it using the Model Checking Contest 2023 [18] benchmark with a focus on challenging queries that challenge the state-of-the-art tool. We show that we save both memory and time when implemented in the CTL algorithm of TAPAAL [10].

Related work Partial-order reductions include many similar techniques such as ample sets [17,24], persistent sets [14], and stubborn sets [14,27]. Each preserves different kinds of properties, but all share the idea that not all interleavings need to be searched. Recently, stubborn reductions have been made available for reachability games [5] and systems with time [3,4]. Our technique shares similarities with identification of stubborn sets [7,14,19]. However, our technique

---

[1] Removing tokens that inhibit transitions may result in more behavior, but inhibitor arcs are often few, and in the rare cases where our technique uninhibits transitions, they are always excluded through stubborn reductions anyway.

is coarser in some ways, as it (i) is based on visible effects instead of just visible transitions, (ii) limits visibility propagation by considering impossible transition firings and effects, and (iii) is only guaranteed to preserve the shortest traces to satisfying markings. Moreover, we simplify the marking rather than the set of considered transitions. In our early experiments, we applied the coarser marking-dependent *up-set* from [19] when determining which places in the query needed change. However, it did not provide any positive effect on the benchmark.

Structural reductions of Petri nets [7,22,26] have been around almost since the introduction of Petri nets. Structural reductions modify the Petri net itself [22,26]. Many possible transformations exist, some even incorporate SMT solvers [26]. Our technique is comparable to a combination of structural reduction rules I and M found in TAPAAL [7]. However, in addition to the refinements (i)-(iii) mentioned earlier, we modify only the marking instead of the net structure. We are aware of only one structural reduction that does so, and it simulates firing transitions in the initial marking [26]. The fact that we only modify the marking allows us to use our technique on-the-fly without allocating memory for several reduced versions of the Petri net.

CTL is a branching-time temporal logic used to specify properties of concurrent systems [8]. It allows for the expression of temporal properties by quantifying over paths in a system's state-transition graph. Note that verifying CTL properties of Petri nets even without inhibitor arcs is generally undecidable [6] and reachability problems have recently been proved to be Ackermann-complete [9]. These undecidability/complexity results do not affect the correctness of our techniques, and the technique can be applied to any reachability problem directly or to subproblems of CTL about reachability. In [20], the authors also explore subproblem-specific reductions in CTL model checking [20], however, the way we reduce markings by token elimination has not been studied before.

Structure of the Paper. In Section 2 we present the Petri net formalism and the reachability problem. In Section 3 we present our techniques and their correctness. Our experiments and results are shown in Section 4, and we conclude on our findings in Section 5.

2   Petri Nets and the Reachability Problem

We shall first introduce the necessary definitions.

Definition 1 (Transition System). *Given a set Π of atomic propositions, a transition system (TS) over Π is a 4-tuple $\mathcal{T} = \langle \mathcal{S}, \mathcal{A}, \rightarrow, L \rangle$ such that $\mathcal{S}$ is a set of states, $\mathcal{A}$ is a finite set of actions, $\rightarrow \subseteq \mathcal{S} \times \mathcal{A} \times \mathcal{S}$ is a transition relation, and $L : \mathcal{S} \rightarrow 2^{\Pi}$ is a labeling function assigning each state to a set of propositions.*

We write $s \xrightarrow{a} s'$ whenever $\langle s, a, s' \rangle \in \rightarrow$. We write $s \xrightarrow{a}$ whenever $\langle s, a, s' \rangle \in \rightarrow$ for some $s' \in \mathcal{S}$ and say that a is *enabled* in s. We write $s \rightarrow s'$ if $\langle s, a, s' \rangle \in \rightarrow$ for some $a \in \mathcal{A}$ and write $s \nrightarrow$ if $\langle s, a, s' \rangle \notin \rightarrow$ for any $a \in \mathcal{A}, s' \in \mathcal{S}$. We extend the notion $\xrightarrow{a}$ inductively to traces $w \in \mathcal{A}^*$ such that $s \xrightarrow{\epsilon} s$ for all $s \in \mathcal{S}$ and

$s \xrightarrow{wa} s'$ if $s \xrightarrow{w} s''$ and $s'' \xrightarrow{a} s'$. Finally, $\rightarrow^*$ is the reflexive and transitive closure of $\rightarrow$.

Definition 2 (Reachability and State Properties). *Given a set Π of atomic propositions, $EF\varphi$ is a reachability property where state property φ (in negation normal form) is defined inductively by the grammar $\varphi ::= \pi \mid \neg\pi \mid \varphi_1 \wedge \varphi_2 \mid \varphi_1 \vee \varphi_2$ where $\pi \in \Pi$. Let Φ be the set of all state properties in negation normal form.*

We assume standard semantics and write $s \vDash \varphi$ if the state s satisfies φ, and we write $s \vDash EF\varphi$ if $s \rightarrow^* s'$ and $s' \vDash \varphi$. The reachability problem involves checking whether a reachability property holds in a given state. For this paper, it is necessary to know that reachability properties are a strict subset of the branching-time logic known as computation tree logic (CTL) but we refer to [8] for further details on CTL.

Definition 3 (Petri Net with Inhibitor Arcs). *A Petri net with inhibitor arcs (PN) is a 4-tuple $N = \langle P, T, W, I \rangle$ where*

- *P is a finite set of places,*
- *T is a finite set of transitions such that $P \cap T = \emptyset$,*
- *$W : (P \times T) \cup (T \times P) \rightarrow \mathbb{N}_0$ is an incidence matrix, and*
- *$I : P \times T \rightarrow \mathbb{N} \cup \{\infty\}$ is an inhibitor weight matrix.*

Definition 4 (Marking). *For a PN N with places P, a marking $M : P \rightarrow \mathbb{N}_0$ is a function that assigns to each place a number of tokens present in the place. The set $\mathcal{M}(N)$ is the set of all markings of PN N.*

The effect matrix $E : T \times P \rightarrow \mathbb{Z}$ is a function defined as $E(t, p) = W(t, p) - W(p, t)$. We also use the following notation where $p \in P$ and $t \in T$:

$${}^\bullet p = \{t' \in T \mid W(t', p) > 0\} \text{ is the preset of } p,$$
$$p^\bullet = \{t' \in T \mid W(p, t') > 0\} \text{ is the postset of } p,$$
$${}^\bullet t = \{p' \in P \mid W(p', t) > 0\} \text{ is the preset of } t,$$
$$t^\bullet = \{p' \in P \mid W(t, p') > 0\} \text{ is the postset of } t,$$
$${}^+p = \{t' \in {}^\bullet p \mid E(t', p) > 0\} \text{ is the increasing preset of } p,$$
$$p^- = \{t' \in p^\bullet \mid E(t', p) < 0\} \text{ is the decreasing postset of } p,$$
$$t^+ = \{p' \in t^\bullet \mid E(t, p') > 0\} \text{ is the increased postset of } t,$$
$${}^-t = \{p' \in {}^\bullet t \mid E(t, p') < 0\} \text{ is the decreased preset of } t,$$
$$p^\circ = \{t' \in T \mid I(p, t') \neq \infty\} \text{ is the inhibited postset of } p,$$
$${}^\circ t = \{p' \in P \mid I(p', t) \neq \infty\} \text{ is the inhibiting preset of } t.$$

We extend the notation to sets such that for a set X of places or transitions, ${}^\bullet X = \bigcup_{x \in X} {}^\bullet x$ and likewise for the other preset and postset operators.

For PNs, without loss of generality, we consider atomic proposition $\pi \in \Pi$ to be of the form $k \leq \sum_p v_p p$ where $k, v_p \in \mathbb{Z}$. Marking M satisfies atomic proposition π, written $M \vDash \pi$, if the inequality holds when all occurrences of places $p \in P$ in π are replaced with $M(p)$. For example, if $p_1, p_2, p_3 \in P$ then

EF $3 \leq p_1 \wedge 1 \leq p_2 - p_3$ asserts that it is possible to reach a marking, where p_1 contains at least 3 tokens and there is at least 1 more token in p_2 than in p_3. The negation of π is achieved by negating all weights v_p and replacing k with $-k + 1$.

A PN N defines a TS $\mathcal{T}(N) = \langle \mathcal{S}, \mathcal{A}, \rightarrow, L \rangle$ over Π where $S = \mathcal{M}(N)$, $\mathcal{A} = T$, and $M \overset{t}{\rightarrow} M'$ if for all $p \in P$ we have $M(p) \geq W(p,t)$ and $M(p) < I(p,t)$ and $M'(p) = M(p) + E(t,p)$. Finally, $\pi \in L(M)$ iff $M \models \pi$ where $\pi \in \Pi$.

Definition 5 (Increasing and Decreasing Support). *The* increasing support *is a function* places$_\Uparrow : \Phi \rightarrow 2^P$ *defined inductively as:*

$$\text{places}_\Uparrow(k \leq \sum_p v_p p) = \{p \in P \mid v_p > 0\}$$

$$\text{places}_\Uparrow(\varphi_1 \wedge \varphi_2) = \text{places}_\Uparrow(\varphi_1) \cup \text{places}_\Uparrow(\varphi_2)$$

$$\text{places}_\Uparrow(\varphi_1 \vee \varphi_2) = \text{places}_\Uparrow(\varphi_1) \cup \text{places}_\Uparrow(\varphi_2) \, .$$

The decreasing support *is a function* places$_\Downarrow : \Phi \rightarrow 2^P$ *defined inductively as:*

$$\text{places}_\Downarrow(k \leq \sum_p v_p p) = \{p \in P \mid v_p < 0\}$$

$$\text{places}_\Downarrow(\varphi_1 \wedge \varphi_2) = \text{places}_\Downarrow(\varphi_1) \cup \text{places}_\Downarrow(\varphi_2)$$

$$\text{places}_\Downarrow(\varphi_1 \vee \varphi_2) = \text{places}_\Downarrow(\varphi_1) \cup \text{places}_\Downarrow(\varphi_2) \, .$$

Finally, we let $\text{places}(\varphi) = \text{places}_\Uparrow(\varphi) \cup \text{places}_\Downarrow(\varphi)$ *be the* support *of the state property* φ.

The intuition is that places$_\Uparrow(\varphi)$ (resp. places$_\Downarrow(\varphi)$) denote the set of places where more (resp. fewer) tokens are potentially needed for φ to be satisfied if not already satisfied. The set $\text{places}(\varphi)$ is also said to be *directly visible* to φ, because it is not possible to go from a marking where φ is not satisfied to one where φ is satisfied without firing a transitions that affects one of these places in the appropriate direction. Formally:

Lemma 1. *Let* $N = \langle P, T, W, I \rangle$ *be a PN, $M, M' \in \mathcal{M}(N)$ markings, φ a state property, and $t \notin {}^+\text{places}_\Uparrow(\varphi) \cup \text{places}_\Downarrow(\varphi)^-$ a transition. If $M \not\models \varphi$ and $M \overset{t}{\rightarrow} M'$, then $M' \not\models \varphi$.*

3   Token Elimination

We now introduce our token elimination technique, which aims to identify (in a dynamic or static way) a set of places where the number of tokens in any reachable marking can be reset to zero while preserving a given reachability property.

We say that elements (places, transitions, tokens, or effects) are *invisible* if they do not affect whether the reachability property holds, i.e. our techniques identify invisible tokens. They do so by computing an over-approximation of the visible transitions and visible effects. Remark that we will often describe the content of our over-approximation as *visible* even though some of it may be *invisible* in practice. We first present the static technique focusing on intuition and then the dynamic technique with full proofs (of which static is a simplified case). For the rest of this section, let us fix a PN $N = \langle P, T, W, I \rangle$ and reachability property $\mathrm{EF}\varphi$.

3.1 Static Token Elimination

Our static token-elimination technique computes two sets of places: $S_\Uparrow^\varphi$ and $S_\Downarrow^\varphi$ that exhibit the following properties. If $M, M' \in \mathcal{M}(N)$ are markings such that $M \to^* M'$ and $M' \vDash \varphi$ and $w \in T^*$ is one of the shortest sequences of transitions such that $M \xrightarrow{w} M'$ (there can be more than one such sequence) then:

- if $p \in \mathrm{places}_\Uparrow(\varphi)$ or there exists a transition t in w that consumes from p, then $p \in S_\Uparrow^\varphi$, and
- if $p \in \mathrm{places}_\Downarrow(\varphi)$ or there exists a transition t in w that is inhibited by p, then $p \in S_\Downarrow^\varphi$.

In other words, $S_\Uparrow^\varphi$ is a superset of places where we need more tokens and positive effects are visible. Similarly, $S_\Downarrow^\varphi$ is a superset of places where we need fewer tokens and where negative effects are visible. We compute $S_\Uparrow^\varphi$ and $S_\Downarrow^\varphi$ inductively as the least fixed point of the following constraints:

(S1) if $p \in \mathrm{places}_\Uparrow(\varphi)$ then $p \in S_\Uparrow^\varphi$,
(S2) if $p \in \mathrm{places}_\Downarrow(\varphi)$ then $p \in S_\Downarrow^\varphi$,
(S3) if $p \in S_\Uparrow^\varphi$ then $^{\bullet+}p \subseteq S_\Uparrow^\varphi$,
(S4) if $p \in S_\Uparrow^\varphi$ then $^{\circ+}p \subseteq S_\Downarrow^\varphi$,
(S5) if $p \in S_\Downarrow^\varphi$ then $(^{\bullet}(p^-) \setminus \{p\}) \subseteq S_\Uparrow^\varphi$,
(S6) if $p \in S_\Downarrow^\varphi$ then $^{\circ}(p^-) \subseteq S_\Downarrow^\varphi$,
(S7) if $p \in S_\Downarrow^\varphi$ and $\exists t \in p^- . W(p, t) > 1$ then $p \in S_\Uparrow^\varphi$.

We briefly give the intuition for these constraints:

- **(S1)**, **(S2)**: If a place is in $\mathrm{places}_\Uparrow(\varphi)$ or $\mathrm{places}_\Downarrow(\varphi)$, then effects of the appropriate direction are (directly) visible to the satisfaction of φ.
- **(S3)**, **(S4)**: If increases are visible in p, then any transition t with positive effect on p is visible, and hence effects that enable t are also visible. That is, increases in the preset of the positive preset of p are visible, and decreases in the inhibiting preset of the positive preset of p are visible.
- **(S5)**, **(S6)**, **(S7)**: Similarly, if decreases are visible in p, then any transition t with negative effect on p is visible, and hence effects that enable t are also visible. However, since we are interested in decreases to p, adding tokens to

p would be counter-productive, which is why we do not require p in $S_\Uparrow^\varphi$ in (**S5**). However, this logic does not hold if some $t \in p^-$ must consume more than one token from p to fire, in which case we may have to add tokens to p before we can empty it with t. Hence, (**S7**).

Finally, let $T_{\text{sta}}^\varphi = {}^+(S_\Uparrow^\varphi) \cup (S_\Downarrow^\varphi)^-$ be the set of transitions that have a visible effect, and let $P_{\text{sta}}^\varphi = \text{places}(\varphi) \cup {}^\bullet T_{\text{sta}}^\varphi \cup {}^\circ T_{\text{sta}}^\varphi$ be the set of places with visible tokens. As we shall prove for the corresponding dynamic version of T_{sta}^φ, the shortest trace to a marking satisfying φ does not include transitions outside of this set. Therefore, it does not matter for the satisfaction of $\text{EF}\varphi$ if we modify the marking in a way that disables transitions not in T_{sta}^φ. Hence, we define a reduction that removes these invisible tokens.

Definition 6 (Static Token Elimination). *The static token elimination abstraction* $\alpha_{\text{sta}}^\varphi : \mathcal{M}(N) \to \mathcal{M}(N)$ *is given by*

$$\alpha_{\text{sta}}^\varphi(M)(p) = \begin{cases} M(p) & \text{if } p \in P_{\text{sta}}^\varphi \\ 0 & \text{otherwise .} \end{cases}$$

Theorem 1 ($\alpha_{\text{sta}}^\varphi$ Preserves Reachability). *Let M be a marking and $\text{EF}\varphi$ a reachability property. We have $M \vDash \text{EF}\varphi$ iff $\alpha_{\text{sta}}^\varphi(M) \vDash \text{EF}\varphi$.*

We note that P_{sta}^φ depends only on the structure of the net and φ. Hence, it can be cached based on φ if it is a reoccurring subproblem on the same net. We take advantage of this in our CTL algorithm implementation.

3.2 Dynamic Token Elimination

The dynamic token elimination is a refinement of the static technique. In addition to visible effects, we shall now also consider whether the effects are possible from the current marking. Let us fix a current marking M. The set $C_\Uparrow^M$ (resp. $C_\Downarrow^M$) is a set of places that may potentially have their number of tokens increased (resp. decreased) in a future marking. Additionally, the set C_F^M contains transitions that may be enabled in a future marking. We define $C_\Uparrow^M$, $C_\Downarrow^M$, and C_F^M inductively as the least fixed point of the following constraint:

(**C**) If $t \in T$ and for all $p \in P$, we have $(W(p, t) \leq M(p)$ or $p \in C_\Uparrow^M)$ and $(I(p, t) > M(p)$ or $p \in C_\Downarrow^M)$, then $t \in C_F^M$ and $t^+ \subseteq C_\Uparrow^M$ and ${}^-t \subseteq C_\Downarrow^M$.

We now state the properties of the sets defined by this constraint.

Lemma 2. *Let $p \in P$ be a place and $t \in T$ be a transition.*

- *If $p \notin C_\Uparrow^M$ then $M'(p) \leq M(p)$ for all M' s.t. $M \to^* M'$,*
- *If $p \notin C_\Downarrow^M$ then $M'(p) \geq M(p)$ for all M' s.t. $M \to^* M'$,*
- *If $t \notin C_F^M$ then $M' \not\xrightarrow{t}$ for all M' s.t. $M \to^* M'$.*

We can now use $C_\Uparrow^M$, $C_\Downarrow^M$, and C_F^M to find refinements of $S_\Uparrow^\varphi$ and $S_\Downarrow^\varphi$. The refined sets $D_\Uparrow^{\varphi,M}$ and $D_\Downarrow^{\varphi,M}$ contain places where positive and negative effects, respectively, are possible and visible. We define $D_\Uparrow^{\varphi,M}$ and $D_\Downarrow^{\varphi,M}$ inductively as the least fixed point of the following constraints:

(D1) if $p \in \text{places}_\Uparrow(\varphi) \cap C_\Uparrow^M$ then $p \in D_\Uparrow^{\varphi,M}$

(D2) if $p \in \text{places}_\Downarrow(\varphi) \cap C_\Downarrow^M$ then $p \in D_\Downarrow^{\varphi,M}$

(D3) if $p \in D_\Uparrow^{\varphi,M}$ then $({}^\bullet({}^+p \cap C_F^M) \cap C_\Uparrow^M) \subseteq D_\Uparrow^{\varphi,M}$

(D4) if $p \in D_\Uparrow^{\varphi,M}$ then $({}^\circ({}^+p \cap C_F^M) \cap C_\Downarrow^M) \subseteq D_\Downarrow^{\varphi,M}$

(D5) if $p \in D_\Downarrow^{\varphi,M}$ then $({}^\bullet(p^- \cap C_F^M) \cap (C_\Uparrow^M \setminus \{p\})) \subseteq D_\Uparrow^{\varphi,M}$

(D6) if $p \in D_\Downarrow^{\varphi,M}$ then $({}^\circ(p^- \cap C_F^M) \cap C_\Downarrow^M) \subseteq D_\Downarrow^{\varphi,M}$

(D7) if $p \in D_\Downarrow^{\varphi,M}$ and $\exists t \in p^- \cap C_F^M.W(p,t) > 1$ and $p \in C_\Uparrow^M$ then $p \in D_\Uparrow^{\varphi,M}$

The constraints correspond to **(S1)-(S7)**, but propagation is now limited using $C_\Uparrow^M$, $C_\Downarrow^M$, and C_F^M. Next, let

$$T_{\text{dyn}}^{\varphi,M} = ({}^+(D_\Uparrow^{\varphi,M}) \cup (D_\Downarrow^{\varphi,M})^-) \cap C_F^M \tag{1}$$

be the set of fireable transitions with visible effects.

Lemma 3. *Let $M \to^* M'$ such that $M' \vDash \varphi$. If $w \in T^*$ is some shortest sequence of transitions (there can be more than one) such that $M \xrightarrow{w} M'$ then necessarily $w \in (T_{\text{dyn}}^{\varphi,M})^*$.*

Proof. Let $w = t_1 \ldots t_n \in T^*$ be some shortest sequence such that $M \xrightarrow{w} M'$ with $M' \vDash \varphi$. If $n = 0$, then $M = M'$ and the claim holds trivially. If $n = 1$ and hence $w = t \in T$, then $M \nvDash \varphi$, otherwise w would be shorter. By contraposition of Lemma 1, we have that $t \in {}^+\text{places}_\Uparrow(\varphi) \cup \text{places}_\Downarrow(\varphi)^-$, otherwise it is not possible that $M' \vDash \varphi$. Since t is enabled, we know $t \in C_F^M$. By **(D1)**, we know $\text{places}_\Uparrow(\varphi) \subseteq D_\Uparrow^{\varphi,M}$, so if $t \in {}^+\text{places}_\Uparrow(\varphi)$ then also $t \in T_{\text{dyn}}^{\varphi,M}$ by definition of $T_{\text{dyn}}^{\varphi,M}$. Alternatively, by **(D2)**, we know $\text{places}_\Downarrow(\varphi) \subseteq D_\Downarrow^{\varphi,M}$, so if $t \in \text{places}_\Downarrow(\varphi)^-$ then again $t \in T_{\text{dyn}}^{\varphi,M}$. Thus, $t = w \in (T_{\text{dyn}}^{\varphi,M})^*$ as required. Now, let $n > 1$. For the sake of contradiction, let us assume that there exists an i such that $t_i \notin T_{\text{dyn}}^{\varphi,M}$ and let us assume that i is the largest index with this property. Clearly, t_i does not have any effect on the support $\text{places}(\varphi)$, otherwise we can use the same argument as when $n = 1$ and show that $t_i \in T_{\text{dyn}}^{\varphi,M}$. Now, since w is a shortest trace, it must be the case that t_i enables t_j for some $i < j \leq n$. That is, t_i adds tokens to ${}^\bullet t_j$ and/or removes tokens from ${}^\circ t_j$. Let us consider each case:

1. If t_i removes tokens from ${}^\circ t_j$, then there exists $p \in {}^- t_i \cap {}^\circ t_j \cap C_\Downarrow^M$. Since j is greater than i (the last index such that $t_i \notin T_{\text{dyn}}^{\varphi,M}$) we have that $t_j \in T_{\text{dyn}}^{\varphi,M}$ which implies that $t_j \in {}^+D_\Uparrow^{\varphi,M}$ and/or $t_j \in (D_\Downarrow^{\varphi,M})^-$ by definition of $T_{\text{dyn}}^{\varphi,M}$. Let us consider each sub-case:

(a) If $t_j \in {}^+D_\Uparrow^{\varphi,M}$ then there exists $p' \in D_\Uparrow^{\varphi,M}$ such that $t_j \in {}^+p'$. By **(D4)** we have that ${}^\circ t_j \cap C_\Downarrow^M \subseteq D_\Downarrow^{\varphi,M}$ which in turn implies $p \in D_\Downarrow^{\varphi,M}$. Since $t_i \in p^-$, then $t_i \in (D_\Downarrow^{\varphi,M})^-$ and thus $t_i \in T_{\text{dyn}}^{\varphi,M}$ creating a contradiction.

(b) Hence, it must be the case that $t_j \in (D_\Downarrow^{\varphi,M})^-$. Similarly, this implies that there exists $p' \in D_\Downarrow^{\varphi,M}$ such that $t_j \in p'^-$. Now by **(D6)** we have that ${}^\circ t_j \cap C_\Downarrow^M \subseteq D_\Downarrow^{\varphi,M}$ which in turn implies $p \in D_\Downarrow^{\varphi,M}$. Again, since $t_i \in p^-$, then $t_i \in (D_\Downarrow^{\varphi,M})^-$ and thus $t_i \in T_{\text{dyn}}^{\varphi,M}$ creating a contradiction.

2. Hence, it must be the case that t_i adds tokens to ${}^\bullet t_j$, that is, there exists $p \in t_i^+ \cap {}^\bullet t_j \cap C_\Uparrow^M$. Again, since j is greater than i we have that $t_j \in T_{\text{dyn}}^{\varphi,M}$ which implies that $t_j \in {}^+D_\Uparrow^{\varphi,M}$ and/or $t_j \in (D_\Downarrow^{\varphi,M})^-$:

(a) If $t_j \in {}^+D_\Uparrow^{\varphi,M}$, then there exists $p' \in D_\Uparrow^{\varphi,M}$ such that $t_j \in {}^+p'$. So by **(D3)** we have that ${}^\bullet t_j \cap C_\Uparrow^M \subseteq D_\Uparrow^{\varphi,M}$ which in turn implies $p \in D_\Uparrow^{\varphi,M}$. Since $t_i \in {}^+p$, then $t_i \in {}^+D_\Uparrow^{\varphi,M}$ and thus $t_i \in T_{\text{dyn}}^{\varphi,M}$ creating a contradiction.

(b) Hence, it must be the case that $t_j \in (D_\Downarrow^{\varphi,M})^-$. This implies that there exists $p' \in D_\Downarrow^{\varphi,M}$ such that $t_j \in p'^-$. Now by **(D5)** we have that ${}^\bullet t_j \cap C_\Uparrow^M \setminus \{p'\} \subseteq D_\Uparrow^{\varphi,M}$, so unless $p = p'$, it must be the case that $p \in D_\Uparrow^{\varphi,M}$. Since $t_i \in {}^+p$, then $t_i \in {}^+D_\Uparrow^{\varphi,M}$ and thus $t_i \in T_{\text{dyn}}^{\varphi,M}$ creating a contradiction. Now finally, if $p = p'$ for all $p' \in D_\Downarrow^{\varphi,M}$ where $t_j \in p'^-$, then we shall use following facts:

- $p \notin {}^\circ t_j$ (follows from case 1.)
- $p \notin D_\Uparrow^{\varphi,M}$ (follows from case 2.a)
- $W(p, t_j) = 1$, otherwise **(D7)** would imply $p \in D_\Uparrow^{\varphi,M}$
- $p \notin \text{places}_\Uparrow(\varphi)$, otherwise $p \in D_\Uparrow^{\varphi,M}$ by **(D1)**

We can thus conclude that $p \in \text{places}_\Downarrow(\varphi)$. This follows from the fact that $D_\Downarrow^{\varphi,M}$ is a least fixed point and the only remaining possible way for $p \in D_\Downarrow^{\varphi,M}$ is **(D2)**. Since none of the other cases applied, we can also conclude that t_j only appears in w in order to remove tokens from p. Moreover, t_i only appears in w in order to enable t_j by adding tokens to p. However, since $W(p, t_j) = 1$, this is always redundant for the purpose of satisfying φ and contradicts that w is some shortest trace.

As none of the cases above is possible, our original assumption that $t_i \notin T_{\text{dyn}}^{\varphi,M}$ is wrong, which implies that $w \in (T_{\text{dyn}}^{\varphi,M})^*$.   □

Finally, let

$$P_{\text{dyn}}^{\varphi,M} = \text{places}(\varphi) \cup {}^\bullet T_{\text{dyn}}^{\varphi,M} \cup {}^\circ T \tag{2}$$

be a refined set of places with visible tokens. We remark that T is the set of all transitions and every inhibiting place must be preserved to uphold the invariant properties of the C-sets. We now consider the following abstraction.

Definition 7 (Dynamic Token Elimination). *The* dynamic token elimination *abstraction* $\alpha_{\text{dyn}}^{\varphi,M} : \mathcal{M}(N) \to \mathcal{M}(N)$ *is given by*

$$\alpha_{\text{dyn}}^{\varphi,M}(M)(p) = \begin{cases} M(p) & \text{if } p \in P_{\text{dyn}}^{\varphi,M} \\ 0 & \text{otherwise .} \end{cases}$$

Theorem 2 ($\alpha_{\text{dyn}}^{\varphi,M}$ Preserves Reachability). *Let M be a marking and $\text{EF}\varphi$ a reachability property. We have $M \vDash \text{EF}\varphi$ iff $\alpha_{\text{dyn}}^{\varphi,M}(M) \vDash \text{EF}\varphi$.*

In the example, Figure 1, we show all intermediary sets computed for the dynamic method on the depicted PN. In this example, the dynamic method will remove the tokens of p_1 while static method will not. The difference arises from the static method incorrectly assuming that t_1 is fireable in a future marking.

The following corollary is essential for the applicability of our technique in on-the-fly model-checking algorithms as it implies that our technique can be applied to any marking reached during traditional state-space exploration. The corollary follows directly from Lemma 3 and Theorem 2.

Corollary 1. *Given marking M_0 and reachability property $\text{EF}\varphi$, then $M_0 \vDash \text{EF}\varphi$ if and only if there exist markings $M_1, \ldots, M_n$ such that $M_n \vDash \varphi$ and $\alpha_{\text{dyn}}^{\varphi,M_{i-1}}(M_{i-1}) \xrightarrow{t_{i-1}} M_i$ and $t_{i-1} \in T_{\text{dyn}}^{\varphi,M_{i-1}}$ for all $1 \le i \le n$.*

The same corollary holds for the static abstraction $\alpha_{\text{sta}}^{\varphi}$, since the only difference is the sets $C_{\Uparrow}^M$, $C_{\Downarrow}^M$, and C_F^M restricting visibility propagation in the defining constraints.

4 Experimental Evaluation

We implemented our methods in the untimed engine of TAPAAL[2] [11] called verifypn[3] [2,7,10]. The methods are used in both the reachability and CTL algorithm. The reachability algorithm is a simple state-space exploration with heuristics [15] and here our method is applied to all successor states right before they are inserted into the frontier. The CTL algorithm is a top-down on-the-fly algorithm called CERTAINZERO [10]. The algorithm recursively breaks problems down into subproblems and structures them in a dependency graph [12,21] where each node consists of a marking and a sub-property. An example dependency graph is seen in Figure 2. The graph is explored in an on-the-fly manner until a conclusion for the root node is found. Starting from the initial assignment of false to all nodes, whenever all target nodes of a hyperedge have the value true, the source of the edge is assigned true. This continues until the root is assigned true or the process stabilizes at minimum fixed-point assignment on a fully-explore dependency graph. Note that a hyperedge with an empty set of

---

[2] TAPAAL is available at www.tapaal.net.
[3] verifypn is open-source on GitHub: https://github.com/TAPAAL/verifypn.

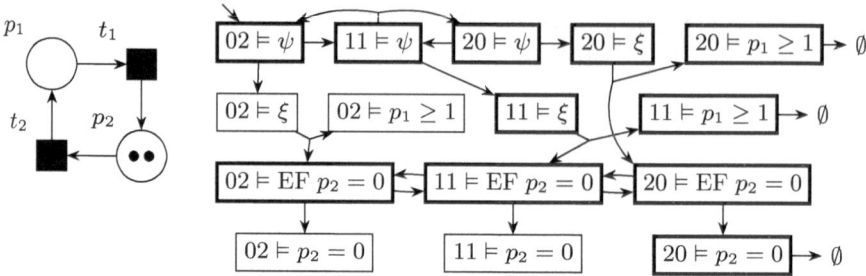

Fig. 2: Left: A Petri net with initial marking 02 (0 tokens in p_1, 2 tokens in p_2). Right: The full dependency graph generated by `verifypn` for the CTL property $\psi \equiv \mathrm{AF}\,\xi$ where $\xi \equiv (p_1 \geq 1 \wedge \mathrm{EF}\,p_2 = 0)$. The nodes that are assigned true in the minimum fixed-point assignment are drawn with thick borders.

target nodes always propagates the value true to its source. During the on-the-fly fixed-point computation, whenever a node containing a reachability property is generated, we apply the token elimination method to the associated marking. In Figure 2, the method would be applied to each node with the sub-property $\mathrm{EF}\,p_2 = 0$. Our techniques provide no benefits in this tiny example, but in other dependency graphs several reachability nodes may be simplified by our token elimination into the same node. Additionally, the simplified node likely has fewer dependencies due to the reduced number of successors, resulting in a smaller dependency graph.

Our tests use the Model Checking Contest (MCC) 2023 benchmark [18] that contains 131 different models. Most models are parameterized, amounting to 1 426 different instances of Petri nets[4]. For each instance, the benchmark provides 32 CTL properties and 32 reachability properties. This gives us 45 632 queries per category where 19 698 of the CTL queries contain a reachability subproperty.

We compare our implementations against the most recent version of TAPAAL (`verifypn` without our methods) since TAPAAL has consistently dominated the CTL category in the recent editions of the MCC competition [18]. We also briefly compare with the latest version of ITS-TOOLS [25] which got second place in MCC 2023. Each query is run with a timeout of 30 minutes and a memory limit of 15 GB on an AMD EPYC 7642 CPU. All experiments use the default settings of TAPAAL, except for the search strategy which is set to random depth-first search (RDFS). We refer to the three versions of `verifypn` as different methods with TAPAAL being the baseline. A reproducibility package containing binaries, data, and plotting scripts is available on Zenodo [16].

4.1   Results

As expected, our methods achieve multiple improvements in the CTL category, but marginal improvements in the reachability category of MCC. This is ex-

---

[4] The MCC2023 benchmark does not contain any Petri net with inhibitor arcs.

	Tapaal	Dynamic	Static	ITS-Tools
CTL (all)	32272	32392 (+120)	32319 (+47)	22998 (−9274)
CTLCardinality	16831	16923 (+92)	16849 (+18)	12056 (−4775)
CTLFireability	15441	15469 (+28)	15470 (+29)	10942 (−4499)

Table 1: Answers found by each method, per category. The numbers in parentheses show the difference to Tapaal.

pected since our methods are similar to the existing stubborn set reductions and structural reduction rules I and M in Tapaal [7], and those (together with all other optimization methods) are enabled. Similarly to our methods, structural reduction rules I and M maintain reachability properties. However, these two reductions alter the net's structure. Therefore, these rules are unsuitable for verifying reachability sub-properties of CTL properties unless we accept the overhead of allocating one or more new Petri nets. Our approach, on the other hand, only changes the immediate marking by removing tokens. This makes it applicable to reachability sub-properties of a CTL property without requiring extra allocations. Our CTL results are hence more interesting to examine and will be the main topic of discussion for the rest of this section.

The number of CTL answers found by each method and ITS-Tools is shown in Table 1. The dynamic method finds 120 more answers than Tapaal, whereas the static finds 47 more. When we distinguish between the cardinality and fireability subcategories, we see that the dynamic method finds more cardinality answers than the static one, but their additional answers with respect to Tapaal are similar for fireability. ITS-Tools finds 9274 fewer answers than Tapaal overall. As a result, we consider a comparison with ITS-Tools to be uninformative and we will exclude it in the following. The number of new answered queries may seem small compared to the size of the benchmark. However, a large portion of the queries in the MCC benchmark are straightforward to solve since the queries are randomly generated [18] and the state spaces of some models are small. For example, Tapaal solves 8275 queries using just query rewriting [2] and linear equations [13,22], and 29608 queries are solved in less than 30 seconds. However, some queries are too complex for any tool due to the extreme size of the state space [6]. For this reason, we shall from now on focus on queries where at least one of the three methods spends at least 2 minutes or 1 GB of memory. We classify such queries as *challenging*. There are 13,863 challenging queries in total, and 782 are answered by at least one of the three methods. A similar projection to challenging queries was made in [1], but our projection is not biased towards queries where our methods provide improvements, as it also includes queries where our method causes slowdowns.

The cactus plots in Figure 3 depict the time and memory usage on the challenging queries. In both plots, the static method curve resembles that of Tapaal but is shifted to the right, indicating that static often performs comparatively to Tapaal, but for some cases, it achieves major savings. The dynamic method

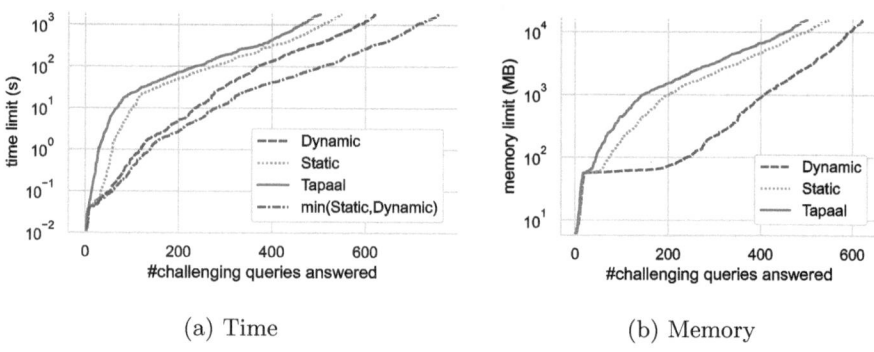

(a) Time   (b) Memory

Fig. 3: Cactus plots showing the number of challenging queries that can be answered within the depicted time/memory limit. The plots are created by ordering the queries independently of the method (on x-axis) by the verification time or peak memory (on y-axis).

provides notable reductions in time and, especially, memory usage. The dynamic method solves more than 200 challenging queries within a 10-second limit, indicating that many queries that challenge TAPAAL become significantly easier with the dynamic method. Regarding memory, TAPAAL answers 144 challenging queries using less than 1 GB, while our dynamic method answers 405.

The dynamic and static methods answer different queries due to their different performance characteristics. For this reason, we also depict the minimum time of the static and dynamic method in Figure 3a which for each query considers the fastest time of our two methods. This is thus an approximation of running both methods in parallel. As shown, this version outperforms all the others by about 120 answers. The results indicate that the static and dynamic methods complement each other despite their similar definitions, and it may be useful to investigate strategies for selecting when to apply which in future work.

The number of configurations in the dependency graph explored by the CTL algorithm of verifypn has been significantly reduced by the dynamic method. Across all queries answered by all three methods, TAPAAL explores 880K configurations on average, the static method explores 866K (-1.7%), and dynamic method explores 807K (-8.3%). On the challenging queries answered by all three methods, TAPAAL explores 16.7M configurations on average, static explores 15.3M (-7.8%), and dynamic explores 10.1M (-39.3%).

Next, we examine the impact of our methods on a query-by-query basis using the challenging queries. To compare queries where one method finds an answer while the other does not, we consider two scenarios: (i) a pessimistic one where we assume that the unanswered queries require infinite time and memory, and (ii) an optimistic one where we assume that the unanswered queries use exactly the time/memory limit of our experiments. Both scenarios are shown on the ratio plots in Figure 4, where a value of 0.5 means that the methods used the same amount of time/memory on the same query. A value of 0.75 means that our

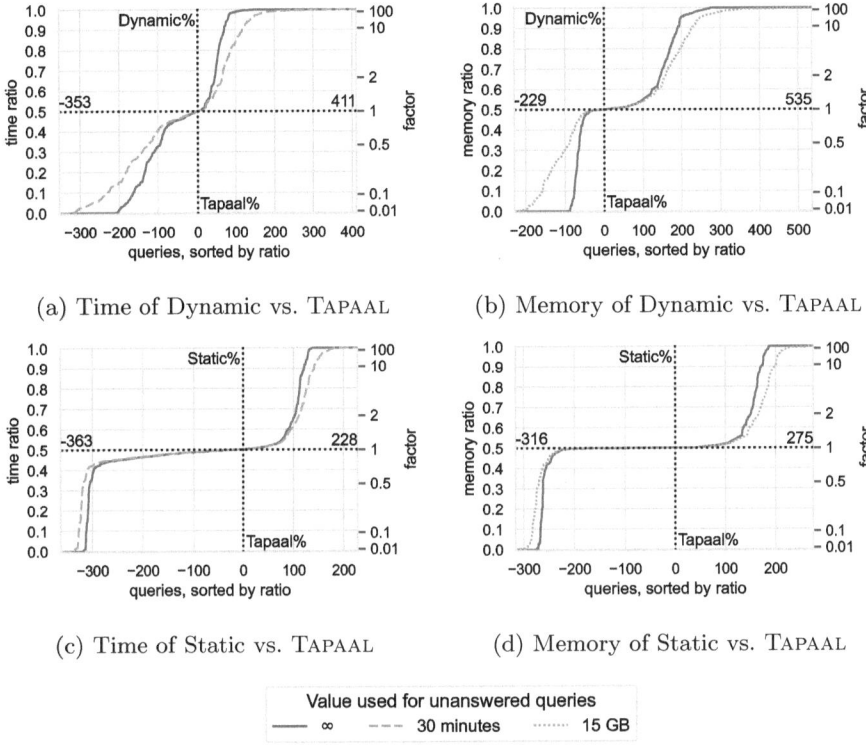

(a) Time of Dynamic vs. TAPAAL

(b) Memory of Dynamic vs. TAPAAL

(c) Time of Static vs. TAPAAL

(d) Memory of Static vs. TAPAAL

Fig. 4: Query-to-query comparison of time and memory usage on the challenging queries, showing the ratio between the TAPAAL baseline and one of our methods, i.e. $\frac{\text{TAPAAL}}{\text{TAPAAL+Ours}}$. Queries are sorted by the ratio and then offset such that 0 on the x-axis is where the methods perform equally. Hence, queries on the left (negative) are queries where TAPAAL performs the best and queries on the right (positive) are where our method performs the best. Each plot includes a pessimistic scenario (solid) where the unanswered queries require infinite resources and an optimistic (dashed or dotted) where unanswered queries require the resource limit of our tests. The axis on the right-hand side shows the ratio as a factor. I.e. a factor of 2 in subfigure (a) means our method was twice as fast.

method only used 25% of the summed time/memory while TAPAAL used 75%. We find that the performance impact of the dynamic method is generally more extreme in magnitude. It provides speedups for about half the queries. The dynamic method is 10 times faster (ratio of ≥ 0.9 on the graph) at 290 queries in the optimistic scenario and 341 queries in the pessimistic scenario, however, it is also 10 times slower than TAPAAL (ratio of ≤ 0.1) at 115 queries in the optimistic scenario and at 186 queries in the pessimistic scenario. When it comes to memory comparison in Figure 4b, the dynamic method provides many significant savings, matching what was concluded earlier. The dynamic method

Speed-up	All models ($N = 1426$)			Challenging models ($N = 473$)		
factor	Dynamic	Static	min(Dyn,Stat)	Dynamic	Static	min(Dyn,Stat)
≤ 0.01	122	45	23	41	17	8
≤ 0.1	224	59	30	64	18	8
≤ 0.5	544	91	57	139	22	13
≥ 2	449	313	488	106	69	119
≥ 10	271	115	287	83	38	86
≥ 100	222	85	236	78	34	81

Table 2: Number of models where at least one of the associated queries saw the given speedup or slowdown w.r.t. the TAPAAL baseline.

occasionally finds answers with degraded memory efficiency. Most degradations are likely attributed to the randomness of the search strategy, as the dynamic method does not accumulate memory usage. Alternatively, the query may have timed out, leading to inflated memory usage. The static method provides a time and memory efficiency almost identical to that of TAPAAL for a majority of the challenging queries. On Figure 4c, if we focus on queries where the methods have a significant performance difference, i.e. a ratio ≥ 0.6 or ≤ 0.4, equating to a 3:2=150% time usage by one of the methods, then the numbers favor the static method. The static method has 131 queries above 0.6 while TAPAAL has 82 queries below 0.4. This implies that the static method has some overhead, but it does not significantly impair its overall benefits. The memory plot in Figure 4d shows a small advantage of the static method over TAPAAL with about half of the queries having very similar peak memory usage, and of the remaining queries a larger portion sees significant memory savings with the static method (shown on the right of the plot).

Our method relies on the structure of the Petri nets, so we investigate whether the performance improvements are concentrated on a certain subset of the models. First, we extend the notion of *challenging* from queries to models. A model is *challenging* if at least 1/4th of its queries are challenging. In Table 2, we group queries by model and check whether at least one query in the group exceeds a speedup or slowdown factor of 2, 10, and 100. Out of the 1426 models, 222 (15.6%) feature a query solved two orders of magnitude faster by the dynamic method compared to TAPAAL, and similar speedups occur on 85 models (6.0%) when using the static method. The static method has significantly fewer queries that see slowdowns, especially small slowdowns to ≤ 0.5 speed (91 compared to the dynamic method's 544). Slowdowns occur on 122 (8.6%) of all models when using the dynamic method, about half as frequent as the two orders of magnitude speedups. On the 329 challenging models, we have 78 models (23.7%) that find a two-order-of-magnitude speedup for at least one query when using the dynamic method. These 78 models belong to 34 different families (a group of similar models scaled to various sizes) out of 131 in total. Again, we also consider the minimum of the dynamic and static methods as if they were run in parallel, and we see that the dynamic and static method complement each other. The number of models with slowdowns is significantly reduced—only half as many as the static method alone which is otherwise the method with fewest slowdowns. Meanwhile, there are also a few additional models with high speedups than when considered individually.

Overall, it is clear that our methods amplify the verification of CTL properties through their reductions of the state space, often leading to time and, especially, memory savings compared to the state-of-the-art methods implemented in TAPAAL. Since they only modify the immediate markings, we can use them in situations where other methods are not applicable.

5   Conclusion

We presented a new token elimination technique to reduce the state-space size in Petri net model checking. Our technique has two phases. First, we approximate sets of impossible transition firings and effects and then we compute sets of visible effects based on the possible firings and effects. This allows us to identify a set of transitions, such that the shortest trace to any goal marking consists exclusively of transitions from this set. Based on this, we derive a set of places where all tokens can be removed without affecting the satisfaction of a given reachability property. We also presented a static instance of our technique that, in contrast to the dynamic one, is computationally cheaper as it does not require recomputations based on the current marking. Since our technique only modifies the marking it can be used in contexts where other reductions are unsuitable while providing similar benefits.

We implemented our techniques in the state-of-the-art CTL algorithm of TAPAAL, winner of the recent editions of the Model Checking Contest in the CTL category. Our implementation eliminates tokens in every reachability node according to the computed visible effects. Through experiments on the Model Checking Contest 2023 benchmark, we showed that our technique improves the performance of CTL model checking. The static technique improves time and memory usage, while the dynamic technique provides even greater time and memory savings at the cost of occasionally high overhead. Due to their different performance characteristics, running them in parallel is also a viable option, avoiding some of the time overhead.

While our experiments focus on the CTL properties, our technique can be adapted to other kinds of properties such as UpperBound queries which ask for the count of a maximum number of tokens in a given set of places. Not all tokens may be relevant to determine such upper bounds when using a state space search. Similarly, it can be used for liveness checks, as this can be rewritten to the CTL query asking if AG EF $enabled(t)$ for all t. Further applications of the token elimination technique to other types of logics are part of the future work.

References

1. Amat, N., Dal Zilio, S., Le Botlan, D.: Project and Conquer: Fast Quantifier Elimination for Checking Petri Net Reachability. In: Verification, Model Checking, and Abstract Interpretation: 25th International Conference, VMCAI 2024, London, United Kingdom, January 15–16, 2024, Proceedings, Part I. LNCS, vol. 14499, p. 101–123. Springer-Verlag, Berlin, Heidelberg (2024). https://doi.org/10.1007/978-3-031-50524-9_5

2. Bønneland, F., Dyhr, J., Jensen, P.G., Johannsen, M., Srba, J.: Simplification of CTL Formulae for Efficient Model Checking of Petri Nets. In: Khomenko, V., Roux, O.H. (eds.) Application and Theory of Petri Nets and Concurrency. LNCS, vol. 10877, pp. 143–163. Springer International Publishing, Cham (2018). https://doi.org/10.1007/978-3-319-91268-4_8

3. Bønneland, F.M., Jensen, P.G., Larsen, K.G., Muñiz, M., Srba, J.: Stubborn Set Reduction for Timed Reachability and Safety Games. In: Dima, C., Shirmohammadi, M. (eds.) Formal Modeling and Analysis of Timed Systems. LNCS, vol. 12860, pp. 32–49. Springer International Publishing, Cham (2021). https://doi.org/10.1007/978-3-030-85037-1_3

4. Bønneland, F.M., Jensen, P.G., Larsen, K.G., Muñiz, M., Srba, J.: Start Pruning When Time Gets Urgent: Partial Order Reduction for Timed Systems. In: Chockler, H., Weissenbacher, G. (eds.) Computer Aided Verification. LNCS, vol. 10981, pp. 527–546. Springer International Publishing, Cham (2018). https://doi.org/10.1007/978-3-319-96145-3_28

5. Bønneland, F., Jensen, P., Larsen, K., Muñiz, M., Srba, J.: Stubborn Set Reduction for Two-Player Reachability Games. In: Logical Methods in Computer Science. vol. 17. International Federation for Computational Logic (Mar 2021). https://doi.org/10.23638/LMCS-17(1:21)2021

6. Burkart, O., Esparza, J.: More Infinite Results. In: Electronic Notes in Theoretical Computer Science. vol. 5, p. 29 (1997). https://doi.org/10.1016/S1571-0661(05)80680-2

7. Bønneland, F.M., Dyhr, J., Jensen, P.G., Johannsen, M., Srba, J.: Stubborn Versus Structural Reductions for Petri Nets. In: Journal of Logical and Algebraic Methods in Programming. vol. 102, pp. 46–63 (2019). https://doi.org/10.1016/j.jlamp.2018.09.002

8. Clarke, E.M., Henzinger, T.A., Veith, H., Bloem, R., et al.: Handbook of Model Checking, vol. 10. Springer (2018). https://doi.org/10.1007/978-3-319-10575-8

9. Czerwiński, W., Orlikowski, L.: Reachability in Vector Addition Systems is Ackermann-complete. In: Foundations of Computer Science. vol. 62, pp. 1229–1240. IEEE (2022). https://doi.org/10.1109/FOCS52979.2021.00120

10. Dalsgaard, A.E., Enevoldsen, S., Fogh, P., Jensen, L.S., Jepsen, T.S., Kaufmann, I., Larsen, K.G., Nielsen, S.M., Olesen, M.C., Pastva, S., Srba, J.: Extended Dependency Graphs and Efficient Distributed Fixed-Point Computation. In: van der Aalst, W., Best, E. (eds.) Application and Theory of Petri Nets and Concurrency. LNCS, vol. 10258, pp. 139–158. Springer International Publishing, Cham (2017). https://doi.org/10.1007/978-3-319-57861-3_10

11. David, A., Jacobsen, L., Jacobsen, M., Jørgensen, K.Y., Møller, M.H., Srba, J.: TAPAAL 2.0: Integrated Development Environment for Timed-Arc Petri Nets. In: Flanagan, C., König, B. (eds.) Tools and Algorithms for the Construction and Analysis of Systems. LNCS, vol. 7214, pp. 492–497. Springer Berlin Heidelberg, Berlin, Heidelberg (2012). https://doi.org/10.1007/978-3-642-28756-5_36

12. Enevoldsen, S., Larsen, K., Srba, J.: Abstract Dependency Graphs and Their Application to Model Checking. In: Proceedings of the 25th International Conference on Tools and Algorithms for the Construction and Analysis of Systems (TACAS'19). LNCS, vol. 11427, pp. 316–333. Springer-Verlag (2019). https://doi.org/10.1007/978-3-030-17462-0_18

13. Esparza, J., Melzer, S.: Verification of Safety Properties Using Integer Programming: Beyond the State Equation. vol. 16, pp. 159–189. Kluwer Academic Publishers (2000). https://doi.org/10.1023/A:1008743212620

14. Godefroid, P.: Partial-Order Methods for the Verification of Concurrent Systems, LNCS, vol. 1032. Springer Berlin, Heidelberg, 1 edn. (1996). https://doi.org/10.1007/3-540-60761-7

15. Jensen, J.F., Nielsen, T., Oestergaard, L.K., Srba, J.: TAPAAL and Reachability Analysis of P/T Nets, LNCS, vol. 9930, pp. 307–318. Springer Berlin Heidelberg, Berlin, Heidelberg (2016). https://doi.org/10.1007/978-3-662-53401-4_16

16. Jensen, N.Ø., Guldstrand Larsen, K., Srba, J.: Token Elimination in Model Checking of Petri Nets Reproducibility Package (Jan 2025). https://doi.org/10.5281/zenodo.14608439

17. Katz, S., Peled, D.: An Efficient Verification Method for Parallel and Distributed Programs. In: de Bakker, J.W., de Roever, W.P., Rozenberg, G. (eds.) Linear Time, Branching Time and Partial Order in Logics and Models for Concurrency. LNCS, vol. 354, pp. 489–507. Springer Berlin Heidelberg, Berlin, Heidelberg (1989). https://doi.org/10.1007/BFb0013032

18. Kordon, F., Bouvier, P., Garavel, H., Hulin-Hubard, F., Amat., N., Amparore, E., Berthomieu, B., Donatelli, D., Dal Zilio, S., Jensen, P., Jezequel, L., Paviot-Adet, E., Srba, J., Thierry-Mieg, Y.: Complete Results for the 2023 Edition of the Model Checking Contest. https://mcc.lip6.fr/2023/results.php (April 2023)

19. Kristensen, L.M., Schmidt, K., Valmari, A.: Question-Guided Stubborn Set Methods for State Properties. In: Formal Methods in System Design. vol. 29, pp. 215–251. Springer Science+Business Media (2006). https://doi.org/10.1007/s10703-006-0006-1

20. Liebke, T., Wolf, K.: Taking Some Burden Off an Explicit CTL Model Checker. In: Donatelli, S., Haar, S. (eds.) Application and Theory of Petri Nets and Concurrency. LNCS, vol. 11522, pp. 321–341. Springer International Publishing, Cham (2019). https://doi.org/10.1007/978-3-030-21571-2_18

21. Liu, X., Smolka, S.A.: Simple Linear-Time Algorithms for Minimal Fixed Points. In: Larsen, K.G., Skyum, S., Winskel, G. (eds.) Automata, Languages and Programming. LNCS, vol. 1443, pp. 53–66. Springer Berlin Heidelberg, Berlin, Heidelberg (1998). https://doi.org/10.1007/BFb0055040

22. Murata, T.: Petri Nets: Properties, Analysis and Applications. Proceedings of the IEEE **77**(4), 541–580 (1989). https://doi.org/10.1109/5.24143

23. Pastor, E., Cortadella, J., Roig, O.: Symbolic Analysis of Bounded Petri Nets. IEEE Transactions on Computers **50**(5), 432–448 (2001). https://doi.org/10.1109/12.926158

24. Peled, D.: All From One, One for All: On Model Checking using Representatives. In: Courcoubetis, C. (ed.) Computer Aided Verification. LNCS, vol. 697, pp. 409–423. Springer Berlin Heidelberg, Berlin, Heidelberg (1993). https://doi.org/10.1007/3-540-56922-7_34

25. Thierry-Mieg, Y.: Symbolic Model-Checking Using ITS-Tools. In: Baier, C., Tinelli, C. (eds.) Tools and Algorithms for the Construction and Analysis of Systems. LNCS, vol. 9035, pp. 231–237. Springer Berlin Heidelberg, Berlin, Heidelberg (2015). https://doi.org/10.1007/978-3-662-46681-0_20

26. Thierry-Mieg, Y.: Structural Reductions Revisited. In: Janicki, R., Sidorova, N., Chatain, T. (eds.) Application and Theory of Petri Nets and Concurrency. pp. 303–323. Springer International Publishing, Cham (2020). https://doi.org/10.1007/978-3-030-51831-8_15

27. Valmari, A.: A Stubborn Attack on State Explosion. In: Formal Methods in System Design. vol. 1, pp. 297–322. Kluwer Academic Publishers (1992). https://doi.org/10.1007/BF00709154

LTL

SemML: Enhancing Automata-Theoretic LTL Synthesis with Machine Learning

Jan Křetínský[1,2] , Tobias Meggendorfer[3(✉)] , Maximilian Prokop[1,2(✉)] ,
and Ashkan Zarkhah[1]

[1] Masaryk University, Brno, Czech Republic
jan.kretinsky@fi.muni.cz
[2] Technical University of Munich, Munich, Germany
prokopm@in.tum.de
[3] Lancaster University Leipzig, Leipzig, Germany

Abstract. Synthesizing a reactive system from specifications given in linear temporal logic (LTL) is a classical problem, finding its applications in safety-critical systems design. We present our tool SEmML, which won this year's LTL realizability tracks of SYNTCOMP, after years of domination by STRIX. While both tools are based on the automata-theoretic approach, ours relies heavily on (i) SEM*antic labelling*, additional information of logical nature, coming from recent LTL-to-automata translations and decorating the resulting parity game, and (ii) M*achine-L earning* approaches turning this information into a guidance oracle for on-the-fly exploration of the parity game (whence the name SEmML). Our tool fills the missing gaps of previous suggestions to use such an oracle and provides an efficeint implementation with additional algorithmic improvements. We evaluate SEmML both on the entire set of SYNTCOMP as well as a synthetic data set, compare it to STRIX, and analyze the advantages and limitations. As SEmML solves more instances on SYNTCOMP and does so significantly faster on larger instances, this demonstrates for the first time that machine-learning-aided approaches can out-perform state-of-the-art tools in real LTL synthesis.

1 Introduction

Synthesis of finite systems from their logical specifications has been one of the central topics of theoretical computer science since the times of Church [7] and Büchi [5], being closely linked to developments of the automata theory [39]. Indeed, the logical formula would be translated to an automaton, in fact a game over this automaton played by the environment and system players, where the strategy of the latter corresponds to an implementation of the specified system.

Since Pnueli's suggestion to use Linear Temporal Logic (LTL) [30] for describing relevant properties of reactive systems, *LTL synthesis* [31] has become an appealing alternative to manual implementation followed by LTL model checking. Indeed, the tedious and error-prone implementation and debugging could be circumvented by automated construction of systems or their controllers, which

This research was funded in part by the DFG project 427755713 GOPro and the MUNI Award in Science and Humanities (MUNI/I/1757/2021) of the Grant Agency of Masaryk University.

A. Gurfinkel and M. Heule (Eds.): TACAS 2025, LNCS 15696, pp. 233–253, 2025.
https://doi.org/10.1007/978-3-031-90643-5_12

are then correct "by construction". Nevertheless, the 2-EXPTIME-completeness of LTL synthesis, stemming from the doubly exponentially sized parity automata for the LTL formulae, has been challenging the practical applicability of the whole concept. Fortunately, this has also led to numerous advances, such as identification of subclasses of properties for which the problem becomes easier, e.g. [2,29,3], or methods avoiding the notoriously expensive step of determinizing the automata, e.g. [24,40] or employing antichain-based methods, e.g. [4,6].

The breakthrough of directly constructing deterministic automata orders of magnitudes *smaller* [18,13] has brought the classical automata-theoretic approach back on the stage, and indeed as the most efficient approach available. This is witnessed by STRIX [26], a synthesis tool based on the translations of Rabinizer/OWL[23,22] tools, winning the LTL tracks of the main synthesis competition SYNTCOMP[16].

Semantic Labelling and Previous Work. The dramatic improvements in the size came with an interesting side-effect. In contrast to determinization of Safra [35] and others [28,36], the new constructions are following the logical structure of the formula. Consequently, the states of the generated automaton/game are labelled by this additional information. It consists of the formula describing the property yet to be satisfied, i.e. monitoring the progress of satisfaction of the original formula, and formulae capturing progress of all its subformulae. For example, an input formula $\neg a \vee \mathbf{G}\,\mathbf{F}(a \wedge \mathbf{X}\,b)$ labels the initial state of the automaton together with the sub-goal $a \wedge \mathbf{X}\,b$ to be satisfied infinitely often, see Fig. 1. After reading a, the successor state is labelled by the remaining goal $\mathbf{G}\,\mathbf{F}(a \wedge \mathbf{X}\,b)$ as well as the progressing sub-goal b left to be satisfied. Under b the automaton then moves to the state with the first component remaining forever the same goal $\mathbf{G}\,\mathbf{F}(a \wedge \mathbf{X}\,b)$, but the second component, now being satisfied fully, signals that one repetition of the sub-goal has been successfully finished.

$$\rightarrow \boxed{\neg a \vee \mathbf{G}\,\mathbf{F}(a \wedge \mathbf{X}\,b); a \wedge \mathbf{X}\,b} \xrightarrow{a} \boxed{\mathbf{G}\,\mathbf{F}(a \wedge \mathbf{X}\,b); b} \xrightarrow{b} \boxed{\mathbf{G}\,\mathbf{F}(a \wedge \mathbf{X}\,b); \mathrm{tt}}$$

Fig. 1. An example of a part of an automaton with semantic labelling

While this labelling was left unused for years, it clearly offers additional information. Indeed, for instance, seeing $\neg a \vee \mathbf{G}\,\mathbf{F}(a \wedge \mathbf{X}\,b)$ as a goal, it seems easier to choose $\neg a$ in order to satisfy it than to take care of the infinitely repeating sub-goal. Similarly, if progress is made in satisfying $a \wedge \mathbf{X}\,b$ by choosing an a, it seems wasteful not to follow with a b, although the overall goal of $\mathbf{G}\,\mathbf{F}(a \wedge \mathbf{X}\,b)$ remains unaffected either way. Such a guidance can be used to explore the automaton/game on-the-fly and possibly finding a winning strategy before the whole state space is constructed. In contrast, from the traditional perspective of solving games on graphs, one can either solve the whole game, or possibly explore it on-the-fly "blindly" since there is no observable difference between taking a transition, say, to the left or right. Note that the guidance need not be reliable, the correctness is still guaranteed by solving (a part of) the game, hinting at possible use of machine learning.

In [19], two attempts have been made to explore the automaton/game in a profitable order using this additional information. Firstly, the first component is subject to a naïve heuristic called *trueness*, estimating the ease to satisfy a formula (by considering every formula as a Boolean combination, ignoring the temporal structure, and counting the percentage of satisfying assignments), and then transitions with higher trueness are explored first. Secondly, reinforcement learning has been used with rewards being related to satisfying sub-goals in the second component. While the former is also implemented in STRIX, both are ad-hoc heuristics with limitations. In [20], a machine-learning approach has been suggested, which learns from solving games for other formulae estimating which transition is more often "winning" than others. This allows for superior precision, also dealing natively with more convoluted choices where the hand-written heuristic struggles. However, only this oracle was implemented, not a (competitive) synthesis procedure.

Our Contribution. In the present tool paper, we show how we incorporate this approach into the whole synthesis pipeline, closing the gaps explicitly left open. Besides, we report on our tool efficiently implementing the approach and, even in a preliminary version, winning this year's edition of the realizability track[1] of the SYNTCOMP competition. In more detail, our contribution is as follows:

- We implement a machine-learning heuristic guiding the on-the-fly exploration. In contrast to [20] using SVM, we evaluate various models and choose the most adequate option. Besides, we adapt it to the state-of-the-art semantic labelling.
- We incorporate it into our synthesis pipeline, which improves over the approach of STRIX in several (traditionally algorithmic) aspects.
- We report on the performance of our tool SEMML (short for SEMantic-labelling-based Machine Learning) and analyze why it performs better than STRIX. It is worth noting that SEMML is faster on the SYNTCOMP benchmark set while being trained only on synthetic data. On this synthetic data, it is even an order of magnitude faster.

Note that other lines of research that use LTL synthesis solvers as blackbox, e.g. LTL modulo theories synthesis [34] or portfolio solvers such as NEUROSYNT [8], directly profit from these improvements.

Further Related Work. Besides STRIX, the closest to our work is, on the one hand, SPOT (with `ltlsynt`) [33], following the same automata-theoretic approach, but constructing the whole automaton; and on the other hand, purely machine-learning approaches such as the deep-learning-based [37,9], implemented in NEUROSYNT [8], which guesses circuits using ML, falling back to STRIX to achieve completeness. Before the automata-theoretic approach, further winning approaches included bounded synthesis, e.g. [11,14], or even earlier safraless

---

[1] For realizability, the task is to determine whether a system satisfying the specification exists; its implementation, however, is only required in the synthesis track, where our tool did not participate. Competitively small representations of computed strategies require numerous (known) techniques, which are orthogonal to the advancements our tool is bringing into the area of machine-learning-aided solving of LTL games.

implementations [17]. As mentioned, all of these are significantly out-performed by STRIX in SYNTCOMP.

2   Tool Description

In this section, we provide an overview of our tool SEMML. We formally state the problem it is solving, describe how to use the tool, and its high-level approach.

2.1   Problem Description: LTL Synthesis and Realizability

The problem of LTL reactive synthesis is defined as follows. We are given an LTL [30] formula ϕ over a set of atomic propositions AP together with a partition of AP into *environment* and *system* propositions $AP = AP_{ENV} \cup AP_{SYS}$. The environment and system generate an infinite word as follows. In each step i, the environment chooses $e_i \subseteq AP_{ENV}$ and then[2] the system chooses $s_i \subseteq AP_{SYS}$, generating a sequence $e_1, s_1, e_2, s_2, \ldots$. The combined word over AP is then $e_1 \cup s_1, e_2 \cup s_2, \ldots$ and the system wins if this word satisfies ϕ. The central question is whether the system has a *winning strategy*, i.e. a way to choose s_i based on the current prefix so that the combined word always satisfies the given formula.[3] In that case, the instance is called *realizable* and *unrealizable* otherwise. For example, the formula $\phi = \mathbf{G}(r \Leftrightarrow \mathbf{X} g)$ with $AP_{SYS} = \{r\}$ and $AP_{ENV} = \{g\}$ prescribes that whenever the environment sends a *request*, the system should in the next step *grant* the request, and only then. This formula is realizable, and a winning strategy is to remember whether the environment sent a request in the previous step.

Deciding whether a formula is realizable or not is called *LTL realizability*. In synthesis in the narrower sense, we want to output such a strategy for the winning player, i.e. a procedure that at every step outputs the next choice, typically in the form of a finite state machine, e.g. a *Mealy machine* or an *AIGER circuit* [1]. While our tool can output the strategy in a straightforward way, we refrain from discussing it further, as it neither the focus of the tool nor of our advancements.

2.2   Functionality

Inputs/Outputs SEMML accepts the standard format TLSF [15] (used in SYNT-COMP), converted to LTL using `syfco`, as well as explicit input, i.e. an LTL formula together with a partition of the atomic propositions. It supports both realizability and synthesis (with the strategy encoded as AIGER circuit).

Usage To streamline interaction, SEMML is invoked through a Python wrapper. For TLSF input, use `main.py --tlsf <path to tlsf file>`, and for explicit input `main.py --ins=<ins> --outs=<outs> -f=<formula>`, where `ins`

---

[2] The convention that the environment chooses first and the system, observing the environment's choice, goes second is called *Mealy* semantics.

[3] Formally, a function $f : (2^{AP_{ENV}})^* \to 2^{AP_{SYS}}$ so that $e_1 f(e_1) e_2 f(e_1 e_2) \ldots \models \phi$.

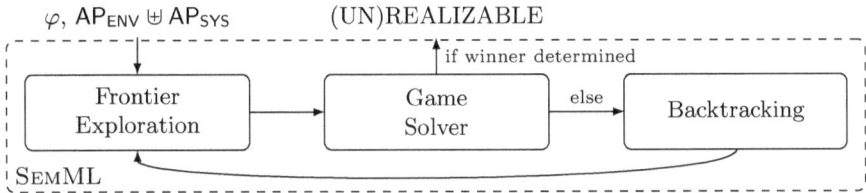

Fig. 2. High level architecture of SEMML.

and `outs` are the atomic propositions owned by environment and system, respectively. The tool then solves the synthesis problem and outputs the witness strategy. If desired, append `--realizability` to only solve the realizability problem. The tool then simply outputs `REALIZABLE` or `UNREALIZABLE`.

2.3 High-Level Architecture

In line with the automata-theoretic approach, SEMML employs *on-the-fly* construction of the corresponding parity game. In SEMML, this process comprises three main components, namely frontier exploration, partial game solving, and backtracking, also outlined in Fig. 2. In a nutshell, starting from an empty game, SEMML explores a "minimal" frontier. Here, we employ a sophisticated machine-learning (ML) guidance that, based on the semantic labelling, decides which parts of the game to explore first. Then, our parity game solver tries to find a solution, interpreting unexplored states as losing for either player. If the solver finds a solution, we are done. If not, we need to explore more of the game. We refer to a backtracking heuristic to identify candidate states and, starting from there, go back to frontier exploration. In this setup, the main purpose of the new ML component is to tackle hard cases, where the automaton is too large to be constructed in its entirety, by trying to identify a small part where one of the players already wins.

3 Advancements in Detail

In this section we describe the major advancements of SEMML. Recall that our technical goal is to employ ML to guide on-the-fly synthesis towards "easily winning" regions and thus improve scalability. To describe our approach and contributions, we first discuss the state of the art. Here, we consider the tool STRIX, which is currently the only implementation of this approach competitive on the standard SYNTCOMP benchmarks, and [20], which provides the first ML-based approach to exploiting the semantic labelling. In particular, we discuss their individual shortcomings and incompatibilities. Then, we outline how we solve these issues, and describe our solution approach in detail.

3.1 State of the Art and its Shortcomings

STRIX alternates between exploring the parity game and trying to solve the explored part. To decide which states to explore, STRIX uses a global double-ended priority queue (one end for each player) to track every state that can be explored further. STRIX simply works on both ends of that queue while checking for solvability in fixed intervals until a winner is identified. This comes with two major problems. Firstly, the states are ordered by (a variant of) the rather naïve trueness [19] of formulae, which roughly corresponds to the percentage of *propositionally* satisfying assignments, completely disregarding the temporal structure. This is particularly problematic for formulas which comprise lots of temporal behaviour (such as $\mathbf{X}\,\mathbf{X}\,\phi$). Secondly, the exploration is not "demand-driven", meaning it can fail because one successor of an important state has not been explored (and thus is considered losing), but during the subsequent exploration phase, that successor is not touched either because other states have more extreme scores (or many states have the same score).

The approach of [20] uses the semantic labelling to predict winning choices locally through a simple learning approach with hand-crafted features. These are then used as the starting point for a parity game solver, ensuring that potential imprecisions of the ML model are detected and fixed. However, (i) they do not provide an implementation competitive w.r.t. the actual runtime, and (ii) adapting their approach to STRIX (or any other tool) is difficult for a variety of reasons. Firstly, STRIX is fundamentally designed to work with a "global" ranking, i.e. picking states to explore from one priority queue, while [20] gives "local" recommendations, specific to a concrete state. Note that combining the two approaches by first picking a state similarly to STRIX and then following [20] in that state does not solve STRIX's lack of demand-driven guidance. Secondly, [20] employs complex features and evaluating them is too time consuming. The timing constraints on evaluating the guidance heuristic are quite strict, since we need to be able to give hundreds of recommendations per second to remain competitive. Finally, [20] uses an outdated automaton construction (via LDBA [38,12]), while STRIX uses a newer, practically more efficient variant. This is particularly relevant, as the automaton construction usually is the biggest bottleneck of LTL synthesis.

Summary. In order to reap the benefits of ML for on-the-fly synthesis, we thus first have to design a novel exploration approach (and adapt all subsequent machinery) capable of processing *local advice* in the spirit of [20]. While this is a pre-requisite for using ML guidance, it is also interesting in its own right, as it allows for a more targeted, deep exploration instead of exploring multiple equally promising directions simultaneously. Then, at the same time, our guidance must be much more efficient than [20], so that it does not add too much overhead, which would negate any performance gained by giving good recommendations. Finally, it also needs to be designed for a modern automaton construction.

We proceed to explain how we tackled these problems. We introduce our locally guided approach to on-the-fly LTL synthesis, describe how we use machine learning to guide the exploration, and finally outline general engineering improvements.

3.2   Locally Guided Exploration

Recall that the overall approach is to alternate between exploring parts of the parity game and checking whether there exists a winning strategy in the current part of the game already, as depicted in Fig. 2. For the exploration, our aim is to follow "good" choices for one player that work well against all options of its opponent. As such, we run the exploration for both "perspectives" separately, and regularly switch between them (further motivation and details in Sec. 3.4). In the following, we take the perspective of the system (aiming to prove realizability); the dual part for the environment is analogous.

As hinted in Sec. 2.3, our exploration approach comprises two parts, namely frontier exploration and backtracking. The components of frontier exploration and its interplay with both backtracking and the game solver is depicted in Fig. 3. During frontier exploration, the core idea is to only explore a necessary minimum so that a strategy of the system can be at all properly defined. In particular, we want to reach a point where every known system state has *at least one* of its successors explored and every known environment state has *all* of its successors explored. If that is the case, we call the (partial) parity game *closed*. Clearly, to obtain a closed game, we repeatedly need to explore states. To this end, we maintain a queue of automaton states (the current frontier) which we still need to explore. After taking a state from the queue, we compute the immediate automaton successors, using an adapted implementation of Owl, and split this automaton transition (under a subset of AP) into the two moves of the players under a subset of AP_{ENV} and AP_{SYS}, respectively. While we hardly have a choice for environment states (we need to explore all successors in the game), in system states we can select which successor to explore. Thus, in these states we ask our exploration heuristic for advice, and add all newly reached states to the queue. For this local guidance, we employ the new ML-based approach, which we later explain in depth. For an example, see Fig. 3 (bottom). From left to right, we obtain a state q_0 from the queue and construct its successors q_1 and q_2 in the automaton. Splitting it into the game introduces the two system states s_1 and s_2. In both states, the exploration heuristic recommends going towards q_2, and we only add that state to the frontier queue.

Overall, we repeat this process until the current game is closed, and then attempt to solve it. If we cannot determine a winner, then in at least one of the system states a "wrong" successor was chosen (the system cannot win the current partial game). Thus, subsequently, we ask the backtracking oracle which states might have been "wrong". Concretely, we heuristically choose a subset of all non-fully explored states with the highest trueness. For each of these, we explore their next best successors according to our heuristics. Now, the game might not be closed, and thus we switch back to frontier exploration. We repeat this process until a winner is found (which always happens, as eventually the entire game is explored).

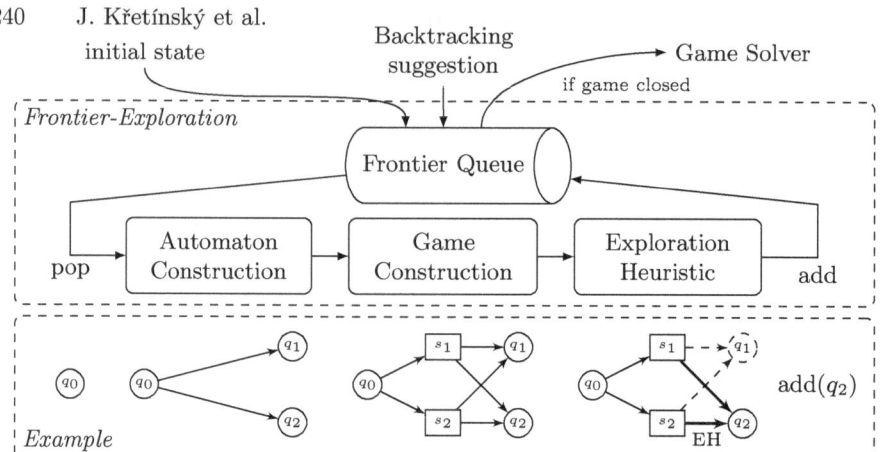

Fig. 3. Illustration of the exploration process together with an example for each step.

3.3   Exploration Guidance Through Machine Learning

In this section, we describe our ML approach used to guide the frontier exploration. Recall that for a given state the exploration heuristic is supposed to give a ranking preferring "good" edges which lead to a winning strategy: Initially, we follow the highest ranked choice, then, when backtracking in this state, the second one, and so on. Thus, we would like this heuristic to prefer edges that can be part of a winning strategy. Additionally, as we also want to obtain small games, among the possibly winning edges we would like to prefer edges leading to smaller strategies (hence exploring a smaller part of the game). Note that one can also employ handcrafted heuristics instead, e.g. the score computed by STRIX (which we also implement and evaluate).

Similar to [20], we employ a supervised learning approach. As usual for ML, we start by describing the dataset used to train our models. We then discuss the overall architecture of the model(s), how we obtain the ground truth, and how we extract features. Finally, we discuss the training method. Of course, our approach is not the only possible way to tackle this problem. Yet, while designing it, we discovered several subtle pitfalls and tried alternative approaches which proved to be suboptimal. We provide further details within this section.

Data Our explicit aim is to exploit structure in real-world formulae. Here, existing datasets such as the SYNTCOMP set seem a natural choice. However, we want to evaluate our approach on the entire SYNTCOMP set (in order to faithfully replicate the SYNTCOMP evaluation). Thus, "showing" any part of it during learning could introduce an unfair advantage. This leaves us with hardly any realistic data sets.

This problem has already been observed by [37]. As a solution, they note that in practice, specifications often follow specific *patterns* and combinations thereof [10]. Thus, randomly combining such patterns should yield numerous formulae that resemble some structure one might expect in practice. To this end, [37] identified over 150 *assumptions* and over 1500 *guarantees* which intuitively limit the behaviour of the environment and system respectively. From this set of "building blocks", they generate formulae by sampling assumptions and guarantees and assemble them in the form of "conjunction of assumptions implies conjunction of guarantees", which adds some comprehensible structure. Formulae of this kind can be interpreted as "if the environment adheres to one behaviour profile, the system should adhere to another".

We extend this idea a bit further by sampling several options for system and environment, which diversifies the formulae while maintaining comprehensibility. In particular, we sample multiple sets of assumptions and guarantees and assemble a formula in the form of "DNF of assumptions implies DNF of guarantees". Intuitively, these formulae mean "If the environment follows one of these behaviour profiles, the system should adhere to one of their behaviour profiles". In particular, this introduces options for the system to which behaviour profile it should adhere to, which in turn might depend on the profile the environment chooses.

We filter our generated data into two groups depending on the size of the corresponding automaton. The training and validation group consists of 1000 formulae where the automaton has at most 500 states. We introduce this limitation to keep the ground truth and feature computation feasible (described later). While 1000 formulae may seem like a small data set, note that we learn from the local decisions in each state of the 1000 associated parity games, which give several million data points in total. For evaluation, we also identified 200 formulae of which the automaton size is not known except that it is larger than 20,000 states.

While this yields a decent data foundation for our venture, the synthetic data definitely is quite different from SYNTCOMP. Thus, for practical purposes, one should consider including SYNTCOMP and other data during learning. Since this is orthogonal to the evaluation in this paper (including any part of SYNTCOMP in our training data would introduce unwanted biases), we deliberately do not include this.

Model Architecture Similar to [20], we rank outgoing edges through all pairwise comparisons. Formally, we employ a *pair classifier* $p : E \times E \to \mathbb{R}$ where the sign denotes whether the first or second edge is preferred and the magnitude denotes the confidence in that prediction. In a state, every pair of edges is compared and each edge is ranked according to the sum of confidences in its favour. However, since this scales quadratically in the number of outgoing edges, we approximate the above for states with more than 16 edges. For them, a number of *pivot edges* are chosen that every other edge is compared to, in order to obtain a "first guess" at a ranking. From that guess, the best 8 are selected to enter the second round which now is a full round of comparisons. The final ranking comprises the ranking among the top 8 followed by the other edges according to the first ranking.

Moreover, similar to [20], we pre-classify states into groups with conceptual differences and train a separate model for each group. Intuitively, we distinguish (i) whether a state is owned by the system or the environment, and (ii) whether the long-term goals are trivially structured, e.g. a single liveness condition, which simplifies some decisions; leading to 4 models in total. We discuss the concrete implementation of the pair classifier in the "Training" section below.

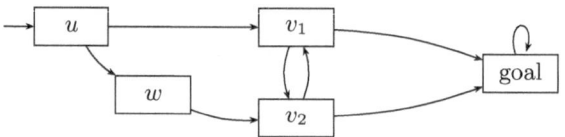

Fig. 4. A simple game to illustrate two challenges for the ground truth. For simplicity, all states are controlled by one player. Clearly, all states are winning.

Ground Truth For the supervised learning of our models, we need meaningful labels that denote the quality of an edge so that we can determine the better one of any given pair. But which edges are "good"? At first, this may seem obvious – simply take all edges which are part of a winning strategy. This however is problematic for multiple reasons, as already outlined in [20].

First, parity games do not allow for *maximally permissive* strategies. This means that there simply is no one "local truth"; whether an edge is good or bad may depend on decisions in other states, as we exemplify in Fig. 4. While the edges leading to the goal from v_1 and v_2 are always winning choices, edge $\overline{v_1 v_2}$ is only winning if the goal-edge is chosen in v_2 (and vice-versa for $\overline{v_2 v_1}$). Consequently, different solution approaches may yield different sets of winning edges, and just considering one of them would bias the model to behave alike to *that concrete solution method* and not to "understand" semantically labelled parity games in general. Relating to the previous example, even though $\overline{v_1 v_2}$ and $\overline{v_2 v_1}$ are symmetric, a solver may only mark one of them as winning, but never both. As such, using the output of one solver would actively try to make our model believe that one of the two is better and imitate that solver's bias.

Secondly, even if multiple edges are indeed winning, this does not inform us about the "complexity" required to win after playing one of them. For example, consider two edges where one leads to a trivially winning sink within two steps and the other leads to a large and complicated, but ultimately also winning region. Qualitatively, both edges are equivalent, but we prefer the former as it yields smaller solutions and requires fewer correct decisions in the future. We also provide an illustration in Fig. 4. There, both choices in u are winning, however we prefer moving to v_1 over moving to w, as we can win "faster".

Thus, in order to determine the quality of any given edge of the game, we analyze the game tree after playing said edge. Constructing the entire game tree and applying min-max is practically infeasible already for rather small instances. Therefore, we apply an improved version of the decayed Monte Carlo tree search suggested in [20]. In particular, we only deeply expand the tree for critical paths (the ones where either player fancies their chances) and thus can identify longer shortest winning paths. Conveniently, we thereby no longer require the "optimal stalling" strategy that [20] uses for the opponent, as the opponent prefers longer losing paths over shorter ones by default due to the decay. In the end, we effectively get a score between -1 and 1 for each edge in the game which indicates the "quality" of this edge. Intuitively, an edge directly leading to tt gets a 1. An edge leading to a region where the system can win but may require a lot of steps to do so yields a small, positive value, while edges after which the environment can quickly force a losing cycle yield a score close to -1.

Feature Extraction The feature extraction transforms a transition in the game into a vector of numbers so that it can be processed by an ML model. The features are based on all the information that is available at the time of deciding which edge to explore further. In particular, this includes the semantic labelling of the transition's source and target, the colour/priority, and also labelling associated to its sibling transitions.

We deliberately aimed at manually designing a (large) set of features derived from the semantics and then prune it via feature selection. While automatic feature extraction is a powerful tool, in our use case the feature extraction needs to be extremely efficient, since we need to call it hundreds of times per second to remain even remotely viable. (Recall that we need to extract the features for every edge in the game and already the games obtained from reasonably simple formulae can easily reach thousands of states and significantly more edges.)

State Features We first introduce twelve "formula features", which transform a single LTL formula into a number. Intuitively, they can be thought of as proxies for higher level concepts. These concepts include *formula-complexity* (syntactic properties such as height and size of the syntax tree), *formula-sat-difficulty* (how "difficult" is it to satisfy the formula, capturing variants of *trueness* [19]), or *formula-controllability* (how much influence does a player have on the truth value of the formula with only their variables). Formula features are then aggregated for a *state* (which comprises several formulae) in one of two ways. Either, we select a single formula of the labelling and yield the value of the base feature on the selected formula as the state's overall value (e.g. selecting the formula that maximizes the value of another base feature). Or, we apply the base feature to all formulae of the semantic labelling and aggregate the results in several ways, exploiting the non-trivial structure of the state labelling. Intuitively, this captures the respective concept (e.g. controllability) over the entire state.

Edge Features Edge features are obtained from state features by either taking the state feature of the edge's successor or the change of the feature along the edge, i.e. the difference of the feature in the successor and predecessor. Further, we can compare that value against the value of all other edges of the same state by normalizing the feature to the $[0,1]$-interval, so that a normalized value of 1 denotes that it is the highest among its sibling edges. This may help learning relative comparisons, but loses all information on the absolute value of the feature. As confirmed in our final models, a mixture of normalized and non-normalized features seems to be desirable. Aside from features derived from states, we also consider features based on the edge priority as suggested by [20]. However, we include the parity information in an "ML-friendly" way, for example by mapping it to a linear scale.

In total, we obtain well above 150k different features for edges. These include, for example, the change in the syntax tree height of the most controllable formula or the aggregated trueness, normalized across all successors. For more details on the features we refer to the appendix of [21].

Training Applying ground truth and feature methods to the generated formulae yields a dataset for supervised learning with way over a million samples for every state class. We bootstrap these down to roughly 100k samples per state class in order to make the training take reasonable amounts of time. The following procedure was done for every state class individually.

Feature Elimination As using our entire set of thousands of features is absolutely impractical in several regards, especially with our performance constraints in mind, we perform multiple stages of feature elimination. First, we randomly select between 50 an 100 features per major category and add some hand-picked features. This leaves us at an algorithmically manageable, yet practically infeasible amount of about 700 features. For further reductions, we perform a variant of recursive feature elimination, adjusted to our pairwise setting (see [21] for details). As different features might be more or less important for different model types and state classes, we ran a separate feature elimination for each of these. For details on what kind of features remained after the elimination, we refer to [21].

Models As for model types, we evaluated (kernel-)SVMs, neural networks, random forests, and gradient boosted trees. The input for each model is the concatenation of the two feature vectors of the respective edges that we want to compare pairwise. For tree models, we additionally concatenated the pointwise differences of the features in order to allow them to compare the same feature of both edges in one decision node. For every model type, we performed several smaller runs to obtain suitable hyper-parameters for the large scale feature elimination.

Ultimately, gradient boosted trees proved to be the best choice for implementing our pair classifier in all four state classes. Together with random forests, they clearly outperformed the non-tree methods like SVM or NN. However, in contrast to random forests, they required less features (3-10, depending on state class) to do so. Further details on this experiment can be found in [21].

3.4   Engineering

To conclude, we provide details on our implementation and engineering improvements. First and foremost, as a major practical improvement, SEMML is implemented in pure Java (built on top of OWL). In contrast, STRIX is developed as a hybrid between Rust and Java, with native compilation of Java through GraalVM, and a complex interplay between the two code bases. This adds, among others, complexity due to working with two languages, subtle performance overheads when crossing language boundaries, and setup difficulties due to requiring a rather particular set of tools. As such, SEMML is significantly easier to use, maintain, and extend. For easy incorporation of third party tools such as syfco, we also include a Python wrapper. For learning, we use the Python library SKLEARN [27], and store our models in the established PMML format.

Aside from structural improvements and pure-Java implementation, we also added several engineering changes compared to the approaches of STRIX and [20], of which we list a few notable ones.

State Merging In parity games, states are fully determined by their set of edges, i.e. if two system states transition to the same successor for every system assignment while emitting the same priority, they are equivalent and can be merged. This equivalence check is very efficient due to our internal representation of states. Interestingly, by applying this reduction we observed a decrease of game sizes by up to two orders of magnitude.

Dual Perspectives As mentioned in Sec. 3.2, our approach alternates between the perspectives of both players. While this is not required for correctness, it helps in practice, as, for example, we can quickly find a small winning region for the environment even if the system player explores in a different direction.

Exploration Scheduling Usually, we switch perspectives whenever the game is closed and the solver is consulted. However, when following a "bad" edge leads the algorithm off the track, we might spend a lot of time trying to close the game. Instead of insisting on continuing this process to the end, we also switch to the other perspective after too many states have been explored without closing the game.

Result Sharing We re-use information discovered from one "perspective" for the other part, where appropriate, for example already constructed parts of the automaton. Moreover, if one side finds a set of states to be winning for them, the exploration of the other side directly treats them as losing.

Caching We trade memory for time by caching all computed features.

BDD We implemented complement edges and several further engineering improvements in the underlying pure-Java BDD library JBDD [25].

4   Experimental Evaluation

In this section, we evaluate the two central research questions of interest, namely:

RQ1 Can SEMML solve LTL realizability more efficiently than state-of-the-art tools, in particular STRIX?

RQ2 How much of the improvements are caused by algorithmic and engineering changes and how much by employing ML-guided exploration?

We first introduce considered tools, metrics of interest, and our benchmark sets. Then, we present our results and discuss each research question separately.

Tools We consider our tool SEMML and the state-of-the-art tool STRIX[4]. To further distinguish algorithmic and engineering improvements from those due to the ML-based exploration heuristic, we also consider SEM~~ML~~ ("SEMML without ML"), which uses the exploration score of STRIX as guidance instead.

Note that both SEMML and STRIX internally construct a strategy even when "only" solving LTL realizability. The problem of exporting the (already constructed) strategy into a particular format, e.g. AIGER circuits, is completely orthogonal. Thus, we explicitly focus on the time to find the solution (i.e. let the tools run in their "realizability" configuration).

---

[4] With its best-performing configuration `--exploration=minmax --lookahead=0`.

Remark 1. When only focusing on the number of solved instances, the portfolio solver NEUROSYNT [8] is a more powerful tool than STRIX. This is to be expected, as it runs multiple approaches (including STRIX) in parallel. However, to clearly compare our specific approach to the state-of-the-art, we deem a direct comparison of SEMML to STRIX (the state-of-the-art of "single-approach"-solvers) more relevant. A more detailed discussion and comparison of SEMML with NEUROSYNT can be found in the appendix of [21].

Metrics Primarily, we are interested in which tool can solve more benchmarks within a given time constraint (the main metric used for SYNTCOMP). Additionally, for the instances solved by multiple tools, we are interested in which tool solves them faster. For that matter, we compute the ratios of (wallclock) time for all samples that both tools were able to solve and aggregate them by computing the geometric mean.[5] We exclude simple instances to account for constant time overheads caused by, e.g., JVM startup and loading of ML models. We treat an instance as simple if both compared tools solve them faster than a given threshold (usually 5s; later we also consider larger values to focus on the most complicated instances).

Benchmarks We consider two classes of benchmarks. First, our evaluation set as described in Sec. 3.3, called Synthetic. Here, we expect the ML-based guidance to shine, as the inputs are of a similar structure as the training data (just much larger). Additionally, we consider the entire set of SYNTCOMP 2024.

We highlight some peculiarities of the SYNTCOMP data set. First, as we observe in our experiments, the vast majority of instances are trivial, i.e. solved within a few seconds. As such, a small constant time overhead has a large (relative) impact. Second, SYNTCOMP mainly comprises parametrized families of formulae, where incrementing the parameter often more than doubles the size of the state space. As such, for many families a lot of their instances are simple, very few are interesting-but-solvable, and then many more are completely out of reach. This results in a rather small set of benchmarks where a notable difference can be expected, and solving one more sample of a family already marks significant improvement. Finally, there are subtle biases and asymmetries that may limit the possible improvement of exploration guidance. On the one hand, several of the realizable families are arbiters (or variants thereof), where, by design, (nearly) the entire state space needs to be explored. In particular, any attempt of guidance is useless and any effort spent on it costs overall performance. On the other hand, many unrealizable families are constructed by taking a realizable family and introducing a contradiction at a parametrized depth of the execution. This class may be more suitable for employing targeted guidance, as one only needs to find that single contradiction in the state space to prove unrealizability. However, these unrealizable families tend to be dominant in numbers while not providing much diversity. Thus, if a heuristic by chance adapts well or badly to a single family or a particular kind of contradiction, this effect alone can dominate the

---

[5] As is customary, the geometric mean is preferable for runtime ratios: For example, for 0.5x and 2x speed-ups it yields 1x instead of 1.25x with an arithmetic mean.

Table 1. Comparison of SEMML to STRIX on SYNTCOMP and synthetic data. We show how many instances are solved by both, by only one, or none of the tools. Note that 815 instances of SYNTCOMP are solved by both tools in under 10 seconds.

| SYNTCOMP | SEMML | | Synthetic | SEMML | |
	solved	unsolved		solved	unsolved
STRIX solved	951	27	STRIX solved	30	0
STRIX unsolved	49	84	STRIX unsolved	53	117

Table 2. Average runtime ratios between STRIX and SEMML for all instances where at least one tool required more than n seconds (where n is in the top row) and both tools found a solution. We also give the number of instances that satisfy these two criteria. A ratio > 1 indicates that SEMML is faster on average.

SYNTCOMP	0	5	30	300	Synthetic	0	5	30	300
ratio	0.09	1.37	2.08	3.58	ratio	8.56	8.56	9.48	13.44
count	951	148	89	30	count	30	30	28	14

overall evaluation. As such, the results on SYNTCOMP, should be interpreted carefully, especially when comparing guidance heuristics.

Experimental Setup Our experiments were conducted on an AMD Epyc 7443 24-Core CPU and 188GB of RAM. Each invocation was limited to 30 minutes and 60GB memory, mimicking SYNTCOMP conditions.

4.1 RQ1: Comparing SEMML to STRIX

Our main results are summarized in Tables 1 and 2 and displayed in Fig. 5. On SYNTCOMP, we solve $49 - 27 = 22$ instances more than STRIX which, considering the difficulty scale of SYNTCOMP, marks a major achievement. Further, we observe significant speed-up compared to STRIX, especially as the instances get larger. For the ratio over entire SYNTCOMP, we mention that there are about 600 instances that STRIX solves (nearly) instantly whereas SEMML requires about a second to start the JVM and load ML parameters.

Investigating the unique solves of both tools in more detail, we observe that on many *realizable* families, SEMML is able to solve one more instance than STRIX within the timeout, sometimes even within a minute. In particular, there are three families (`amba_gr`, `amba_decomposed_lock`, `collector_v3`), where two or even more extra instances were solved, marking a major improvement. The instances only solved by STRIX turned out to be mostly from variants of the `ltl2dba` families. Here, we conjecture that our guidance takes a "bad turn", never reached closure, and thus never reconsidered its steps, while the less guided, broader exploration of STRIX has a higher chance of exploring the right parts.

For *unrealizable* formulae, most of our unique solves were of the discussed form of injecting a fault into some arbiter and our targeted exploration was able to localize these faults deep into the state space. STRIX's unique solves are again mostly unrealizable variants of `ltl2dba` and `detector_unreal` formulae.

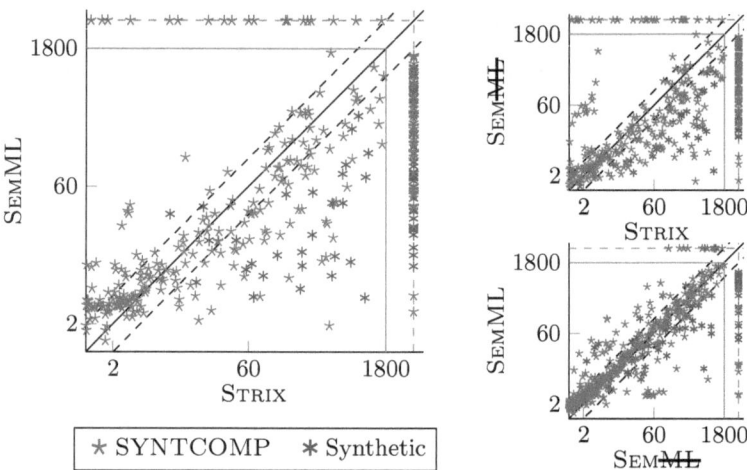

Fig. 5. Scatter plots of the runtimes of SEMML, STRIX, and SEM~~ML~~ on SYNTCOMP. A point (x, y) denotes that tool X and tool Y needed x and y seconds, respectively. If a point is above/below the diagonal, tool X is faster/slower. Plots are on logarithmic scale, dashed diagonals indicate that one tool is twice as fast. Timeouts are pushed to the orthogonal dashed line. The axes start at 1 second.

On the Synthetic dataset, SEMML outperforms STRIX by an order of magnitude, solving all instances STRIX is able to solve, and even 53 additional ones. On the 30 instances that both tools solved, SEMML is 8.56 times faster, and this factor increases to 13.44 when considering the most challenging instances.

4.2 RQ2: Effects of Machine Learning and Algorithmic Changes

We proceed to investigate the impact of our algorithmic and engineering changes and ML heuristic individually. For that matter, we first compare STRIX to SEM~~ML~~ and then proceed with comparing SEM~~ML~~ to SEMML.

STRIX *vs.* SEM~~ML~~ Especially on SYNTCOMP, a significant part of the improvements is caused by our algorithmic changes. For example, the game for `collectorv1_14` has over 19M states in STRIX while SEMML keeps it at a manageable 60k states due merging of game states. This allowed SEMML to solve `collectorv1_15` as well, whereas STRIX could not. Similarly, we also observed the concrete impact of the BDD improvements as well as the demand-guided exploration. The former is more prominent for realizable, while the latter shows significant impact mostly (but not exclusively) for unrealizable instances. Concretely, 24 of 30 SEM~~ML~~'s unique solves of unrealizable instances are fault-injected-arbiters. Here, our deep, targeted exploration was able to localize the fault, even when only following the exploration score of STRIX. STRIX's broader exploration could not reach these regions despite following the same score, likely because it tried to follow multiple "leads" at once, due to its global view. On the Synthetic set, the effects are even more pronounced. Here, already SEM~~ML~~ solves all instances that STRIX solves and 37 more, with a speed-up of 9.1.

SEMML *vs.* SEMML Despite our algorithmic changes already yielding significant improvements, ML still adds performance on top. For SYNTCOMP, our guidance is able to identify solutions much quicker on several families (e.g. `01-13.tlsf` or `collector_v3`), resulting in a speed-up factor of 1.25 (with lower threshold of 30 seconds to focus on complicated instances) and 2 more unique solves on realizable samples. On unrealizable formulae, SEMML solves 7 further instances (mainly from `full_arbiter_unreal`), but fails on 8 instances (mainly from `round_robin_arbiter_unreal`). We conjecture that this is due to bad generalization, and due to the fact that exploration towards a deep fault comes with more opportunities for a ML model to "mess up", whereas SEMML's score is stable. Overall however, SEMML is competitive with SEMML on SYNTCOMP, which is positive, considering the discussed structure of SYNTCOMP and, especially, that our model was not even trained on similar inputs.

Turning our attention to the Synthetic set (in line with the training data), we see that SEMML has significant 20 unique solves compared to 4 for SEMML and a speed-up of 1.57 on complicated instances (threshold of 30 seconds). Based on this, we conjecture that SYNTCOMP likely is "out-of-distribution" for our model and, consequently, training with both synthetic as well as SYNTCOMP samples would add even more improvements for real-world formulae.

Remark 2. To conclude, we stress that our ML models are deliberately kept small, since we need to be able to evaluate them extremely quickly. As such, we only considered quite simple features and small models. Concretely, the final models for all state classes are comprised of 15 trees of depth 2. We also evaluated larger models with more complex and meaningful features. These performed significantly better in terms of pure accuracy on the pair classification, but added so much overhead that ultimately fewer instances were solved.

5   Conclusion and Future Work

We presented our tool SEMML, which combines algorithmic and engineering improvements together with tailored machine-learning heuristics to arrive at a highly performant tool for reactive synthesis. Our experimental evaluation confirms the impact of both our improvements. In particular, SEMML significantly outperforms the state-of-the-art tool STRIX, which dominated the reactive synthesis competition since its first appearance.

For future work, we identify several avenues. In terms of algorithmic improvements, both the backtracking heuristic and our parity game solver can be significantly improved by a tighter integration with the exploration heuristic. Further, we intend to implement – as well as develop new – state of the art methods for extracting and representing solutions efficiently to practically make use of the solutions we are now able to identify. For users of the tool, we want to provide a variant of SEMML that is also trained on SYNTCOMP formulae, unfair for academic evaluation but useful for actual industrial synthesis. We also want to investigate hierarchical oracles, i.e. include more accurate (but slower) oracles, which are only consulted when the basic oracle has low confidence.

Data availability statement. The models, tools, and scripts to reproduce our experimental evaluation are archived and available at [32].

References

1. The reactive synthesis competition: SYNTCOMP 2018 results. http://www.syntcomp.org/syntcomp-2018-results/ (2018), http://www.syntcomp.org/syntcomp-2018-results/
2. Alur, R., Torre, S.L.: Deterministic generators and games for ltl fragments. ACM Trans. Comput. Log. **5**(1), 1–25 (2004). https://doi.org/10.1145/963927.963928
3. Bansal, S., Giacomo, G.D., Stasio, A.D., Li, Y., Vardi, M.Y., Zhu, S.: Compositional safety LTL synthesis. In: Lal, A., Tonetta, S. (eds.) Verified Software. Theories, Tools and Experiments - 14th International Conference, VSTTE 2022, Trento, Italy, October 17-18, 2022, Revised Selected Papers. Lecture Notes in Computer Science, vol. 13800, pp. 1–19. Springer (2022). https://doi.org/10.1007/978-3-031-25803-9_1, https://doi.org/10.1007/978-3-031-25803-9_1
4. Bohy, A., Bruyère, V., Filiot, E., Jin, N., Raskin, J.: Acacia+, a tool for LTL synthesis. In: Madhusudan, P., Seshia, S.A. (eds.) Computer Aided Verification - 24th International Conference, CAV 2012, Berkeley, CA, USA, July 7-13, 2012 Proceedings. Lecture Notes in Computer Science, vol. 7358, pp. 652–657. Springer (2012). https://doi.org/10.1007/978-3-642-31424-7_45
5. Büchi, J.: On a decision method in restricted second-order arithmetic. In: Nagel, E., Suppes, P., Tarski, A. (eds.) Proceedings of the First International Congress on Logic, Methodology, and Philosophy of Science 1960 (1962)
6. Cadilhac, M., Pérez, G.A.: Acacia-bonsai: A modern implementation of downset-based LTL realizability. In: Sankaranarayanan, S., Sharygina, N. (eds.) Tools and Algorithms for the Construction and Analysis of Systems - 29th International Conference, TACAS 2023, Held as Part of the European Joint Conferences on Theory and Practice of Software, ETAPS 2022, Paris, France, April 22-27, 2023, Proceedings, Part II. Lecture Notes in Computer Science, vol. 13994, pp. 192–207. Springer (2023). https://doi.org/10.1007/978-3-031-30820-8_14
7. Church, A.: Application of recursive arithmetic to the problem of circuit synthesis. Journal of Symbolic Logic (1963)
8. Cosler, M., Hahn, C., Omar, A., Schmitt, F.: Neurosynt: A neuro-symbolic portfolio solver for reactive synthesis. In: Finkbeiner, B., Kovács, L. (eds.) Tools and Algorithms for the Construction and Analysis of Systems - 30th International Conference, TACAS 2024, Held as Part of the European Joint Conferences on Theory and Practice of Software, ETAPS 2024, Luxembourg City, Luxembourg, April 6-11, 2024, Proceedings, Part III. Lecture Notes in Computer Science, vol. 14572, pp. 45–67. Springer (2024). https://doi.org/10.1007/978-3-031-57256-2_3
9. Cosler, M., Schmitt, F., Hahn, C., Finkbeiner, B.: Iterative circuit repair against formal specifications. In: The Eleventh International Conference on Learning Representations, ICLR 2023, Kigali, Rwanda, May 1-5, 2023. OpenReview.net (2023), https://openreview.net/forum?id=SEcSahl0Q1
10. Dwyer, M.B., Avrunin, G.S., Corbett, J.C.: Property specification patterns for finite-state verification. In: Proceedings of the Second Workshop on Formal Methods in Software Practice. p. 7–15. FMSP '98, Association for Computing Machinery, New York, NY, USA (1998). https://doi.org/10.1145/298595.298598

11. Ehlers, R.: Unbeast: Symbolic bounded synthesis. In: Abdulla, P.A., Leino, K.R.M. (eds.) Tools and Algorithms for the Construction and Analysis of Systems - 17th International Conference, TACAS 2011, Held as Part of the Joint European Conferences on Theory and Practice of Software, ETAPS 2011, Saarbrücken, Germany, March 26-April 3, 2011. Proceedings. Lecture Notes in Computer Science, vol. 6605, pp. 272–275. Springer (2011). https://doi.org/10.1007/978-3-642-19835-9_25

12. Esparza, J., Kretínský, J., Raskin, J., Sickert, S.: From linear temporal logic and limit-deterministic büchi automata to deterministic parity automata. Int. J. Softw. Tools Technol. Transf. **24**(4), 635–659 (2022). https://doi.org/10.1007/s10009-022-00663-1

13. Esparza, J., Kretínský, J., Sickert, S.: A unified translation of linear temporal logic to ω-automata. J. ACM **67**(6), 33:1–33:61 (2020). https://doi.org/10.1145/3417995

14. Faymonville, P., Finkbeiner, B., Tentrup, L.: Bosy: An experimentation framework for bounded synthesis. In: Majumdar, R., Kuncak, V. (eds.) Computer Aided Verification - 29th International Conference, CAV 2017, Heidelberg, Germany, July 24-28, 2017, Proceedings, Part II. Lecture Notes in Computer Science, vol. 10427, pp. 325–332. Springer (2017). https://doi.org/10.1007/978-3-319-63390-9_17

15. Jacobs, S., Klein, F., Schirmer, S.: A high-level LTL synthesis format: TLSF v1.1. In: Piskac, R., Dimitrova, R. (eds.) Proceedings Fifth Workshop on Synthesis, SYNT@CAV 2016, Toronto, Canada, July 17-18, 2016. EPTCS, vol. 229, pp. 112–132 (2016). https://doi.org/10.4204/EPTCS.229.10

16. Jacobs, S., Pérez, G.A., Abraham, R., Bruyère, V., Cadilhac, M., Colange, M., Delfosse, C., van Dijk, T., Duret-Lutz, A., Faymonville, P., Finkbeiner, B., Khalimov, A., Klein, F., Luttenberger, M., Meyer, K.J., Michaud, T., Pommellet, A., Renkin, F., Schlehuber-Caissier, P., Sakr, M., Sickert, S., Staquet, G., Tamines, C., Tentrup, L., Walker, A.: The reactive synthesis competition (SYNTCOMP): 2018-2021. CoRR **abs/2206.00251** (2022). https://doi.org/10.48550/arXiv.2206.00251

17. Jobstmann, B., Bloem, R.: Optimizations for LTL synthesis. In: Formal Methods in Computer-Aided Design, 6th International Conference, FMCAD 2006, San Jose, California, USA, November 12-16, 2006, Proceedings. pp. 117–124. IEEE Computer Society (2006). https://doi.org/10.1109/FMCAD.2006.22

18. Kretínský, J., Esparza, J.: Deterministic automata for the (f, g)-fragment of LTL. In: Madhusudan, P., Seshia, S.A. (eds.) Computer Aided Verification - 24th International Conference, CAV 2012, Berkeley, CA, USA, July 7-13, 2012 Proceedings. Lecture Notes in Computer Science, vol. 7358, pp. 7–22. Springer (2012). https://doi.org/10.1007/978-3-642-31424-7_7

19. Kretínský, J., Manta, A., Meggendorfer, T.: Semantic labelling and learning for parity game solving in LTL synthesis. In: Chen, Y., Cheng, C., Esparza, J. (eds.) Automated Technology for Verification and Analysis - 17th International Symposium, ATVA 2019, Taipei, Taiwan, October 28-31, 2019, Proceedings. Lecture Notes in Computer Science, vol. 11781, pp. 404–422. Springer (2019). https://doi.org/10.1007/978-3-030-31784-3_24

20. Kretínský, J., Meggendorfer, T., Prokop, M., Rieder, S.: Guessing winning policies in LTL synthesis by semantic learning. In: Enea, C., Lal, A. (eds.) Computer Aided Verification - 35th International Conference, CAV 2023, Paris, France, July 17-22, 2023, Proceedings, Part I. Lecture Notes in Computer Science, vol. 13964, pp. 390–414. Springer (2023). https://doi.org/10.1007/978-3-031-37706-8_20

21. Kretinsky, J., Meggendorfer, T., Prokop, M., Zarkhah, A.: Semml: Enhancing automata-theoretic ltl synthesis with machine learning (2025), https://arxiv.org/abs/2501.17496

22. Kretínský, J., Meggendorfer, T., Sickert, S.: Owl: A library for ω-words, automata, and LTL. In: Lahiri, S.K., Wang, C. (eds.) Automated Technology for Verification and Analysis - 16th International Symposium, ATVA 2018, Los Angeles, CA, USA, October 7-10, 2018, Proceedings. Lecture Notes in Computer Science, vol. 11138, pp. 543–550. Springer (2018). https://doi.org/10.1007/978-3-030-01090-4_34

23. Kretínský, J., Meggendorfer, T., Sickert, S., Ziegler, C.: Rabinizer 4: From LTL to your favourite deterministic automaton. In: Chockler, H., Weissenbacher, G. (eds.) Computer Aided Verification - 30th International Conference, CAV 2018, Held as Part of the Federated Logic Conference, FloC 2018, Oxford, UK, July 14-17, 2018, Proceedings, Part I. Lecture Notes in Computer Science, vol. 10981, pp. 567–577. Springer (2018). https://doi.org/10.1007/978-3-319-96145-3_30

24. Kupferman, O., Piterman, N., Vardi, M.Y.: Safraless compositional synthesis. In: Ball, T., Jones, R.B. (eds.) Computer Aided Verification, 18th International Conference, CAV 2006, Seattle, WA, USA, August 17-20, 2006, Proceedings. Lecture Notes in Computer Science, vol. 4144, pp. 31–44. Springer (2006). https://doi.org/10.1007/11817963_6

25. Meggendorfer, T.: JBDD: A java BDD library. https://github.com/incaseoftrouble/jbdd (2017)

26. Meyer, P.J., Sickert, S., Luttenberger, M.: Strix: Explicit reactive synthesis strikes back! In: Chockler, H., Weissenbacher, G. (eds.) Computer Aided Verification - 30th International Conference, CAV 2018, Held as Part of the Federated Logic Conference, FloC 2018, Oxford, UK, July 14-17, 2018, Proceedings, Part I. Lecture Notes in Computer Science, vol. 10981, pp. 578–586. Springer (2018). https://doi.org/10.1007/978-3-319-96145-3_31

27. Pedregosa, F., Varoquaux, G., Gramfort, A., Michel, V., Thirion, B., Grisel, O., Blondel, M., Prettenhofer, P., Weiss, R., Dubourg, V., Vanderplas, J., Passos, A., Cournapeau, D., Brucher, M., Perrot, M., Duchesnay, E.: Scikit-learn: Machine learning in Python. Journal of Machine Learning Research **12**, 2825–2830 (2011)

28. Piterman, N.: From nondeterministic buchi and streett automata to deterministic parity automata. In: 21th IEEE Symposium on Logic in Computer Science (LICS 2006), 12-15 August 2006, Seattle, WA, USA, Proceedings. pp. 255–264. IEEE Computer Society (2006). https://doi.org/10.1109/LICS.2006.28

29. Piterman, N., Pnueli, A., Sa'ar, Y.: Synthesis of reactive(1) designs. In: Emerson, E.A., Namjoshi, K.S. (eds.) Verification, Model Checking, and Abstract Interpretation, 7th International Conference, VMCAI 2006, Charleston, SC, USA, January 8-10, 2006, Proceedings. Lecture Notes in Computer Science, vol. 3855, pp. 364–380. Springer (2006). https://doi.org/10.1007/11609773_24

30. Pnueli, A.: The temporal logic of programs. In: 18th Annual Symposium on Foundations of Computer Science, Providence, Rhode Island, USA, 31 October - 1 November 1977. pp. 46–57. IEEE Computer Society (1977). https://doi.org/10.1109/SFCS.1977.32

31. Pnueli, A., Rosner, R.: On the synthesis of an asynchronous reactive module. In: Ausiello, G., Dezani-Ciancaglini, M., Rocca, S.R.D. (eds.) Automata, Languages and Programming, 16th International Colloquium, ICALP89, Stresa, Italy, July 11-15, 1989, Proceedings. Lecture Notes in Computer Science, vol. 372, pp. 652–671. Springer (1989). https://doi.org/10.1007/BFb0035790

32. Prokop, M.: Artifact for "semml: Enhancing automata-theoretic ltl synthesis with machine learning" (Jan 2025). https://doi.org/10.5281/zenodo.14587814, https://doi.org/10.5281/zenodo.14587814

33. Renkin, F., Schlehuber-Caissier, P., Duret-Lutz, A., Pommellet, A.: Dissecting ltlsynt. Formal Methods Syst. Des. **61**(2), 248–289 (2022). https://doi.org/10.1007/S10703-022-00407-6
34. Rodríguez, A., Sánchez, C.: Boolean abstractions for realizability modulo theories. In: Enea, C., Lal, A. (eds.) Computer Aided Verification. pp. 305–328. Springer Nature Switzerland, Cham (2023)
35. Safra, S.: On the complexity of omega-automata. In: 29th Annual Symposium on Foundations of Computer Science, White Plains, New York, USA, 24-26 October 1988. pp. 319–327. IEEE Computer Society (1988). https://doi.org/10.1109/SFCS.1988.21948
36. Schewe, S.: Tighter bounds for the determinisation of büchi automata. In: de Alfaro, L. (ed.) Foundations of Software Science and Computational Structures, 12th International Conference, FOSSACS 2009, Held as Part of the Joint European Conferences on Theory and Practice of Software, ETAPS 2009, York, UK, March 22-29, 2009. Proceedings. Lecture Notes in Computer Science, vol. 5504, pp. 167–181. Springer (2009). https://doi.org/10.1007/978-3-642-00596-1_13
37. Schmitt, F., Hahn, C., Rabe, M.N., Finkbeiner, B.: Neural circuit synthesis from specification patterns. In: Ranzato, M., Beygelzimer, A., Dauphin, Y.N., Liang, P., Vaughan, J.W. (eds.) Advances in Neural Information Processing Systems 34: Annual Conference on Neural Information Processing Systems 2021, NeurIPS 2021, December 6-14, 2021, virtual. pp. 15408–15420 (2021), https://proceedings.neurips.cc/paper/2021/hash/8230bea7d54bcdf99cdfe85cb07313d5-Abstract.html
38. Sickert, S., Esparza, J., Jaax, S., Křetínský, J.: Limit-deterministic büchi automata for linear temporal logic. In: Chaudhuri, S., Farzan, A. (eds.) Computer Aided Verification - 28th International Conference, CAV 2016, Toronto, ON, Canada, July 17-23, 2016, Proceedings, Part II. Lecture Notes in Computer Science, vol. 9780, pp. 312–332. Springer (2016). https://doi.org/10.1007/978-3-319-41540-6_17
39. Thomas, W.: On the synthesis of strategies in infinite games. In: Mayr, E.W., Puech, C. (eds.) STACS 95, 12th Annual Symposium on Theoretical Aspects of Computer Science, Munich, Germany, March 2-4, 1995, Proceedings. Lecture Notes in Computer Science, vol. 900, pp. 1–13. Springer (1995). https://doi.org/10.1007/3-540-59042-0_57
40. Tomita, T., Ueno, A., Shimakawa, M., Hagihara, S., Yonezaki, N.: Safraless LTL synthesis considering maximal realizability. Acta Informatica **54**(7), 655–692 (2017). https://doi.org/10.1007/S00236-016-0280-3

Formally Verifying a Transformation from MLTL Formulas to Regular Expressions

Zili Wang[1]($\boxtimes$)(iD), Katherine Kosaian[2](iD), and Kristin Yvonne Rozier[1](iD)

[1] Iowa State University, Ames, IA, USA
ziliw1@iastate.edu, kyrozier@iastate.edu
[2] University of Iowa, Iowa City, IA, USA
katherine-kosaian@uiowa.edu

Abstract. Mission-time Linear Temporal Logic (MLTL), a widely used subset of popular specification logics like STL and MTL, is often used to model and verify real world systems in safety-critical contexts. As the results of formal verification are only as trustworthy as their input specifications, the WEST tool was created to facilitate writing MLTL specifications. Accordingly, it is vital to demonstrate that WEST itself works correctly. To that end, we verify the WEST algorithm, which converts MLTL formulas to (logically equivalent) regular expressions, in the theorem prover Isabelle/HOL. Our top-level result establishes the correctness of the regular expression transformation; we then generate a code export from our verified development and use this to experimentally validate the existing WEST tool. To facilitate this, we develop some verified support for checking the equivalence of two regular expressions.

Keywords: MLTL · Regular Expressions · Interactive Theorem Proving · Isabelle/HOL · Code Generation · Tool Validation

1 Introduction

As formal methods tools become increasingly integrated into system development life cycles, it is necessary to offer stronger demonstrations of their correct implementation than piecemeal code analysis and experimental validation. After all, these are the tools justifying and verifying, e.g., the certification of systems; these tools must obey a higher standard for correctness. This starts with their input languages and specification validation.

Many formal methods tools, such as model checkers and runtime verification engines, reason over behavior specifications in LTL or related linear-time logics that extend LTL, e.g., to add intervals on the temporal operators like Signal Temporal Logic (STL) [32], Metric Temporal Logic (MTL) [1], and Metric Interval Temporal Logic (MITL) [2]. Mission-time Linear Temporal Logic (MLTL) [40,30] represents a commonly used subset of these timed logics, and has a conversion to LTL [30]. Several tools use MLTL as a core specification language; these include the Formal Requirements Elicitation Tool (FRET) [19,34,4], the

A. Gurfinkel and M. Heule (Eds.): TACAS 2025, LNCS 15696, pp. 254–275, 2025.
https://doi.org/10.1007/978-3-031-90643-5_13

Realizable Responsive Unobtrusive Unit (R2U2) [40,43,23], and the Ogda runtime monitoring tool [37,35,36]. Popular symbolic model checker NUXMV [9] supports a subset of MLTL [25] by allowing bounds on the Globally and Future operators (but not on Until or Release). The WEST tool [17,51] transforms MLTL formulas into logically equivalent (and easier to analyze) regular expressions and facilitates the validation of MLTL specifications with an interactive GUI. Since WEST validates specifications, which are the fundamental basis for formal verification, it is especially critical to rigorously establish its correctness.

The research community has long recognized that specification is the biggest bottleneck in formal methods [42]; to that end LTL is formalized in Coq [14], in PVS [38], and in Isabelle/HOL [47], along with many algorithms for its use in formal verification [48,45,46,44,18]. Libraries for related linear-time logics were inspired by, or directly built upon those for LTL, including formalizations of MTL in Coq [10] and PVS [12,50]; a PVS formalization of MITL [41]; and Isabelle formalizations of the 3-valued variant LTL3 [3] and MLTL [27]. Further, the importance of ensuring correctness of formal methods tools naturally prompts using these formalizations to generate tools. For instance, an Isabelle/HOL formalization of the VeriMon tool for monitoring metric first-order temporal logic (MFOTL) generates (via code export) VeriMon's codebase [8]. An Isabelle/HOL formalization of a metric dynamic logic (MDL) runtime monitoring algorithm also generated the Vydra tool [39].[3] In Coq, a formalization of monitoring past-time MTL generates an OCaml monitoring engine [11].

We enrich this space by formalizing the WEST algorithm for specification validation. Building on an existing MLTL library in Isabelle/HOL [27,26], we formally prove that the WEST algorithm generates regular expressions that are logically equivalent to the input MLTL formulas, filling in details omitted from the original tool's correctness proofs. From our formalized algorithms, we generate a new implementation of WEST to validate the (unverified) implementations of WEST: the proof-of-concept original [17] and a highly optimized refactoring [51]. As WEST validates other MLTL tools, most notably the runtime verification engine R2U2 [40], our work helps to foster trust in a safety-critical space. Our experiments also show that our Isabelle-generated code is (in aggregate) close in performance to the optimized, unverified version of WEST.

Section 2 recaps the existing Isabelle/HOL MLTL library [27,26], introduces the trace regular expressions fundamental to the WEST algorithm, and sets up the definitions underlying our formalization. Section 3 presents our formalization of the WEST algorithm. Section 4 gathers our formalization insights to inform future efforts that build on our contributions. Section 5 experimentally evaluates the new version of WEST generated via Isabelle's code export utility in comparison with two previous, hand-coded versions [17,51], while Section 6 concludes with a discussion. Our formalization (totaling ≈ 7400 lines of code) is available on the Archive of Formal Proofs (AFP) [52].

---

[3] Vydra also reasons with regular expressions in the input language, rather than using regular expression to represent the input, as WEST does.

2   MLTL and Regular Expressions

In this section, we present the syntax and semantics of MLTL and explain our formalization of the WEST regular expressions used by the WEST tool, highlighting some key datatypes; when appropriate, we intersperse mathematical definitions with Isabelle/HOL code. We also introduce some useful functions that are important in the correctness proofs later on.

Other works formalize regular expressions in different contexts. An algorithm for matching extended regular expressions via symbolic derivatives was formalized in Lean [56], and the Myhill-Nerode theorem was restated in Isabelle/HOL using regular expressions (instead of automata, which is more common) [54]. There has also been work formalizing decision procedures to check equivalence of regular expressions in Rocq [13] and Isabelle/HOL [29]. The latter is particularly relevant; we are interested in potentially incorporating it in future work to improve our (currently naive) regular expression checking procedure.

2.1   Syntax and Semantics of MLTL

Let AP be a finite set of atomic propositions. Let $p \in$ AP be an atomic proposition, and $a, b \in \mathbb{N}$ be natural numbers such that $a \leq b$; MLTL formulas are defined by the following grammar; the temporal operators $\mathsf{F}, \mathsf{G}, \mathsf{U}, \mathsf{R}$ denote "Future", "Globally", "Until", and "Release", respectively.

$$\phi, \psi := \texttt{True} \mid \texttt{False} \mid \mathsf{p} \mid \neg\phi \mid \phi \wedge \psi \mid \phi \vee \psi \mid \mathsf{F}_{[a,b]}\phi \mid \mathsf{G}_{[a,b]}\phi \mid \phi\mathsf{U}_{[a,b]}\psi \mid \phi\mathsf{R}_{[a,b]}\psi.$$

A **trace** π is a finite sequence $\pi = \pi[0], \pi[1], \ldots$ of sets of atomic propositions, where $\pi[i] \subseteq$ AP for all i. We refer to the i-th element of a trace π as the i-th state of the trace, and intuitively interpret $\pi[i]$ as the set of propositions that are true at time i. We denote the length of a trace π by $|\pi|$, and the suffix of a trace π starting at time i by π_i; that is, $\pi_i = \pi[i], \pi[i+1], \ldots$ and $\pi_0 = \pi$. The existing MLTL library in Isabelle/HOL [26] encodes a trace as a list of sets of natural numbers; each set represents the atomic propositions that are true at each timestep. For example, the trace $\pi = \{p_0, p_1\}, \{p_0\}$ is encoded in Isabelle as the `[{0, 1}, {0}]`, which has type `nat set list`.

A trace π satisfies an MLTL formula ϕ, denoted $\pi \models \phi$, as follows [40,30], where ψ is another MLTL formula:

$\pi \models p$ iff $p \in \pi[0]$ $\qquad\qquad\qquad$ $\pi \models \neg\phi$ iff $\pi \not\models \phi$

$\pi \models \phi \wedge \psi$ iff $\pi \models \phi$ and $\pi \models \psi$ $\qquad$ $\pi \models \phi \vee \psi$ iff $\pi \models \phi$ or $\pi \models \psi$

$\pi \models \mathsf{F}_{[a,b]}\phi$ iff $|\pi| > a$ and $\exists i \in [a,b].\ \pi_i \models \phi$

$\pi \models \mathsf{G}_{[a,b]}\phi$ iff $|\pi| \leq a$ or $\forall i \in [a,b].\ \pi_i \models \phi$

$\pi \models \phi\,\mathsf{U}_{[a,b]}\psi$ iff $|\pi| > a$ and $\exists i \in [a,b].\ (\pi_i \models \psi$ and $\forall j \in [a, i-1].\ \pi_j \models \phi)$

$\pi \models \phi\,\mathsf{R}_{[a,b]}\psi$ iff $|\pi| \leq a$ or $(\forall i \in [a,b].\ \pi_i \models \psi)$ or $\exists j \in [a, b-1].\ (\pi_j \models \phi$ and $\forall k \in [a,j]\ \pi_k \models \psi)$

2.2   Trace Regular Expressions

The WEST algorithm [17] takes an MLTL formula as input and recursively computes a WEST regular expression representing exactly the set of traces that satisfy that formula. Intuitively, we can think of this as happening in two steps. First, we represent traces as **bit strings**; here, instead of encoding each state in a trace as a set, we encode each state as a bit string of length n (where n is the number of variables in the formula). Next, we define **WEST regular expressions (WEST regexes)** as a compact way to represent a set of traces.

More precisely, we assume that $\mathrm{AP} = \{p_0, p_1, \ldots, p_{n-1}\}$ and impose (without loss of generality) an ordering on these atomic propositions; we use this ordering to construct the **bit string** of a trace π of length m as the length mn string of 0's and 1's such that the value of atomic proposition p_k at timestep i corresponds to the $(ni + k)$-th character of the bit string [17, Definition 2]. We visualize an example in Fig. 1. We encode bit strings in Isabelle as lists of lists.

In Isabelle/HOL, we obtain an ordering on our set of atomic propositions by constraining them to be natural numbers, of type **nat**. Following WEST's implementation [51], we choose not to fix n globally (which we could accomplish using a locale [6,7]) but instead pass the number of variables as an argument to the helper functions in the WEST algorithm (in the top-level function, we compute the right value to pass to the helper functions).

We then collate these bit string representations in **trace regular expressions**,[4] or trace regexes for short, which are strings

$\mathrm{AP} = \{p_0, p_1\}$

Time: 0   1   2   3

Trace: $\{p_0\}$ $\{p_0, p_1\}$ $\{\}$ $\{p_1\}$
BitStr: 10   11   00   01
Isa: [[1,0], [1,1], [0,0], [0,1]]

Fig. 1: For $\mathrm{AP} = \{p_0, p_1\}$, the bit string of trace $\{p_0\}, \{p_0, p_1\}, \{\}, \{p_1\}$ is 10,11,00,01 (following the source material [17], we use commas to separate timesteps for readability) which is encoded in Isabelle as [[1,0], [1, 1], [0, 0], [0, 1]] (type **nat list list**).

consisting of 0, 1, and S, where S is a shorthand for the regular expression 0|1. For example, fixing the number of atomic propositions to be $n = 3$, the trace regex 10S matches only the two bit strings 101 and 100 (each representing a trace of length 1), and the trace regex S00,0S0 matches the four bit strings (each representing a length 2 trace) "100,010", "100,000", "000,010", and "000,000".

In Isabelle/HOL, trace regexes have type *WEST_bit list list*, where our custom datatype *WEST_bit* is comprised by *Zero*, *One*, and *S*. We represent trace regexes with *WEST_bit list list* and not *WEST_bit list* because the number of atomic propositions, n, is critical for the interpretation of traces from their bit string representations. We must ensure that each *WEST_bit list*, referred to as a *state regex*, has length n in the overall list; having a list of lists facilitates this check. For this, we define the function *trace_regex_of_vars* which takes as inputs trace regex r and the number of atomic propositions n, and checks that each state regex in r has length n. Here, *!* is Isabelle/HOL syntax for the i-th element of L.

---

[4] Also called temporal regular expressions [17, Definition 4].

```
definition trace_regex_of_vars:: "trace_regex ⇒ nat ⇒ bool"
   where "trace_regex_of_vars r n = (∀ i<length r. length (r!i) = n)"
```

Then, we build a list of trace regexes as a `WEST_regex` of type `WEST_bit list list list`, the final return type of the WEST algorithm. A WEST regex `L` is well-defined for n atomic propositions if each trace regex r in `L` satisfies `trace_regex_of_vars r n`. We summarize the datatypes of objects in our encoding in Table 1. While the nested lists may seem unwieldy at first glance, they ensure modularity in the implementation and, more crucially, in the correctness proofs. We turn to an example of this modularity now, as we build up to formalizing the notion of a WEST regex matching a trace.

Terminology	Description	Isabelle Type
WEST bit	Custom Isabelle datatype	`WEST_bit`
state regex	List of WEST bits that encodes states as bit strings	`WEST_bit list`
trace regex	List of WEST states that represents sets of traces compactly as regular expressions	`WEST_bit list list`
WEST regex	List of WEST traces that represents the union of all sets of traces represented by the WEST traces	`WEST_bit list list list`

Table 1: Summary of the datatypes of each object in our encoding.

2.3   Useful Definitions

The notion of matching is foundational to the WEST algorithm because it is crucial for connecting the semantics of MLTL formulas to the semantics of WEST regexes. We define that a state regex r **matches** a state if r equals the bit string representation of the state or if r generalizes the bit string by replacing some characters in the bit string with S's. This notion lifts to traces: a trace regex r matches a trace π iff r matches the bit string representation of π. Furthermore, we may lift this to WEST regexes. For trace regexes $r_1, r_2, ..., r_k$, we can combine them by alternations as $r_1|r_2|...|r_k$; we abbreviate this as the WEST regex $L = [r_1, r_2, ..., r_k]$, and define that L matches a trace π iff some r_i matches π.

We contribute a formal mathematical definition of the notion of matching, which previous work [17] supplied only an intuition for. We do this in three steps. First, we define matching a state regex (of type `WEST_bit list`) to a state in a trace (of type `nat set`) in the definition `match_timestep`:

```
definition match_timestep:: "nat set ⇒ state_regex ⇒ bool"
      where "match_timestep state r = (∀ i < length r.
      (r ! i = One ⟶ i ∈ state) ∧ (r ! i = Zero ⟶ i ∉ state))"
```

This definition checks that for all i, `r!i` equaling `One` implies the i-th atomic proposition p_i holds at the input state (i.e., $p_i \in$ `state`), and `r!i` equaling `Zero` implies p_i does not hold at this state. If `r!i` is S, then p_i can be either true or false at this state. For example, the state regex $[0, 1, S]$ matches $\{1\}$ and $\{1, 2\}$.

Next we define matching a trace regex (of type `WEST_bit list list`) to a trace (of type `nat set list`) in the definition `match_regex`:

definition `match_regex::` `"trace` $\Rightarrow$ `trace_regex` $\Rightarrow$ `bool"`
   where `"match_regex` π `r` `=` `((`$\forall$ `time<length r.`
   `(match_timestep` `(`π `!` `time)` `(r` `!` `time)))`$\wedge$`(length` π $\geq$ `length r))"`

This definition takes as input a trace π and a trace regex r, and checks that `match_timestep` holds for all regex states in `trace` (i.e., for all `r ! time`) on the corresponding state in the trace (π `! time`). It also checks that the length of π is at least the length of r (a well-definedness condition, as we need to access π `! time` for all time up to the length of r).

Finally, we define matching a WEST regex (of type `WEST_bit list list list`) to a trace (of type `nat set list`) in the definition `match`:

definition `match::` `"trace` $\Rightarrow$ `WEST_regex` $\Rightarrow$ `bool"`
   where `"match` π `L` `=` `(`$\exists$`i` `<` `length L.` `match_regex` π `(L` `!` `i))"`

This definition checks that `match_regex` holds for some trace regex `L ! i` in L and the trace π. We may intuitively view WEST regexes as compactly representing the behavior of a set of traces; then, the WEST algorithm transforms a given MLTL formula into a WEST regex that captures the set of satisfying traces.

Another important function, `WEST_num_vars`, counts the number of atomic propositions in a given MLTL formula by recursively computing the maximum number of atomic propositions in all subformulas. For example, `WEST_num_vars` of an atomic proposition p is $p+1$ (as atomic propositions are indexed from 0), and `WEST_num_vars` of `And_mltl` φ ψ is the maximum of `WEST_num_vars` φ and `WEST_num_vars` ψ. This function is used frequently in our correctness results.

3   Formalizing the WEST Algorithm

Intuitively, the WEST algorithm recursively computes a list of trace regexes for the subformulas of an MLTL formula, and then combines these lists using the `WEST_and` and `WEST_or` operations for taking intersections and unions of sets of traces. The finite semantics of MLTL formulas ensures that all existential and universal quantifiers can be translated to a finite number of `WEST_and` and `WEST_or` operations on trace regexes; thus the WEST algorithm directly defines the temporal operators in terms of `WEST_and` and `WEST_or`. For these temporal operators, we also need a *shifting* operation, `shift`, which the source material [17] implicitly uses but does not explicitly define. Intuitively, `shift` ensures that we are analyzing the locations

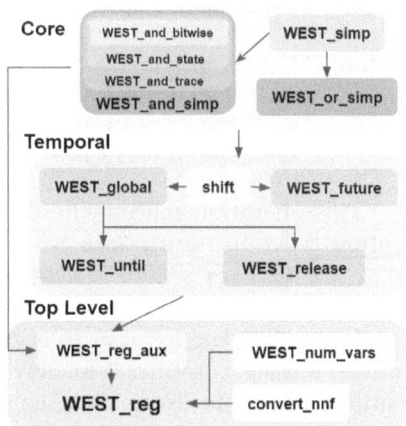

Fig. 2: High-level overview of key components in our formalization of the WEST algorithm.

in the trace specified by the temporal operators; we will see this in an example in Sect. 3.2. Fig. 2 visualizes the overall structure of the WEST algorithm.

We first discuss our formalization of the core operators `WEST_and` and `WEST_or` along with our formalization of an important simplification step in Sect. 3.1. Then, we present how the temporal operators are built on top of these core operators in Sect. 3.2, using the `shift` operation. Finally, we discuss the top-level WEST algorithm `WEST_reg` and our overall correctness result in Sect. 3.3.

3.1 The Core Operations of WEST

The `WEST_or` operation simply combines two WEST regexes (i.e., lists of trace regexes) into one WEST regex. We implement this in Isabelle/HOL using the built-in @ operator for list concatenation. The top-level correctness theorem shows that for two WEST regexes `L1` and `L2`, `L1` matches a trace π or `L2` matches π iff `L1@L2` matches π. We formally state this as the `WEST_or_correct` lemma.

> **lemma** `WEST_or_correct`:
>   **fixes** π::"trace" **and** `L1 L2`::"WEST_regex"
>   **shows** "match π (L1@L2) $\longleftrightarrow$ (match π L1) $\vee$ (match π L2)"

Next, the `WEST_and` operation takes as input two lists of trace regexes and computes a list of trace regexes representing the intersection of the sets of traces represented by the input lists. We visualize the intended semantics of this operation in Fig. 3. One notable point here is that `WEST_and Zero One` is `None`, because it is impossible for a bit in a trace regex to simultaneously equal `Zero` and `One`. In Isabelle/HOL, we formalize `WEST_and` in four steps: first we define an operation between two bits, then between two regex states, then between two trace regexes, and finally between two WEST regexes.

The lowest-level operation between two bits (each of type `WEST_bit`) is defined in the function `WEST_and_bitwise` as follows:

> **fun** `WEST_and_bitwise`:: "WEST_bit $\Rightarrow$ WEST_bit $\Rightarrow$ WEST_bit option" **where**
>   "WEST_and_bitwise b One = (if b=Zero then None else Some One)"
> | "WEST_and_bitwise b Zero = (if b=One then None else Some Zero)"
> | "WEST_and_bitwise b S = Some b"

This operation reflects the desired semantics visualized in Fig. 3 by using option types to return `None` when the set intersection is empty. For example, `WEST_and_bitwise S Zero` is `Some Zero`, while `WEST_and_bitwise One Zero` is `None`.

This operation is then lifted to two regex states in `WEST_and_state`; here, we apply `WEST_and_bitwise` to each pair of corresponding bits in the two regex states. If `None` is returned for any pair, then the function returns `None` for the entire regex state. Note that the lengths of the two regex states must be the same (i.e., equal to n, the number of atomic propositions), and this operation returns `None` if they are not. Then, we again lift `WEST_and_state` to operate on two trace regexes in the function `WEST_and_trace` by applying `WEST_and_state` to each pair of corresponding regex states in the two trace regexes, returning `None` if any of the calls to *WEST_and_state* returns *None*. The input trace regexes are allowed to have different lengths, and the shorter trace regex is treated as if the missing regex states are all *S*, following [17, Definition 4, Pad]. The full formal definitions can be found in our formalization [52].

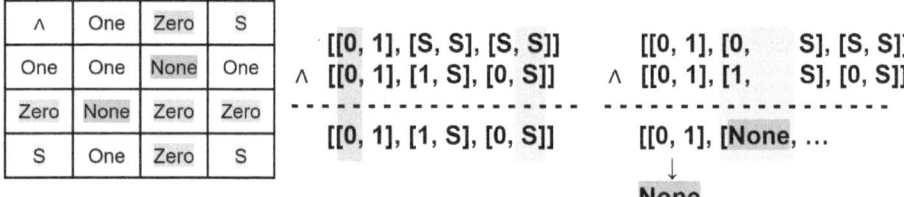

Fig. 3: Operations table for *WEST_and_bit* operation for bits (left), and two examples of *WEST_and* between regex states and traces (middle and right).

To establish the correctness of *WEST_and*, we prove the following lemma:

> **lemma** *WEST_and_correct:*
>   **fixes** π::*"trace"* **and** *L1 L2*:: *"WEST_regex"*
>   **assumes** *L1_of_num_vars*: *"WEST_regex_of_vars L1 n"*
>   **assumes** *L2_of_num_vars*: *"WEST_regex_of_vars L2 n"*
>   **shows** *"(match π L1 $\wedge$ match π L2) $\longleftrightarrow$ match π (WEST_and L1 L2)"*

This shows that for input WEST regexes *L1* and *L2*, both *L1* and *L2* match trace π iff the *WEST_and* of *L1* and *L2* matches π. In other words, the set of traces that the *WEST_and* of *L1* and *L2* matches is exactly the intersection between the set of traces that *L1* matches and the set of traces that *L2* matches. The assumptions on *L1* and *L2* are well-definedness conditions that ensure all state regexes have length n (the number of atomic propositions), as required by *WEST_and_state*.

To keep the sizes of WEST regexes small, WEST implements an additional simplification step which collects together related trace regexes. If two trace regexes differ only by a single bit, then they may be combined into one trace regex where the differing bit is *S*. For example, fixing the number of atomic propositions to $n = 2$, the WEST regex *[[[0,0],[0,1]], [[0,0],[0,0]], [[0,1],[0,S]]]* may first be reduced (by combining the first two trace regexes) to *[[[0,0],[0,S]], [[0,1],[0,S]]]*, and then to *[[[0,S],[0,S]]]*. This is crucial for improving the tool performance, as it helps to mitigate blowup in the length of the list of trace regexes during the *WEST_and* and *WEST_or* operations [17, Section 4].

The underlying idea is straightforward: greedily simplify pairs of regexes until no more pairs can be simplified; we implement this in the *WEST_simp* function. It is crucial that the simplification step does not change the set of traces that a WEST regex matches. The following lemma shows that, for a well-defined WEST regex *L*, a trace π matches *L* iff π matches the simplification of *L*:

> **lemma** *WEST_simp_correct:*
>   **fixes** *L*::*"WEST_regex"* **and** π::*"trace"* **and** *n*::*"nat"*

```
    assumes "WEST_regex_of_vars L n"
    shows "match π (WEST_simp L n) ⟷ match π L"
```

Finally, we define the functions `WEST_and_simp` and `WEST_or_simp` by passing the output of `WEST_and` and `WEST_or` (respectively) to `WEST_simp`. The correctness of `WEST_and_simp` and `WEST_or_simp` follows directly from the correctness results for `WEST_and`, `WEST_or`, and `WEST_simp`.

3.2   Temporal Operators

Our formalization of the temporal operators in the WEST algorithm uses the `WEST_and_simp` and `WEST_or_simp` operators. It also uses an operation to shift regular expressions to later timesteps, which we call `shift`. Though the source material never explicitly defines this `shift` operation, it uses it implicitly and defines an analogous operation [17, Definition 5]. We formalize `shift` as follows:

```
fun shift:: "WEST_regex ⇒ nat ⇒ nat ⇒ WEST_regex"
    where "shift L n t = map (λtrace. (arbitrary_trace n t)@trace) L"
```

Here, we refer to a state regex of all `S`'s as an *arbitrary state*, and we refer to a trace regex of all arbitrary states as an *arbitrary trace* [17, Section 6]. In this snippet, `arbitrary_trace n t` constructs an arbitrary trace regex containing `t` arbitrary states of length `n`. Then, `shift` takes as input a WEST regex `L`, and appends an arbitrary trace of `t` arbitrary states to the front of each trace regex in `L`. As intuitively named, `shift` shifts all trace regexes in `L` by `t` timesteps.

For example, fixing the number of atomic propositions at $n = 2$, the WEST regex `L = [[[1,1]], [[0,0], [0,0]]]` captures that either p_0 and p_1 both need to be true at timestep 0, or p_0 and p_1 both need to be false at timesteps 0 and 1. If instead we want to delay this behavior for p_0 and p_1 by 3 timesteps, we can compute `shift L 2 3`, which returns `[[[S,S],[S,S],[S,S],[1,1]], [[S, S],[S,S],[S,S],[0,0],[0,0]]]`. The following lemma formalizes the connection between the `shift` operation for WEST regexes and the suffix of a trace:

```
lemma shift_match_property:
    assumes "length π ≥ t"
    shows "match (drop t π) L ⟷ match π (shift L num_vars t)"
```

More precisely, `shift_match_property` establishes that a sufficiently long trace π matches a WEST regex `L` shifted by `t` timesteps iff the suffix of π with `t` states removed, denoted `drop t π`, matches `L`.

Now, we demonstrate how the temporal operators are built on top of the core WEST operators. We provide for an example `WEST_global`, defined as follows:

```
fun WEST_global:: "WEST_regex ⇒ nat ⇒ nat ⇒ nat ⇒ WEST_regex"
    where "WEST_global L a b n = (if (a = b) then (shift L n a)
    else (if (a < b) then (WEST_and_simp (shift L n b)
```

```
            (WEST_global L a (b-1) n) n) else [])))"
```

WEST_global takes as input a WEST regex `L`, lower and upper interval bounds `a` and `b`, and the number of atomic propositions `n`. **WEST_global** then uses the `shift` operation to shift the input regex `L` by `b` timesteps, and computes the **WEST_and** of the shifted `L` and **WEST_global** with `b-1`. Intuitively, `L` captures a set of traces specifying some behavior at timestep 0, and the successive `shift` and **WEST_and** operations ensures that `L`'s behavior happens at all timesteps between `a` and `b`. The remaining temporal operators are defined in a similar manner, using `shift` and the core WEST operators.

We establish the correctness of the **WEST_global** operator as follows:

lemma `WEST_global_correct`:
    fixes `L::"WEST_regex"` **and** φ`::"nat mltl"` **and** π`::"trace"`
    assumes `semantics_`φ`: "`$\bigwedge\pi$`. (length` π $\geq$ `complen_mltl` φ $\longrightarrow$
                       `(match` π `L` $\longleftrightarrow$ `semantics_mltl` π φ`))"`
    assumes `L_vars: "WEST_regex_of_vars L n"`
    assumes φ`_vars: "WEST_num_vars` φ $\leq$ `n" and "a`$\leq$`b"`
    assumes `trace_len: "length` π $\geq$ `(complen_mltl` φ`) + b"`
    shows `"match` π `(WEST_global L a b n)` $\longleftrightarrow$
        `semantics_mltl` π `(Global_mltl` φ `a b)"`

This lemma says that for a WEST regex `L` over `n` variables (assumption `L_vars`) that captures the semantics of an MLTL formula φ of at most `n` variables (assumption `semantics_`φ and φ`_vars`), and a trace π of sufficient length, **WEST_global** φ `a b n` matches π iff π satisfies the semantics of `Global_mltl` φ `a b` (representing the formula $G_{[a,b]}\phi$).

Likewise, each of the remaining temporal operators has a correctness lemma that establishes the connection between the WEST regex it computes and its corresponding temporal operator. The correctness lemmas for the temporal operators totaled about 850 lines of code.

3.3   Top-Level Algorithm and Correctness

The WEST algorithm takes as input an MLTL formula ϕ in negation normal form (NNF) and recursively computes the WEST regex representing the set of traces with length at least the computation length of φ that satisfy the formula. The existing Isabelle/HOL MLTL library [27] already formalizes the computation length[5] of ϕ, denoted `complen`(ϕ), which intuitively measures how much time is needed to decide the satisfiability of ϕ [17,24,27].

We formalize the WEST algorithm in the function `WEST_reg` as follows:

---

[5] This is also known as the *worst-case propagation delay* in the context of runtime verification [24,55].

```
fun WEST_reg:: "nat mltl ⇒ WEST_regex"
    where "WEST_reg φ = (let nnf_φ = convert_nnf φ in
                    WEST_reg_aux nnf_φ (WEST_num_vars φ))"
```

Although input formulas to the WEST algorithm must be in NNF, we allow formulas of all shapes as input and apply the `convert_nnf` function from the existing MLTL formalization [27] to transform the input formula to NNF. The resultant NNF formula `nnf_φ` and the number of atomic propositions, computed as `WEST_num_vars` φ, are then passed to the auxiliary function `WEST_reg_aux`. This auxiliary function takes two inputs (a `nat mltl` formula φ and a natural number n for the number of atomic propositions) and cases on the structure of φ to apply the appropriate core operators and return a WEST regex.

We consider here a few representative cases: `True`, `Prop_mltl`, `And_mltl`, and `Global_mltl` (corresponding to the cases of `True`, an atomic proposition, a conjunction, and the global operator). Mathematically, these cases are defined in the source material as follows [17]: $\text{reg}(\text{True}) = S^n$, $\text{reg}(p_k) = S^k 1 S^{n-k-1}$, and $\text{reg}(\phi \wedge \psi) = \text{reg}(\phi) \wedge \text{reg}(\psi)$. The global operation, $\text{reg}(\mathsf{G}_{[a,b]}\phi)$ computes (recursively) the `WEST_and` of $\text{reg}(\phi)$ shifted by i timesteps for all i with $a \leq i \leq b$ (note this is essentially what `WEST_global` computes). In Isabelle/HOL, we have:

```
WEST_reg_aux:: "(nat) mltl ⇒ nat ⇒ WEST_regex"
    where "WEST_reg_aux True_mltl n = [[(map (λ j. S) [0 ..< n])]]"
    | "WEST_reg_aux (Prop_mltl p) n =
        [[(map (λj. (if (p=j) then One else S)) [0 ..< n])]]"
    | "WEST_reg_aux (And_mltl φ ψ) n = (WEST_and_simp
        (WEST_reg_aux φ n) (WEST_reg_aux ψ n) n)"
    | "WEST_reg_aux (Global_mltl φ a b) n =
        WEST_global (WEST_reg_aux φ n) a b n"
```

Here, `map f L` applies a function `f` on every element of a list `L`, so the base case for `True_mltl` creates a WEST regex containing a trace regex of all `S`'s. In the case `Prop_mltl p`, the map function takes as input `j` and returns `One` if the propositional variable `p` equals the index `j`, and otherwise `S`. In `And_mltl`, we directly call the `WEST_and` operator; likewise in `Global_mltl`.

Top-Level Correctness. A central contribution of our work is proving (and even slightly generalizing) the correctness of the `WEST_reg_aux` function and elucidating many of the details omitted in the original proof of correctness. Theorem 2 in the source material states the correctness result as follows: for a MLTL formula ϕ in negation normal form, a trace π with length $\text{complen}(\phi)$ satisfies ϕ iff π matches $\text{reg}(\phi)$ [17]. We formalize this in the theorem `WEST_reg_aux_correct`:

```
theorem WEST_reg_aux_correct:
    fixes π::"trace" and φ::"nat mltl" and n::"nat"
    assumes π_long_enough: "length π ≥ complen_mltl φ"
    assumes is_nnf: "∃ ψ. φ = (convert_nnf ψ)"
    assumes φ_nv: "WEST_num_vars φ ≤ n"
```

```
    assumes "intervals_welldef φ"
    shows "match π (WEST_reg_aux φ n) ⟷ semantics_mltl π φ"
```

This theorem states that for MLTL formula φ in NNF (assumption `is_nnf`) with at most n variables (assumption `φ_nv`) and well-defined interval bounds (assumption `intervals_welldef φ`) and a trace π of length at least `complen`(φ) (assumption `π_long_enough`), the trace π satisfies φ iff the trace π matches the WEST regex computed by `WEST_reg_aux φ n`. Here, the functions `convert_nnf`, `complen_mltl`, and `intervals_welldef` are from the existing MLTL formalization [26]. The `φ_nv` is an implicit assumption in the source material, which globally fixes the number of atomic propositions.[6] We slightly generalize the original correctness result, as our formal result holds for all traces of length at least the computation length of φ rather than just the traces of length equal to the computation length of φ.

We prove this by structural induction on the input formula φ. The `is_nnf` assumption allows us to use the custom induction rule `nnf_induct` from the existing MLTL formalizing [26], simplifying the induction proof. The base cases are straightforward, and the inductive cases are proven by applying the inductive hypothesis on the subformulas and using the correctness lemmas for the core WEST operators. For instance, for input formula φ = `Global_mltl` ψ a b (which is $G_{[a,b]}\psi$), the inductive hypothesis gives us that the trace π satisfies ψ iff the WEST regex L computed by `WEST_reg_aux ψ n` matches π. Next, in order to apply the correctness result of the `WEST_global` operator, we need to show that L is a WEST regex over n atomic propositions (i.e., each state regex in each trace regex in L is of length n). For this, we prove the lemma `WEST_reg_aux_num_vars`:

```
lemma WEST_reg_aux_num_vars:
    fixes φ::"nat mltl"
    assumes is_nnf: "∃ ψ. φ = (convert_nnf ψ)"
    assumes "WEST_num_vars φ ≤ n" and "intervals_welldef φ"
    shows "WEST_regex_of_vars (WEST_reg_aux φ n) n"
```

This lemma states that, for a formula φ in NNF with at most n atomic propositions, the WEST regex computed by `WEST_reg_aux φ n` is a WEST regex over n atomic propositions. With this, we can apply the correctness result of the `WEST_global` operator on L and complete the proof of the `Global_mltl` case.

Finally, we present the top-level correctness result for the WEST algorithm:

```
theorem WEST_reg_correct:
    fixes φ::"nat mltl" and π::"trace"
    assumes "intervals_welldef φ"
    assumes π_long_enough: "length π ≥ complen_mltl φ"
    shows   "match π (WEST_reg φ) ⟷ semantics_mltl π φ"
```

---

[6] Note that we crucially assume that the number of variables of φ is $\leq n$ instead of $= n$ in order to satisfy the inductive hypothesis in our (inductive) proof.

This theorem states that for any MLTL formula φ with well-defined interval bounds [27] and any trace π of length at least the computation length of φ, π satisfies φ iff the WEST regex `WEST_reg` φ matches π. The correctness of the top-level WEST algorithm took about 600 LOC in Isabelle/HOL compared to the 60 or so lines of proof sketches in the source material [17, Appendix III].[7]

4   Formalization Insights

Retrospectively viewing our formalization at a high level, we highlight a few notable points. First, our modular definitions did considerably streamline our correctness proofs. Many proofs have relatively similar structures, which helped guide the formalization at a high level. However, we also found that relatively short proofs in the source material became lengthy in the formalization, in part because they often split into many subcases. For example, the notion of a WEST regex matching a trace is intuitively simple, but the formalization used several helper functions. As another example, the proof of `WEST_and_correct` is approximately 15 lines of a proof sketch in the source material [17, Theorem 4]. However, our formal development took approximately 1800 LOC to state and prove this result level by level, starting from the correctness of the **and** operation on state regexes, then on trace regexes, and finally on WEST regexes. Although these proofs had structural similarities, subtle differences between the operators complicated the low-level details of the proofs; for instance, the option types of `WEST_and_state` required careful analysis in the correctness proofs.

Second, our formalization makes *all* details explicit, including details omitted in the source material. Many of our formal proofs are by induction; setting up the "right" inductive structure in a formal setting requires careful analysis that is often glossed over in source material. For instance, the top-level correctness theorem required making a mathematically implicit assumption on `num_vars` explicit. Setting up this assumption in the wrong way leads to an ineffective inductive structure. As another example, in the proof of `WEST_simp_correct`, we perform a tricky induction on the difference between the length of the input WEST regex and the output simplified WEST regex. Additionally, we are required to prove that all functions terminate. For many functions, Isabelle/HOL proves this automatically [28], but we occasionally ran into cases where we had to explicitly construct a measure to prove termination. For example, the `WEST_reg_aux` function and the `WEST_simp` function required such manual termination proofs. Intuitively, `WEST_reg_aux` recurses on all subformulas in NNF, converting subformulas to NNF as necessary; accordingly, we use a termination measure that is similar to the number of nodes in the abstract syntax tree (AST) of the formula, but weighs nodes that are not in NNF more heavily. This allows us to prove that `WEST_reg_aux` terminates, as this measure strictly decreases on every recursive call. Further, for `WEST_simp`, the length of the input list is not strictly decreasing, but the list of candidate pairs for simplification will be exhausted at some point,

---

[7] The results leading up to this top-level theorem required an additional $\approx$ 5300 LOC.

so we use a measure that combines the length of the input list with the length of remaining candidate pairs.

Overall, integrating `WEST_simp` into our formalization was rather involved. Our initial formalization did not include `WEST_simp`, but we ultimately realized that it is crucial for speed and thus also important for tool validation. While the modular nature of our formalization easily allowed us to add in this function to the algorithm, its correctness proofs were intricate. Similarly to `WEST_and`, we proved the correctness of `WEST_simp` level by level, totaling around 1300 LOC.

As a final interesting point, we found during our tool validation that `WEST_reg` and the (unverified) WEST tool sometimes produce trace regexes that differ only by a string of `S`'s at the end. In such cases, because these trace regexes have different length, our equivalence checking methods spuriously identify a mismatch. The WEST tool always produces trace regexes that have the same length as the computation length of the input formula, while `WEST_reg` does not.[8] To account for this, we define a function `simp_pad_WEST_reg` which pads trace regexes to this computation length (and then simplifies). We extend the top-level correctness theorem from `WEST_reg` to `simp_pad_WEST_reg`; in our experiments, we work with `simp_pad_WEST_reg` so as to eliminate these spurious mismatches.

5   Experiments

The functions `simp_pad_WEST_reg` and `naive_equivalence` are executable in Isabelle/HOL, and we use Isabelle/HOL's code generator [20] to export these functions to Haskell.[9] We choose Haskell both to facilitate our experimental setup and because the GHC compiler [33] produces reasonably fast native machine code. We use our code export to validate two versions of the WEST tool—the initial version of WEST [17], and also a more recent version that has been highly optimized [51]. We also compare the different implementations for speed. We run all of our experiments in WSL2 on a Windows machine with an 11th generation Intel Core i7 processor and 32GB of RAM. We use an unverified parsing script to transform input MLTL formulas into the format required by our code export.[10]

Previous Validation Efforts. The most recent (and fastest) version of WEST was validated against several MLTL tools [51]: ① the original version of WEST [17], ② the runtime verification engine R2U2 [43,24,23] ③ a direct C++ implementation of MLTL semantics [51], and ④ translating MLTL formulas to propositional logic [21] and applying a BDD based AllSAT solver. The validation works by analyzing, for each formula in the test suite, whether the trace

---

[8] This is because we implicitly treat shorter trace regexes to have all `S`'s at the end (recall our discussion of the `WEST_and_trace` operator in Sect. 3.1).

[9] Note that, although Isabelle/HOL's code generator is not yet fully verified, exporting a formalized function is more trustworthy than simply coding a function. Additionally, some work has considered verifying Isabelle's code generator [22].

[10] There has been some recent work [49] on improving support for verified parsing in Isabelle/HOL, so verifying this parsing step might be an interesting future direction.

set of regexes produced by WEST is equivalent to the set of satisfying traces produced by other tools. The equivalence checking is a crucial step performed between outputs that can be in different formats (depending on the output format of each tool). The test suite of 1662 MLTL formulas was designed to capture every possible combination of MLTL operators [17].

5.1 Verified Equivalence Checking

Our tool validation is set up to check the outputs of our verified implementation of WEST against the two existing implementations. For this, we need to be able to check equivalences between WEST regexes. It is not always enough to merely check set equality, as implementation differences can lead to different (but logically equivalent) outputs. For instance, the two WEST regexes $[[[S, S]]]$ and $[[[S, 1]], [[1, S]], [[0, 0]]]$ are equivalent, but `WEST_simp` does not simplify the second into the first. The order in which `WEST_simp` simplifies pairs of trace regexes within a WEST regex is what causes these differences.

Developing a fully verified and optimized equivalence checking algorithm is out of scope of our work, but we still wanted a lightweight trustworthy implementation of regex equivalence checking. Accordingly, we formalize a naive equivalence checking function for WEST regexes, called `naive_equivalence`. This function works by explicitly enumerating all the trace regexes that each WEST regex produces and then checking set equality.

We then prove the experimentally relevant direction of correctness: If two WEST regexes are equivalent under our (executable) naive equivalence checking function, then they are indeed equivalent under the (non-executable) mathematical definition. Formally, we have the following lemma:

```
lemma regex_equivalence_correct:
  fixes A B::"WEST_regex"
  shows "(naive_equivalence A B) ⟶ (∀π. match π A = match π B)"
```

The proof was approximately 1150 lines of code. Although establishing both directions of equivalence here (i.e, ⟷ instead of ⟶) is theoretically desirable, the direction we verify is the experimentally significant one, since we encounter no instances where `naive_equivalence` failed in our test suite. More specifically, `naive_equivalence` holds on all but 4 of the 1662 input formulas and times out (after 4 hours) on the remaining 4 formulas. Often the outputs are identical; for example, the Isabelle implementation and the optimized WEST tool produced identical WEST regexes on 1547 of the formulas. We additionally ran the previous (unverified) equivalence checking procedure, which succeeded on all of the formulas. Collectively, these results establish strong confidence in the correctness of the (unverified) WEST tools [17,51].

5.2 Speed Comparison

The original C++ version of WEST [17] performed string-based operations, and the optimized version of WEST takes advantage of highly parallelized computations by using bitsets [51]. Although fast performance is not our primary goal, preliminary experiments demonstrate how our formalized code compares to the two unverified versions of WEST. Overall, we find that the optimized version of WEST is fast (as expected). Our Isabelle implementation also performs quite

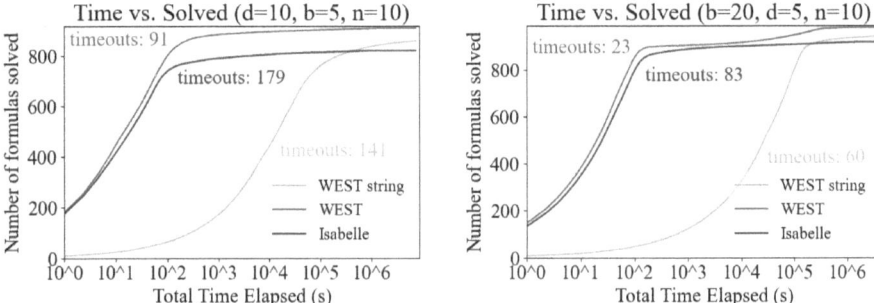

Fig. 4: Two cactus plots, each comparing the three WEST implementations on 1000 random formulas of varying nesting depth d, interval bounds b, and number of atomic propositions n. The number of total solved instances is shown on the y-axis, and the cumulative time taken is shown on the x-axis, with the number of timeouts labeled.

respectably; it is, in aggregate, close in performance to the optimized version of WEST. We perform extensive experiments to compare the performance of the three tools on large randomly generated benchmark sets. We use a script to generate random MLTL formulas [51], varying the parameters of the maximum depth and the maximum interval time bounds. Our results are in Fig. 4. As the primary focus of our work is tool validation, we do not envision our contribution as replacing the WEST tool, but its relative efficiency is encouraging nonetheless.

However, we did find that, on individual examples, our code export has somewhat unpredictable behavior (whereas the optimized version of WEST appears to be uniformly fast), and our code export seems to incur timeouts more frequently than the unverified WEST implementations. For example, in Fig. 5, we evaluate the speed of the three tools based on varying values of d, the depth of the formula, while fixing the number of atomic propositions at $n = 5$ and the maximum interval bound at $b = 2$. Here, we observe that the Isabelle implementation begins to timeout much more frequently than the other two tools when $d = 4$ and $d = 5$.

Additional results, including aggregate cactus plots on easier but larger test suites, an extension of Fig. 5 on higher values of formula depth d, and experiments where we vary the value of maximum interval bound b (instead of d), can be found in Appendix A of the full version of this paper [53].

6 Conclusion

Our work produces a third, open-source, freely available implementation of the WEST algorithm, this time *formally verified* [52]. Given the popularity of MLTL as a formal specification language for safety-critical applications [24,15,31,16,5],

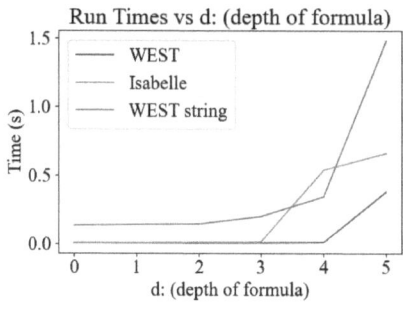
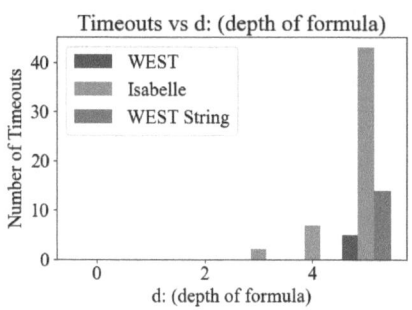

Fig. 5: Results for $n = 5$, $b = 2$, and varying values of d from 0 to 5, with a batch size of 300 formulas per value of d. The Isabelle implementation is faster than the unoptimized WEST tool on most values of d, but times out on many formulas for $d = 5$.

verifying significant algorithms like WEST, which facilitates MLTL specification, is well-justified. We build on an existing formalization of MLTL in Isabelle/HOL [27] to further develop the library of verified MLTL algorithms and properties, which could help facilitate future verified developments in this space. Our development validates the existing (unverified) WEST tool [17,51] on benchmarks from the literature, bringing us a step closer to validating other MLTL tools like R2U2 [40,23]. Though our primary focus was not on speed, the aggregate performance of our Isabelle-generated code is promising, and optimizing our formalization could be interesting future work. It would be particularly beneficial to further optimize (and verify the reverse direction of) our naive WEST regex equivalence checking, possibly using existing work [29] which verifies regex equivalence checking in a general setting. Verified parsing (to transform input formulas into the syntax required by our code export) would also be welcome. Additionally, a deeper analysis of the performance of the WEST tools and of our verified code on different classes of benchmarks could inform future verified tool generation efforts. For example, it would be interesting to experimentally compare a code export to some of the other languages supported by Isabelle/HOL, like SML and OCaml, to see if a different target language could help avoid timeouts. Importantly, our formalization of MLTL rewriting, equivalence checking, and regular expression manipulation could serve as a basis for formalizing similar utilities in logics like MTL and STL that extend MLTL.

Acknowledgments. Thanks to NSF CAREER Award CNS-1552934, NSF CCRI-2016592, and GRFP-2024364991 for supporting this work. We thank the anonymous TACAS reviewers as well as Alec Rosentrater and Laura Gamboa Guzman for their helpful feedback on the paper, and the TACAS artifact evaluators for their time.

References

1. Alur, R., Henzinger, T.A.: Real-time Logics: Complexity and Expressiveness. In: LICS. pp. 390–401. IEEE (1990)

2. Alur, R., Feder, T., Henzinger, T.A.: The Benefits of Relaxing Punctuality. In: Logrippo, L. (ed.) Proceedings of the Tenth Annual ACM Symposium on Principles of Distributed Computing, Montreal, Quebec, Canada, August 19-21, 1991. pp. 139–152. ACM (1991). https://doi.org/10.1145/112600.112613, https://doi.org/10.1145/112600.112613

3. Amjad, R., van Glabbeek, R., O'Connor, L.: Definitive set semantics for LTL3. Archive of Formal Proofs (August 2024), https://isa-afp.org/entries/LTL3_Semantics.html, Formal proof development

4. Anastasia Mavridou: Capturing and Analyzing Requirements with FRET. Presentation, nasa formal methods symposium, https://github.com/NASA-SW-VnV/fret, National Aeronautics and Space Agency, Pasadena, California, USA (May 2022)

5. Aurandt, A., Jones, P., Rozier, K.Y.: Runtime Verification Triggers Real-time, Autonomous Fault Recovery on the CySat-I. In: Proceedings of the 14th NASA Formal Methods Symposium (NFM 2022). Lecture Notes in Computer Science (LNCS), vol. 13260. Springer, Cham, Caltech, California, USA (May 2022). https://doi.org/10.1007/978-3-031-06773-0_45

6. Ballarin, C.: Locales and locale expressions in Isabelle/Isar. In: Berardi, S., Coppo, M., Damiani, F. (eds.) TYPES. LNCS, vol. 3085, pp. 34–50. Springer (2003). https://doi.org/10.1007/978-3-540-24849-1_3, https://doi.org/10.1007/978-3-540-24849-1_3

7. Ballarin, C.: Locales: A module system for mathematical theories. J. Autom. Reason. 52(2), 123–153 (2014). https://doi.org/10.1007/S10817-013-9284-7, https://doi.org/10.1007/s10817-013-9284-7

8. Basin, D.A., Dardinier, T., Hauser, N., Heimes, L., y Munive, J.J.H., Kaletsch, N., Krstic, S., Marsicano, E., Raszyk, M., Schneider, J., Tirore, D.L., Traytel, D., Zingg, S.: VeriMon: A formally verified monitoring tool. In: Seidl, H., Liu, Z., Pasareanu, C.S. (eds.) ICTAC. LNCS, vol. 13572, pp. 1–6. Springer (2022). https://doi.org/10.1007/978-3-031-17715-6_1, https://doi.org/10.1007/978-3-031-17715-6_1

9. Cavada, R., Cimatti, A., Dorigatti, M., Griggio, A., Mariotti, A., Micheli, A., Mover, S., Roveri, M., Tonetta, S.: The nuXmv symbolic model checker. In: Biere, A., Bloem, R. (eds.) CAV. LNCS, vol. 8559, pp. 334–342. Springer (2014). https://doi.org/10.1007/978-3-319-08867-9_22, https://doi.org/10.1007/978-3-319-08867-9_22

10. Chattopadhyay, A., Mamouras, K.: A Verified Online Monitor for Metric Temporal Logic with Quantitative Semantics. In: Runtime Verification: 20th International Conference, RV 2020, Los Angeles, CA, USA, October 6–9, 2020, Proceedings. p. 383–403. Springer-Verlag, Berlin, Heidelberg (2020). https://doi.org/10.1007/978-3-030-60508-7_21, https://doi.org/10.1007/978-3-030-60508-7_21

11. Chattopadhyay, A., Mamouras, K.: A verified online monitor for metric temporal logic with quantitative semantics. In: Deshmukh, J., Ničković, D. (eds.) Runtime Verification. pp. 383–403. Springer International Publishing, Cham (2020)

12. Conrad, E., Titolo, L., Giannakopoulou, D., Pressburger, T., Dutle, A.: A compositional proof framework for FRETish requirements. In: Popescu, A., Zdancewic, S. (eds.) CPP '22: 11th ACM SIGPLAN International Conference on Certified Programs and Proofs, Philadelphia, PA, USA, January 17 - 18, 2022. pp. 68–81. ACM (2022). https://doi.org/10.1145/3497775.3503685, https://doi.org/10.1145/3497775.3503685

13. Coquand, T., Siles, V.: A Decision Procedure for Regular Expression Equivalence in Type Theory. In: Jouannaud, J., Shao, Z. (eds.) CPP. LNCS, vol. 7086, pp. 119–134. Springer (2011). https://doi.org/10.1007/978-3-642-25379-9_11, https://doi.org/10.1007/978-3-642-25379-9_11

14. Coupet-Grimal, S.: An axiomatization of linear temporal logic in the calculus of inductive constructions. J. Log. Comput. **13**(6), 801–813 (2003). https://doi.org/10.1093/LOGCOM/13.6.801, https://doi.org/10.1093/logcom/13.6.801

15. Dabney, J.B., Badger, J.M., Rajagopal, P.: Adding a verification view for an autonomous real-time system architecture. In: Proceedings of SciTech Forum. p. Online. 2021-0566, AIAA (January 2021). https://doi.org/https://doi.org/10.2514/6.2021-0566

16. Dabney, J.B., Rajagopal, P., Badger, J.M.: Using assume-guarantee contracts for developmental verification of autonomous spacecraft. Flight Software Workshop (FSW) Online: https://www.youtube.com/watch?v=HFnn6TzblPg (February 2022)

17. Elwing, J., Gamboa-Guzman, L., Sorkin, J., Travesset, C., Wang, Z., Rozier, K.Y.: Mission-time LTL (MLTL) formula validation via regular expressions. In: Herber, P., Wijs, A. (eds.) iFM. LNCS, vol. 14300, pp. 279–301. Springer (2023). https://doi.org/10.1007/978-3-031-47705-8_15, https://doi.org/10.1007/978-3-031-47705-8_15

18. Esparza, J., Lammich, P., Neumann, R., Nipkow, T., Schimpf, A., Smaus, J.G.: A fully verified executable LTL model checker. Archive of Formal Proofs (May 2014), https://isa-afp.org/entries/CAVA_LTL_Modelchecker.html, Formal proof development

19. Giannakopoulou, D., Mavridou, A., Rhein, J., Pressburger, T., Schumann, J., Shi, N.: Formal requirements elicitation with FRET. In: International Working Conference on Requirements Engineering: Foundation for Software Quality (REFSQ-2020). No. ARC-E-DAA-TN77785 (2020)

20. Haftmann, F.: Code generation from specifications in higher-order logic. Ph.D. thesis, Technical University Munich (2009), http://mediatum2.ub.tum.de/node?id=886023

21. Hariharan, G., Jones, P.H., Rozier, K.Y., Wongpiromsarn, T.: Maximum satisfiability of Mission-time Linear Temporal Logic. In: Petrucci, L., Sproston, J. (eds.) FORMATS. LNCS, vol. 14138, pp. 86–104. Springer (2023). https://doi.org/10.1007/978-3-031-42626-1_6, https://doi.org/10.1007/978-3-031-42626-1_6

22. Hupel, L., Nipkow, T.: A Verified Compiler from Isabelle/HOL to CakeML. In: Ahmed, A. (ed.) ESOP. LNCS, vol. 10801, pp. 999–1026. Springer (2018). https://doi.org/10.1007/978-3-319-89884-1_35, https://doi.org/10.1007/978-3-319-89884-1_35

23. Johannsen, C., Jones, P., Kempa, B., Rozier, K.Y., Zhang, P.: R2U2 Version 3.0: Re-Imagining a Toolchain for Specification, Resource Estimation, and Optimized Observer Generation for Runtime Verification in Hardware and Software. In: Enea, C., Lal, A. (eds.) Computer Aided Verification. pp. 483–497. Springer Nature Switzerland, Cham (2023)

24. Kempa, B., Zhang, P., Jones, P.H., Zambreno, J., Rozier, K.Y.: Embedding Online Runtime Verification for Fault Disambiguation on Robonaut2. In: FORMATS. pp. 196–214. LNCS, Springer, Vienna, Austria (September 2020), http://research.temporallogic.org/papers/KZJZR20.pdf

25. Kessler, F.B.: nuXmv 1.1.0 (2016-05-10) Release Notes. https://es-static.fbk.eu/tools/nuxmv/downloads/NEWS.txt (2016)

26. Kosaian, K., Wang, Z., Sloan, E.: Mission-time linear temporal logic. Archive of Formal Proofs (January 2025), `https://isa-afp.org/entries/Mission_Time_LTL.html`, Formal proof development

27. Kosaian, K., Wang, Z., Sloan, E., Rozier, K.: Formalizing MLTL formula progression in Isabelle/HOL (2024), `https://arxiv.org/abs/2410.03465`

28. Krauss, A.: Automating Recursive Definitions and Termination Proofs in Higher-Order Logic. Ph.D. thesis, Technische Universität München (2009)

29. Krauss, A., Nipkow, T.: Proof Pearl: Regular Expression Equivalence and Relation Algebra. J. Autom. Reason. **49**(1), 95–106 (2012). `https://doi.org/10.1007/S10817-011-9223-4`, `https://doi.org/10.1007/s10817-011-9223-4`

30. Li, J., Vardi, M.Y., Rozier, K.Y.: Satisfiability Checking for Mission-Time LTL. In: Proceedings of 31st International Conference on Computer Aided Verification (CAV 2019). LNCS, Springer, New York, NY, USA (July 2019)

31. Luppen, Z., Jacks, M., Baughman, N., Hertz, B., Cutler, J., Lee, D.Y., Rozier, K.Y.: Elucidation and Analysis of Specification Patterns in Aerospace System Telemetry. In: Proceedings of the 14th NASA Formal Methods Symposium (NFM 2022). Lecture Notes in Computer Science (LNCS), vol. 13260. Springer, Cham, Caltech, California, USA (May 2022). `https://doi.org/10.1007/978-3-031-06773-0_28`

32. Maler, O., Nickovic, D.: Monitoring temporal properties of continuous signals. In: Formal Techniques, Modelling and Analysis of Timed and Fault-Tolerant Systems, pp. 152–166. Springer (2004)

33. Marlow, S., Jones, S.L.P.: The Glasgow Haskell Compiler (2012), `https://api.semanticscholar.org/CorpusID:35370`

34. NASA Technology Transfer Program: FRET : Formal Requirements Elicitation Tool (ARC-18066-1). Online: `https://software.nasa.gov/software/ARC-18066-1` (2024)

35. Perez, I.: Runtime verification with ogma. In: Invited Talk to University of California (2023)

36. Perez, I., Goodloe, A.: OGMA. `https://github.com/nasa/ogma` (2021)

37. Perez, I., Mavridou, A., Pressburger, T., Goodloe, A., Giannakopoulou, D.: Automated translation of natural language requirements to runtime monitors. In: Fisman, D., Rosu, G. (eds.) Tools and Algorithms for the Construction and Analysis of Systems. pp. 387–395. Springer International Publishing, Cham (2022)

38. Pnueli, A., Arons, T.: TLPVS: A PVS-based LTL verification system. In: Dershowitz, N. (ed.) Verification: Theory and Practice, Essays Dedicated to Zohar Manna on the Occasion of His 64th Birthday. LNCS, vol. 2772, pp. 598–625. Springer (2003). `https://doi.org/10.1007/978-3-540-39910-0_26`, `https://doi.org/10.1007/978-3-540-39910-0_26`

39. Raszyk, M., Basin, D., Traytel, D.: Multi-head monitoring of metric dynamic logic. In: International Symposium on Automated Technology for Verification and Analysis. pp. 233–250. Springer (2020)

40. Reinbacher, T., Rozier, K.Y., Schumann, J.: Temporal-logic based runtime observer pairs for system health management of real-time systems. In: Proceedings of the 20th International Conference on Tools and Algorithms for the Construction and Analysis of Systems (TACAS). Lecture Notes in Computer Science (LNCS), vol. 8413, pp. 357–372. Springer-Verlag (April 2014)

41. Roohi, N., Viswanathan, M.: Revisiting MITL to fix decision procedures. In: Dillig, I., Palsberg, J. (eds.) VMCAI. LNCS, vol. 10747, pp. 474–494. Springer (2018). `https://doi.org/10.1007/978-3-319-73721-8_22`, `https://doi.org/10.1007/978-3-319-73721-8_22`

42. Rozier, K.Y.: Specification: The biggest bottleneck in formal methods and autonomy. In: Proceedings of 8th Working Conference on Verified Software: Theories, Tools, and Experiments (VSTTE 2016). LNCS, vol. 9971, pp. 1–19. Springer-Verlag, Toronto, ON, Canada (July 2016). https://doi.org/10.1007/978-3-319-48869-1_2

43. Rozier, K.Y., Schumann, J.: R2U2: Tool Overview. In: Proceedings of International Workshop on Competitions, Usability, Benchmarks, Evaluation, and Standardisation for Runtime Verification Tools (RV-CUBES). vol. 3, pp. 138–156. Kalpa Publications, Seattle, WA, USA (September 2017), https://easychair.org/publications/paper/Vncw

44. Schimpf, A., Lammich, P.: Converting linear-time temporal logic to generalized Büchi automata. Archive of Formal Proofs (May 2014), https://isa-afp.org/entries/LTL_to_GBA.html, Formal proof development

45. Seidl, B., Sickert, S.: A compositional and unified translation of LTL into ω-automata. Archive of Formal Proofs (April 2019), https://isa-afp.org/entries/LTL_Master_Theorem.html, Formal proof development

46. Sickert, S.: Converting linear temporal logic to deterministic (generalized) Rabin automata. Archive of Formal Proofs (September 2015), https://isa-afp.org/entries/LTL_to_DRA.html, Formal proof development

47. Sickert, S.: Linear temporal logic. Archive of Formal Proofs (March 2016), https://isa-afp.org/entries/LTL.html, Formal proof development

48. Sickert, S.: An efficient normalisation procedure for linear temporal logic: Isabelle/HOL formalisation. Archive of Formal Proofs (May 2020), https://isa-afp.org/entries/LTL_Normal_Form.html, Formal proof development

49. Tilscher, S., Wimmer, S.: LL(1) parser generator. Archive of Formal Proofs (May 2024), https://isa-afp.org/entries/LL1_Parser.html, formal proof development

50. Titolo, L., Conrad, E., Giannakopoulou, D., Pressburger, T., Dutle, A.: FRET Proof Framework. https://lauratitolo.github.io/project/fret-proof-framework/ (2022)

51. Wang, Z., Gamboa-Guzman, L.P., Rozier, K.Y.: WEST: Interactive Validation of Mission-time Linear Temporal Logic (MLTL) (2024), https://temporallogic.org/research/WEST/

52. Wang, Z., Kosaian, K.: Mission-time linear temporal logic to regular expressions. Archive of Formal Proofs (January 2025), https://isa-afp.org/entries/Mission_Time_LTL_to_Regular_Expression.html, Formal proof development

53. Wang, Z., Kosaian, K., Rozier, K.Y.: Formally verifying a transformation from MLTL formulas to regular expressions (2025), https://arxiv.org/abs/2501.17444

54. Wu, C., Zhang, X., Urban, C.: A formalisation of the Myhill-Nerode theorem based on regular expressions (proof pearl). In: van Eekelen, M., Geuvers, H., Schmaltz, J., Wiedijk, F. (eds.) Interactive Theorem Proving. pp. 341–356. Springer Berlin Heidelberg, Berlin, Heidelberg (2011)

55. Zhang, P., Aurandt, A.A., Dureja, R., Jones, P.H., Rozier, K.Y.: Model predictive runtime verification for cyber-physical systems with real-time deadlines. In: Petrucci, L., Sproston, J. (eds.) Formal Modeling and Analysis of Timed Systems - 21st International Conference, FORMATS 2023, Antwerp, Belgium, September 19-21, 2023, Proceedings. Lecture Notes in Computer Science, vol. 14138, pp. 158–180. Springer (2023). https://doi.org/10.1007/978-3-031-42626-1_10, https://doi.org/10.1007/978-3-031-42626-1_10

56. Zhuchko, E., Veanes, M., Ebner, G.: Lean formalization of extended regular expression matching with lookarounds. In: Proceedings of the 13th ACM SIGPLAN International Conference on Certified Programs and Proofs. p. 118–131. CPP 2024, Association for Computing Machinery, New York, NY, USA (2024). `https://doi.org/10.1145/3636501.3636959`, `https://doi.org/10.1145/3636501.3636959`

Learning Real-Time One-Counter Automata Using Polynomially Many Queries

Prince Mathew[1]([✉]) [iD], Vincent Penelle[2], and A. V. Sreejith[1]

[1] Indian Institute of Technology Goa, Ponda, India
{prince, sreejithav}@iitgoa.ac.in
[2] Univ. Bordeaux, CNRS, Bordeaux INP, LaBRI, UMR 5800, 33400 Talence, France
vincent.penelle@u-bordeaux.fr

Abstract. In this paper, we introduce a novel method for active learning of deterministic real-time one-counter automata (DROCA). The existing techniques for learning a DROCA rely on observing the behaviour of the DROCA up to exponentially large counter values. Our algorithm eliminates this need and requires only a polynomial number of queries. Additionally, our method differs from existing techniques as we learn a minimal counter-synchronous DROCA, resulting in much smaller counter-examples on equivalence queries. Learning a minimal counter-synchronous DROCA cannot be done in polynomial time unless $P = NP$, even in the case of visibly one-counter automata. We use a SAT solver to overcome this difficulty. The solver is used to compute a minimal separating DFA from a given set of positive and negative samples.
We prove that the equivalence of two counter-synchronous DROCAs can be checked significantly faster than that of general DROCAs. For visibly one-counter automata, we have discovered an even faster algorithm for equivalence checking. We implemented the proposed learning algorithm and tested it on randomly generated DROCAs. Our evaluations show that the proposed method outperforms the existing techniques on the test set.

Keywords: One-counter automata · Active learning · SAT solver.

1 Introduction

The problem of identifying a model from a given dataset is an area of interest in various fields of computer science, like formal verification and machine learning. However, inferring the right model from labelled samples is challenging. For instance, finding a minimal separating DFA – a DFA that accepts a given set of positive samples and rejects a given set of negative samples – is known to be NP-complete [9]. Angluin [2] introduced an active learning framework called L^*, involving a learner and a teacher. The learner can ask membership and equivalence queries to the teacher. Angluin showed that DFA can be learnt in polynomial time with respect to the size of the minimal DFA.

This document contains numerous links to enhance its usability. Terms and concepts defined within the document are directly linked to their definitions as hyperlinks.

© The Author(s) 2025
A. Gurfinkel and M. Heule (Eds.): TACAS 2025, LNCS 15696, pp. 276–294, 2025.
https://doi.org/10.1007/978-3-031-90643-5_14

In this paper, we are interested in active learning of a deterministic real-time one-counter automaton (DROCA). These are finite-state machines equipped with a non-negative integer counter that can be incremented or decremented on reading an input symbol. The counter adds expressive power, enabling a DROCA to recognise certain non-regular context-free languages (e.g., $\{a^n b^n \mid n > 0\}$). However, this added power also introduces significant challenges in learning.

Our contribution. We introduce the notion of counter-synchronous DROCAs – two DROCAs are counter-synchronous if, for any word, the counter value reached on reading that word is the same on both machines. Given two DROCAs with K states, we give an $\mathcal{O}(K^6)$ time[4] algorithm that solves the following two problems (see Theorem 3): (1) check if they are counter-synchronous, and (2) check whether they are equivalent, if they are counter-synchronous. For visibly one-counter automata (DROCA where the input alphabet determines the counter-actions), we have devised an even faster $\mathcal{O}(\alpha(K^3)K^3)$ algorithm for checking equivalence (see Theorem 4).

The main result of this paper is a novel approach for active learning of DROCAs. However, the active learning framework differs from that introduced by Angluin in a few crucial aspects (see Section 4). Similar to the work by Bruyère et al. [4], we use an additional query called counter value query. This allows the learner to ask for the counter value reached on reading a word in the DROCA. Furthermore, the learner has access to a minimal synchronous-equivalence query on the DROCA. The teacher returns true for an equivalence query if the learnt DROCA is counter-synchronous and equivalent to the teacher's DROCA. Otherwise, it returns a minimal word that violates this property.

In this framework, we give an algorithm that learns a minimal counter-synchronous DROCA. A key innovation in our approach is the use of a SAT solver for solving the NP-hard problem of finding a minimal separating DFA from a set of positive and negative samples. The solver, in conjunction with a modified version of L*, learns a characteristic DFA (see Definition 6). Subsequently, we use this characteristic DFA to construct a minimal counter-synchronous DROCA. Our algorithm requires only a polynomial number of queries to the SAT solver and the teacher. Consequently, our algorithm is in $\mathsf{P^{NP}}$.

Justification for using a SAT solver. We argue that unless $\mathsf{P} = \mathsf{NP}$, learning a minimal visibly one-counter automaton (VOCA) cannot be done in polynomial time. This follows from the fact that minimisation of VOCA can be reduced to learning a minimal VOCA. Furthermore, It was pointed out by Michaliszyn and Otop [15] that minimising VOCA is NP-complete. This follows from the result by Gauwin et al.[8] that minimising VPDA is NP-complete.

Comparison with existing methods. From a complexity theoretical perspective, DROCAs can be learned with polynomial space and exponential time with a straightforward brute-force approach. This method entails enumerating all conceivable DROCAs, starting with a one-state DROCA, and submitting equivalence

---

[4] For all practical applications, one can consider α as a constant (see Section 3).

queries for each. This approach, without a doubt, entails an exponential number of equivalence queries. All existing algorithms for learning DROCAs, including the algorithm by Fahmy and Roos [7], the algorithm by Bruyère et al. [4], and the algorithm for learning VOCAs by Neider and Löding [17] require exponential time and an exponential number of queries with respect to the number of states of a minimal DROCA recognising the language. All these algorithms share the idea of learning the initial portion of an infinite behavioural graph and then seek to identify a repetitive structure in it. However, in the worst-case scenario, this repetitive structure becomes apparent only after learning an exponentially large portion of the graph. In this case, the learnt DROCA will be exponentially large. Consequently, learning this exponential-sized behaviour necessitates exponentially many queries. Moreover, the equivalence queries also run on these exponentially large DROCAs, making it even more infeasible. Bruyère et al. [4] were the first to pursue a practical learning application of learning DROCAs. However, due to the difficulty in checking the equivalence of DROCAs, they had to use a weaker form of equivalence query that checks for counter-examples up to some random counter value. Their equivalence check might say two non-equivalent DROCAs are equivalent if the minimal counter-example is large.

Our approach (MinOCA) differs fundamentally from these existing methods by eliminating the need to observe the automaton's behaviour up to exponentially large counter values. We propose an algorithm for learning DROCAs using only a polynomial number of queries. This sets it apart from existing techniques that require exponentially many queries for learning. One significant bottleneck in learning DROCAs is the equivalence test by the teacher. Given two DROCAs with number of states less than some $K \in \mathbb{N}$, the equivalence check takes $\mathcal{O}(K^{26})$ time[5]. This is impractical for real-world applications. To mitigate this, we use the synchronous-equivalence check that runs in $\mathcal{O}(K^6)$ time. We obtain significantly smaller counter-examples while using this equivalence check. Our equivalence queries are also on models whose size is less than or equal to a minimal counter-synchronised DROCA. Furthermore, unlike existing techniques that learn exponentially large DROCAs, our algorithm always learns an equivalent counter-synchronous DROCA with the minimal number of states.

Experiments. We evaluate an implementation of our algorithm and compare the results obtained with the existing technique by Bruyère et al. [4]. Experiments were conducted on randomly generated DROCAs with number of states ranging from 2 to 15 and the input alphabet size varying from 2 to 5. The results indicate that the proposed method outperforms the existing one [4].

The remainder of this paper is organised as follows: Section 2 gives the definitions and preliminaries. Section 3 gives equivalence results of counter-synchronised DROCAs. Section 4 details our learning algorithm for DROCAs, Section 5 covers the implementation details and presents our experimental results. Finally, Section 6 summarises our work and suggests future research directions.

---

[5] This polynomial is derived from the algorithm given in [3].

2   Definitions and Preliminaries

For any finite set S, $|S|$ denotes its cardinality. Non-negative numbers are denoted by $\mathbb{N}$, and $[i, j]$ denote the interval $\{i, i + 1, \ldots, j\} \subseteq \mathbb{N}$. For any $d \in \mathbb{N}$, the sign of d (denoted by $sign(d)$) is defined as $sign(d) = 0$ if $d = 0$ and is 1 otherwise. Let $w = a_0 a_1 a_2 \ldots a_n \in \Sigma^*$. For $j, k \in [0, n]$, with $j < k$, we use $w[j]$ to denote the letter a_j and $w_{[j \ldots k]}$ to denote the factor $a_j a_{j+1} \cdots a_k$.

Definition 1. *A deterministic real-time one-counter automaton* (DROCA) $\mathcal{A} = (Q, \Sigma, q_0, \delta_0, \delta_1, F)$, *where Q is a finite nonempty set of states, Σ is the input alphabet, $q_0 \in Q$ is the initial state, $\delta_0 : Q \times \Sigma \to Q \times \{0, +1\}$ and $\delta_1 : Q \times \Sigma \to Q \times \{0, +1, -1\}$ are the transition functions, and $F \subseteq Q$ is the set of final states.*

We use $|\mathcal{A}|$ to denote the size of $\mathcal{A}$, which we consider to be $|Q|$. A configuration c of a DROCA is a pair $(q, n) \in Q \times \mathbb{N}$, where $q \in Q$ denotes the current state and $n \in \mathbb{N}$ is the counter value. The configuration $c_0 = (q_0, 0)$ is called the *initial configuration* of $\mathcal{A}$. Let $p, q \in Q, n \in \mathbb{N}, e \in \{-1, 0, +1\}$ and $a \in \Sigma$. A *transition* between two configurations (p, n) and $(q, n + e)$ on the symbol a is defined, if $\delta_{sign(n)}(p, a) = (q, e)$. We use $(p, n) \xrightarrow{a} (q, n + e)$ to denote this. A run on a word $w = a_1 \ldots a_n$ from a configuration (p_1, m_1) is the sequence of transitions $(p_1, m_1) \xrightarrow{a_1} (p_2, m_2) \xrightarrow{a_2} (p_3, m_3) \xrightarrow{a_3} \ldots \xrightarrow{a_{n-1}} (p_n, m_n)$ where $p_i \in Q$ and m_is are counter values. In this case, we denote the run by $(p_1, m_1) \xrightarrow{w} (p_n, m_n)$. Note that the counter values always stay non-negative, implying a decrement is not permitted from a configuration with zero counter value.

Let $q \in Q$, $n \in \mathbb{N}$, and $w \in \Sigma^*$ with $(q_0, 0) \xrightarrow{w} (q, n)$. We use $\mathsf{ce}_\mathcal{A}(w) = n$ to denote the counter value reached on reading w from the initial configuration. We call $\mathsf{ce}_\mathcal{A}(w)$ the *counter-effect* of w. We denote by $height_\mathcal{A}(w)$ the maximal counter-effect of the prefixes of w in $\mathcal{A}$. We drop the subscript $\mathcal{A}$ when the DROCA under consideration is evident. $\mathcal{A}$ is deterministic (resp. complete) if, for any word w, there is at most (resp. at least) one run on w starting from any configuration. We say that a word w is accepted by $\mathcal{A}$ if and only if $(q_0, 0) \xrightarrow{w} (q_f, m)$ for some $q_f \in F$ and $m \in \mathbb{N}$. The language of $\mathcal{A}$, denoted by $\mathcal{L}(\mathcal{A})$, is the set of all words accepted by $\mathcal{A}$. For convenience, we use $\mathcal{A}(w) = 1$ if $w \in \mathcal{L}(\mathcal{A})$ and $\mathcal{A}(w) = 0$ otherwise. Two DROCAs $\mathcal{A}$ and $\mathcal{B}$ are *equivalent* if $\mathcal{L}(\mathcal{A}) = \mathcal{L}(\mathcal{B})$.

There are no ϵ-transitions in a DROCA. We consider only complete DROCAs in this paper. Every incomplete DROCA can be made complete without changing its language by directing all the undefined transitions to a new non-final sink state.

Definition 2. *We say that two DROCAs $\mathcal{A}$ and $\mathcal{B}$ are* counter-synchronised *if for all $w \in \Sigma^*$, $\mathsf{ce}_\mathcal{A}(w) = \mathsf{ce}_\mathcal{B}(w)$.*

3   Equivalence of Counter-Synchronised DROCAs

The equivalence of DROCAs was shown to be in NL by Böhm and Göller [3]. They show that there exists a $\mathcal{O}(K^{26})$ length word that distinguishes two non-equivalent DROCAs of size K. However, this is not suitable for practical applications.

We give an efficient $\mathcal{O}(K^6)$ algorithm to check the equivalence of counter-synchronised DROCAs. If two DROCAs are not counter-synchronised, then our algorithm outputs the smallest word for which they reach different counter values. If they are counter-synchronised and not equivalent, then our algorithm outputs the smallest word that is accepted by one and rejected by the other. In both these cases, the length of the counter-example is $\mathcal{O}(K^5)$.

In Theorem 4, we can treat α as a constant since $\alpha(j) \leq 4$ for all $j < 2^{1000}$ (see [1]). Hopcroft and Karp [11] showed that equivalence checking of two DFAs of size n can be done in $\mathcal{O}(\alpha(n)n)$ time.

Theorem 3. *Let $\mathcal{A}$ and $\mathcal{B}$ be DROCAs where $|\mathcal{A}|, |\mathcal{B}| \leq K$. If $\mathcal{A}$ is not counter-synchronised and equivalent to $\mathcal{B}$, then there is a minimal word w where $|w| \leq 2K^5$, $height_\mathcal{A}(w)$, $height_\mathcal{B}(w) \leq K^4$, and either $ce_\mathcal{A}(w) \neq ce_\mathcal{B}(w)$ or $\mathcal{A}(w) \neq \mathcal{B}(w)$. There is an $\mathcal{O}(K^6)$ time algorithm to output this word if it exists.*

sketch. Let $\mathcal{A}$ and $\mathcal{B}$ be counter-synchronous but not equivalent. The equivalence of $\mathcal{A}$ and $\mathcal{B}$ reduces to reachability in their product DROCA. From [5], the height of a minimal word that reaches a configuration is K^4 for a DROCA of size K^2.

Let $\mathcal{A}$ and $\mathcal{B}$ be not counter-synchronous and w be the minimal word where $ce_\mathcal{A}(w) \neq ce_\mathcal{B}(w)$. Let $w = w_1 a$ for some w_1 and $a \in \Sigma$. Since w is minimal, $ce_\mathcal{A}(w') = ce_\mathcal{B}(w')$ for all prefixes of w' of w_1. The synchronous run of w_1 can be seen as the run of a DROCA with K^2 states. From [5], $height_\mathcal{A}(w_1) \leq K^4$.

In both cases, it suffices to search for words of height less than K^4. We construct DFAs of size K^5 corresponding to the configuration graph of $\mathcal{A}$ and $\mathcal{B}$ up to counter value K^4. We conclude by doing a DFA equivalence check.   □

A visibly one-counter automaton (VOCA) is a (DROCA) where the input alphabet is $\Sigma = (\Sigma_+, \Sigma_-, \Sigma_0)$. The counter value is incremented (resp. decremented, not changed) on reading a symbol from Σ_+ (resp. Σ_-, Σ_0). Note that VOCAs over the same alphabet are counter-synchronous by definition as the word itself defines the counter value reached. For VOCAs, we give a faster $\mathcal{O}(\alpha(K^3)K^3)$ time algorithm for equivalence checking using ideas from [14].

Theorem 4. *Let $\mathcal{A}$ and $\mathcal{B}$ be VOCAs where $|\mathcal{A}|, |\mathcal{B}| \leq K$. If $\mathcal{A}$ and $\mathcal{B}$ are not equivalent, then there is a word w where $A(w) \neq B(w)$, $|w| \leq 4K(K + K^2)$, and $height_\mathcal{A}(w) \leq 2(K + K^2)$. An $\mathcal{O}(\alpha(K^3)K^3)$ algorithm can find this w if it exists.*

Proof. Let $\mathcal{A} = (P, \Sigma, p_\iota, \delta_0^1, \delta_1^1, F_1)$ and $\mathcal{B} = (Q, \Sigma, q_\iota, \delta_0^2, \delta_1^2, F_2)$ be two non-equivalent VOCAs. Let $P = \{p_1, \ldots, p_{|\mathcal{A}|}\}$ and $Q = \{q_1, \ldots, q_{|\mathcal{B}|}\}$. For any word w, $ce_\mathcal{A}(w) = ce_\mathcal{B}(w)$. Let $ce(w)$ denote this value. Similary, let $height(w)$ denote $height_\mathcal{A}(w) = height_\mathcal{B}(w)$. For states $p_i \in P$ and $q_j \in Q$, we define the row vector $\mathbf{x}_{(p_i, q_j)} \in \{0, 1\}^{|\mathcal{A}|+|\mathcal{B}|}$ as: $\mathbf{x}_{(p_i, q_j)}[k] = 1$ if and only if $k = i$ or $k = |\mathcal{A}|+j$. We also define the row vector $\boldsymbol{\eta} \in \{-1, 0, 1\}^{|\mathcal{A}|+|\mathcal{B}|}$ where $\boldsymbol{\eta}[k] = 1$ if $k \leq |\mathcal{A}|$ and $p_k \in F_1$, $\boldsymbol{\eta}[k] = -1$, if $k > |\mathcal{A}|$ and $q_{k-|\mathcal{A}|} \in F_2$, and $\boldsymbol{\eta}[k] = 0$ otherwise. Therefore, $\mathbf{x}_{(p,q)}\boldsymbol{\eta}^\top \neq 0$, if exactly one among p and q is a final state.

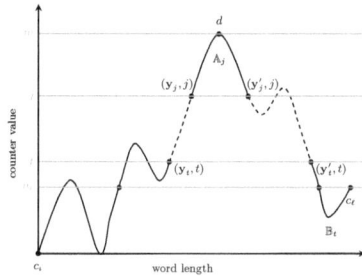

Fig. 1: The figure shows the synchronous run of a word on two VOCAs such that it reaches a final state in one VOCA and a non-final state in the other. The dashed line denotes the part of the synchronous run that can be removed.

We consider the synchronous run of $\mathcal{A}$ and $\mathcal{B}$. A configuration pair of this synchronous run is $(\mathbf{x}_{(p,q)}, n)$ where $p \in P, q \in Q$, and $n \in \mathbb{N}$. The initial configuration pair is $c_\iota = (\mathbf{x}_{(p_\iota, q_\iota)}, 0)$. Given two configuration pairs $c_1 = (\mathbf{x}_{(p,q)}, n)$ and $c_2 = (\mathbf{x}_{(p',q')}, m)$, $c_1 \xrightarrow{u} c_2$ denotes $(p, n) \xrightarrow{u} (p', m)$ and $(q, n) \xrightarrow{u} (q', m)$. The transition matrix on u from c_1 is $\mathbb{M} \in \{0, 1\}^{(|\mathcal{A}| + |\mathcal{B}|)^2}$ where $\mathbb{M}[i, j] = 1$ if and only if $(p_i, n) \xrightarrow{u} (p_j, m)$ or $(q_{i - |\mathcal{A}|}, n) \xrightarrow{u} (q_{j - |\mathcal{A}|}, m)$. Hence, $\mathbf{x}_{(p,q)} \mathbb{M} = \mathbf{x}_{(p',q')}$. Claims 1 to 3 follow.

Claim 1. *For any $p, p' \in P$, $q, q' \in Q$ and word w, the transition matrix of w from $(\mathbf{x}_{(p,q)}, n)$ is the same as the transition matrix of w from $(\mathbf{x}_{(p',q')}, n)$.*

Claim 2. *Let w be such that $ce(w') > 0$ for all prefixes w' of w. Then, the transition matrix of w from $(\mathbf{x}_{(p,q)}, n)$ is the same as the transition matrix of w from $(\mathbf{x}_{(p',q')}, m)$ for any $p, p' \in P$ and $q, q' \in Q$ and $m, n > 0$.*

Claim 3. *Any set of $|\mathcal{A}|^2 + |\mathcal{B}|^2 + 1$ transition matrices is linearly dependent.*

Let w be a minimal word such that $\mathcal{A}(w) \neq \mathcal{B}(w)$. Let $c_\ell = (\mathbf{x}_\ell, n_\ell)$ be such that $c_\iota \xrightarrow{w} c_\ell$. Hence, $\mathbf{x}_\ell \boldsymbol{\eta}^\top \neq 0$. Note that there is no configuration pair that repeats during the run of w. Otherwise, we can remove the run between the repetitions to get a shorter word. This will contradict the minimality of w.

Claim 4. *$height(w) \leq n_\ell + |\mathcal{A}|^2 + |\mathcal{B}|^2$.*

Proof. Assume for contradiction that $height(w) = m$ and $m > n_\ell + |\mathcal{A}|^2 + |\mathcal{B}|^2$. There is a factorisation of $w = w_1 w_2$ such that $c_\iota \xrightarrow{w_1} (\mathbf{z}, m) \xrightarrow{w_2} c_\ell$. For an $i \in [n_\ell, m]$, let $(\mathbf{y}_i, i)$ (resp. $(\mathbf{y}'_i, i)$) be the configuration pair where the counter value i is encountered for the last (resp. first) time during the run of w_1 (resp. w_2). Let $\mathbb{A}_i$ and $\mathbb{B}_i$ denote the transition matrices where $\mathbf{y}_i \mathbb{A}_i = \mathbf{y}'_i$ and $\mathbf{y}'_i \mathbb{B}_i = \mathbf{x}_\ell$. Let $w = x_i y_i z_i$ where $c_\iota \xrightarrow{x_i} (\mathbf{y}_i, i) \xrightarrow{y_i} (\mathbf{y}'_i, i) \xrightarrow{z_i} c_\ell$. See Figure 1. Consider the matrices $\mathbb{A}_{m-1}, \mathbb{A}_{m-2}, \ldots, \mathbb{A}_{n_\ell}$ in order. From Claim 3, there exists $t \in [n_\ell, m - 1]$ where $\mathbb{A}_t$ is linearly dependent on $\mathbb{A}_{m-1}, \cdots, \mathbb{A}_{t+1}$. Since $\mathbf{y}_t \mathbb{A}_t \mathbb{B}_t \boldsymbol{\eta}^\top \neq 0$, $\mathbf{y}_t (r_{t+1} \mathbb{A}_{t+1} + \cdots + r_{m-1} \mathbb{A}_{m-1}) \mathbb{B}_t \boldsymbol{\eta}^\top \neq 0$ for integers $r_{t+1}, \ldots, r_{m-1}$. Hence there is a $j > t$ where $\mathbf{y}_t \mathbb{A}_j \mathbb{B}_t \boldsymbol{\eta}^\top \neq 0$. We show $x_t y_j z_t$ is accepted exactly by one of $\mathcal{A}$ and $\mathcal{B}$ contradicting minimality of w. It suffices to show $c_\iota \xrightarrow{x_t} (\mathbf{y}_t, t) \xrightarrow{y_j} (\mathbf{y}_t \mathbb{A}_j, t) \xrightarrow{z_t} (\mathbf{y}_t \mathbb{A}_j \mathbb{B}_t, n_\ell)$. From Claim 2, the transition matrix of y_j from $(\mathbf{y}_t, t)$ is $\mathbb{A}_j$ and from Claim 1, the transition matrix of z_t from $(\mathbf{y}_t \mathbb{A}_j, t)$ is $\mathbb{B}_t$. $\square_{Claim:4}$

Claim 5. $n_\ell \leq |\mathcal{A}| + |\mathcal{B}|$.

Proof. Assume for contradiction that $n_\ell > |\mathcal{A}| + |\mathcal{B}|$. For $i \in [1, n_\ell]$, let $(\mathbf{z}_i, i)$ denote the configuration pair where counter value i is encountered the last time during the run of w. Let $w = x_i z_i$ where $c_\iota \xrightarrow{x_i} (\mathbf{z}_i, i) \xrightarrow{z_i} c_\ell$ and $\mathbb{C}_i$ be such that $\mathbf{z}_i \mathbb{C}_i = \mathbf{x}_\ell$. From the fundamental theorem of vector spaces, there exists $t \leq (|\mathcal{A}| + |\mathcal{B}|) + 1$ such that $\mathbf{z}_t$ is a linear combination of $\mathbf{z}_1, \ldots, \mathbf{z}_{t-1}$. Since $\mathbf{z}_t \mathbb{C}_t \boldsymbol{\eta}^\top \neq 0$, there exists $j < t$ such that $\mathbf{z}_j \mathbb{C}_t \boldsymbol{\eta}^\top \neq 0$. From Claim 2, the transition matrix of z_t from $(\mathbf{z}_j, j)$ is $\mathbb{C}_t$. The word $x_j z_t$ contradicts the minimality of w. $\square_{Claim:5}$

Let $\mathsf{K} \in \mathbb{N}$ such that $|\mathcal{A}|, |\mathcal{B}| < \mathsf{K}$. From Claim 4 and Claim 5, we get that $height(w) \leq 2(\mathsf{K} + \mathsf{K}^2)$. Similar to that in Theorem 3, we reduce the problem of finding the distinguishing word to equivalence check of DFAs of size $\mathcal{O}(\mathsf{K}^3)$. $\square$

4   Learning DROCAs

In this section, we give an L*-like algorithm for active learning of DROCAs using polynomially many queries with the help of a SAT solver. In this framework, we have a *learner* and a *teacher*. The learner aims to construct a DROCA that recognises the same language as the teacher's DROCA (call it $\mathcal{A}$). The teacher answers the following types of queries by the learner.

- membership queries $\mathsf{MQ}_\mathcal{A}$: the learner provides a word $w \in \Sigma^*$. The teacher returns 1 if $w \in \mathcal{L}(\mathcal{A})$, and 0 if $w \notin \mathcal{L}(\mathcal{A})$.
- counter value queries $\mathsf{CV}_\mathcal{A}$: the learner asks the counter value reached on reading word w. The teacher returns the counter value. i.e., $\mathsf{ce}_\mathcal{A}(w)$.
- minimal synchronous-equivalence queries $\mathsf{MSQ}_\mathcal{A}$: the learner asks whether a DROCA $\mathcal{C}$ is equivalent and counter-synchronous to $\mathcal{A}$. The teacher returns *yes* if $\mathcal{C}$ and $\mathcal{A}$ are counter-synchronous and equivalent. Otherwise, the teacher provides a minimal counter-example $z \in \Sigma^*$ such that $\mathcal{C}(z) \neq \mathcal{A}(z)$ or $\mathsf{ce}_\mathcal{A}(z) \neq \mathsf{ce}_\mathcal{C}(z)$.

The requirement for the teacher to return a counter-example z such that the counter values reached on reading z in the teachers and learners DROCAs are different can be removed. But in that case, we have to use the equivalence check for DROCAs (not necessarily counter-synchronous). The number of queries needed will be polynomial in the length of the minimal counter-example that distinguishes two DROCAs. Including this additional condition allows the use of the counter-synchronous equivalence check (see Theorem 3), which is much faster. The assumption of the teacher returning a minimal counter-example can be removed if we use partial-equivalence queries. A *partial-equivalence query* takes two DROCAs and a limit as inputs and determines whether the two DROCAs are equivalent for all words whose length does not exceed the limit. If they are not, then it returns a distinguishing word whose length is less than the limit. Neider and Löding [17] and Bruyère et al. [4] used partial-equivalence queries to learn the behaviour of DROCAs up to a certain counter value. One can simulate the teacher returning a minimal counter-example by a polynomial number of partial-equivalence queries. Similarly, a partial-equivalence query can be replaced with an equivalence query that returns a minimal counter-example.

		ce	ϵ		a	
			$Memb$	$Actions$	$Memb$	$Actions$
$\mathcal{P}$	ϵ	0	0	$(0,+1,+1)$	0	$(1,+1,-1)$
	a	1	0	$(1,+1,-1)$	0	$(1,+1,-1)$
	ab	0	0	$(0,0,+1)$	1	$(0,+1,+1)$
	aba	0	1	$(0,+1,+1)$	0	$(1,+1,+1)$
	b	1	0	$(1,+1,+1)$	0	$(1,+1,+1)$
$\mathcal{PΣ}$	aa	2	0	$(1,+1,-1)$	0	$(1,+1,-1)$
	abb	1	0	$(1,+1,+1)$	0	$(1,+1,+1)$
	abaa	1	0	$(1,+1,+1)$	0	$(1,+1,+1)$
	abab	1	0	$(1,+1,+1)$	0	$(1,+1,+1)$
	ba	2	0	$(1,+1,+1)$	0	$(1,+1,+1)$
	bb	2	0	$(1,+1,+1)$	0	$(1,+1,+1)$

Table 1: An observation table of the DROCA given in Figure 2a recognising the language $\{a^n b^n a \mid n > 0\}$. Here, $\mathcal{P} = \{\epsilon, a, ab, aba\}$ and $\mathcal{S} = \{\epsilon, a\}$.

4.1 Observation Table

Our algorithm maintains an *observation table* C over the input alphabet $\Sigma = \{\sigma_1, \sigma_2, \ldots, \sigma_k\}$ for some $k \in \mathbb{N}$. $C = (\mathcal{P}, \mathcal{S}, Memb, \text{ce} \upharpoonright_{\mathcal{P} \cup \mathcal{P}\Sigma}, Actions)$, where $\mathcal{P} \subseteq \Sigma^*$ is a nonempty prefix-closed set of strings, $\mathcal{S} \subseteq \Sigma^*$ is a nonempty suffix-closed set of strings, $Memb : (\mathcal{P} \cup \mathcal{P}\Sigma)\mathcal{S} \to \{0,1\}$ is a function that indicates whether words belong to the language, $\text{ce} \upharpoonright_{\mathcal{P} \cup \mathcal{P}\Sigma} : \mathcal{P} \cup \mathcal{P}\Sigma \to \mathbb{N}$ is the function ce with domain restricted to the set $\mathcal{P} \cup \mathcal{P}\Sigma$, and $Actions : (\mathcal{P} \cup \mathcal{P}\Sigma)\mathcal{S} \to \{0,1\} \times \{0,1,-1\}^k$ is a function representing the sign of the counter value reached and the counter-actions on every letter after reading a word. Given $w \in (\mathcal{P} \cup \mathcal{P}\Sigma)\mathcal{S}$, $Memb(w)$ is equal to 0 (resp. 1) if $\mathcal{A}(w)$ is equal to 0 (resp. 1), and $Actions(w) = (sign(\text{ce}(w)), \text{ce}(w\sigma_1) - \text{ce}(w), \ldots, \text{ce}(w\sigma_k) - \text{ce}(w))$. Given $w_1, w_2 \in (\mathcal{P} \cup \mathcal{P}\Sigma)\mathcal{S}$, we say that $Actions(w_1)$ is not similar to $Actions(w_2)$ if and only if $sign(\text{ce}(w_1)) = sign(\text{ce}(w_2))$ and $Actions(w_1) \neq Actions(w_2)$. We use $Actions(w_1) \not\sim Actions(w_2)$ to denote this. The observation table initially has $\mathcal{P} = \mathcal{S} = \{\epsilon\}$ and is augmented as the algorithm runs.

An observation table can be viewed as a two-dimensional array with rows labelled with elements of $\mathcal{P} \cup \mathcal{P}\Sigma$, columns labelled by elements of S and an additional column labelled ce. The column ce contains the counter value reached on reading the word labelling a row (see Table 1). For any $p \in \mathcal{P} \cup \mathcal{P}\Sigma$ and $s \in \mathcal{S}$, the entry in row p and column s is equal to $(Memb(ps), Actions(ps))$ and $cell(p)$ denotes the finite function f_p from $\mathcal{S}$ to $\{0,1\} \times \{0,1\} \times \{0,1,-1\}^k$ defined by $f_p(s) = (Memb(ps), Actions(ps))$. We use $row(p)$ to denote $(\mathsf{ce}(p), cell(p))$. For $p, p' \in \mathcal{P} \cup \mathcal{P}\Sigma$, we say $row(p)$ is equal to $row(p')$ (denoted by $row(p) = row(p')$), if $cell(p) = cell(p')$ and $\mathsf{ce}(p) = \mathsf{ce}(p')$.

Now, we introduce the notion of d-closed and d-consistent observation tables for any $d \in \mathbb{N}$. This is similar to the notion of closed and consistency used by Angluin [2], but it also takes into account the counter values.

Definition 5. Let $(\mathcal{P}, \mathcal{S}, Memb, \mathsf{ce} \restriction_{\mathcal{P} \cup \mathcal{P}\Sigma}, Actions)$ be an observation table and $d \in \mathbb{N}$.

1. The observation table is not d-closed if there exist $p \in \mathcal{P}$ and $a \in \Sigma$ such that $\mathsf{ce}(pa) \leq d$ and for all $p' \in \mathcal{P}$, $row(pa) \neq row(p')$.
2. The observation table is not d-consistent if there exist $p, q \in \mathcal{P}$ and $a \in \Sigma$ such that $\mathsf{ce}(p) = \mathsf{ce}(q) \leq d$, $row(p) = row(q)$, and $row(pa) \neq row(qa)$.

Consider the observation table given in Table 1. This table is 1-closed but not 2-closed. This is because of the presence of the words aa, ba and bb in $\mathcal{P}\Sigma$. The given table is trivially 1-consistent as there are no equal rows in $\mathcal{P}$.

4.2   Constructing a DROCA from an Observation Table

We introduce the notion of a characteristic DFA. Given an alphabet Σ, we define the modified alphabet $\widetilde{\Sigma} = \bigcup_{a \in \Sigma}\{a^0, a^1\}$. For a DROCA $\mathcal{A}$, we define a function $\mathrm{Enc}_{\mathcal{A}} : \Sigma^* \to \widetilde{\Sigma}^*$ as follows: For $w \in \Sigma^+$, $\mathrm{Enc}_{\mathcal{A}}(w) = \tilde{w}$, such that for all $i \in [0, |w| - 1]$, $\tilde{w}[i] = w[i]^{sign(\mathsf{ce}_{\mathcal{A}}(w_{[0 \cdots i-1]}))}$. Also $\mathrm{Enc}_{\mathcal{A}}(\epsilon) = \epsilon$.

Definition 6. Let $\mathcal{A} = (Q, \Sigma, q_0, \delta_0, \delta_1, F)$ be a DROCA. The characteristic DFA $\mathcal{D}_{\mathcal{A}}$ of $\mathcal{A}$ over the modified alphabet $\widetilde{\Sigma}$ is $\mathcal{D}_{\mathcal{A}} = (Q, \widetilde{\Sigma}, q_0, \delta, F)$ where, for all $q \in Q$ and $a \in \Sigma$, $\delta(q, a^0) = p$ (resp. $\delta(q, a^1) = p$) if and only if $\delta_0(q, a) = (p, c)$ (resp. $\delta_1(q, a) = (p, c)$) for some $p \in Q$ and $c \in \{0, 1, -1\}$.

Figure 2b shows the characteristic DFA over the modified alphabet $\widetilde{\Sigma}$ corresponding to the DROCA given in Figure 2a. Note that in a characteristic DFA, the counter information is not present. If we have access to the counter-actions, then we can construct a DROCA from this characteristic DFA.

Constructing a Characteristic DFA Using a SAT Solver: Let $C = (\mathcal{P}, \mathcal{S}, Memb, \mathsf{ce} \restriction_{\mathcal{P} \cup \mathcal{P}\Sigma}, Actions)$ be an observation table. We give C as input to a procedure ConstructAutomaton and obtain a DFA $\mathcal{D}_C$ over the modified alphabet $\widetilde{\Sigma}$ as output. The DFA $\mathcal{D}_C$ satisfies the following two properties:

1. for all $p \in \mathcal{P} \cup \mathcal{P}\Sigma$ and $s \in \mathcal{S}$, $\mathrm{Enc}_{\mathcal{A}}(ps) \in \mathcal{L}(\mathcal{D}_C)$ if and only if $Memb(ps) = 1$.

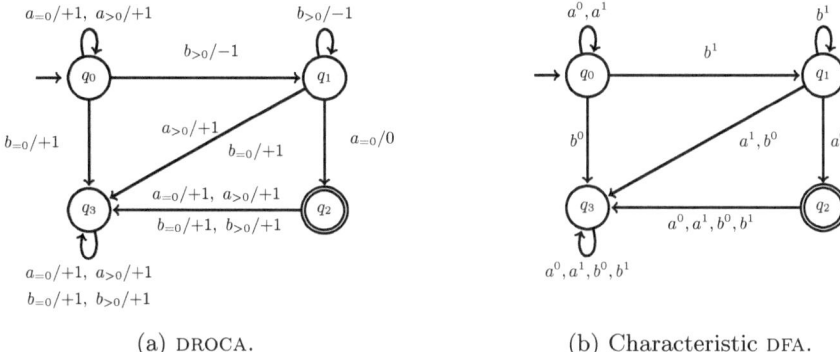

(a) DROCA.

(b) Characteristic DFA.

Fig. 2: A DROCA recognising the language $\{a^n b^n a \mid n > 0\}$ is given in Figure 2a. The characteristic DFA corresponding to this DROCA is shown in Figure 2b.

2. for any $p_1, p_2 \in \mathcal{P} \cup \mathcal{P}\Sigma$ and $s_1, s_2 \in \mathcal{S}$, if the run on $\text{Enc}_{\mathcal{A}}(p_1 s_1)$ and $\text{Enc}_{\mathcal{A}}(p_2 s_2)$ reaches the same state in $\mathcal{D}_C$ then $Actions(p_1 s_1)$ is similar to $Actions(p_2 s_2)$.

We outline the operations performed by the function $\texttt{ConstructAutomaton}$. First, we create two sets of words, Pos and Neg. For any $p \in \mathcal{P} \cup \mathcal{P}\Sigma$ and $s \in \mathcal{S}$, we add $\text{Enc}_{\mathcal{A}}(ps)$ to Pos (resp. Neg) if and only if $Memb(ps) = 1$ (resp. 0). The DFA $\mathcal{D}_C$ will accept all words in Pos and reject all words in Neg. This ensures condition 1. Observe that not all words over $\widetilde{\Sigma}$ correspond to encodings of words over Σ. To ensure condition 2, we add words over a larger alphabet $\widetilde{\Sigma} \cup Operations$, where $Operations = \{Actions(w) \mid w = ps$ for some $p \in \mathcal{P}$ and $s \in \mathcal{S}\}$. For any $p \in \mathcal{P} \cup \mathcal{P}\Sigma$ and $s \in \mathcal{S}$, we add $\text{Enc}_{\mathcal{A}}(ps) \cdot Actions(ps)$ to Pos and for all $op \in Operations$ where $Actions(ps) \not\sim op$, we add $\text{Enc}_{\mathcal{A}}(ps) \cdot op$ to Neg. We find the minimal separating DFA for the sets Pos and Neg. The transitions labelled by the letters from $Operations$ are removed from this minimal separating DFA to obtain $\mathcal{D}_C$.

Given an observation table, the sets Pos and Neg can be constructed in polynomial time. Every state of $\mathcal{A}$ can add two elements to the set $Operations$ – one corresponding to the counter-actions on reading letters from counter value zero and the other for reading letters from positive counter value. Hence, the cardinality of this set is at most $2|\mathcal{A}|$. In our implementation, we use the algorithm by Dell'Erba et al. [6] that uses a SAT solver to find a minimal separating DFA. However, any algorithm that finds a minimal separating DFA suffices [10,12,16]. In the next subsection, we observe that $\mathcal{D}_C$ is a characteristic DFA.

Constructing a DROCA from a Characteristic DFA: Let the input alphabet be $\Sigma = \{\sigma_1, \ldots, \sigma_k\}$ and $C = (\mathcal{P}, \mathcal{S}, Memb, \text{ce} \upharpoonright_{\mathcal{P} \cup \mathcal{P}\Sigma}, Actions)$ be an observation table over Σ. The following lemma states that we can construct a DROCA $\mathcal{B}_C$ from C such that it agrees with the observation table C. The idea is to use the observation table to assign counter-actions to transitions of $\mathcal{D}_C$.

Lemma 7. *Given an observation table C, we can construct a DROCA $\mathcal{B}_C$ with $|\mathcal{B}_C| \leq |\mathcal{A}|$ such that for all $p \in \mathcal{P} \cup \mathcal{P}\Sigma$ and $s \in \mathcal{S}$, $\mathcal{B}_C(ps) = Memb(ps)$ and $ce_{\mathcal{B}_C}(ps) = ce_{\mathcal{A}}(ps)$.*

Proof. Let the function `ConstructAutomaton` for input C return a DFA $\mathcal{D}_C = (Q, \Sigma, q_0, \delta, F)$. For all $p \in \mathcal{P} \cup \mathcal{P}\Sigma$ and $s \in \mathcal{S} \cup \mathcal{S}\Sigma$, we can find $ce(ps)$ from C. We define the DROCA $\mathcal{B}_C = (Q, \Sigma, q_0, \delta_0, \delta_1, F)$ where δ_0 and δ_1 are specified as follows. For all $q \in Q$, $a \in \Sigma$, $\delta_0(q, a) = (\delta(q, a^0), c)$ for some $c \in \{0, 1\}$, if there exists $p \in \mathcal{P} \cup \mathcal{P}\Sigma$ and $s \in \mathcal{S}$ such that $\mathcal{D}_C$ on reading $Enc_{\mathcal{A}}(ps)$ reaches the state q with $ce(ps) = 0$ and $ce(psa) = c$. Similarly, for all $q \in Q$, $a \in \Sigma$, $\delta_1(q, a) = (\delta(q, a^1), c)$ for some $c \in \{0, 1, -1\}$, if there exists $p \in \mathcal{P} \cup \mathcal{P}\Sigma$ and $s \in \mathcal{S}$ such that $\mathcal{D}_C$ on reading $Enc_{\mathcal{A}}(ps)$ reaches the state q with $ce(ps) > 0$ and $ce(psa) = c$. If there are any transitions that do not have a counter-action, it means that there is no word in the observation table that took that transition. One can assign any arbitrary counter-action for these transitions.

We know that for any word $w, w' \in \Sigma^*$, if $\mathcal{D}_C$ on reading w and w' reaches the same state, then $Actions(w)$ is similar to $Actions(w')$. In our construction, we are assigning counter-actions to transitions from a state in $\mathcal{B}_C$ based on the counter-actions of words that reach that state in $\mathcal{D}_C$. Since all words that reach a state have similar counter-actions, this assignment will be consistent. By construction, for all $p \in \mathcal{P} \cup \mathcal{P}\Sigma$ and $s \in \mathcal{S}$, $ce_{\mathcal{B}_C}(ps) = ce_{\mathcal{A}}(ps)$. This also ensures that $Enc_{\mathcal{A}}(ps) = Enc_{\mathcal{B}_C}(ps)$. Note that, $\mathcal{D}_C$ on reading $Enc_{\mathcal{A}}(ps)$ reaches a final state if and only if $ps \in \mathcal{L}(\mathcal{A})$. Since $Enc_{\mathcal{A}}(ps) = Enc_{\mathcal{B}_C}(ps)$, we get that $\mathcal{B}_C$ reaches a final state on reading ps if and only if $ps \in \mathcal{L}(\mathcal{A})$. Therefore, for all $p \in \mathcal{P} \cup \mathcal{P}\Sigma$ and $s \in \mathcal{S}$, $\mathcal{B}_C(ps) = 1$ if and only if $Memb(ps) = 1$. □

4.3   MinOCA: The Learning Algorithm

Algorithm 1 learns a DROCA that is equivalent to an input DROCA $\mathcal{A}$. Initially, it sets up an observation table using empty strings and incrementally refines this table to distinguish states of the unknown DROCA. The process iteratively increases an integer value d and uses membership and counter value queries to construct a d-closed and d-consistent observation table $C = (\mathcal{P}, \mathcal{S}, Memb, ce \restriction_{\mathcal{P} \cup \mathcal{P}\Sigma}, Actions)$ (see lines 4 – 14 of Algorithm 1). This part resembles the L^* algorithm. Making the table d-closed adds new rows to $\mathcal{P}$, and making it d-consistent adds new columns to $\mathcal{S}$. We construct a DROCA from a d-closed and d-consistent observation table C using Lemma 7 and ask a minimal synchronous-equivalence query. If the teacher provides a counter-example, then all its prefixes are added to $\mathcal{P}$, and the value of d is updated to the height of the counter-example, if it is more than d. The table is then extended until it becomes d-closed and d-consistent. This process continues until the correct DROCA is learnt.

Analysis: The correctness of Algorithm 1 follows from the fact that whenever the teacher replies yes to a minimal synchronous-equivalence query, the learnt DROCA recognises the target language. Now, we show that the algorithm terminates after polynomially many queries.

Require: The teacher knowing a DROCA $\mathcal{A}$.
Ensure : A DROCA accepting the same language as $\mathcal{A}$ is returned.

1 Initialise $\mathcal{P}$ and $\mathcal{S}$ to $\{\epsilon\}$, and d to 0.
2 Initialise the observation table $C = (\mathcal{P}, \mathcal{S}, Memb, \mathsf{ce} \restriction_{\mathcal{P} \cup \mathcal{P}\Sigma}, Actions)$.
3 **repeat**
4   **while** C *is not d-closed or not d-consistent* **do**
5   **if** C *is not d-closed* **then**
6   Find $p \in \mathcal{P}$, $a \in \Sigma$ such that $\mathsf{ce}(pa) \leq d$, $row(pa) \neq row(p')$ for all $p' \in \mathcal{P}$.
7   Add pa to $\mathcal{P}$.
8   **end**
9   **if** C *is not d-consistent* **then**
10   Find $p, q \in \mathcal{P}$, $a \in \Sigma$, $s \in \mathcal{S}$ such that $\mathsf{ce}(p) = \mathsf{ce}(q) \leq d$, $row(p) = row(q)$, and $(Memb(pas) \neq Memb(qas)$ or $Actions(pas) \neq Actions(qas))$.
11   Add as to $\mathcal{S}$.
12   **end**
13   Extend $Memb$ and $Actions$ to $(\mathcal{P} \cup \mathcal{P}\Sigma)\mathcal{S}$, using membership and counter value queries.
14   **end**
15   Construct a DROCA $\mathcal{B}_C$ from C using Lemma 7.
16   Ask minimal synchronous-equivalence query $\mathsf{MSQ}_{\mathcal{A}}(\mathcal{B}_C)$.
17   **if** *teacher gives a counter-example z* **then**
18   Add z and all its prefixes to $\mathcal{P}$ and extend $Memb$ and $Actions$ to $(\mathcal{P} \cup \mathcal{P}\Sigma)\mathcal{S}$ using membership and counter value queries.
19   **if** $height_{\mathcal{A}}(z) > d$ **then**
20             $d = height_{\mathcal{A}}(z)$.
21   **end**
22   **end**
23 **until** *teacher replies yes to a minimal synchronous-equivalence query*;
24 Halt and output $\mathcal{B}_C$.

Algorithm 1: MinOCA: DROCA learning algorithm.

Similar to [17], we define a refined Myhill-Nerode congruence $\simeq \,\subseteq\, \Sigma^* \times \Sigma^*$ as follows: for $u, v \in \Sigma^*$, $u \simeq v$ if and only if for all $z \in \Sigma^*$, $\mathcal{A}(uz) = \mathcal{A}(vz)$ and $\mathsf{ce}_{\mathcal{A}}(uz) = \mathsf{ce}_{\mathcal{A}}(vz)$. For all $w \in \Sigma^*$, let $[w]$ denote the equivalence class of w under $\simeq$. The behaviour graph of a DROCA is an infinite state automaton induced by this refined congruence $\simeq$. Each equivalence class under this refined congruence corresponds to a state of the behaviour graph, and the transitions between them are defined based on the equivalence class of the resultant words. i.e., for $u \in \Sigma^*$ and $a \in \Sigma$ there is a transition from the state corresponding to $[u]$ to the state corresponding to $[ua]$ on reading the symbol a. The state corresponding to an equivalence class $[u]$ will be marked as a final state in the behaviour graph if and only if $\mathcal{A}(u) = 1$.

Let $\simeq|_C$ denote the restriction of $\simeq$ to the entries in the observation table C. i.e., for all $p, p' \in \mathcal{P} \cup \mathcal{P}\Sigma$ and $s, s' \in \mathcal{S}$, $ps \simeq|_C p's'$ if and only if for all $z \in \Sigma^*$ where both psz and $p's'z$ are in $(\mathcal{P} \cup \mathcal{P}\Sigma)\mathcal{S}$, $\mathcal{A}(psz) = \mathcal{A}(p's'z)$ and $ce_\mathcal{A}(psz) = ce_\mathcal{A}(p's'z)$. Given an observation table C, we can construct a partial behavioural graph BG_C induced by $\simeq|_C$ in a similar fashion. Note that for all $p \in \mathcal{P} \cup \mathcal{P}\Sigma$ and $s \in \mathcal{S}$, the counter value corresponding to the equivalence class reached on reading ps and the membership of ps in BG_C is the same as the counter value reached and membership of ps in C.

Proposition 1. *Given* $p, p' \in \mathcal{P}$, *if* $p \simeq p'$, *then* $row(p) = row(p')$.

In the next proposition, C is an observation table and $\mathcal{B}_C$ the DROCA learnt by the learner from C (in Line 15 of Algorithm 1).

Proposition 2. *Let* z *be a counter-example, with* $height_\mathcal{A}(z) = d$, *returned by* $\mathsf{MSQ}_\mathcal{A}(\mathcal{B}_C)$. *Let* C' *be the observation table obtained by adding the prefixes of* z *to* $\mathcal{P}$ *in* C *and making it* d-*closed and* d-*consistent. Then the number of distinct rows with counter value less than or equal to* d *in* C' *is more than that of* C.

sketch. Let $z = \mathsf{MSQ}_\mathcal{A}(\mathcal{B}_C)$ be a counter-example with $height_\mathcal{A}(z) = d$. Let C' be the observation table obtained by adding the prefixes of z to $\mathcal{P}$ in C and making it d-closed and d-consistent. Assume for contradiction that the number of distinct rows with counter value less than or equal to d in C' is the same as that of C. From Proposition 1, we get that BG_C and $BG_{C'}$ are the same in this case. From Lemma 7 for all $p \in \mathcal{P} \cup \mathcal{P}\Sigma$ and $s \in \mathcal{S}$, the counter values reached and membership of ps are the same in $\mathcal{B}_C$ and C. We also know that the counter value corresponding to the equivalence class reached on reading ps and membership of ps in BG_C is the same as the counter value reached and membership of ps in C. Since $BG_C = BG_{C'}$, the membership and counter values reached by all prefixes of z in $\mathcal{A}$ should also match $\mathcal{B}_C$ contradicting the assumption that z is a counter-example.   □

Proposition 3. *For any* $d \in \mathbb{N}$, *at most* $d \times |\mathcal{A}|$ *many counter-examples of height less than or equal to* d *is returned by the minimal synchronous-equivalence query.*

sketch. Fix a $d' \in \mathbb{N}$. There are at most $|\mathcal{A}|$ many configurations of $\mathcal{A}$ with counter value d'. We know that for $p, p' \in \mathcal{P}$, if $row(p) \neq row(p')$, then $p \not\simeq p'$. Hence, there are at most $|\mathcal{A}|$ distinct rows in the observation table with counter value d'. Consequently, there are at most $d \times |\mathcal{A}|$ distinct rows with counter values $d' \leq d$. The claim now follows from Proposition 2.   □

Proposition 4. *At most* $|\mathcal{A}|^5 + 1$ *many minimal synchronous-equivalence queries are executed during the run of Algorithm 1.*

Proof. Assume for contradiction that more than $|\mathcal{A}|^5 + 1$ minimal synchronous-equivalence queries are executed. Hence, more than $|\mathcal{A}|^5$ counter-examples are returned by these queries. From Proposition 3, it follows that at least one counter-example is of height greater than $|\mathcal{A}|^4$. However, from Theorem 3, we know that the height of the minimal counter-example that distinguishes two DROCAs of size $|\mathcal{A}|$ is at most $|\mathcal{A}|^4$. This is a contradiction, since by Lemma 7, $|\mathcal{B}_C| \leq |\mathcal{A}|$ for any observation table C during the run of the algorithm.   □

Theorem 8. *Given a* DROCA $\mathcal{A}$, *a minimal counter-synchronous* DROCA *recognising the same language can be learnt with at most* $|\mathcal{A}|^5 + 1$ *queries to the SAT solver,* $|\mathcal{A}|^5 + 1$ *minimal synchronous-equivalence queries and polynomially many membership and counter value queries.*

We can adapt the learning algorithm for DROCAs for learning VOCAs. A minimal VOCA can be learnt using at most $2|\mathcal{A}|^3 + 1$ equivalence queries from Theorem 4. For VOCAs, we do not require the counter value queries. Also, there are words that do not have a valid run. i.e., the counter goes below zero during the run. These words will not have a corresponding entry in the observation table and will be treated as don't care. In this case, Algorithm 1 can be simplified further as we don't have to create the set *Operations* to encode the counter actions, as the actions on the counter are already determined by the input alphabet.

Corollary 9. *Given a* VOCA $\mathcal{A}$, *a minimal* VOCA *recognising the same language can be learnt using at most* $\mathcal{O}(|\mathcal{A}|^3)$ *queries to the SAT solver,* $\mathcal{O}(|\mathcal{A}|^3)$ *minimal synchronous-equivalence queries and polynomially many membership queries.*

5   Implementation

The proposed method, henceforth denoted as `MinOCA`, was implemented in Python[6] and is tested against a set of randomly generated DROCAs. In this section, we discuss the implementation details and compare `MinOCA` with the method by Bruyère et al. [4], hereafter referred to as `BPS`.

Equivalence Query: Even though there is a polynomial time algorithm to check the equivalence of two DROCAs [3], the polynomial is so large that it is not suitable for practical applications. In `MinOCA`, we construct a DROCA that is counter-synchronised with the DROCA to be learnt. The equivalence is checked by a breadth-first search on the configuration graph up to the counter value and length obtained from Theorem 3. The minimal synchronous-equivalence query either returns a word for which the constructed DROCA and DROCA to be learnt reach different counter values or returns a word that is accepted by one and rejected by the other. In our implementation, after each equivalence query, we increment the value of d and make the table is d-closed and d-consistent.

One major distinction between `MinOCA` and `BPS` is that the latter employs an approximate equivalence query, while the former uses an exact equivalence query. This implies that the DROCA returned by `BPS` after learning may not be correct. On the other hand, the DROCA returned by `MinOCA` is always correct.

Finding a Minimal-Separating DFA: We utilise the Python library `DFAMiner` by Dell'Erba et al. [6] that uses a SAT solver to find a minimal separating DFA from a given set of positive and negative samples. Various other techniques for computing a minimal separating automaton can be found in [12,16,18].

---

[6] The implementation of `MinOCA`, the datasets used, and the complete results generated can be found in the following link: https://doi.org/10.5281/zenodo.14604419 [13].

Random Generation of DROCAs: We follow a procedure similar to that by Bruyère et al. [4] to randomly generate DROCAs with a given number of states.

Let $n \in \mathbb{N}$ be the number of states of the DROCA to be generated. The procedure GenerateDROCA used to generate random DROCAs is as follows. First, we initialise the set of states $Q = \{q_1, q_2, \ldots, q_n\}$. For all $q \in Q$, we add q to the set of final states F with probability 0.5. If $Q = F$ or $F = \emptyset$ after this step, then we restart the procedure. Otherwise, for all $q \in Q$ and $a \in \Sigma$, we assign $\delta_0(q, a) = (p, c)$ (resp. $\delta_1(q, a) = (p, c)$), with p a random state in Q and c a random counter operation in $\{0, +1\}$ (resp. $\{0, +1, -1\}$). The constructed DROCA is $\mathcal{A} = (Q, \Sigma, \{q_1\}, \delta_0, \delta_1, F)$. If the number of reachable states of $\mathcal{A}$ from the initial configuration is not n, then we discard $\mathcal{A}$ and restart the whole procedure. Otherwise, we output $\mathcal{A}$.

Dataset for comparing MinOCA *and* BPS. A dataset containing a total of 5600 DROCAs was generated, with the input alphabet size varying from 2 to 5 and the number of states ranging from 2 to 15. For each combination of input alphabet size and number of states, 100 random DROCAs were generated. The notion of acceptance in BPS is by final state and zero counter value. MinOCA employs the widely accepted notion of acceptance with the final state only. For comparison, we generated random DROCAs where both acceptance conditions coincide. In order to achieve this, we use the procedure GenerateDROCA with an added condition that mandates that the final states can only be reached by transitions that read a symbol from counter value of zero and do not modify the counter value.

Experimental Results: We implemented MinOCA in Python and used the Java implementation of BPS. The computations were performed on an Apple M1 chip with 8GB of RAM, running macOS Sonoma Version 14.3. MinOCA spends most of the time in finding a minimal separating DFA. The scalability of our algorithm is hence dependent on the scalability of finding a minimal separating DFA.

A timeout of 5 minutes was allotted for both BPS and MinOCA for learning each DROCA. If the algorithm times out, we discard that sample and process the next one. The number of languages successfully learned by MinOCA and BPS for different input sizes is depicted in Figure 3. Notice that MinOCA outperforms BPS in terms of the number of successfully learnt DROCAs.

Figure 4 shows the average length of the longest counter-examples. MinOCA provides a smaller counter-example on average. Figure 5 shows the average number of states in the learnt DROCAs. The number of states of the automaton learnt by MinOCA is always less than or equal to the input size. Figure 6 shows the average number of equivalence queries used for successfully learning the input DROCAs. The number of equivalence queries is smaller for MinOCA in all cases.

In Figures 7 and 8, MinOCA learns a minimal counter-synchronised DROCA equivalent to the input. However, the DROCA learnt by BPS is equivalent but is not counter-synchronous with respect to the input. It is also not complete.

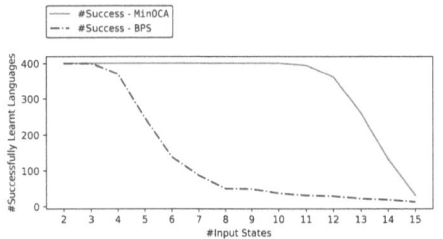

Fig. 3: Number of successfully learnt languages by MinOCA and BPS.

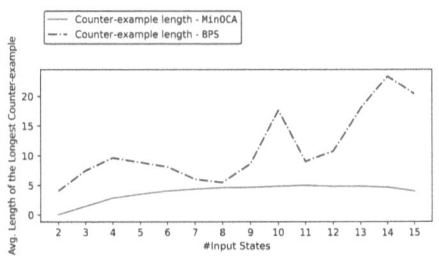

Fig. 4: The average length of the longest counter-example.

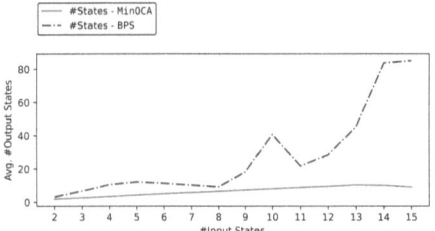

Fig. 5: Average number of states in the learnt DROCAs.

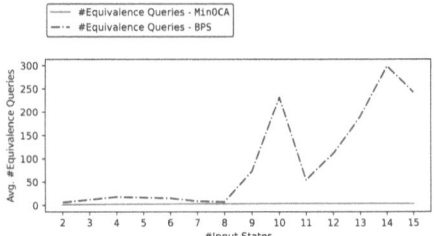

Fig. 6: Average number of equivalence queries used by MinOCA and BPS.

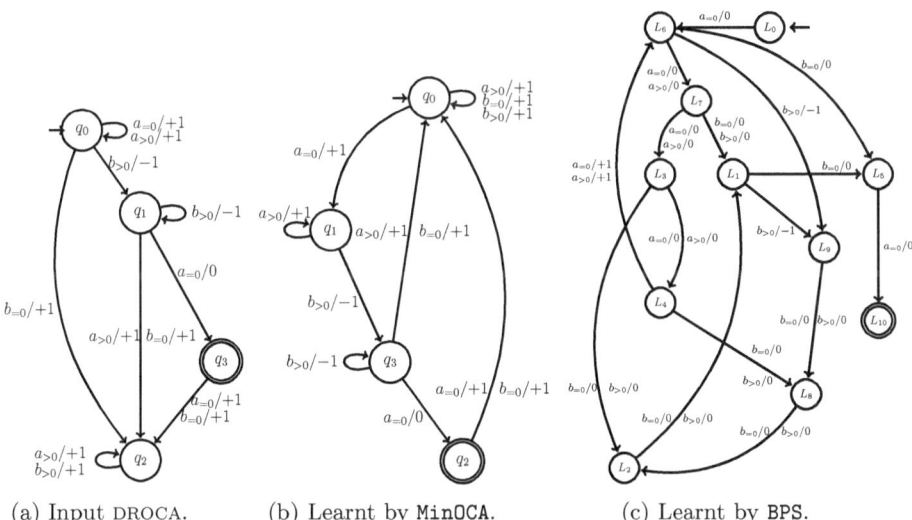

(a) Input DROCA. (b) Learnt by MinOCA. (c) Learnt by BPS.

Fig. 7: The input DROCA recognises the language $\{a^n b^n a \mid n > 0\}$.

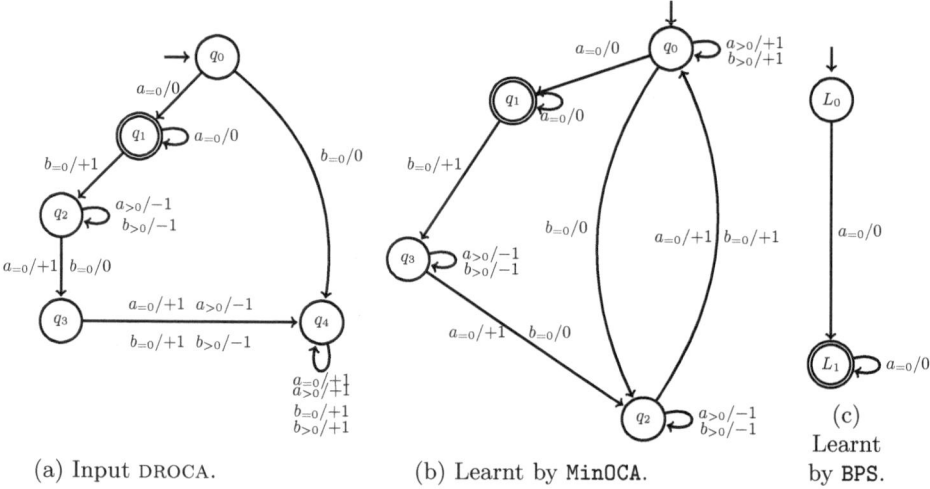

(a) Input DROCA.   (b) Learnt by MinOCA.   (c) Learnt by BPS.

Fig. 8: The input DROCA recognises $\{w \in \{a, b\}^* \mid w$ does not contain a $b\}$.

6   Conclusion

In this paper, we presented a novel approach for active learning of DROCAs. We showed that a DROCAs can be learnt using polynomially many queries with the help of a SAT solver. This is in contrast to the existing techniques that require exponentially many queries. Our algorithm learns a minimal counter-synchronous DROCA, which results in significantly smaller counter-examples on equivalence queries. Additionally, the development of a specialised equivalence-checking algorithm for counter-synchronous DROCAs, with a time complexity of $\mathcal{O}(n^6)$, further contributes to the feasibility of our approach. For VOCAs, we optimised this equivalence-checking process to $\mathcal{O}(n^3)$, enabling efficient learning. We evaluated our algorithm against randomly generated DROCAs. The results indicate that our method significantly outperforms the existing method by Bruyère et al. [4].

In future work, the proposed algorithm can be improved by finding better methods for identifying the minimal separating DFA. The algorithm can also be applied to learn VOCAs, and the scalability of this approach warrants further investigation. Additionally, extending these ideas to learn more general models, such as visibly pushdown automata, represents a valuable direction for further research. Another open problem is to determine whether active learning of DROCAs can be done in polynomial time. This problem is open, even in the case of VOCAs. However, learning a minimal VOCA cannot be done in polynomial time unless $P = NP$. Exploring the possibility of finding a polynomial-time algorithm to obtain a polynomial approximation is worthy of further study.

Acknowledgments. A.V. Sreejith would like to acknowledge the support by SERB for the project "Probabilistic Pushdown Automata" [MTR/2021/000788].

References

1. Marco Almeida, Nelma Moreira, and Rogério Reis. Testing the equivalence of regular languages. *J. Autom. Lang. Comb.*, 15(1/2):7–25, 2010. `doi:10.25596/JALC-2010-007`.
2. Dana Angluin. Learning regular sets from queries and counterexamples. *Inf. Comput.*, 75(2):87–106, 1987. `doi:10.1016/0890-5401(87)90052-6`.
3. Stanislav Böhm and Stefan Göller. Language equivalence of deterministic real-time one-counter automata is nl-complete. In Filip Murlak and Piotr Sankowski, editors, *Mathematical Foundations of Computer Science 2011 - 36th International Symposium, MFCS 2011, Warsaw, Poland, August 22-26, 2011. Proceedings*, volume 6907 of *Lecture Notes in Computer Science*, pages 194–205. Springer, 2011. `doi:10.1007/978-3-642-22993-0\_20`.
4. Véronique Bruyère, Guillermo A. Pérez, and Gaëtan Staquet. Learning realtime one-counter automata. In Dana Fisman and Grigore Rosu, editors, *Tools and Algorithms for the Construction and Analysis of Systems - 28th International Conference, TACAS 2022, Held as Part of the European Joint Conferences on Theory and Practice of Software, ETAPS 2022, Munich, Germany, April 2-7, 2022, Proceedings, Part I*, volume 13243 of *Lecture Notes in Computer Science*, pages 244–262. Springer, 2022. `doi:10.1007/978-3-030-99524-9\_13`.
5. Dmitry Chistikov, Wojciech Czerwinski, Piotr Hofman, Michal Pilipczuk, and Michael Wehar. Shortest paths in one-counter systems. *Log. Methods Comput. Sci.*, 15(1), 2019. `doi:10.23638/LMCS-15(1:19)2019`.
6. Daniele Dell'Erba, Yong Li, and Sven Schewe. Dfaminer: Mining minimal separating dfas from labelled samples. In André Platzer, Kristin Yvonne Rozier, Matteo Pradella, and Matteo Rossi, editors, *Formal Methods - 26th International Symposium, FM 2024, Milan, Italy, September 9-13, 2024, Proceedings, Part II*, volume 14934 of *Lecture Notes in Computer Science*, pages 48–66. Springer, 2024. `doi:10.1007/978-3-031-71177-0\_4`.
7. Amr F. Fahmy and Robert S. Roos. Efficient learning of real time one-counter automata. In Klaus P. Jantke, Takeshi Shinohara, and Thomas Zeugmann, editors, *Algorithmic Learning Theory, 6th International Conference, ALT '95, Fukuoka, Japan, October 18-20, 1995, Proceedings*, volume 997 of *Lecture Notes in Computer Science*, pages 25–40. Springer, 1995. `doi:10.1007/3-540-60454-5\_26`.
8. Olivier Gauwin, Anca Muscholl, and Michael Raskin. Minimization of visibly pushdown automata is np-complete. *Log. Methods Comput. Sci.*, 16(1), 2020. `doi:10.23638/LMCS-16(1:14)2020`.
9. E. Mark Gold. Complexity of automaton identification from given data. *Inf. Control.*, 37(3):302–320, 1978. `doi:10.1016/S0019-9958(78)90562-4`.
10. Marijn Heule and Sicco Verwer. Exact DFA identification using SAT solvers. In José M. Sempere and Pedro García, editors, *Grammatical Inference: Theoretical Results and Applications, 10th International Colloquium, ICGI 2010, Valencia, Spain, September 13-16, 2010. Proceedings*, volume 6339 of *Lecture Notes in Computer Science*, pages 66–79. Springer, 2010. `doi:10.1007/978-3-642-15488-1\_7`.
11. John E. Hopcroft and Richard M. Karp. A linear algorithm for testing equivalence of finite automata. *Technical Report, University of California*, pages 71–114, 1971.
12. Martin Leucker and Daniel Neider. Learning minimal deterministic automata from inexperienced teachers. In Tiziana Margaria and Bernhard Steffen, editors, *Leveraging Applications of Formal Methods, Verification and Validation. Technologies for Mastering Change - 5th International Symposium, ISoLA 2012,*

Heraklion, Crete, Greece, October 15-18, 2012, Proceedings, Part I, volume 7609 of *Lecture Notes in Computer Science*, pages 524–538. Springer, 2012. `doi:10.1007/978-3-642-34026-0\_39`.

13. Prince Mathew. princemathew07/minoca: Minoca v1.0.0, January 2025. `doi:10.5281/zenodo.14604419`.

14. Prince Mathew, Vincent Penelle, Prakash Saivasan, and A. V. Sreejith. Weighted one-deterministic-counter automata. In Patricia Bouyer and Srikanth Srinivasan, editors, *43rd IARCS Annual Conference on Foundations of Software Technology and Theoretical Computer Science, FSTTCS 2023, December 18-20, 2023, IIIT Hyderabad, Telangana, India*, volume 284 of *LIPIcs*, pages 39:1–39:23. Schloss Dagstuhl - Leibniz-Zentrum für Informatik, 2023. `doi:10.4230/LIPICS.FSTTCS.2023.39`.

15. Jakub Michaliszyn and Jan Otop. Learning deterministic visibly pushdown automata under accessible stack. In Stefan Szeider, Robert Ganian, and Alexandra Silva, editors, *47th International Symposium on Mathematical Foundations of Computer Science, MFCS 2022, August 22-26, 2022, Vienna, Austria*, volume 241 of *LIPIcs*, pages 74:1–74:16. Schloss Dagstuhl - Leibniz-Zentrum für Informatik, 2022. `doi:10.4230/LIPICS.MFCS.2022.74`.

16. Daniel Neider. Computing minimal separating DFAs and regular invariants using SAT and SMT solvers. In Supratik Chakraborty and Madhavan Mukund, editors, *Automated Technology for Verification and Analysis - 10th International Symposium, ATVA 2012, Thiruvananthapuram, India, October 3-6, 2012. Proceedings*, volume 7561 of *Lecture Notes in Computer Science*, pages 354–369. Springer, 2012. `doi:10.1007/978-3-642-33386-6\_28`.

17. Daniel Neider and Christof Löding. Learning visibly one-counter automata in polynomial time. *Technical Report, RWTH Aachen*, AIB-2010-02, 2010.

18. Marcell Vazquez-Chanlatte, Vint Lee, and Ameesh Shah. DFA-identify, August 2021. URL: `https://github.com/mvcisback/dfa-identify`.

LydiaSyft: A Compositional Symbolic Synthesis Framework for LTL$_f$ Specifications

Shufang Zhu[1(✉)] and Marco Favorito[2]

[1] University of Liverpool, Liverpool, UK
shufang.zhu@liverpool.ac.uk
[2] Banca d'Italia, Rome, Italy
marco.favorito@bancaditalia.it

Abstract. There has been a massive interest in utilizing Linear Temporal Logic on finite traces (LTL$_f$) as a specification language in the last decade, particularly in reactive synthesis. This highlights the need for a unified and efficient framework to fulfil the increasing demand for easy-to-use implementations of synthesis (and reasoning) algorithms for LTL$_f$. To that end, we introduce LydiaSyft, an open-source compositional symbolic synthesis framework that integrates efficient data structures and techniques focused on LTL$_f$ specifications. LydiaSyft supports both explicit-DFA and symbolic-DFA construction from LTL$_f$ formulas, essential DFA manipulations, and offers an extensible framework for reactive synthesis of LTL$_f$ specifications, accommodating more complex synthesis scenarios. We demonstrate this feasibility by supporting LTL$_f$ synthesis as well as LTL$_f$ synthesis with LTL environment specifications expressed in various forms. LydiaSyft is highly efficient and versatile, providing user-friendly C++ interfaces and extensive benchmarks that cater to a diverse audience, including computer scientists, practitioners, students, and the reactive synthesis research community.

Keywords: Reactive synthesis · Linear Temporal Logic on finite traces · Symbolic synthesis · Open-source framework

1 Introduction

Recently, there has been massive interest in reactive synthesis for specifications expressed in Linear Temporal Logic on finite traces (LTL$_f$) [12]. The first LTL$_f$ synthesizer Syft demonstrated the practical scalability of LTL$_f$ synthesis [25], which opened the door to a whole dimension of utilizing LTL$_f$ in various domains such as planning [11], robotics [16], and reinforcement learning [6]. This massive interest in LTL$_f$ led to an increasing demand for easy-to-use implementations of synthesis and reasoning algorithms for LTL$_f$ specifications.

We introduce LydiaSyft, an open-source software framework for LTL$_f$ reasoning and synthesis. The reasoning component leverages LTL$_f$-to-DFA construction, reducing LTL$_f$ reasoning to automata-based reasoning. LydiaSyft adopts the

S. Zhu and M. Favorito—Equal contribution.

A. Gurfinkel and M. Heule (Eds.): TACAS 2025, LNCS 15696, pp. 295–302, 2025.
https://doi.org/10.1007/978-3-031-90643-5_15

compositional automata construction technique from Lydia [9], providing both explicit-state DFA and symbolic-state DFA construction and manipulation. Unlike Lydia and Syft, which handle only standard LTL$_f$ synthesis (though Lydia introduces a novel compositional LTL$_f$-to-DFA construction technique), LydiaSyft supports a broader range of synthesis settings for LTL$_f$ specifications, including LTL$_f$ synthesis [13,25], maximally permissive strategy of LTL$_f$ synthesis [24], LTL$_f$ synthesis with simple Stability or Fairness environment specification [23], and LTL$_f$ synthesis with Generalized-Reachability(1) environment specification [7,8]. LydiaSyft leverages the symbolic game-solving techniques from Syft [25] to deal with the synthesis problems and offers reusable C++ libraries of two-player game solvers. These solvers support customization, enabling users to create and efficiently solve custom games, e.g., the reachability game solver used in robotics task planning [16].

The primary goal of LydiaSyft is to provide an easy-to-extend platform for LTL$_f$ reasoning and synthesis, focusing on usability and extensibility over peak performance optimizations, such as those for standard LTL$_f$ synthesis [21,10,15,22]. Despite this focus, LydiaSyft features an efficient, modular C++ implementation of core data structures and synthesis techniques, earning it **2nd** place in the LTL$_f$ synthesis track of SYNTCOMP 2024. Due to space constraints, additional experimental results and further technical details are provided in the Appendix.

LydiaSyft is available at https://github.com/whitemech/LydiaSyft, and the documentation at https://whitemech.github.io/LydiaSyft/index.html. The peer-reviewed artifact is available at https://zenodo.org/records/13927906.

2   Architecture

The main components of LydiaSyft's architecture are depicted in Figure 1 (All the techniques implemented in LydiaSyft also support Linear Dynamic Logic on finite traces (LDL$_f$) [12] specifications). LydiaSyft accepts LTL$_f$ formulas written in a syntax following the TLSF format [18]. Depending on the synthesis task, LydiaSyft takes additional inputs capturing safety (expressed in LTL$_f$), simple Fairness, simple Stability, and Generalized-Reactivity(1) specifications [23,7,8].

Explicit-state DFA construction. LydiaSyft leverages the compositional LTL$_f$-to-DFA construction techniques from Lydia [9] to build an *explicit-state DFA* of the input LTL$_f$ specification. This process involves a fully compositional technique that aggressively minimizes partial results so that the state space of the DFA is kept at the minimum. A novel contribution of our integration is to provide a better code interface to handle automata, enhancing interoperability with other modules and, potentially, with external tools.

Symbolic-state DFA construction. The constructed explicit-state DFA is then transformed into a *symbolic-state DFA*, both the state space and the transitions of which are represented symbolically in BDDs. This provides a compact form of the DFA, facilitating subsequent computational steps. In particular, the data structure used is known in the literature as *partitioned* DFA representation [25]. LydiaSyft provides novel implementations for representing and manipulating symbolic DFAs using the same interface used for explicit-state DFAs.

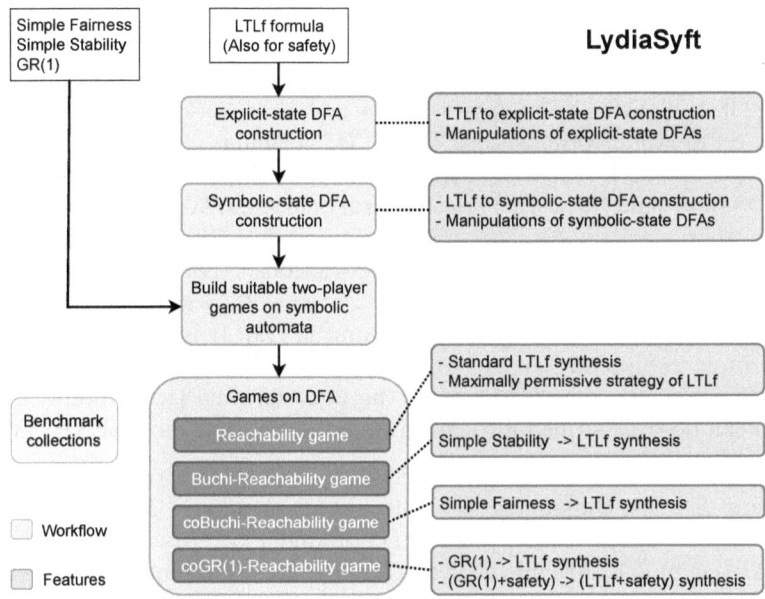

Fig. 1: An architecture overview of LydiaSyft.

Game construction. On top of the symbolic automata, LydiaSyft builds a two-player game data structure, possibly incorporating additional specifications like GR(1). These games form the backbone of the synthesis process, where the agent has to find a strategy that wins the game against the environment. LydiaSyft also supports adaptable player orders: agent-first or environment-first. We default to an agent-first setting in the rest of the paper, as in [13].

Games on DFA for synthesis. LydiaSyft supports various synthesis scenarios for LTL$_f$ specifications through reducing to games on DFA, addressing diverse problems: (*i*) *reachability game*, for LTL$_f$ synthesis [13,25] (*ii*) *maxset reachability game*, for computing the maximally permissive strategy of LTL$_f$ synthesis [24]. (*iii*) *Büchi-Reachability game*, for LTL$_f$ synthesis with simple Stability environment specifications [23]. (*iv*) *coBüchi-Reachability game*, for LTL$_f$ synthesis with simple Fairness environment specifications [23]. (*vi*) *coGR(1)-Reachability game*, for LTL$_f$ synthesis with GR(1) environment specifications, and possible additional safety conditions to both the environment and the agent [7,8]. A computed winning strategy, if it exists, can be printed in DOT format.

3   Compositional LTL$_f$-to-DFA Construction

The basic building block for LydiaSyft is the LTL$_f$-to-DFA construction. This section details how the explicit-state/symbolic-state DFA construction parts work and which data structures and procedures have been used.

LTL$_f$ **Basics.** *Linear Temporal Logic on finite traces* (LTL$_f$) [12] is a specification language expressing temporal properties on finite, nonempty traces. In particular, LTL$_f$ shares syntax with LTL, which is instead interpreted over infinite traces [20]. LydiaSyft also supports the variant that works for empty traces [4]. Given a set of atomic propositions *Prop*, LTL$_f$ formulas are generated as follows: $\varphi ::= tt \mid a \mid \varphi \wedge \varphi \mid \neg\varphi \mid O\varphi \mid \varphi \mathcal{U} \varphi$, where *tt* is the tautology, $a \in Prop$ is an *atom*, O (*Next*) and $\mathcal{U}$ (*Until*) are temporal operators. We make use of standard Boolean abbreviations, e.g., *ff* $\equiv \neg tt$, $\vee$ (or) and $\rightarrow$ (implies), *true* and *false*. In addition, we define the following abbreviations: *Weak Next* $\bullet\varphi \equiv \neg O\neg\varphi$, *Eventually* $\Diamond\varphi \equiv true\, \mathcal{U}\, \varphi$ and *Always* $\Box\varphi \equiv false\, \mathcal{R}\, \varphi$, where $\mathcal{R}$ is for *Release*. The detailed semantics of LTL$_f$ can be found in [12]. It is shown that, for every LTL$_f$ formula φ, one can construct a Deterministic Finite Automaton (DFA) that accepts exactly the same language as the LTL$_f$ formula [12]. Notably, an LTL$_f$ formula can be transformed into an equivalent DFA in at most 2EXPTIME [12].

Build explicit-state DFA. An explicit-state DFA [17] is a tuple $\mathcal{A} = \langle \Sigma, S, s_0, \delta, F \rangle$, where: Σ is the alphabet, S is a finite set of states, $s_0 \in S$ is the initial state, $\delta : S \times \Sigma \rightarrow S$ is a total transition function and $F \subseteq S$ is the set of accepting states. Given an LTL$_f$ formula φ, LydiaSyft leverages the compositional DFA construction in Lydia [9], which inductively applies a transformation procedure to each subformula of φ. This construction is "bottom-up", computing the DFAs of subformulas and combining them based on the LTL$_f$ operator under transformation. LydiaSyft extends Lydia's DFA library, which represents explicit-state DFAs using *Shared Multi-terminal Binary Decision Diagrams* (ShMTBDDs) [5,19]. To ensure compatibility with subsequent symbolic-state DFA construction, LydiaSyft provides convenient wrappers for these libraries. Notably, LydiaSyft enhances explicit-state DFA manipulation by offering operations such as complement, product, state and transition restrictions, and printing.

Build symbolic-state DFA. Given an explicit-state DFA $\mathcal{A} = (2^{\mathcal{X} \cup \mathcal{Y}}, S, s_0, \delta, F)$, the corresponding symbolic-state DFA is defined as $\mathcal{D} = (\mathcal{X}, \mathcal{Y}, \mathcal{Z}, \iota, \eta, f)$, where $\mathcal{X}$ and $\mathcal{Y}$ are as in $\mathcal{A}$, and $\mathcal{Z}$ is a set of $\lceil \log_2 |S| \rceil$ propositions, with each state $s \in S$ corresponding to an interpretation $Z \in 2^{\mathcal{Z}}$. The initial state s_0 is represented by $\iota \in 2^{\mathcal{Z}}$. The transition function $\eta = \{\eta_0, \eta_1, \cdots, \eta_k\}$ ($|\eta| = |\mathcal{Z}|$) maps interpretations $X \in 2^{\mathcal{X}}$, $Y \in 2^{\mathcal{Y}}$ and $Z \in 2^{\mathcal{Z}}$ to the successor state $\delta(s, X \cup Y)$ such that $\eta_i(X, Y, Z) = 1$ iff the value of $z_i \in \mathcal{Z}$ is 1 in the interpretation $Z' \in 2^{\mathcal{Z}}$ corresponding to $\delta(s, X \cup Y)$. Finally, the set of accepting states f is a Boolean formula over $\mathcal{Z}$, satisfied by Z iff it corresponds to an accepting state $s \in F$ [25]. LydiaSyft utilizes the same symbolic-state DFA representation as Syft, which represents a symbolic-state DFA $\mathcal{D}$ as a sequence of BDDs. However, while Syft manually converts explicit-state DFAs (represented as ShMTBDDs) into symbolic-state DFAs by traversing the ShMTBDD and generating propositional evaluations for each explicit state, LydiaSyft takes a different approach. It employs Algebraic Decision Diagrams (ADDs) [2] as an intermediate step, leveraging the BDD/ADD library CUDD-3.0.0. We first convert a ShMTBDD to a sequence of ADDs, and then use the rich API functions, in particular BddIthBit, provided by CUDD to obtain the BDD sequence, avoiding the manual conversion.

Additionally, LydiaSyft supports a range of symbolic-state DFA manipulations, including complement, product, state and transition restrictions, and printing.

4   Synthesis Settings for LTL$_f$ Specifications

This section outlines the synthesis settings for LTL$_f$ specifications supported by LydiaSyft. Let $\mathcal{X}$ and $\mathcal{Y}$ be Boolean variables, with $\mathcal{X}$ controlled by the environment and $\mathcal{Y}$ controlled by the agent. An *agent strategy* is a function σ_{agn} : $(2^{\mathcal{X}})^* \to 2^{\mathcal{Y}}$, and an environment strategy is a function σ_{env} : $(2^{\mathcal{Y}})^+ \to 2^{\mathcal{X}}$. An agent strategy *induces* a trace $\pi = (X_0 \cup Y_0)(X_1 \cup Y_1)\cdots \in (2^{\mathcal{X}\cup\mathcal{Y}})^\omega$ if $\sigma_{agn}(\epsilon) = Y_0$ and $\sigma_{agn}(X_0 X_1 \cdots X_j) = Y_{j+1}$ for every $j \geq 0$. An environment strategy *induces* a trace $\pi \in (2^{\mathcal{X}\cup\mathcal{Y}})^\omega$ if $\sigma_{env}(Y_0 Y_1 \cdots Y_j) = X_j$ for every $j \geq 0$. The unique trace induced by an agent strategy σ_{agn} and an environment strategy σ_{env} is denoted by $\mathsf{play}(\sigma_{agn}, \sigma_{env})$ or simply π when clear from the context.

LTL$_f$ **Synthesis.** The problem is described as a tuple $\mathcal{P} = (\mathcal{X}, \mathcal{Y}, \varphi)$, where φ is an LTL$_f$ formula over $\mathcal{X} \cup \mathcal{Y}$. Realizability of $\mathcal{P}$ checks whether $\exists\sigma_{agn}\forall\sigma_{env} : \exists k \geq 0.\mathsf{play}^k(\sigma_{agn}, \sigma_{env}) \models \varphi$. Synthesis of $\mathcal{P}$ computes a strategy σ_{agn} if exists [13]. LydiaSyft integrates the preprocessing techniques for LTL$_f$ synthesis introduced in [21] for effective *realizability check* and *unrealizability check*. If preprocessing fails, LydiaSyft constructs a symbolic-state DFA $\mathcal{D}_\varphi$ for φ, and builds a reachability game $G = (\mathcal{D}_\varphi, \mathtt{Reach}(t))$, where t is a set of target states. LydiaSyft follows the symbolic synthesis technique presented in [25] to solve $G = (\mathcal{D}_\varphi, \mathtt{Reach}(t))$, providing a C++ library Reachability.h.

LTL$_f$ **MaxSet Synthesis.** LTL$_f$ maxset synthesis $\mathcal{P} = (\mathcal{X}, \mathcal{Y}, \varphi)$ aims at computing the maximally permissive strategy (MaxSet), which represents the set of all agent winning strategies [24]. As shown in [24], MaxSet for $\mathcal{P} = (\mathcal{X}, \mathcal{Y}, \varphi)$ can be solved by reasoning about the maxset reachability game on $\mathcal{D}_\varphi$. LydiaSyft provides a C++ library ReachabilityMaxSet.h, which takes the reachability game $G = (\mathcal{D}_\varphi, \mathtt{Reach}(t))$ as input and computes two nondeterministic strategies characterizing MaxSet, if there is at least one winning strategy.

LTL$_f$ **Synthesis with Simple Stability/Fairness Env. Specs.** We now outline the LydiaSyft-supported synthesis settings for LTL$_f$ specifications involving two-player games on DFAs that extend beyond reachability, focusing specifically on LTL$_f$ synthesis with environment specifications. Following [1], we specify the environment behaviour by an LTL formula *env* and call it *environment specification*, and the agent goal is an LTL$_f$ formula φ. Formally, given an LTL formula *env*, we say that an environment strategy *enforces env*, written $\sigma_{env} \rhd env$, if for every agent strategy σ_{agn} we have $\mathsf{play}(\sigma_{agn}, \sigma_{env}) \models env$. The problem of LTL$_f$ *synthesis with environment specifications* is to find an agent strategy σ_{agn} such that $\exists\sigma_{agn}\forall\sigma_{env} \rhd env : \exists k.\mathsf{play}^k(\sigma_{agn}, \sigma_{env}) \models \varphi$.

An LTL formula *env* is considered as a simple Stability specification if it is of the form $\Diamond\Box(\alpha)$, and a simple Fairness specification if it is of the form $\Box\Diamond(\alpha)$, where α is a Boolean formula involving only environment variables [23]. As shown in [23], LTL$_f$ synthesis with simple Stability/Fairness environment specification can be reduced to Büchi-Reachability and coBüchi-Reachability games on $\mathcal{D}_\varphi$, respectively. LydiaSyft provides a C++ library BuchiReachability.h, which takes a constructed Büchi-Reachability game $G = (\mathcal{D}_\varphi, \texttt{BuchiReach}(t, \beta))$ as input, performs a nested fixpoint computation to solve the game. The library coBuchiReachability.h supports coBüchi-Reachability game solving.

LTL$_f$ **Synthesis with Generalized Reachability(1) Env. Specs.** GR(1) is a syntactic fragment of LTL, providing a powerful notion of fairness [3]. The problem of LTL$_f$ synthesis with GR(1) environment specifications introduced in [7,8] successfully brought the advances of GR(1) synthesis and LTL$_f$ synthesis. LydiaSyft employs the solution proposed in [7,8] reducing the synthesis problem to a coGR(1)-Reachability game. LydiaSyft also allows adding additional safety conditions to both the environment and the agent, expressed in LTL$_f$ formulas, as in [7,8]. It provides a C++ library coGR1Reachability.h, which takes a coGR(1)-Reachability game (with possible safety conditions) as input, reduces it further to a GR(1) game and uses Slugs [14] to solve it.

An example of using LydiaSyft as a CLI tool for LTL$_f$ synthesis is shown in Listing 1.1.

Listing 1.1: Example CLI Commands for LTL$_f$ Synthesis

```
#Usage:
> LydiaSyft synthesis --help
solve a classical LTLf synthesis problem
Usage: LydiaSyft synthesis [OPTIONS]

Options:
  -h,--help                   Print this help message and exit
  --help-all                  Expand all help
  -f,--spec-file TEXT:FILE REQUIRED
                              Specification file
  -s,--syfco-path TEXT:FILE   Path to Syfco binary
#Example of usage:
> LydiaSyft synthesis -f examples/test.tlsf    # UNREALIZABLE
> LydiaSyft synthesis -f examples/test1.tlsf   # REALIZABLE
```

5   Conclusion and Future Works

In this paper, we presented LydiaSyft, an open-source synthesis framework that integrates efficient data structure and synthesis techniques, focusing on agent goals expressed in LTL$_f$ specifications. We believe that LydiaSyft provides a significant foundation to address the increasing demand for synthesis and reasoning of LTL$_f$ specifications. LydiaSyft offers researchers, practitioners, and students convenient access to flexible automata construction from LTL$_f$ specifications, and various synthesis settings. Furthermore, it provides a unified and accessible approach for reproducibility. We are actively working on the framework to integrate further and future synthesis settings into LydiaSyft. Using the permissive MIT license, we hope that LydiaSyft will be used and extended by various communities that are closely connected to LTL$_f$ synthesis, such as reactive synthesis, AI planning, and task planning in robotics.

References

1. Aminof, B., De Giacomo, G., Murano, A., Rubin, S.: Planning under LTL environment specifications. In: ICAPS. pp. 31–39 (2019)
2. Bahar, R., Frohm, E., Gaona, C., Hachtel, G., Macii, E., Pardo, A., Somenzi, F.: Algebraic decision diagrams and their applications. In: ICCAD. pp. 188–191 (1993)
3. Bloem, R., Jobstmann, B., Piterman, N., Pnueli, A., Sa'ar, Y.: Synthesis of Reactive(1) designs. J. Comput. Syst. Sci. **78**(3), 911–938 (2012)
4. Brafman, R.I., De Giacomo, G., Patrizi, F.: LTL_f/LDL_f non-markovian rewards. In: AAAI. pp. 1771–1778 (2018)
5. Bryant, R.E.: Symbolic Boolean Manipulation with Ordered Binary-Decision Diagrams. ACM Comput. Surv. **24**(3) (1992)
6. Camacho, A., Icarte, R.T., Klassen, T.Q., Valenzano, R.A., McIlraith, S.A.: LTL and beyond: Formal languages for reward function specification in reinforcement learning. In: IJCAI. pp. 6065–6073 (2019)
7. De Giacomo, G., Di Stasio, A., M. Tabajara, L., Y. Vardi, M., Zhu, S.: Finite-trace and generalized-reactivity specifications in temporal synthesis. In: IJCAI. pp. 1852–1858 (2021)
8. De Giacomo, G., Di Stasio, A., Tabajara, L.M., Vardi, M.Y., Zhu, S.: Finite-trace and generalized-reactivity specifications in temporal synthesis. In: Formal Methods Syst. Des. (2023)
9. De Giacomo, G., Favorito, M.: Compositional approach to translate LTL_f/LDL_f into deterministic finite automata. In: ICAPS. pp. 122–130 (2021)
10. De Giacomo, G., Favorito, M., Li, J., Vardi, M.Y., Xiao, S., Zhu, S.: Ltl$_f$ synthesis as AND-OR graph search: Knowledge compilation at work. In: IJCAI. pp. 2591–2598 (2022)
11. De Giacomo, G., Fuggitti, F.: FOND4LTL: FOND Planning for LTL/PLTL Goals as a Service (2021)
12. De Giacomo, G., Vardi, M.Y.: Linear Temporal Logic and Linear Dynamic Logic on Finite Traces. In: IJCAI. pp. 854–860 (2013)
13. De Giacomo, G., Vardi, M.Y.: Synthesis for LTL and LDL on Finite Traces. In: IJCAI. pp. 1558–1564 (2015)
14. Ehlers, R., Raman, V.: Slugs: Extensible GR(1) synthesis. In: CAV. Lecture Notes in Computer Science, vol. 9780, pp. 333–339 (2016)
15. Favorito, M.: Forward LTL_f synthesis: DPLL at work. In: IPS-RCRA-SPIRIT@AIxIA. vol. 3585 (2023)
16. He, K., Wells, A.M., Kavraki, L.E., Vardi, M.Y.: Efficient Symbolic Reactive Synthesis for Finite-Horizon Tasks. In: ICRA. pp. 8993–8999 (2019)
17. Hopcroft, J.E., Motwani, R., Ullman, J.D.: Introduction to automata theory, languages, and computation, 3rd Edition. Pearson international edition, Addison-Wesley (2007)
18. Jacobs, S., Perez, G.A., Schlehuber-Caissier, P.: The temporal logic synthesis format tlsf v1.2 (2023)
19. Morten, B., Nils, K., Theis, R.: Mona: decidable arithmetic in practice (demo). In: FTRTFT. pp. 459–462 (1996)
20. Pnueli, A.: The temporal logic of programs. In: FOCS. pp. 46–57 (1977)
21. Xiao, S., Li, J., Zhu, S., Shi, Y., Pu, G., Y. Vardi, M.: On-the-fly synthesis for LTL over finite traces. In: AAAI. pp. 6530–6537 (2021)
22. Xiao, S., Li, Y., Huang, X., Xu, Y., Li, J., Pu, G., Strichman, O., Vardi, M.Y.: Model-guided synthesis for LTL over finite traces. In: VMCAI. pp. 186–207 (2024)

23. Zhu, S., Giacomo, G.D., Pu, G., Vardi, M.Y.: LTL$_f$ synthesis with fairness and stability assumptions. In: AAAI. pp. 3088–3095 (2020)
24. Zhu, S., De Giacomo, G.: Synthesis of maximally permissive strategies for LTL$_f$ specifications. In: IJCAI. pp. 2783–2789 (2022)
25. Zhu, S., Tabajara, L.M., Li, J., Pu, G., Vardi, M.Y.: Symbolic LTL$_f$ Synthesis. In: IJCAI. pp. 1362–1369 (2017)

Automating the Analysis of Quantitative Automata with QuAK

Marek Chalupa[1], Thomas A. Henzinger[1], Nicolas Mazzocchi[2],
and N. Ege Saraç[1(✉)]

[1] Institute of Science and Technology Austria (ISTA), Klosterneuburg, Austria
{mchalupa,tah,esarac}@ista.ac.at
[2] Slovak University of Technology in Bratislava, Slovak Republic
nicolas.mazzocchi@stuba.sk

Abstract. Quantitative automata model beyond-boolean aspects of systems: every execution is mapped to a real number by incorporating weighted transitions and value functions that generalize acceptance conditions of boolean ω-automata. Despite the theoretical advances in systems analysis through quantitative automata, the first comprehensive software tool for quantitative automata (Quantitative Automata Kit, or QuAK) was developed only recently. QuAK implements algorithms for solving standard decision problems, e.g., emptiness and universality, as well as constructions for safety and liveness of quantitative automata. We present the architecture of QuAK, which reflects that all of these problems reduce to either checking inclusion between two quantitative automata or computing the highest value achievable by an automaton—its so-called top value. We improve QuAK by extending these two algorithms with an option to return, alongside their results, an ultimately periodic word witnessing the algorithm's output, as well as implementing a new safety-liveness decomposition algorithm that can handle nondeterministic automata, making QuAK more informative and capable.

Keywords: quantitative automata · automata-based analysis · quantitative safety · quantitative liveness

1 Introduction

Traditional system behavior analysis categorizes system behaviors as correct or incorrect. However, modern systems require more nuanced approaches to address performance and robustness criteria. Quantitative automata generalize boolean ω-automata by adding rational-valued weights to their transitions and using value functions (instead of acceptance conditions) that accumulate infinite weight sequences into single values. Common value functions include Inf, Sup, LimInf, and LimSup (respectively generalizing safety, reachability, co-Büchi and Büchi acceptance conditions), as well as DSum (discounted sum), LimInfAvg, and LimSupAvg (limit average a.k.a. mean payoff).

This work was supported in part by the ERC-2020-AdG 101020093.

A. Gurfinkel and M. Heule (Eds.): TACAS 2025, LNCS 15696, pp. 303–312, 2025.
https://doi.org/10.1007/978-3-031-90643-5_16

Decision problems for boolean automata extend naturally to quantitative automata. For example, a quantitative automaton $\mathcal{A}$ is nonempty with respect to a rational number v iff $\mathcal{A}$ maps some infinite word w to a value at least v [13]. These problems are closely related to game theory [21] and enable reasoning about quantitative system aspects. Although quantitative automata have been extensively studied from a theoretical perspective [16,5,8,34,35,4,26,24,25,6] and these works could significantly impact their practical verification, until recently, there was no general software tool for their analysis.

Quantitative Automata Kit (QuAK) [11] is the first general tool for quantitative automata analysis. It currently supports several automaton types (Inf, Sup, LimInf, LimSup, LimInfAvg, LimSupAvg) and provides decision procedures for fundamental problems such as emptiness, universality, inclusion, and safety.

We present an improved version of QuAK: (i) the safety-liveness decompositions are extended to handle nondeterministic automata, and (ii) the inclusion and top value algorithms are extended with capabilities to return a witness—an ultimately periodic word explaining the algorithm's output. For checking inclusion, i.e., whether $\mathcal{A}(w) \leq \mathcal{B}(w)$ for all words w, the witness $\hat{w}$ is a word such that $\mathcal{A}(\hat{w}) > \mathcal{B}(\hat{w})$. For computing top value, i.e., $\top_{\mathcal{A}} = \sup_{w \in \Sigma^\omega} \mathcal{A}(w)$, the witness $\hat{w}$ is a word such that $\mathcal{A}(\hat{w}) = \top_{\mathcal{A}}$. Since all the other procedures are reduced to either inclusion checking or top value computation, these extensions significantly improve QuAK's informativeness for analyzing quantitative automata.

Several approaches extend system modeling beyond boolean aspects. One uses multi-valued truth domains [9,15], while another relies on weighted automata [36], where numerical weights are assigned to transitions and accumulated via semiring operations. Tools such as Vaucanson [32], Vcsn [18], and Awali [31] support weighted automata analysis. Other approaches address digital-analog interactions [2,1,22], with tools like UPPAAL [30] and HyTech [23]. Signal temporal logic [33] allows reasoning about specification satisfaction degrees, as implemented in Breach [19], S-TaLiRo [3], and RTAMT [37]. Probabilistic verification handles uncertainties, as implemented in PRISM [29] and STORM [17].

2 Quantitative Automata

Let Σ be a finite alphabet of letters. We denote by Σ^* (resp. Σ^ω) the set of all finite (resp. infinite) words over Σ. For $w \in \Sigma^\omega$ and $u \in \Sigma^*$, we write $u \prec w$ when u is a prefix of w. A *value domain* $\mathbb{D}$ is a nontrivial complete lattice. A *quantitative property* is a total function $\Phi : \Sigma^\omega \to \mathbb{D}$.

We study quantitative automata, which define a subset of quantitative properties on totally-ordered value domains. Formally, a *nondeterministic quantitative automaton* (or simply an *automaton*) is a tuple $\mathcal{A} = (\Sigma, Q, s, \delta)$ where Σ is a finite alphabet, Q is a finite nonempty set of states, $s \in Q$ is the initial state, and $\delta : Q \times \Sigma \to 2^{\mathbb{Q} \times Q}$ is a finite transition function over weight-state pairs [13]. A *transition* is a tuple $(q, \sigma, x, q') \in Q \times \Sigma \times \mathbb{Q} \times Q$ such that $(x, q') \in \delta(q, \sigma)$, denoted $q \xrightarrow{\sigma:x} q'$. The weight of a transition $t = (q, \sigma, x, q')$ is denoted by $\gamma(t) = x$. An automaton $\mathcal{A}$ is *deterministic* when $|\delta(q, a)| = 1$ for every $q \in Q$ and $a \in \Sigma$,

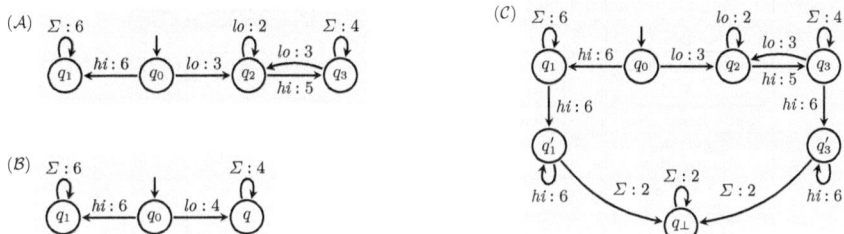

Fig. 1: A nondeterministic LimInfAvg-automaton $\mathcal{A}$ over the alphabet $\Sigma = \{hi, lo\}$, modeling the power consumption of a device where starting with high-power mode is not reversible, its safety closure $\mathcal{B}$, and its liveness component $\mathcal{C}$ in a corresponding decomposition [7].

and it is *total* (a.k.a. *complete*) when $|\delta(q, a)| \geq 1$ for every $q \in Q$ and $a \in \Sigma$. We require quantitative automata to be total.

A run of $\mathcal{A}$ on an infinite word $w = a_0 a_1 \ldots$ is an infinite sequence $\rho = q_0 \xrightarrow{a_0 : x_0} q_1 \xrightarrow{a_1 : x_1} q_2 \ldots$ of transitions where $q_0 = s$ and $(x_i, q_{i+1}) \in \delta(q_i, a_i)$ for each integer $i \geq 0$. Since each transition has a weight, a run $\rho = t_0 t_1 \ldots$ produces an infinite sequence $\gamma(\rho) = \gamma(t_0)\gamma(t_1) \ldots$ of weights. A value function $\mathsf{Val} : \mathbb{Q}^\omega \to \mathbb{R}$ maps infinite weight sequences to real values. A Val-automaton is a quantitative automaton equipped with the value function Val, i.e., where each run ρ is mapped to the value obtained by applying Val to its weight sequence $\gamma(\rho)$. Given a Val-automaton $\mathcal{A}$, the value of an infinite word w is $\mathcal{A}(w) = \sup\{\mathsf{Val}(\gamma(\rho)) \mid \rho \text{ is a run of } \mathcal{A} \text{ on } w\}$. The *top value* of an automaton $\mathcal{A}$ is $\top_\mathcal{A} = \sup_{w \in \Sigma^\omega} \mathcal{A}(w)$, and its *bottom value* is $\bot_\mathcal{A} = \inf_{w \in \Sigma^\omega} \mathcal{A}(w)$. We consider the below value functions over an infinite sequence $x = x_0 x_1 \ldots$ of rational weights.

- $\mathsf{Inf}(x) = \inf_{n \geq 0} x_n$
- $\mathsf{LimInf}(x) = \liminf_{n \to \infty} x_n$
- $\mathsf{LimInfAvg}(x) = \liminf_{n \to \infty} \left(\dfrac{1}{n} \sum_{i=0}^{n-1} x_i \right)$

- $\mathsf{Sup}(x) = \sup_{n \geq 0} x_n$
- $\mathsf{LimSup}(x) = \limsup_{n \to \infty} x_n$
- $\mathsf{LimSupAvg}(x) = \limsup_{n \to \infty} \left(\dfrac{1}{n} \sum_{i=0}^{n-1} x_i \right)$

- For a discount factor $\lambda \in \mathbb{Q} \cap (0, 1)$, $\mathsf{DSum}_\lambda(x) = \sum_{i \geq 0} \lambda^i x_i$

The automaton $\mathcal{A}$ in Figure 1 shows a LimInfAvg automaton modeling the long-term average power consumption of a device with two operating modes.

Quantitative Automata Problems We describe the standard decision problems of quantitative automata as well as the problems related to their safety and liveness. The complexity results are summarized in Table 1.

An automaton $\mathcal{A}$ is *nonempty* (resp. *universal*) with respect to a threshold $v \in \mathbb{Q}$ iff $\mathcal{A}(w) \geq v$ for some (resp. all) $w \in \Sigma^\omega$. Nonemptiness (resp. universality) is closely related to computing an automaton's top value (resp. bottom value): $\mathcal{A}$ is nonempty (resp. universal) with respect to $v \in \mathbb{Q}$ iff $\top_\mathcal{A} \geq v$ (resp. $\bot_\mathcal{A} \geq v$).

	Inf	Sup, LimInf, LimSup	LimInfAvg, LimSupAvg	DSum
Nonemptiness check	PTIME			
Universality check	PSPACE-complete		Undecidable	Open
Inclusion check	PSPACE-complete		Undecidable	Open
Equivalence check	PSPACE-complete		Undecidable	Open
Top value computation	PTIME			
Safety closure construction	$O(1)$	PTIME		$O(1)$
Safety-liveness decomposition	$O(1)$	PTIME		$O(1)$
Safety check	$O(1)$	PSPACE-complete	EXPSPACE; PSPACE-hard	$O(1)$
Liveness check	PSPACE-complete			
Constant-function check	PSPACE-complete			

Table 1: The complexity of performing the operations on the left column with respect to nondeterministic automata with the value function on the top. The decidability results in the top five rows are shown in [28,13] and undecidability in [16,12,27]. All the results in the bottom five rows are shown in [7]. All the operations are computable in PTIME for deterministic automata.

An automaton $\mathcal{A}$ is *included in* (resp. *equivalent to*) an automaton $\mathcal{B}$ iff $\mathcal{A}(w) \leq \mathcal{B}(w)$ (resp. $\mathcal{A}(w) = \mathcal{B}(w)$) for all $w \in \Sigma^\omega$. An automaton $\mathcal{A}$ is *constant* iff there exists $c \in \mathbb{R}$ such that $\mathcal{A}(w) = c$ for all $w \in \Sigma^\omega$. This problem is closely related to safety and liveness of quantitative automata, as we discuss below.

Quantitative safety generalizes the boolean view by considering membership hypotheses in the form of lower bound queries: a property is safe iff every wrong membership hypothesis has a finite witness for the violation. Formally, a quantitative property $\Phi : \Sigma^\omega \to \mathbb{D}$ is *safe* iff for every $w \in \Sigma^\omega$ and $v \in \mathbb{D}$ with $\Phi(w) \not\geq v$, there exists a finite prefix $u \prec w$ such that $\sup_{w' \in \Sigma^\omega} \Phi(uw') \not\geq v$ [25]. Moreover, an automaton $\mathcal{A}$ is safe iff the quantitative property defined by $\mathcal{A}$ is safe. Given a quantitative property $\Phi : \Sigma^\omega \to \mathbb{D}$, its *safety closure* is defined as $SafetyCl(\Phi)(w) = \inf_{u \prec w} \sup_{w' \in \Sigma^\omega} \Phi(uw')$ and is the least safety property that bounds Φ from above [25]. As expected, a property Φ is safe iff $\Phi(w) = SafetyCl(\Phi)(w)$ for all $w \in \Sigma^\omega$, and we can compute the safety closure of an automaton $\mathcal{A}$—the automaton $SafetyCl(\mathcal{A})$ that expresses the safety closure of the property defined by $\mathcal{A}$. While this characterization is useful for some classes of quantitative automata, the equivalence problem is undecidable for LimInfAvg and LimSupAvg automata. For these, the safety problem is still decidable by a reduction to their constant-function problem [6].

Quantitative liveness extends the membership-based view: a quantitative property $\Phi : \Sigma^\omega \to \mathbb{D}$ is live iff for every word (whose value is less than $\top = \sup \mathbb{D}$) there exists a wrong membership hypothesis without a finite witness for the violation. Formally, a quantitative property $\Phi : \Sigma^\omega \to \mathbb{D}$ is *live* iff for all $w \in \Sigma^\omega$, if $\Phi(w) < \top$, then there exists a value $v \in \mathbb{D}$ such that $\Phi(w) \not\geq v$ and for all prefixes $u \prec w$, we have $\sup_{w' \in \Sigma^\omega} \Phi(uw') \geq v$ [25]. Moreover, an automaton $\mathcal{A}$ is live iff the quantitative property defined by $\mathcal{A}$ is live. For the common classes of quantitative automata, deciding liveness reduces to

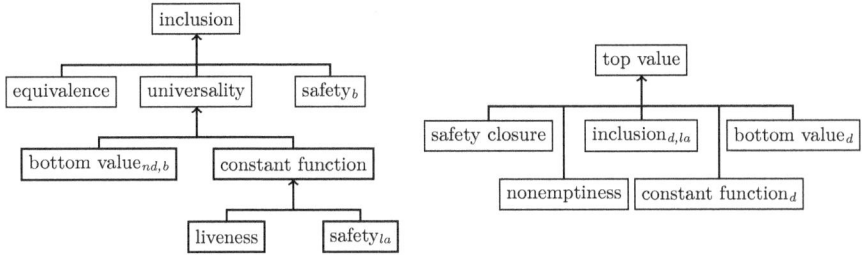

Fig. 2: Reductions of quantitative automata problems in QuAK. The subscript b stands for basic (i.e., $\mathsf{Val} \in \{\mathsf{Inf}, \mathsf{Sup}, \mathsf{LimInf}, \mathsf{LimSup}\}$), la for limit-average (i.e., $\mathsf{Val} \in \{\mathsf{LimInfAvg}, \mathsf{LimSupAvg}\}$), d for deterministic, and nd for nondeterministic. For example, checking safety of limit-average automata (safety_{la}) reduces to their constant-function problem, which reduces to universality of LimInf automata.

the constant-function problem: an automaton $\mathcal{A}$ is live iff $SafetyCl(\mathcal{A})$ is constant [6]. Just like every boolean property is the intersection of its safety closure and a liveness property, every quantitative property is the pointwise minimum of its safety closure and a liveness property [25]. Recently, it was proved that all the common classes of automata can be decomposed into its safety closure and a liveness property [7]. Consider the automaton $\mathcal{A}$, its safety closure $\mathcal{B}$, and its liveness part $\mathcal{C}$ as defined in Figure 1. In $\mathcal{B}$, each strongly connected component (SCC) of $\mathcal{A}$ is assigned the highest value achievable within the component, representing the greatest among the lower bound hypotheses that cannot be refuted by any finite prefix. The liveness part $\mathcal{C}$ consists of three components: the upper part is a copy of $\mathcal{A}$ (ensuring $\mathcal{C}$ can have runs with the same value as $\mathcal{A}$); the middle part contains a $\top_{\mathcal{A}}$-weighted copy of the highest-valued cycle in each SCC (enabling $\mathcal{C}$ to achieve high-valued runs when $\mathcal{A}$ and $\mathcal{B}$ agree); and the lower part includes a sink state looping with the lowest weight of $\mathcal{A}$ (allowing $\mathcal{C}$ to "escape" the middle part and realize a value using the upper part).

3   QuAK Overview and Usage

QuAK is written in C++ using the standard library, and the source code is available online [10]. It can be used both as a C++ library and a stand-alone tool through the command-line interface – see our project repository for instructions. For Inf, Sup, LimInf, LimSup, $\mathsf{LimInfAvg}$, and $\mathsf{LimSupAvg}$ automata, QuAK implements the operations listed in Table 1 and a monitoring procedure where the monitor maintains the maximal and minimal possible values or a running average. The problems handled in QuAK reduce to either the inclusion problem or the top value computation, as shown in Figure 2. For the details of these reductions, we refer the reader to [7,11,13].

We improve over QuAK's initial version [11] in two ways. First, a safety-liveness decomposition for nondeterministic automata is implemented, following a new result that provides a decomposition for nondeterministic automata with prefix-independent value functions, namely, LimInf, LimSup, $\mathsf{LimInfAvg}$, and

```
Word* witEmpt, witSafe;
Automaton* A = new Automaton("A.txt");
Automaton* B = safetyClosure(A, LimInfAvg);
Automaton* C = livenessComponent(A, LimInfAvg);
bool flagEmpt = A->isNonEmpty(LimInfAvg, 5, &witEmpt);
bool flagSafe = A->isSafe(LimInfAvg, &witSafe);
```

Fig. 3: An example usage of QuAK as a C++ library. The functions `isNonEmpty` and `isSafe` now take an additional (optional) parameter for storing the stem and the period of the ultimately periodic word witnessing the algorithms' outputs.

LimSupAvg automata [7, Thm. 9.5]. Second, the inclusion-checking and the top-value computation algorithms are extended with an option to return a witness (for negative instance of inclusion and all instances of top value). Since all other problems reduce to these two (see Figure 2), the ability to generate witnesses makes QuAK more informative for analyzing quantitative automata. Inclusion checking, a central component of QuAK, is implemented using an antichain-based algorithm, extending FORKLIFT for Büchi automata [20], with details and performance benefits discussed in [11]. As this algorithm systematically searches for counterexamples, it inherently supports witness construction for negative instances. Top value computation is based on graph-theoretic algorithms [13], with witness generation achieved via backtracking pointers. These improvements, along with other features of QuAK, were validated through unit testing, random testing, and cross-validation with existing implementations.

QuAK reads and constructs automata from text files. Each automaton is represented as a list of transitions of the format `a : v, q -> p` which encodes a transition from state q to state p with letter a and weight v. The initial state of the input automaton is the source state of the first transition in its text file.

Recall the nondeterministic limit-average automaton $\mathcal{A}$ and its safety-liveness decomposition from Figure 1. The first three lines of the code snippet in Figure 3 construct the automata $\mathcal{A}$, $\mathcal{B}$, and $\mathcal{C}$ as presented in Figure 1. The nonemptiness check returns `false`, and `witEmpt` points to an array storing $u = hi$ and $v = hi$ as $\top_{\mathcal{A}} = \mathcal{A}(hi^\omega) = 6$. Similarly, the safety check returns `false` and `witSafe` points to an array storing $u = v = lo$ as $\mathcal{B}(lo^\omega) = 4$ and $\mathcal{A}(lo^\omega) = 2$.

4   Conclusion

We presented an improved version of QuAK, our software tool for automating quantitative automata analysis, which extends the functionality introduced in [11]. Future work aims to improve the tool's scalability and applicability while exploring more efficient verification methods. One promising avenue is the development of symbolic approaches to efficiently manage large state spaces. Another key direction involves extending the tool to support additional formalisms, such as various types of discounted-sum automata [4], mean-payoff automaton expressions [12], and nested quantitative automata [14]. In parallel with these efforts, developing novel verification methods specifically tailored to the safety fragments of expressive quantitative formalisms presents an exciting research direction.

References

1. Alur, R., Dill, D.L.: A theory of timed automata. Theor. Comput. Sci. **126**(2), 183–235 (1994). https://doi.org/10.1016/0304-3975(94)90010-8
2. Alur, R., Henzinger, T.A.: Real-time logics: Complexity and expressiveness. Inf. Comput. **104**(1), 35–77 (1993). https://doi.org/10.1006/INCO.1993.1025
3. Annpureddy, Y., Liu, C., Fainekos, G., Sankaranarayanan, S.: S-taliro: A tool for temporal logic falsification for hybrid systems. In: Abdulla, P.A., Leino, K.R.M. (eds.) Tools and Algorithms for the Construction and Analysis of Systems - 17th International Conference, TACAS 2011, Held as Part of the Joint European Conferences on Theory and Practice of Software, ETAPS 2011, Saarbrücken, Germany, March 26-April 3, 2011. Proceedings. Lecture Notes in Computer Science, vol. 6605, pp. 254–257. Springer (2011). https://doi.org/10.1007/978-3-642-19835-9_21
4. Boker, U.: Discounted-sum automata with real-valued discount factors. In: Sobocinski, P., Lago, U.D., Esparza, J. (eds.) Proceedings of the 39th Annual ACM/IEEE Symposium on Logic in Computer Science, LICS 2024, Tallinn, Estonia, July 8-11, 2024. pp. 15:1–15:14. ACM (2024). https://doi.org/10.1145/3661814.3662090
5. Boker, U., Henzinger, T.A.: Exact and approximate determinization of discounted-sum automata. Log. Methods Comput. Sci. **10**(1) (2014). https://doi.org/10.2168/LMCS-10(1:10)2014
6. Boker, U., Henzinger, T.A., Mazzocchi, N., Saraç, N.E.: Safety and liveness of quantitative automata. In: Pérez, G.A., Raskin, J. (eds.) 34th International Conference on Concurrency Theory, CONCUR 2023, September 18-23, 2023, Antwerp, Belgium. LIPIcs, vol. 279, pp. 17:1–17:18. Schloss Dagstuhl - Leibniz-Zentrum für Informatik (2023). https://doi.org/10.4230/LIPICS.CONCUR.2023.17
7. Boker, U., Henzinger, T.A., Mazzocchi, N., Saraç, N.E.: Safety and liveness of quantitative properties and automata. Log. Methods Comput. Sci. **21**(2) (2025). https://doi.org/10.46298/lmcs-21(2:2)2025, https://lmcs.episciences.org/13149. ISSN 1860-5974
8. Boker, U., Henzinger, T.A., Otop, J.: The target discounted-sum problem. In: 30th Annual ACM/IEEE Symposium on Logic in Computer Science, LICS 2015, Kyoto, Japan, July 6-10, 2015. pp. 750–761. IEEE Computer Society (2015). https://doi.org/10.1109/LICS.2015.74
9. Bruns, G., Godefroid, P.: Model checking partial state spaces with 3-valued temporal logics. In: Halbwachs, N., Peled, D.A. (eds.) Computer Aided Verification, 11th International Conference, CAV '99, Trento, Italy, July 6-10, 1999, Proceedings. Lecture Notes in Computer Science, vol. 1633, pp. 274–287. Springer (1999). https://doi.org/10.1007/3-540-48683-6_25
10. Chalupa, M., Henzinger, T.A., Mazzocchi, N., Saraç, N.E.: QuAK - Quantitative Automata Kit (2024), maintained at https://github.com/ista-vamos/QuAK
11. Chalupa, M., Henzinger, T.A., Mazzocchi, N., Saraç, N.E.: Quak: Quantitative automata kit (2024), https://arxiv.org/abs/2409.03569
12. Chatterjee, K., Doyen, L., Edelsbrunner, H., Henzinger, T.A., Rannou, P.: Mean-payoff automaton expressions. In: Gastin, P., Laroussinie, F. (eds.) CONCUR 2010 - Concurrency Theory, 21th International Conference, CONCUR 2010, Paris, France, August 31-September 3, 2010. Proceedings. Lecture Notes in Computer Science, vol. 6269, pp. 269–283. Springer (2010). https://doi.org/10.1007/978-3-642-15375-4_19
13. Chatterjee, K., Doyen, L., Henzinger, T.A.: Quantitative languages. ACM Trans. Comput. Log. **11**(4), 23:1–23:38 (2010). https://doi.org/10.1145/1805950.1805953

14. Chatterjee, K., Henzinger, T.A., Otop, J.: Nested weighted automata. ACM Trans. Comput. Log. **18**(4), 31:1–31:44 (2017). https://doi.org/10.1145/3152769

15. Chechik, M., Gurfinkel, A., Devereux, B.: chi-chek: A multi-valued model-checker. In: Brinksma, E., Larsen, K.G. (eds.) Computer Aided Verification, 14th International Conference, CAV 2002,Copenhagen, Denmark, July 27-31, 2002, Proceedings. Lecture Notes in Computer Science, vol. 2404, pp. 505–509. Springer (2002). https://doi.org/10.1007/3-540-45657-0_41

16. Degorre, A., Doyen, L., Gentilini, R., Raskin, J., Torunczyk, S.: Energy and mean-payoff games with imperfect information. In: Dawar, A., Veith, H. (eds.) Computer Science Logic, 24th International Workshop, CSL 2010, 19th Annual Conference of the EACSL, Brno, Czech Republic, August 23-27, 2010. Proceedings. Lecture Notes in Computer Science, vol. 6247, pp. 260–274. Springer (2010). https://doi.org/10.1007/978-3-642-15205-4_22

17. Dehnert, C., Junges, S., Katoen, J., Volk, M.: A storm is coming: A modern probabilistic model checker. In: Majumdar, R., Kuncak, V. (eds.) Computer Aided Verification - 29th International Conference, CAV 2017, Heidelberg, Germany, July 24-28, 2017, Proceedings, Part II. Lecture Notes in Computer Science, vol. 10427, pp. 592–600. Springer (2017). https://doi.org/10.1007/978-3-319-63390-9_31, https://doi.org/10.1007/978-3-319-63390-9_31

18. Demaille, A., Duret-Lutz, A., Lombardy, S., Sakarovitch, J.: Implementation concepts in vaucanson 2. In: Konstantinidis, S. (ed.) Implementation and Application of Automata - 18th International Conference, CIAA 2013, Halifax, NS, Canada, July 16-19, 2013. Proceedings. Lecture Notes in Computer Science, vol. 7982, pp. 122–133. Springer (2013). https://doi.org/10.1007/978-3-642-39274-0_12

19. Donzé, A.: Breach, A toolbox for verification and parameter synthesis of hybrid systems. In: Touili, T., Cook, B., Jackson, P.B. (eds.) Computer Aided Verification, 22nd International Conference, CAV 2010, Edinburgh, UK, July 15-19, 2010. Proceedings. Lecture Notes in Computer Science, vol. 6174, pp. 167–170. Springer (2010). https://doi.org/10.1007/978-3-642-14295-6_17

20. Doveri, K., Ganty, P., Mazzocchi, N.: Forq-based language inclusion formal testing. In: Shoham, S., Vizel, Y. (eds.) Computer Aided Verification - 34th International Conference, CAV 2022, Haifa, Israel, August 7-10, 2022, Proceedings, Part II. Lecture Notes in Computer Science, vol. 13372, pp. 109–129. Springer (2022). https://doi.org/10.1007/978-3-031-13188-2_6

21. Fijalkow, N., Bertrand, N., Bouyer-Decitre, P., Brenguier, R., Carayol, A., Fearnley, J., Gimbert, H., Horn, F., Ibsen-Jensen, R., Markey, N., Monmege, B., Novotný, P., Randour, M., Sankur, O., Schmitz, S., Serre, O., Skomra, M.: Games on graphs. CoRR **abs/2305.10546** (2023). https://doi.org/10.48550/ARXIV.2305.10546, https://doi.org/10.48550/arXiv.2305.10546

22. Henzinger, T.A.: The theory of hybrid automata. In: Proceedings, 11th Annual IEEE Symposium on Logic in Computer Science, New Brunswick, New Jersey, USA, July 27-30, 1996. pp. 278–292. IEEE Computer Society (1996). https://doi.org/10.1109/LICS.1996.561342

23. Henzinger, T.A., Ho, P.: HYTECH: the cornell hybrid technology tool. In: Antsaklis, P.J., Kohn, W., Nerode, A., Sastry, S. (eds.) Hybrid Systems II, Proceedings of the Third International Workshop on Hybrid Systems, Ithaca, NY, USA, October 1994. Lecture Notes in Computer Science, vol. 999, pp. 265–293. Springer (1994). https://doi.org/10.1007/3-540-60472-3_14

24. Henzinger, T.A., Mazzocchi, N., Saraç, N.E.: Abstract monitors for quantitative specifications. In: Dang, T., Stolz, V. (eds.) Runtime Verification - 22nd Inter-

national Conference, RV 2022, Tbilisi, Georgia, September 28-30, 2022, Proceedings. Lecture Notes in Computer Science, vol. 13498, pp. 200–220. Springer (2022). https://doi.org/10.1007/978-3-031-17196-3_11

25. Henzinger, T.A., Mazzocchi, N., Saraç, N.E.: Quantitative safety and liveness. In: Kupferman, O., Sobocinski, P. (eds.) Foundations of Software Science and Computation Structures - 26th International Conference, FoSSaCS 2023, Held as Part of the European Joint Conferences on Theory and Practice of Software, ETAPS 2023, Paris, France, April 22-27, 2023, Proceedings. Lecture Notes in Computer Science, vol. 13992, pp. 349–370. Springer (2023). https://doi.org/10.1007/978-3-031-30829-1_17

26. Henzinger, T.A., Saraç, N.E.: Quantitative and approximate monitoring. In: 36th Annual ACM/IEEE Symposium on Logic in Computer Science, LICS 2021, Rome, Italy, June 29 - July 2, 2021. pp. 1–14. IEEE (2021). https://doi.org/10.1109/LICS52264.2021.9470547

27. Hunter, P., Pauly, A., Pérez, G.A., Raskin, J.: Mean-payoff games with partial observation. Theor. Comput. Sci. **735**, 82–110 (2018). https://doi.org/10.1016/J.TCS.2017.03.038, https://doi.org/10.1016/j.tcs.2017.03.038

28. Kupferman, O., Lustig, Y.: Lattice automata. In: Cook, B., Podelski, A. (eds.) Verification, Model Checking, and Abstract Interpretation, 8th International Conference, VMCAI 2007, Nice, France, January 14-16, 2007, Proceedings. Lecture Notes in Computer Science, vol. 4349, pp. 199–213. Springer (2007). https://doi.org/10.1007/978-3-540-69738-1_14

29. Kwiatkowska, M.Z., Norman, G., Parker, D.: PRISM: probabilistic symbolic model checker. In: Field, T., Harrison, P.G., Bradley, J.T., Harder, U. (eds.) Computer Performance Evaluation, Modelling Techniques and Tools 12th International Conference, TOOLS 2002, London, UK, April 14-17, 2002, Proceedings. Lecture Notes in Computer Science, vol. 2324, pp. 200–204. Springer (2002). https://doi.org/10.1007/3-540-46029-2_13

30. Larsen, K.G., Pettersson, P., Yi, W.: UPPAAL in a nutshell. Int. J. Softw. Tools Technol. Transf. **1**(1-2), 134–152 (1997). https://doi.org/10.1007/S100090050010

31. Lombardy, S., Marsault, V., Sakarovitch, J.: Awali, a library for weighted automata and transducers (version 2.3) (2022), software available at http://vaucanson-project.org/Awali/2.3/

32. Lombardy, S., Poss, R., Régis-Gianas, Y., Sakarovitch, J.: Introducing VAUCANSON. In: Ibarra, O.H., Dang, Z. (eds.) Implementation and Application of Automata, 8th International Conference, CIAA 2003, Santa Barbara, California, USA, July 16-18, 2003, Proceedings. Lecture Notes in Computer Science, vol. 2759, pp. 96–107. Springer (2003). https://doi.org/10.1007/3-540-45089-0_10

33. Maler, O., Nickovic, D.: Monitoring temporal properties of continuous signals. In: Lakhnech, Y., Yovine, S. (eds.) Formal Techniques, Modelling and Analysis of Timed and Fault-Tolerant Systems, Joint International Conferences on Formal Modelling and Analysis of Timed Systems, FORMATS 2004 and Formal Techniques in Real-Time and Fault-Tolerant Systems, FTRTFT 2004, Grenoble, France, September 22-24, 2004, Proceedings. Lecture Notes in Computer Science, vol. 3253, pp. 152–166. Springer (2004). https://doi.org/10.1007/978-3-540-30206-3_12

34. Michaliszyn, J., Otop, J.: Approximate learning of limit-average automata. In: Fokkink, W.J., van Glabbeek, R. (eds.) 30th International Conference on Concurrency Theory, CONCUR 2019, August 27-30, 2019, Amsterdam, the Netherlands. LIPIcs, vol. 140, pp. 17:1–17:16. Schloss Dagstuhl - Leibniz-Zentrum für Informatik (2019). https://doi.org/10.4230/LIPICS.CONCUR.2019.17

35. Michaliszyn, J., Otop, J.: Minimization of limit-average automata. In: Zhou, Z. (ed.) Proceedings of the Thirtieth International Joint Conference on Artificial Intelligence, IJCAI 2021, Virtual Event / Montreal, Canada, 19-27 August 2021. pp. 2819–2825. ijcai.org (2021). https://doi.org/10.24963/IJCAI.2021/388
36. Schützenberger, M.P.: On the definition of a family of automata. Inf. Control. **4**(2-3), 245–270 (1961). https://doi.org/10.1016/S0019-9958(61)80020-X
37. Yamaguchi, T., Hoxha, B., Nickovic, D.: RTAMT - runtime robustness monitors with application to CPS and robotics. Int. J. Softw. Tools Technol. Transf. **26**(1), 79–99 (2024). https://doi.org/10.1007/S10009-023-00720-3, https://doi.org/10.1007/s10009-023-00720-3

Verification 1

Neural Network Verification with Branch-and-Bound for General Nonlinearities

Zhouxing Shi[1]([✉]), Qirui Jin[2], Zico Kolter[3], Suman Jana[4],
Cho-Jui Hsieh[1], and Huan Zhang[5]

[1] University of California, Los Angeles, Los Angeles, USA
z.shi@ucla.edu
[2] University of Michigan, Ann Arbor, USA
qiruijin@umich.edu
[3] Carnegie Mellon University, Pittsburgh, USA
[4] Columbia University, New York, USA
[5] University of Illinois Urbana-Champaign, Champaign, USA
huan@huan-zhang.com

Abstract. Branch-and-bound (BaB) is among the most effective techniques for neural network (NN) verification. However, existing works on BaB for NN verification have mostly focused on NNs with piecewise linear activations, especially ReLU networks. In this paper, we develop a general framework, named GenBaB, to conduct BaB on general nonlinearities to verify NNs with general architectures, based on linear bound propagation for NN verification. To decide which neuron to branch, we design a new branching heuristic which leverages linear bounds as shortcuts to efficiently estimate the potential improvement after branching. To decide nontrivial branching points for general nonlinear functions, we propose to pre-optimize branching points, which can be efficiently leveraged during verification with a lookup table. We demonstrate the effectiveness of our GenBaB on verifying a wide range of NNs, including NNs with activation functions such as Sigmoid, Tanh, Sine and GeLU, as well as NNs involving multi-dimensional nonlinear operations such as multiplications in LSTMs and Vision Transformers. Our framework also allows the verification of general nonlinear computation graphs and enables verification applications beyond simple NNs, particularly for AC Optimal Power Flow (ACOPF). GenBaB is part of the latest α,β-CROWN[6], the winner of the 4th and the 5th International Verification of Neural Networks Competition (VNN-COMP 2023 and 2024). Code for reproducing the experiments is available at https://github.com/shizhouxing/GenBaB. Appendices can be found at http://arxiv.org/abs/2405.21063.

Keywords: Neural network verification · Branch-and-bound · Linear relaxation.

---

[6] https://github.com/Verified-Intelligence/alpha-beta-CROWN

Z. Shi and Q. Jin—Equal contribution.

© The Author(s) 2025
A. Gurfinkel and M. Heule (Eds.): TACAS 2025, LNCS 15696, pp. 315–335, 2025.
https://doi.org/10.1007/978-3-031-90643-5_17

1 Introduction

Neural network (NN) verification aims to formally verify whether a neural network satisfies certain properties, such as safety or robustness properties, prior to its deployment in safety-critical applications. Existing NN verifiers typically compute certified bounds for the output given a pre-defined input region and check the desired properties on the output bounds. As computing exact bounds is NP-complete [18], it becomes crucial to relax the bound computation to improve the efficiency. Bound propagation methods [10, 15, 34, 40, 43, 48] have been commonly used, which relax nonlinearities in NNs into linear lower and upper bounds which can be efficiently propagated to finally bound the output of an entire NN.

To obtain tighter verified bounds, Branch-and-Bound (BaB) has been widely utilized [4, 5, 7, 11, 23, 41, 46] in state-of-the-art NN verifiers, where BaB iteratively *branches* the bounds of intermediate neurons, such that subproblems of verification are created and tighter *bounds* can be computed for each subproblem. However, previous works mostly focused on ReLU networks due to the simplicity of ReLU from its piecewise linear nature. Branching a ReLU neuron only requires branching at 0, and it immediately becomes linear in either branch around 0. Conversely, handling NNs with nonlinearities beyond ReLU introduces additional complexity as the convenience of piecewise linearity diminishes. It is important for verifying many models with non-ReLU nonlinearities, including: NNs with non-ReLU activation functions; more complex NNs such as LSTMs [17] and Transformers [38] which have nonlinearities including multiplication and division beyond activation functions; applications such as AC Optimal Power Flow (ACOPF) [14] where the verification problem is defined on a computational graph consisting of a NN and also several nonlinear operators encoding the nonlinear constraints to be verified. Although some previous works have considered BaB for NNs beyond ReLU networks, e.g., [15, 44] considered BaB on networks with S-shaped activations such as Sigmoid, these works still often specialize in specific and relatively simple types of nonlinearities. A more principled framework for handling general nonlinearities is lacking, leaving ample room for further advancements in verifying non-ReLU NNs.

In this paper, we propose **GenBaB**, a principled neural network verification framework with BaB for general nonlinearities. To enable BaB for general nonlinearities beyond ReLU, we first formulate a general BaB framework, and we introduce general branching points, where we may branch at points other than 0 for nonlinear functions, which is needed when the nonlinearity is not piecewise linear around 0. We then propose a new branching heuristic named "Bound Propagation with Shortcuts (BBPS)" for branching general nonlinearities, which carefully leverages the linear bounds from bound propagation as shortcuts to efficiently and effectively estimate the bound improvement from branching a neuron. Moreover, we propose to decide nontrivial branching points by pre-optimizing branching points, according to the tightness of the resulted linear relaxation, and we save the optimized branching points into a lookup table to be efficiently used when verifying an entire NN with different data instances.

We demonstrate the effectiveness of our GenBaB on a variety of networks, including feedforward networks with Sigmoid, Tanh, Sine, or GeLU activations, as well as LSTMs and Vision Transformers (ViTs). These models involve various nonlinearities including S-shaped activations, periodic trigonometric functions, and also multiplication and division which are multi-dimensional nonlinear operations beyond activation functions. We also enable verification on models for the AC Optimal Power Flow (ACOPF) application [14]. GenBaB is generally effective and outperforms existing baselines. The improvement from GenBaB is particularly significant for models involving functions with stronger nonlinearity. For example, on a 4×100 network with the Sine activation, GenBaB improves the verification from 4% to 60% instances verified (NNs with the Sine activation have been proposed for neural representations and neural rendering in Sitzmann et al. [35]).

2   Background

The NN verification problem. Let $f : \mathbb{R}^d \to \mathbb{R}^K$ be a neural network taking input $\mathbf{x} \in \mathbb{R}^d$ and outputting $f(\mathbf{x}) \in \mathbb{R}^K$. Suppose $\mathcal{C}$ is the input region to be verified, and $s : \mathbb{R}^K \to \mathbb{R}$ is an output specification function, $h : \mathbb{R}^d \mapsto \mathbb{R}$ is the function that combines the NN and the output specification as $h(\mathbf{x}) = s(f(\mathbf{x}))$. NN verification can typically be formulated as verifying if $h(\mathbf{x}) > 0, \forall \mathbf{x} \in \mathcal{C}$ provably holds. A commonly adopted special case is robustness verification given a small input region, where $f(\mathbf{x})$ is a K-way classifier and $h(\mathbf{x}) := \min_{i \neq c}\{f_c(\mathbf{x}) - f_i(\mathbf{x})\}$ checks the worst-case margin between the ground-truth class c and any other class i. The input region is often taken as a small ℓ_∞-ball with radius ϵ around a data point $\mathbf{x}_0$, i.e., $\mathcal{C} := \{\mathbf{x} \mid \|\mathbf{x} - \mathbf{x}_0\|_\infty \leq \epsilon\}$. This is a succinct and useful problem for provably verifying the robustness properties of a model and also for benchmarking NN verifiers, although there are other NN verification problems beyond robustness [3]. We mainly focus on this setting for its simplicity following prior works.

Linear bound propagation. We develop our GenBaB based on linear bound propagation [45, 48] for computing the verified bounds of each subproblem during the BaB. Linear bound propagation can lower bound $h(\mathbf{x})$ by propagating linear bounds w.r.t. the output of one or more intermediate layers as $h(\mathbf{x}) \geq \sum_i \mathbf{A}_i \hat{\mathbf{x}}_i + \mathbf{c}$ ($\forall \mathbf{x} \in \mathcal{C}$), where $\hat{\mathbf{x}}_i$ ($i \leq n$) is the output of intermediate layer i in the network $f(\mathbf{x})$ with n layers, $\mathbf{A}_i$ are the coefficients w.r.t. layer i, and $\mathbf{c}$ is a bias term. In the beginning, the linear bound is simply $h(\mathbf{x}) \geq \mathbf{I} \cdot h(\mathbf{x}) + \mathbf{0}$ which is actually an equality. In the bound propagation, $\mathbf{A}_i \hat{\mathbf{x}}_i$ is recursively substituted by the linear bound of $\hat{\mathbf{x}}_i$ w.r.t its input. For simplicity, suppose layer $i - 1$ is the input to layer i and $\hat{\mathbf{x}}_i = h_i(\hat{\mathbf{x}}_{i-1})$, where $h_i(\cdot)$ is the computation for layer i. And suppose we have the linear bounds of $\hat{\mathbf{x}}_i$ w.r.t its input $\hat{\mathbf{x}}_{i-1}$ as:

$$\underline{\mathbf{a}}_i \hat{\mathbf{x}}_{i-1} + \underline{\mathbf{b}}_i \leq \hat{\mathbf{x}}_i = h_i(\hat{\mathbf{x}}_{i-1}) \leq \overline{\mathbf{a}}_i \hat{\mathbf{x}}_{i-1} + \overline{\mathbf{b}}_i, \tag{1}$$

with parameters $\underline{\mathbf{a}}_i, \underline{\mathbf{b}}_i, \overline{\mathbf{a}}_i, \overline{\mathbf{b}}_i$ for the linear bounds, and "$\leq$" holds elementwise. Then $\mathbf{A}_i \hat{\mathbf{x}}_i$ can be substituted and lower bounded by $\mathbf{A}_i \hat{\mathbf{x}}_i \geq \mathbf{A}_{i-1} \hat{\mathbf{x}}_{i-1} + (\mathbf{A}_{i,+} \underline{\mathbf{b}}_i + \mathbf{A}_{i,-} \overline{\mathbf{b}}_i)$, where $\mathbf{A}_{i-1} = \mathbf{A}_{i,+} \underline{\mathbf{a}}_i + \mathbf{A}_{i,-} \overline{\mathbf{a}}_i$, ("+" and "−" in the subscripts denote taking positive and negative elements, respectively). In this way, the linear bounds are propagated from layer i to layer $i - 1$. Ultimately, the linear bounds can be propagated to the input of the network $\mathbf{x}$ as $h(\mathbf{x}) \geq \mathbf{A}_0\mathbf{x} + \mathbf{c}$ ($\mathbf{A}_0 \in \mathbb{R}^{1 \times d}$), where the input can be viewed as the 0-th layer. Depending on $\mathcal{C}$, this linear bound can be concretized into a lower bound without $\mathbf{x}$. We focus on settings where $\mathcal{C}$ is an ℓ_∞-ball as mentioned above, and thereby we have:

$$\forall \|\mathbf{x} - \mathbf{x}_0\|_\infty \leq \epsilon, \quad \mathbf{A}_0\mathbf{x} + \mathbf{c} \geq \mathbf{A}_0\mathbf{x}_0 - \epsilon\|\mathbf{A}_0\|_1 + \mathbf{c}. \tag{2}$$

To obtain Eq. (1), if h_i is a linear operator, we simply have $\underline{\mathbf{a}}_i\hat{\mathbf{x}}_{i-1} + \underline{\mathbf{b}}_i = \overline{\mathbf{a}}_i\hat{\mathbf{x}}_{i-1} + \overline{\mathbf{b}}_i = h_i(\hat{\mathbf{x}}_{i-1})$ which is h_i itself. Otherwise, linear relaxation is used, which relaxes a nonlinearity and bound the nonlinearity by linear functions. An intermediate bound on $\hat{\mathbf{x}}_{i-1}$ as $\mathbf{l}_{i-1} \leq \hat{\mathbf{x}}_{i-1} \leq \mathbf{u}_{i-1}$ is usually required for the relaxation, which can be obtained by treating the intermediate layer as the output of a network and running additional bound propagation.

3   Method

3.1   Overall Framework

Notations. Although in Section 2, we considered a feedforward NN for simplicity, linear bound propagation has been generalized to NNs with general architectures and general computational graphs [45]. In our work, we also consider a general computational graph $h(\mathbf{x})$ for input region $\mathbf{x} \in \mathcal{C}$. Instead of a feedforward network with n *layers* in Section 2, we consider a computational graph with n *nodes*, where each node i computes some function $h_i(\cdot)$ which may either correspond to a linear layer in the NN or a nonlinearity. We use $\hat{\mathbf{x}}_i$ to denote the output of node i, which may contain many neurons, and we use $\hat{\mathbf{x}}_{i,j}$ to denote the output of the j-th neuron in node i. Intermediate bounds of node i may be needed to relax and bound $h_i(\cdot)$, and we use $\mathbf{l}_{i,j}, \mathbf{u}_{i,j}$ to denote the intermediate lower and upper bound respectively. We use $\mathbf{l}$ and $\mathbf{u}$ to denote all the intermediate lower bounds and upper bounds, respectively, for the entire computational graph.

Overview of GenBaB. Our GenBaB is a general branch-and-bound framework to handle NNs with general nonlinearities, for NN verification with linear bound propagation. Note that our contributions focus on the *branching* part for general nonlinearities, while *bounding* for individual subdomains during BaB follows existing linear bound propagation which has supported general models [45].

We conduct an initial verification using linear bound propagation before entering BaB. We proceed to BaB only if the initial verification is not sufficient for a successful verification, and we aim to use BaB to enhance the verification for such hard cases. In our BaB, we branch the intermediate bounds of neurons connected to general nonlinearities. We maintain a dynamic pool of intermediate bound domains, $\mathcal{D} = \{(\mathbf{l}^{(i)}, \mathbf{u}^{(i)})\}_{i=1}^m$, where each domain $(\mathbf{l}^{(i)}, \mathbf{u}^{(i)})$ ($1 \leq i \leq m$) denotes the intermediate bounds of a subproblem in the BaB, $m = |\mathcal{D}|$ is the number of current domains, and initially we have $\mathcal{D} = \{(\mathbf{l}, \mathbf{u})\}$ with the intermediate bounds from the initial verification. Then in each iteration of BaB, we pop a domain from $\mathcal{D}$, and we select a neuron to branch and a branching point between the intermediate bounds of the selected neuron. To support general nonlinearities, we formulate a new and general branching framework in Section 3.2, where we introduce general branching points, in contrast to branching ReLU at 0 only, and we also support more complicated networks architectures where a nonlinearity can involve multiple input nodes or output nodes. To decide nontrivial branching points, in Section 3.3, we propose to pre-optimize the branching points, which aims to produce the tightest linear relaxation after taking the optimized branching point. And in order to decide which neuron we choose to branch, we propose a new branching heuristic in Section 3.4 to estimate the potential improvement for each choice of a branched neuron, where we carefully leverage linear bounds as an efficient shortcut for a more precise estimation.

Each branching step generates new subdomains. For the new subdomains, we update $\mathbf{l}, \mathbf{u}$ for the branched neurons according to the branching points, and the branching decision is also encoded into the bound propagation as additional constraints by Lagrange multipliers following Wang et al. [41]. For each new subdomain, given updated $\mathbf{l}, \mathbf{u}$, we use $V(h, \mathcal{C}, \mathbf{l}, \mathbf{u})$ to denote a new verified bound computed with new intermediate bounds $\mathbf{l}, \mathbf{u}$. Subdomains with $V(h, \mathcal{C}, \mathbf{l}, \mathbf{u}) > 0$ are verified and discarded, otherwise they are added to $\mathcal{D}$ for further branching. We repeat the process until no domain is left in $\mathcal{D}$ and the verification succeeds, or when the timeout is reached and the verification fails. In the implementation, our BaB is batched where many domains are handled in parallel on a GPU with the batch size dynamically tuned to fit the GPU memory.

3.2   Branching for General Nonlinearities

As illustrated in Figure 1, branching for general nonlinearities on general computational graphs is more complicated, in contrast to BaB for ReLU networks. For general nonlinearities, we need to consider branching at points other than 0. In addition, unlike typical activation functions, some nonlinearities may take more than one inputs and thereby have multiple input nodes that can be branched, such as multiplication in LSTM ("$f_{t+1} \odot c_t$" in Figure 1) or Transformers [17, 38]. On general computational graphs, a node can also be followed by multiple nonlinearities, as appeared in LSTMs (such as "c_t" in Figure 1), and then branching the intermediate bounds of this node can affect multiple nonlinearities.

To resolve these challenges, we propose a more general formulation for branching on general computational graphs with general nonlinearities. Each time, we consider branching the intermediate bounds of a neuron j in a node i, namely $[\mathbf{l}_{i,j}, \mathbf{u}_{i,j}]$, if node i is the input of some nonlinearity. We consider branching the concerned neuron into 2 branches with a nontrivial branching point $\mathbf{p}_{i,j}$, as $[\mathbf{l}_{i,j}, \mathbf{u}_{i,j}] \rightarrow [\mathbf{l}_{i,j}, \mathbf{p}_{i,j}], [\mathbf{p}_{i,j}, \mathbf{u}_{i,j}]$. Here we consider branching from the perspective of each node i which is the input to at least one nonlinearity and decide if we branch the intermediate bounds $[\mathbf{l}_i, \mathbf{u}_i]$ of this node. This consideration allows us to conveniently support nonlinearities with multiple input nodes or multiple nonlinearities sharing an input node. On the contrary, if we consider branching from the perspective of each nonlinearity, the considered nonlinearity may share

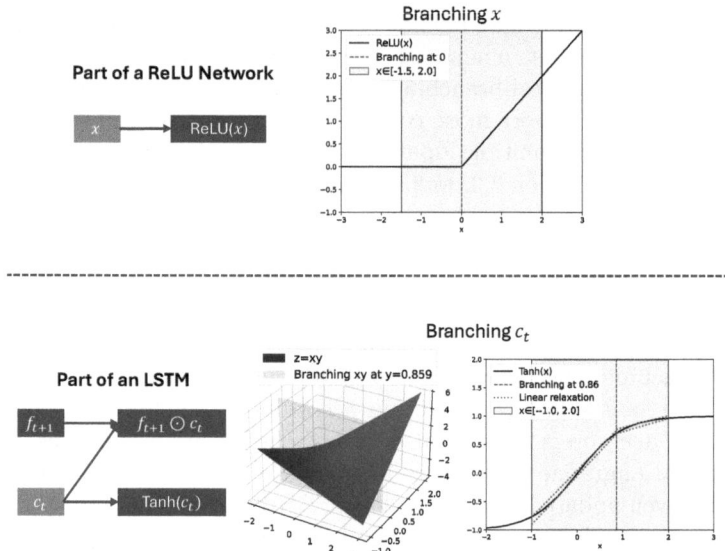

Fig. 1: Illustration of the more complicated nature of branching for general nonlinearities (branching a ReLU activation v.s. branching for nonlinearities in an LSTM). Notations for part of an LSTM follows PyTorch's documentation (https://pytorch.org/docs/stable/generated/torch.nn.LSTM.html). Nodes in orange are being branched. For general nonlinearities, branching points can be non-zero (0.86 in the LSTM example here), a nonlinearity can take multiple input nodes ($f_{t+1} \odot c_t$ here), and a node can also be followed by multiple nonlinearities (c_t is followed by a multiplication and also Tanh, and branching c_t affects both two nonlinearities).

some input node with another nonlinearity and thus other nonlinearities can also be affected.

3.3   Where to Branch? New Considerations for General Nonlinear Functions

The more complex nature of general nonlinear functions also brings flexibility on choosing branching points, compared to the ReLU activation where only branching at 0 is reasonable. A straightforward way is to branch in the middle between the intermediate lower and upper bounds, as shown in Figure 2a. However, this can be suboptimal for many nonlinear functions. Intuitively, as tighter linear relaxation can often lead to tighter verified bounds [24, 46], we aim to choose a branching point such that the linear relaxation for both sides after the branching can be as tight as possible. Therefore, we propose to *pre-optimize branching points* for each case of nonlinearity in the model, before actually running BaB on different data instances. We enumerate all pairs of possible intermediate bounds within a certain range with a step size, where we set a small step size which defines the

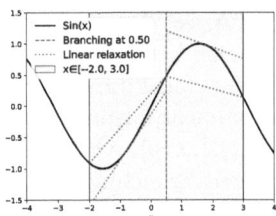 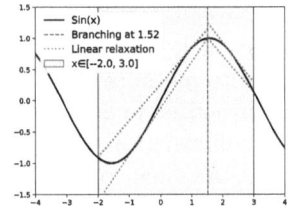 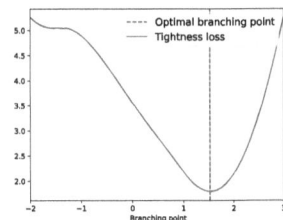

(a) Branching a Sine activation in the middle.

(b) Branching a Sine at our pre-optimized branching point.

(c) The tightness loss defined in Eq. (3) for different branching points.

Fig. 2: Illustration of branching the intermediate bounds of a neuron connected to the Sine activation [35].

gap between the adjacent enumerated intermediate bounds. And we save the optimized branching points into a lookup table. During verification, for each pair of intermediate bounds we actually encounter, we efficiently query the lookup table and take the branching point for the closest intermediate bound pair in the lookup table (if no valid branching point is obtained from the lookup table, we try branching in the middle instead as a backup). An example of pre-optimized branching points is shown in Figure 2b. We only need to pre-optimize branching points once for each new model, and the produced lookup table can be used on an arbitrary number of data instances, and thus the time cost of the pre-optimization is negligible for the overall verification.

We now formulate the objective of the pre-optimization. For simplicity here, we mainly assume that we have a unary nonlinear function $q(x)$, although our method supports functions with any number of inputs in practice. Suppose the input intermediate bounds for $q(x)$ is $l \leq x \leq u$, we aim to find a branching point $p = P(l, u)$ such that the overall tightness of the linear relaxation for input range $[l, p]$ and $[p, u]$, respectively, is the best. Suppose the linear relaxation for input range $[l, p]$ is $\underline{a}_1 x + \underline{b}_1 \leq q(x) \leq \overline{a}_1 x + \overline{b}_1$, and similarly $\underline{a}_2 x + \underline{b}_2 \leq q(x) \leq \overline{a}_2 x + \overline{b}_2$ for input range $[p, u]$. Following previous works such as Shi et al. [31], we use the integral of the gap between the lower linear relaxation and the upper linear relaxation to measure the tightness (the linear relaxation is considered as tighter when the gap is smaller). We define it as a *tightness loss* $P(q(x), l, u, p)$ for nonlinearity $q(x)$ with input range $[l, u]$ and branching point p:

$$P(q(x), l, u, p) = \int_l^p \left((\overline{a}_1 x + \overline{b}_1) - (\underline{a}_1 x + \underline{b}_1) \right) dx + \int_p^u \left((\overline{a}_2 x + \overline{b}_2) - (\underline{a}_2 x + \underline{b}_2) \right) dx,$$
(3)

where the parameters for the linear relaxation $(\underline{a}_1, \overline{a}_1, \underline{b}_1, \overline{b}_1, \underline{a}_2, \overline{a}_2, \underline{b}_2, \overline{b}_2)$ all depend on p. We take the best branching point p ($l < p < u$) which minimizes $P(q(x), l, u, p)$. Figure 2c plots the tightness loss for the Sine activation. This problem can be solved by gradient descent, or an enumeration over a number of potential branching points if the nonlinear function only has one or two inputs.

Moreover, we also support a generalized version of Eq. (3) for nonlinear functions with multiple inputs (such as multiplication involving two inputs), where we use a multiple integral to measure the tightness for multi-dimensional nonlinearities. And when a branched node has multiple nonlinear output nodes, we take the sum for multiple nonlinearities as $\sum_{q \in \mathcal{Q}} P(q(x), l, u, p)$, where $\mathcal{Q}$ is the set of output nonlinearities. As such, our pre-optimized branching points support general computational graphs.

3.4   Which Neuron to Branch? A New Branching Heuristic

Since a NN usually contains many neurons where branching can potentially occur, typically a branching heuristic is used to efficiently decide a neuron to branch, so that the time cost of each BaB iteration is moderate to allow more BaB iterations within the time budget. The branching heuristic is essentially a scoring function for estimating the new verified bound after branching at each neuron, in order to choose a good neuron which potentially leads to a good improvement after the branching. We propose a new branching heuristic to support general nonlinearities.

Specifically, we design a function $\tilde{V}(\mathbf{l}, \mathbf{u}, i, j, k, \mathbf{p}_{i,j})$ which estimates the new bound of the k-th ($1 \leq k \leq 2$) branch, after branching neuron j in node i using branching points $\mathbf{p}_{i,j}$. We use $B(\mathbf{l}, \mathbf{u}, i, j, k, \mathbf{p}_{i,j})$ to denote the updated intermediate bounds after this branching, and essentially we aim to use $\tilde{V}(\mathbf{l}, \mathbf{u}, i, j, k, \mathbf{p}_{i,j})$ to efficiently estimate $V(h, \mathcal{C}, B(\mathbf{l}, \mathbf{u}, i, j, k, \mathbf{p}_{i,j}))$ which is the actual verified bound after the branching, but it is too costly to directly compute an actual verified bound for each branching option.

Suppose we consider branching a neuron j in node i and we aim to estimate $V(\cdot)$ for each branch k. In the linear bound propagation, when the bounds are propagated to node i, we have:

$$h(\mathbf{x}) \geq \mathbf{A}_{i,j}^{(k)} \hat{\mathbf{x}}_{i,j} + \mathbf{c}^{(k)} \geq V(h, \mathcal{C}, B(\mathbf{l}, i, j, k, \mathbf{p}_{i,j})), \tag{4}$$

where we use $\mathbf{A}_{i,j}^{(k)}$ and $\mathbf{c}^{(k)}$ to denote the parameters in the linear bounds for the k-th branch, and here $\mathbf{c}^{(k)}$ a bias term accumulated on all the neurons. Since we do not update the intermediate bounds except for the branched neurons during BaB for efficiency following Wang et al. [41], branching a neuron in node i only affects the linear relaxation of nonlinear nodes immediately after node i (i.e., output nodes of i). Therefore, $\mathbf{A}_{i,j}^{(k)}$ and $\mathbf{c}^{(k)}$ can be computed by only propagating the linear bounds from the output nodes of i, using previously stored linear bounds, rather than from the final output of $h(\mathbf{x})$.

For a more efficient estimation, instead of propagating the linear bounds towards the input of the network step by step, we propose a new branching heuristic named *Bound Propagation with Shortcuts (BBPS)*, where we use a shortcut to directly propagate the bounds to the input. Specifically, we save the linear bounds of all the potentially branched intermediate nodes during the initial verification. For every neuron j in intermediate node i, we record:

$$\forall \mathbf{x} \in \mathcal{C}, \quad \underline{\mathbf{A}}_{ij}\mathbf{x} + \underline{\hat{\mathbf{c}}}_{ij} \leq \hat{\mathbf{x}}_{ij} \leq \overline{\mathbf{A}}_{ij}\mathbf{x} + \overline{\mathbf{c}}_{ij}, \tag{5}$$

where $\hat{\mathbf{A}}_{ij}, \hat{\underline{\mathbf{c}}}_{ij}, \overline{\mathbf{A}}_{ij}, \overline{\mathbf{c}}_{ij}$ are parameters for the linear bounds. These are obtained when linear bound propagation is used for computing the intermediate bounds $[\mathbf{l}_{i,j}, \mathbf{u}_{i,j}]$ and the linear bounds are propagated to the input $\mathbf{x}$. We then use Eq. (5) to compute a lower bound for $\mathbf{A}_{i,j}^{(k)}\hat{\mathbf{x}}_{i,j} + \mathbf{c}^{(k)}$:

$$\mathbf{A}_{i,j}^{(k)}\hat{\mathbf{x}}_{i,j} + \mathbf{c}^{(k)} \geq (\mathbf{A}_{i,j,+}^{(k)}\hat{\underline{\mathbf{A}}}_{ij} + \mathbf{A}_{i,j,-}^{(k)}\overline{\mathbf{A}}_{ij})\mathbf{x} + \mathbf{A}_{i,j,+}^{(k)}\hat{\underline{\mathbf{c}}}_{ij} + \mathbf{A}_{i,j,-}^{(k)}\overline{\mathbf{c}}_{ij} + \mathbf{c}^{(k)}. \quad (6)$$

The right-hand-side can be concretized by Eq. (2) to serve as an approximation for $V(\cdot)$ after the branching. In this way, the linear bounds are directly propagated from node i to input $\mathbf{x}$ and concretized using a shortcut. We thereby take the concretized bound as $\tilde{V}(\mathbf{l}, \mathbf{u}, i, j, k, \mathbf{p}_{i,j})$ for our BBPS heuristic score.

This computation is efficient, and it does not affect the time complexity of BaB as the time complexity is mainly dominated by the bound computation after each branching. Our branching heuristic is also generally formulated. We leverage updates on the linear relaxation of any nonlinearity, and general branching points and general number of inputs nodes are supported when we update the linear relaxation. Node i can also have multiple nonlinear output nodes, as we accumulate the linear bounds propagated from all the output nodes to produce Eq. (4).

Comparison to branching heuristics in previous works. Existing branching heuristics from previous works [4, 5, 7, 23] are more restrictive, as they mostly focused on branching ReLU neurons with a fixed branching point (0 for ReLU) and their heuristic is specifically formulated for ReLU, unlike our general formulation above. Even if we directly generalize their branching heuristic to support general nonlinearities, we also empirically find they are often not precise enough for general nonlinearities due to their more aggressive approximation. In the existing BaBSR heuristic originally for ReLU networks [4], they essentially propagate the bounds only to the node before the branched one with an early stop, and they then ignore the coefficients ($\mathbf{A}_{i-1,j}^{(k)}$ for a feedforward NN) without propagating further. In contrast, in our BBPS heuristic, we carefully utilize a shortcut to propagate the bounds to the input as Eq. (6) rather than discard linear terms early. Therefore, we expect our BBPS heuristic to be more precise and effective.

4 Experiments

4.1 Settings

Implementation and additional experimental details are provided in Appendix D.

Models and Data. We focus on verifying NNs with nonlinearities beyond ReLU, and we experiment on models with various nonlinearities as shown in Table 1. We mainly consider the commonly used ℓ_∞ robustness verification specification on image classification. We use the term *instance* to refer to a data example along with the corresponding verification specification. We adopt some MNIST [22] models with Sigmoid and Tanh activation functions from previous works [27, 33, 34], along with their data instances. Besides, to test our method on more models with various nonlinearities using a consistent training setting for all the models, we train many new models with various nonlinearities on CIFAR-10 [21] by PGD adversarial training [25], using an ℓ_∞ perturbation with $\epsilon = 1/255$ in both training and verification. The models we train on CIFAR-10 include models with Sigmoid, Tanh, Sine, and GeLU activation functions, respectively, as well as LSTM [17] and ViT [8]. We adopt PGD adversarial training, because NNs trained without robust training are known to be highly vulnerable to tiny adversarial perturbations [13, 36] and formal verification is not possible unless ϵ is much smaller. For these CIFAR-10 models, we first run vanilla CROWN [45, 47] (linear bound propagation without optimized linear relaxation [24, 46] or BaB [41, 46]), to remove instances which are too easy where vanilla CROWN already succeeds. We also remove instances where PGD attack succeeds, as such instances are impossible to verify. We only retain the first 100 instances if there are more instances left. We set a timeout of 300 seconds for our BaB in all these experiments. In addition, we adopt an NN verification benchmark for verifying properties in the Machine Learning for AC Optimal Power Flow (ML4ACOPF) problem [14][7] which is beyond robustness verification.

Baselines. We compare our GenBaB with the previous α,β-CROWN which did not support BaB on non-ReLU nonlinearities. We also compare with several other baselines, including Deep-Poly [34], PRIMA [27], VeriNet [15], PROVER [29], DeepT [1], Wu et al. [44], Wei et al. [42], on the models they support, respectively. Among these baselines, only VeriNet and Wu et al. [44] support BaB on Sigmoid or Tanh models, and none of the baseline supports BaB on general nonlinearities. While the original BaBSR heuristic in Bunel et al. [4] only supported ReLU networks, we also implemented a generalized version of BaBSR for nonlinearities beyond ReLU for an empirical comparison in Table 3, based on the difference in treating the linear term discussed in Section 3.4.

Table 1: List of models with various nonlinearities in our experiments.

Model	Nonlinearities in the model
Feedforward	sigmoid, tanh, sin, GeLU
LSTM	sigmoid, tanh, xy
ViT with ReLU	ReLU, xy, x/y, x^2, $\sqrt{x}$, $\exp(x)$
ML4ACOPF	ReLU, sigmoid, sin, xy, x^2

4.2   Main Results

Experiments on Sigmoid and Tanh networks for MNIST. We first experiment on Sigmoid networks and Tanh networks for MNIST and show the results in Table 2. On 6 out of the 8 models, our GenBaB is able to verify more instances over α,β-CROWN without BaB and also outperforms all the non-CROWN baselines.

---

[7] Benchmark: `https://github.com/AI4OPT/ml4acopf_benchmark`.

Table 2: Number of verified instances out of the first 100 test examples on MNIST for several Sigmoid networks and Tanh networks along with their ϵ. The settings are the same as those in PRIMA [27]. "$L \times W$" in the network names denote a fully-connected NN with L layers and W hidden neurons in each layer. The upper bounds in the last row are computed by PGD attack [25], as a sound verification should not verify instances where PGD can successfully find counterexamples.

Method	Sigmoid Networks				Tanh Networks			
	6×100 $\epsilon=0.015$	6×200 $\epsilon=0.012$	9×100 $\epsilon=0.015$	ConvSmall $\epsilon=0.014$	6×100 $\epsilon=0.006$	6×200 $\epsilon=0.002$	9×100 $\epsilon=0.006$	ConvSmall $\epsilon=0.005$
DeepPoly[a][b]	30	43	38	30	38	39	18	16
PRIMA[a]	53	73	56	51	61	68	52	30
VeriNet[c]	65	81	56	-	31	30	16	-
Marabou [44][?]	65	75	96[?]	63	-	-	-	-
Vanilla CROWN[b]	53	63	49	65	18	24	44	55
α,β-CROWN (w/o BaB)	62	81	**62**	84	**65**	72	58	69
GenBaB (ours)	**71**	**83**	**62**	**92**	**65**	**78**	**59**	**75**
Upper bound	93	99	92	97	94	97	96	98

[a] Results for DeepPoly and PRIMA are directly from Müller et al. [27].
[b] While DeepPoly and CROWN are thought to be equivalent on ReLU networks [27], these two works adopt different relaxation for Sigmoid and Tanh, which results in different results here.
[c] Results for VeriNet are obtained by running the tool (https://github.com/vas-group-imperial/VeriNet) by ourselves. VeriNet depends on the FICO Xpress commercial solver which requires a license for models that are relatively large. FICO Xpress declined the request we submitted for an academic license due to the lack of a course tutor. Thus, results on ConvSmall models are not available.
[?] We found that the result Wu et al. [44] reported on the Sigmoid 9×100 model exceeds the upper bound by PGD attack ($96 > 92$), and thus the result tends to be not fully valid (also reported in Zhou et al. [51]).

We find that improving on Sigmoid 9×100 and Tanh 6×100 networks by BaB is harder, as the initial bounds are typically too loose on the unverifiable instances before BaB, possibly due to these models being trained without robustness consideration.

Experiments on feedforward NNs with various activation functions for CIFAR-10. In Table 3, we show results for models on CIFAR-10. On all the models, GenBaB verifies much more instances compared to α,β-CROWN without BaB. We also conduct ablation studies to investigate the effect of our BBPS heuristic and branching points, with results shown in the last three rows of Table 3. Comparing "Base BaB" and " + BBPS", on most of the models, we find that our BBPS heuristic significantly improves over directly generalizing the BaBSR heuristic [4] used in "Base BaB". Comparing "+ BBPS" and "+ BBPS, + pre-optimized", we find that our pre-optimized branching points achieve a noticeable improvement on many models over always branching in the middle. The results demonstrate the effectiveness of our GenBaB with our BBPS heuristic and pre-optimized branching points. GenBaB also exhibits much better scalability, where we compare the

Table 3: Number of verified instances out of 100 filtered instances on CIFAR-10 with $\epsilon = 1/255$ for feedforward NNs with various activation functions. The last three rows contain results for the ablation study, where "Base BaB" does not use our BBPS heuristic or pre-optimized branching points, but it uses a generalized BaBSR heuristic [4] and always branches intermediate bounds in the middle.

Method	Sigmoid Networks				Tanh Networks		Sine Networks			GeLU Networks		
	4×100	4×500	6×100	6×200	4×100	6×100	4×100	4×200	4×500	4×100	4×200	4×500
PRIMA[a]	0	0	0	0	0	0	-	-	-	-	-	-
Vanilla CROWN[b]	0	0	0	0	0	0	0	0	0	0	0	0
α,β-CROWN w/o BaB[c]	28	16	43	39	25	6	4	2	4	44	33	27
GenBaB (ours)	**58**	**24**	**64**	**50**	**49**	**10**	**60**	**35**	**22**	**82**	**65**	**39**
Ablation Studies												
Base BaB	34	19	44	41	34	8	9	8	7	64	54	39
+ BBPS	57	24	63	49	48	10	56	34	21	74	59	36
+ BBPS, + pre-optimized	58	24	64	50	49	10	60	35	22	82	65	39

[a]Results for PRIMA are obtained by running ERAN (https://github.com/eth-sri/eran) which contains PRIMA. PRIMA does not support Sine or GeLU activations.
[b]We have extended its support to GeLU, as discussed in Appendix B.3.
[c]We have extended optimizable linear relaxation in α,β-CROWN to Sine and GeLU, as discussed in Appendix B.

model size each method can handle w.r.t. a threshold on the number of verified instances. For example, if our threshold is 20 verified instances, GenBaB can at least scale to 4×500 (22 instances verified) while α,β-CROWN w/o BaB cannot even scale to 4×100 (likely even much smaller, as only 4 instances are verified for 4×100).

For PRIMA and vanilla CROWN, as we only use relatively hard instances for verification here, these two methods are unable to verify any instance in this experiment. For VeriNet, all the models here are too large without a license for the FICO Xpress solver (an academic license was not available to us as mentioned in Table 2); we have not obtained the code to run Wu et al. [44] on these models. Thus, we do not include the results for VeriNet or Wu et al. [44].

Experiments on LSTMs. Next, we experiment on LSTMs containing more complex nonlinearities, including both Sigmoid and Tanh activations, as well as multiplication as $\text{sigmoid}(x)\tanh(y)$ and $\text{sigmoid}(x)y$. We compare with PROVER [29] which is a specialized verifier for RNNs and it outperforms earlier works [19]. While there are other works on verifying RNN and LSTM, such as [9, 26, 28], we have not obtained their code, and we also make orthogonal contributions compared to them on improving the relaxation for RNN verification which can also be combined with our BaB. We take the hardest model, an LSTM for MNIST, from the main experiments of PROVER (other models can be verified by PROVER on more than 90% instances and are thus omitted), where each 28×28 image is sliced into 7 frames for LSTM. We also have two LSTMs trained by ourselves on CIFAR-10, where we linearly map each 32×32 image into 4 patches as the input tokens, similar to ViTs with patches [8]. Table 4 shows the results.

Table 4: Number of verified instances out of 100 instances on LSTMs and ViTs. The MNIST model is from PROVER [29] with $\epsilon = 0.01$, and the CIFAR-10 models are trained by ourselves with $\epsilon = 1/255$. "LSTM-7-32" indicates an LSTM with 7 input frames and 32 hidden neurons, similar for the other two models. "ViT-*L-H*" stands for *L* layers and *H* heads. Some models have fewer than 100 instances, after filtering out easy or impossible instances, as shown in "upper bounds". Results for PROVER are obtained by running the tool (https://github.com/eth-sri/prover). Results for DeepT are obtained by running the tool (https://github.com/eth-sri/DeepT). PROVER and DeepT specialize in RNNs and ViTs, respectively.

| Method | MNIST Model | CIFAR-10 Models | | | | | |
	LSTM-7-32	LSTM-4-32	LSTM-4-64	ViT-1-3	ViT-1-6	ViT-2-3	ViT-2-6
PROVER	63	8	3	-	-	-	-
DeepT	-	-	-	0	1	0	1
α,β-CROWN w/o BaB	82	16	9	1	3	11	7
GenBaB (ours)	**84**	**20**	**14**	**49**	**72**	**65**	**56**
Upper bound	98	100	100	67	92	72	69

α,β-CROWN without BaB can already outperform PROVER with specialized relaxation for RNN and LSTM. Our GenBaB outperforms both PROVER and α,β-CROWN without BaB.

Experiments on ViTs. We also experiment on ViTs which contain more other nonlinearities, as shown in Table 1. For ViTs, we compare with DeepT [1] which is specialized for verifying Transformers without BaB. We show the results in Table 4, where our methods outperform DeepT, and our GenBaB effectively improves the verification. Moreover, in Appendix C.2, we compare with Wei et al. [42] which supports verifying attention networks but not the entire ViT, and we experiment on models from Wei et al. [42] and find that our GenBaB also outperforms Wei et al. [42].

Experiments on ML4ACOPF. Finally, we experiment on models for the Machine Learning for AC Optimal Power Flow (ML4ACOPF) problem [14], and we adopt the ML4ACOPF neural network verification benchmark, a standardized benchmark in the 2023 International Verification of Neural Networks Competition (VNN-COMP'23). The benchmark consists of a NN with power demands as inputs, and the output of the NN gives an operation plan of electric power plants. Then, the benchmark aims to check for a few nonlinear constraint violations of this plan, such as power generation and balance constraints. These constraints, as part of the computational graph to verify, involve many nonlinearities including Sine, Sigmoid, multiplication, and square function. Our work is the first to support this verification problem. Among the 23 benchmark instances, PGD attack finds a counterexample on one instance, and our GenBaB verifies all the remaining 22 instances. Only 16 instances can be verified if BaB is disabled. This experiment

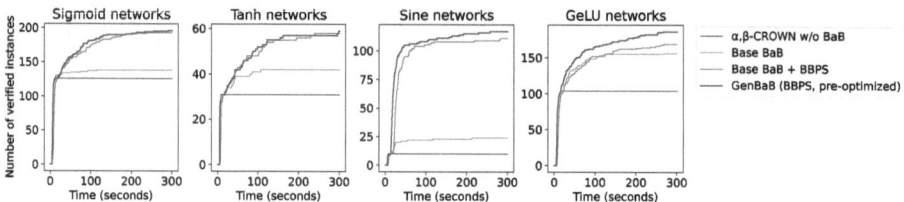

Fig. 3: Total number of verified instances against running time threshold on feedforward networks for CIFAR-10 with various activation functions. "Base BaB" means that in the most basic BaB setting, we use a generalized BaBSR heuristic and always branch in the middle point of intermediate bounds. "Base + BBPS" uses our BBPS heuristic. Our full GenBaB uses both BBPS and pre-optimized branching points.

shows a more practical application of our work and further demonstrates the effectiveness of our framework.

4.3 Time Cost

Table 5: Time cost of pre-optimizing the branching points for models with different nonlinearities. We only need to run pre-optimization once for each model. The cost is thus negligible as we have many data instances to verify.

Model	Sigmoid	Tanh	Sin	GeLU	LSTM	ViT
Time cost (seconds)	49	55	112	82	761	746

In this section, we analyze the time cost of our method. Our GenBaB aims to verify additional instances which cannot be verified without BaB, for models with general nonlinearities. Average time is not a suitable metric here [41], because different methods verify different numbers of instances, and a stronger verifier which can verify more hard instances requiring more time cost will naturally have a larger average time compared to a weak verifier which can only verify the easiest instances quickly. Instead, we plot the number of verified instances against different time thresholds in Figure 3. Such plots, a.k.a. "cactus plots", are commonly adopted in previous works [3, 41]. The plots show that our GenBaB enables the verification of more instances as more time budget is allowed for BaB. While the baseline without BaB can verify some relatively easy instances within a short running time (GenBaB can also verify these easy instances during the initial verification with the same time cost if BaB is not needed), the baseline cannot utilize the remaining time budget to verify more instances. Time cost for LSTM and ViT models are shown in Appendix C.1. In Table 5, we also show the time cost of pre-optimizing the branching points. Overall, the pre-optimization can be done quickly. As explained in Section 3.3, this time cost is negligible for the overall verification, as we only need to run the pre-optimization once for each model and the produced lookup table of branching points can be used to verify an arbitrary number of instances.

4.4   Comparison with BaB on ReLU for Models Containing ReLU

Table 6: Number of verified instances by GenBaB compared to BaB on ReLU only, for certain models containing ReLU. For BaB on ReLU only, we show results for two different branching heuristic (FSB [7] and our BBPS).

Method	ViT-1-3	ViT-1-6	ViT-2-3	ViT-2-6	ML4ACOPF
BaB on ReLU only (FSB)	47	70	63	55	18
BaB on ReLU only (BBPS)	47	70	63	55	21
GenBaB	**49**	**72**	**65**	**56**	**22**
Upper bound	67	92	72	69	22

Although our focus is on BaB on non-ReLU nonlinearities, some of the relatively complicated models involved in our experiments still contain ReLU, and thus we compare our GenBaB with BaB on ReLU only for these models. Specifically, only ViT and ML4ACOPF models in our experiments contain ReLU, although they also contain many other nonlinearities. We show results in Table 6. The results demonstrate that our GenBaB which branches on general nonlinearities outperforms BaB on ReLU only for the models containing ReLU. And many other models with other nonlinearities do not even contain ReLU. Threfore, our GenBaB is important for the BaB on models with general nonlinearities. We also observe that when we only conduct BaB on ReLU for ML4ACOPF, our BBPS heuristic also outperforms the FSB heuristic [7] which is the default branching heuristic adopted by α,β-CROWN for ReLU (FSB is improved from BaBSR [4] and enhanced with a filtering mechanism to compute actual verified bounds for a shortlist of neurons), and our GenBaB which considers all the nonlinearities can verify more instances (all the 22 possible instances are verified) compared to BaB on ReLU only.

5   Related Work

Due to the NP-complete nature of the NN verification [18], linear bound propagation [34, 43, 48] has been proposed to relax nonlinearities in a NN network using linear lower and upper bounds and then propagate the linear relationship between different layers, so that tractable output bounds can be efficiently computed for much larger NNs with various architectures [2, 19, 31, 45]. A limitation of using linear bound propagation only is that the linear relaxation, which depends on the output bounds of intermediate layers, can often have a limited tightness as the intermediate bounds gradually become looser in later layers. Therefore, branch-and-bound (BaB) has been an essential technique in state-of-the-art verifiers [5, 7, 16, 20, 23, 30, 39, 41, 44, 46] leveraging linear relaxation, which iteratively branches the intermediate bounds of selected neurons to enable tight linear relaxation and compute tighter output bounds. However, most of the existing works on the BaB for NN verification have focused on ReLU networks with the piecewise-linear ReLU activation function, and they are not directly applicable to NNs with nonlinearities beyond ReLU. Nevertheless, there are several previous works on the BaB for verifying NNs with nonlinearities other than ReLU. Henriksen and Lomuscio [15] conducted BaB on Sigmoid and Tanh networks, but their framework depends on a commercial LP solver which has been argued as less effective than recent NN verification methods using linear bound propagation [41]. Besides, Wu et al. [44] studied verifying Sigmoid networks with counter-example-guided abstraction refinement. These works have focused on S-shaped activations such as Sigmoid and Tanh, and there still lacks a general framework supporting general nonlinearities beyond a particular type of activation functions, which we address in this paper.

Orthogonal to our contributions on BaB for general nonlinearities, many works studied the verification of NNs with various nonlinearities without considering BaB, by improving the linear relaxation or extending the support of verification to various architectures or specifications: Sigmoid and Tanh networks [2, 6, 48], RNNs and LSTMs [9, 19, 26, 29, 37, 49], Transformers [1, 32, 42, 50], general computational graphs [45], and specifications on activation patterns instead of input [12]. Contributions along these lines may be combined with our work, as our BaB is independent from the underlying linear relaxation adopted. Moreover, some works improved the branching heuristic for verifying ReLU networks: Lu and Mudigonda [23] proposed to use a Graph Neural Network for the branching heuristic; De Palma et al. [7] proposed Filtered Smart Branching (FSB) which filters initial candidates by a heuristic score and then uses a more accurate bound computation to select an optimal neuron from a shortlist; Ferrari et al. [11] considered the effect of a tighter multi-neuron relaxation in the branching heuristic. These insights originally for ReLU networks may inspire future improvement of the BaB for general nonlinearities.

6   Conclusion

To conclude, we propose a general BaB framework for NN verification involving general nonlinearities in general computational graphs. We also propose a new branching heuristic for deciding branched neurons and a pre-optimization procedure for deciding branching points. Experiments on verifying NNs with various nonlinearities demonstrate the effectiveness of our method.

Acknowledgments

This project is supported in part by NSF 2048280, 2331966, 2331967 and ONR N00014-23-1-2300:P00001. Huan Zhang is supported in part by the AI2050 program at Schmidt Sciences (Grant #G-23-65921).

Bibliography

[1] Bonaert, G., Dimitrov, D.I., Baader, M., Vechev, M.: Fast and precise certification of transformers. In: Proceedings of the 42nd ACM SIGPLAN International Conference on Programming Language Design and Implementation, pp. 466–481 (2021)

[2] Boopathy, A., Weng, T., Chen, P., Liu, S., Daniel, L.: Cnn-cert: An efficient framework for certifying robustness of convolutional neural networks. In: The Thirty-Third AAAI Conference on Artificial Intelligence, pp. 3240–3247 (2019), https://doi.org/10.1609/aaai.v33i01.33013240

[3] Brix, C., Bak, S., Liu, C., Johnson, T.T.: The fourth international verification of neural networks competition (vnn-comp 2023): Summary and results. arXiv preprint arXiv:2312.16760 (2023)

[4] Bunel, R., Mudigonda, P., Turkaslan, I., Torr, P., Lu, J., Kohli, P.: Branch and bound for piecewise linear neural network verification. Journal of Machine Learning Research **21**(2020) (2020)

[5] Bunel, R., Turkaslan, I., Torr, P.H.S., Kohli, P., Mudigonda, P.K.: A unified view of piecewise linear neural network verification. In: Advances in Neural Information Processing Systems, pp. 4795–4804 (2018)

[6] Choi, S.W., Ivashchenko, M., Nguyen, L.V., Tran, H.D.: Reachability analysis of sigmoidal neural networks. ACM Transactions on Embedded Computing Systems (2023)

[7] De Palma, A., Bunel, R., Desmaison, A., Dvijotham, K., Kohli, P., Torr, P.H., Kumar, M.P.: Improved branch and bound for neural network verification via lagrangian decomposition. arXiv preprint arXiv:2104.06718 (2021)

[8] Dosovitskiy, A., Beyer, L., Kolesnikov, A., Weissenborn, D., Zhai, X., Unterthiner, T., Dehghani, M., Minderer, M., Heigold, G., Gelly, S., Uszkoreit, J., Houlsby, N.: An image is worth 16x16 words: Transformers for image recognition at scale. In: International Conference on Learning Representations (2021)

[9] Du, T., Ji, S., Shen, L., Zhang, Y., Li, J., Shi, J., Fang, C., Yin, J., Beyah, R., Wang, T.: Cert-rnn: Towards certifying the robustness of recurrent neural networks. In: Proceedings of the 2021 ACM SIGSAC Conference on Computer and Communications Security, p. 516–534, CCS '21 (2021), ISBN 9781450384544, https://doi.org/10.1145/3460120.3484538

[10] Dvijotham, K., Stanforth, R., Gowal, S., Mann, T.A., Kohli, P.: A dual approach to scalable verification of deep networks. In: Proceedings of the Thirty-Fourth Conference on Uncertainty in Artificial Intelligence, UAI 2018, Monterey, California, USA, August 6-10, 2018, pp. 550–559 (2018)

[11] Ferrari, C., Mueller, M.N., Jovanović, N., Vechev, M.: Complete verification via multi-neuron relaxation guided branch-and-bound. In: International Conference on Learning Representations (2021)

[12] Geng, C., Le, N., Xu, X., Wang, Z., Gurfinkel, A., Si, X.: Towards reliable neural specifications. In: International Conference on Machine Learning, pp. 11196–11212, PMLR (2023)

[13] Goodfellow, I.J., Shlens, J., Szegedy, C.: Explaining and harnessing adversarial examples. In: International Conference on Learning Representations (2015)

[14] Guha, N., Wang, Z., Wytock, M., Majumdar, A.: Machine learning for ac optimal power flow. arXiv preprint arXiv:1910.08842 (2019)

[15] Henriksen, P., Lomuscio, A.: Efficient neural network verification via adaptive refinement and adversarial search. In: ECAI 2020, pp. 2513–2520, IOS Press (2020)

[16] Henriksen, P., Lomuscio, A.: Deepsplit: An efficient splitting method for neural network verification via indirect effect analysis. In: IJCAI, pp. 2549–2555 (2021)

[17] Hochreiter, S., Schmidhuber, J.: Long short-term memory. Neural computation **9**(8), 1735–1780 (1997)

[18] Katz, G., Barrett, C., Dill, D.L., Julian, K., Kochenderfer, M.J.: Reluplex: An efficient smt solver for verifying deep neural networks. In: International Conference on Computer Aided Verification, pp. 97–117 (2017)

[19] Ko, C., Lyu, Z., Weng, L., Daniel, L., Wong, N., Lin, D.: POPQORN: quantifying robustness of recurrent neural networks. In: International Conference on Machine Learning, Proceedings of Machine Learning Research, vol. 97, pp. 3468–3477 (2019)

[20] Kouvaros, P., Lomuscio, A.: Towards scalable complete verification of relu neural networks via dependency-based branching. In: IJCAI, pp. 2643–2650 (2021)

[21] Krizhevsky, A., Hinton, G., et al.: Learning multiple layers of features from tiny images. Technical Report TR-2009 (2009)

[22] LeCun, Y., Cortes, C., Burges, C.: Mnist handwritten digit database. ATT Labs [Online]. Available: http://yann.lecun.com/exdb/mnist **2** (2010)

[23] Lu, J., Mudigonda, P.: Neural network branching for neural network verification. In: Proceedings of the International Conference on Learning Representations (ICLR 2020), Open Review (2020)

[24] Lyu, Z., Ko, C., Kong, Z., Wong, N., Lin, D., Daniel, L.: Fastened CROWN: tightened neural network robustness certificates. In: The Thirty-Fourth AAAI Conference on Artificial Intelligence, pp. 5037–5044 (2020)

[25] Madry, A., Makelov, A., Schmidt, L., Tsipras, D., Vladu, A.: Towards deep learning models resistant to adversarial attacks. In: International Conference on Learning Representations (2018)

[26] Mohammadinejad, S., Paulsen, B., Deshmukh, J.V., Wang, C.: Diffrnn: Differential verification of recurrent neural networks. In: Formal Modeling and Analysis of Timed Systems: 19th International Conference, FORMATS 2021, Paris, France, August 24–26, 2021, Proceedings 19, pp. 117–134, Springer (2021)

[27] Müller, M.N., Makarchuk, G., Singh, G., Püschel, M., Vechev, M.: Prima: general and precise neural network certification via scalable convex hull approx-

imations. Proceedings of the ACM on Programming Languages **6**(POPL), 1–33 (2022)

[28] Paulsen, B., Wang, C.: Linsyn: Synthesizing tight linear bounds for arbitrary neural network activation functions. In: Tools and Algorithms for the Construction and Analysis of Systems: 28th International Conference, TACAS 2022, Held as Part of the European Joint Conferences on Theory and Practice of Software, ETAPS 2022, Munich, Germany, April 2–7, 2022, Proceedings, Part I, pp. 357–376, Springer (2022)

[29] Ryou, W., Chen, J., Balunovic, M., Singh, G., Dan, A., Vechev, M.: Scalable polyhedral verification of recurrent neural networks. In: International Conference on Computer Aided Verification, pp. 225–248 (2021)

[30] Shi, Z., Wang, Y., Zhang, H., Kolter, J.Z., Hsieh, C.J.: Efficiently computing local lipschitz constants of neural networks via bound propagation. Advances in Neural Information Processing Systems **35**, 2350–2364 (2022)

[31] Shi, Z., Zhang, H., Chang, K., Huang, M., Hsieh, C.: Robustness verification for transformers. In: International Conference on Learning Representations (2020)

[32] Shi, Z., Zhang, H., Chang, K.W., Huang, M., Hsieh, C.J.: Robustness verification for transformers. In: International Conference on Learning Representations (2019)

[33] Singh, G., Ganvir, R., Püschel, M., Vechev, M.T.: Beyond the single neuron convex barrier for neural network certification. In: Advances in Neural Information Processing Systems, pp. 15072–15083 (2019)

[34] Singh, G., Gehr, T., Püschel, M., Vechev, M.: An abstract domain for certifying neural networks. Proceedings of the ACM on Programming Languages **3**(POPL), 41 (2019)

[35] Sitzmann, V., Martel, J., Bergman, A., Lindell, D., Wetzstein, G.: Implicit neural representations with periodic activation functions. Advances in Neural Information Processing Systems **33**, 7462–7473 (2020)

[36] Szegedy, C., Zaremba, W., Sutskever, I., Bruna, J., Erhan, D., Goodfellow, I.J., Fergus, R.: Intriguing properties of neural networks. In: International Conference on Learning Representations (2014)

[37] Tran, H.D., Choi, S.W., Yang, X., Yamaguchi, T., Hoxha, B., Prokhorov, D.: Verification of recurrent neural networks with star reachability. In: Proceedings of the 26th ACM International Conference on Hybrid Systems: Computation and Control, pp. 1–13 (2023)

[38] Vaswani, A., Shazeer, N., Parmar, N., Uszkoreit, J., Jones, L., Gomez, A.N., Kaiser, L., Polosukhin, I.: Attention is all you need. In: Advances in Neural Information Processing Systems 30: Annual Conference on Neural Information Processing Systems 2017, December 4-9, 2017, Long Beach, CA, USA, pp. 5998–6008 (2017)

[39] Wang, S., Pei, K., Whitehouse, J., Yang, J., Jana, S.: Efficient formal safety analysis of neural networks. In: Advances in Neural Information Processing Systems, pp. 6369–6379 (2018)

[40] Wang, S., Pei, K., Whitehouse, J., Yang, J., Jana, S.: Formal security analysis of neural networks using symbolic intervals. In: 27th {USENIX} Security Symposium ({USENIX} Security 18), pp. 1599–1614 (2018)

[41] Wang, S., Zhang, H., Xu, K., Lin, X., Jana, S., Hsieh, C.J., Kolter, J.Z.: Beta-crown: Efficient bound propagation with per-neuron split constraints for neural network robustness verification. Advances in Neural Information Processing Systems **34**, 29909–29921 (2021)

[42] Wei, D., Wu, H., Wu, M., Chen, P.Y., Barrett, C., Farchi, E.: Convex bounds on the softmax function with applications to robustness verification. In: International Conference on Artificial Intelligence and Statistics, pp. 6853–6878, PMLR (2023)

[43] Wong, E., Kolter, J.Z.: Provable defenses against adversarial examples via the convex outer adversarial polytope. In: International Conference on Machine Learning, Proceedings of Machine Learning Research, vol. 80, pp. 5283–5292 (2018)

[44] Wu, H., Tagomori, T., Robey, A., Yang, F., Matni, N., Pappas, G., Hassani, H., Pasareanu, C., Barrett, C.: Toward certified robustness against real-world distribution shifts. arXiv preprint arXiv:2206.03669 (2022)

[45] Xu, K., Shi, Z., Zhang, H., Wang, Y., Chang, K., Huang, M., Kailkhura, B., Lin, X., Hsieh, C.: Automatic perturbation analysis for scalable certified robustness and beyond. In: Advances in Neural Information Processing Systems (2020)

[46] Xu, K., Zhang, H., Wang, S., Wang, Y., Jana, S., Lin, X., Hsieh, C.: Fast and complete: Enabling complete neural network verification with rapid and massively parallel incomplete verifiers. In: International Conference on Learning Representations (2021)

[47] Zhang, H., Chen, H., Xiao, C., Gowal, S., Stanforth, R., Li, B., Boning, D.S., Hsieh, C.: Towards stable and efficient training of verifiably robust neural networks. In: International Conference on Learning Representations (2020)

[48] Zhang, H., Weng, T., Chen, P., Hsieh, C., Daniel, L.: Efficient neural network robustness certification with general activation functions. In: Advances in Neural Information Processing Systems, pp. 4944–4953 (2018)

[49] Zhang, Y., Du, T., Ji, S., Tang, P., Guo, S.: Rnn-guard: Certified robustness against multi-frame attacks for recurrent neural networks. arXiv preprint arXiv:2304.07980 (2023)

[50] Zhang, Y., Shen, L., Guo, S., Ji, S.: Galileo: General linear relaxation framework for tightening robustness certification of transformers. In: Proceedings of the AAAI Conference on Artificial Intelligence, vol. 38, pp. 21797–21805 (2024)

[51] Zhou, X., Xu, H., Xu, A., Shi, Z., Hsieh, C.J., Zhang, H.: Testing neural network verifiers: A soundness benchmark with hidden counterexamples. arXiv preprint arXiv:2412.03154 (2024)

CYCLONE: A Heterogeneous Tool for Verifying Infinite Descent

Liron Cohen[1]([✉])(ID), Reuben N. S. Rowe[2](ID), and Matan Shaked[1](ID)

[1] Ben-Gurion University, Beer-Sheva, Israel
cliron@bgu.ac.il, shakedma@post.bgu.ac.il
[2] Royal Holloway, University of London, Egham, UK
reuben.rowe@rhul.ac.uk

Abstract. The Infinite Descent property underpins key verification techniques, such as size-change program termination and cyclic proofs. Deciding whether the Infinite Descent property holds of a given program or cyclic deduction is PSPACE-complete, with several exponential time algorithms in the literature. In this paper, we consider algorithms with better time complexity but which are (necessarily) *incomplete*. Concretely, we formulate and evaluate a number of alternative algorithms for semi-deciding Infinite Descent. Our aim is to improve average runtime performance by utilising more efficient algorithms for specific subclasses of input. We present CYCLONE, a tool integrating these algorithms with an existing (complete) decision procedure. We evaluate CYCLONE on a large suite of examples harvested from the Cyclist theorem prover, finding that the incomplete algorithms achieve extremely high coverage and afford substantial runtime improvement in practice. We thus believe that the CYCLONE tool will foster broader adoption of techniques based on Infinite Descent and expand their practical applications.

Keywords: Infinite descent · Cyclic proof · Program termination

1 Introduction

Infinite Descent is an ω-regular liveness property that has important practical applications in the verification of software. For instance, it underpins the size-change framework for checking program termination [15], in which a program's call-graph is used to produce an abstraction recording when the values manipulated by the program (e.g. numbers) decrease as they are passed between function calls. Infinite Descent then states that along all infinite paths through this call-graph, we can trace a value that (strictly) decreases infinitely often. If the call-graph satisfies this property then we know the program must terminate, since the order used to interpret the decrease of values is well-founded. This technique is used, for example, in the termination checker for the Agda proof assistant [1].

Infinite Descent also plays a crucial role in cyclic proof-theoretical techniques for reasoning about inductive (and coinductive) properties [6,9,10,11,12,21,23].

© The Author(s) 2025
A. Gurfinkel and M. Heule (Eds.): TACAS 2025, LNCS 15696, pp. 336–354, 2025.
https://doi.org/10.1007/978-3-031-90643-5_18

$$
\cfrac{
  \cfrac{
    \cfrac{
      \cfrac{
        \cfrac{
          \cfrac{6:\ N(x) \vdash O(x), E(x)}{5:\ N(y) \vdash O(y), E(y)}\ \text{SUBST}
        }{4:\ N(y) \vdash O(y), O(s(y))}\ \text{INTRO}_{,s}
      }{3:\ N(y) \vdash E(s(y)), O(s(y))}\ \text{INTR}_{E,s}
    }{
      \cfrac{2:\ \vdash E(0), O(0)}{}\ \text{INTR}_{E,0}
      \qquad
    }
  }{1:\ N(x) \vdash E(x), O(x)}\ \text{SPLIT}_N
}{0:\ N(x) \vdash E(x) \vee O(x)}\ \vee\text{R}
$$

Fig. 1: A cyclic proof that every natural number is either even or odd. The blue trace witnesses the Infinite Descent, with progress marked by the blue circle.

Instead of using inference rules in which a (co)inductive invariant must be explicitly provided, the invariants can be 'discovered' by repeatedly decomposing a goal into subgoals that are either provable or reducible back to the original goal, forming a cycle in the proof. The Infinite Descent condition is then used to justify the soundness of such a cyclic proof graph. In proof-theoretic settings, the notion of 'decrease' is usually called 'progress', and commonly corresponds to particular logic-specific steps that 'unfold' instances of (co)inductive definitions.

For example, Fig. 1 shows a cyclic proof of the fact that every natural number is either even or odd, in a system for first-order logic with inductive predicates. The natural numbers predicate N is (inductively) defined via the rules $N(0)$ and $N(s(x)) \Leftarrow N(x)$ (where s stands for the successor). The predicates E and O denote even and odd numbers, respectively, and are mutually defined via the rules $E(0)$, $O(s(x)) \Leftarrow E(x)$ and $E(s(x)) \Leftarrow O(x)$. The SPLIT$_N$ rule performs a case split on the predicate instance $N(x)$, guided by the defining rules for N, which substitutes 0 and $s(y)$ for x in the left- and right-hand premises, respectively. In the latter, y is a fresh variable (denoting the predecessor of x) for which we know from the definition of N that $N(y)$ must hold. The other steps of the proof unfold the E and O predicate instances, and perform substitutions. A cyclic proof has the structure of a tree with 'backlinks', i.e. a tree in which some of the leaves (called *buds*) have an edge to another node (called its *companion*). In Fig. 1, node 6 is a bud whose companion is (the syntactically equal) node 1. When all buds link to an ancestor node (as in this case), the proof is said to be (in) *cycle normal (form)*. However, this need not be the case in general. The proof satisfies the Infinite Descent property since along the infinite path traversing the cycle, we can trace a value (the instances of the N predicate) that *progresses* (i.e. is unfolded by the SPLIT$_N$ rule) infinitely often.

This kind of cyclic reasoning has been employed widely to create both theoretical frameworks for program verification and inductive theorem proving (e.g., [3,4,20,24,25,27,17]), as well the Cypress program synthesis tool [13] and the automatic theorem provers Cyclist [5], Songbird [7], Inductor [22] and CycleQ [14]. Since the problem of deciding the Infinite Descent property is PSPACE-complete [15,18], in practice these tools all implement one of a number of known algorithms that have worst-case exponential runtimes [8]. Although this worst-case performance is not often encountered 'in the wild', these tools still rely on deciding large numbers of problem instances. Therefore any speed up of the Infinite Descent check has the potential to provide significant benefits in practice.

Our goal is to advance the state-of-the-art for deciding Infinite Descent and thus push forward the practical use of automated cyclic reasoning and termination checking. Our approach is to identify more efficient algorithms that only *semi*-(co)decide Infinite Descent, along with (efficiently decidable) characterisations of the subclass of instances on which they may return a definite answer. The idea is that, since they do not need to uniformly treat all problem instances, these algorithms may utilise particular structure in the input to return an answer more quickly than the full decision procedures. We then heuristically combine these semi-decision procedures into a heterogeneous pipeline, defaulting to a uniform decision procedure in case none of them can return an answer.

In this paper we describe three such algorithms. The first decides an existing criterion, proposed by Brotherston [2], called the Trace Manifold condition. The other two decide novel criteria that we have formulated and call "Flat Cycles" and "Descending Unicycles", respectively. We analyse the coverage of these algorithms by harvesting a large database of problem instances generated by the test suites of the Cyclist theorem prover, which comprise inductive entailments of First-Order Logic and Separation Logic. Guided by the analysis of these algorithms, we combine and implement them within a new tool dubbed CYCLONE [19], which we integrate into Cyclist. We present an evaluation of our tool's performance on our harvested database, comparing it to the performance of the existing decision procedures. We found that CYCLONE demonstrates significant runtime improvements, sometimes of several orders of magnitude.

Paper Outline. Sec. 2 formally defines the Infinite Descent problem, in a general form, and summarises the existing decision procedures. Sec. 3 describes the database of problem instances that we harvested for evaluating our new algorithms. Sec. 4 then describes our novel semi-decision procedures. In Sec. 5 we present the implementation of our tool, CYCLONE, and compare its performance to the existing methods implemented in Cyclist. Finally, Sec. 6 concludes.

2   Infinite Descent for Sloped Graphs

We begin by formally defining the Infinite Descent property in the abstract setting of *sloped graphs*, following [8], which captures the essence of the Infinite Descent problem in an application-independent way. That is, the formulation of Infinite Descent in size-change termination, or some given cyclic logical proof system, are special instances of the abstract definition we give here.

Infinite Descent tracks the ordering relationship between (abstract) values along paths in a graph. The following definition of *sloped graphs* thus augments the standard notion of a directed graph by associating with each node, or vertex, a collection of abstract *positions*, and with each edge a relation assigning (flat or downward) *slopes* between the positions associated with its end-points.

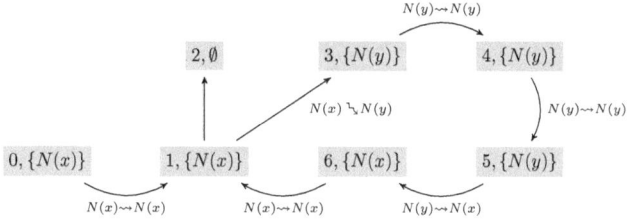

Fig. 2: Sloped graph from Example 1

Definition 1 (Sloped graphs). *We assume a set* Pos *of positions and a set* S = {⤳, ⬃} *of slopes, whose elements are called* flat *and* downward, *respectively.*
- *A* sloped relation $R \subseteq$ Pos × Pos × S *is a partial function from pairs of positions to slopes.*
- *A* sloped graph *SG is a tuple* $(V, E, Ps, (R_{v,v'})_{(v,v') \in E})$ *such that:*
  (1) (V, E) *is a directed graph with nodes V and edges E;*
  (2) $Ps : V \to \wp(\text{Pos})$ *is a function assigning a set of positions to every node;*
  (3) $(R_{v,v'})_{(v,v') \in E}$ *is a family of sloped relations $R_{v,v'} \subseteq Ps(v) \times Ps(v') \times$ S indexed by edges.*
We call the quantity $\max \{|Ps(v)| \mid v \in V\}$ *the* (vertex) width *of SG.*

Example 1. The cyclic proof shown in Fig. 1 can be abstracted by the sloped graph $SG = (V, E, Ps, (R_{v,v'})_{(v,v') \in E})$ defined as follows, and depicted in Fig. 2, where we use inductive predicate instances as positions.
- $V = \{0, 1, 2, 3, 4, 5\}$.
- $E = \{(0,1), (1,2), (1,3)(3,4), (4,5), (5,6), (6,1)\}$.
- $Ps(0) = Ps(1) = Ps(6) = \{N(x)\}$, $Ps(3) = Ps(4) = Ps(5) = \{N(y)\}$, $Ps(2) = \emptyset$.
- $R_{0,1} = R_{6,1} = \{(N(x), N(x), ⤳)\}$, $R_{1,3} = \{(N(x), N(y), ⬃)\}$, $R_{3,4} = R_{4,5} = \{(N(y), N(y), ⤳)\}$, and $R_{5,6} = \{(N(y), N(x), ⤳)\}$.

Since a sloped graph is a form of directed graph, we also adopt the graph-theoretic notions of (finite and infinite) *paths* through the graph, which we denote by $(v_i)_{i<\alpha}$ where $\alpha \le \omega$ is (the ordinal that is) the length of the path.

A trace along a path in a sloped graph selects a position from each node in the path, making sure that each position is related to the next by the sloped relations associated with the edges that are traversed.

Definition 2 (Traces). *A trace along a (possibly infinite) path $(v_i)_{i<\alpha}$ in a sloped graph $SG = (V, E, Ps, (R_{v,v'})_{(v,v') \in E})$ is a (possibly infinite) sequence of positions $\tau = (p_i)_{i<\alpha}$ such that, for every $i < \alpha$, both $p_i \in Ps(v_i)$ and $R_{v_i,v_{i+1}}(p_i, p_{i+1}, s)$ for some (necessarily unique) slope s. When $s = ⬃$ we call i a* progressing point *in the trace. We may also write $\tau(v_i)$ to denote the ith position, p_i. A trace is* decreasing *if it has infinitely many progressing points. An infinite path is* descending *if it has a tail along which there is a decreasing trace.*

Definition 3 (Infinite Descent). *A sloped graph is said to satisfy Infinite Descent if all of its infinite paths are descending.*

Algorithm	Time Complexity Upper Bound
VLA	$\mathcal{O}(n^5 \cdot w^2 \cdot 2^{2nw \log(2nw)})$
SLA	$\mathcal{O}(n^2 \cdot w \cdot \min(n^4, 3^{2w^2}) \cdot 2^{2w \log(2w)})$
FWK	$\mathcal{O}(n \cdot w^4 \cdot 3^{3w^2} + n^3 \cdot w^4 \cdot 3^{2w^2})$
OR	$\mathcal{O}(n^3 \cdot w^4 \cdot 3^{2w^2})$

Table 1: Time complexity bounds for Infinite Descent decision procedures

The problem of deciding whether a given sloped graph satisfies Infinite Descent is PSPACE-complete [15,18]. There are two basic approaches for deciding the Infinite Descent property described in the literature.

Automata-theoretic: One approach is to encode the problem as an inclusion between ω-automata: a 'path' automaton that recognises words corresponding to all infinite paths in the sloped graph and a 'trace' automaton that recognises words corresponding to all potential descending traces. A sloped graph satisfies Infinite Descent if and only if the former automaton is included in the latter. The problem can be encoded using ω-words over either the vertices or the sloped relations of the sloped graph. We call these encodings the *Vertex-Language Automata* (VLA) and the *Slope-Language Automata* (SLA) encodings, respectively.

Ramsey-theoretic: An alternative approach is to compute for each pair of nodes the collection of sloped relations consisting of the compositions of the sloped relations along (finite) paths between the two nodes, with slopes combined according to the ordering $\rightsquigarrow \; < \; \searrow$. Once this 'composition closure' is computed, checking Infinite Descent amounts to verifying the presence of certain downward slopes in the relations representing loops in the sloped graph. This encoding is an instance of the algebraic path problem and can be solved using the Floyd-Warshall-Kleene (FWK) algorithm [16]. By taking advantage of the specific symmetric nature of the Infinite Descent setting, a so-called *order-reduced* (OR) optimisation of this procedure is possible [8].

All of these algorithms exhibit exponential worst-case runtime, but the complexity profile of each method depends, in varying proportions, on two parameters of the sloped graph: the number of nodes n, and the vertex width w. The worst-case complexity bounds are summarised in Table 1. A comprehensive account of these methods and their comparative performance can be found in [8].

3   A Database of Sloped Graphs

In order to support our goal of identifying useful classes of sloped graphs for which Infinite Descent can be (semi-)decided (more) efficiently, we generated a large database of sloped graphs using the Cyclist automated theorem prover [5], which we believe to be representative of problem instances arising in real-world applications. Cyclist implements a generic engine for cyclic proof search, supporting arbitrary (cyclic) logical systems by exposing an API to this engine. It currently features a number of logics with inductively defined predicates, includ-

	Satisfies Infinite Descent	Does not satisfy Infinite Descent	(all)
FOL	260	6437	6697
SL	42692	27694	70386
(all)	42952	34131	77083

Table 2: Aggregated numbers of sloped graphs in our database

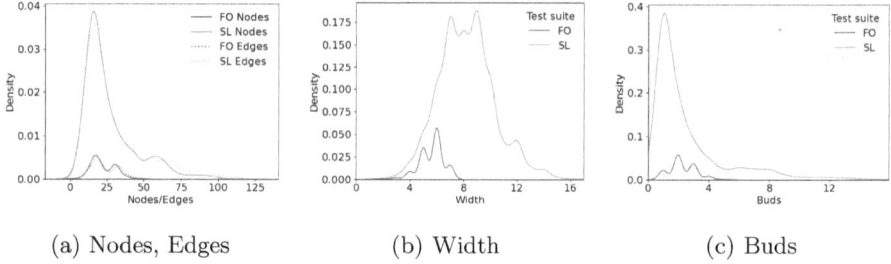

(a) Nodes, Edges   (b) Width   (c) Buds

Fig. 3: Distribution of various sloped graph metrics

ing first-order logic (FOL) and Separation Logic (SL), which come with test suites of representative (valid and invalid) logical entailments. During a search for a cyclic proof of a given entailment, Cyclist runs the Infinite Descent check for each intermediate (partial) candidate proof it encounters. We modified Cyclist to output a JSON representation of the corresponding sloped graphs. (Note that Cyclist also employs a preprocessing procedure for minimizing the proof graphs, which we discuss in Sec. 5.2.)

In total, we collected over 77,000 sloped graphs. Table 2 shows the numbers of sloped graphs aggregated by the logic they were generated from and whether or not they satisfy Infinite Descent. We also collated statistics pertaining to various metrics of sloped graphs, namely the number of nodes, edges, buds, and vertex width. Again aggregated by the logic, Fig. 3 shows the density functions of these metrics. Across the database, per graph, the number of nodes is at most 107 and the number of edges is at most 120, with graphs most frequently having around 20 nodes/edges. Additionally, graphs have a vertex width of at most 17, with the most frequent quantity being around 8. We see a maximum of 16 buds in any graph, with most of the graphs having around 2 buds. We observe that the vertex width is not particularly correlated with the number of edges/nodes and, in general, the width is low compared to the number of nodes. In contrast, in both test suites, we can see a high correlation between the number of nodes and edges with the two metrics being almost identical. We also see that, in general, the more nodes/edges in a graph, the more buds. However, the number of buds is generally *much* lower than the number of nodes. This is not surprising given that the graphs are (proof) trees with (few) backlinks, rather than generally highly connected graphs.

4   Effective Semi-algorithms for Infinite Descent

We now present the novel (incomplete) semi-decision procedures that we developed. Concretely we present the following heuristics, analysing their runtime complexity and coverage (the number of graphs in our database for which it returns a definitive answer, i.e. "yes" or "no"):

Trace Manifold (TM): a criterion from [2], for which we provide a novel algorithm and implementation. This heuristic returns "yes"/"don't know".

Flat Cycles (FC): a novel criterion based on the notion of a *flat projection* of a sloped graph. This heuristic returns "no"/"don't know".

Descending Unicycles (DU): a novel criterion based on *non-overlapping cycles* in a sloped graph. This heuristic returns "yes"/"no"/"don't know".

We began by implementing the Trace Manifold criterion, but we found the coverage of this method on our database to be very low. This prompted us to formulate the other two criteria, which have better runtime complexity and verify Infinite Descent on a much larger class of sloped graphs.

4.1   The Trace Manifold Criterion

The *Trace Manifold* criterion (TM) is a property of basic cycles in a sloped graph, SG, that is a cycle normal tree with backlinks. In such graphs, a basic cycle can be identified with a bud B, being the unique path in the graph leading to B from its companion, denoted $\mathcal{R}(B)$. A *structural connectivity* relation, $\leq_{SG}$, over the buds can also be defined by relating two buds B_1 and B_2 precisely when $\mathcal{R}(B_1)$ lies along the basic cycle associated with B_2.

A trace manifold comprises a set of traces for basic cycles.

Definition 4 (Trace Manifold). *A set of (finite) traces is a trace manifold for a sloped graph $SG = (V, E, Ps, (R_{v,v'})_{(v,v')\in E})$ when it is of the form*

$$\{\tau_{S,B} \mid S \text{ a strongly connected subgraph of } SG, B \in S \text{ is a bud}\}$$

and satisfies the following.

(1) Each $\tau_{S,B} = p_1 \ldots p_n$ is a trace along the basic cycle of B such that there is some slope s for which $(p_n, p_1, s) \in R_{B,\mathcal{R}(B)}$.

(2) For all τ_{S,B_1} and τ_{S,B_2}, if $B_1 \leq_{SG} B_2$ then $\tau_{S,B_1}(\mathcal{R}(B_1)) = \tau_{S,B_2}(\mathcal{R}(B_1))$.

(3) For every strongly connected subgraph, S, of SG there is a bud $B \in S$ such that $\tau_{S,B} = p_1 \ldots p_n$ has a progressing point or $(p_n, p_1, \searrow) \in R_{B,\mathcal{R}(B)}$.

The properties of a trace manifold entail that its constituent traces can be combined to yield descending traces for each infinite path.

Proposition 1 (Trace Manifold Criterion [2, Prop. 7.2.3]). *If a (cycle normal) sloped graph has a trace manifold, then it satisfies Infinite Descent.*

To our knowledge, we are the first to implement a concrete algorithm to decide the trace manifold criterion. Ultimately, however, given its low coverage and potentially exponential runtime, we decided not to include it in CYCLONE's final pipeline.

Algorithm. Firstly, check if the sloped graph, SG, is in cycle normal form, returning "don't know" if not. Otherwise, compute each possible trace along the basic cycles. Then, for each strongly connected subgraph, containing buds $B_1, \ldots, B_n$, check for some possible combination of traces $\tau_1, \ldots, \tau_n$ along their respective basic cycles, with at least one trace progressing, satisfying $\tau_i(\mathcal{R}(B_i)) = \tau_j(\mathcal{R}(B_i))$ for each pair of buds such that $B_i \leq_{SG} B_j$. This check succeeds iff a trace manifold exists. So, return "yes" in this case, otherwise return "don't know".

Complexity and Practical Runtime Evaluation. The algorithm described above is exponential in both the number of buds and the number of nodes of the sloped graph: quantification over all strongly-connected subgraphs leads to the exponential dependency on the number of buds, and the quantification over all traces following basic cycles leads to the exponential dependency in the number of (sloped graph) nodes. Note that, given the set of buds (information that is provided by Cyclist), checking whether a graph is in cycle normal form takes only polynomial time.

Evaluating the implementation of our algorithm we discovered that, despite its high worst-case complexity, its runtime performance on the instances in our database of sloped graphs is, on average, significantly better than the state-of-the-art *complete* method (OR). This is because the number of traces in each of these instances is usually fairly small. We observed that the more edges in the input sloped graph, the faster our implementation of TM compared to that of OR. Our implementation was at most 29% slower than OR, and up to 1,970% faster. However, despite its favourable runtime performance it only covered 31.2% of the sloped graphs in our database that satisfy Infinite Descent, and thus only 17.38% of the database overall. Moreover, although 48.4% of graphs in the database are in cycle normal form, TM returns an answer on only 35.9% of these. Interestingly, though, almost all cycle normal graphs in our database satisfying Infinite Descent also satisfy TM.

4.2   Flat Cycles

This section presents a novel linear runtime method for checking if a sloped graph does *not* satisfy Infinite Descent. For this, we first define the notion of the *flat projection graph*, which is the underlying directed graph retaining only edges whose associated sloped relation contains no downward slope.

Definition 5 (Flat projection graph). *The* Flat Projection Graph *of a sloped graph* $SG = (V, E, Ps, (R_{v,v'})_{(v,v') \in E})$ *is the graph* $SG^{\rightsquigarrow} = (V, E^{\rightsquigarrow})$, *where*

$$E^{\rightsquigarrow} = \{(u, v) \mid (u, v) \in E \wedge \forall p \in Ps(u) \; \forall q \in Ps(v). \, (p, q, \searrow) \notin R_{u,v}\}$$

Proposition 2 (Flat Cycles criterion (FC)). *Let* SG *be a sloped graph. If* $SG^{\rightsquigarrow}$ *has a cycle then* SG *does not satisfy Infinite Descent.*

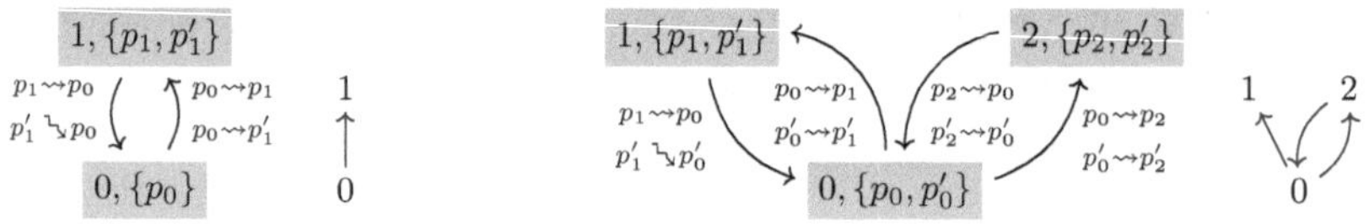

(a) Does not satisfy FC   (b) Satisfies FC

Fig. 4: Sloped graphs and their Flat Projection graphs (in blue)

Algorithm 1 Infinite Descent by the Flat Cycles Criterion

Input: Sloped Graph $SG = (V, E, Ps, (R_{v,v'})_{(v,v') \in E})$, vertex width $= w$
Output: "no" if SG has a flat cycle and "don't know" otherwise
1: $E^{\rightsquigarrow} := \emptyset$
2: **for all** $(u, v) \in E$ **do**   ▷ $|E|$ iterations
3:     **if** $(p, q, \searrow) \notin R_{u,v}$ for all $p \in Ps(u), q \in Ps(v)$ **then**   ▷ $\mathcal{O}(w^2)$
4:         $E^{\rightsquigarrow} \leftarrow E^{\rightsquigarrow} \cup \{(u, v)\}$ ▷ $\mathcal{O}(1)$
5: **if** DFS$(V, E^{\rightsquigarrow})$ detects a cycle **then return** "no"   ▷ $\mathcal{O}(|V| + |E^{\rightsquigarrow}|)$
6: **else return** "don't know"

Example 2. Fig. 4 shows two examples of sloped graphs: one that does not satisfy the flat cycles criterion and one that does. Fig. 4a presents a sloped graph with two nodes: node 0 with one position, p_0, and node 1 with two positions, p_1, p'_1. Since there is a downward slope in $R_{1,0}$, $(1, 0) \notin E^{\rightsquigarrow}$ and therefore the flat projection graph of this sloped graph (presented in blue) does not contain a cycle. This, in turn, entails that FC does not yield a decision on this graph. On the other hand, Fig. 4b presents a sloped graph with three nodes: node 0 having one position and nodes 1, 2, having two positions each. Again, $(1, 0) \notin E^{\rightsquigarrow}$ because there is a downward slope in $R_{1,0}$. However, because there is no downward slope in either $R_{0,2}$ or $R_{2,0}$, we get that $(0, 2) \in E^{\rightsquigarrow}$ and $(2, 0) \in E^{\rightsquigarrow}$, thus, there is a cycle in the flat projection graph (presented in blue), which means that the sloped graph satisfies the flat cycles criterion. Indeed, the sloped graph portrayed in Fig. 4b does not satisfy Infinite Descent, as Prop. 2 entails.

While FC may seem like a strong condition, requiring an entire cycle in the graph with no downward slopes on any of its edges, in practice it is very frequent and covers 80.77% of the graphs in the database that do not satisfy Infinite Descent, and thus 35.76% of the entire database.

Algorithm. Algo. 1 checks if a sloped graph satisfies Infinite Descent using the FC criterion. It generates the flat projection graph and checks it for cycles using a depth-first search (DFS). If there is a cycle, we know from Prop. 2 that the sloped graph does not satisfy Infinite Descent and so return "no". Otherwise, the algorithm returns "don't know".

Complexity and Practical Runtime Evaluation. The algorithm goes over all edges in the sloped graph ($|E|$ iterations) and for each one it checks, in time

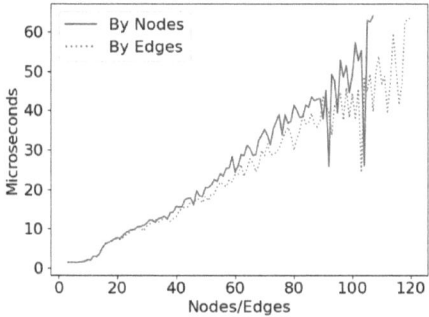

Fig. 5: Flat Cycles Runtime by Nodes and Edges

quadratic in the vertex width of the input graph, whether its associated sloped relation has no downward slope. If the relation has no downward slope we add the edge to the flat edges set, which can be done in $\mathcal{O}(1)$ if we store this set as an adjacency linked list for every node in the graph. Then we perform a DFS on the flat projection graph which has runtime complexity of $\mathcal{O}(|V| + |E^{\leadsto}|)$. Since $E^{\leadsto} \subseteq E$, in the worst case $|E^{\leadsto}| = \mathcal{O}(|E|)$, which makes the worst-case runtime $\mathcal{O}(|E| \cdot w^2 + |V| + |E|) = \mathcal{O}(|V| + |E| \cdot (w^2 + 1))$.

Fig. 5 shows the runtime of checking the criterion as a function of either the number of nodes or the number of edges in the graph. The values in the figure are an average of the runtime among all sloped graphs with each number of nodes/edges. We can see a linear growth in the runtime in both graphs, as expected from the runtime complexity analysis.

4.3 Descending Unicycles

Having defined in the previous section a linear-time algorithm that covers a significant amount of the graphs in the database that *do not* satisfy Infinite Descent, in this section, we present a novel, polynomial-time criterion that covers a significant amount of the graphs that also *do* satisfy Infinite Descent.

We first identify a class of sloped graphs we call *unicycles graphs*. We say that a path from cycle c to cycle c' is any path $v_0, ..., v_n$ such that $v_0 \in c$ and $v_n \in c'$.

Definition 6 (Unicycles graph). *A directed graph $G = (V, E)$ is a unicycles graph if for every two distinct basic cycles c, c' in G, if there is a path from c to c', then there is no path from c' to c.*

Note that a unicycles graph necessarily does not contain any overlapping cycles, i.e., two cycles with some shared node(s). Thus, e.g., the graph in Fig. 4b is not a unicycles graph since there is a path in both directions through the node 0. However, the graph in Fig. 4a is a unicycles graph because it has just one cycle. The graphs in Fig. 6 are unicycles graphs because, in both cases, although there is a path from $c_1 = 0, 1$ to $c_2 = 2, 3$, there is no path from c_2 to c_1.

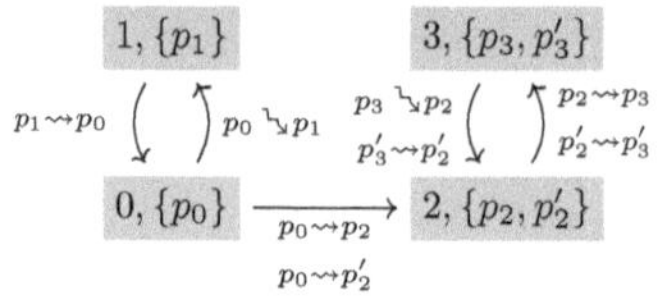

(a) Satisfies DU 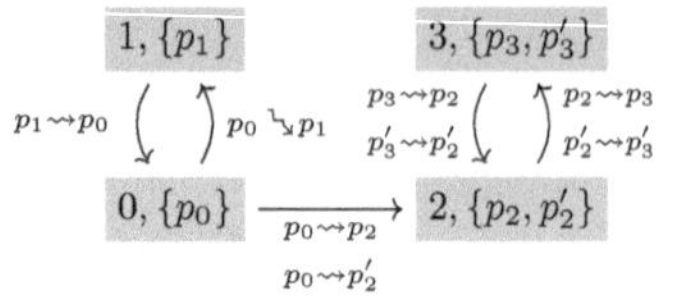   (b) Does not satisfy DU

Fig. 6: Unicycles Graphs

The key insight is that if a sloped graph is a unicycles graph, then the infinite paths in the sloped graph are of the form $\pi = v_0, \ldots, v_m, (u_0, \ldots, u_k)^\omega$, with $u_0, \ldots, u_k$ a basic cycle in the graph. This means that checking Infinite Descent on unicycles graphs amounts to checking whether, for every basic cycle c in the graph, the path c^ω has a progressing trace. We next formalize this requirement.

Definition 7 (Simply descending graph). *We define the following, given a sloped graph* $SG = (V, E, Ps, (R_{v,v'})_{(v,v') \in E})$.
(1) The positions graph induced by a path $\pi = v_1, \ldots, v_m$ *in SG, denoted* SG_π^{pos}, *is a directed graph* (V_π, E_π) *with a distinguished subset of* progressing *edges* $Prog_\pi \subseteq E_\pi$, *defined by:*
  - $V_\pi = \{(v_i, p) \mid 1 \le i \le m \text{ and } p \in Ps(v_i)\}$
  - $E_\pi = \{((v_i, p), (v_{i+1}, q)) \mid 1 \le i < m \text{ and } \exists s.(p, q, s) \in R_{v_i, v_{i+1}}\}$
  - $Prog_\pi = \{((v_i, p), (v_{i+1}, q)) \mid 1 \le i < m \text{ and } (p, q, \searrow) \in R_{v_i, v_{i+1}}\}$
(2) A basic cycle c *in SG is said to be* descending *if* SG_c^{pos} *has a basic cycle with at least one progressing edge (i.e., an edge in* $Prog_c$*).*
(3) We say that SG is simply descending *if every basic cycle in SG is descending.*

Example 3. The graph SG in Fig. 4a is simply descending because the basic cycle $(0, p_0), (1, p'_1)$ of $SG_{(0,1)}^{pos}$ has a progressing edge. The graph SG in Fig. 4b is not simply descending, because its positions graph $SG_{(0,2)}^{pos}$ has no progressing edge, and thus its basic cycle $0, 2$ is not descending. Fig. 6 illustrates two sloped graphs with the same underlying directed graph. The graph in Fig. 6a is simply descending because both $c_1 = (0, 1)$ and $c_2 = (2, 3)$ are descending cycles. However, the graph in Fig. 6b is not simply descending because c_2 is not descending.

For unicycles graphs, the simply descending criterion is both sound *and* complete for Infinite Descent.

Proposition 3 (Descending Unicycles criterion (DU)). *If SG is a unicycles sloped graph, then SG satisfies Infinite Descent iff it is simply descending.*

Like the FC criterion, the DU criterion seems to be a strong condition in requiring that cycles in the sloped graph do not overlap. However, again, in practice, this requirement is satisfied in 90.69% of all graphs in our database, which makes for almost complete coverage of the database. However, unlike the FC criterion, it can return both a definite "yes" and a definite "no" answer.

Algorithm 2 Infinite Descent by the Descending Unicycles Criterion

---

Input: Sloped Graph $SG = (V, E, Ps, (R_{v,v'})_{(v,v')\in E})$, vertex width $= w$

Output: "don't know" if SG is not a unicycles graph, "yes" if Descending
    Unicycles holds for SG and "no" otherwise

1: $SCCs, backedgesLowLinks \leftarrow \mathsf{Tarjan}(V, E)$ $\triangleright\ \mathcal{O}(|V| + |E|)$

2: **if** $\mathsf{hasDuplicates}(backedgesLowLinks)$ **then** $\triangleright\ \mathcal{O}(|V|)$

3:     **return** "don't know"

4: **for all** $SCC \in SCCs$ **do** $\triangleright\ \mathcal{O}(|V|)$ iterations

5:     **if not** $\mathsf{isDescendingCycle}(SCC, SG)$ **then** $\triangleright\ \mathcal{O}(w^2 \cdot |SCC|)$

6:         **return** "no"

7: **return** "yes"

Algorithm. Algo. 2 checks if a sloped graph that is a tree with backlinks satisfies Infinite Descent using the DU criterion. First, it calculates the strongly connected components (SCCs) of the graph, together with the low link of each bud's destination using Tarjan's algorithm [26]. Note that a graph has overlapping cycles if and only if there are two buds whose destination nodes have equal low links. That is because two cycles overlap if and only if they form a strongly connected set and because the buds' destination nodes have the same low link if and only if they are in the same SCC. Thus, if there are duplicates in this *backedgesLowLinks* list, then the graph is not a unicycles graph and we return a "don't know". Otherwise, the graph *is* a unicycles graph, which means that every strongly connected component is a basic cycle. Then, we go over all SCCs and check if they are descending cycles of SG. If and only if so, by Prop. 3 we get that SG satisfies Infinite Descent. Checking if a cycle c is a descending cycle amounts to running Tarjan's algorithm on SG_c^{pos} while also checking with each edge if it is progressing. We find a strongly connected component with a progressing edge in SG_c^{pos} if and only if c is a descending cycle in SG. That is because the progressing edge must be a part of a basic cycle and because every basic cycle is a part of a SCC.

Complexity and Practical Runtime Evaluation. Line 1 uses Tarjan's algorithm, which has a runtime complexity of $\mathcal{O}(|V| + |E|)$. It also returns some of the low links that are generated by Tarjan's algorithm, of which there are $\mathcal{O}(|V|)$. Line 2 looks for duplicates in the returned low links list, which is done in $O(|V|)$ (on average) by generating a hash set from the list and comparing its size to the low links list's size. Finally, line 4 iterates over all SCCs and for each one checks if it is descending using Tarjan's algorithm on SG_{SCC}^{pos}. SG is a unicycles graph, and so in any SCC of SG the number of nodes is equal to the number of edges. Further, since each edge in a strongly connected component SCC has $\mathcal{O}(w^2)$ corresponding edges in SG_{SCC}^{pos}, Tarjan's algorithm on SG_{SCC}^{pos} has runtime complexity of $\mathcal{O}(|SCC| + w^2 \cdot |SCC|)$. Since the SCCs of a graph are a partition of its nodes, the runtime complexity of the loop in Line 4 is $\mathcal{O}(|V| + w^2 \cdot |V|)$. Overall, then, the runtime complexity of Algo. 2 is $\mathcal{O}((|V| + |E|) + |V| + (|V| + w^2 \cdot |V|)) = O(w^2 \cdot |V| + |E|)$.

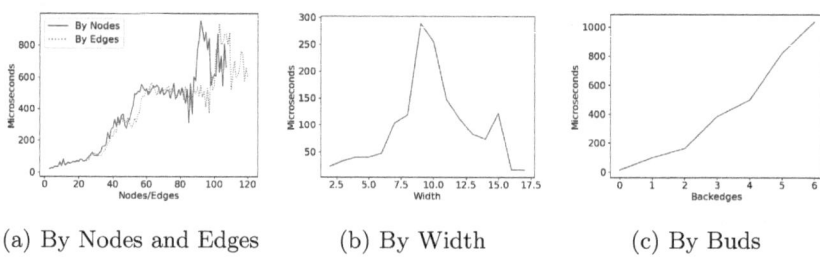

(a) By Nodes and Edges   (b) By Width   (c) By Buds

Fig. 7: Descending Unicycles Runtime

Fig. 7 shows the runtime of checking the DU criterion as a function of the number of nodes, edges, and buds, as well as the vertex width of the graph, with each point in the figure averaging the runtime among all sloped graphs with the associated number of nodes/edges/buds or vertex width. Because of the high correlation between the number of nodes and edges in a sloped graph, we plot both metrics in a single graph. In Fig. 7b, we see the highest runtimes around width 10 because the graphs that have the most amount of nodes/edges in our database also all have a width of around 10. The trend in Fig. 7a is only somewhat linear because the algorithm only traverses the positions of nodes in cycles. A clear linear trend is observed in Fig. 7c which plots the runtime as a function of the number of buds in the graph, which, in unicycles graphs, is the number of cycles. This indicates that the algorithm performs what seems to be a constant amount of work for each cycle in the sloped graphs from our database. This implies that cycles have a consistent size, and together with Fig. 7a we can infer that as the size of cyclic pre-proofs grow, so does the number of cycles.

5   The CYCLONE Verifier and its Evaluation

Having reported above on the individual runtime performance of our implementations of each of the incomplete methods, we now present our integrated tool, CYCLONE, which combines these into a pipeline that defaults to a complete method (specifically, OR) for cases not covered by our new methods. We also present the results of our experimental evaluation, comparing CYCLONE with each of the complete decision procedures alone as they are implement in [8]. We implemented each of our new algorithms, as well as CYCLONE itself, in C++ and integrated into the Cyclist prover framework [5]. A corresponding artifact, containing our implementation and experimental data, is available on Zenodo [19]. The experiments we report on, both in the current and previous section, were all performed on an Apple M1 CPU with 8GB of RAM, running macOS Sonoma.

5.1   Composing the Methods in CYCLONE

The composition of the methods that CYCLONE uses is presented in Algo. 3. As mentioned in sec. 4.1, we do not use the TM method: CYCLONE only uses the FC and DU methods. It first applies the FC criterion to try and return a very fast "no". If FC returns a "don't know", it then uses the DU criterion to try and

Algorithm 3 Cyclone

Input: Sloped Graph $SG = (V, E, Ps, (R_{v,v'})_{(v,v')\in E})$
Output: "yes" if SG satisfies Infinite Descent and "no" otherwise
1: **if** InfDescByFC$(SG) = $ "no" **then return** "no"
2: $DU \leftarrow$ InfDescByDU(SG)
3: **if** $DU \neq$ "don't know" **then return** DU
4: **return** InfDescByOR(SG)

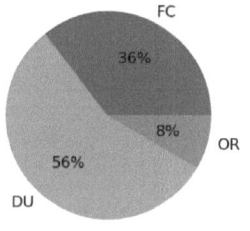

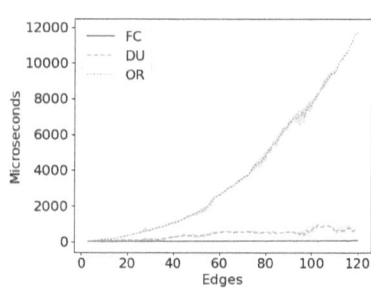

(a) Method Usage Distribution   (b) Method Runtime

Fig. 8: Cyclone Methods Distribution and Runtime

return a (not as) fast "yes" or a "no". Finally, if DU also returns "don't know", CYCLONE resorts to using the existing, complete and exponential OR algorithm to obtain a definitive answer.

Fig. 8a shows the distribution of methods from which CYCLONE derived its answer when run on our database. Fig. 8b presents the average runtime of the different methods used in CYCLONE, aggregated by number of edges, as well as the interquartile ranges. We plot the runtimes only as a function of the number of edges since we observed that the other parameters of the complexity analysis have a high correlation with this parameter. The FC method is considerably faster than the other two, with what appears to be a constant line. The DU method appears to be slower than the FC but is still much faster than OR, which looks at least polynomial. Note that the faster the method the lower its coverage, and recall that FC covers 35.76% of the graphs in the database, whilst DU covers 90.69%. The OR method, which has a complete coverage of the database, is the slowest method. We run the methods in ascending order of runtimes because even when FC returns a "don't know", this still happens fast enough that the overhead does not noticeably affect the overall runtime. The same is true for the DU method compared to the runtime of OR.

We did experiment with an implementation that runs the various methods in parallel, rather than the sequential pipeline described above. However we found that, since the graphs in our database are rather small, the system overheads involved in introducing parallelism were detrimental to the overall performance compared to the sequential pipeline.

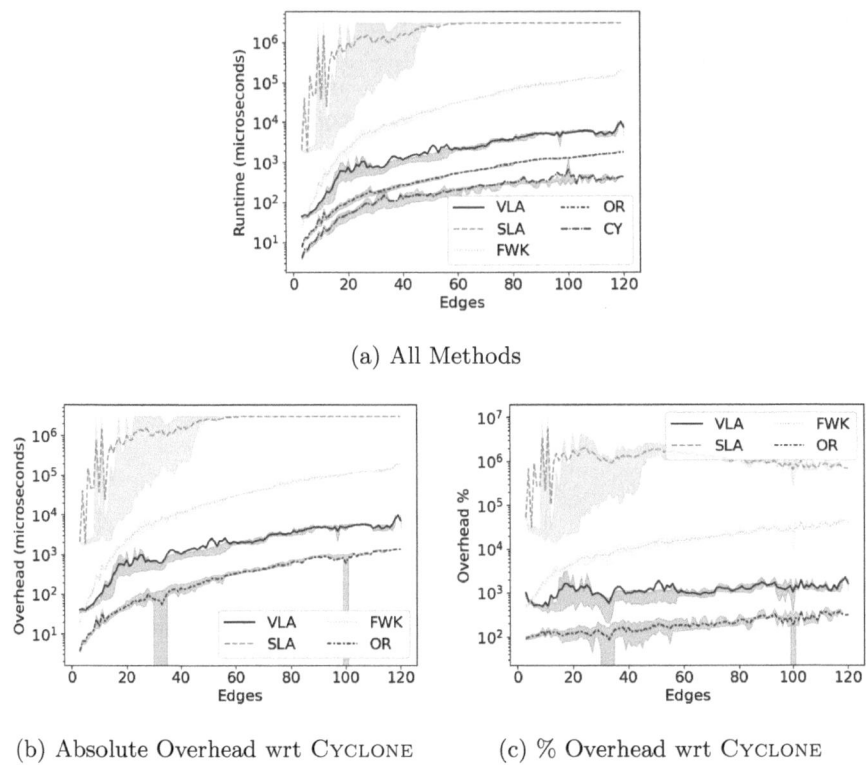

(a) All Methods

(b) Absolute Overhead wrt CYCLONE   (c) % Overhead wrt CYCLONE

Fig. 9: Methods Runtime Comparison

Fig. 8a shows that CYCLONE decides Infinite Descent in polynomial time on around 92% of the sloped graphs in our database. This high coverage, together with the polynomial complexity of our incomplete methods, is what enables the high performance of CYCLONE. Furthermore, as mentioned, even on the remaining 8% of graphs, the overhead of running them is so low compared to the runtime of the complete method that the overall performance is unaffected.

5.2 Comparison with State-of-the-Art Methods

We now report on our evaluation of CYCLONE against the state-of-the-art methods (VLA, SLA, FWK, and OR) for deciding Infinite Descent using the database described in Sec. 3. The figures in this section again present aggregated average runtime of each method by the number of edges, and the interquartile ranges. Additionally, we compare the runtime overhead of each of the existing methods with CYCLONE as the baseline.

Fig. 9a plots the runtime of all methods using a logarithmic scale. It shows a clear difference in the various methods' runtimes and, most importantly, that CYCLONE is the fastest among them. The runtime of every method grows somewhat sub-exponentially with the number of edges in the sloped graph. This might be because the sloped graphs in the database do not have many edges, so the exponential trend of the runtime does not yet manifest itself experimentally.

Fig. 9b and Fig. 9c present, respectively, the absolute overhead in milliseconds and the percentage overhead of each complete method with respect to CYCLONE. Apart from the SLA method, the average percentage overhead increases as the graph size increases. This shows that the runtime complexity difference of the methods indeed manifests itself in the experimental results. Observe that CYCLONE is between around 80% to around 350% faster than the fastest method (OR), between around 480% to around 2200% faster than VLA, between 480% and 43,000% faster than FWK.

Finally, looking at the SLA method we can see a constant line in the runtime. This is because we used a timeout of 3 seconds in our tests, and SLA seems to hit this timeout after a certain size of input. This explains why, in contrast with the other methods, the percentage overhead for SLA decreases as the number of edges increases. The timeout limit notwithstanding, we can still see a tremendous advantage to CYCLONE, which is between around $3 \times 10^4\%$ and $5 \times 10^6\%$ faster than the SLA method. These results show that CYCLONE significantly improves the practical runtime of the Infinite Descent check on real-world sloped graphs.

As noted in Sec. 3, our database contains the sloped graphs that Cyclist produced directly from concrete cyclic pre-proofs. However, Cyclist also pre-processes each sloped graph before handing it to the Infinite Descent check. This consists of pruning nodes that do not lie along cycles and collapsing non-branching paths, which considerably reduces the size of the graphs whilst maintaining the structure necessary for checking Infinite Descent. We also collected these minimised forms of the sloped graphs generated by Cyclist, and then evaluated CYCLONE against the state-of-the-art methods on this preprocessed dataset. Here, CYCLONE is still 90% to 170% faster than the best performing other method, which again is the OR method.

6   Conclusion

We introduced CYCLONE, an efficient and general tool for deciding the Infinite Descent property, implemented by combining with existing exponential decision procedures two novel, incomplete but polynomial-time algorithms exploiting statistically significant structural properties of sloped graphs. We demonstrated, on real-world data, CYCLONE's superior runtime performance compared to existing approaches. Moreover, the CYCLONE tool is open-ended in that it may incorporate additional semi-decision procedures as they are developed.

We evaluated Cyclone on a dataset generated by the Cyclist prover, consisting of graphs corresponding to cyclic pre-proofs from its test suites. To broaden coverage of real-world use cases, we plan to expand the dataset. In particular, since verifying Infinite Descent supports program termination verification via the size-change principle, we aim to create a dataset of termination instances, generated from, e.g. Agda's termination checker, for future evaluation. We also plan to explore preprocessing methods other than Cyclist's minimisation, which may better align with our methods and further improve CYCLONE's performance.

Acknowledgments. This research was partially supported by the Israel Science Foundation (Grant No. 790/21).

References

1. Agda Developers: Agda, https://agda.readthedocs.io/
2. Brotherston, J.: Sequent Calculus Proof Systems for Inductive Definitions. Ph.D. thesis, University of Edinburgh (November 2006), https://era.ed.ac.uk/handle/1842/1458
3. Brotherston, J., Bornat, R., Calcagno, C.: Cyclic Proofs of Program Termination in Separation Logic. In: Necula, G.C., Wadler, P. (eds.) Proceedings of the 35th ACM SIGPLAN-SIGACT Symposium on Principles of Programming Languages, POPL 2008, San Francisco, California, USA, January 7-12, 2008. pp. 101–112. ACM (2008). https://doi.org/10.1145/1328438.1328453
4. Brotherston, J., Gorogiannis, N.: Cyclic Abduction of Inductively Defined Safety and Termination Preconditions. In: Müller-Olm, M., Seidl, H. (eds.) Static Analysis - 21st International Symposium, SAS 2014, Munich, Germany, September 11-13, 2014. Proceedings. Lecture Notes in Computer Science, vol. 8723, pp. 68–84. Springer (2014). https://doi.org/10.1007/978-3-319-10936-7_5
5. Brotherston, J., Gorogiannis, N., Petersen, R.L.: A Generic Cyclic Theorem Prover. In: Jhala, R., Igarashi, A. (eds.) Programming Languages and Systems - 10th Asian Symposium, APLAS 2012, Kyoto, Japan, December 11-13, 2012. Proceedings. Lecture Notes in Computer Science, vol. 7705, pp. 350–367. Springer (2012). https://doi.org/10.1007/978-3-642-35182-2_25
6. Brotherston, J., Simpson, A.: Sequent Calculi for Induction and Infinite Descent. Journal of Logic and Computation **21**(6), 1177–1216 (2010). https://doi.org/10.1093/logcom/exq052
7. Cheng, K.S., Ngan, C.W., Trung, T.Q., Chanh, L.T., Sivaraman, A., Toan, N.T.: Songbird Prover (2016), https://songbird-prover.github.io/
8. Cohen, L., Jabarin, A., Popescu, A., Rowe, R.N.S.: The Complex(ity) Landscape of Checking Infinite Descent. Proceedings of the ACM on Programming Languages **8**(POPL), 1352–1384 (Jan 2024). https://doi.org/10.1145/3632888
9. Cohen, L., Rowe, R.N.S.: Non-Well-Founded Proof Theory of Transitive Closure Logic. ACM Trans. Comput. Logic **21**(4) (Aug 2020). https://doi.org/10.1145/3404889
10. Das, A.: On The Logical Complexity of Cyclic Arithmetic. Log. Methods Comput. Sci. **16**(1) (2020). https://doi.org/10.23638/LMCS-16(1:1)2020
11. Dax, C., Hofmann, M., Lange, M.: A Proof System for the Linear Time μ-Calculus. In: Arun-Kumar, S., Garg, N. (eds.) FSTTCS 2006: Foundations of Software Technology and Theoretical Computer Science, 26th International Conference, Kolkata, India, December 13-15, 2006, Proceedings. Lecture Notes in Computer Science, vol. 4337, pp. 273–284. Springer (2006). https://doi.org/10.1007/11944836_26
12. Doumane, A.: Constructive Completeness for the Linear-time μ-calculus. In: Proceedings of the 32nd Annual ACM/IEEE Symposium on Logic in Computer Science, LICS 2017. pp. 1–12 (2017). https://doi.org/10.1109/LICS.2017.8005075
13. Itzhaky, S., Peleg, H., Polikarpova, N., Rowe, R.N.S., Sergey, I.: Cyclic Program Synthesis. In: Freund, S.N., Yahav, E. (eds.) PLDI '21: 42nd ACM SIGPLAN International Conference on Programming Language Design and Implementation,

Virtual Event, Canada, June 20-25, 2021. pp. 944–959. ACM (2021). https://doi.org/10.1145/3453483.3454087

14. Jones, E., Ong, C.H.L., Ramsay, S.: CycleQ: An Efficient Basis for Cyclic Equational Reasoning. In: Proceedings of the 43rd ACM SIGPLAN International Conference on Programming Language Design and Implementation. pp. 395–409. PLDI 2022, Association for Computing Machinery, New York, NY, USA (2022). https://doi.org/10.1145/3519939.3523731

15. Lee, C.S., Jones, N.D., Ben-Amram, A.M.: The Size-Change Principle for Program Termination. In: Proceedings of the 28th ACM SIGPLAN-SIGACT symposium on Principles of programming languages. POPL01, ACM (Jan 2001). https://doi.org/10.1145/360204.360210

16. Lehmann, D.J.: Algebraic Structures for Transitive Closure. Theor. Comput. Sci. **4**(1), 59–76 (1977). https://doi.org/10.1016/0304-3975(77)90056-1

17. Lepigre, R., Raffalli, C.: Practical Subtyping for Curry-Style Languages. ACM Trans. Program. Lang. Syst. **41**(1), 5:1–5:58 (2019). https://doi.org/10.1145/3285955

18. Nollet, R., Saurin, A., Tasson, C.: PSPACE-Completeness of a Thread Criterion for Circular Proofs in Linear Logic with Least and Greatest fixed points. In: Cerrito, S., Popescu, A. (eds.) Automated Reasoning with Analytic Tableaux and Related Methods - 28th International Conference, TABLEAUX 2019, London, UK, September 3-5, 2019, Proceedings. Lecture Notes in Computer Science, vol. 11714, pp. 317–334. Springer (2019). https://doi.org/10.1007/978-3-030-29026-9_18

19. Rowe, R., Cohen, L., Shaked, M.: Cyclone: A Heterogeneous Tool for Checking Infinite Descent (Software Artifact) (2025). https://doi.org/10.5281/zenodo.14743891

20. Rowe, R.N.S., Brotherston, J.: Automatic Cyclic Termination Proofs for Recursive Procedures in Separation Logic. In: Bertot, Y., Vafeiadis, V. (eds.) Proceedings of the 6th ACM SIGPLAN Conference on Certified Programs and Proofs, CPP 2017, Paris, France, January 16-17, 2017. pp. 53–65. ACM (2017). https://doi.org/10.1145/3018610.3018623

21. Santocanale, L.: A Calculus of Circular Proofs and Its Categorical Semantics. In: Nielsen, M., Engberg, U. (eds.) Proceedings of the 5th International Conference on Foundations of Software Science and Computation Structures, FOSSACS 2002. pp. 357–371. Berlin, Heidelberg (2002). https://doi.org/10.1007/3-540-45931-6_25

22. Serban, C., Iosif, R.: An Entailment Checker for Separation Logic with Inductive Definitions. Electronic Communications of the EASST **76** (May 2019). https://doi.org/10.14279/tuj.eceasst.76.1073

23. Sprenger, C., Dam, M.: A Note on Global Induction in a mu-calculus with Explicit Approximations. In: Ésik, Z., Ingólfsdóttir, A. (eds.) Fixed Points in Computer Science, FICS 2002, Copenhagen, Denmark, 20-21 July 2002, Preliminary Proceedings. BRICS Notes Series, vol. NS-02-2, pp. 22–24. University of Aarhus (2002), https://www.brics.dk/NS/02/2/

24. Ta, Q., Le, T.C., Khoo, S., Chin, W.: Automated Mutual Explicit Induction Proof in Separation Logic. In: Fitzgerald, J.S., Heitmeyer, C.L., Gnesi, S., Philippou, A. (eds.) FM 2016: Formal Methods - 21st International Symposium, Limassol, Cyprus, November 9-11, 2016, Proceedings. Lecture Notes in Computer Science, vol. 9995, pp. 659–676 (2016). https://doi.org/10.1007/978-3-319-48989-6_40

25. Ta, Q., Le, T.C., Khoo, S., Chin, W.: Automated Lemma Synthesis in Symbolic-heap Separation Logic. Proc. ACM Program. Lang. **2**(POPL), 9:1–9:29 (2018). https://doi.org/10.1145/3158097

26. Tarjan, R.: Depth-first Search and Linear Graph Algorithms. SIAM Journal on Computing **1**(2), 146–160 (Jun 1972). https://doi.org/10.1137/0201010

27. Tellez, G., Brotherston, J.: Automatically Verifying Temporal Properties of Pointer Programs with Cyclic Proof. J. Autom. Reason. **64**(3), 555–578 (2020). https://doi.org/10.1007/s10817-019-09532-0

Extracting Linear Relations from Gröbner Bases for Formal Verification of And-Inverter Graphs

Daniela Kaufmann[1][(✉)] [iD] and Jérémy Berthomieu[2] [iD]

[1] TU Wien, Vienna, Austria
`daniela.kaufmann@tuwien.ac.at`
[2] Sorbonne Université, CNRS, LIP6, Paris, France
`jeremy.berthomieu@lip6.fr`

Abstract. Formal verification techniques based on computer algebra have proven highly effective for circuit verification. The circuit, given as an and-inverter graph, is encoded using polynomials that automatically generate a Gröbner basis with respect to a lexicographic term ordering. Correctness of the circuit is derived by computing the polynomial remainder of the specification. However, the main obstacle is the monomial blow-up during the reduction, as the degree can increase.

In this paper, we investigate an orthogonal approach and focus the computational effort on rewriting the Gröbner basis itself. Our goal is to ensure the basis contains linear polynomials that can be effectively used to rewrite the linearized specification. We first prove the soundness and completeness of this technique and then demonstrate its practical application. Our implementation of this method shows promising results on benchmarks related to multiplier verification.

Keywords: Algebraic Reasoning, Gröbner Basis, Hardware Verification

1 Introduction

Formal verification techniques based on algebraic reasoning have emerged as highly effective tools for verifying hardware, particularly in the context of verifying arithmetic circuits on the gate-level. As digital systems become more complex, ensuring the correctness of such circuits is paramount, especially in safety-critical applications like cryptography and signal processing to prevent a repetition of infamous failures, such as the Pentium FDIV bug [32]. Established methods based on satisfiability solving (SAT) [4], or binary decision diagrams (BDDs) [7] often struggle with the complex non-linear structure of arithmetic circuits. In contrast, formal verification techniques based on theorem provers [33] or computer algebra, specifically those leveraging Gröbner bases, offer an effective alternative and have made significant progress in recent years [18,21,22,29].

In the algebraic method, circuits are given as and-inverter graphs (AIG) [23]. The graph is encoded as a set of polynomials, which are sorted according to a lexicographic term ordering, where for each gate in the circuit the output variable is always greater than the input variables of the gate. Hence, the leading terms of the polynomial equations consist of single variables that are mutually disjoint. This property is called *unique monic leading term* (UMLT) in [18].

© The Author(s) 2025
A. Gurfinkel and M. Heule (Eds.): TACAS 2025, LNCS 15696, pp. 355–374, 2025.
https://doi.org/10.1007/978-3-031-90643-5_19

If such an ordering is chosen, the polynomials automatically form a Gröbner basis [5]. Informally said, a Gröbner basis is a mathematical construct that offers a decision procedure that guarantees soundness and completeness of the verification process. The correctness of the circuit is determined by computing the unique polynomial remainder of the specification polynomial, which represents the intended functionality of the circuit, modulo the Gröbner basis. The circuit fulfills the specification if, and only if, the final remainder is zero [19].

However, a major practical obstacle in using a lexicographic term ordering is the significant computational effort during the reduction process, as the degree can increase. More precisely the size of the intermediate reduction results generally increases, since the tails of the polynomials in the Gröbner basis have a higher degree than their leading terms. This is often deferred to as *monomial blow-up*. A study in [28] showed that the intermediate reduction results for 16-bit multipliers can have more than 10^6 monomials. To address this challenge, various preprocessing and rewriting algorithms have been developed, which syntactically or semantically analyze the input circuit to remove redundant information from the polynomial encoding, ultimately optimizing the reduction process and improving the efficiency of the verification.

Related Work. Advanced reduction engines designed for the automatic algebraic verification of multipliers given as AIGs are implemented in tools such as DYNPHASEORDEROPT [21], DYPOSUB [29], and AMULET2 [17,18], including its variant TELUMA [15]. In [17,18] SAT solving is used to rewrite certain parts of the multiplier before applying an incremental column-wise verification algorithm. In a follow-up work [15] the usage of the external SAT solver could be removed by using a sophisticated algebraic encoding that also takes the polarity of literals into account. These techniques have been further enhanced by parallelization [26] and equivalence checking-based verification [24].

In [29], the authors present a dynamic rewriting approach. They decide on the reduction order on the fly and backtrack if the size of intermediate reduction results exceeds a predetermined threshold. In [21], the authors revisit and improve upon [29] by incorporating mixed signals in their encoding.

While all of the discussed approaches employ various preprocessing and rewriting techniques, they share a common characteristic: they all rely on a lexicographic term ordering. *None of the related works have explored alternative term orderings, such as those that prioritize degree-based sorting to limit the degree during the reduction process.*

Our contribution. In this paper, we propose an alternative, orthogonal strategy that shifts the focus of the computational effort from rewriting the specification to rewriting the Gröbner basis itself. We impose a different term ordering that takes their degree into account. The approach is based on the following observation:

> *If the specification polynomial is linear, a Gröbner basis with respect to a degree reverse lexicographic term ordering contains linear polynomials that suffice to derive correctness of the circuit.*

Our first contribution is to derive the theoretical foundations of this observation, including a technical theorem that proves its soundness and completeness.

However, the computation of a single Gröbner basis for the whole circuit is practically infeasible due to the large number of variables and more importantly the *degree of the underlying ideal.* Our second contribution is a practical algorithm that splits the computation of the Gröbner basis into multiple smaller more manageable sub-problems. We evaluate our approach on a set of benchmarks for multiplier verification. The experimental results are promising and indicate that our approach offers a valuable addition to existing algebraic verification techniques.

The remainder of the paper is organized as follows. In Section 2 we introduce the necessary preliminaries. In Section 3 we show the theory of our approach and prove the soundness and completeness. We present a practical verification algorithm in Section 4, and discuss its implementation and the experimental evaluation in Section 5 before we conclude the paper in Section 6.

2   Preliminaries

In the first part of the preliminaries, Section 2.1, we introduce the theory of Gröbner bases following [5,6,8] and discuss key properties that are important for our approach. In the second part, Section 2.2, we present the necessary background on AIGs and how we can encode these graphs using polynomial equations.

2.1   Gröbner Basis

Definition 1 (Term, Monomial, Polynomial, see [8, Chap. 2, Sec. 2, Def. 7]). *Let $X = (x_1, \ldots, x_n)$ be a set of variables and $\mathbb{K}$ be a field. A monomial is a product of the form $x_1^{e_1} \cdots x_n^{e_n}$, with exponents $e_1, \ldots, e_n \in \mathbb{N}_0$. The set of all monomials is represented by $[X]$. A term is a monomial multiplied by a constant, written as $\alpha x_1^{e_1} \cdots x_n^{e_n}$ with $\alpha \in \mathbb{K}$. A polynomial p is a finite sum of such terms. We denote the number of terms in p by* $\mathrm{size}(p)$.

Throughout this section let $\mathbb{K}[X] = \mathbb{K}[x_1, \ldots, x_n]$ denote the ring of polynomials in variables $x_1, \ldots, x_n$ with coefficients in the field $\mathbb{K}$. We write polynomials in their canonical form. That is, monomials with equal monomials are merged by adding their coefficients; and terms with coefficients equal to zero are removed.

Definition 2 (Degree). *The degree of a monomial $\sigma = x_1^{e_1} \cdots x_n^{e_n}$ is the sum of its exponents, i.e., $\deg(\sigma) = |\sigma| = \sum_{i=1}^{n} e_i$. The degree of a polynomial is the maximum degree of its terms.*

The terms within a polynomial are sorted according to a total order to ensure a consistency for algebraic operations.

Definition 3 (Monomial Order). *A monomial order is a total order $\prec$ such that for all distinct monomials σ_1, σ_2 we have (i) $\sigma_1 \prec \sigma_2$ or $\sigma_2 \prec \sigma_1$, (ii) every non-empty set of monomials has a smallest element and (iii) $\sigma_1 \prec \sigma_2 \Rightarrow \tau\sigma_1 \prec \tau\sigma_2$ for any term τ.*

Definition 4 (Lexicographic Order, see [8, Chap. 2, Sec. 2, Def. 3]). *Let* $\sigma_1 = x_1^{u_1} \cdots x_n^{u_n}$ *and* $\sigma_2 = x_1^{v_1} \cdots x_n^{v_n}$ *be two monomials. We say that* $\sigma_1 \prec_{\text{lex}} \sigma_2$, *if there exists an index* i *such that with* $u_j = v_j$ *for all* $1 \leq j < i$, *and* $u_i < v_i$.

Definition 5 (Degree Reverse Lexicographic Order, see [8, Chap. 2, Sec. 2, Def. 6]). *Let* $\sigma_1 = x_1^{u_1} \cdots x_n^{u_n}$ *and* $\sigma_2 = x_1^{v_1} \cdots x_n^{v_n}$ *be two monomials. We say that* $\sigma_1 \prec_{\text{drl}} \sigma_2$, *if* $|\sigma_1| < |\sigma_2|$ *or if* $|\sigma_1| = |\sigma_2|$ *and there exists an index* i *such that* $u_j = v_j$ *for all* $i < j \leq n$, *and* $u_i > v_i$.

Since every polynomial $p \in \mathbb{K}[X]$ contains only a finite number of monomials, and these terms are sorted according to a fixed total order, we can identify the largest monomial in p. This is referred to as the *leading monomial* of p and denoted as $\text{lm}(p)$. If $p = c\tau + \cdots$ and $\text{lm}(p) = \tau$, then $\text{lc}(p) = c$ is called the *leading coefficient* and $\text{lt}(p) = \text{lc}(p) \text{lm}(p) = c\tau$ is called the *leading term* of p. The *tail* of p is defined by $\text{tail}(p) = p - \text{lt}(p)$.

Definition 6 (Ideal). *A nonempty subset* $I \subseteq \mathbb{K}[X]$ *is called an* ideal *if*

$$\forall\, u, v \in I : u + v \in I \quad \text{and} \quad \forall\, w \in \mathbb{K}[X]\ \forall\, u \in I : wu \in I.$$

If $I \subseteq \mathbb{K}[X]$ is an ideal, then a set $G = \{g_1, \ldots, g_m\} \subseteq \mathbb{K}[X]$ is called a *basis* of I if $I = \{h_1 g_1 + \cdots + h_m g_m \mid h_1, \ldots, h_m \in \mathbb{K}[X]\}$, i.e., if I consists of all the linear combinations of g_i with polynomial coefficients. We denote this by $I = \langle G \rangle$ and say I is generated by G.

An ideal $I = \langle G \rangle \subseteq \mathbb{K}[X]$ can be interpreted as an equational theory, where the basis $G = \{g_1, \ldots, g_m\}$ serves as the set of axioms. The ideal $I = \langle G \rangle$ consists of precisely those polynomials f for which the equation $f = 0$ can be derived from the axioms $g_1 = \cdots = g_m = 0$ through repeated application of the rules $u = 0 \wedge v = 0 \Rightarrow u + v = 0$ and $u = 0 \Rightarrow wu = 0$.

To check whether a polynomial $f \in \mathbb{K}[X]$ is contained in an ideal I, we want to solve the so-called *ideal membership problem*: Given a polynomial $f \in \mathbb{K}[X]$ and an ideal $I = \langle G \rangle \subseteq \mathbb{K}[X]$, determine if $f \in I$.

Definition 7 (Remainder). *The process of finding a remainder with respect to a set of polynomials* G *is equal to computing the remainder of a polynomial division, but extended to multiple divisors, until no further division is possible. The result is a polynomial that represents the equivalent class modulo the ideal generated by* G. *We write* $p \rightarrow_G g$ *to denote that* g *is the polynomial remainder of* p *modulo* G *and we also say "p is reduced by G".*

In general, an ideal I has many bases that generate I. We are particularly interested in bases with certain structural properties that allow to uniquely answer the ideal membership problem. Such bases are called *Gröbner bases* [5].

Lemma 1 (see [8, Chap. 2, Sec. 5, Cor. 6]). *Every ideal* $I \subseteq \mathbb{K}[X]$ *has a Gröbner basis w.r.t. a fixed total order.*

Given an arbitrary basis of an ideal, a Gröbner basis can be computed using Buchberger's algorithm that repeatedly computes so-called S-Polynomials. These S-Polynomials are reduced by the polynomials that are already in the current basis, i.e., calculating the remainder of polynomial division, and non-zero remainders are added to the ideal basis. These steps are repeated until the basis is saturated. If all S-Polynomials reduce to zero the set of ideal generators is a Gröbner basis [5]. Generally, Buchberger-like algorithms for computing Gröbner bases, such as Buchberger's seminal algorithm [5] or Faugère's F_4 [9] algorithm, have a worst-case time complexity double exponential in the number of variables, because of the size of the output [30]. Still, in practice, these algorithms behave in general way better for $\prec_{drl}$ than for other monomial orders, such as $\prec_{lex}$.

We will not introduce this process more formally, as we will treat the computation of a Gröbner basis as a black-box technique in our approach. The following properties are more important for us.

Lemma 2 (see [8, Chap. 2, Sec. 6, Prop. 1]). *If $G = \{g_1, \ldots, g_m\}$ is a Gröbner basis, then every $f \in \mathbb{K}[X]$ has a unique polynomial remainder r with respect to G. Furthermore, it holds that $f - r \in \langle G \rangle$, which implies that f is contained in the ideal $I = \langle G \rangle$ if, and only if, $f \to_G 0$.*

Depending on the information one seeks, some Gröbner bases are more useful than others. Gröbner bases w.r.t. $\prec_{lex}$ are the tool of choice for solving polynomial systems but are, in general, more expensive to compute than degree-based Gröbner bases. Yet, *change of order* algorithms, such as the seminal FGLM one [11] can convert a Gröbner basis into another one for different order. In our setting of verifying AIG the complexity would be in $O(n2^{3n})$, where n is the number of input variables of the AIG. Hence, for large n, this is impractical. Variants of FGLM exploiting the structure of the input and output Gröbner bases under some genericity assumptions exist, we can mention [2,10,12,31], but they are mostly designed for solving polynomial systems. As a consequence, they consider the input Gröbner basis to be for a degree-based order, such as $\prec_{drl}$, and the output Gröbner basis to be for $\prec_{lex}$.

2.2 And-Inverter Graphs

An *and-inverter graph* (AIG) [23] is a special case of a directed acyclic graph (DAG). They are useful tools to represent Boolean functions and logic circuits and provide a compact and efficient way to describe logical expressions.

Definition 8 (AIG). *An AIG operates over Boolean variables. Every node expresses a logical conjunction between its two input variables, which are depicted by incoming edges in the lower part of the node. We distinguish two types of inputs, primary inputs (of the graph) and intermediate nodes. Outputs of the node are represented by an edge in the upper half. If an edge is marked, it indicates that the variable is negated.*

Definition 9 (Specification). *The specification of an AIG is a polynomial equation $\mathcal{S} \in \mathbb{K}[X]$ that relates the outputs of an AIG to its primary inputs.*

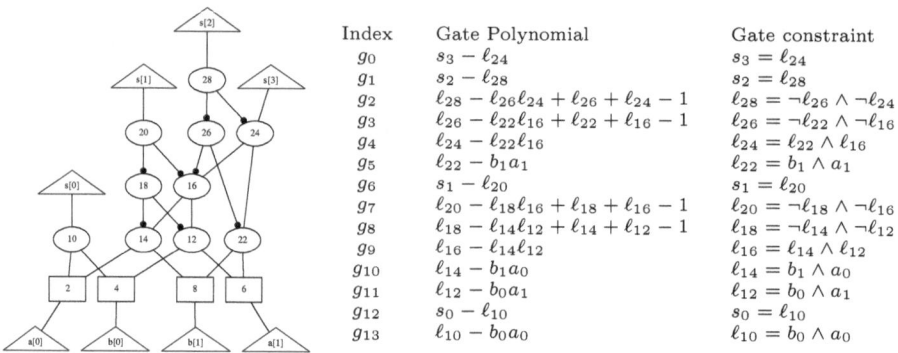

Index	Gate Polynomial	Gate constraint
g_0	$s_3 - \ell_{24}$	$s_3 = \ell_{24}$
g_1	$s_2 - \ell_{28}$	$s_2 = \ell_{28}$
g_2	$\ell_{28} - \ell_{26}\ell_{24} + \ell_{26} + \ell_{24} - 1$	$\ell_{28} = \neg\ell_{26} \wedge \neg\ell_{24}$
g_3	$\ell_{26} - \ell_{22}\ell_{16} + \ell_{22} + \ell_{16} - 1$	$\ell_{26} = \neg\ell_{22} \wedge \neg\ell_{16}$
g_4	$\ell_{24} - \ell_{22}\ell_{16}$	$\ell_{24} = \ell_{22} \wedge \ell_{16}$
g_5	$\ell_{22} - b_1 a_1$	$\ell_{22} = b_1 \wedge a_1$
g_6	$s_1 - \ell_{20}$	$s_1 = \ell_{20}$
g_7	$\ell_{20} - \ell_{18}\ell_{16} + \ell_{18} + \ell_{16} - 1$	$\ell_{20} = \neg\ell_{18} \wedge \neg\ell_{16}$
g_8	$\ell_{18} - \ell_{14}\ell_{12} + \ell_{14} + \ell_{12} - 1$	$\ell_{18} = \neg\ell_{14} \wedge \neg\ell_{12}$
g_9	$\ell_{16} - \ell_{14}\ell_{12}$	$\ell_{16} = \ell_{14} \wedge \ell_{12}$
g_{10}	$\ell_{14} - b_1 a_0$	$\ell_{14} = b_1 \wedge a_0$
g_{11}	$\ell_{12} - b_0 a_1$	$\ell_{12} = b_0 \wedge a_1$
g_{12}	$s_0 - \ell_{10}$	$s_0 = \ell_{10}$
g_{13}	$\ell_{10} - b_0 a_0$	$\ell_{10} = b_0 \wedge a_0$

Boolean Input Polynomials: $a_1^2 - a_1, a_0^2 - a_0, b_1^2 - b_1, b_0^2 - b_0$

Spec $\mathcal{S}$: $\sum_{i=0}^{3} 2^i s_i = (\sum_{i=0}^{1} 2^i a_i)(\sum_{i=0}^{1} 2^i b_i) = 8s_3 + 4s_2 + 2s_1 + s_0 - 4a_1b_1 - 2a_1b_0 - 2a_0b_1 - a_0b_0$

Fig. 1. AIG and polynomial encoding of a 2-bit multiplier in the ring $\mathbb{Q}[X]$.

Together with the specification polynomial, we fix the polynomial ring $\mathbb{K}[X]$ of the encoding. Although the nodes in an AIG compute logical conjunction over Boolean variables, the specification can encode richer relations. Hence, the encoding is not restricted to the Boolean ring $\mathbb{B}[X]$, but may include different coefficient domains, such as integers or rationals.

Definition 10 (Gate Polynomials). *Each node in an AIG can be encoded by a corresponding polynomial equation that models the logical conjunction. Nodes in an AIG raise four types of equations, depending if either none, the first, the second, or both inputs are negated. Let g be an AIG node with inputs a, b:*

Gate constraint		Gate polynomial
$g = a \wedge b$	$\Rightarrow$	$g - ab = 0$
$g = \neg a \wedge b$	$\Rightarrow$	$g - (1 - a)b = g + ab - b = 0$
$g = a \wedge \neg b$	$\Rightarrow$	$g - a(1 - b) = g + ab - a = 0$
$g = \neg a \wedge \neg b$	$\Rightarrow$	$g - (1 - a)(1 - b) = g - ab + b + a - 1 = 0$

The correctness of the encoding can easily be checked by truth tables. Furthermore, observe that the degree of the gate polynomials is always two.

Definition 11 (Boolean Input Polynomial). *For every primary input a_i of the AIG we define a corresponding* Boolean input polynomial $a_i(a_i - 1) = a_i^2 - a_i = 0$ *that encodes that the variable can only take the values 0 and 1.*

As we will only consider polynomial equations with right hand side zero, we will from now on shorten our notation and write "f" instead of "$f = 0$".

Example 1. Figure 1 shows an AIG representing a 2-bit multiplier. We denote the primary inputs by a_0, a_1, b_0, b_1 and outputs by s_0, s_1, s_2, s_3. The internal nodes are denoted by ℓ_i, with subscript i corresponding to the number of the respective AIG node. The right hand side of Figure 1 lists the gate constraints as well as the corresponding gate polynomials, which are derived using the encoding presented in Def. 10. We furthermore list the Boolean input polynomials (Def. 11) and the specification polynomial $S \in \mathbb{Q}[X]$, which relates that $S = A \cdot B$, for $S = \sum_{i=0}^{3} 2^i s_i$, $A = \sum_{i=0}^{1} 2^i a_i$, and $B = \sum_{i=0}^{1} 2^i b_i$.

3 Verification using Degree Reverse Lexicographic Order

In this section we will lay out the theoretical foundation of our proposed approach for extracting linear relations from the Gröbner basis that is used for reduction.

Existing algebraic verification techniques for acyclic graphs encode the circuit as a polynomial using a lexicographic term ordering where the variables are sorted according to a reverse topological term ordering (RTTO) [27]. This has the benefit that due to repeated application of Buchberger's product criterion, see [8, Chap. 2, Sec. 10, Prop. 1], the set of gate polynomials together with the Boolean input polynomials automatically form a Gröbner basis [19]. Since the leading terms of the gate polynomials consist of one single variable, polynomial division comes down to substitution. The variables in the specification are substituted by the corresponding tails of the gate polynomials until no further rewriting is possible. The graph fulfills its specification if, and only if, the final result is zero.

Generally, this implies that the degree of the intermediate reduction results increases, since the tails of the gate polynomials have a higher degree than their linear leading terms. Substituting those variables in non-linear monomials has the potential to lead to a monomial blow-up during the reduction.

Example 2. Consider again the polynomials of Example 1. Initially size($\mathcal{S}$) = 8 and deg($\mathcal{S}$) = 2. After four rewriting steps we have the following intermediate reduction result: $\mathcal{S} \rightarrow_{\{g_1,g_2,g_3,g_4\}} 4\ell_{24}\ell_{22}\ell_{16} - 4\ell_{24}\ell_{22} - 4\ell_{24}\ell_{16} + 8\ell_{24} - 4\ell_{22}\ell_{16} + 4\ell_{22} + 2s_1 + 4\ell_{16} + s_0 - 4a_1b_1 - 2a_1b_0 - 2a_0b_1 - a_0b_0$ which has degree 3 and consists of 13 monomials.

We will now impose a different ordering on the set of gate polynomials that takes the degree of the polynomials into account. That is, we compute a Gröbner basis based on the degree reverse lexicographic monomial ordering, where the monomials in a polynomial are first sorted according to their degree.

Our approach is based on the following result that we prove in Theorem 1: *If the specification polynomial is linear, then the ideal membership of the specification can be decided using only the linear polynomials of the Gröbner basis.*

We linearize the specification by replacing all non-linear monomials σ_i in $\mathcal{S}$ with new extension variables t_i. For each replacement we generate a new polynomial constraint $t_i - \sigma_i$ and add it to the set of gate polynomials. The idea of linearization is, for instance, already used in [25] in the context of cutting planes.

The next lemma proves that if the specification $\mathcal{S}$ is contained in the ideal generated by the gate polynomials, then the linearized specification $\mathcal{S}_{\text{lin}}$ is contained in the ideal generated by the gate polynomials and *extension polynomials*.

Lemma 3. *Let* $p \in \mathbb{K}[X]$, $I \subseteq \mathbb{K}[X]$. *Let* $\Sigma = \{t_i - \sigma_i \mid t_i \notin X \wedge \sigma_i \in p \wedge \deg(\sigma_i) > 1\}$. *Let* p_{lin} *be the polynomial where every non-linear monomial of* p *is replaced by a corresponding extension variable* t_i. *Then we have* $p \in I$ *if, and only if,* $p_{\text{lin}} \in I + \langle \Sigma \rangle$.

Proof. Let $p = \sum_{\sigma_i \in p} c_i \sigma_i$, where the c_i's are in $\mathbb{K}$. By definition, we can write $p_{\text{lin}} = \sum_{\sigma_i \in p} c_i t_i$. Thus, $p_{\text{lin}} = \sum_{\sigma_i \in p} c_i (t_i - \sigma_i) + \sum_{\sigma_i \in p} c_i \sigma_i$. By hypothesis, the first sum is in $\langle \Sigma \rangle$ and the second one, which is p, only depends in variables X. Therefore, if $p \in I$, then $p_{\text{lin}} \in I + \langle \Sigma \rangle$. Conversely, if $p_{\text{lin}} \in I + \langle \Sigma \rangle$, then $p \in (I + \langle \Sigma \rangle) \cap \mathbb{K}[X] = I$ by construction of $I + \langle \Sigma \rangle$.

We now show soundness and completeness of our observation. That is, if we want to show ideal membership of a linear polynomial, the Gröbner basis of the ideal contains a set of linear polynomials G_1 that suffice for deriving the ideal membership, all non-linear polynomials of the Gröbner basis can be neglected. This will shift the computational difficulties from the reduction to the Gröbner basis generation.

Theorem 1. *Let* $p \in \mathbb{K}[X]$ *with* $\deg(p) = 1$, $I \subseteq \mathbb{K}[X]$ *be an ideal. Let* G *be a Gröbner basis of* I *with respect to* $\prec_{\text{drl}}$ *and let* $G_1 = \{g \in G \mid \deg(g) \leq 1\}$. *We have* $p \in I$ *if, and only if,* $p \to_{G_1} 0$. *In particular,* $p = \alpha_1 g_1 + \cdots + \alpha_m g_m$ *with* $g_i \in G_1$, $\alpha_i \in \mathbb{K}$.

Proof. First, let us observe that if G_1 contains a non-zero constant polynomial, then $I = \mathbb{K}[X]$ and p necessarily reduces to 0 by G_1.

We now assume that G_1 only contains polynomials of degree 1. For $g \in G_1$, we write $g = \text{lt}(g) + \text{tail}(g)$. Because polynomials in G_1 are ordered with respect to $\prec_{\text{drl}}$, we have $\deg(\text{lm}(g)) = 1$ and $\deg(\text{tail}(g)) \leq 1$. Since $\deg(\text{lm}(p)) = 1$ the division algorithm for computing the reduction of p by G, see [8, Chap. 2, Sec. 3], will only select polynomials in G whose leading monomials also have degree 1, i.e. those in G_1. The reduction step will replace p by $p - \alpha_i g_i = \text{tail}(p) - \alpha_i \text{tail}(g_i)$, for $\alpha_i \in \mathbb{K}^*$ and some g_i, which has degree less or equal to 1.

Since $p \in I$ if, and only if, $p \to_G 0$, we have $p \in I$ if, and only if, $p \to_{G_1} 0$.

We emphasize that the theory, and in particular the result of Theorem 1, can be applied to general DAGs. The key property of the graph is that it must be acyclic. If it has cycles one cannot canonically compare the variables, hence it is not possible to derive a total term order and compute a Gröbner basis.

The conclusion of Theorem 1 moreover shows that we can significantly simplify the algorithm for checking the ideal membership of $\mathcal{S}$. Instead of repeated polynomial substitution, with potential non-linear intermediate reduction results, we pick $g_i \in G_1$, such that $\text{lm}(g_i) = \text{lm}(\mathcal{S})$, multiply g_i by a constant α_i such that $\text{lc}(\mathcal{S}) = -\alpha_i \text{lc}(g_i)$ and add those two polynomials. Hence, we have replaced polynomial division by linear polynomial operations.

Therefore, we can apply the following approach to verify that an AIG fulfills its specification, see Alg. 1. We first encode the graph as a set of polynomials G_{init} (line 1), and linearize the specification (line 2) as described in Lemma 3.

Algorithm 1: Linear Gröbner basis reduction

    Input   : Circuit C in AIG format, Specification polynomial $\mathcal{S}$

    Output: Determine whether C fulfills the specification

1 $G_{\text{init}} \leftarrow$ Gate-Polynomials$(C) \cup$ Boolean-Input-Polynomials(C);

2 $\mathcal{S}_{\text{lin}}, G_{\text{ext}} \leftarrow$ Linearize$(\mathcal{S})$;

3 $G_{\text{drl}} \leftarrow$ Compute-$\prec_{\text{drl}}$-Gröbner-Basis$(G_{\text{init}} \cup G_{\text{ext}})$;

4 $G_1 \leftarrow \{g \mid g \in G_{\text{drl}} \wedge \deg(g) \leq 1\}$;

5 **while** $\text{lm}(\mathcal{S}_{\text{lin}}) \in \{\text{lm}(g) | g \in G_1\}$ **do**

6 $p_{\text{lin}} \leftarrow g \in G_1$ such that $\text{lm}(g) = \text{lm}(\mathcal{S}_{\text{lin}})$;

7   **if** $\nexists\, p_{\text{lin}}$ **then return** $\bot$;

8 $\mathcal{S}_{\text{lin}} \leftarrow$ Linear-Reduce$(\mathcal{S}_{\text{lin}}, p_{\text{lin}})$;

9 **end**

10 **return** $\mathcal{S}_{\text{lin}} = 0$

The set G_{ext} contains the extension polynomials. In the next step we compute a Gröbner basis w.r.t. $\prec_{\text{drl}}$ (line 3) and extract the linear polynomials G_1 (line 4). We calculate the remainder of the specification modulo the linear elements of the Gröbner basis (lines 5–8) until no further reduction is possible and return whether the final result is zero. The correctness of Alg. 1 follows from Theorem 1.

Example 3. Consider again the AIG of Example 1. First of all we define four extension variables t_{ij} to encode the non-linear terms $a_i b_j$ for $i, j \in \{0, 1\}$ and rewrite the specification to $8s_3 + 4s_2 + 2s_1 + s_0 - 4t_{11} - 2t_{10} - 2t_{01} - t_{00}$. The four polynomial equations $t_{ij} - a_i b_j$ are added to the set of gate polynomials and we compute a Gröbner basis w.r.t. $\prec_{\text{drl}}$. The full Gröbner basis consists of 52 polynomials. Important for us are the first thirteen elements of the Gröbner basis, as those are the linear polynomials G_1:

$$
\begin{aligned}
g_1 &= \ell_{10} - t_{00} & g_8 &= \ell_{22} - t_{11} \\
g_2 &= s_0 - \ell_{10} & g_9 &= \ell_{24} - \ell_{16} \\
g_3 &= \ell_{12} - t_{10} & g_{10} &= \ell_{26} - \ell_{24} + \ell_{16} + t_{11} - 1 \\
g_4 &= \ell_{14} - t_{01} & g_{11} &= \ell_{28} + 2\ell_{24} - \ell_{16} - t_{11} \\
g_5 &= \ell_{18} - \ell_{16} + t_{01} + t_{10} - 1 & g_{12} &= s_2 - \ell_{28} \\
g_6 &= \ell_{20} + 2\ell_{16} - t_{01} - t_{10} & g_{13} &= s_3 - \ell_{24} \\
g_7 &= s_1 - \ell_{20}
\end{aligned}
$$

We derive that $\mathcal{S} \in \langle G_1 \rangle$ as $\mathcal{S} = 8g_{13} + 4g_{12} + 4g_{11} + 2g_7 + 2g_6 + g_2 + g_1$.

In practice, however line 3 of Alg. 1 turns out to be a bottleneck, since computing a single $\prec_{\text{drl}}$-Gröbner basis does not scale for larger AIGs.

We have also seen in Example 1 that 39 out of 52 polynomials in the computed Gröbner basis are non-linear. While these polynomials are needed to compute the full Gröbner basis of the ideal, they are not required for solving the ideal membership problem of the linear specification. Furthermore, from the 13 linear polynomials, only 7 are used to generate the specification. Hence, our generated Gröbner basis contains redundant and/or useless information. We will now discuss a method to reduce the overhead by computing local Gröbner bases.

Algorithm 2: Verification-via-Locally-extracting-Linear-Polynomials

---

    Input : Circuit C in AIG format, Specification polynomial $\mathcal{S}$

    Output: Determine whether C fulfills the specification

1 $G_{\text{init}} \leftarrow$ Row-Wise-RTTO-Polynomial-Encoding(C);

2 $\mathcal{S}_{\text{lin}}, G_{\text{ext}} \leftarrow$ Linearize-Spec-wrt-AIG$(\mathcal{S}, G_{\text{init}})$;

3 $G \leftarrow$ Preprocessing(G_{ext}) ▷See Section 4.1

4 while $\text{lm}(\mathcal{S}_{\text{lin}}) \in \{\text{lm}(g) | g \in G\}$ **do**

5 | $p \leftarrow g \in G$ such that $\text{lm}(g) = \text{lm}(\mathcal{S}_{\text{lin}})$;

6 | $p_{\text{lin}} \leftarrow$ Linearize-Single-Polynomial(p, G) ▷See Section 4.2

7 | **if** $\nexists p_{\text{lin}}$ **then return** $\perp$;

8 | $\mathcal{S}_{\text{lin}} \leftarrow$ Linear-Reduce$(\mathcal{S}_{\text{lin}}, p_{\text{lin}})$;

9 end

10 return $\mathcal{S}_{\text{lin}} = 0$

---

4   Locally extracting Linear Polynomials

The core idea of the optimized approach is to start from a $\prec_{\text{lex}}$-Gröbner basis and incrementally extract linear polynomials from a smaller set of gate polynomials instead of computing a single full $\prec_{\text{drl}}$-Gröbner basis for the whole input AIG. The algorithm is outlined in Alg. 2 and will be explained in more detail throughout the remainder of this section.

In a nutshell, we first encode the circuit using a lexicographic term ordering (line 1) and linearize the specification polynomial (line 2) with respect to the given circuit. After some preprocessing where we extract easily derivable linear polynomials (line 3), we rewrite the specification by generating linear polynomials on the fly (lines 4–9). We pick the gate polynomial p that has the same leading term as the intermediate reduction result (line 5) and compute a $\prec_{\text{drl}}$-Gröbner basis for a sub-circuit of C that includes p (line 6) to receive the linearized polynomial p_{lin} that we use for reducing the specification (line 7). Let us now go into more detail of every step.

Encoding. The AIG is encoded using gate polynomials and Boolean input polynomials as described in Definitions 10 and 11 using a lexicographic term ordering. We choose a row-wise variable ordering that sorts variables based on their distance to the inputs. If nodes have an equal distance, we sort according to the value of the AIG node. For example, we would sort the variables in Example 1 as $a_0 \prec_{\text{lex}} b_0 \prec_{\text{lex}} a_1 \prec_{\text{lex}} b_1 \prec_{\text{lex}} \ell_{10} \prec_{\text{lex}} \ell_{12} \prec_{\text{lex}} \ell_{14} \prec_{\text{lex}} \ell_{22} \prec_{\text{lex}} s_0 \prec_{\text{lex}} \ell_{16} \prec_{\text{lex}} \ell_{18} \prec_{\text{lex}} \ell_{20} \prec_{\text{lex}} \ell_{24} \prec_{\text{lex}} \ell_{26} \prec_{\text{lex}} \ell_{28} \prec_{\text{lex}} s_1 \prec_{\text{lex}} s_3 \prec_{\text{lex}} s_2$. In this order the output variable of a gate is always greater than its input variables, which automatically generates a $\prec_{\text{lex}}$-Gröbner basis.

Theorem 4 in [19] has shown that we can locally rewrite elements of the $\prec_{\text{lex}}$-Gröbner basis without jeopardizing the Gröbner basis property as long as the leading monomials remain the same. We apply the same technique and locally rewrite gate polynomials from quadratic to linear polynomials that will be used in the reduction.

Algorithm 3: Preprocessing

Input : Set of poynomial encodings of gate constraints G
Output: Rewritten Set of Polynomial encodings G
1 $G \leftarrow$ Merge-Nodes-with-Equal-Inputs(G);
2 $G \leftarrow$ Eliminate-Positive-Nodes(G);
3 $G \leftarrow$ Propagating-Equivalent-Nodes(G);
4 **return** G;

Linearization of the Specification. Lemma 3 provides us with a methodology on how to linearize the specification S by introducing extension variables to represent non-linear terms. However, some of the terms might already be contained in the polynomial encoding of the circuit. For those terms we can simply use the corresponding leading term in the specification. We first swipe through the set of gate polynomials and check whether the non-linear tail of a gate polynomial is contained in the specification. If this is the case, we replace the non-linear term by the corresponding leading term.

For instance, in Example 3 we have the gate polynomial $\ell_{22} - a_1 b_1$. Hence, we do not require the extension variable t_{11} to linearize S. This equality $\ell_{22} = t_{11}$ is also contained as polynomial g_8 in the computed $\prec_{\text{drl}}$-Gröbner basis.

All non-linear terms of S that cannot be linearized using gate polynomials we introduce extension variables as described in Section 3.

At this point, our encoding consists of a linear specification polynomial and a set of quadratic gate polynomials and Boolean input polynomials that generate a Gröbner basis w.r.t. a lexicographic term ordering. The following subsections present how we linearize elements of the Gröbner basis.

4.1 Preprocessing

The goal of preprocessing is to eliminate variables and derive linear polynomials in the $\prec_{\text{lex}}$-Gröbner basis that can be identified using simple heuristics. We employ three steps of rewriting, depicted in Alg. 3.

Merge Nodes with Equal Inputs. If multiple AIG nodes ℓ_i, ℓ_j have the same inputs a, b, we can express one gate polynomial using the other. For instance, in our running Example 1 the nodes $\ell_{24} = \ell_{22}\ell_{16}$ and $\ell_{26} = (1 - \ell_{22})(1 - \ell_{16})$ would be such a set of AIG nodes.

Every gate polynomial of an AIG node has degree two, and the quadratic term is the product of the input nodes. Hence, the non-linear term in those gate polynomials that have the same inputs is the same. We remove the non-linear term of the topologically larger polynomial by adding or subtracting the smaller polynomial. For instance, we derive $\ell_{26} - \ell_{24} + \ell_{22} + \ell_{16} - 1$.

Furthermore, assume two gates ℓ_i and ℓ_j both have input variables a, b. If at least one input has a different polarity in ℓ_i and ℓ_j, we immediately can derive that the product $\ell_i\ell_j$ is equal to zero. To see this, let $\ell_i - \bar{a}\bar{b}$, $\ell_j - \hat{a}\hat{b}$ be the corresponding gate polynomials, where $\bar{a}$ and $\hat{a}$ represent the polarity of a. We have $\ell_i\ell_j = \bar{a}\bar{b}\hat{a}\hat{b} = 0$, since $(\bar{a} = 1 - \hat{a}) \vee (\bar{b} = 1 - \hat{b})$ holds. Thus, we can always remove the term $\ell_i\ell_j$ in a possible parent node, for instance the monomial $\ell_{26}\ell_{24}$ in ℓ_{28} in Example 1 can be removed.

Eliminate Positive Nodes. In this step we eliminate nodes which are only non-negated inputs to other nodes in the graph. This heuristic was already considered in [15] to introduce a possible sharing of nodes. Since this heuristic is only applied on positive inputs, we can simply replace every occurrence of the node by the corresponding tail in the gate polynomial of the parent node. This will increase the degree of the parent polynomial, but will not increase the number of terms. We can check whether parts of the new tail term of the parent are equal to the tail term of another gate polynomial. If yes, we can reduce the tail term and include the leading term. This will decrease the temporal increase of the polynomial degree and furthermore will impose a node sharing which will be useful in later Gröbner basis computations. For instance, consider polynomials $f - da, e - ca, d - cb$. We can derive $f - cba = f - eb$.

Propagating Equivalent Nodes. If at any point in the rewriting we derive a linear polynomial of the form $\ell_i - \ell_j$ or $\ell_i + \ell_j - 1$ we know that ℓ_i is equal to either ℓ_j or to its negation $1 - \ell_j$. We propagate this information by eliminating the topologically larger node ℓ_i from the polynomial encoding. We choose to eliminate ℓ_i and not ℓ_j in order to not mess up the reverse topological term ordering for parent nodes of ℓ_j. Propagation of equivalent nodes may not directly lead to linear gate polynomials, but helps to reduce the overall number of variables.

4.2   Linear Reduction

After preprocessing we repeatedly rewrite the linearized specification by the polynomial p in the Gröbner basis that has the same leading monomial as the specification (line 5 in Alg. 2). For doing so, we need to linearize p. The pseudo-code is listed in Alg. 4. By Theorem 1, we know that a full $\prec_{\mathrm{drl}}$-Gröbner basis of a circuit C must contain a linear polynomial p_{lin} with the same leading monomial as p. If this condition is not met, then the circuit does not satisfy the specification, as we cannot further reduce $\mathcal{S}$.

However, we do not want to compute a full $\prec_{\mathrm{drl}}$ Gröbner basis. Our goal is to make the Gröbner basis just big enough such that it contains a linear polynomial p_{lin} with leading term v. Let $v = \mathrm{lm}(p)$. We aim to compute a Gröbner basis w.r.t. a $\prec_{\mathrm{drl}}$-ordering for a sub-circuit $C_{v,d}$ of C. The sub-circuit $C_{v,d}$ is constructed by including v and all children nodes of v up to a maximum distance d. Initially, we set $d = 3$. The motivation for this threshold is that our preprocessing techniques already generates most linear polynomials detectable with $d = 2$. On the other hand we do not want to start with a larger value for d to keep the initial Gröbner basis computation as small as possible. If we encounter a child node that already has a linear polynomial representation, we do not further add its children. This

---

Algorithm 4: Linearize-Single-Polynomial

    Input : Polynomial p, Polynomial system G
    Output: Linear polynomial p_{lin} or $\emptyset$

1 $v \leftarrow \text{lm}(p); d \leftarrow 3$;
2 **while** $d \leq \text{dist}(v)$ **do**
3      $C_v \leftarrow \{v\} \cup \{\text{Children-up-to-Distance}(v, d)\} \cup \{\text{Siblings}(v)\}$;
4      $C_v \leftarrow C_v \cup \{\text{Parents}(C_v)\}$;
5      $G_v \leftarrow \text{Gate-Polynomials}(C_v, G) \cup \text{Boolean-Input-Polynomials}(C_v)$;
6      $G_{\text{drl}} \leftarrow \text{Compute-}\prec_{\text{drl}}\text{-Gröbner-Basis}\ (G_v)$;
7   **if** $\exists p_{\text{lin}} \in G_{\text{drl}}$ *such that* $\deg(p_{\text{lin}}) = 1 \wedge \text{lm}(p_{\text{lin}}) = v$ **then return** p_{lin};
8      $d \leftarrow d + 1$;
9 **end**
10 **return** $\emptyset$;

---

allows us to avoid unnecessary computations by excluding parts of the circuit that have already been simplified. Additionally, we include all smaller sibling nodes of v. Siblings are nodes that share at least one child with v. Moreover, we collect all parent nodes whose children are already included in the collected set of nodes. This ensures that all relevant dependencies in the sub-circuit are captured. This set of nodes represents the part of the circuit on which we will compute a local $\prec_{\text{drl}}$-Gröbner basis.

If this local Gröbner basis does not contain the expected linear polynomial, it suggests that the sub-circuit $C_{v,d}$ is insufficient to capture the desired behavior. In such cases, we repeat the process for the sub-circuit $C_{v,d+1}$, where we increase the distance d to add more nodes. Theoretically it would be very beneficial to cache the calls and reuse the computed Gröbner basis for $C_{v,d}$ for the Gröbner basis computation of $C_{v,d+1}$, however in practice most available Gröbner basis engines cannot exploit that a subset of the inputs is already Gröbner basis.

We continue with the iterative process of increasing d until either a linear polynomial is found, or, in the worst case we have computed a full $\prec_{\text{drl}}$-Gröbner basis for all gate polynomials that are topologically smaller than v. If we still did not find a linear polynomial at this point, we know that the circuit is incorrect. This follows from Theorem 1.

While our approach guarantees the completeness of the verification process, it comes with a practical limitation: computational complexity. If the sub-circuit grows too large (i.e., if too many nodes need to be added to C_v), the computation of the $\prec_{\text{drl}}$-Gröbner basis becomes infeasible in practice.

5 Experimental Evaluation

We evaluate our proposed approach on a set of multiplier benchmarks for different input bit-widths n. For all the circuits we have $\mathcal{S} = \sum_{i=0}^{2n+1} 2^i s_i - (\sum_{i=0}^{n} 2^i a_i) \cdot (\sum_{i=0}^{n} 2^i b_i)$, hence choose $\mathbb{K} = \mathbb{Q}$. Since all the leading coefficients of the gate polynomials are 1, the computation will stay in the ring $\mathbb{Z}[X] \subseteq \mathbb{Q}[X]$ [18].

5.1   Implementation

We implement Alg. 2 in our tool MULTILING [14, 16], written in C++. We employ the following features:

- MULTILING uses the polynomial arithmetic module from AMULET2 [17], which is targeted towards polynomial arithmetic where the variables represent Boolean values and the coefficients are integer values. In particular, the arithmetic engine automatically includes reasoning over the Boolean input polynomials, by reducing exponents, i.e., it calculates $x \cdot x = x$ internally.
- We sort the variables based on their minimum distance to the primary inputs to sort all extension variables next to the primary inputs, which gave us better practical results than the column-wise variable order from AMULET2.
- As a consequence of the row-wise order, we do not apply an incremental column-wise reduction algorithm [19], but rewrite the complete specification.
- For computing the $\prec_{\mathrm{drl}}$-Gröbner basis, we use the MSOLVE [3] library. Since MSOLVE is designed for general purposes, we have to explicitly provide the Boolean input polynomials.
- If the distance of a node to the primary inputs is below six and the linearization of the individual polynomial fails, we switch to non-linear rewriting as a fall-back option. This threshold allows us to capture Booth encoding in our multiplier benchmarks. We empirically noticed that the linearization of Booth encodings requires a rather large $\prec_{\mathrm{drl}}$-Gröbner basis and it is computationally cheaper to use non-linear rewriting instead. However, switching to non-linear rewriting leads to a non-linear intermediate reduction result, meaning that we have to use non-linear rewriting also for the remainder of the circuit to maintain completeness.
- In contrast to AMULET2, we do not support proof logging in MULTILING at the moment, as we have not yet instrumented MSOLVE to produce proofs in the PAC [20] format. This missing implementation is part of future work.

5.2   Setup

We run our experiments on a Intel i7-1260P CPU. The time is listed in rounded seconds (wall-clock time). We set the time limit to 300 s and the memory limit to 10 000 MB. We compare MULTILING against the algebraic approaches of AMULET2 [17], TELUMA [15], and DYNPHASEORDEROPT (DPOO) [21]. The tools of related works [26] and [24] are not publicly available.

Benchmarks.   We evaluate our approach on integer multiplier circuits. Multipliers consist of three main components: partial product generation (PPG), partial product accumulation (PPA), and a final-stage adder (FSA). Each component has optimized architectures to reduce space and delay.

Two encodings are frequently used for PPG: simple AND-gate-based generation or Booth encoding. In the former case, every partial product $a_i b_j$ is explicitly computed, hence we do not require extension variables in our approach.

ABC-benchmarks			Related work			Preprocess		Time (s)		MSOLVE Calls						
n	Synth	Nodes	[15]	[17]	[21]	MergedN	PosN	Total	MSOLVE	#	d = 3 (s)		d = 4 (s)		d = 5 (s)	
32	resyn	7840	0.1	TO	0.2	1948	1	1.7	0.2	7	4	0.03	2	0.03	1	0.04
32	resyn2	7840	0.1	TO	0.3	1948	1	1.3	0.2	6	4	0.03	1	0.03	1	0.04
32	resyn3	7840	0.1	0.01	0.3	1952	0	0.8	0.0	0	0			0		0	
32	dc2	7840	0.1	0.01	0.2	1952	0	1.0	0.0	0	0			0		0	
32	comp	7839	EE	TO	0.2	1948	0	1.5	0.2	6	4	0.03	1	0.03	1	0.04
64	resyn	32064	0.3	TO	1.0	7996	1	11.0	0.2	7	4	0.03	2	0.03	1	0.04
64	resyn2	32064	0.2	TO	1.0	7996	1	11.7	0.2	6	4	0.03	1	0.03	1	0.04
64	resyn3	32064	0.3	0.2	1.0	8000	0	11.2	0.0	0	0			0		0	
64	dc2	32064	0.2	0.3	1.0	8000	0	11.1	0.0	0	0			0		0	
64	comp	32063	EE	TO	1.0	7996	0	12.2	0.2	6	4	0.03	1	0.03	1	0.04
128	resyn	129664	1.2	TO	5.7	32380	1	228.6	0.2	7	4	0.03	2	0.04	1	0.04
128	resyn2	129664	1.2	TO	6.4	32380	1	232.7	0.2	6	4	0.03	1	0.03	1	0.04
128	resyn3	129664	1.2	TO	7.7	32384	0	228.9	0.0	0	0			0		0	
128	dc2	129664	1.1	TO	6.6	32384	0	229.4	0.0	0	0			0		0	
128	comp	129663	EE	TO	5.8	32380	0	230.4	0.2	6	4	0.04	1	0.04	1	0.04

Table 1. Results on n-bit ABC benchmarks.   TO := > 300 s; EE := segfault.

For Booth encoding, we require extension variables as the partial products are internally combined. During PPA, partial products are accumulated, with the final two layers summed in the FSA.

In structured circuits, PPG, PPA, and FSA are clearly defined, benefiting tools like AMULET2 and TELUMA that require a clear cut between PPA and FSA to simplify the FSA. In synthesized circuits, gates are merged and rewritten to optimize the circuit, which blurs these component boundaries, and complicates direct verification. We consider two sets of benchmarks:

- *aoki-multipliers* [13]: This set of benchmarks is generated by combining different architectures for PPG, PPA, and FSA [1] , yielding 192 non-synthesized multiplier architectures with an input bit-width 64.
- *optimized* ABC *multipliers* [1]: We generate multipliers in ABC consisting of a simple PPG, an array PPA and a ripple-carry adder as FSA for bit-widths 32, 64, and 128, and optimize all of them within ABC using five different types of standard synthesis scripts: *resyn, resyn2, resyn3, dc2.* We include a *complex* script that combines several synthesis techniques[2]. We include these 15 optimized benchmarks to demonstrate the robustness of our presented approach. Optimized benchmarks are particularly challenging as they cannot be fully decomposed into their building blocks.

All benchmarks model correct multipliers, i.e., the circuits fulfill the specification.

5.3   Results

The results for the optimized ABC multipliers are shown in Table 1. The heuristics of AMULET2 and TELUMA are not robust for these benchmarks and produce time outs. DPOO and our tool MULTILING are both able to solve all

---

[1] PPG: simple (sp), Booth encoding (bp); PPA: Array (ar), Wallace tree (wt), Balanced delay tree (bd), Overturned-stairs tree (os), Dadda tree (dt), (4;2) compressor tree (ct), (7,3) counter tree (cn), Red. binary addition tree (ba); FSA: Ripple-carry (rc), Carry look-ahead (cl), Ripple-block carry look-ahead (rb), Block carry look-ahead (bc), Ladner-Fischer (lf), Kogge-Stone (ks), Brent-Kung (bk), Han-Carlson (hc), Conditional sum (cn), Carry select (cs), Carry-skip fix size (csf), Carry-skip var. size (csv)

[2] -c "logic; mfs2 -W 20; ps; mfs; st; ps; dc2 -l; ps; resub -l -K 16 -N 3 -w 100; ps; logic; mfs2 -W 20; ps; mfs; st; ps; iresyn -l; ps; resyn; ps; resyn2; ps; resyn3; ps; dc2 -l; ps;"

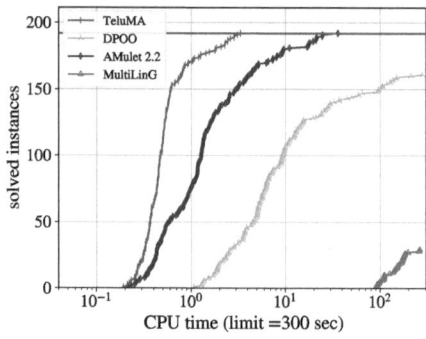
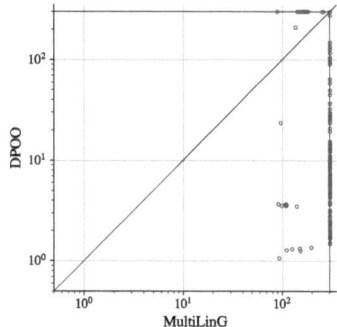

Fig. 2. Results of aoki-benchmarks   **Fig. 3.** MULTILInG versus DPOO

benchmarks within the time limit. We provide statistics on MULTILInG and show how often nodes with equal inputs are merged ("MergedN"), the number of eliminated positive nodes ("PosN"). We explicitly measure the time that is required by MSOLVE. This time is included in the total computation time. Additionally we provide statistics on the MSOLVE calls and list the total number ("#"), as well as the number of calls for each depth d and the *average* computation time per depth. For "resyn3" and "dc2" everything could be linearized via merging nodes. This is in high contrast to the aoki benchmarks, see Table 2 and we believe this is due to dense structure of the ABC graphs, which involve a higher sharing of nodes leading to more node pairs with equal children.

Figure 2 shows the results on the aoki-benchmarks. Both, TELUMA and AMULET2, are able to solve the complete benchmark set. DPOO solves 163 out of 192 benchmarks, whereas our approach is only able to solve 29 benchmarks. 106 benchmarks exceed the memory limit and 57 benchmarks exceed the time limit. Details on the solved instances are given in Table 2.

Although the number of solved instances is low for MULTILInG, we are able to solve 13 benchmarks that DPOO does not cover, see Figure 3. All those instances use a carry-lookahead adder (cl) as FSA, which includes sequences of OR-gates that lead to a monomial blow-up when rewritten. AMULET2 and TELUMA solve these benchmarks using either a SAT solver or polynomial rewriting to replace the FSA with an equivalent ripple-carry adder. In our approach these circuits benefit from rewriting positive nodes.

Table 2 provides additional insights and shows that for multipliers using a simple PPG between 65–86% of the computation time is spent in MSOLVE. For multipliers using a Booth encoding (bp) this percentage is lower, as we switch to non-linear rewriting during the reduction. Column "Nlin" provides the percentage of "Nodes" that are reduced using non-linear rewriting.

Summarizing, AMULET2 and TELUMA are highly efficient on the structured circuits but are not robust on optimized benchmarks. DPOO and MULTILInG are both robust and complement each other on complex multiplier designs. Hence our proposed approach is a valuable addition to the algebraic verification landscape and will be even more powerful when combined with existing methods.

Benchmarks		Preprocess		Time (s)		MSOLVE Calls					Nlin
Name	Nodes	Mrg	PosN	Total	MSOLVE (%)	#	d=3 (s)	d=4 (s)	d=5 (s)	d=6 (s)	%
sparrc	48000	8000	3968	92.7	79.5 (86.0)	3968	3968 0.02	0	0	0	0.0
sparcl	53733	8000	7749	96.2	79.4 (82.8)	3969	3969 0.02	0	0	0	0.0
spwtrc	49312	8332	3964	152.3	119.2 (78.4)	4004	3990 0.03	14 0.03	0	0	0.0
spwtcl	68747	8332	16845	176.2	122.6 (69.8)	4003	3990 0.03	13 0.03	0	0	0.0
spbdrc	49116	8281	3966	110.0	87.3 (79.8)	3968	3967 0.02	1 0.02	0	0	0.0
spbdcl	69240	8281	17305	142.5	101.5 (71.7)	3966	3966 0.03	0	0	0	0.0
sposrc	49392	8350	3966	125.3	97.2 (78.1)	3968	3967 0.02	1 0.02	0	0	0.0
sposcl	71291	8350	18485	151.8	105.5 (69.9)	3966	3966 0.03	0	0	0	0.0
spdtrc	48000	8000	3968	149.6	116.3 (78.1)	3968	3968 0.03	0	0	0	0.0
spdtcl	71000	8000	19219	174.6	115.1 (66.1)	3968	3968 0.03	0	0	0	0.0
spctrc	41248	8194	208	196.2	162.9 (83.3)	7763	3996 0.02	1884 0.02	1883 0.03	0	0.0
spctcl	62428	8194	14249	257.4	171.9 (66.9)	7761	3995 0.02	1883 0.02	1883 0.03	0	0.0
spcnrc	47236	8076	3060	136.6	105.7 (77.6)	3037	3037 0.04	0	0	0	0.0
spcncl	70236	8076	18311	173.3	111.3 (64.7)	3037	3037 0.04	0	0	0	0.0
bparrc	38311	6794	2137	98.7	38.8 (39.6)	2112	2108 0.02	2 0.02	1 0.05	1 0.05	38.2
bpwtrc	37315	6550	2134	91.2	43.6 (47.9)	2139	2125 0.02	12 0.02	1 0.06	1 0.06	39.3
bpwtcl	57556	6550	15589	159.1	46.6 (29.5)	2137	2124 0.02	11 0.03	1 0.05	1 0.06	25.5
bpbdrc	37365	6561	2135	110.0	49.0 (44.9)	2110	2106 0.02	2 0.03	1 0.05	1 0.05	39.2
bpbdcl	58309	6561	16058	181.0	44.7 (24.8)	2109	2106 0.02	1 0.03	1 0.05	1 0.06	25.1
bposrc	37459	6584	2136	105.8	41.3 (39.4)	2111	2107 0.02	2 0.03	1 0.06	1 0.06	39.1
bposcl	58759	6584	16296	170.9	49.5 (29.1)	2109	2106 0.02	1 0.04	1 0.06	1 0.06	24.9
bpdtrc	36044	6237	2114	108.5	47.2 (43.6)	2087	2084 0.02	1 0.03	1 0.05	1 0.05	40.6
bpdtcl	59169	6237	17489	167.5	52.4 (31.5)	2087	2084 0.03	1 0.03	1 0.06	1 0.06	24.7
bpctrc	32951	6428	193	139.7	101.9 (73.1)	3991	2112 0.02	939 0.02	939 0.04	1 0.04	44.5
bpctcl	54251	6428	14353	254.2	115.3 (45.6)	3991	2112 0.02	939 0.03	939 0.04	1 0.06	27.0
bpcnrc	35557	6300	1616	89.0	39.1 (44.0)	1609	1606 0.02	1 0.03	1 0.05	1 0.05	41.2
bpcncl	58682	6300	16991	170.1	50.3 (29.6)	1609	1606 0.03	1 0.03	1 0.06	1 0.06	24.9
bpbarc	38141	6590	2330	108.6	46.8 (43.2)	2322	2314 0.02	6 0.03	1 0.05	1 0.05	38.7
bpbacl	61768	6590	18080	182.2	54.9 (30.3)	2321	2313 0.02	6 0.02	1 0.04	1 0.04	23.9

Table 2. Results on *solved* aoki benchmarks.

6 Conclusion

In this paper we have presented a novel technique to verify directed acyclic graphs using computer algebra. Our first contribution is a theoretical theorem that shows how we can perform the ideal membership test of a specification polynomial using only linear polynomial operations. Secondly, we discuss how we can apply this theorem in practice to overcome the overhead of computing a full Gröbner basis. We present a technique that incrementally computes Gröbner bases for small sub-graphs to extract the linear information of the polynomials. We have demonstrated the potential of our approach on a set of multiplier circuits that have been challenging to verify so far.

In the future we aim to turn the black-box Gröbner basis approach into a white-box and explore how we can derive the linear polynomials without the computation of a full Gröbner basis. We also envision equivalence checking as a potential application, as this restricts the computation to Boolean polynomials.

Acknowledgments. This research was supported by the Austrian Science Fund (FWF) [10.55776/ESP666], the joint ANR-FWF ANR-19-CE48-0015 ECARP and ANR-22-CE91-0007 EAGLES projects, the ANR-19-CE40-0018 DE RERUM NATURA project, and grants DIMRFSI 2021-02–C21/1131 of the Paris Île-de-France Region and FA8665-20-1-7029 of the EOARD-AFOSR.

References

1. Berkeley Logic Synthesis and Verification Group: ABC: A System for Sequential Synthesis and Verification. http://www.eecs.berkeley.edu/~alanmi/abc/ (2019), bitbucket Version 1.01

2. Berthomieu, J., Neiger, V., Safey El Din, M.: Faster Change of Order Algorithm for Gröbner Bases under Shape and Stability Assumptions. In: ISSAC. pp. 409–418. ACM (2022). https://doi.org/10.1145/3476446.3535484

3. Berthomieu, J., Eder, C., Safey El Din, M.: msolve: A Library for Solving Polynomial Systems. In: ISSAC. pp. 51–58. ACM (2021). https://doi.org/10.1145/3452143.3465545

4. Biere, A.: Collection of Combinational Arithmetic Miters Submitted to the SAT Competition 2016. In: SAT Competition 2016. Dep. of Computer Science Report Series B, vol. B-2016-1, pp. 65–66. University of Helsinki (2016)

5. Buchberger, B.: Ein Algorithmus zum Auffinden der Basiselemente des Restklassenringes nach einem nulldimensionalen Polynomideal. Ph.D. thesis, University of Innsbruck (1965)

6. Buchberger, B., Kauers, M.: Gröbner basis. Scholarpedia **5**(10), 7763 (2010), http://www.scholarpedia.org/article/Groebner_basis

7. Chen, Y., Bryant, R.E.: Verification of Arithmetic Circuits with Binary Moment Diagrams. In: DAC. pp. 535–541. ACM (1995). https://doi.org/10.1145/217474.217583

8. Cox, D., Little, J., O'Shea, D.: Ideals, Varieties, and Algorithms. Springer-Verlag New York (1997)

9. Faugère, J.Ch.: A New Efficient Algorithm for Computing Gröbner bases (F4). Journal of Pure and Applied Algebra **139**(1), 61–88 (1999). https://doi.org/10.1016/S0022-4049(99)00005-5

10. Faugère, J.Ch., Gaudry, P., Huot, L., Renault, G.: Sub-Cubic Change of Ordering for Gröbner Basis: A Probabilistic Approach. In: ISSAC. pp. 170–177. ACM (2014). https://doi.org/10.1145/2608628.2608669

11. Faugère, J.Ch., Gianni, P., Lazard, D., Mora, T.: Efficient Computation of Zero-dimensional Gröbner Bases by Change of Ordering. J. Symbolic Comput. **16**(4), 329–344 (1993). https://doi.org/10.1006/jsco.1993.1051

12. Faugère, J.Ch., Mou, C.: Sparse FGLM algorithms. Journal of Symbolic Computation **80**(3), 538–569 (2017). https://doi.org/10.1016/j.jsc.2016.07.025

13. Homma, N., Watanabe, Y., Aoki, T., Higuchi, T.: Formal Design of Arithmetic Circuits Based on Arithmetic Description Language. IEICE Trans. Fundam. Electron. Commun. Comput. Sci. **89-A**(12), 3500–3509 (2006). https://doi.org/10.1093/IETFEC/E89-A.12.3500

14. Kaufmann, D.: MultiLinG (2025), https://www.github.com/d-kfmnn/multiling

15. Kaufmann, D., Beame, P., Biere, A., Nordström, J.: Adding dual variables to algebraic reasoning for gate-level multiplier verification. In: DATE. pp. 1431–1436. IEEE (2022). https://doi.org/10.23919/DATE54114.2022.9774587

16. Kaufmann, D., Berthomieu, J.: MultiLinG - Extracting Linear Relations from Gröbner Bases for Formal Verification of And-Inverter Graphs (Artifact) (2025). https://doi.org/10.5281/zenodo.14609934

17. Kaufmann, D., Biere, A.: Amulet 2.0 for verifying multiplier circuits. In: TACAS (2). LNCS, vol. 12652, pp. 357–364. Springer (2021). https://doi.org/10.1007/978-3-030-72013-1_19

18. Kaufmann, D., Biere, A., Kauers, M.: Verifying Large Multipliers by Combining SAT and Computer Algebra. In: FMCAD 2019. pp. 28–36. IEEE (2019). https://doi.org/10.23919/FMCAD.2019.8894250
19. Kaufmann, D., Biere, A., Kauers, M.: Incremental Column-wise verification of arithmetic circuits using computer algebra. Formal Methods Syst. Des. **56**(1), 22–54 (2020). https://doi.org/10.1007/S10703-018-00329-2
20. Kaufmann, D., Fleury, M., Biere, A., Kauers, M.: Practical Algebraic Calculus and Nullstellensatz with the Checkers Pacheck and Pastèque and Nuss-Checker. Formal Methods Syst. Des. **64**(1), 73–107 (2022). https://doi.org/10.1007/s10703-022-00391-x
21. Konrad, A., Scholl, C.: Symbolic Computer Algebra for Multipliers Revisited - It's All About Orders and Phases. In: FMCAD 2024. pp. 261–271. TU Wien Academic Press (2024). https://doi.org/10.34727/2024/isbn.978-3-85448-065-5_32
22. Konrad, A., Scholl, C., Mahzoon, A., Große, D., Drechsler, R.: Divider verification using symbolic computer algebra and delayed don't care optimization. In: FMCAD. pp. 1–10. IEEE (2022). https://doi.org/10.34727/2022/ISBN.978-3-85448-053-2_17
23. Kuehlmann, A., Paruthi, V., Krohm, F., Ganai, M.: Robust Boolean reasoning for equivalence checking and functional property verification. IEEE TCAD **21**(12), 1377–1394 (2002). https://doi.org/10.1109/TCAD.2002.804386
24. Li, R., Li, L., Yu, H., Fujita, M., Jiang, W., Ha, Y.: Refscat: Formal verification of logic-optimized multipliers via automated reference multiplier generation and sca-sat synergy. IEEE TCAD pp. 1–1 (2024). https://doi.org/10.1109/TCAD.2024.3442987
25. Liew, V., Beame, P., Devriendt, J., Elffers, J., Nordström, J.: Verifying Properties of Bit-vector Multiplication Using Cutting Planes Reasoning. In: FMCAD 2020. FMCAD, vol. 1, pp. 194–204. TU Vienna Academic Press (2020). https://doi.org/10.34727/2020/ISBN.978-3-85448-042-6_27
26. Liu, H., Liao, P., Huang, J., Zhen, H.L., Yuan, M., Ho, T.Y., Yu, B.: Parallel gröbner basis rewriting and memory optimization for efficient multiplier verification. In: DATE. pp. 1–6 (2024). https://doi.org/10.23919/DATE58400.2024.10546568
27. Lv, J., Kalla, P., Enescu, F.: Efficient Gröbner Basis Reductions for Formal Verification of Galois Field Arithmetic Circuits. IEEE TCAD **32**(9), 1409–1420 (2013). https://doi.org/10.1109/TCAD.2013.2259540
28. Mahzoon, A., Große, D., Drechsler, R.: PolyCleaner: Clean your Polynomials before Backward Rewriting to verify Million-gate Multipliers. In: ICCAD 2018. pp. 129:1 – 129:8. ACM (2018). https://doi.org/10.1145/3240765.3240837
29. Mahzoon, A., Große, D., Scholl, C., Drechsler, R.: Towards formal verification of optimized and industrial multipliers. In: DATE. pp. 544–549. IEEE (2020). https://doi.org/10.23919/DATE48585.2020.9116485
30. Mayr, E.W., Meyer, A.R.: The complexity of the word problems for commutative semigroups and polynomial ideals. Advances in Mathematics **46**(3), 305–329 (1982). https://doi.org/10.1016/0001-8708(82)90048-2
31. Neiger, V., Schost, É.: Computing syzygies in finite dimension using fast linear algebra. Journal of Complexity **60**, 101502 (2020). https://doi.org/10.1016/j.jco.2020.101502
32. Sharangpani, H., Barton, M.L.: Statistical analysis of floating point flaw in the pentium processor (1994)
33. Temel, M.: Vescmul: Verified implementation of s-c-rewriting for multiplier verification. In: TACAS (1). LNCS, vol. 14570, pp. 340–349. Springer (2024). https://doi.org/10.1007/978-3-031-57246-3_19

Implicit Rankings for Verifying Liveness Properties in First-Order Logic

Raz Lotan$^{(\boxtimes)}$ and Sharon Shoham

Tel Aviv University, Tel Aviv, Israel
lotanraz@gmail.com

Abstract. Liveness properties are traditionally proven using a ranking function that maps system states to some well-founded set. Carrying out such proofs in first-order logic enables automation by SMT solvers. However, reasoning about many natural ranking functions is beyond reach of existing solvers. To address this, we introduce the notion of implicit rankings — first-order formulas that soundly approximate the reduction of some ranking function without defining it explicitly. We provide recursive constructors of implicit rankings that can be instantiated and composed to induce a rich family of implicit rankings. Our constructors use quantifiers to approximate reasoning about useful primitives such as cardinalities of sets and unbounded sums that are not directly expressible in first-order logic. We demonstrate the effectiveness of our implicit rankings by verifying liveness properties of several intricate examples, including Dijkstra's k-state, 4-state and 3-state self-stabilizing protocols.

1 Introduction

Liveness properties of a system assert that some desirable behavior eventually happens in all executions of the system. The most common approach to proving liveness properties is based on the notion of a well-founded ranking. Such a proof goes by finding a ranking function f from the set of states of the system to some well-founded set $(A, <)$ such that for any transition of the system from state s to state s' where the desired behavior does not yet occur, the ranking is reduced, i.e., $f(s') < f(s)$. Thus, well-foundedness of A ensures that there is no infinite execution that does not eventually satisfy the property.

Many recent works use first-order logic (FOL) for verifying safety and liveness properties [26, 31, 35–37, 39, 43, 48]. FOL has been established as a useful tool for modeling and verifying systems, mostly due to the success of automatic solvers that answer complicated satisfiability queries in seconds. One challenge that arises when proving liveness properties in FOL is that well-foundedness is not directly expressible in FOL. Additionally, many common primitives that are useful for defining ranking functions, such as cardinality of sets, and sums over unbounded domains, cannot be directly captured in FOL.

We present an approach that overcomes these hurdles and facilitates carrying out proofs based on ranking functions in FOL. Our approach utilizes the observation that it suffices to encode the reduction in the ranking function without

© The Author(s) 2025
A. Gurfinkel and M. Heule (Eds.): TACAS 2025, LNCS 15696, pp. 375–395, 2025.
https://doi.org/10.1007/978-3-031-90643-5_20

explicitly encoding the ranking function itself. Furthermore, the reduction need not be encoded precisely, but can be soundly approximated. For this purpose, we define the notion of an *implicit ranking*, which can be soundly used in liveness proofs in place of explicit ranking functions. An implicit ranking consists of a reduction formula, $\varphi_<$, and a conservation formula, $\varphi_\le$. These are two-state first-order formulas for which there exists *some* ranking function f mapping the states to elements of *some* well-founded set $(A, <)$ such that whenever states s and s' satisfy $\varphi_<$ we have $f(s') < f(s)$ and whenever s, s' satisfy $\varphi_\le$ we have $f(s') \le f(s)$. Conservation is needed, for example, in proof rules for verifying liveness under fairness assumptions.

We then introduce recursive constructors for implicit rankings that can be instantiated and composed to induce a rich family of implicit rankings. Our constructors are based on familiar notions from order theory, such as pointwise ordering and lexicographic ordering, which can be used to lift and aggregate orders in various ways, adapted to the first-order setting. A key component of our approach is the introduction of domain-based constructors that use quantification over the domain of a state to express aggregation of rankings. For example we can express a pointwise aggregation of given rankings, or a lexicographic aggregation based on a given order on the elements in the domain. When composed, such aggregations can capture complex ranking arguments that are unattainable by existing methods.

Implicit rankings produced by domain-based constructors are sound for finite, albeit unbounded, domains. Such domains are common when reasoning about distributed protocols, concurrent systems, arrays, etc. where the set of nodes, array indices, etc. is finite but not fixed. In fact, liveness of such systems often depends on the finiteness of the domain. Thus, such constructors allow us to utilize finiteness of the domain in liveness proofs, even though finiteness itself is not definable in FOL.

As notable examples, we use our constructors to produce implicit rankings for the self-stabilization property of Dijkstra's k-state, 4-state and 3-state protocols [13]. In these examples, domain-based constructors are able to replace reasoning about unbounded sums and set cardinalities in novel ways. We use the implicit rankings within a sound proof rule to verify the examples, where the premises of the rule are discharged automatically by an SMT solver. To the best of our knowledge, this is the first SMT-based verification of the more challenging 3-state and 4-state protocols, and it is simpler than existing proofs for such protocols [1, 3, 8, 12, 14, 19, 20, 23, 25, 34].

Contributions.

- We define *implicit rankings*, which soundly approximate reduction and conservation of some ranking function in FOL, and show how these implicit rankings can be used in liveness proofs (Section 4).
- We introduce constructors of implicit rankings based on familiar notions from order theory, including domain-based constructors that are sound for finite but unbounded domains and can sometimes replace reasoning about unbounded summations and set cardinalities (Section 5).

– We implement the proposed constructors in a tool for verifying liveness properties of first-order transition systems, and demonstrate the power of our constructors by verifying a set of examples of liveness properties, including Dijkstra's self-stabilizing protocols (Section 6).

In the next section we present two examples that motivate our approach. Section 3 then provides the necessary background for Sections 4 to 6 and Section 7 discusses related work and concludes the paper.

Full Version. The full version of the paper is available at [27].

2   Motivating Examples

Example 1. As a first motivating example (Figure 1), we consider an abstraction of a self-stabilizing protocol. In a self-stabilizing protocol privileges are initially distributed arbitrarily in a network, but eventually the protocol converges to a stable state where only one machine holds a privilege. The protocol we consider abstracts the movement of privileges in Dijkstra's k-state protocol [13]. While the abstraction does not enjoy stabilization, it suffices for showing a property that is used in the proof of stabilization for Dijkstra's protocol.

In this protocol, the network consists of a finite number of machines, arranged in a ring, with one machine, called the bottom machine (bot), being distinguished. Every machine i has a field i.next which directs to its right-hand neighbor in the ring. At any moment any machine may be privileged or not. Initially, privileges are assigned arbitrarily, with the guarantee that at least one machine is privileged. At each iteration, an arbitrary privileged machine is scheduled, the scheduled machine loses its privilege and its right-hand neighbor becomes privileged (whether it was already privileged or not). The property we wish to prove is that machine bot is eventually scheduled: $\Diamond(\mathsf{skd} = \mathsf{bot})$. In the original protocol, the steps of machine bot are different from all other machines (this difference is lost in the abstraction) and, in particular, they take the state of the network closer to stabilization.

Next, we describe a ranking function for proving the liveness property. To present the ranking function we denote the number of machines by n and think of the machines as indexed by $0, 1, \ldots, n-1$ according to their order in the ring, with $\mathsf{bot} = 0$. Now, a natural ranking function is: $\mathrm{Rk} = \sum_{i \neq 0 : \mathrm{priv}(i)} n - i$. Intuitively, the value $n - i$ can be seen as the number of steps required for the privilege of machine i to reach machine 0 (if no other privileges are present). We can now verify that in any transition from s to s', if the eventuality does not occur in either s or s', the rank is reduced. Indeed, for any transition, if $\mathsf{skd} = 0$ the eventuality is satisfied in s; otherwise, skd loses its privilege, decreasing Rk by $n-\mathsf{skd}$, and $\mathsf{skd}+1$ gains a privilege, (possibly) increasing Rk by $n-(\mathsf{skd}+1)$, ultimately decreasing Rk by 1 (or more, if $\mathsf{skd} + 1$ was already privileged).

While this ranking function is natural, it is not clear how to reason about it with existing automated solvers due to the unbounded sum operation which is not directly expressible in FOL (without induction). Next, we show how we can

```
machine bot
relation priv(machine)
function next(machine) : machine
while(exists m. priv(m)):
    skd = *
    assume(priv(skd))
    priv(skd) = false
    priv(next(skd)) = true
```

```
index ptr = n - 1
array(index) a = [1 for i in 0,...,n-1]
while (ptr >= 0):
    if a[ptr] == 0:
        a[ptr] = 1 ; ptr = ptr - 1
    else:
        a[ptr] = 0 ; ptr = n - 1
```

Fig. 1. Toy Stabilization

Fig. 2. Binary Counter

express this ranking argument in FOL by an implicit ranking which encodes a sound approximation of the reduction in the ranking function. To do this, we show that we can replace reasoning about set cardinalities and unbounded sums by reasoning about other aggregations that are expressible in FOL.

To avoid combining arithmetic reasoning with quantifiers, we use an uninterpreted sort to model the machines, and instead of relying on numbers, we model the ring structure with a strict order on machines, lt, such that bot is minimal in that order, and the next field corresponds to the successor function in the order lt, except for the maximal element which points to bot.

Now, we observe that in our model, the expression $n - i$ used in the ranking function above for a privileged machine i is the cardinality of the set of machines that are greater or equal to i in the order lt. Further, we can sum over all machines by pushing the condition on i into the set definition. Thus, Rk $= \sum_i |\{j : \mathsf{priv}(i) \wedge i \neq 0 \wedge (\mathsf{lt}(i,j) \vee i = j)\}|$. In order to express reduction in the sum, we recall that in a transition, the summands are unchanged for all machines except for skd, skd $+ 1$; the contribution of skd $+ 1$ to the sum after the transition is smaller than the contribution of skd before the transition and the contribution of skd to the sum after the transition is 0 (because it loses its privilege) and therefore, smaller or equal to that of skd $+1$ before the transition. Therefore we can use an adaption of a pointwise argument which "permutes" skd and skd $+ 1$ to capture the reduction in the sum over all machines.

Next, we need to express reduction (or conservation) in the summands (either of the same machine i or of different machines) along transitions. The summands are cardinalities of sets of machines j. Thus, we observe that it suffices to show strict set inclusion. This amounts to a pointwise argument over all machines j, showing reduction (or conservation) in the binary predicate $\alpha(i,j) = \mathsf{priv}(i) \wedge i \neq 0 \wedge (\mathsf{lt}(i,j) \vee i = j)$ that defines membership of j in the set of i. The reduction in the binary predicate, the pointwise reduction and the permuted-pointwise reduction, can all be encoded in FOL. Thus, the overall approximation of the reduction in the ranking function can be expressed (and hence verified automatically) by the following first-order formula, where unprimed symbols represent the pre-state of a transition and primed variables represent the post-state:

$$\forall j. \ (\alpha'(\mathsf{next}(\mathsf{skd}), j) \rightarrow \alpha(\mathsf{skd}, j)) \wedge \exists j. \ (\neg\alpha'(\mathsf{next}(\mathsf{skd}), j) \wedge \alpha(\mathsf{skd}, j)) \wedge$$
$$\forall j. \ (\alpha'(\mathsf{skd}, j) \rightarrow \alpha(\mathsf{next}(\mathsf{skd}), j)) \wedge$$
$$\forall i. \ ((i \neq \mathsf{skd} \wedge i \neq \mathsf{next}(\mathsf{skd}) \rightarrow \forall j. \ (\alpha'(i, j) \rightarrow \alpha(i, j)))$$

Example 2. As a second motivating example (Figure 2), we look at a binary counter implemented in an array, taken from [24]. For simplicity of the presentation, we consider a version of the counter that counts down. The counter is implemented by an array $a[0], \ldots, a[n-1]$ with $a[0]$ as the most significant bit and $a[n-1]$ as the least significant bit, initialized with all 1s. A pointer ptr traverses the array starting at index $n-1$ (the lsb) until it sees the first 1, replacing at each step any 0 it sees with a 1. When reaching the first cell with a 1, it sets that cell to a 0 and returns ptr to index $n-1$. We wish to prove that eventually the array holds all 0s: $\Diamond(\forall x.a[x] = 0)$.

To find a ranking function, we notice that the reduction in the counter value happens between states of the program where ptr $= n-1$. Such states partition the execution to "intervals". For a state inside an interval, we can derive the value of the counter at the beginning of the interval (i.e., when ptr was last $n-1$) by $a_{\mathsf{old}}[i] = 0 \iff a[i] = 0 \vee i >$ ptr. Within an interval, the counter values stored by a_{old} do not change but ptr is reduced; and when a new interval starts, the value of a_{old} is reduced (and ptr is set back to $n-1$). This lends itself to a ranking function in the form of a lexicographic pair $\mathrm{Rk} = (\mathrm{val}(a_{\mathsf{old}}), \mathsf{ptr})$.

Unfortunately, it is not clear how to encode the value of the counter in FOL. In fact, most existing techniques for encoding ranking functions in FOL are limited to polynomial ranking functions, while the counter requires an exponential ranking function. Fortunately, we realize that a reduction in the counter value corresponds to a lexicographic reduction in the sequence of bits stored in the array representing the counter based on the order on array indices.

To encode the ranking argument in FOL we model the indices of the array, as in Example 1, by an uninterpreted index sort and a strict order lt on it, with the maximal index acting as $n-1$. The content of the array is modeled using a unary relation $a(\cdot)$ that records the cells with value 1. Then, a_{old} is recorded by $a_{\mathsf{old}}(i) = a(i) \wedge (\mathsf{lt}(i, \mathsf{ptr}) \vee i = \mathsf{ptr})$. With this encoding, reduction in ptr is measured by the order on indices lt and reduction in a_{old} is measured lexicographically, based on the same order lt on indices, where for every index i, the values of cell i are ordered by implication on the derived predicate $a_{\mathsf{old}}(i)$. Overall, the reduction in rank can be encoded in FOL by the formula:

$$\exists i. \, (\neg a'_{\mathsf{old}}(i) \wedge a_{\mathsf{old}}(i) \wedge \forall j. \, \mathsf{lt}(j, i) \rightarrow (a'_{\mathsf{old}}(j) \rightarrow a_{\mathsf{old}}(j))) \vee$$
$$((\forall i. \, a'_{\mathsf{old}}(i) \leftrightarrow a_{\mathsf{old}}(i)) \wedge \mathsf{lt}(\mathsf{ptr}', \mathsf{ptr}))$$

Section 4 formally defines the notion of an implicit ranking which the reduction formulas above exemplify. The crux of our work is in Section 5, where we present constructors of implicit rankings. As we show in Section 6, the implicit rankings for both motivating examples can be built using our constructors.

3   Preliminaries

First-Order Logic. We consider uninterpreted FOL with equality, without theories. For simplicity, we present our results for a single-sorted version of FOL.

The extension of the results to many-sorted logic, which we use in practice, is natural. A first-order signature Σ contains relation, constant and function symbols. A term t over Σ is a variable x, a constant c, the application of a function on a sequence of terms $f(t)$ or an if-then-else term $\text{ite}(\alpha, t_1, t_2)$. Formulas α over Σ are defined recursively: atomic formulas are either $t_1 = t_2$ or $r(t)$ where r is a relation symbol. Non-atomic formulas are built using connectives $\neg, \wedge, \vee, \rightarrow$ and quantifiers $\forall, \exists$. We write $\alpha(x_1, \ldots, x_k)$ to denote that the free variables in α are contained in $x_1, \ldots, x_k$. Given sequences of terms $t_1, \ldots, t_k$ we then use the notation $\alpha(t_1, \ldots, t_k)$ to denote the formula obtained from α by substituting each x_j with t_j. For a signature Σ we use subscripts and superscripts $\ddagger$ to denote disjoint copies of Σ defined by $\Sigma\ddagger = \{a\ddagger \mid a \in \Sigma\}$, assumed to satisfy $\Sigma \cap \Sigma\ddagger = \emptyset$. For a formula α over Σ, we denote by $\alpha\ddagger$ the formula over $\Sigma\ddagger$ obtained by substituting each symbol $a \in \Sigma$ with $a\ddagger \in \Sigma\ddagger$.

First-order formulas are evaluated over pairs of structures and assignments. A structure for Σ is a pair $s = (\mathcal{D}, \mathcal{I})$ where $\mathcal{D}$ is a non-empty set called the domain, and $\mathcal{I}$ is an interpretation that maps each relation, constant and function symbol to an appropriate construct over $\mathcal{D}$. We denote by $\text{struct}(\Sigma, \mathcal{D})$ the set of all structures over $\mathcal{D}$. An assignment v from a sequence of variables x to a domain $\mathcal{D}$ is a function $v : x \rightarrow \mathcal{D}$. We denote the set of all assignments from x to $\mathcal{D}$ by $\text{assign}(x, \mathcal{D})$. We denote the concatenation of two sequences of variables x, y by $x{\cdot}y$. For two assignments u, v without shared variables, we denote by $u{\cdot}v$ the disjoint union of u and v. We call a pair (s, v) of a structure and an assignment an a-structure. For a domain $\mathcal{D}$ and a sequence of variables x we denote the set of all a-structures by $\text{a-struct}(\Sigma, x, \mathcal{D})$. For a formula α and an a-structure (s, v) we write $(s, v) \models \alpha$ to denote that (s, v) satisfies α.

Transition Systems in First-Order Logic. We consider transition systems given by a first-order specification $\mathcal{T} = (\Sigma, \iota, \tau)$ where Σ is a signature, ι is a closed formula over Σ that specifies initial states, and τ is a formula over a double signature $\Sigma \uplus \Sigma'$ that specifies transitions, where the symbols in Σ represent the pre-state and the symbols in Σ' represent the post-state of a transition. A trace of $\mathcal{T}$ is an infinite sequence of structures $(s_i)_{i=0}^{\infty}$ over the same domain such that s_0 is an initial state and for all $i \in \mathbb{N}$, there is a transition from s_i to s_{i+1}.

Well-Founded Partial Orders. A binary relation $\leq$ on a set A is a partial order if it is reflexive, antisymmetric and transitive. For a partial order we write $a_1 < a_2$ for $a_1 \leq a_2$ and $a_1 \neq a_2$. A partial order $\leq$ is called well-founded if there is no sequence $a_0, a_1, \ldots$ such that $a_{i+1} < a_i$ for all $i \in \mathbb{N}$. We then refer to $\leq$ as a wfpo for short[1]. If $\leq$ is a partial order on A and A is finite, then $\leq$ is a wfpo.

4 Expressing Ranking in First-Order Logic

In this section we introduce the notion of *implicit ranking*. To motivate our definition, we start by considering the way rankings are typically used.

---

[1] This is a different (weaker) notion from a partial-well-order (an antisymmetric well-quasi-order), which requires no infinite decreasing chains and no infinite antichains.

4.1   Using Ranking for Liveness Proofs

Well-founded rankings are useful for proving liveness properties of transition systems. A typical proof rule that uses rankings is based on two notions: a conservation of the ranking, corresponding to $\leq$, and a reduction in the ranking, corresponding to $<$. As an example, we examine proving liveness properties of the form $\mathcal{P} = \Box \Diamond r \rightarrow \Diamond q$. A transition system $\mathcal{T} = (\Sigma, \iota, \tau)$ satisfies $\mathcal{P}$ if every trace of $\mathcal{T}$ that satisfies r infinitely often eventually satisfies q (r can be understood as a fairness assumption). We can prove such a property by finding a ranking function f from states of the system to a set A with a wfpo $\leq$ and a formula ϕ, and validating the following premises: (i) $\iota \wedge \neg q \rightarrow \phi$ (ii) $\phi \wedge \tau \wedge \neg q' \rightarrow \phi'$ (iii) $\phi \wedge \tau \wedge \neg q' \rightarrow \varphi_{\leq}$ (iv) $\phi \wedge \tau \wedge \neg q' \wedge r \rightarrow \varphi_{<}$, where $\varphi_{\leq}, \varphi_{<}$ are formulas that encode conservation and reduction of f. (i) and (ii) assert that ϕ holds in all states in a trace as long as q does not hold. (iii) guarantees that in every transition that does not visit q we have conservation of f. (iv) states that in every transition following a visit to r we have a reduction in f. If all premises are valid, r cannot be visited infinitely often without eventually satisfying q, as that would induce an infinitely decreasing chain in f. We use a similar proof rule for more general liveness properties in our evaluation (Section 6).

   The structure of the proof rule above reveals that for soundness, $\varphi_{\leq}$ and $\varphi_{<}$ do not need to precisely capture conservation and reduction in the ranking. Instead, because $\varphi_{\leq}, \varphi_{<}$ appear only positively, it suffices that they *underapproximate* them, such that whenever a pair of states satisfies $\varphi_{\leq}$, the value of f is conserved between them, and whenever a pair of states satisfies $\varphi_{<}$, the value of f is reduced between them. The implication in the other direction is not needed for soundness. This observation is key for encoding complex ranking arguments in FOL. It allows flexibility in encoding conservation and reduction, which is crucial in cases where these relations (as well as the ranking function itself) are not directly expressible in FOL, but their underapproximations are.

4.2   Implicit Ranking

This section formalizes the notion of an *implicit ranking*— a pair of formulas $\varphi_{\leq}, \varphi_{<}$ which, for every domain $\mathcal{D}$, encode underapproximations of conservation and reduction of some implicitly defined ranking function on structures with domain $\mathcal{D}$. For compositionality, we generalize this concept to pairs of a-structures.

Notation. The definition of an implicit ranking uses formulas that reason about a pair of a-structures. To that end, given a signature Σ and a sequence of variables $\boldsymbol{x} = (x_i)_{i=1}^m$, we consider a double signature $\Sigma_0 \uplus \Sigma_1$ and two copies of the variables $\boldsymbol{x}_b = (x_{b,i})_{i=1}^m$ for $b \in \{0,1\}$. Intuitively, Σ_0 and $\boldsymbol{x}_0$ represent a "lower ranked" a-structure and Σ_1 and $\boldsymbol{x}_1$ represent a "higher ranked" a-structure. For a term t with variables $\boldsymbol{x}$, we denote by t_b the term obtained by substituting Σ_b for Σ and $\boldsymbol{x}_b$ for $\boldsymbol{x}$. With abuse of notation, we consider a structure $s = (\mathcal{D}, \mathcal{I})$ for Σ as a structure for Σ_b where $\mathcal{I}(a_b) = \mathcal{I}(a)$ for every $a_b \in \Sigma_b$ and an assignment to $\boldsymbol{x}$ as an assignment to $\boldsymbol{x}_b$ by defining $v(x_{b,i}) = v(x_i)$. For a formula φ over $\Sigma_0 \uplus \Sigma_1$

with free variables x_0, x_1 and a-structures $(s_0, v_0), (s_1, v_1) \in$ a-struct$(\Sigma, x, \mathcal{D})$, we write $(s_0, v_0), (s_1, v_1) \models \varphi$ to denote satisfaction of φ when for $b \in \{0, 1\}$, the interpretation of Σ_b is taken from s_b, and the assignment to x_b is taken from v_b.

Definition 1 (Implicit Ranking). *Let $\varphi_\leq, \varphi_<$ be two formulas over $\Sigma_0 \uplus \Sigma_1$. We say that* Rk $= (\varphi_\leq, \varphi_<)$ *is an* implicit ranking *with parameters x, if the free variables in $\varphi_\leq$ and $\varphi_<$ are confined to x_0, x_1 and for any domain $\mathcal{D}$, there exist a set A, a wfpo $\leq$ on A and a function $f :$ a-struct$(\Sigma, x, \mathcal{D}) \rightarrow A$, such that:*

$$(s_0, v_0), (s_1, v_1) \models \varphi_\leq(x_0, x_1) \implies f(s_0, v_0) \leq f(s_1, v_1)$$
$$(s_0, v_0), (s_1, v_1) \models \varphi_<(x_0, x_1) \implies f(s_0, v_0) < f(s_1, v_1)$$

For an implicit ranking Rk *and a domain $\mathcal{D}$, we call $(A, \leq)$ a ranking range for $\mathcal{D}$ and f a ranking function for $\mathcal{D}$. If x is empty, we call* Rk *a closed implicit ranking. If the existence of $A, \leq$ and f is ensured only for finite domains $\mathcal{D}$, we call* Rk *an implicit ranking for finite domains.*

The formulas $\varphi_\leq, \varphi_<$ encode relations between a-structures, which means that they let us compare specific elements in one state with possibly different elements in another state. Technically, this is achieved by the free variables in $\varphi_\leq$ and $\varphi_<$. In proof rules, we only need to compare structures and thus only allow the use of closed implicit rankings. The use of free variables is needed for the construction of these rankings. In Section 5 we introduce constructors that create new implicit rankings from existing rankings, some of which eliminate free variables.

Definition 1 ensures that for each domain $\mathcal{D}$, the formulas $\varphi_\leq$ and $\varphi_<$ underapproximate conservation and reduction of some ranking function over a-structures. The ranking function f and the corresponding ranking range are not explicitly encoded. As explained above, this allows us to find such formulas even if the exact conservation and reduction of f are not readily expressible in FOL. For example, for a function f that maps s to the number of elements in $\mathcal{D}$ that satisfy a predicate $\alpha(x)$, there is no formula that precisely captures the conservation of f, but it can be approximated, say, by the formula $\forall x.\alpha_0(x) \rightarrow \alpha_1(x)$.

Closed implicit rankings can be used in proof rules such as the one above by substituting Σ' (the post-state signature) for Σ_0 and Σ (the pre-state signature) for Σ_1. While implicit rankings ensure reduction/conservation in a possibly different function for each domain, they are sound to use as all states along a trace of a transition system share a domain. In the case of implicit rankings for finite domains, soundness is guaranteed for systems where the domain is finite in each trace, but still unbounded.

5   Constructions of Implicit Rankings

We introduce several constructors for implicit rankings, that can be instantiated and composed to create a rich family of implicit rankings. Our constructors essentially encode standard constructions of partial orders. Each constructor has its own arguments, which may themselves be implicit rankings. Some constructors only construct implicit rankings for finite domains. These are called finite-domain constructors. For other constructors, whether the constructed implicit ranking is for arbitrary or finite domains is inherited from the implicit rankings used as arguments for the constructor. We provide the following guarantees.

Theorem 1. *All constructors defined in this section are* sound *in the sense that (i) if the arguments of a constructor satisfy their assumptions, then the output of the constructor is an implicit ranking (for finite domains if the constructor is finite-domain), and (ii) for constructors that receive implicit rankings as arguments, if at least one of the arguments is an implicit ranking for finite domains, so is the constructed implicit ranking.*

Due to space considerations we defer soundness proofs to [27]. We give only the crux of the proofs: the definitions of ranking range and ranking function for the constructed implicit ranking given these notions for the arguments of the constructor.

5.1 Base Constructors

We start by introducing two non-recursive constructors, which are used as the base in recursive constructions of implicit rankings.

Binary Constructor. The first constructor we define captures a binary ranking function, mapping each a-structure (s, v) to 0 or 1 (ordered $0 \leq 1$) by checking whether (s, v) satisfies a formula α. In this case, reduction is obtained if α holds in the higher-ranked a-structure and does not hold in the lower-ranked a-structure. Conservation also includes the case where α holds in both or in neither.

Constructor 1. *The* binary constructor *receives a formula $\alpha(x)$ over Σ. It returns an implicit ranking* $\mathrm{Bin}(\alpha) = (\varphi_\leq, \varphi_<)$ *with parameters x defined by:*

$$\varphi_\leq(x_0, x_1) = \alpha_0(x_0) \to \alpha_1(x_1) \qquad \varphi_<(x_0, x_1) = \alpha_1(x_1) \wedge \neg\alpha_0(x_0)$$

Example 3. Continuing with Example 1, for $\alpha(i, j) = \mathrm{priv}(i) \wedge \mathrm{lt}(i, j)$, $\mathrm{Bin}(\alpha)$ is an implicit ranking with parameters i, j, capturing reduction and conservation in the ranking between a pair of machines (i_1, j_1) in the higher-ranked structure and a potentially different pair (i_0, j_0) in the lower-ranked structure. The need for comparing different pairs in different structures is demonstrated in Example 1.

Position-in-Order Constructor. The second base constructor, which is a finite-domain constructor, utilizes an already existing (possibly derived) partial order in the system itself, building on the observation that a partial order over a *finite* domain is always well-founded. The order is defined by a single signature formula $\ell(y_0, y_1)$, which allows comparing two (tuples of) elements. To guarantee soundness we must verify that $\ell(\boldsymbol{y}_0, \boldsymbol{y}_1)$ defines a strict order, and that it is immutable, i.e., does not change between the ranked structures, encoded by:

$$\text{order}(\ell) := (\forall \boldsymbol{y}^1, \boldsymbol{y}^2.\ell_0(\boldsymbol{y}^1, \boldsymbol{y}^2) \leftrightarrow \ell_1(\boldsymbol{y}^1, \boldsymbol{y}^2)) \wedge$$
$$(\forall \boldsymbol{y}^1, \boldsymbol{y}^2.\ell_0(\boldsymbol{y}^1, \boldsymbol{y}^2) \rightarrow \neg \ell_0(\boldsymbol{y}^2, \boldsymbol{y}^1)) \wedge$$
$$(\forall \boldsymbol{y}^1, \boldsymbol{y}^2, \boldsymbol{y}^3.\ell_0(\boldsymbol{y}^1, \boldsymbol{y}^2) \wedge \ell_0(\boldsymbol{y}^2, \boldsymbol{y}^3) \rightarrow \ell_0(\boldsymbol{y}^1, \boldsymbol{y}^3))$$

If $s_0, s_1 \models \text{order}(\ell)$ the interpretation of ℓ in s_0 coincides with its interpretation in s_1 and both define a strict partial order on the set $\text{assign}(\boldsymbol{y}, \mathcal{D})$, where $\mathcal{D}$ is the domain of s_0 and s_1. Then, if $\mathcal{D}$ is finite, this order is a wfpo. The position-in-order constructor uses ℓ to create an implicit ranking that compares the valuation of the same term (or sequence of terms) $\boldsymbol{t}$ in the two structures. The term may include free variables, allowing to compare valuations under different assignments in the two structures. The underlying ranking function maps an a-structure to its interpretation of ℓ together with the valuation it assigns to $\boldsymbol{t}$.

Constructor 2. *The* position-in-order constructor *receives a formula* $\ell(\boldsymbol{y}_0, \boldsymbol{y}_1)$ *over* Σ *and a sequence of terms* $\boldsymbol{t}(\boldsymbol{y})$ *over* Σ *with* $|\boldsymbol{t}| = |\boldsymbol{y}|$. *It returns an implicit ranking for finite domains* $\text{Pos}(\boldsymbol{t}, \ell) = (\varphi_\leq, \varphi_<)$ *with parameters* $\boldsymbol{y}$ *defined by:*

$$\varphi_\leq(\boldsymbol{y}_0, \boldsymbol{y}_1) = \text{order}(\ell) \wedge (\ell_0(\boldsymbol{t}_0, \boldsymbol{t}_1) \vee \boldsymbol{t}_0 = \boldsymbol{t}_1) \qquad \varphi_<(\boldsymbol{y}_0, \boldsymbol{y}_1) = \text{order}(\ell) \wedge \ell_0(\boldsymbol{t}_0, \boldsymbol{t}_1)$$

Example 4. Continuing with Example 2, define $\ell(i_0, i_1) = \text{lt}(i_0, i_1)$, and $t = \text{ptr}$. Then $\text{Pos}(t, \ell)$ is a closed implicit ranking for finite domains, where the ranking is based on the position of the pointer in the different structures.

5.2   Constructors for Aggregation of Finitely Many Rankings

We now present constructors which receive as input a finite number of implicit rankings and create an implicit ranking that mimics aggregation of the underlying ranking ranges and functions. These constructors are based on standard ways to lift partial orders on sets to a partial order on their Cartesian product.

Pointwise Constructor. For partially-ordered sets $A_1, \dots, A_m$ with partial orders $\leq_1, \dots, \leq_m$ respectively, the pointwise partial order $\leq_{\text{pw}}$ on the set $A_1 \times \cdots \times A_m$ is defined by $(a_1, \dots, a_m) \leq_{\text{pw}} (b_1, \dots, b_m) \iff \bigwedge_i a_i \leq_i b_i$. If the orders $\leq_1, \dots, \leq_m$ are wfpos then so is $\leq_{\text{pw}}$. The following constructor encodes this in FOL to aggregate rankings. A corresponding ranking function is defined by $f(s, v) = (f_1(s, v), \dots, f_m(s, v))$, where f_i is a ranking function to A_i.

Constructor 3. *The* pointwise constructor *receives implicit rankings* $\text{Rk}^i = (\varphi^i_\leq, \varphi^i_<)$ *for* $i = 1, \dots, m$, *each with parameters* $\boldsymbol{x}$. *It returns an implicit ranking* $\text{PW}(\text{Rk}^1, \dots, \text{Rk}^m) = (\varphi_\leq, \varphi_<)$ *with parameters* $\boldsymbol{x}$ *defined by:*

$$\varphi_\leq(\boldsymbol{x}_0, \boldsymbol{x}_1) = \bigwedge_i \varphi^i_\leq(\boldsymbol{x}_0, \boldsymbol{x}_1) \qquad \varphi_<(\boldsymbol{x}_0, \boldsymbol{x}_1) = \varphi_\leq(\boldsymbol{x}_0, \boldsymbol{x}_1) \wedge \bigvee_i \varphi^i_<(\boldsymbol{x}_0, \boldsymbol{x}_1)$$

Lexicographic Constructor. A different partial order on $A = A_1 \times \cdots \times A_m$ can be defined by the lexicographic ordering: $(a_1, \ldots, a_m) \leq_{\text{lex}} (b_1, \ldots, b_m) \iff \bigvee_i (a_i <_i b_i \wedge \bigwedge_{j<i} (a_j \leq_j b_j)) \vee (\bigwedge_i a_i \leq_i b_i)$. Again, if $\leq_i$ are all wfpos, then so is $\leq_{\text{lex}}$. The Lexicographic Constructor encodes this idea in FOL. A corresponding ranking function is defined as for the pointwise constructor.

Constructor 4. *The* lexicographic constructor *receives implicit rankings* $\text{Rk}^i = (\varphi^i_\leq, \varphi^i_<)$ *for* $i = 1, \ldots, m$, *each with parameters* $\boldsymbol{x}$. *It returns an implicit ranking* $\text{Lex}(\text{Rk}^1, \ldots, \text{Rk}^m) = (\varphi_\leq, \varphi_<)$ *with parameters* $\boldsymbol{x}$ *defined by:*

$$\varphi_<(\boldsymbol{x}_0, \boldsymbol{x}_1) = \bigvee_i (\varphi^i_<(\boldsymbol{x}_0, \boldsymbol{x}_1) \wedge \bigwedge_{j<i} \varphi^j_\leq(\boldsymbol{x}_0, \boldsymbol{x}_1))$$
$$\varphi_\leq(\boldsymbol{x}_0, \boldsymbol{x}_1) = \varphi_<(\boldsymbol{x}_0, \boldsymbol{x}_1) \vee \bigwedge_i \varphi^i_\leq(\boldsymbol{x}_0, \boldsymbol{x}_1)$$

5.3   Constructors for Domain-Based Aggregations of Rankings

We now turn to present constructors that encode domain-based aggregations of rankings. As demonstrated in Example 1, such aggregations can sometimes replace summations and cardinalities of sets in ranking arguments. These are constructors that receive as input an implicit ranking $(\varphi_\leq, \varphi_<)$ with parameters $\boldsymbol{x}$, partitioned to $\boldsymbol{x} = \boldsymbol{y} \cdot \boldsymbol{z}$. and return an implicit ranking with parameters $\boldsymbol{z}$, for which the conservation and reduction depend on the aggregation of the results of $\varphi_\leq$ and $\varphi_<$ for different values of $\boldsymbol{y}$ in the domain. This is established by quantifying over $\boldsymbol{y}$. To do so, we use generalizations of the partial-order constructions we saw in Section 5.2 to sets of functions. Due to the nature of these constructions, the soundness of the produced rankings depends on the finiteness of the domain, so these constructors are *finite-domain constructors*.

Domain-Pointwise Constructor. For a partially-ordered set $(A, \leq_A)$ and a set Y, we can lift $\leq_A$ to a pointwise partial order on the set of functions $Y \to A$: for any $a, b \in Y \to A$ we have $a \leq_{\text{pw}} b \iff \forall y \in Y.a(y) \leq_A b(y)$. If the order $\leq_A$ is a wfpo and Y is finite then $\leq_{\text{pw}}$ is a wfpo. In our case the set Y is the set of assignments to $\boldsymbol{y}$ over some finite domain. The next constructor encodes this idea in FOL in a straight-forward way: conservation of the aggregated ranking occurs when we have conservation of the input ranking for all values of $\boldsymbol{y}$, and reduction is achieved when, additionally, there is some value of $\boldsymbol{y}$ for which we have reduction of the input rank. A corresponding ranking function to assign$(\boldsymbol{y}, \mathcal{D}) \to A$ is defined by $f(s, v) = \lambda u \in \text{assign}(\boldsymbol{y}, \mathcal{D}).f_A(s, u \cdot v)$ where f_A is a ranking function to A.

Constructor 5. *The* domain-pointwise constructor *receives an implicit ranking* $\text{Rk}^\circ = (\varphi^\circ_\leq, \varphi^\circ_<)$ *with parameters* $\boldsymbol{x} = \boldsymbol{y} \cdot \boldsymbol{z}$. *It returns an implicit ranking for finite domains* $\text{DomPW}(\text{Rk}^\circ, \boldsymbol{y}) = (\varphi_\leq, \varphi_<)$ *with parameters* $\boldsymbol{z}$ *defined by:*

$$\varphi_\leq(\boldsymbol{z}_0, \boldsymbol{z}_1) = \forall \boldsymbol{y}.\varphi^\circ_\leq(\boldsymbol{y} \cdot \boldsymbol{z}_0, \boldsymbol{y} \cdot \boldsymbol{z}_1)$$
$$\varphi_<(\boldsymbol{z}_0, \boldsymbol{z}_1) = \varphi_\leq(\boldsymbol{z}_0, \boldsymbol{z}_1) \wedge (\exists \boldsymbol{y}.\varphi^\circ_<(\boldsymbol{y} \cdot \boldsymbol{z}_0, \boldsymbol{y} \cdot \boldsymbol{z}_1))$$

Next we demonstrate how DomPW can be used to approximate set cardinalities.

Example 5. For a formula with one free variable $\alpha(x)$, if we take $\mathrm{Rk}^\circ = \mathrm{Bin}(\alpha)$, the implicit ranking for finite domains $\mathrm{Rk} = \mathrm{DomPW}(\mathrm{Rk}^\circ, x) = (\varphi_\le, \varphi_<)$ approximates the cardinality of the set of elements that satisfy α: if structures s_0, s_1 are such that $s_0, s_1 \models \varphi_<$, we have that the set of elements that satisfy α in s_0 is a strict subset of that in s_1, and so we have reduction in cardinality. This does not capture cardinality precisely, and we can encode a more precise approximation using Const. 6.

Example 6. Taking $\mathrm{Rk}^\circ = \mathrm{Bin}(\mathrm{priv}(i) \wedge \mathrm{lt}(i, j))$ from Example 3, the implicit ranking for finite domains $\mathrm{DomPW}(\mathrm{Rk}^\circ, j) = (\varphi_\le, \varphi_<)$ aggregates over j but still has i as a parameter. This lets us compare cardinalities of the sets of machines associated with two different machines described by i_0 and i_1.

Domain Permuted-Pointwise Constructor. The following constructor is a relaxation of Const. 5, based on the notion of a permuted pointwise order, meant to capture cases where two functions are almost pointwise-ordered but some permutation of the inputs is required. For a set Y, a partially-ordered set A, and two functions $a, b \in Y \to A$, we say that $a \le_{\mathrm{perm}} b$ if there exists a bijection σ on Y such that $a \le_{\mathrm{pw}} b \circ \sigma$. The result, $\le_{\mathrm{perm}}$, is a *preorder* on $Y \to A$. It induces a partial order on the quotient set of $Y \to A$ w.r.t. $\equiv_{\mathrm{perm}}$ in the usual way. If $(A, \le_A)$ is a wfpo and Y is finite, $\le_{\mathrm{perm}}$ is a wfpo on the quotient set of $Y \to A$. In our case $Y = \mathrm{assign}(\boldsymbol{y}, \mathcal{D})$ and a ranking function f_A to A can be lifted to a ranking function to the quotient set of $\mathrm{assign}(\boldsymbol{y}, \mathcal{D}) \to A$ by defining $f(s, v) = [\lambda u \in \mathrm{assign}(\boldsymbol{y}, \mathcal{D}).f_A(s, u \cdot v)]_{\equiv_{\mathrm{perm}}}$.

The above order is not directly first-order definable — we cannot capture the existence of a permutation σ as this would require second order quantification. Instead, the permuted-pointwise constructor under-approximates and encodes only the cases where σ is composed of transpositions of at most a constant number k of pairs of elements $\boldsymbol{y}^1_\to, \boldsymbol{y}^1_\leftarrow, \ldots, \boldsymbol{y}^k_\to, \boldsymbol{y}^k_\leftarrow$ as follows: $\sigma(\boldsymbol{y}^i_\to) = \boldsymbol{y}^i_\leftarrow$ and $\sigma(\boldsymbol{y}^i_\leftarrow) = \boldsymbol{y}^i_\to$ for $i = 1, \ldots, k$ and $\sigma(\boldsymbol{y}) = \boldsymbol{y}$ for any other $\boldsymbol{y}$. To ensure that σ is a well-defined permutation we require that for every $i \ne j$ we have $\boldsymbol{y}^i_\to \ne \boldsymbol{y}^j_\to, \boldsymbol{y}^i_\leftarrow \ne \boldsymbol{y}^j_\leftarrow$ and $\boldsymbol{y}^i_\to \ne \boldsymbol{y}^j_\leftarrow$. We can then capture $\sigma(\boldsymbol{y})$ for any $\boldsymbol{y}$ by a term $\boldsymbol{y}_\sigma$ (see below), and encode reduction or conservation according to σ by comparing $\boldsymbol{y}$ to $\boldsymbol{y}_\sigma$ with the input implicit ranking. (Notably, this is the only constructor that uses the input implicit ranking to compare different elements.) While this is only an approximation, we have found it captures several interesting cases, such as the one needed to verify Example 1.

Constructor 6. *The* domain permuted-pointwise constructor *receives an implicit ranking* $\mathrm{Rk}^\circ = (\varphi^\circ_\le, \varphi^\circ_<)$ *with parameters* $\boldsymbol{x} = \boldsymbol{y} \cdot \boldsymbol{z}$, *and* $k \in \mathbb{N}$. *It returns an implicit ranking for finite domains* $\mathrm{DomPerm}(\mathrm{Rk}^\circ, \boldsymbol{y}, k) = (\varphi_\le, \varphi_<)$ *with parameters* $\boldsymbol{z}$ *defined by:*

$$\varphi_\le(\boldsymbol{z}_0, \boldsymbol{z}_1) = \tilde{\exists}\sigma. \, \forall \boldsymbol{y}. \, \varphi^\circ_\le(\boldsymbol{y} \cdot \boldsymbol{z}_0, \boldsymbol{y}_\sigma \cdot \boldsymbol{z}_1)$$
$$\varphi_<(\boldsymbol{z}_0, \boldsymbol{z}_1) = \tilde{\exists}\sigma. \, \forall \boldsymbol{y}. \, \varphi^\circ_\le(\boldsymbol{y} \cdot \boldsymbol{z}_0, \boldsymbol{y}_\sigma \cdot \boldsymbol{z}_1) \wedge \exists \boldsymbol{y}. \, \varphi^\circ_<(\boldsymbol{y} \cdot \boldsymbol{z}_0, \boldsymbol{y}_\sigma \cdot \boldsymbol{z}_1)$$

where: $\boldsymbol{y}_\sigma = \mathrm{ite}(\boldsymbol{y} = \boldsymbol{y}^1_\to, \, \boldsymbol{y}^1_\leftarrow, \, \mathrm{ite}(\boldsymbol{y} = \boldsymbol{y}^1_\leftarrow, \, \boldsymbol{y}^1_\to, \, \ldots,$
$$\mathrm{ite}(\boldsymbol{y} = \boldsymbol{y}^k_\to, \, \boldsymbol{y}^k_\leftarrow, \, \mathrm{ite}(\boldsymbol{y} = \boldsymbol{y}^k_\leftarrow, \, \boldsymbol{y}^k_\to, \, \boldsymbol{y}))))$$
$$\tilde{\exists}\sigma. \, \alpha := \exists \boldsymbol{y}^1_\to, \boldsymbol{y}^1_\leftarrow, \ldots, \boldsymbol{y}^k_\to, \boldsymbol{y}^k_\leftarrow. \, \textstyle\bigwedge_{i<j}(\boldsymbol{y}^i_\to \ne \boldsymbol{y}^j_\to \wedge \boldsymbol{y}^i_\leftarrow \ne \boldsymbol{y}^j_\leftarrow \wedge \boldsymbol{y}^i_\to \ne \boldsymbol{y}^j_\leftarrow) \wedge \alpha$$

Next, we demonstrate how DomPerm can approximate sums over unbounded sets and weighted set cardinalities. We expand on the relation to sums in [27].

Example 7. Continuing with Example 6, taking $\text{Rk}^\circ = \text{DomPW}(\text{Bin}(\text{priv}(i) \wedge \text{lt}(i,j)), j)$, $\text{Rk} = \text{DomPerm}(\text{Rk}^\circ, i, 1)$ is an implicit ranking that captures the reduction argument described in Example 1. In particular, the aggregation captured by the permuted-pointwise constructor replaces an unbounded summation. The reduction formula listed in Example 1 is slightly simplified compared to Rk produced by DomPerm above: it includes only the nontrivial disjuncts of the ite expressions, and it uses $\text{skd}, \text{skd} + 1$ in place of the existential quantifier.

Example 8. Consider a ranking function $|\{x \mid \alpha(x)\}| + 2|\{x \mid \beta(x)\}|$, where α and β are two predicates, and consider the case where conservation of ranking between states s_0, s_1 holds due to 'mixing' of the predicates, for example "exchanging" one element x^0 that satisfies β in s_0 with two elements x^1, x^2 that satisfy α in s_1. We can use the DomPerm constructor to capture such a ranking argument. We first add to the signature of the transition system an enumerated sort **type** with three values: $\text{type}_\alpha, \text{type}_\beta^1, \text{type}_\beta^2$. We then define the unified predicate $\gamma(x, ty) = (ty = \text{type}_\alpha \wedge \alpha(x)) \vee ((ty = \text{type}_\beta^1 \vee ty = \text{type}_\beta^2) \wedge \beta(x))$. This can be understood as introducing one copy of the domain for α and two copies for β, and interpreting each of α and β over the copies relevant to them. Finally, we consider $\text{Rk} = \text{DomPerm}(\text{Bin}(\gamma), (x, ty), 2) = (\varphi_\leq, \varphi_<)$. To see that the aforementioned pair of states indeed satisfies the resulting conservation formula, i.e., $(s_0, s_1) \models \varphi_\leq$, consider the permutation defined by $y_\leftarrow^1 = (x^0, \text{type}_\beta^1), y_\leftarrow^2 = (x^0, \text{type}_\beta^2), y_\rightarrow^1 = (x^1, \text{type}_\alpha), y_\rightarrow^2 = (x^2, \text{type}_\alpha)$.

Remark 1. Our decision to focus on permutations obtained by transpositions in our first-order encoding was motivated by examples such as Example 8. There are of course other classes of permutations that can be encoded in first-order logic and would also result in a sound approximation of $\leq_{\text{perm}}$.

Note that Const. 5 (domain-pointwise) can be understood as a special case of Const. 6 obtained by considering the degenerate case $k = 0$.

Domain-Lexicographic Constructor. The following constructor is an analog of Const. 4, where instead of aggregation based on the order of indices of the given rankings, we aggregate based on a partial order on $\text{assign}(y, \mathcal{D})$. To that end we rely on an already-existing order in the system, encoded by a single signature formula $\ell(y_0, y_1)$, and axiomatized as in Const. 2.

For a partially-ordered set A with a partial order $\leq_A$ and a set Y with a wfpo $\leq_Y$, the set of functions $Y \to A$ can be ordered by the lexicographic partial order: for any $a, b \in Y \to A$ we have $a \leq_{\text{lex}} b \iff a(y) \leq_A b(y)$ for all minimal elements of the set $\{y \in Y \mid a(y) \neq b(y)\}$ (for $a \neq b$, this set is not empty, because $\leq_Y$ is a wfpo). Equivalently, for every $y \in Y$ such that $a(y) \not\leq_A b(y)$ there exists y^* such that $y^* <_Y y$ with $a(y^*) <_A b(y^*)$. Additionally, if $\leq_A$ is a wfpo and Y is finite, $\leq_{\text{lex}}$ is a wfpo. The constructor encodes this in a straight-forward way: the set Y is $\text{assign}(y, \mathcal{D})$ and $<_Y$ is given by ℓ. A corresponding ranking function can be defined by the interpretation of ℓ as in Const. 2 combined with $\lambda u \in \mathrm{assign}(\boldsymbol{y}, \mathcal{D}).f_A(s, u \cdot v)$ as in Const. 5.

Constructor 7. *The* domain-lexicographic constructor *receives an implicit ranking* $\mathrm{Rk}^\circ = (\varphi^\circ_\leq, \varphi^\circ_<)$ *with parameters* $\boldsymbol{x} = \boldsymbol{y} \cdot \boldsymbol{z}$, *and a formula* $\ell(\boldsymbol{y}_0, \boldsymbol{y}_1)$ *over* Σ. *It returns an implicit ranking for finite domains* $\mathrm{DomLex}(\mathrm{Rk}^\circ, \boldsymbol{y}, \ell) = (\varphi_\leq, \varphi_<)$ *with parameters* $\boldsymbol{z}$ *defined by:*

$$\varphi_\leq(\boldsymbol{z}_0, \boldsymbol{z}_1) = \mathrm{order}(\ell) \wedge \forall \boldsymbol{y}.(\varphi^\circ_\leq(\boldsymbol{y} \cdot \boldsymbol{z}_0, \boldsymbol{y} \cdot \boldsymbol{z}_1) \vee \exists \boldsymbol{y}^*.(\ell_0(\boldsymbol{y}^*, \boldsymbol{y}) \wedge \varphi^\circ_<(\boldsymbol{y}^* \cdot \boldsymbol{z}_0, \boldsymbol{y}^* \cdot \boldsymbol{z}_1)))$$

$$\varphi_<(\boldsymbol{z}_0, \boldsymbol{z}_1) = \varphi_\leq(\boldsymbol{z}_0, \boldsymbol{z}_1) \wedge (\exists \boldsymbol{y}.\varphi^\circ_<(\boldsymbol{y} \cdot \boldsymbol{z}_0, \boldsymbol{y} \cdot \boldsymbol{z}_1))$$

Example 9. Continuing with Example 2, define a formula $\alpha(i)$ which is set to true if the array holds a 1 in index i, and take $\mathrm{Rk}^\circ = \mathrm{Bin}(\alpha)$. Take, as in Example 4, $\ell(i_0, i_1) = \mathrm{lt}(i_0, i_1)$. Then, $\mathrm{Rk} = \mathrm{DomLex}(\mathrm{Rk}^\circ, i, \ell)$ captures lexicographic reduction of values in the array, akin to reduction in a binary counter. Compared to the formula given above, the reduction formula in Example 2 is simplified by the fact that the order given by ℓ is total, which need not be the case in general.

Note that Const. 5 (domain-pointwise) can be understood as a special case of Const. 7 obtained by considering the degenerate case $\ell(\boldsymbol{y}_0, \boldsymbol{y}_1) = \mathrm{false}$.

6   Implementation and Evaluation

To explore the power of the implicit rankings defined by our constructors we implemented a deductive verification procedure for liveness properties of the form $(\bigwedge_i \forall \boldsymbol{x}.\Box \Diamond r_i(\boldsymbol{x})) \rightarrow \Box(p \rightarrow \Diamond q)$ where r_i are parameterized fairness assumptions, based on a proof rule given in [27]. Our implementation, available at [28], is based on the Z3 [32] Python API. It takes as input a first-order transition system, a liveness property, a closed implicit ranking defined using the constructors of Section 5 and the other formulas required for applying the proof rule. Given the above, we automatically construct the implicit ranking formulas $\varphi_<, \varphi_\leq$ defined by the constructors and use Z3 to validate the premises of the rule. Some of the domain-based constructors create formulas with quantifier alternations, which may be challenging for solvers. We thus allow the user to provide *hint terms* for the existential quantifiers in the declaration of such constructors. We replace the existential quantification with disjunction over formulas substituted with these terms in the solver queries (this is sound since the implicit ranking formulas appear only positively in the proof rule and in recursive constructors).

Results. We evaluate our tool on a suite of examples from previous works, listed below. We use Z3 version 4.12.2.0, run on a laptop running Windows with a Core-i7 2.8 GHz CPU. All examples are successfully verified within 10 minutes. Below we describe the examples. For each, we note whether the validation of the premises required user-provided hint terms for the existential quantifiers introduced by the constructors. In all examples we use finite-domain constructors, which assume a finite (but unbounded) semantics for the domain of the relevant sorts. In some examples, such as our two motivating examples, there are no fairness assumptions, in which case we use $\Box\Diamond$true as a fairness assumption; this amounts to assuming totality of the transition relation, which indeed holds in these examples. Some of the more complicated examples additionally require some abstraction techniques. We expand more on each example and these technical details in the full version of the paper [27].

Toy Stabilization (Example 1). The ranking argument described in Section 2 is captured by an implicit ranking defined by DomPerm(DomPW(Bin)).

Binary Counter (Example 2). The ranking argument described in Section 2 is captured by an implicit ranking defined using Lex(DomLex(Bin),Pos).

Token Ring. A mutual exclusion protocol [15] where a token moves around a ring, allowing its holder to enter the critical section. We show that every machine that tries to enter the critical section eventually does. We use an implicit ranking defined by DomLex(Lex(Bin,Bin,Bin)) capturing the linear movement of the token along the ring and changes in local state of the token's holder.

Leader Ring. The Chang-Roberts algorithm for leader election in a ring [5], with first-order modeling and invariants based on [17, 38]. The liveness property is that eventually a leader is elected. We use an implicit ranking defined by Lex(DomPW(Bin),DomLex(Bin)), where DomPW(Bin) is used to track the cardinality of the set of machines that did not yet send their id, and DomLex(Bin) tracks the movement of messages around the ring.

SAT Backtracking. We verify termination of a naive backtracking search algorithm for solving boolean satisfiability. The implicit ranking is given by Lex(DomLex(Bin),PW(DomPW(Bin),DomPW(Bin))) keeping track of the current assignment that is reduced lexicographically when we change assignment, and the number of steps required until progressing to the next assignment which corresponds to the number of variables that are yet to be assigned true, and those that are yet to be assigned false.

SAT Backjumping. Termination of an abstraction of the CDCL algorithm for solving boolean satisfiability [2, 30], taken from [33]. The algorithm non-deterministically applies decisions, unit propagations, backjumping and learning. We use an implicit ranking, based on the proof in [33] defined by $Lex(Rk^1, Rk^2)$ where $Rk^1 = DomLex(DomPW(Bin))$ tracks for each decision level the number of assignments made in it, and $Rk^2 = DomPW(Bin)$ tracks the number of assigned variables.

Self-Stabilization Protocols. We verify several self-stabilizing protocols [13]. In these protocols, a set of machines is organized in a line/ring. Each machine holds some local value(s). Privileges are assigned to machines according to relations between a machine's values and its neighbors' values. In every transition a privileged machine changes its local values, such that it loses its privilege and a new privilege may be created for one of its neighbors. The protocols differ in how the privileges are defined and updated. For each protocol we show that eventually a unique privilege is present (stabilization) and that starting with a unique privilege, every machine gets a privilege infinitely often (fairness).

Dijkstra's k-State Protocol. In this protocol a designated machine bot can introduce new values into the ring. We prove stabilization by proving three lemmas (based on [19,23]): (1) machine bot is eventually scheduled, (2) if bot is scheduled infinitely often then eventually bot holds a unique value in the ring and (3) if bot holds a unique value in the ring eventually there is a unique privilege in the ring. The implicit ranking required for properties (1) and (3) is the same and has structure DomLex(Bin), tracking the movement of privileges towards bot according to the ring order. The implicit ranking for property (2) has structure DomPW(Bin), aggregating over values to capture the distance between bot's value and a new value. Fairness is proven similarly to (1).

Dijkstra's 4-State Protocol. In this protocol two kinds of privileges can be derived for every machine. The different privileges move in different directions. We base our proof on [12]. The implicit ranking for proving stabilization is given by a lexicographic pair $\text{Lex}(\text{Rk}^1, \text{Rk}^2)$ where Rk^1 has structure Dom-Perm(Bin), capturing the number of privileges of both kinds. Rk^2 has structure DomPerm(PW(DomPW(Bin),DomPW(Bin))) which captures a bound on the number of moves required from all machines until a privilege is lost. For this implicit ranking we used simple hint terms as described above, replacing existential quantification with instantiation of skd, skd.next or skd.prev. The structure of implicit ranking we use for fairness is $\text{Lex}(\text{Rk}^1, \text{Rk}^2, \text{Rk}^3)$ with each Rk^i tracking a movement of some privilege in some direction using DomLex(Bin).

Ghosh's 4-State Protocol. A simplification of Dijkstra's 4-state protocol [20]. The implicit ranking we use is an appropriate modification of the above.

Dijkstra's 3-State Protocol. The implicit ranking we use for proving stabilization is a direct encoding of the ranking function given in [25] (See also [14]) This ranking is a 4-argument lexicographic ranking $\text{Lex}(a, b, c, d)$. a captures a weighted sum of set cardinalities by DomPerm(Bin) with $k = 4$ as in Example 8. This generates premises with 18 existential quantifiers requiring complicated hints to validate. b and c are DomPerm(Bin) capturing set cardinalities and d captures the number of steps until reduction in either a, b, or c, encoded using composition of DomPerm and DomPW. The ranking for fairness is similar.

7   Related Work and Concluding Remarks

Numerous approaches for liveness verification have been proposed in the literature, including abstraction techniques [6,23], liveness to safety reductions [4,10, 35,36], rich proof structures [11,16,39,47], and more [21,42]. Our work considers verification based on the classical notion of ranking functions [18,44]. Many proof rules based on ranking functions have been suggested, e,g., [7,15,29,31,41]. As explained in Section 4.1, our constructions of implicit rankings can be used in any rule that requires conservation and reduction of rank. In contrast to [9, 22,40,45,46,48] which automate the search for ranking functions, we focus on expanding the class of ranking functions that can be used and leave automation for future work. We now turn to expand on the most relevant recent works.

The closest work to ours is [31], which uses *relational rankings* or fixed-size lexicographic tuples of them as ranking functions in liveness proofs for first-order transition systems. Relational rankings count the number of elements that satisfy some predicate, and their reduction and conservation are measured approximately in a pointwise fashion. Relational rankings can be captured by our constructors, specifically DomPW(Bin), but our constructors induce a richer family of rankings and offer more expressiveness, sometimes, at the expense of more complex quantifier structure. On the other hand, [31] does not assume finiteness, but proves that the set considered is finite at any time. Generalizing our finite-domain constructors to this setting is not trivial, and is a subject for future work. The proof rule of [31] also allows modular temporal reasoning. The definition of implicit ranking we offer can also be used in such a proof rule.

The approach of [48] focuses on automating the search for a ranking function for protocols modeled in FOL. They automatically synthesize integer-valued polynomial ranking functions from integer variables that appear in the protocol specification, fairness variables, and cardinalities of sets defined by predicates (some of which are user-provided). Similarly to our domain-based aggregations, they assume finiteness of certain domains. While we use the assumption implicitly, they introduce integer variables that bound the finite cardinalities. In both [31] and [48], only rankings that are polynomial in the cardinality of the domain can be used, which cannot capture Example 2. Additionally, their domain-based aggregations, which are limited to cardinalities of sets, cannot be recursively composed, which is needed for examples such as Example 1.

The approach of [35, 36] is based on a liveness-to-safety reduction that uses a dynamic finite abstraction to reduce liveness to acyclicity of traces. The reduction is encoded via a monitor that augments the original system. Liveness is established by showing an arbitrary monitored state called the saved state is never revisited. While very general, the approach is difficult to use since one has to find an invariant of the augmented system that justifies that the current state is never equal to the saved state. Our implicit rankings can be understood as a natural way to describe such two-state invariants instead of reasoning about an augmented system. This also makes them more amenable to automation.

Acknowledgement We thank Neta Elad and Eden Frenkel for helpful discussions. The research leading to these results has received funding from the European Research Council under the European Union's Horizon 2020 research and innovation programme (grant agreement No [759102-SVIS]). This research was partially supported by the Israeli Science Foundation (ISF) grant No. 2117/23.

References

1. Altisen, K., Corbineau, P., Devismes, S.: Certification of an exact worst-case self-stabilization time. Theor. Comput. Sci. **941**, 262–277 (2023), https://doi.org/10.1016/j.tcs.2022.11.019
2. Bayardo Jr, R.J., Schrag, R.: Using csp look-back techniques to solve real-world sat instances. In: Aaai/iaai. pp. 203–208. Citeseer (1997)

3. Beauquier, J., Bérard, B., Fribourg, L., Magniette, F.: Proving convergence of self-stabilizing systems using first-order rewriting and regular languages. Distributed Comput. **14**(2), 83–95 (2001). https://doi.org/10.1007/PL00008931

4. Biere, A., Artho, C., Schuppan, V.: Liveness checking as safety checking. In: Cleaveland, R., Garavel, H. (eds.) 7th International ERCIM Workshop in Formal Methods for Industrial Critical Systems, FMICS 2002, ICALP 2002 Satellite Workshop, Málaga, Spain, July 12-13, 2002. Electronic Notes in Theoretical Computer Science, vol. 66, pp. 160–177. Elsevier (2002), https://doi.org/10.1016/S1571-0661(04)80410-9

5. Chang, E.J.H., Roberts, R.: An improved algorithm for decentralized extrema-finding in circular configurations of processes. Commun. ACM **22**(5), 281–283 (1979), https://doi.org/10.1145/359104.359108

6. Cook, B., Podelski, A., Rybalchenko, A.: Abstraction refinement for termination. In: Hankin, C., Siveroni, I. (eds.) Static Analysis, 12th International Symposium, SAS 2005, London, UK, September 7-9, 2005, Proceedings. Lecture Notes in Computer Science, vol. 3672, pp. 87–101. Springer (2005), https://doi.org/10.1007/11547662_8

7. Cook, B., Podelski, A., Rybalchenko, A.: Termination proofs for systems code. In: Schwartzbach, M.I., Ball, T. (eds.) Proceedings of the ACM SIGPLAN 2006 Conference on Programming Language Design and Implementation, Ottawa, Ontario, Canada, June 11-14, 2006. pp. 415–426. ACM (2006). https://doi.org/10.1145/1133981.1134029

8. Courtieu, P.: Proving self-stabilization with a proof assistant. In: 16th International Parallel and Distributed Processing Symposium (IPDPS 2002), 15-19 April 2002, Fort Lauderdale, FL, USA, CD-ROM/Abstracts Proceedings. IEEE Computer Society (2002). https://doi.org/10.1109/IPDPS.2002.1016619

9. Cousot, P.: Proving program invariance and termination by parametric abstraction, lagrangian relaxation and semidefinite programming. In: Cousot, R. (ed.) Verification, Model Checking, and Abstract Interpretation, 6th International Conference, VMCAI 2005, Paris, France, January 17-19, 2005, Proceedings. Lecture Notes in Computer Science, vol. 3385, pp. 1–24. Springer (2005). https://doi.org/10.1007/978-3-540-30579-8_1

10. Daniel, J., Cimatti, A., Griggio, A., Tonetta, S., Mover, S.: Infinite-state liveness-to-safety via implicit abstraction and well-founded relations. In: Chaudhuri, S., Farzan, A. (eds.) Computer Aided Verification - 28th International Conference, CAV 2016, Toronto, ON, Canada, July 17-23, 2016, Proceedings, Part I. Lecture Notes in Computer Science, vol. 9779, pp. 271–291. Springer (2016), https://doi.org/10.1007/978-3-319-41528-4_15

11. Dietsch, D., Heizmann, M., Langenfeld, V., Podelski, A.: Fairness modulo theory: A new approach to LTL software model checking. In: Kroening, D., Pasareanu, C.S. (eds.) Computer Aided Verification - 27th International Conference, CAV 2015, San Francisco, CA, USA, July 18-24, 2015, Proceedings, Part I. Lecture Notes in Computer Science, vol. 9206, pp. 49–66. Springer (2015). https://doi.org/10.1007/978-3-319-21690-4_4

12. Dijkstra, E.W.: Self-stabilization with four-state machines (Oct 1973), http://www.cs.utexas.edu/users/EWD/ewd03xx/EWD392.PDF, circulated privately

13. Dijkstra, E.W.: Self-stabilizing systems in spite of distributed control. Commun. ACM **17**(11), 643–644 (nov 1974), https://doi.org/10.1145/361179.361202

14. Dijkstra, E.W.: A belated proof of self-stabilization. Distributed Comput. **1**(1), 5–6 (1986), https://doi.org/10.1007/BF01843566

15. Fang, Y., Piterman, N., Pnueli, A., Zuck, L.D.: Liveness with invisible ranking. Int. J. Softw. Tools Technol. Transf. **8**(3), 261–279 (2006). https://doi.org/10.1007/S10009-005-0193-X

16. Farzan, A., Kincaid, Z., Podelski, A.: Proving liveness of parameterized programs. In: Grohe, M., Koskinen, E., Shankar, N. (eds.) Proceedings of the 31st Annual ACM/IEEE Symposium on Logic in Computer Science, LICS '16, New York, NY, USA, July 5-8, 2016. pp. 185–196. ACM (2016). https://doi.org/10.1145/2933575.2935310

17. Feldman, Y.M.Y., Padon, O., Immerman, N., Sagiv, M., Shoham, S.: Bounded quantifier instantiation for checking inductive invariants. Log. Methods Comput. Sci. **15**(3) (2019), https://doi.org/10.23638/LMCS-15(3:18)2019

18. Floyd, R.W.: Assigning Meanings to Programs, pp. 65–81. Springer Netherlands, Dordrecht (1993). https://doi.org/10.1007/978-94-011-1793-7_4

19. Fokkink, W.J., Hoepman, J., Pang, J.: A note on k-state self-stabilization in a ring with k=n. Nord. J. Comput. **12**(1), 18–26 (2005)

20. Ghosh, S.: An alternative solution to a problem on self-stabilization. ACM Trans. Program. Lang. Syst. **15**(4), 735–742 (1993), https://doi.org/10.1145/155183.155228

21. Hawblitzel, C., Howell, J., Kapritsos, M., Lorch, J.R., Parno, B., Roberts, M.L., Setty, S.T.V., Zill, B.: Ironfleet: proving safety and liveness of practical distributed systems. Commun. ACM **60**(7), 83–92 (2017), https://doi.org/10.1145/3068608

22. Heizmann, M., Hoenicke, J., Leike, J., Podelski, A.: Linear ranking for linear lasso programs. In: Hung, D.V., Ogawa, M. (eds.) Automated Technology for Verification and Analysis - 11th International Symposium, ATVA 2013, Hanoi, Vietnam, October 15-18, 2013. Proceedings. Lecture Notes in Computer Science, vol. 8172, pp. 365–380. Springer (2013). https://doi.org/10.1007/978-3-319-02444-8_26

23. Hong, C., Lin, A.W.: Regular abstractions for array systems. Proc. ACM Program. Lang. **8**(POPL), 638–666 (2024), https://doi.org/10.1145/3632864

24. Ish-Shalom, O., Itzhaky, S., Rinetzky, N., Shoham, S.: Run-time complexity bounds using squeezers. In: Programming Languages and Systems. pp. 320–347. Springer International Publishing, Cham (2021)

25. Kessels, J.L.W.: An exercise in proving self-stabilization with a variant function. Inf. Process. Lett. **29**(1), 39–42 (1988), https://doi.org/10.1016/0020-0190(88)90131-7

26. Lotan, R., Frenkel, E., Shoham, S.: Proving cutoff bounds for safety properties in first-order logic. In: Akshay, S., Niemetz, A., Sankaranarayanan, S. (eds.) Automated Technology for Verification and Analysis. ATVA 2024. LNCS, vol. 15054, pp. 135–159. Springer, Cham (2025). https://doi.org/10.1007/978-3-031-78709-6_7

27. Lotan, R., Shoham, S.: Implicit rankings for verifying liveness properties in first-order logic (full version) (2024), https://arxiv.org/abs/2412.13996

28. Lotan, R., Shoham, S.: Implicit-rankings-fol (2025). https://doi.org/10.5281/zenodo.14584594

29. Manna, Z., Pnueli, A.: Completing the temporal picture. Theor. Comput. Sci. **83**(1), 91–130 (1991). https://doi.org/10.1016/0304-3975(91)90041-Y

30. Marques Silva, J., Sakallah, K.: Grasp-a new search algorithm for satisfiability. In: Proceedings of International Conference on Computer Aided Design. pp. 220–227 (1996). https://doi.org/10.1109/ICCAD.1996.569607

31. McMillan, K.L.: Toward liveness proofs at scale. In: Gurfinkel, A., Ganesh, V. (eds.) Computer Aided Verification - 36th International Conference, CAV 2024, Montreal, QC, Canada, July 24-27, 2024, Proceedings, Part I. Lecture Notes in Computer Science, vol. 14681, pp. 255–276. Springer (2024). https://doi.org/10.1007/978-3-031-65627-9_13

32. de Moura, L.M., Bjørner, N.S.: Z3: an efficient SMT solver. In: Tools and Algorithms for the Construction and Analysis of Systems, 14th International Conference, TACAS 2008, Budapest, Hungary, March 29-April 6, 2008. Proceedings. Lecture Notes in Computer Science, vol. 4963, pp. 337–340. Springer (2008). https://doi.org/10.1007/978-3-540-78800-3_24

33. Nieuwenhuis, R., Oliveras, A., Tinelli, C.: Abstract DPLL and abstract DPLL modulo theories. In: Baader, F., Voronkov, A. (eds.) Logic for Programming, Artificial Intelligence, and Reasoning, 11th International Conference, LPAR 2004, Montevideo, Uruguay, March 14-18, 2005, Proceedings. Lecture Notes in Computer Science, vol. 3452, pp. 36–50. Springer (2004). https://doi.org/10.1007/978-3-540-32275-7_3, https://doi.org/10.1007/978-3-540-32275-7_3

34. Oehlerking, J., Dhama, A., Theel, O.E.: Towards automatic convergence verification of self-stabilizing algorithms. In: Herman, T., Tixeuil, S. (eds.) Self-Stabilizing Systems, 7th International Symposium, SSS 2005, Barcelona, Spain, October 26-27, 2005, Proceedings. Lecture Notes in Computer Science, vol. 3764, pp. 198–213. Springer (2005). https://doi.org/10.1007/11577327_14

35. Padon, O., Hoenicke, J., Losa, G., Podelski, A., Sagiv, M., Shoham, S.: Reducing liveness to safety in first-order logic. Proc. ACM Program. Lang. 2(POPL), 26:1–26:33 (2018). https://doi.org/10.1145/3158114

36. Padon, O., Hoenicke, J., McMillan, K.L., Podelski, A., Sagiv, M., Shoham, S.: Temporal prophecy for proving temporal properties of infinite-state systems. Formal Methods Syst. Des. 57(2), 246–269 (2021). https://doi.org/10.1007/S10703-021-00377-1

37. Padon, O., Losa, G., Sagiv, M., Shoham, S.: Paxos made epr: decidable reasoning about distributed protocols. Proc. ACM Program. Lang. 1(OOPSLA) (oct 2017). https://doi.org/10.1145/3140568

38. Padon, O., McMillan, K.L., Panda, A., Sagiv, M., Shoham, S.: Ivy: Safety verification by interactive generalization. In: PLDI '16: Proceedings of the 37th ACM SIGPLAN Conference on Programming Language Design and Implementation. pp. 614–630 (Jun 2016). https://doi.org/10.1145/2908080.2908118

39. Peyras, Q., Bodeveix, J., Brunel, J., Chemouil, D.: Sound verification procedures for temporal properties of infinite-state systems. In: Silva, A., Leino, K.R.M. (eds.) Computer Aided Verification - 33rd International Conference, CAV 2021, Virtual Event, July 20-23, 2021, Proceedings, Part II. Lecture Notes in Computer Science, vol. 12760, pp. 337–360. Springer (2021). https://doi.org/10.1007/978-3-030-81688-9_16, https://doi.org/10.1007/978-3-030-81688-9_16

40. Podelski, A., Rybalchenko, A.: A complete method for the synthesis of linear ranking functions. In: Steffen, B., Levi, G. (eds.) Verification, Model Checking, and Abstract Interpretation, 5th International Conference, VMCAI 2004, Venice, Italy, January 11-13, 2004, Proceedings. Lecture Notes in Computer Science, vol. 2937, pp. 239–251. Springer (2004). https://doi.org/10.1007/978-3-540-24622-0_20

41. Podelski, A., Rybalchenko, A.: Transition invariants. In: 19th IEEE Symposium on Logic in Computer Science (LICS 2004), 14-17 July 2004, Turku, Finland, Proceedings. pp. 32–41. IEEE Computer Society (2004). https://doi.org/10.1109/LICS.2004.1319598

42. Sun, X., Ma, W., Gu, J.T., Ma, Z., Chajed, T., Howell, J., Lattuada, A., Padon, O., Suresh, L., Szekeres, A., Xu, T.: Anvil: Verifying liveness of cluster management controllers. In: Gavrilovska, A., Terry, D.B. (eds.) 18th USENIX Symposium on Operating Systems Design and Implementation, OSDI 2024, Santa Clara, CA,

USA, July 10-12, 2024. pp. 649–666. USENIX Association (2024), https://www.usenix.org/conference/osdi24/presentation/sun-xudong

43. Taube, M., Losa, G., McMillan, K.L., Padon, O., Sagiv, M., Shoham, S., Wilcox, J.R., Woos, D.: Modularity for decidability of deductive verification with applications to distributed systems. SIGPLAN Not. **53**(4), 662–677 (jun 2018). https://doi.org/10.1145/3296979.3192414

44. Turing, A.: Checking a large routine, p. 70–72. MIT Press, Cambridge, MA, USA (1989)

45. Urban, C., Gurfinkel, A., Kahsai, T.: Synthesizing ranking functions from bits and pieces. In: Chechik, M., Raskin, J. (eds.) Tools and Algorithms for the Construction and Analysis of Systems - 22nd International Conference, TACAS 2016, Eindhoven, The Netherlands, April 2-8, 2016, Proceedings. Lecture Notes in Computer Science, vol. 9636, pp. 54–70. Springer (2016). https://doi.org/10.1007/978-3-662-49674-9_4

46. Urban, C., Miné, A.: An abstract domain to infer ordinal-valued ranking functions. In: Shao, Z. (ed.) Programming Languages and Systems - 23rd European Symposium on Programming, ESOP 2014, Grenoble, France, April 5-13, 2014, Proceedings. Lecture Notes in Computer Science, vol. 8410, pp. 412–431. Springer (2014). https://doi.org/10.1007/978-3-642-54833-8_22

47. Vardi, M.Y.: An automata-theoretic approach to linear temporal logic. In: Moller, F., Birtwistle, G.M. (eds.) Logics for Concurrency - Structure versus Automata (8th Banff Higher Order Workshop, Banff, Canada, August 27 - September 3, 1995, Proceedings). Lecture Notes in Computer Science, vol. 1043, pp. 238–266. Springer (1995). https://doi.org/10.1007/3-540-60915-6_6

48. Yao, J., Tao, R., Gu, R., Nieh, J.: Mostly automated verification of liveness properties for distributed protocols with ranking functions. Proc. ACM Program. Lang. **8**(POPL), 1028–1059 (2024). https://doi.org/10.1145/3632877

Author Index

A. Gurfinkel and M. Heule (Eds.): TACAS 2025, LNCS 15696, pp. 397–399, 2025.
https://doi.org/10.1007/978-3-031-90643-5